European Yearbook of International Economic Law

EYIEL Monographs - Studies in European and International Economic Law

Volume 28

EYIEL Monographs is a subseries of the European Yearbook of International Economic Law (EYIEL). It contains scholarly works in the fields of European and international economic law, in particular WTO law, international investment law, international monetary law, law of regional economic integration, external trade law of the EU and EU internal market law. The series does not include edited volumes. EYIEL Monographs are peer-reviewed by the series editors and external reviewers.

Tobias Naef

Data Protection without Data Protectionism

The Right to Protection of Personal Data and Data Transfers in EU Law and International Trade Law

Springer

Tobias Naef
Faculty of Law
University of Zurich
Zurich, Switzerland

Dissertation of the Faculty of Law of the University of Zurich to obtain the degree of Doktor der Rechtswissenschaft (Doctor of Law, PhD)
Approved at the request of Prof. Dr. Matthias Oesch and Prof. Dr. Christine Kaufmann
The Faculty of Law hereby authorizes the printing of this dissertation, without indicating an opinion of the views expressed in the work.
Zurich, 10 March 2021
The Dean: Prof. Dr. Thomas Gächter

ISSN 2364-8392 ISSN 2364-8406 (electronic)
European Yearbook of International Economic Law
ISSN 2524-6658 ISSN 2524-6666 (electronic)
EYIEL Monographs - Studies in European and International Economic Law
ISBN 978-3-031-19892-2 ISBN 978-3-031-19893-9 (eBook)
https://doi.org/10.1007/978-3-031-19893-9

The pre-press stage and the publication were supported by the Swiss National Science Foundation (SNSF).

This Springer imprint is published by the registered company Springer Nature Switzerland AG
The registered company address is: Gewerbestrasse 11, 6330 Cham, Switzerland

To my parents

Acknowledgments

This book is based on my dissertation that was developed during my tenure as a research associate at the Law Faculty of the University of Zurich and written during my research stays in Lund; Amsterdam; Cambridge, UK; and Washington D.C. It was finalized back again in Zurich. Writing this book has been an incredible journey and I wish to thank my supervisor Prof. Matthias Oesch for all the support I received over the years. His academic guidance, diligent advice, and encouraging words were a steady constant through the ups and downs of finishing my dissertation. I would also like to thank Prof. Christine Kaufmann for preparing the second opinion on this dissertation. The Faculty of Law of the University of Zurich accepted my dissertation in 2021 with the predicate *summa cum laude*.

The research for this book was partly funded with scholarships from the League of European Research Universities, the Swiss National Science Foundation, and the Europe Institute at the University of Zurich. I am grateful for the opportunities provided by these scholarships. I would also like to thank Prof. Xavier Groussot for hosting me at Lund University; Dr. Kristina Irion for welcoming me at the Institute for Information Law at the University of Amsterdam; Prof. Eyal Benvenisti for hosting me at the Lauterpacht Centre for International Law at the University of Cambridge; and Jane Harman for inviting me to the Woodrow Wilson Center for International Scholars in Washington D.C.

It would have been impossible for me to write this book without the support I received from colleagues, friends, and family, some of whom I would like to mention here. Prof. Anupam Chander at Georgetown Law and Dr. Thomas Streinz at NYU Law for their inspiring discussions on data protection and trade law; Dr. Zachary Reyna for a meticulous job editing this book; Dr. Anja Trautmann from Springer for guiding me through the intricacies of the publishing process, the research associates at the University of Zurich and the Lauterpacht Centre—in particular, Dr. Rika Koch and Dr. Nina Hadorn—for their company on this journey; my friends for all the distractions along the way; and my sister for always having my back. A very special thanks goes to Dr. Barbara Kammermann. Her love and patience gave me the strength and capacity to see this project through.

Finally, I wish to thank my parents. Their support and uncompromising faith in me have allowed me to follow a path that was not open to them. This book is dedicated to them.

Zurich, Switzerland
2022

Tobias Naef

Contents

Part II International Trade Law

List of Abbreviations

AA	Association Agreement
AB	Appellate Body
AG	Advocate General
ARIO	Draft Articles on the Responsibility of International Organizations
ASD	Australian Signals Directorate
BCR	Binding Corporate Rules
BDSG	Bundesdatenschutzgesetz
BEUC	Bureau Européen des Unions de Consommateurs
BILETA	British and Irish Law Education Technology Association
BND	Bundesnachrichtendienst
BVerfGE	Bundesverfassungsgericht
CARIFORUM	Caribbean Forum
CBC	Canadian Broadcasting Corporation
CCIN	Commission de Contrôle des Informations Nominatives
CETA	EU-Canada Comprehensive Economic and Trade Agreement
CFR, Charter	Charter of Fundamental Rights of the European Union
CIA	Central Intelligence Agency
CNIL	Commission Nationale de l'Informatique et des Libertés
CoE	Council of Europe
Cp.	Compare
CPCprov	Provisional Central Product Classification
CPTPP	Comprehensive and Progressive Agreement for the Trans-Pacific Partnership
CRID	Research Centre on IT and Law
CRS	Congressional Research Service
CTIVD	Dutch Review Committee for Intelligence and Security Services
DisCo	Disruptive Competition Project
DPA	Data Protection Authority
DPC	Data Protection Commissioner
DPD	Data Protection Directive

DRD	Data Retention Directive
DSK	Datenschutzkonferenz der Datenschutzbeauftragten des Bundes und der Länder
DSU	Dispute Settlement Understanding
EC	European Communities
ECHR	European Charter of Human Rights
ECIPE	European Centre for International Political Economy
ECJ	European Court of Justice
ECtHR	European Court of Human Rights
ed./eds	Editor/s
EDPB	European Data Protection Board
EDPS	European Data Protection Supervisor
EEA	European Economic Area
EESC	European Economic and Social Committee
EGC	General Court of the European Union
EO	Executive Order
EPA	Economic Partnership Agreement
ESF	European Services Forum
et al.	et alteris, and others
ETS	European Treaty Series
EU	European Union
FAQ	Frequently Asked Questions
FISA	Foreign Intelligence Surveillance Act
fn.	footnote
FRA	European Union Agency for Fundamental Rights
FTC	Federal Trade Commission
GATS	General Agreement on Trade in Services
GATT	General Agreement on Tariffs and Trade
GCHQ	Government Communications Headquarters
GDPR	General Data Protection Regulation
GMO	Genetically Modified Organism
GNS	Group of Negotiations on Services
GUE/NGL	European United Left/Nordic Green Left
HM	Her Majesty's
HRC	Human Rights Committee
i.e.	id est, in other words
IaaS	Infrastructure as a Service
IAPP	International Association of Privacy Professionals
Ibid.	ibidem, in the same place
ICC	International Chamber of Commerce
ICCPR	International Covenant on Civil and Political Rights
ICJ	International Court of Justice
ICO	Information Commissioner's Office
ICTSD	International Centre for Trade and Sustainable Development

IDB	Inter-American Development Bank
IHC	Irish High Court
IIF	Institute of International Finance
ILC	International Law Commission
IMCO	European Parliament Committee on the Internal Market and Consumer Protection
IMF	International Monetary Fund
IO	International Organizations
IoT	Internet of Things
IP	Internet Protocol
ISP	Internet Service Provider
IT	Information Technology
ITA	Information Technology Agreement
ITIF	The Information Technology & Innovation Foundation
ITU	International Telecommunication Union
IvIR	Institute for Information Law
JEEPA	EU-Japan Economic Partnership Agreement
KORUS	US-Korea Free Trade Agreement
LIBE	European Parliament Committee on Civil Liberties, Justice and Home Affairs
MERCOSUR	Mercado Común del Sur
MFN	Most-favored nation
NAFTA	North American Free Trade Agreement
noyb	none of your business
NSA	National Security Agency
NYT	The New York Times
OCT	Overseas Countries and Territories
OECD	Organization for Economic Cooperation and Development
OED	Oxford English Dictionary
OJ	Official Journal of the European Union
OMR	Outermost Regions
PaaS	Platform as a Service
para.	Paragraph
paras	Paragraphs
PCLOB	Privacy and Civil Liberties Oversight Board
PIIE	Peterson Institute for International Economics
PNR	Passenger Name Records
PPD	Presidential Policy Directive
RDV	Recht der Datenverarbeitung
RGF	Really Good Friends
RGPD	Règlement Général sur la Protection des Données
SaaS	Software as a Service
SARK	Swedish Ministry of Defense Committee on the Vulnerability of Computer Systems

SORM	Systema Operativno-Rozysknikh Meropriatiy, System of Operative Search Measures
SWIFT	Society for Worldwide Interbank Financial Telecommunications
TCP	Transmission Control Protocol
TEU	Treaty on European Union
TFEU	Treaty on the Functioning of the European Union
TiSA	Trade in Services Agreement
TNC	Trade Negotiations Committee
TTIP	Transatlantic Trade and Investment Partnership
TPP	Trans-Pacific Partnership
UCLA	University of California
UK	United Kingdom
UN	United Nations
UNCTAD	United Nations Conference on Trade and Development
UNGA	United Nations General Assembly
UNTS	United Nations Treaty Series
US	United States
USITC	United States International Trade Commission
USMCA	United States-Mexico-Canada Agreement
USTR	United States Trade Representative
VCLT	Vienna Convention on the Law of Treaties
W/120	Service Sectoral Classification List
WP	Working Party
WTO	World Trade Organization

Chapter 1
Introduction

1.1 Framing

Data protection is an area where fundamental rights collide with trade policy. Personal data has become an essential asset for the digital economy.[1] Consequently, the free flow of personal data across borders has been described as a "new battleground" for states trying to protect their vital economic and non-economic interests—especially now that trade negotiations are shifting to digital trade.[2]

The conflict over data protection and trade first crystallized in the transatlantic relations between Europe and the United States (US). From the outset, the US has been concerned with trade barriers erected by rules regulating the cross-border flow of personal data in European countries. As early as 1978, the Director of the White House Office of Telecommunications Policy, John Eger, wrote that "there is the danger, of course, that these new laws will be used not only to protect just privacy but also to protect domestic economic interests."[3] As efforts to harmonize data protection within the European Communities (EC) progressed, the US rhetoric about its motives has been ratcheted up.[4] Ira Magaziner, who was responsible for electronic commerce issues in the administration of US President Bill Clinton, stated in 1998 that "we in the U.S. don't recognize an extraterritorial attempt to shut down

[1] See UNCTAD (2019), pp. 29–30, for a description of the monetization of personal data including cross-border data flows.

[2] Burri (2017b), p. 408. The *Financial Times* referred to "EU trade data flows" as the new GMOs, referring to a long-lasting and high-profile trade dispute between the US and the EC over the European moratorium on the approval of genetically modified biotech products. See Beatie (2017).

[3] Eger (1979), p. 1066.

[4] Bennett and Raab (2006), p. 87; Madsen (1992), p. 26.

T. Naef, *Data Protection without Data Protectionism*, EYIEL Monographs - Studies in European and International Economic Law 28,
https://doi.org/10.1007/978-3-031-19893-9_1

the electronic flow of data between countries. According to the principles of international trade, I think that's a violation of WTO rules."[5]

Spiros Simitis—one of the pioneers of European regulatory policy in the field of data protection and the first titled "data protection officer"—famously countered these allegations in an interview with the *New York Times* in 1999 by referring to another high-profile trade dispute between the US and the EC over the European banana import regime: "Americans still have the illusion that they can change the [data protection] directive, but they can't ... *This is not bananas we are talking about* ... This is about what we consider a fundamental claim to privacy, and therefore there is a limit to compromise."[6] Nevertheless, US political attacks on EU data protection has not subsided, even after Edward Snowden revealed in 2013 the extent of US mass surveillance.[7] In the runup to the adoption of the General Data Protection Regulation (GDPR)[8] in 2016, US President Barack Obama said in an interview with *Re/code* that EU "roadblocks" for cross-border flows of personal data to the US are not always entirely sincere because European countries intend to displace US companies with European companies.[9] In essence, the US narrative has always been that EU data protection rules are a form of data protectionism.[10]

In spite—or maybe because—of this, the EU began to express disapproval of impediments to the free flow of data across borders.[11] EU Commissioner for Trade Cecilia Malström noted in 2016 that "in the digital age, restrictions on cross-border data flows inhibit trade of all kinds, and may amount to 'digital protectionism'."[12] However, the EU's opposition to digital or data protectionism is on a wholly

[5]See Shaffer (2000), p. 56; Farrell (2002), p. 116; Swire and Litan (1998), p. 189, who refer to comments of Ira Magaziner at a conference of the Brookings Institution and the Cato Institute on 6 February 1998 as reported by Declan McCullagh for the Netly News.

[6]The remark is cited in Edmund (1999) [emphasis added].

[7]The journalists Glenn Greenwald, Ewen MacAskill, Barton Gellman and Laura Poitras broke the story on 7 June 2013. See Greenwald and MacAskill (2013); Gellman and Poitras (2013).

[8]Regulation (EU) 2016/679 of the European Parliament and of the Council of 27 April 2016 on the protection of natural persons with regard to the processing of personal data and on the free movement of such data, and repealing Directive 95/46/EC (General Data Protection Regulation) [2016] OJ L 119/1.

[9]Kara Swisher Interviews President Barack Obama on Cyber Security, Privacy and His Relationship With Silicon Valley. Swisher (2015).

[10]Aaronson (2019), pp. 557–562; Schwartz and Pfeifer (2017), p. 118; Farrell and Newman (2016); Aaronson (2015), p. 674; USITC (2013), pp. 5-1, 5-2. However, there are other voices as well in the US. Former Commissioner of the FTC Julie Brill stated that "in some quarters in the United States, there has been suspicion that discussions about privacy in Europe were veiled attempts at protectionism. I believe the *Schrems* decision should put those suspicions to rest. The decision crystallizes what has been clear—or should have been clear—for a long time about privacy in Europe: it is a fundamental right that Europeans and their Court take very seriously." Brill (2015), p. 4.

[11]In a communication on digital trade from 2015, the European Commission contended that "European companies still face significant barriers around the world, such as non-transparent rules, government interference, unjustified data localization and data storage requirements." European Commission (2015), p. 7.

[12]European Commission (2016).

different trajectory than its regard for the fundamental right to data protection. The European Commission has been careful to exclude its data protection regime from a protectionism narrative. In a communication from 2017 on exchanging and protecting personal data in a globalized world, the Commission highlighted that "European companies operating in some third countries are increasingly faced with protectionist restrictions that cannot be justified with legitimate privacy considerations."[13] Nonetheless, this reference to "legitimate considerations" highlights that even from a European perspective, privacy and data protection are sometimes used as a disguise for protectionist policies.[14] In the end, while many states recognize, at least on paper, that data protection and privacy are important values, they diverge quite jarringly on what the correct level or design of such protection should be.[15] There is a deep disagreement about when data protection should be considered data protectionism. This research explores EU-style data protection, its application to cross-border flows of personal data, and its consequences.

The key to legally explaining the conflict over data protection and trade in the EU is the right to data protection enshrined in Article 8 Charter of Fundamental Rights (Charter, CFR).[16] This research provides a new account of the right to data protection with regard to cross-border flows of personal data. Crucially, the right to data protection has an extraterritorial dimension that is independent from the legal data transfer mechanisms provided by secondary Union law. I suggest that there is an unwritten constituent part of the right to data protection in Article 8 CFR, which mandates continuous protection of all personal data transferred from the EU to third countries. This extraterritorial dimension of the right to data protection also requires a new investigation of the restrictions placed on the free flow of personal data by the EU.

Even if restrictions on the free flow of personal data are deeply rooted in the protection of fundamental rights, they can still constitute barriers to international trade as regulated by the World Trade Organization (WTO). So far, data protection has not been subject to dispute settlement proceedings at the WTO. Consequently, this research also provides a precise legal assessment of the EU's fundamental rights-based regulation of data transfers and its resulting restrictions on cross-border flows of personal data in a *hypothetical challenge* at the WTO. I argue that the scope for regulating data protection in accordance with WTO law is wider than expected from the previous jurisprudence of the WTO's adjudicative bodies on other public policy objectives.[17] Nevertheless, I also show that even a delicately crafted and rule-

---

[13] European Commission (2017), p. 3.

[14] See Burri (2017b), p. 448; Chander and Le (2015), p. 448.

[15] Yakovleva (2020), p. 476; Schwartz and Peifer (2017), pp. 178–179; Aaronson (2015), pp. 682–683.

[16] Charter of Fundamental Rights of the European Union [2012] OJ C 326/391.

[17] So far, only one of all the cases that reached the adjudicative stage of WTO dispute settlement satisfied all the standards of the general exceptions. See WTO Panel Report, *EC – Asbestos*, para. 8.240; cp. Public Citizen (2015), pp. 5–6.

based system of data transfers must be carefully managed in order to comply with the rules of the WTO.

Given its importance for digital trade, the free flow of personal data across borders is the subject of multiple, current negotiations in international trade law.[18] While multilateral trade negotiations at the WTO move slow and compromise is increasingly more difficult, bilateral and regional trade agreements have become an important forum in which topics such as cross-border flows of personal data can be addressed. Indeed, bilateral and regional trade agreements have compensated in several ways the lack of progress at the WTO.[19] The challenge for the EU is to safeguard its fundamental rights-based regulation of data transfers in these negotiations. This research also explores and offers the legal requirements for a data flow clause in EU trade agreements. I ultimately suggest four possible designs for such a data flow clause in EU trade agreements. All in all, the intention of this research is to show—using the example of EU law—where the line between data protection and data protectionism in international trade law currently is, and how it can, or should be redrawn.

1.2 Questions

The right to data protection in Article 8 CFR has been in force since 2009. Many aspects of this innovative fundamental right have yet to be extensively explored.[20] One of the topics that has received little attention to date is the relationship between the right to data protection in Article 8 CFR and cross-border flows of personal data. The existing research is often limited to short explanations of how the legal mechanisms for the transfer of personal data in the GDPR, or its predecessor Directive 95/46/EC,[21] should be interpreted in light of Article 8 CFR.[22] Commentaries on the Charter do not usually address the implications of the right to data protection for the cross-border free flow personal data.[23] Consequently, the first question this research

[18] On 25 January 2019, 76 members of the WTO started negotiations on electronic commerce. See WTO (2019). The parties to these negotiations include countries that have different domestic policy priorities and approaches to data protection. Sen (2018), pp. 339–341.

[19] Burri (2017a), p. 101.

[20] González Fuster (2014), p. 205.

[21] Directive 95/46/EC of the European Parliament and Council of 24 October 1995 on the protection of individuals with regard to the processing of personal data and on the free movement of such data [1995] OJ L 281/31.

[22] See, e.g., Kuner (2020), p. 757, 802; Drechsler (2019), para. 10; Wagner (2018), p. 323.

[23] See Riesz (2019), pp. 196–224; Knecht (2019), pp. 3392–3394; Johlen (2016), pp. 214–223; Kranenborg (2014), pp. 241–259; Bernsdorff (2014), pp. 243–249; the issue is briefly addressed by Tinière (2018), pp. 198–199; but cp. Lock (2019a), p. 2126.

seeks to answer is: Does the right to data protection in Article 8 CFR protect individuals in the EU in cases in which their personal data is transferred to third countries for processing?

The second research question focuses on the effect of the protection afforded by the right to data protection in Article 8 CFR for cross-border flows of personal data. Chapter V GDPR includes multiple different legal mechanisms for enabling the transfer of personal data to third countries. These include: adequacy decisions from the European Commission according to Article 45 GDPR, instruments providing appropriate safeguards in Article 46 GDPR, and the derogations in Article 49 GDPR. The use of these mechanisms must fully incorporate the protection afforded by Article 8 CFR, which can lead to restrictions on the free flow of personal data from the EU to third countries. The research question is thus what kind of restrictions are imposed on cross-border flows of personal data because of Article 8 CFR and the legal mechanisms for data transfers in Chapter V GDPR?

The conflict over data protection and trade is not new. Both data protection law and WTO law have been around for more than 20 years. The coexistence of these two legal disciplines has been subject so some scholarly debate.[24] However, little attention has been paid to the intricacies of EU-style data protection. It mostly circled around the now defunct Safe Harbor Agreement between the EU and the US.[25] Corresponding to the rising prominence of data protection law, the issue has been taken up more frequently in recent years.[26] Nevertheless even here, the importance of the fundamental right to data protection in Article 8 CFR has not been sufficiently analyzed in the EU regulation of data transfers as the subject of the analysis under WTO law. The third research question thus relates to the coexistence of EU data protection law and WTO law on trade in services: Is the fundamental rights-based regulation of data transfers in the EU compatible with the obligations of WTO members in the General Agreement on Trade in Services (GATS)?[27]

The fourth and final research question addresses the coexistence of EU data protection law and data flow clauses in bilateral and regional trade agreements. The inclusion of provisions regulating the cross-border flow of personal data in trade agreements has not yet been studied systematically. The issue is usually mentioned briefly as part of explanations of the challenges for the regulation of digital trade in bilateral and regional trade agreements, but the discussion is minimal.[28] Some

---

[24] Peng (2011), pp. 756–757; Wunsch-Vincent (2008), pp. 504–505, 518; Shaffer (2000), pp. 46–54; Bloss (2000), pp. 654–660; Swire and Litan (1998), pp. 189–196.

[25] Shapiro (2003), pp. 2782–2783; Perez Asinari (2003), pp. 3–5; Reidenberg (2001), pp. 737–739.

[26] Velli (2019), pp. 884–889; Ruotolo (2018), pp. 21–28; Saluzzo (2017), p. 819; Yakovleva and Irion (2016), pp. 202–207; Irion et al. (2016), pp. 26–39; Weber (2012), pp. 36–39; Reyes (2011), pp. 13–34; Keller (2011), pp. 352–353; with regard to Korean data protection law MacDonald and Streatfield (2014), pp. 629–650.

[27] General Agreement on Trade in Services of 15 April 1994, Marrakesh Agreement Establishing the World Trade Organization, Annex 1B, 1869 UNTS 183.

[28] Gasser and Palfrey (2012), p. 145; Meltzer (2019), pp. 43–46; Wu (2017), pp. 22–24; Burri (2017a), pp. 106–110.

examples include: studies that briefly discuss the difficulties of including data protection in trade agreements;[29] studies addressing regulatory cooperation for the protection of personal data in trade agreements;[30] and studies that focus on the different positions during the negotiations of the so-called "mega-regional trade agreements" such as the Transatlantic Trade and Investment Partnership (TTIP), the Trade in Services Agreement (TiSA) or the Trans-Pacific Partnership (TPP).[31] Yet, there has been no analysis of the legal requirements for data flow clauses included in EU trade agreements and there have been no alternative suggestions for the design of such clauses. In addition, the EU horizontal model data flow clauses, which the European Commission endorsed in 2018, have not been the subject of much scientific debate either.[32] The final research question is thus how the fundamental rights-based regulation of data transfers in the EU can be accommodated in the bilateral and regional trade agreements of the EU?

1.3 Structure

In terms of the structure, this book consists of two main parts. The first part is dedicated to EU data protection law while the second part covers international trade law. The two parts are both further divided into two main chapters each (plus a preliminary chapter in the form of this introduction and a final chapter in the form of an epilogue). The four main chapters each address one of the four research questions raised above.

Chapter Two discusses the global reach of the right to data protection in Article 8 CFR. It outlines the substance of the right to data protection and introduces the extraterritorial dimension of this fundamental right as an unwritten constituent part of Article 8 CFR. The chapter then focuses on foreign internet surveillance, which is the most important field of application for the extraterritorial dimension of the right to data protection. Chapter Three explores the restrictions imposed on cross-border flows of personal data by the EU. It describes the legal mechanisms for the transfer of personal data in the GDPR and sets out how the extraterritorial dimension of the right to data protection must be applied to the three legal mechanisms set out in the GDPR. Chapter Four assesses the compatibility of the EU's fundamental rights-based regulation of data transfers with WTO law. The chapter explains why international trade in services requires cross-border flows of data, and—against this background—shows where the regulation of data transfers in the

[29] Willemyns (2020), pp. 237–238; Wolfe (2019), pp. 79–81; Yakovleva (2018), pp. 487–499; Berka (2017), pp. 185–186; Branstetter (2016), p. 321; Yijun (2016), pp. 387–389; Greenleaf (2018), pp. 203–212.

[30] Mancini (2020), pp. 192–203; Irion (2018), pp. 9–11.

[31] Streinz (2019), pp. 330–340; Berka (2017), pp. 176–182; Park (2017), pp. 363–370.

[32] Yakovleva (2020), pp. 494–496; Streinz (2019), p. 336; Velli (2019), pp. 890–893.

EU constitutes a trade barrier, and whether such barriers can be justified according to the GATS. Finally, Chapter Five investigates how data flow clauses can be integrated in EU bilateral and regional trade agreements. The chapter offers four suggestions for the design of data flow clauses that entail a commitment to the cross-border flow of personal data while respecting the EU's fundamental rights. The chapter also criticizes the horizontal data flow clauses that were adopted by the European Commission in 2018 as a model for future trade agreements of the EU. Chapter Six concludes the book with an epilogue.

1.4 Method

The book applies the doctrinal legal research method.[33] This method can be defined as "research which provides a systematic exposition of the rules governing a particular legal category, analyses the relationship between rules, explains areas of difficulty and, perhaps, predicts future developments."[34] In practice, the analysis of the case law of the competent courts and adjudicative bodies is of the utmost importance. In the field of EU law, the relevant case law primarily comes from the European Court of Justice (ECJ). The opinions of the Advocates General (AG), which are produced before the ECJ makes its decision and serve as an orientation for the Court, are also crucial.[35] AG opinions often provide further analysis of the legal issues at stake and provide valuable insights for doctrinal legal research.[36] Where necessary, the case law of the European Court of Human Rights (ECtHR) is also taken into account. The ECtHR deals with data protection—in the absence of a specific right to data protection enshrined in the European Convention of Human Rights (ECHR)[37]—under the right to private life in Article 8 ECHR.[38] The case law on Article 8 ECHR of the ECtHR is relevant for EU law because the Charter contains an identical right to private life in Article 7 CFR. According to Article 52(3) CFR, as long as the Charter contains rights that correspond to rights guaranteed by the ECHR, then the meaning and scope of those rights should be the same as those laid down by the ECHR.[39] In the field of international trade law, the relevant case

[33] For an overview of the doctrinal legal research method see Bhat (2020), pp. 143–168; Hutchinson and Duncan (2012), pp. 110–119; Smits (2017), pp. 207–228.

[34] Hutchinson and Duncan (2012), p. 101.

[35] See for the role of AG opinions Albors-Llorens (2020), pp. 284–285; Schütze (2018), p. 206; Craig and de Búrca (2017), p. 61; Solanke (2015), pp. 113-116; Dashwood et al. (2011), p. 62.

[36] Albors Llorens (2020), p. 284; Solanke (2015), p. 115.

[37] Convention for the Protection of Human Rights and Fundamental Freedoms of 4 November 1953, ETS 5, 213 UNTS 221.

[38] See, e.g., ECtHR, *Amann v. Switzerland*, para. 56; ECtHR, *S. and Marper v. the United Kingdom*, para. 103; Lynskey (2014), pp. 581–587; Kokott and Sobotta (2013), p. 223.

[39] Lock (2019b), pp. 2255–2256; Schütze (2018), pp. 466–468; Craig and de Búrca (2017), p. 398; Solanke (2015), pp. 258–259.

law comes from WTO panels and the Appellate Body (AB). It must be noted, however, that the reports of WTO panels and the AB are only legally binding on the parties involved in the litigation and do not constitute binding precedents for other disputes, even if the same question of WTO law arises in the future.[40] In short, there is no rule of *stare decisis* in WTO dispute settlement that can bind the adjudicative bodies in subsequent cases.[41] Nevertheless, the AB has underlined that the fact that AB reports are only legally binding on the parties to a dispute "does not mean that subsequent panels are free to disregard the legal interpretations and the *ratio decidendi* contained in previous Appellate Body reports."[42] The reports of WTO panels and the AB therefore provide relevant guidance to address the research question concerning WTO law.

Where the meaning of rules must be determined in this book, the appropriate instruments for interpreting the law are applied. In the interpretation of EU law, the four classical methods of interpretation can be used: historical interpretation, literal interpretation, systematic interpretation, and teleological interpretation.[43] The ECJ emphasizes that "in interpreting a provision of EU law, it is necessary not only to refer to its wording but also to consider its context and the objectives of the legislation of which it forms part, and in particular the origin of that legislation."[44] There is no formal hierarchy among the methods of interpretation in EU law, but it is evident from the case law of the ECJ and extrajudicial writings of AGs and judges of the ECJ that the Court often gives high importance to teleological considerations.[45] The importance of teleological interpretation for EU law is reflected in this book.

The interpretation of terms in international law follows the customary rules of interpretation in Article 31 and Article 32 Vienna Convention on the Law of Treaties (VCLT).[46] In the realm of WTO law, Article 3.2 Dispute Settlement Understanding (DSU) refers to these customary rules of interpretation.[47] Article 31(1) VCLT provides the general rule of interpretation and requires that a treaty must be interpreted in good faith in accordance with the ordinary, contextual meaning of the terms of the

[40] Van Damme (2009), p. 197.

[41] Matsushita et al. (2015), pp. 89–90.

[42] WTO AB Report, *US – Stainless Steel (Mexico)*, para. 158.

[43] Lenaerts and Gutiérrez-Fons (2014), p. 6; Schütze (2018), p. 211; Itzcovich (2009), pp. 539–540. In addition, Albertina Albors Llorens describes the comparative method of interpretation in the EU. See Albors Llorens (1999), p. 375, 380.

[44] ECJ, *La Quadrature du Net*, para. 105.

[45] See former ECJ judge Pescatore (1972), p. 325; former AG Fennelly (1996), p. 664; ECJ judge Lenaerts and Gutiérrez-Fons (2014), p. 36; see also Schütze (2018), p. 212; Albors Llorens (1999), p. 382.

[46] Vienna Convention on the Law of Treaties of 23 May 1969, 1155 UNTS 331.

[47] Understanding on the Rules and Procedures Governing the Settlement of Disputes of 15 April 1994, Marrakesh Agreement Establishing the World Trade Organization, Annex 2, 1869 UNTS 401. See Van den Bossche and Zdouc (2017), pp. 190–198; Matsushita et al. (2015), pp. 63–87.

treaty and in the light of the treaty's object and purpose.[48] Article 32 VCLT states that recourse to supplementary means of interpretation, including the preparatory work of the treaty and the circumstances of its conclusion, may be used when the interpretation according to Article 31 VCLT leaves the meaning ambiguous or obscure, or leads to a result which is manifestly absurd or unreasonable.[49] While the purpose, or teleology of the law, is of paramount importance for the interpretation of EU law, a sovereignty-oriented reading with a focus on the literal interpretation is essential in international law.[50] That does not mean, however, that the interpretation of WTO law does not offer any flexibility for new developments. The AB specifically held that

> WTO rules are not so rigid or so inflexible as not to leave room for reasoned judgments in confronting the endless and ever-changing ebb and flow of real facts in real cases in the real world. They will serve the multilateral trading system best if they are interpreted with that in mind.[51]

This book critically examines the essential features of the legal rules in question and the corresponding case law to provide alternative interpretations of those rules where appropriate, and then to combine and synthesize the relevant elements to establish an arguably correct and complete statement of the law.[52] In addition, three methodological specifics deserve mention:

First, the right to data protection in Article 8 CFR is examined in the context of the historical development of legal data protection in Europe. Here, the project benefits significantly from the research by Gloria González Fuster, whose work has described the emergence of personal data protection as a fundamental right of the EU in great detail.[53] Given this historical context, the need for an interpretation of this fundamental right in the light of technological developments becomes apparent. This need can also be found in the Preamble of the Charter. An interpretation in the light of technological developments is of central importance for the construction of the extraterritorial dimension of the right to data protection. In the age of the internet, when personal data flows across territorial borders on an unprecedented scale, this need is even more important. Furthermore, this book identifies the underpinning values of data protection and shows that they are equally applicable to the protection of personal data in a transnational context.

---

[48] See generally Dörr (2018a), pp. 559–616; Sorel and Boré Eveno (2011), pp. 804–837; Villiger (2009), pp. 415–441.

[49] See generally Dörr (2018b), pp. 617–633; le Bouthillier (2011), pp. 841–837; Villiger (2009), pp. 442–449.

[50] Ammann (2020), pp. 199–202; Gardiner (2015), pp. 181–196; Van Damme (2009), pp. 221–235; Fernández de Casadevante y Rom (2007), pp. 37–38.

[51] WTO AB Report, *Japan – Alcoholic Beverages II*, paras 122–123.

[52] Cp. Hutchinson (2018), p. 13.

[53] See particularly the research on the surfacing of national norms on data processing in Europe. González Fuster (2014), pp. 55–71.

Second, this research conducts a fundamental rights compatibility analysis of data transfers based on the different legal mechanisms in Chapter V GDPR. This analysis demonstrates and explains the restrictions that are required by the EU on cross-border flows of personal data from the perspective of fundamental rights. The requirements for limitations on fundamental rights in EU law can be found in Article 52(1) CFR:

> Any limitation on the exercise of the rights and freedoms recognised by this Charter must be provided for by law and respect the essence of those rights and freedoms. Subject to the principle of proportionality, limitations may be made only if they are necessary and genuinely meet objectives of general interest recognised by the Union or the need to protect the rights and freedoms of others.[54]

The analysis offered in this book is more detailed than the analysis by the ECJ in the data transfer case *Schrems 2*.[55] An important difference with the analysis of the ECJ results from my argument that the interference with the right to data protection in Article 8 CFR should be legally located in the EU when personal data is transferred to a third country, rather than in the rules, measures, and actions of the third countries.[56] This changes the analysis insofar as the interference with the right to data protection—i.e., the transfer of personal data in question—cannot be justified with the same objectives of general interest or the same need to protect the rights and freedoms of others as is possible when the interference is found, for example, in the access of foreign intelligence agencies to transferred personal data.

Third, this research project makes concrete proposals *de lege ferenda* on how to design data flow clauses for future EU trade agreements. The four proposals each include a commitment to cross-border flows of personal data. For this reason, these proposals stand in contrast to the model data flow clauses endorsed by the European Commission in 2018.[57] The underlying assumptions these proposals rest on—which is also reflected in title of this book—are: first, cross-border flows of personal data are important for the global economy and are of benefit to individuals and the larger society, but the fundamental rights-based regulation of data transfers and the resulting restrictions on data transfers are equally important to protect and guarantee the privacy of individuals, their right to informational self-determination, the transparency of data processing operations, and democracy. Second, international cooperation in the field of data protection and international commitments to cross-border flows of personal data are important both to strengthen data protection and to combat data protectionism as long as data flow clauses in trade agreements leave enough room for genuine data protection considerations. This is why my proposals all respect the extraterritorial dimension of the right to data protection in Article 8 CFR and accommodate the legal mechanisms for data transfers in Chapter V GDPR.

---

[54] Spaventa (2020), pp. 267-268; Lock (2019b), pp. 2249–2254; Schütze (2018), pp. 461–466; Peers and Sacha (2014), pp. 1469–1486.

[55] ECJ, *Schrems* 2, paras 174–185.

[56] Ibid., para. 165; ECJ, *Schrems*, para. 87.

[57] European Commission (2018).

References

Bibliography

Aaronson SA (2015) Why trade agreements are not setting information free: the lost history and reinvigorated debate over cross-border data flows, human rights, and national security. World Trade Rev 14(4):671–700

Aaronson SA (2019) What are we talking about when we talk about digital protectionism? World Trade Rev 18(4):541–577

Albors Llorens A (1999) The European court of justice, more than a teleological court. Cambridge Yearb Eur Legal Stud 2:373–398

Albors Llorens A (2020) Judicial protection before the court of justice of the European Union. In: Barnard C, Peers S (eds) European Union law, 3rd edn. Oxford University Press, Oxford, pp 283–333

Ammann O (2020) Domestic courts and the interpretation of international law. Methods and reasoning based on the Swiss example. Brill, Leiden

Beattie A (2017) EU trade data flows are becoming the new GMOs. Financial Times, 4 December 2017. https://www.ft.com/content/9da22968-d8ee-11e7-a039-c64b1c09b482. Accessed 10 April 2022

Bennett CJ, Raab CD (2006) The governance of privacy: policy instruments in global perspectives. MIT Press, Cambridge

Berka W (2017) CETA, TTIP, TiSA and data protection. In: Griller S, Obwexer W, Vranes E (eds) Mega-regional trade agreements: CETA, TTIP, and TiSA: new orientations for EU external economic relations. Oxford University Press, Oxford, pp 175–186

Bernsdorff N (2014) Artikel 8 Schutz personenbezogener Daten. In: Meyer J (ed) Charta der Grundrechte der Europäischen Union, 4th edn. Nomos, Baden-Baden, pp 239–250

Bhat PI (2020) Idea and methods of legal research. Oxford University Press, Oxford

Bloss K (2000) Raising or razing the E-curtain: the EU directive on the protection of personal data. Minnesota J Int Law 9(2):645–661

Branstetter L (2016) TPP and digital trade. In: Cimino-Isaacs C, Schott JJ (eds) Trans-Pacific partnership: an assessment. Columbia University Press, Washington DC, pp 309–322

Brill J (2015) Transatlantic Privacy After Schrems: Time for An Honest Conversation. Keynote Address at the Amsterdam Privacy Conference. 23 October 2015

Burri M (2017a) The governance of data and data flows in trade agreements: the pitfalls of legal adaptation. UC Davis Law Rev 51(1):65–133

Burri M (2017b) The regulation of data flows through trade agreements. Georgetown Int Law J 48(1):407–448

Chander A, Le UP (2015) Data nationalism. Emory Law J 64(3):677–739

Craig P, de Búrca G (2017) EU Law, 6th edn. Oxford Academic, Oxford

Dashwood A, Dougan M, Rodger B et al (2011) European Union law, 6th edn. Hart, Oxford

Dörr O (2018a) Article 31. General rule of interpretation. In: Dörr O, Schmalenbach K (eds) Vienna Convention on the law of treaties. A commentary, 2nd edn. Springer, Heidelberg, pp 559–616

Dörr O (2018b) Article 32. Supplementary means of interpretation. In: Dörr O, Schmalenbach K (eds) Vienna convention on the law of treaties. A commentary, 2nd edn. Springer, Heidelberg, pp 617–633

Drechsler L (2019) What is Equivalent? A Probe into GDPR Adequacy based on EU Fundamental Rights. Jusletter IT. 21 February 2019

Edmund A (1999) Europe and U.S. Are Still at Odds over Privacy. New York Times. 27 May 1999

Eger JM (1979) Emerging restrictions on transnational data flows: privacy protection or non-tariff trade barriers. Law Policy Int Bus 10(4):1055–1104

Farrell H (2002) Negotiating privacy across arenas: the EU-U.S. "safe harbour" discussions. In: Héritier A (ed) Common goods. Reinventing European and international governance. Rowman and Littlefield, Lanham, pp 105–126
Farrell H, Newman A (2016) The Transatlantic Data War. Europe Fights Back Against the NSA. Foreign Affairs January/February 2016. https://www.foreignaffairs.com/articles/united-states/2015-12-14/transatlantic-data-war. Accessed 3 January 2021
Fennelly N (1996) Legal interpretation at the European court of justice. Fordham Int Law J 20(3):656–679
Fernández de Casadevante y Rom C (2007) Sovereignty and interpretation of international norms. Springer, Heidelberg
Gardiner R (2015) Treaty interpretation, 2nd edn. Oxford University Press, Oxford
Gasser U/Palfrey J (2012) Fostering innovation and trade in the global information society: the different facets and roles of interoperability. In: Burri M, Cottier T (eds) Trade governance in the digital age. Cambridge University Press, Cambridge, p. 123–154
Gellman B, Poitras L (2013) U.S., British intelligence mining data from nine U.S. Internet companies in broad secret program. The Washington Post, 7 June 2013. https://www.washingtonpost.com/investigations/us-intelligence-mining-data-from-nine-us-internet-companies-in-broad-secret-program/2013/06/06/3a0c0da8-cebf-11e2-8845-d970ccb04497_story.html. Accessed 3 January 2021
González Fuster G (2014) The emergence of personal data protection as a fundamental right of the EU. Springer, Heidelberg
Greenleaf G (2018) Free trade agreements and data privacy. Future perils of Faustian bargains. In: Svantesson DJB, Kloza D (eds) Trans-Atlantic data privacy relations as a challenge for democracy. Intersentia, Cambridge, pp 181–212
Greenwald G, MacAskill E (2013) NSA Prism program taps into user data of Apple, Google and others. The Guardian, 7 June 2013. https://www.theguardian.com/world/2013/jun/06/us-tech-giants-nsa-data. Accessed 3 January 2021
Hutchinson T (2018) Doctrinal research. Researching the jury. In: Watkins D, Burton M (eds) Research methods in law, 2nd edn. Routledge, London, pp 8–39
Hutchinson T, Duncan N (2012) Defining and describing what we do: doctrinal legal research. Deakin Law Rev 17(1):83–120
Irion K (2018) Public Security Exception in the Area of non-personal Data in the European Union. Research paper commissioned by the European Parliament Committee on the Internal Market and Consumer Protection. Amsterdam
Irion K, Yakovleva S, Bartl M (2016) Trade and Privacy: Complicated Bedfellows? How to achieve data protection-proof free trade agreements. Independent study commissioned by BEUC et al. Amsterdam
Itzcovich G (2009) The interpretation of community law by the European Court of Justice. German Law J 10(5):537–560
Johlen H (2016) Art. 8. Schutz personenbezogener Daten. In: Stern K, Sachs M (eds) GRCh Europäische Grundrechte-Charta. Kommentar. Beck, München, pp 207–223
Keller P (2011) European and international media law: Liberal democracy, trade, and the new media. Oxford University Press, Oxford
Knecht M (2019) Artikel 8 Schutz personenbezogener Daten. In: Becker U, Hatje A, Schoo J, Schwarze J (eds) EU-Kommentar. Schwarze, Baden-Baden, pp 3390–3394
Kokott J, Sobotta C (2013) The distinction between privacy and data protection in the jurisprudence of the CJEU and the ECtHR. Int Data Priv Law 3(4):222–228
Kranenborg H (2014) Article 8. In: Peers S, Hervey T, Kenner J, Ward A (eds) The EU charter of fundamental rights. A commentary. Bloomsbury, Oxford, pp 223–265
Kuner C (2020) Chapter V transfers of personal data to third countries or international organisations (Articles 44-50). In: Kuner C, Bygrave L, Docksey C (eds) The EU general data protection regulation (GDPR). Oxford University Press, Oxford p, pp 755–862

Le Bouthillier Y (2011) Article 32 Convention of 1969. In: Corten O, Klein P (eds) The Vienna Conventions on the law of treaties. A commentary. I Oxford University Press, Oxford, p. 841–863
Lenaerts K, Gutiérrez-Fons JA (2014) To say what the law of the EU is: methods of interpretation and the European Court of Justice. Columbia J Eur Law 20(2):3–61
Lock T (2019a) Article 8 CFR. In: Kellerbauer M, Klamert M, Tomkin J (eds) The EU treaties and the charter of fundamental rights. A commentary. Oxford University Press, Oxford, pp 2121–2127
Lock T (2019b) Article 52 CFR. In: Kellerbauer M, Klamert M, Tomkin J (eds) The EU treaties and the charter of fundamental rights. A commentary. Oxford University Press, Oxford, pp 2248–2260
Lynskey O (2014) Deconstructing data protection: the 'Added-Value' of a right to data protection in the EU legal order. Int Comp Law Q 63(3):569–597
MacDonald D, Streatfeild C (2014) Personal data privacy and the WTO. Houston J Int Law 36:625–653
Madsen W (1992) Handbook of personal data protection. Stockton Press, New York
Mancini I (2020) Deepening trade *and* fundamental rights? Harnessing data protection rights in the regulatory cooperation chapters of EU trade agreements. In: Weiß W, Furculita C (eds) Global politics and EU trade policy. European yearbook of international economic law. Springer, Heidelberg, pp 185–207
Matsushita M, Schoenbaum TJ, Mavroidis PC, Hahn M (2015) The World Trade Organization. Law, practice, and policy, 3rd edn. Oxford University Press, Oxford
Meltzer JP (2019) Governing Digital Trade. World Trade Rev 18(1):23–48
Park N (2017) Data protection in the TPP: more emphasis on the "Use" than the "Protection". In: Chaisse J, Gao H, Lo C-f (eds) Paradigm shift in international economic law rule-making. TPP as a new model for trade agreements? Springer, Singapore pp 363–370
Peers S, Sacha P (2014) Article 52 – scope and interpretation of rights and principles. In: Peers S, Hervey R, Kenner J, Ward A (eds) The EU charter of fundamental rights. A commentary. Oxford University Press, Oxford, pp 1455–1522
Peng S-y (2011) Digitalization of services, the GATS and the protection of personal data. In: Sethe R, Heinemann A, Hilty RM et al (eds) Kommunikation. Stämpfli, Bern, pp 753–769
Perez Asinari MV (2003) The WTO and the Protection of Personal Data. Do EU Measures Fall within GATS Exception? Which Future for Data Protection within the WTO e-commerce Context? Paper presented at the 18th BILETA Conference: Controlling Information in the Online Environment. London
Pescatore P (1972) Les Objectifs de la Communauté Européenne Comme Principes d'Interprétation dans la Jurisprudence de la Cour de Justice. In: Miscellanea (eds) W.J. Ganshof van der Meersch: Studia ab discipulis amicisque in honorem egregii professoris edita. Bruylant, Brussels, p. 325–363
Public Citizen (2015) Only One of 44 Attempts to Use the GATT Article XX/GATS Article XIV "General Exception" Has Ever Succeeded: Replicating the WTO Exception Construct Will Not Provide for an Effective TPP General Exception. Washington DC
Reidenberg JR (2001) E-commerce and trans-Atlantic privacy. Houston Law Rev 38(3):717–749
Reyes CL (2011) WTO-compliant protection of fundamental rights. Lessons from the EU privacy directive. Melbourne J Int Law 12(1):1–36
Riesz T (2019) Schutz personenbezogener Daten. In: Holoubek M, Lienbacher G (eds) GRC Kommentar, 2nd edn. Manz, Wien, pp 155–225
Ruotolo GM (2018) The EU data protection regime and the multilateral trading system. Where dream and day unite. Questions Int Law 51(6):5–29
Saluzzo S (2017) Cross border data flows and international trade law. The relationship between EU data protection law and the GATS. Diritto del Commercio Internazionale 31(4):807–829
Schütze R (2018) European Union law, 2nd edn. Cambridge University Press, Cambridge

Schwartz PM, Peifer K-N (2017) Transatlantic data privacy law. Georgetown Law J 106(1):115–179
Sen N (2018) Understanding the role of the WTO in international data flows: taking the liberalization or the regulatory autonomy path? J Int Econ Law 21(2):323–348
Shaffer G (2000) Globalization and social protection: the impact of EU and international rules in the ratcheting up of U.S. privacy standards. Yale J Int Law 25(1):1–88
Shapiro E (2003) All is not fair in the privacy trade: the Safe Harbor agreement and the World Trade Organization. Fordham Law Rev 71(6):2781–2821
Smits JM (2017) What is legal doctrine? In: van Gestel R, Micklitz H-W, Rubin E-L (eds) Rethinking legal scholarship. A transatlantic dialogue. Cambridge University Press, Cambridge, pp 207–228
Solanke I (2015) EU Law. Pearson, Harlow
Sorel J-M, Boré Eveno V (2011) Article 31 Convention of 1969. In: Corten O, Klein P (eds) The Vienna Conventions on the law of treaties. A commentary, vol I. Oxford University Press, Oxford, pp 804–837
Spaventa E (2020) Fundamental rights in the European Union. In: Barnard C, Peers S (eds) European Union law, 3rd edn. Oxford University Press, Oxford, pp 243–282
Streinz T (2019) Digital Megaregulation uncontested? TPP's model for the global digital economy. In: Kingsbury B, Malone DM, Mertenskötter P et al (eds) Megaregulation contested: global economic ordering after TPP. Oxford University Press, Oxford, pp 312–342
Swire PP, Litan RE (1998) None of your business. World data flows, electronic commerce, and the European privacy directive. Brooking Institution Press, Washington DC
Swisher K (2015) President Obama: The Re/code Interview. Re/code. 13 February 2015. https://www.youtube.com/watch?v=yaylQmnXztU&ab_channel=Recode. Accessed 2 June 2022
Tinière R (2018) Article 8. Protection des données à caractère personnel. In: Picod F, Van Drooghenbroeck S (eds) Charte des droits fondamentaux de l'Union européenne. Commentaire article par article. Bruylant, Brussels, pp 185–204
UNCTAD (2019) Digital Economy Report 2019. Value Creation and Capture: Implications for Developing Countries. United Nations Publishing, New York
USITC (2013) Digital Trade in the U.S. and Global Economies, Part 1. Washington DC
Van Damme I (2009) Treaty interpretation by the WTO appellate body. Oxford University Press, Oxford
Van den Bossche P, Zdouc W (2017) The law and policy of the World Trade Organization, 4th edn. Cambridge University Press, Cambridge
Velli F (2019) The issue of data protection in EU trade commitments: cross-border data transfers in GATS and bilateral free trade agreements. Eur Pap 4(3):881–894
Villiger ME (2009) Commentary on the 1969 Vienna convention on the law of treaties. Brill, Leiden/Boston
Wagner J (2018) The transfer of personal data to third countries under the GDPR. When does a recipient country provide an adequate level of protection? Int Data Priv Law 8(4):318–337
Weber R (2012) Regulatory autonomy and privacy standards under the GATS. Asian J WTO Int Health Law Policy 7(1):25–48
Willemyns I (2020) Agreement forthcoming? A comparison of EU, US, and Chinese RTAs in times of plurilateral E-commerce negotiations. J Int Econ Law 23(1):221–244
Wolfe R (2019) Learning about digital trade: privacy and E-commerce in CETA and TPP. World Trade Rev 18(1):63–84
Wu M (2017) Digital Trade-Related Provisions in Regional Trade Agreements: Existing Models and Lessons for the Multilateral Trade System. ICTSD and IDB Overview Paper. Geneva/Washington DC
Wunsch-Vincent S (2008) Trade rules for the digital age. In: Panizzon M, Pohl N, Sauvé P (eds) GATS and the regulation of international trade in services. Cambridge University Press, Cambridge, pp 497–529

Yakovleva S (2018) Should fundamental rights to privacy and data protection be a part of the EU's international trade 'deals'? World Trade Rev 17(3):477–508
Yakovleva S (2020) Privacy protection(ism): the latest wave of trade constraints on regulatory autonomy. Univ Miami Law Rev 74(2):416–519
Yakovleva S, Irion K (2016) The best of both worlds. Free trade in services and EU law on privacy and data protection. Eur Data Protect Law Rev 2(2):191–208
Yijun TG (2016) Current issues of cross-border personal data protection in the context of cloud computing and trans-Pacific partnership agreement: join or withdraw. Wisconsin Int Law J 34(2):367–408

Jurisprudence

ECJ, *La Quadrature du Net:* ECJ, Judgment of 6 October 2020, *La Quadrature du Net*, C-511/18, C-512/18 and C-520/18, EU:C:2020:791
ECJ, *Schrems:* ECJ, Judgment of 6 October 2015, *Schrems*, C-362/14, EU:C:2015:650
ECJ, *Schrems 2:* ECJ, Judgment of 16 July 2020, *Facebook Ireland and Schrems*, C-311/18, EU:C:2020:559
ECtHR, *Amann v. Switzerland:* ECtHR, Judgment of 16 February 2000, *Amann v. Switzerland*, App no. 27798/95
ECtHR, *S. and Marper v. the United Kingdom:* ECtHR, Judgment of 4 December 2008, *S. and Marper v. the United Kingdom,* App nos. 30562/04 and 30566/04
WTO AB Report, *Japan – Alcoholic Beverages II:* WTO AB Report of 4 October 1996, *Japan – Taxes on Alcoholic Beverages* WT/DS8/AB/R

Documents

European Commission (2015) Communication Trade for All. Towards a more responsible trade and investment policy. COM(2015) 497 final. 14 October 2015
European Commission (2016) Press Release Commissioner Malmström on the Opportunities of Digital Trade. 17 November 2016
European Commission (2017) Communication on Exchanging and Protecting Personal Data in a Globalised World. COM(2017) 7 final. 10 January 2017
European Commission (2018) European Commission endorses provisions for data flows and data protection in EU trade agreements. Daily News. 31 January 2018
WTO (2019) Joint Statement on Electronic Commerce. WT/L/1056. 25 January 2019

Part I
European Union Data Protection Law

Chapter 2
The Global Reach of the Right to Data Protection

The internet as a technology not only revolutionized communication, it also enabled new forms of trade. Digital trade often involves personal data. Information about individuals now travels around the world on an unprecedented and rapidly growing scale. The key to understanding the implications of data protection in the EU for trade with the wider world is the Charter of Fundamental Rights of the EU (Charter, CFR). The Charter has the status of primary Union law and data protection is enshrined as a fundamental right in Article 8 CFR. The first section of this chapter traces the development of the right to data protection from the early data protection laws in Europe to the inclusion of Article 8 into the Charter. It identifies the driving forces behind this development and offers insights into the origins of this new fundamental right (Sect. 2.1). The second section addresses the substance of the right to data protection. It explains the underlying values for the interpretation of the new fundamental right and analyzes the six written constituent parts of Article 8 CFR. It shows that the right to data protection must be distinguished from the right to private life in Article 7 CFR. The second section also explains what counts as an interference with the right to data protection and addresses lawful limitations on the exercise of this new fundamental right (Sect. 2.2). The third section focuses on the extraterritorial dimension of the right to data protection. The jurisprudence of the ECJ reveals an unwritten constituent part of the new fundamental right: the right to continuous protection of personal data. Personal data cannot be exported to third states that do not provide a level of protection for the transferred personal data that is essentially equivalent to that guaranteed within the EU (Sect. 2.3). Certain practices in third states are of particular relevance for the extraterritorial dimension of Article 8 CFR. Foreign internet surveillance often targets personal data that is transferred from the EU to a third country. The fourth section analyzes the requirements for foreign internet surveillance practices emanating from the right to data protection in Article 8 CFR (Sect. 2.4).

T. Naef, *Data Protection without Data Protectionism*, EYIEL Monographs - Studies in European and International Economic Law 28,
https://doi.org/10.1007/978-3-031-19893-9_2

2.1 Development of the Right to Data Protection

The development of the right to data protection in Article 8 CFR is based on, and fueled by, technological progress and the associated new powers of the state. The origins of the right to data protection are important in understanding this relatively new fundamental right. The first data protection rules emerged in Europe in the 1970s (Sect. 2.1.1). These rules inspired international organizations such as the Organization for Economic Cooperation and Development (OECD) and the Council of Europe to dedicate attention to the increasingly important subject of data protection in the 1980s (Sect. 2.1.2). Diverging data protection rules in the member states of the EC created problems for the common market and led to a communitywide harmonization of data protection rules in the 1990s (Sect. 2.1.3). The constitutionalizing process in the EU finally led to the codification of a fundamental rights catalogue that included a new fundamental right to data protection in the 2000s (Sect. 2.1.4).

2.1.1 *Early Data Protection Laws*

Rules on the processing of personal data first surfaced in European countries during the second part of the last century. The German federal state of Hesse adopted the first legal act concerning the use of information about individuals stored on public authorities' files in 1970 (*Hessisches Datenschutzgesetz*).[1] Sweden approved the first national law regulating automated processing of personal information in the public and private sector in 1973 (*Datalag*).[2] Germany was the first member of the EC to pass a national law protecting individuals against the misuse of personal data through data processing operations in 1977 (*Bundesdatenschutzgesetz,* BDSG).[3] France endorsed a law on computers, files and freedoms addressing the collection and processing of personal data in 1978 (*loi relative à l'informatique, aux fichiers et aux libertés*).[4] These four early laws constitute the first period of regulatory activities related to data protection. They all have a similar background. The law in the German federal state of Hesse followed the official setting up of public data processing facilities in Hesse, where the public authorities were particularly active in promoting the automated processing of information on individuals for

---

[1]Hessisches Datenschutzgesetz vom 7. Oktober 1970, Gesetz- und Verordnungsblatt für das Land Hessen Teil I, Nr. 41, 625 vom 12. Oktober 1970.

[2]Datalag av. den 11 maj 1973, Svensk författningssamling 1973:289.

[3]Gesetz zum Schutz vor Missbrauch personenbezogener Daten bei der Datenverarbeitung vom 27. Januar 1977 (Bundesdatenschutzgesetz, BDSG), Bundesgesetzblatt Teil 1, Nr. 7, 201 vom 1. Februar 1997.

[4]Loi n° 78-17 du 6 janvier 1978 relative à l'informatique, aux fichiers et aux libertés, Journal Officiel de la République Française, 227 du 7 janvier 1978.

administrative purposes.[5] The *Datalag* in Sweden was the direct outcome of public concern generated by a population census that gathered personal data to facilitate automated processing of information on Swedish citizens.[6] Sweden had also been developing a system of identification through personal identification numbers since the 1940s. The comparatively early and progressive computerization of the Swedish public administration and its capacity to integrate and connect decentralized information added to the public concern responsible for the adoption of the *Datalag*. In France, a journalism article about a government project named SAFARI (*Système Automatisé pour les Fichiers administratifs et le Répertoire des Individus*) caused great public alarm and spurred legislative action on data protection. SAFARI entailed the linkage of disparate information on French citizens stored by different public authorities.[7] Accordingly, the computerization of public authorities and the collecting and connecting of information about individuals in centralized data banks triggered the first regulatory activities related to data protection in Europe.

Trade concerns did not play a role and human rights played only a minor role in the early development of these data protection rules. The right to private life enshrined in Article 8 ECHR was not mentioned in these laws. In Germany, neither the *Hessische Datenschutzgesetz* nor the BDSG was associated with human rights.[8] The Swedish *Datalag* was advanced to protect the personal integrity of individuals. Only the French law stated in Article 1 that information technology must not infringe human identity, human rights, private life and individual or public freedoms. Thus, it cannot be said that the early data protection laws in Europe were (strongly) associated with human rights.

While these developments unfolded in Germany, Sweden and France, some other European countries were choosing a different path to address the processing of information about individuals: they established constitutional provisions. The Portuguese Constitution of 1976 addressed the use of data processing under the title “Rights, Freedoms and Guarantees”.[9] Article 35 of the 1976 Portuguese Constitution granted all citizens a right to information on the content of all data banks concerning them and a right to access and rectify that data. It prohibited automatic processing of data concerning a person’s political convictions, religious beliefs or private life, except if the data was in non-identifiable form. It also made unconstitutional any

[5] See generally González Fuster (2014a), pp. 56–58; Simitis (2010), p. 1995; Hondius (1975), p. 36.

[6] See generally Klosek (2000), pp. 106–108; Eger (1978), pp. 1068–1073. One of the first and most important data protection cases before the German Constitutional Court (*Bundesverfassungsgericht*) also concerned a population census. BVerfGE, *Volkzählung*, Urteil vom 15. Dezember 1983.

[7] The article written by Philippe Boucher carried the title *“Safari ou la chasse aux Français”* and appeared in Le Monde on 21 March 1974. See González Fuster (2014a), p. 62; Eger (1978), pp. 1074–1078.

[8] Lee Bygrave describes the German *Datenschutzgesetz* as particularly elusive to the interests or values it aimed to substantiate. Bygrave (2002), p. 8.

[9] Constituição da República Portuguesa de 2 de abril de 1976.

attempt to give all Portuguese citizens all-purpose national identification numbers.[10] The Spanish Constitution of 1977 addressed data processing indirectly.[11] Article 18 of the 1977 Spanish Constitution enshrined a right to honor, personal privacy, and family privacy (*intimidad personal y familiar*). It also guaranteed the secrecy of communications. Moreover, it mandated that the law shall limit the use of information technology in order to guarantee the honor, personal privacy, and family privacy of citizens and the full exercise of their rights. Neither the 1976 Portuguese Constitution nor the 1977 Spanish Constitution established a fundamental right to data protection, but they addressed the use of computers and certain data processing operations at the highest level in order to protect citizens. There was no link made to trade in these provisions.

Austria was the first country with a constitutionally protected right to data protection. The federal act on the protection of personal data was adopted in 1978 (*Datenschutzgesetz,* DSG).[12] Article 1 DSG declares that the right to data protection is a fundamental right enjoying constitutional rank and that it may only be restricted under the conditions of Article 8 ECHR.[13] Article 1 DSG further established that everyone is entitled to have personal data kept secret, but only insofar as they have an interest in that data deserving protection, particularly with regard to respect for their private and family life. Even though data protection formally became a fundamental right in Austria, it was not a self-standing right but intrinsically linked to the right to private life.

2.1.2 Materialization in International Instruments

The development of the right to data protection entered a new phase by the beginning of the 1980s, when the OECD and the Council of Europe adopted instruments for the processing of personal information. Two key international instruments were elaborated at this time. First, the Guidelines Governing the Protection of Privacy and Transborder Flows of Personal Data of the OECD (OECD Privacy Guidelines) and second the Convention for the Protection of Individuals with regard to Automatic Processing of Personal Data of the Council of Europe (Convention 108).

The OECD is an international economic organization established in 1961 as the successor of the Organization for European Economic Cooperation to promote

---

[10]Constitutional reviews have later altered the content of Article 35 of the 1976 Portuguese Constitution leading to an extension of the protection. See Dias Venâncio (2008), pp. 244–246.

[11]Constitución Española de 6 de diciembre 1978, Boletin Oficial del Estado, Núm. 311.1, 29313 de 29 diciembre 1978.

[12]Bundesgesetz vom 18. Oktober 1978 über den Schutz personenbezogener Daten (Datenschutzgesetz, DSG), Bundesgesetzblatt Nr. 565/1978, 3619.

[13]In Austria, constitutional protection is granted to fundamental rights contained in statutory regulations enjoying constitutional ranking (*Verfassungsrang*). Prakke (2004), p. 67.

economic development and world trade. The OECD brings together European and non-European countries including the US. During the 1970s, more than a third of the 24 OECD member countries had already enacted laws with elements regulating the processing of information about individuals. The OECD was concerned that differing national laws, superimposed on interconnecting information and communication technology, would result in serious inefficiencies and economic costs, obstacles to the attainment of its institutional objectives, and even divide the global community of free market economies.[14] The US in particular feared that with the advent of automatic data processing, European countries (and their regional institutions such as the EC) might erect legal and economic barriers for privacy reasons. US officials suspected some sort of data protectionism in so far as "legislation, nominally for the purpose of data protection, could actually have such objectives as the protection of domestic employment, local technology and expertise, home industries, national culture, language, and sovereignty."[15] European countries stressed the intrinsic value of their data protection rules and the need to protect their citizens from automatic data processing.[16]

Given the different perspectives, especially on each side of the Atlantic, the OECD tried to resolve this quandary with general principles regulating the processing of personal data. The introduction of these general principles into domestic law, it was hoped, would reduce economic inefficiencies and strengthen citizens' rights regarding their personal information. The OECD Privacy Guidelines thus set minimum standards for data privacy in order to reduce differences between OECD member states and to avoid undue interference with cross-border flows of personal data. The OECD wanted to eliminate reasons that might induce member states to restrict such data flows.[17] The OECD Privacy Guidelines did not explicitly refer to data protection and used instead the words "protection of privacy" and "individual liberties." The Explanatory Memorandum accompanying the OECD Privacy Guidelines conceded that it is common practice in continental Europe to refer to privacy protection laws as data laws, or even as data protection laws.[18]

Not long after the adoption of the OECD Privacy Guidelines, the Council of Europe finalized Convention 108.[19] The Council of Europe is an international

---

[14]This was highlighted by Justice Michael Kirby on the 30th anniversary of the OECD Privacy Guidelines. Justice Kirby was the Chair of the OECD Expert Group on Transborder Data Flows and the Protection of Privacy that prepared the OECD Privacy Guidelines.

[15]Kirby (1980), p. 28.

[16]For European countries, the impairment of personal privacy was not a theoretical danger. It was one deeply remembered from the misuse of information about individuals during World War II. Kirby (2011), pp. 8–9.

[17]Lynskey (2015), p. 48.

[18]OECD (1980), para. 4.

[19]The OECD Expert Group that prepared the OECD Privacy Guidelines was instructed to work in close cooperation and consultation with both the Council of Europe, which had already been active in the field of data protection for some years, and the EC, which was starting to express interest in data protection. Michael (1994), p. 33; Kirby (1980), p. 43.

organization that was established in 1949 to uphold human rights, democracy, and the rule of law in Europe. The Parliamentary Assembly of the Council of Europe issued a recommendation in 1968 that pointed out the need to study and report on the question of whether national legislation in the member states adequately protected the right to privacy—enshrined in Article 8 ECHR—against violations enabled by the use of modern scientific and technical methods.[20] Subsequent resolutions of the Council of Europe covered data banks in the private sector (1973)[21] and in the public sector (1974).[22] Convention 108 (adopted in 1981) was drafted because there were still problematic disparities between data protection regimes across Europe after the adoption of the two resolutions. Unlike the OECD, the Council of Europe was primarily concerned with the protection of human rights. The purpose of Convention 108 was to secure respect for every individual's rights and fundamental freedoms, and in particular the right to privacy, with regard to automatic processing of personal data in the territory of each party.[23]

Shortly before the adoption of Convention 108, the Parliamentary Assembly of the Council of Europe issued a recommendation to examine the desirability of including in the ECHR a provision on the protection of personal data.[24] The reply of the Committee of Ministers, which came after the adoption of Convention 108, referred to the Steering Committee for Human Rights and the European Committee for Legal Cooperation who, in their respective opinions, agreed that it was not appropriate at the time to draft a provision on the protection of personal data for incorporation in the ECHR.[25] They suggested that it was preferable to first acquire more experience with Convention 108. They also highlighted that the ECtHR recently confirmed in *Marckx v. Belgium* that states had positive obligations under the right to private life in Article 8 ECHR and that this possibly implied provisions for the safeguarding of private data from automatic processing.[26] The political discussion did not resume, and the ECtHR expanded its jurisprudence on data protection issues based on Article 8 ECHR.

These two international instruments from the 1980s, put data protection on the global agenda. They shared the ambition to enable cross-border flows of personal data on the basis of common data protection standards. Especially the OECD Privacy Guidelines tried to address allegations of data protectionism in Europe raised by the

[20] While reluctant initially to associate privacy with the right to private life in Article 8 ECHR, the Parliamentary Assembly of the Council of Europe set off to use the word privacy to refer to the content of Article 8 ECHR in Council of Europe, Recommendation 509 (1968), para. 8.1. González Fuster (2014a), pp. 81–84; Bygrave (2002), p. 20.

[21] Council of Europe (1973), p. 22.

[22] Council of Europe (1974), p. 29.

[23] The entanglement between these expressions continued in EU law, where it survived for several decades, and where it is arguably not (yet) completely undone. González Fuster (2014a); see Sect. 2.3.3.

[24] Council of Europe (1980), para. 3.

[25] Council of Europe (1981), Item 10, 27–29.

[26] See ECtHR, *Marckx v. Belgium*, para. 31. Interestingly, such an argument could also have been used to question the need to adopt Convention 108 in the first place.

US. The OECD Privacy Guideline intended to bridge the Atlantic divide to guarantee frictionless flows of personal data. At the same time, Convention 108 associated data protection heavily with human rights protection in Europe.

2.1.3 Harmonization in Community Law

The European Commission stressed in a communication from 1973 the need to become more competitive with the data processing industry in the US.[27] The Commission underlined that common measures for the protection of citizens in the field of data protection are necessary to support the effective application of computer systems on the single market.[28] It seems therefore, that the Commission began to address data protection in the context of economic competition. However, it did so not for protectionist reasons but to prevent inefficiencies on the common market. The Commission also underlined that rules on access to information about individuals in data banks were of constitutional importance despite the fact that in 1973 there were no constitutional provisions on data processing in any European country. The Commission thus warned that it would be better to seek genuine political consensus on this matter than to be obliged to harmonize conflicting national legislation later on.[29]

The European Parliament agreed and stressed that national provisions to protect privacy have a direct influence on the establishment and operation of the common market. It called on the Commission to prepare a proposal for a directive on the harmonization of legislation on data protection that would also provide citizens of the EC with maximum protection.[30] The Commission instead recommended the EC member states to ratify Convention 108 in 1981. It considered this international instrument an appropriate tool to create a harmonized level of data protection in Europe.[31] Despite being reluctant to propose EC legislation on data protection, this recommendation was quite progressive because it also stated that data protection had the quality of a fundamental right.[32]

---

[27] Commission of the European Communities (1973), paras 3–5.

[28] Ibid., para. 39.

[29] Ibid.

[30] European Parliament (1979), paras 2, 4.

[31] Commission of the European Communities (1981).

[32] Ibid. Sect. I Para. 2. With the exception of the English version, all eight other language versions maintain that data protection had the quality of a fundamental right. For example, the German version reads: "*Der Datenschutz ist ein notwendiger Bestandteil des Schutzes des Individuums. Er hat den Charakter eines Grundrechts.*" The English version merely states: "Data protection is a necessary part of the protection of the individual. It is quite fundamental."

Nine years later, the Commission concluded that Convention 108 had failed to reduce the differences between national data protection rules. There was too much leeway in the implementation of the basic principles of Convention 108 and not all EC member states had ratified the international instrument.[33] Moreover, practical experience showed that the differences between national data protection rules endangered the common market. For example, the French national data protection authority blocked the transfer of employee data between the Fiat corporate offices in France and Italy in 1989 arguing that Italy did not have adequate data protection regulation.[34]

The Commission adopted a proposal for a directive concerning the protection of individuals in relation to the processing of personal data in 1990. The first objective in Article 1(1) of the 1990 proposal was the protection of the privacy of individuals in relation to the processing of personal data contained in data files. Privacy was portrayed in Recital (7) of the 1990 proposal as being protected in Article 8 ECHR and in the general principles of Community law. The second objective in Article 1(2) of the 1990 proposal was to prevent restrictions to the free flow of personal data between EC member states. The Commission argued that ensuring a high level of fundamental rights protection within the Community system would remove obstacles to the establishment of the common market based on the approximation of laws rule in Article 100a EC Treaty.[35] Directive 95/46/EC was adopted in 1995. The directive did not formally endorse the notion of data protection although it was widely known as the Data Protection Directive (DPD). The directive referred to the protection of the fundamental rights and freedoms of natural persons, and in particular, their right to privacy with respect to the processing of personal data. Directives are designed to harmonize public policy throughout the EU by expressing an agreed set of goals and principles while granting member states some room to choose the ways to meet those goals and principles. Data protection thus became an obligation under Community law through Directive 95/46/EC.[36]

The Lisbon Treaty of 2009 marked another step for the harmonization of data protection in Europe.[37] The treaty introduced Article 16 TFEU on data protection into EU primary law and officially gave the EU the competence to enact consistent data protection legislation.[38] The Commission subsequently initiated a review process of Directive 95/46/EC. The review process identified three key problems of the framework:[39]

---

[33] European Commission (1990a), p. 3, 15.

[34] Brouwer (2008), p. 187; Simitis (1990), p. 11.

[35] European Commission (1990b).

[36] Bennet (1997), p. 106.

[37] Treaty of Lisbon amending the Treaty on European Union and the Treaty establishing the European Community, signed at Lisbon [2007] OJ C 306/1.

[38] Consolidated version of the Treaty on the Functioning of the European Union [2012] OJ C 326/47. Hielke Hijmans provides an extensive analysis of Article 16 TFEU. Hijmans (2016), p. 4.

[39] European Commission (2011), pp. 3–4; De Hert and Papakonstantinou (2012), p. 131.

- Insufficient protection of the rights of individuals with regard to modern data processing technologies.
- Inadequate level of harmonization of data protection laws in the EU.
- Continuing challenges in the handling of increasing global data flows.

The Commission went on to present a proposal for a GDPR in 2012.[40] Regulations are meant to implement public policy in the EU without granting the member states room to choose the ways to meet the formulated goals and principles. They are directly applicable in all EU member states.[41] The Commission had promised a clear and uniform legislative framework at EU level that would do away with the patchwork of legal regimes across the EU member states and remove barriers for easier trade relations.[42] The GDPR was adopted in 2016.[43] Consequently, data protection is now harmonized and consolidated on the level of the EU.[44] In contrast to earlier legislation, the GDPR does not refer to privacy. Instead, the GDPR sets out in Article 1(2) to protect fundamental rights and freedoms of natural persons and in particular the right to data protection.

2.1.4 *Inclusion in the Charter of Fundamental Rights*

While developing rules on data processing, the EU was also concerned with its approach to fundamental rights. EU institutions discussed possible paths to reinforce their formal commitment to fundamental rights for many decades. After the conclusion of the Amsterdam Treaty in 1997, the European Commission entrusted a group of experts to analyze the possibility of explicitly recognizing a catalogue of fundamental rights in EU law. The Commission was particularly interested in the possibility of including new rights that mirror the challenges of the modern information society.[45] The group of experts was chaired by Spiros Simitis, a renowned specialist in the field of data protection.[46] It was thus no surprise that the group of expert

---

[40] European Commission (2012).

[41] ECJ, *Politi s.a.s. v Ministry for Finance of the Italian Republic*, para. 9.

[42] Reding (2012), p. 128.

[43] The adoption was also fueled by the revelations of former National Security Agency (NSA) analyst Edward Snowden on the scale of surveillance by US intelligence services and their global and European partners in 2013.

[44] De Hert and Papakonstantinou (2016), p. 182.

[45] Expert Group on Fundamental Rights (1999), p. 6. A committee that was appointed by the European Commission in the run-up to the intergovernmental conference in Amsterdam already published a report in 1996 arguing that technological progress is creating many problems in terms of fundamental rights, that the information society may threaten individual privacy, and that it is thus necessary to stimulate the recognition of new rights. See Comité des Sages (1996), pp. 15–16, 41.

[46] Spiros Simitis' career is intertwined with the development of data protection in Europe. He had been one of the drafters of the pioneering German data protection laws, Data Protection Commissioner of the German state of Hesse, data protection expert at the Council of Europe and consultant for the European Commission in matters of data protection.

underlined their critique of the state of fundamental rights protection in EU law with the example of data protection.[47] Their report recommended the explicit recognition of fundamental rights in the EU, including all rights provided in Articles 2 to 13 ECHR, but also the addition of new rights such as the right to determine the use of personal data.[48]

Inspired by the report of the expert group, the European Council decided in 1999 that a charter of fundamental rights should be adopted in order to make the overriding importance and relevance of fundamental rights more visible to the citizens of the Union.[49] The Council formally entrusted the drafting of this charter to a special body composed of representatives of the EU member states' heads of state and government, the President of the European Commission, members of the European Parliament, and members of national parliaments. The body called itself the Convention.[50] The Convention's job was marked by a tension between its mandate to make existing fundamental rights more visible and the possibility to innovate within this mandate. In order to render existing rights more visible, it was necessary to identify rights that were not particularly visible, and there is only a thin line between an invisible right and a non-existing right.[51] The tentative list of rights distributed by the Convention's bureau (called the Praesidium) in January 2000 invited reflection on the possibility of a right to data protection in addition to the right to respect for private life.[52] This list was preceded by a recommendation from the Article 29 WP in 1999 to include a fundamental right to data protection in the charter.[53]

---

[47] The expert group noted that generally accepted data protection principles appeared to be abandoned in the third pillar of the EU (police and judicial cooperation) even though Directive 95/46/EC suggested a link between data protection and fundamental rights. See Expert Group on Fundamental Rights (1999), p. 8.

[48] Ibid., 17.

[49] European Council (1999).

[50] The Convention was very data protection friendly based on the careers of some of its members. The Convention was chaired by the Roman Herzog, former President of the Federal Constitutional Court of Germany. He was particularly familiar with the Federal Constitutional Court's case law on the right to informational self-determination. Guy Braibant was involved in the drafting of the French *loi relative à l'informatique, aux fichiers et aux libertés* in 1978. Jordi Solé has actively contributed to the drafting process of the 1978 Spanish Constitution, and specifically to the discussions on the wording on the provision regarding data protection. Stefano Rodotà was a member of the Expert Group set up in 1978 to draft the OECD Privacy Guidelines and Chairman of the Italian data protection authority as well as a member of the Article 29 WP that had already expressed its full support for the inclusion of a right to data protection in the Charter.

[51] González Fuster (2014a), p. 192.

[52] Presidency Note (2000), p. 5.

[53] Article 29 WP (1999), pp. 2–3. The Article 29 WP was an independent European body with advisory status according to Article 29 Directive 95/46/EC and consisted of representatives of all supervisory authorities of the EU member states. When the GDPR came into force on 25 May 2018, the Article 29 WP was replaced with the European Data Protection Board (EDPB) that carries out the same task. The work of the Article 29 WP was not legally binding, but it carried considerable weight because it reflects the legal interpretation and policy objectives of the supervisory authorities in the EU member states tasked with enforcing data protection rules.

The first draft of Articles 10 to 19 of the charter in February 2000 offered a separate article on data protection: “Every natural person shall have a right to protection for his personal data.”[54] This was not an infringement of the prohibition to innovate because the accompanying comments of the draft claimed that data protection was in any case already an aspect of privacy.[55] The same draft provided an alternative, more comprehensive wording for the article on data protection with additional constituents: “The information must be processed fairly and for specified purposes, and subject to the data subject’s consent or to any other legitimate basis specified by law.”[56] The draft also raised the question of whether oversight by an independent body should be included.[57] It is remarkable that, with the exception of the right of access to personal data and the right to have personal data rectified, this first draft (in its alternative wording) already contained all the constituent parts of the final version.

At some point of the amendment stage, members of the Convention suggested to delete the entire article on data protection and to incorporate instead a reference to data protection under the right to respect for private life.[58] These amendments were ignored in the final draft of the charter in October 2000. The final draft included both Article 7 entailing respect for private and family life and Article 8 enshrining the protection of personal data.[59]

Article 7 Respect for Private and Family Life
Everyone has the right to respect for his or her private and family life, home and communications.

Article 8 Protection of personal data

1. Everyone has the right to the protection of personal data concerning him or her.
2. Such data must be processed fairly for specified purposes and on the basis of the consent of the person concerned or some other legitimate basis laid down by law. Everyone has the right of access to data which has been collected concerning him or her, and the right to have it rectified.
3. Compliance with these rules shall be subject to control by an independent authority.

The comments elaborated under the authority of the Praesidium accompanying the Charter of Fundamental Rights specified that Article 8 was based on Article 286

[54] Praesidium (2000a), p. 5.
[55] Ibid.
[56] Ibid.
[57] Ibid.
[58] Praesidium (2000b), p. 448, 465.
[59] Praesidium (2000c).

EC Treaty, Directive 95/46/EC, Article 8 ECHR, and Convention 108.[60] Moreover, the assertion in the comments that data protection was an aspect of privacy disappeared. However, the reference to the right to private life in Article 8 ECHR still constitutes a weak link between the new right to data protection and privacy. The same is true for the references to Directive 95/46/EC and Convention 108 because they also refer to privacy. The preamble to the Charter declares that it reaffirms rights as they are found in particular constitutional traditions and international obligations common to the EU member states, the TEU, the Community Treaties, the ECHR, the Social Charters adopted by the Community and by the Council of Europe, and the case law of the ECJ and of the ECtHR. The Convention stretched its mandate to render existing rights more visible with the inclusion of data protection in the charter in so far as it was not a self-standing right that could be reaffirmed from the indicated sources.[61] The coexistence of the right to private life and the right to data protection in the Charter might be described as the outcome of an unresolved friction between an established approach and a novel one.[62] This is why some scholars argue that the Convention had manifestly not respected the prohibition to innovate with respect to data protection.[63]

The new fundamental right to data protection established that the protection afforded in the Charter is not exclusively granted to individuals and their personal data in relation to their privacy, but generally whenever their personal data is processed. Ultimately, the inclusion of data protection as a fundamental right in the Charter goes along with another part of the Preamble of the Charter expressing the necessity to strengthen the protection of fundamental rights in light of changes in society, social progress, and scientific and technological developments.[64] The Charter was formally proclaimed by the European Parliament, the Council, and the European Commission on 7 December 2000 in Nice.[65] It came into force on 1 December 2009 and is referenced in Article 6(1) TEU as an independent document, which has the same legal value as the EU Treaties.

---

[60] Explanations relating to the Charter of Fundamental Rights [2007] OJ C303/17, 20.

[61] It is difficult to assert the existence of a common constitutional tradition among EU member states in relation to the right to data protection. González Fuster (2014a), pp. 183–184.

[62] Coudray (2010), p. 290.

[63] González Fuster (2014a), p. 199; Braibant (2001), p. 47.

[64] Rodotà (2009), p. 80. Orla Lynskey argues that the EU has not adequately justified the introduction of the right to data protection in the EU legal order. Lynskey (2014), p. 572.

[65] Charter of Fundamental Rights of the European Union [2000] OJ C364/1. At the same time, it was decided to defer a decision on the Charter's legal status. See European Council (2000), para. 2.

2.1.5 Summary

The right to data protection has its roots in European data protection laws of the early 1970s, which addressed the computerization of public authorities, the collecting and connecting of information about individuals in centralized data banks, and the associated new powers of the state. These laws were not motivated by trade concerns and were not (strongly) associated with human or fundamental rights either. The first constitutional provisions in Europe containing data protection rules in the late 1970s started to connect data protection with the protection of privacy. Two international instruments from the 1980s established a link between data protection and the protection of trade. Similarly, the EC started to regulate data protection because of privacy and trade concerns on the common market. The adoption of Directive 95/46/EC coincided with discussions about a formal commitment to fundamental rights in the EU. It was decided that a charter of fundamental rights should make existing rights more visible in the EU. While it was forbidden to innovate and create new rights, a new right to data protection that is independent from the right to private life was nevertheless included in the Charter. It drew its support from the Preamble of the Charter expressing the necessity to strengthen the protection of fundamental rights in the light of changes in society, social progress, and scientific and technological developments. Protectionism was never a motive for the development of the right to data protection.

2.2 Substance of the Right to Data Protection

The underlying values of data protection are essential for the interpretation of the new fundamental right in Article 8 CFR (Sect. 2.2.1). The right to data protection has six written constituents that provide an indication its scope of protection (Sect. 2.2.2). The new fundamental right comes directly after the right to private life in Article 7 CFR in the order of the Charter. The two rights are distinct, but they share significant overlaps. Moreover, there is an added value of having both rights in the Charter (Sect. 2.2.3). The right to data protection is not absolute and limitations are possible. These limitations are especially relevant in the context of foreign internet surveillance, which is a major problem for cross-border flows of personal data (Sect. 2.2.4).

2.2.1 Foundational Values

Data protection is a catch-all term for a series of rules concerned with the processing of personal data.[66] A plethora of values underpin these rules. The foundational

[66] De Hert and Gutwirth (2009), p. 9.

values of the right to data protection are an essential starting point to interpret this new fundamental right. These values also provide guidance to determine lawful limitations on the exercise of the right to data protection. The most important values are privacy (Sect. 2.2.1.1), informational self-determination (Sect. 2.2.1.2), transparency (Sect. 2.2.1.3), and democracy (Sect. 2.2.1.4).

2.2.1.1 Privacy

There is no direct link between the right to data protection and privacy in the final version of the Charter but it is clear that privacy is a major value that data protection aims to safeguard.[67] Despite its importance, the notion of privacy remains somewhat nebulous and difficult to describe with precision.[68] Privacy is not one thing but a cluster of many distinct yet related things.[69]

Samuel Warren and Louis Brandeis argued in their seminal article from 1890 for the creation of new and explicit legal protection for personal privacy.[70] They sought a legal remedy to balance technological progress:

> Instantaneous photographs and newspaper enterprise have invaded the sacred precincts of private and domestic life; and numerous mechanical devices threaten to make good the prediction that 'what is whispered in the closet shall be proclaimed from the house-tops'.[71]

There is a striking parallelism between their argument for the creation of privacy protection laws and the later development of data protection, which was focused on technological progress and the associated new powers of the state. Warren and Brandeis described privacy as being part of a more general right of the individual "to be let alone."[72] The right to be let alone conceives privacy in terms of non-interference. According to the influential definition of privacy adopted at the Nordic Conference of Jurists convened in 1967, privacy can be understood as "the right to be let alone to live one's own life with the minimum of interference."[73] This includes, among other things, protection against interference with private, family, and home life; the disclosure of irrelevant embarrassing facts relating to private life;

---

[67] McDermott (2017), p. 2; Tzanou (2017a), p. 24; Bygrave (2002), p. 125.

[68] In the words of legal theorist Robert Post: "Privacy is a value so complex, so entangled in competing and contradictory dimensions, so engorged with various and distinct meanings, that I sometimes despair whether it can be usefully addressed at all." Post (2001), p. 2087.

[69] Daniel Solove rejects the idea that privacy is a unitary value. Instead, he regards privacy as a concept that itself protects a plurality of values. He suggests six different types: (1) the right to be let alone, (2) limited access to the self, (3) secrecy, (4) control over personal information, (5) personhood, and (6) intimacy. Solove (2008), pp. 12–13, 40.

[70] Warren and Brandeis (1890), p. 197.

[71] Ibid., 195.

[72] Ibid., 205.

[73] The conference was convened by the International Commission of Jurists. The adopted conclusions are cited in Strömholm (1967), p. 237, see Appendix IV Article 2.

the use of the name, identity or likeness; spying; interference with correspondence; misuse of private communications, written or oral; and disclosure of information given or received in circumstances of professional confidence.

Other theorists have also conceived privacy in terms of degree of access to a person. Ruth Gavison defined privacy as a condition of "limited accessibility."[74] According to Gavison, the condition of limited accessibility consists of three separate elements: secrecy (the extent to which we are known to others), solitude (the extent to which others have physical access to us), and anonymity (the extent to which we are the subject of others' attention). In addition, Sissela Bok underlines that privacy requires protection from unwanted access by others, either physical, mental, or informational.[75] Anita Allen summarizes that privacy denotes a degree of inaccessibility of persons, their mental states, and information about them to the senses and surveillance devices of others.[76]

Technological developments highlight the importance of privacy. The advent of big data enabled surveillance practices on unprecedented scales.[77] Edward Snowden revealed in 2013 the extent of global mass surveillance. He showed how governments were secretly collecting huge quantities of personal data in our communications, including private e-mails, phone locations, web histories, and much more—all of it without consent and grounded on a thin legal basis.[78] The right to be let alone and the concept of limited accessibility establish a sphere for the individual where the state and private parties cannot interfere without justification, including but not limited to surveillance practices. In this regard, the Grand Chamber of the ECJ found that legislation permitting public authorities access to personal data on a generalized basis through the content of electronic communications must be regarded as compromising the essence of the right to private life (privacy).[79]

Data protection rules usually do not prohibit the processing of personal data. Data protection rules regulate, and sometimes limit, the ways in which personal data can legally be processed. Notable exceptions are prohibitions in the GDPR for the processing of sensitive data in order to safeguard the private sphere of individuals.[80] Principles such as purpose limitation, data minimization, storage limitation, and confidentiality in the GDPR are examples of how privacy and its formulations both

[74] Gavison (1980), pp. 428–436.

[75] Bok (1982), pp. 10–11.

[76] Allen (1988), p. 15.

[77] Lyon (2014), pp. 4–5.

[78] The journalists Glenn Greenwald, Ewen MacAskill, Barton Gellman and Laura Poitras broke the story on 7 June 2013. See Greenwald and MacAskill (2013); Gellman and Poitras (2013).

[79] ECJ, *Schrems*, para. 94.

[80] Article 9(1) GDPR prohibits the processing of special categories of personal data ('sensitive data') revealing racial or ethnic origin, political opinions, religious or philosophical beliefs, or trade union membership, and the processing of genetic data, biometric data for the purpose of uniquely identifying a natural person, data concerning health or data concerning a natural person's sex life or sexual orientation. Article 9(2) GDPR contains a list of exceptions when paragraph 1 does not apply. Cp. Rouvroy and Poullet (2009), p. 70. See Recital (10) GDPR.

as a right to be let alone and as limited accessibility of the person are embedded in data protection rules.[81]

2.2.1.2 Informational Self-Determination

Informational self-determination is another value that data protection aims to safeguard.[82] The notion of informational self-determination is deeply rooted in concepts of human dignity, personal liberty, and autonomy. Lewis Hinchman has observed that in contemporary philosophy, the main requirement of autonomy is "that the choices [one makes] be truly one's own, that one must not have been manipulated, gulled, brainwashed, or conditioned into making them."[83] Personal liberty and autonomy are affected when the quantity and quality of personal data offer opportunities for the use and manipulation of individual characteristics.

The German Constitutional Court (*Bundesverfassungsgericht*) noted in a landmark decision from 1984 on the constitutionality of a population census that modern methods of storing information about a person combined with automatic data processing enable the creation of partial or virtually complete personality profiles, the accuracy and application of which the concerned individuals have no sufficient means to control.[84] Today, algorithms can even hold individuals accountable for whatever the combination of their personal data reveals. Such profiles raise concerns about personal liberty and autonomous agency. The German Constitutional Court reflected that the lack of opportunities to control the accuracy and use of these constructed profiles can influence individuals' behavior through the psychological pressure exerted on them.[85] This influence could have a "chilling effect" and impair individuals in the exercise of their personal liberty to make decisions that are truly their own.[86] In reaction, the Constitutional Court developed a right to informational self-determination as an expression of the general right of personality, which, in turn, is based on the general protection of personal liberty and human dignity.[87] The notion of informational self-determination implies that individuals' control over their personal data is a necessary precondition for a life that is governed by free

[81] Article 5(1)(b), (c), (e), (f) and Article 5(2) GDPR.

[82] Some scholars in the US, where the notion of data protection is not widely used, also perceive privacy in terms of information control. For example, Alan Westin holds that privacy "is the claim of individuals [...] to determine for themselves when, how, and to what extent information about them is communicated to others." Westin (1967), p. 7.

[83] Hinchman (1996), p. 488.

[84] BVerfGE, *Volkzählung*, 45. For a detailed account of the decision in English see Hornung and Schnabel (2009).

[85] BVerfGE, *Volkzählung*, 46.

[86] Ibid.; see Wagner DeCew (1997), p. 64.

[87] BVerfGE, *Volkzählung*, 44. This is why human dignity is often cited as the ultimate foundation of data protection (and the overall goal of human rights protection). Tzanou (2017a), p. 29; Lynskey (2015), p. 94; Petersen (2012), p. 1013; ECtHR, *S.W. v. the United Kingdom*, para. 44.

choices.[88] The right to informational self-determination guarantees the ability of individuals to determine for themselves the disclosure and use of their personal data.[89]

Data protection rules empower individuals as data subjects with a bundle of rights.[90] The consent of individuals to the processing of their personal data is one of the important mechanisms in the GDPR to determine when personal data can legally be used.[91] These include rights for individuals to access information about themselves and to have this information rectified.[92] The Grand Chamber of the ECJ has even decided that there must be a right to be forgotten in the case *Google Spain* regarding a Spanish citizen's claim to delete information about him found on Google searches.[93] These rights are examples of how informational self-determination is embedded in data protection rules.

Furthermore, AG Pedro Cruz Villalón explicitly mentioned informational self-determination in relation to data protection in his opinion on *Digital Right Ireland.* He wrote that Directive 2006/24/EC (Data Retention Directive, DRD) applied to personal data necessary to identify users of publicly available electronic communication services or public communications networks and that this data falls within the category of data the disclosure of which is subject to the express authorization of each individual based on the right to informational self-determination.[94]

2.2.1.3 Transparency

Transparency is a third value that data protection aims to safeguard.[95] The processing of personal data bears inherent imbalances. These imbalances are manifest in the asymmetries between the two sides of data processing operations.[96] There is, on the one side, the data subjects whose personal data is processed, and, on the other side, the data controllers who determine the purposes and means of such processing. Helen Nissenbaum describes the situation of data subjects as one in which, "a) there is virtually no limit to the amount of information that can be recorded, b) there is virtually no limit to the scope of analysis that can be done –

---

[88] Rouvroy and Poullet (2009), p. 51.

[89] BVerfGE, *Volkzählung,* 46.

[90] Lynskey (2015), p. 192; Lazaro and Le Métayer (2015), pp. 17–18. Cp. ECJ, AG Opinion, *Digital Rights Ireland*, para. 57.

[91] Article 6(1)(a) GDPR; see Carolan (2016), pp. 463–464; Whitley (2009), p. 156. But see Schermer et al. (2014), pp. 176–178; Tene and Polonetsky (2013), pp. 260–263.

[92] Articles 15 and 16 GDPR.

[93] ECJ, *Google Spain*, para. 97; see also Article 17 GDPR.

[94] ECJ, AG Opinion, *Digital Rights Ireland*, para. 57.

[95] McDermott (2017), pp. 1–7; Tzanou (2017a), p. 26; González Fuster (2014b), pp. 95–99; Schwartz (1995), pp. 589–590; Paul de Hert and Serge Gutwirth even argue that transparency is the core value of data protection. See De Hert and Gutwirth (2006), p. 80.

[96] Tzanou (2017a), p. 26.

bounded only by human ingenuity, and c) the information may be stored virtually forever."[97] Herbert Burkert argues that data protection rules are, in essence, about the (transparent) distribution of power.[98] Paul De Hert and Serge Gutwirth define data protection as a tool of transparency that channels the exercise of power over data subjects.[99] Data protection rules strive to enhance the transparency of data processing operations in order to bring balance between data subjects and data controllers. This is why data protection rules often require that personal data is processed fairly.[100] Fairness is an ambiguous notion. In the context of data protection, it is regularly associated with transparency and implies that the processing of personal data must be clear to the data subject.[101] Recital (38) Directive 95/46/EC was very explicit in this regard:

> Whereas, if the processing of data is to be fair, the data subject must be in a position to learn of the existence of a processing operation and, where data are collected from him, must be given accurate and full information, bearing in mind the circumstances of the collection.

In order to achieve such transparency, the GDPR requires that organizations which process personal data must provide individuals whose data is processed with various kinds of information, such as the identity of the processing organization, the type of data involved, the extent and the purposes of the processing operations, the risks, rules, and safeguards attached to these operations, and the time limit for erasure or periodic review of the data involved.[102] This is a reflection of the attempt to achieve procedural fairness for data processing operations.[103] Transparency ultimately enables individuals to know who knows what about them, as well as when and on what occasions, and, therefore, allows them to act accordingly.

2.2.1.4 Democracy

Democracy is the last value discussed here that data protection aims to safeguard.[104] Priscilla Regan claims that data protection rules serve purposes beyond those that they perform for a particular individual. She distinguishes between the private

---

[97] Nissenbaum (1998), p. 576.

[98] According to his understanding, data protection rules seek to de-legitimize asymmetries of information distribution through transparency (and in the interest of individual freedom and democratic participation). See Burkert (2009), pp. 339–340.

[99] De Hert and Gutwirth (2006), p. 77; Article 29 WP (2017), p. 5. Victor Tadros is critical of the proposition that data protection is merely a tool of transparency and suggests that it should not be seen purely as regulation of legitimate activity, but rather as restraint on the use of information. See Tadros (2006), pp. 116–118.

[100] Cp. Article 5(1)(a) GDPR.

[101] Clifford and Ausloos (2018), p. 139; Bygrave (2002), p. 59.

[102] See Articles 12–14 GDPR; Recital (39) GDPR.

[103] Clifford and Ausloos (2018), p. 163; Tzanou (2013), p. 90.

[104] Boehme-Neßler (2016), p. 228; Schwartz (1995), pp. 589–590; Gavison (1980), p. 455.

purpose of these rules and their public purpose in which they are instrumentally valuable to a democratic political system, securing, for examples, things like freedom of speech and association.[105] Similarly, the ECJ has acknowledged that the retention of traffic and location data as well as data pertaining to mobile communication of individuals is not compatible with the right to data protection and moreover has an effect on the exercise of the freedom of expression, which constitutes one of the essential foundations of a pluralist democratic society.[106]

The German Constitutional Court noted in its 1984 population census decision with regard to the power of modern data processing technology that informational self-determination is essential for the common good because democratic societies rely on individuals that can act and collaborate freely.[107] James Flemming further argues that the integrity of a democratic society rests on individuals' capacity for free decision making and the collective's capacity for free discourse.[108] The power resting in the accumulation, aggregation, and application of personal data has the potential to seriously distort these processes.[109] If individuals cannot oversee and control what information about them is openly accessible in their social environment, and if they cannot appraise the knowledge of possible communication partners about them, then they may be inhibited in their capacity for free decision making.[110] Furthermore, if individuals are unsure whether dissenting behavior is noticed and information is being permanently stored, used, and passed on, they will try to avoid it so as not to attract attention.[111]

Data protection rules thus foster the capacity of individuals for free decision making and secure the conditions that are necessary for sustaining an open collective discourse by shielding participants against intrusive data processing operations, enabling them to control their personal data, and making data processing operations more transparent. Consequently, data protection is a tool for the preservation and promotion of political participation and therefore plays a vital societal role in a functioning democracy.

---

[105] Regan (1995), pp. 221–230. Arthur J. Cockfield argues that legal analysis should recognize the public aspect of these rules. Cockfield (2007), p. 51.

[106] The ECJ highlighted that data, which is retained and subsequently used without informing the individuals concerned, is likely to generate the feeling that their private lives are the subject of constant surveillance. ECJ, *Digital Rights Ireland*, C-293/12 and C-594/12, paras 28, 37; see also ECJ, *Tele2/Watson*, paras 92–93, 101; Krotoszynski Jr. (2016), p. 175.

[107] BVerfGE, *Volkzählungsurteil*, 47.

[108] James Flemming coined the notions of deliberative autonomy and deliberative democracy in his work on constitutional constructivism to describe the necessary capacities of individuals and the collective for a functional democratic society. See Flemming (2004), pp. 1439–1441; Flemming (1995), pp. 7–16.

[109] Totalitarian regimes in Eastern Europe relied on information gathering and storage to weaken the individual's capacities for critical reflection and to repress social movements. Collective human self-determination is fragile in the face of widespread surveillance and data collection. See Schwartz (1994), pp. 1052–1053.

[110] Cp. BVerfGE, *Volkzählungsurteil*, 45.

[111] Cp. ibid.

2.2.2 *Written Constituents of the Right to Data Protection*

The right to data protection in Article 8 CFR is not designed like other fundamental rights. The first paragraph introduces the right to data protection and the two following paragraphs contain six written constituent parts of the fundamental right. The general principle in Article 8(1) CFR includes the concept of personal data and defines the scope of the fundamental right (Sect. 2.2.2.1). The six constituent parts of the right to data protection can be divided into three groups.[112] The first group includes the constituent parts that resemble data protection principles in Article 5 GDPR: fairness, purpose specification, and legitimate basis for a data processing operation (Sect. 2.2.2.2). The second group includes the constituent parts that contain additional rights: the right of access to personal data and the right to have personal data rectified (Sect. 2.2.2.3). Lastly, the constituent part requiring independent supervision constitutes the third group (Sect. 2.2.2.4).

2.2.2.1 General Principle

The first paragraph of Article 8 CFR introduces the general principle of the fundamental right. Everyone has the right to the protection of personal data concerning him or her. The notion of personal data is crucial to the understanding of the right to data protection. Article 4(1) GDPR defines personal data as

> any information relating to an identified or identifiable natural person (the data subject), whereas an identifiable natural person is one who can be identified, directly or indirectly, in particular by reference to an identifier such as a name, an identification number, location data, an online identifier or to one or more factors specific to the physical, physiological, genetic, mental, economic, cultural or social identity of that natural person.[113]

For example, IP addresses are personal data because they allow for the identification of a natural person (the internet user).[114] The definition of personal data is intended to be very broad. Since information can relate to a person in content, purpose or result, the information relating to a person is broader than just the information about that person.[115] Information relates to a person in purpose, for example, when the data is used or is likely to be used with the purpose to evaluate or influence the status or

---

[112] Similarly, González Fuster (2014a), p. 204. Yves Poullet instead refers to four principles: a scope of application covering all personal data, subjective rights, certain limitations imposed on those processing data and the existence of a supervisory authority. See Poullet (2006), p. 216.

[113] The Article 29 WP breaks up the definition of personal data into four elements. Personal data is information (1), relating to (2), an identified or identifiable (3) natural person (4). See Article 29 WP (2007), 6.

[114] ECJ, *Breyer*, paras 38–49; ECJ, *Scarlet Extended*, para. 51; Recital (30) GDPR.

[115] Article 29 WP (2007), pp. 10–11.

behavior of that person.[116] An identified person is a person who is known or distinguished in a group whereas an identifiable person is a person who is not yet identified but his or her identification is possible.[117] To determine whether a person is identifiable, account needs to be taken of all the means reasonably likely to be used.[118] To ascertain whether the means are reasonably likely to be used, all objective factors such as the costs and amount of time required for identification as well as the available technology at the time of the processing and technological developments are relevant. As data processing technologies advance and the pool of data which can be combined grows (combining databases has becomes a daily practice of intelligence agencies), the possibility of linking information to a person increases.[119]

The right in Article 8 CFR protects individuals from the processing of their personal data. The processing of personal data is any operation which is performed on personal data such as collection, recording, organization, structuring, storage, use, combination, sharing, or transfer to another country.[120] Any data processing operation involving personal data of individuals in the EU falls under the scope of the right to data protection and must respect its constituent parts.

2.2.2.2 Fairness, Purpose Specification, and Basis for the Processing of Personal Data

Three constituent parts of the right to data protection can be found in the first sentence of Article 8(2) CFR. They require that personal data is processed fairly, for specified purposes, and on the basis of the consent of the person concerned or some other legitimate basis laid down by law. These constituent parts are linked with transparency.[121]

For processing operations to be fair, the data subject must be in a position to learn of their existence. Secret processing of personal data without a legitimate basis defined by law is considered to interfere with the right to data protection. The French Council of States (*Conseil d'État*) provided an illustrative example in the *Les Pages Jaunes* case. In this case, the French Council of States found that the collection and aggregation of information about individuals from their public social media profiles

[116] Ibid., 10. When increasing amounts of data are gathered in real time from increasingly connected environments, intended to be used in automated decision-making about us, and we do not know how autonomous self-learning and self-managing computers draw meaning from data, we should always reasonably assume that any information is likely to relate to a person, since we cannot eliminate this possibility with certainty. See Purtova (2018), p. 55.

[117] Article 29 WP (2007), pp. 10–11.

[118] ECJ, *Breyer*, paras 41, 46; Recital (26) GDPR.

[119] Tene and Polonetsky (2013) 257–258; Schwartz and Solove (2011) 1836–1847; Ohm (2010), pp. 1716–1731.

[120] Article 4(2) GDPR.

[121] Forgó et al. (2017), pp. 26–28.

for the online directory services of the Les Pages Jaunes was unfair because data subjects were not sufficiently informed that their public profiles would be collected.[122]

Purpose specification reflects the idea that data processing operations should be foreseeable for the data subject and should not go beyond the reasonable expectations of the individuals concerned.[123] This prohibits aimless data collection. The purpose of data processing operations must be specified prior to the collection. Any processing of personal data for purposes that are incompatible with the initially specified purpose must be considered to interfere with the right to data protection.

Data processing operations always require a legal basis. Article 8(2) CRF identifies the consent of the person concerned as a broadly applicable basis for the lawful processing of personal data. The prominent role of consent in data protection is an expression of informational self-determination.[124] Article 4(11) GDPR defines consent as "any freely given, specific, informed and unambiguous indication of the data subject's wishes by which he or she, by a statement or by a clear affirmative action, signifies agreement to the processing of personal data relating to him or her."[125] The consent of the person concerned cannot be valid as a legal basis for data processing operations when power and information asymmetries jeopardize effective informational self-determination.[126] In such circumstances, consent is neither informed nor freely given. The ECJ addressed an illustrative example in the *Schwarz v. Stadt Bochum* case. The ECJ observed that persons are not free to object to the processing of their fingerprints for a passport and that persons applying for passports cannot therefore be deemed to have consented to the processing of their personal data.[127] According to Article 8(2) CFR, other legitimate bases for the processing of personal data can be laid down by law.

2.2.2.3 Right of Access and Right to Rectify

The second sentence of Article 8(2) CFR contains two constituent parts of the right to data protection. Each of the two constituent parts contain a separate right for data subjects: the right of access to personal data that has been collected and the right to rectify that data. These two constituent parts provide further safeguards for the informational self-determination of individuals and the transparency of data

---

[122] Conseil d'État, *Les Pages Jaunes*, para. 9.

[123] Brouwer (2011), p. 279.

[124] The Article 29 WP sees the autonomy of the data subject as a pre-condition and a consequence of consent: it gives data subjects influence over the processing of information concerning them. See Article 29 WP (2011), pp. 8–9.

[125] Eleni Kosta warns that "the role of consent in this era is reduced, as the control of the individual over his personal information is overcome by the facilitation of everyday activities in electronic communications and especially the internet". See Kosta (2013), p. 399.

[126] Bergemann (2018), pp. 122–123; Zanfir (2014), p. 241; Lynskey (2015), pp. 189–190.

[127] ECJ, *Schwarz v. Stadt Bochum*, para. 32.

processing operations. The right of access to personal data enables data subjects to follow data processing operations, to verify the accuracy of their personal data, and to check the lawfulness of data processing operations.[128] The right of access to personal data must relate to past data processing operations.[129] Article 15 GDPR specifies that the data subject has the right to receive an array of information about processing operations involving their personal data including the purpose of the processing, the recipients to whom the data has been or will be disclosed, in particular recipients in third countries, and the envisaged period for which the data will be stored. The right to rectify personal data requires the data controller to rectify inaccurate personal data concerning the data subject. Article 16 GDPR demands that the rectification happens without undue delay. These rights have been framed as enabling the emancipatory engagement of individuals and as a legally supported variation of *sousveillance*.[130]

2.2.2.4 Independent Supervision

The last constituent part of the right to protection of personal data can be found in Article 8(3) CFR. This last constituent part provides that compliance with the rules in Article 8 CFR must be subject to control by an independent authority. The ECJ has repeatedly held that independent supervision is an essential component of the protection of individuals with regard to the processing of personal data.[131] The power asymmetries between data controllers and data subjects require a carefully crafted system of checks-and-balances.[132] The requirement of independent supervision over data protection rules is a safeguard that addresses accountability of informational power in a democratic society. Article 8(3) CFR guarantees individuals a right to lodge claims suing for the protection of their personal data.[133] The authority tasked with supervision must be independent. Article 52 GDPR requires that the independence of this authority must be secured legally and administratively. Article 8(3) CFR precludes that the supervisory authority is subject to directions or any other external influence, which could call the performance of its task into question.[134] The guarantee of independence is intended to ensure the effectiveness and reliability of the monitoring of compliance with data protection rules.[135]

---

128 Cp. Recital (41) Directive 95/46/EC.

129 ECJ, *Rijkeboer*, para. 54.

130 Sousveillance connotes the surveillance of the surveilling entity by the surveilled subjects. Rothmann (2017), p. 225.

131 ECJ, *Tele 2/Watson*, para. 123; ECJ, *Schrems*, para. 41; ECJ, *Commission v. Hungary,* para. 48; ECJ, *Commission v. Austria,* para. 36.

132 Nissenbaum (1998), p. 576.

133 ECJ, *Tele 2/Watson*, para. 123.

134 ECJ, Opinion 1/15, para. 230; ECJ, *Commission v. Germany,* para. 30.

135 ECJ, *Schrems*, para. 41.

The ECJ held in *Schrems* that the powers of the national supervisory authorities in the EU member states concern the processing of personal data carried out on their own territories.[136] With regard to the transfer of personal data from the EU to a third country, the ECJ concluded that it constitutes processing of personal data in an EU member state, and so in accordance with Article 8(3) CFR, the national supervisory authorities are responsible for the monitoring of compliance with data protection rules.[137]

2.2.3 Relationship with the Right to Private Life

The fundamental right to data protection in Article 8 CFR exists alongside and in addition to the right to private life in Article 7 CFR (Sect. 2.2.3.1). The two rights are distinct but share significant overlaps (Sect. 2.2.3.2). The ECJ still struggles to approach the two rights independently (Sect. 2.2.3.3). Nevertheless, the existence of the right to private life provides added value to the right to data protection (Sect. 2.2.3.4).

2.2.3.1 The Right to Private Life

The right to private life enshrined in Article 7 CFR provides that everyone has the right to respect for his or her private and family life, home, and communications.[138] It is first and foremost a defensive right to protect individuals against arbitrary interference by public authorities.[139] The explanations relating to the Charter underline that Article 7 CFR corresponds to Article 8 ECHR.[140] The meaning and scope of the right to private life in Article 7 CFR should therefore be read as the same as the right to private life in Article 8 ECHR according to Article 52(3) CFR. The ECtHR found interferences with Article 8 ECHR in cases concerning the interception and recording of telephone calls,[141] the storing of information relating to the private life of individuals,[142] and the examination of personal data from bulk interception of personal data.[143] The right to private life in Article 8 ECHR has a long history of

[136] Ibid., para. 44.

[137] Ibid., paras 44–47.

[138] The term right to private life is used here to refer to Article 7 CFR or Article 8 ECHR.

[139] The notion of privacy conceptually embraces the different guarantees of Article 7 CFR: The protection of private and family life, the protection of the home and the protection of communications. Rodotà (2009), p. 79.

[140] Explanations relating to the Charter of Fundamental Rights, 20.

[141] ECtHR, *Amman v. Switzerland,* para. 56.

[142] ECtHR, *Rotaru v. Romania*, para. 43.

[143] ECtHR, *Big Brother Watch and others v. United Kingdom*, para. 325.

protecting individuals against the processing of their personal data, especially concerning the surveillance practices of European countries.[144]

2.2.3.2 Distinct But Overlapping Rights

The Charter does not explain the difference or the relationship between the right to private life in Article 7 CFR and the right to data protection in Article 8 CFR. There is a lively debate among scholars regarding the nature of the relationship between these two rights in the Charter. Bart van der Sloot denies a separate function of the right to data protection and argues that data protection rules deserve protection under a fundamental rights framework already covered by the right to private life.[145] Orla Lynskey argues that the right to data protection grants individuals more rights over more personal data than the right to private life alone.[146] Paul de Hert and Serge Gutwirth portray the two rights as having separate functions. They see the right to private life as a tool of opacity that limits the illegitimate and excessive use of power, and have argued that the right to data protection is a tool of transparency directed toward channeling the legitimate use of power.[147] Maria Tzanou, for her part, criticizes this theory because it implies that data protection is not indispensable as a separate fundamental right.[148]

It is important not to lose sight of the systematic reality in this debate. The right to data protection has been enshrined as an independent fundamental right in the Charter. In this context, the right to data protection is considered, or expected, to add something new to the protection of fundamental rights. This was also recognized by the ECJ:

> It should be added, finally, that Article 8 of the Charter concerns a fundamental right which is distinct from that enshrined in Article 7 of the Charter and which has no equivalent in the ECHR.[149]

Orla Lynskey's model for the relationship between Articles 7 and 8 CFR seems to be the most convincing. She argues that the right to data protection overlaps considerably with the right to private life because they both ensure the privacy of individuals concerning their personal data, but that the right to data protection embodies a

144 De Hert and Gutwirth (2009), pp. 23–29.

145 van der Sloot (2017), p. 28.

146 Lynskey (2014), p. 588; Kokott and Sobotta (2013), p. 225.

147 De Hert and Gutwirth (2006), p. 62.

148 Tzanou (2013), p. 92.

149 When the British Court of Appeal (England & Wales) asked whether the scope of Articles 7 and 8 CFR expand beyond that of Article 8 ECHR, the ECJ refused to clarify their exact relationship because "justification for making a request for a preliminary ruling is not for advisory opinions to be delivered on general or hypothetical questions, but rather that it is necessary for the effective resolution of a dispute concerning EU law." ECJ, *Tele 2/Watson*, paras 129–130.

number of values that the right to private life does not include and vice versa.[150] Informational self-determination and transparency are important values that data protection rules aim to safeguard and which may distinguish the right to data protection from the right to private life.[151] Such an understanding is respectful of the development of data protection in Europe where privacy was not always the driving force. The two rights should be understood as distinct but overlapping.[152] The overlapping part of the two rights concerns data privacy. Nevertheless, the two rights construe data privacy differently based on their underlying values.

Almost all forms of processing of personal data fall under the scope of the right to data protection, regardless of any interference with the right to private life. In contrast, whether or not the processing of personal data also falls under the scope of the right to private life depends on the nature of the data and the context of the processing.[153] If a measure falls under the scope of both rights then each right should be independently applied based on their underlying values.

2.2.3.3 Combined Reading of the Two Rights

The jurisprudence of the ECJ does not (entirely) reflect the distinctive character of the right to data protection. The ECJ mentioned the right to data protection for the first time in 2008 in the case *Promusicae*.[154] This was before the Charter became legally binding. The ECJ referred to Article 8 CFR as "the right that guarantees protection of personal data and hence of private life."[155] The right to data protection was essentially perceived as a subset of the right to private life.[156] This perception was cemented in 2009 in the case *Rijkeboer* when the ECJ held that several constituent parts of the right to data protection formed part of the right to private life including the fair and lawful processing of personal data as well as the right of access to personal data and the right to rectify personal data.[157]

After the Charter became legally binding on 1 December 2009, *Schecke* was the first case in which the ECJ had to assess the validity of a secondary EU law in light of the right to data protection. The referring Administrative Court Wiesbaden (*Verwaltungsgericht Wiesbaden*) found that an obligation to publish the personal data of farmers who received agricultural funds on the internet constituted an unjustified interference with the right to data protection without mentioning the

---

[150] Lynskey (2015), pp. 103–104, 130; Kokott and Sobotta (2013), p. 228.

[151] Lynskey (2014), p. 588; ECJ, AG Opinion, *Digital Rights Ireland*, para. 57.

[152] Ferretti (2014), p. 851.

[153] ECJ, *Österreichischer Rundfunk*, para. 74; ECJ, *Digital Rights Ireland*, para. 27.

[154] ECJ, *Promusicae*, para. 64.

[155] Ibid., para. 63.

[156] Paul de Hert and Serge Gutwirth criticize the ECJ of viewing "data protection as privacy, no more no less". de Hert and Gutwirth (2009), p. 33.

[157] ECJ, *Rijkeboer*, paras 49, 64.

right to private life.[158] The ECJ, however, invented a formula expressing the two rights as one "right to respect for private life with regard to the processing of personal data, recognized by Articles 7 and 8 CFR."[159] The ECJ added that the limitations which may lawfully be imposed on the right to data protection correspond to those tolerated in relation to the right to private life enshrined in Article 8 ECHR.[160] These findings created the impression that the right to data protection cannot operate alone without the right to private life.[161]

The ECJ took an important step in 2011 with the case *Scarlet* concerning an injunction requiring internet service providers to install a filtering system that actively monitors all electronic communications on their network in order to prevent infringements of intellectual property rights. The ECJ found that such an injunction may infringe the right to data protection in Article 8 CFR and the freedom to receive or impart information in Article 11 CFR.[162] The ECJ thus abandoned the *Schecke* formula and recognized an independent character of the right to data protection. The Grand Chamber of the ECJ took another step in 2014 with the case *Digital Rights Ireland* concerning the validity of Directive 2006/24/EC (Data Retention Directive, DRD) which obliged providers of publicly available electronic communications services or public communications networks to retain certain types of data and make them available to national authorities for the purposes of fighting serious crime. The ECJ found that Directive 2006/24/EC raised questions relating to the right to private life in Article 7 CFR, the right to data protection in Article 8 CFR, and the right to freedom of expression in Article 11 CFR, and subsequently explained why the retention of traffic and location data under Directive 2006/24/EC affected these three rights.[163] However, the explanations concerning the right to data protection were not very extensive. The ECJ simply stated that Directive 2006/24/EC interfered with the right to data protection because it provided for the processing of personal data without further clarifying which constituents of Article 8 CFR were affected.[164]

The Grand Chamber of the ECJ consolidated that approach in *Tele2/Watson* concerning the compatibility of Swedish and British data retention requirements and in Opinion 1/15 concerning the PNR agreement between the EU and Canada.[165] Contrary to the interferences with Articles 7 and 8 CFR, lawful limitations on the two rights were assessed together. This consolidated approach shows that the ECJ prefers a combined reading of Articles 7 and 8 CFR.[166] The combined reading reflects the fact that there are overlaps between the two distinct fundamental rights.

---

[158] ECJ, *Schecke*, para. 30.

[159] Ibid., para. 52.

[160] Ibid.

[161] Tzanou (2017a), p. 55.

[162] ECJ, *Scarlet Extended*, para. 50.

[163] ECJ, *Digital Rights Ireland*, para. 25.

[164] Ibid., para. 36.

[165] ECJ, *Tele2/Watson*, para. 129; ECJ, Opinion 1/15, paras 125–126.

[166] Hustinx (2017), p. 172.

However, Maria Tzanou argues that this is an unnecessary circumvention of the Charter.[167] In order to validate the constitutional reality as it is found in the Charter, the two rights should be independently applied based on their underlying values. This is also underlined by the fact that the GDPR only refers to the right to data protection.

2.2.3.4 The Added Value of Having Two Fundamental Rights

There is an added value of having both fundamental rights, the right to private life and the right to data protection, recognized in the Charter. From the perspective of the right to data protection, much can be gained from the right to private life. If data processing operations are fair; conducted for the purpose initially specified; have a legitimate basis; and when access to the data is granted, rectification of the data is possible, and independent supervision is in place – in short, when all constituent parts of the right to data protection are respected – the right to private life in Article 7 CFR offers additional protection to individuals in the field of data privacy.

The ECJ specifically determined that the protection of the right to private life in Article 7 CFR requires that derogations from and limitations on the protection of personal data must apply only in so far as is strictly necessary.[168] The strict necessity test superimposed on the protection of personal data by Article 7 CFR offers additional safeguards for data subjects. The jurisprudence of the ECtHR on limitations of the right to private life in Article 8 ECHR is a rich source of inspiration in this regard. The ECJ has found analogies to previous cases of the ECtHR:

- EU legislation must impose minimum safeguards so that the persons whose data have been retained have sufficient guarantees to effectively protect their personal data against the risk of abuse and against any unlawful access and use of that data;[169]
- the need for such safeguards is all the greater where personal data are subjected to automatic processing and where there is a significant risk of unlawful access to those data;[170]
- access, as a general rule, can only be granted to secure the objective of fighting crime if the individual whose data is being processed is suspected of planning,

[167] Tzanou (2017a), p. 41.

[168] ECJ, *Satamedia*, para. 56; ECJ, *Schecke*, para. 77; ECJ, *Digital Rights Ireland*, para. 52; ECJ, *Schrems*, para. 92; ECJ, *Tele2/Watson*, para. 96.

[169] ECJ, *Digital Right Ireland*, para. 54 in analogy, as regards Article 8 ECHR, to ECtHR, *Liberty and Others v. the United Kingdom*, para. 62; ECtHR, *Rotaru v. Romania*, paras 57–59; ECtHR, *S. and Marper v. the United Kingdom*, para. 102.

[170] ECJ, *Digital Right Ireland*, para. 54 in analogy, as regards Article 8 ECHR, to ECtHR, *S. and Marper v. the United Kingdom*, para. 103; ECtHR, *M. K. v. France*, para. 35.

committing or having committed a serious crime or of being implicated in one way or another in such a crime;[171] and
- that, except for cases of validly established urgency, such access has to be subject to a prior review carried out either by a court or by an independent administrative body, and that the decision of that court or body must be made following a reasoned request by the authorities.[172]

The combined reading of Articles 7 and 8 CFR has allowed the ECJ to take the standards of the right to private life into account when deciding cases in the field of data privacy. However, the same result could be achieved when both rights are addressed independently.

2.2.4 Limitations on the Right to Data Protection

The fundamental right to data protection is not absolute. Limitations on the exercise of the right to data protection are possible when they meet certain conditions. There is some confusion as to when an interference with the right to data protection actually takes place (Sect. 2.2.4.1). Any limitation on a fundamental right must respect the essence of the right. The essence of the right to private life (Sect. 2.2.4.2) and the right to data protection (Sect. 2.2.4.3) should be assessed independently. The remaining conditions for lawful limitations on fundamental rights will be addressed afterwards (Sect. 2.2.4.4).

2.2.4.1 Interference with the Right to Data Protection

There is some confusion as to when an interference with the right to data protection actually takes place. It is necessary to first determine whether the right to data protection is enshrined in the first paragraph of Article 8 CFR or in Article 8 CFR taken as a whole. If we consider that the first paragraph entails the right to data protection, any processing of personal data will automatically interfere with the fundamental right in Article 8 CFR. If we accept, however, that the right to data protection is not confined to the first paragraph, but established by all three paragraphs taken together, an interference can only occur when the processing of personal data does not respect one or more of the constituent parts of the fundamental right in Article 8 CFR.

[171] ECJ, *Tele2/Watson*, para. 119 in analogy, as regards Article 8 ECHR, to ECtHR, *Zakharov v. Russia*, para. 260.

[172] ECJ, *Tele2/Watson*, para. 120 in analogy, as regards Article 8 ECHR, to ECtHR, *Szabó and Vissy v. Hungary*, paras 77, 80.

The ECJ has so far followed the former approach.[173] The ECJ seems to assume that there is a tension between the first and the subsequent paragraphs of Article 8 CFR. The Court's approach seems to be that the general principle in the first paragraph contains a prohibition on data processing operations and the other paragraphs contain the conditions for exceptions to this prohibition. For example, the ECJ found in Opinion 1/15 an interference with Article 8(1) CFR because the measure in question involved the processing of personal data.[174] The ECJ concluded that the requirements for a justification of the interference according to Article 52(1) CFR are not fulfilled. Only afterwards did the ECJ address some of the constituent parts of the right to data protection in Article 8(2) and (3) CFR.[175]

The scope of Article 8 CFR—involving all processing of personal data—should not be confused with the question of whether the right to data protection has been interfered with.[176] There are significant reasons to follow the latter approach, which establishes the right to data protection in Article 8 CFR taken as a whole.[177] For example, the approach of the ECJ ends up inflating the right to data protection. Any transfer of personal data outside the EU would constitute an interference with the right to data protection. Such an interpretation is not reconcilable with the development of the right to data protection, which must be seen in light of changes in society, social progress, and scientific and technological developments. Data processing operations are part of everyday life. It would thus undermine the concept of fundamental rights if every data processing operation was viewed as an interference with the right to data protection. Data protection enables data processing operations according to certain rules rather than impeding them. The presumption of the right to data protection should be that data processing operations are allowed and necessary in the digital age.[178] AG Siegbert Alber wrote that "there would be no need for data protection if there were a general prohibition of information disclosure."[179]

I thus argue that an interference with the right to data protection enshrined in Article 8 CFR only takes place if a data processing operation is not fair, is not conducted for the purpose initially specified, does not have a legitimate basis, and when the data subject cannot access or rectify his or her data, or if there is no independent supervision controlling the implementation of these rules. An interference with the right to data protection is thus an interference with one or more of its constituent parts. There are indications that this point of view has slowly begun to influence jurisprudence. AG Henrik Saugmandsgaard Øe wrote in a footnote of his

[173] ECJ, *Schecke*, para. 49; ECJ, *Deutsche Telekom*, para. 51; ECJ, *Digital Rights Ireland*, para. 36; ECJ, Opinion 1/15, para. 126.

[174] ECJ, Opinion 1/15, para. 126.

[175] The ECJ did not address the constituents of fairness and purpose specification in Article 8(2) CFR. See ibid., paras 218, 228.

[176] Hustinx (2017), p. 140.

[177] Ibid., 140–141; Tzanou (2017a), p. 63; González Fuster and Gellert (2012), p. 78.

[178] van der Sloot (2017), p. 22; Floridi (2006), p. 116.

[179] ECJ, AG Opinion, *The Queen v. Minister of Agriculture, Fisheries and Food*, para. 41.

opinion in *Schrems 2* that "[i]nfringement of that right assumes that personal data have been processed in breach of those requirements" by which he referred to the written constituents of the right to data protection.[180] Similarly, the ECJ stated in *Schrems 2* that access to personal data falls within the scope of Article 8 CFR because it constitutes the processing of personal data and, accordingly, must satisfy the requirements laid down in that article.[181] The Court did not automatically find an interference here.

2.2.4.2 The Essence of the Right to Private Life

Any limitation on the exercise of the rights recognized by the Charter must respect the essence of those rights according to Article 52(1) CFR.[182] The essence—sometimes referred to as the minimum, essential, or absolute core of a right—represents the untouchable part of a fundamental right that cannot be limited, diminished, restricted or interfered with. Any interference with the essence of a fundamental right would make the right lose its value for the right holder and for society as a whole.[183] The essence is the absolute barrier for limitations of a fundamental right and affords protection against the most extreme and blatant forms of interference with fundamental rights for which justifications do not exist.[184] This is why interferences with the essence should be identified independently from the assessment of proportionality.[185] The application of the essence is reserved for rare cases in which the assessment of proportionality does not have a grip. The essence of a fundamental right cannot usually be determined in light of the formulation in the Charter.[186] Instead, the identification of the essence is a matter of interpretation and should also reflect the underlying values of a fundamental right. The starting point should be the question of whether the interference with a fundamental right makes it impossible to exercise this right.[187] It then needs to be verified whether the interference calls into question the fundamental right as such.[188]

The ECJ found in *Digital Rights Ireland* that the retention of data required by Directive 2006/24/EC (Data Retention Directive, DRD) was a particularly serious interference but did not adversely affect the essence of Article 7 CFR because the

---

[180] ECJ, AG Opinion, *Schrems 2*, para. 256, fn. 120.

[181] ECJ, *Schrems 2*, para. 170.

[182] The ECHR does not contain any express reference to the essence of human rights, but the jurisprudence of the ECtHR regularly refers to the essence of human rights. See ECtHR, *Mürsel Eren v. Turkey*, para. 44; ECtHR, *Prince Hans-Adam II of Liechtenstein v. Germany*, para. 44.

[183] Brkan (2018), p. 333.

[184] Ojanen (2016), p. 322.

[185] Brkan (2019), p. 867.

[186] Ojanen (2016), p. 326.

[187] Brkan (2019), p. 869.

[188] ECJ, *Puškár*, para. 64; ECJ, *Florescu*, para. 55; ECJ, *Spasic*, para. 58.

DRD "not permit the acquisition of knowledge of the content of the electronic communications as such."[189] The DRD only obliged telecommunication and internet service providers to retain data relating to their users, notably their names and addresses, date, time, duration and type of communication as well as IP addresses (so-called "metadata" referring to the who, when, and where of a communication). The ECJ added in *Schrems* that

> legislation permitting the public authorities to have access on a generalised basis to the content of electronic communications must be regarded as compromising the essence of the fundamental right to respect for private life, as guaranteed by Article 7 of the Charter.[190]

The distinction between the metadata and content of electronic communications has been widely criticized.[191] Thomas Ojanen points out that the difference in value for surveillance proposes between metadata and the content of electronic communications is rapidly fading away in a modern network environment.[192] Maja Brkan reproaches the ECJ for apprehending interferences with the essence of Article 7 CFR as a matter of degree rather than type.[193] Although the ECJ recognized that metadata "is no less sensitive, having regard to the right to privacy, than the actual content of communications" in *Tele2/Watson*, the Court still found that access to such data does not adversely affect the essence of Article 7 CFR.[194] The ECJ added new elements to the interpretation of the essence of the right to private life in Opinion 1/15. The Court found that even though passenger name data may reveal very specific information concerning the private life of a person, the nature of that information is limited to certain aspects of private life (information relating to air travel between Canada and the EU).[195] The ECJ again used a gradual benchmark regarding the number of aspects of the private life covered in order to determine whether an interference with the essence of the right to private life occurred.[196]

2.2.4.3 The Essence of the Right to Data Protection

It is (even) less clear what constitutes an interference with the essence of the right to data protection in Article 8 CFR. The ECJ found in *Digital Rights Ireland* that the retention of data does not adversely affect the essence of Article 8 CFR because the

---

[189] ECJ, *Digital Rights Ireland*, para. 39.

[190] ECJ, *Schrems*, para. 94.

[191] Ojanen (2016), p. 328; Zuiderveen and Arnbak (2015), p. 35; Granger and Irion (2014) 847.

[192] Ojanen (2016), p. 328. "[W]e kill with metadata" is a phrase originally from General Michael Hayden, former director of the NSA and the CIA, and relates to a comment from NSA General Counsel Stewart Baker that "metadata absolutely tells you everything about somebody's life. If you have enough metadata, you don't really need content." See Cole (2014).

[193] Brkan (2019) 869, 872, 875.

[194] ECJ, *Tele2/Watson*, paras 99–101.

[195] ECJ, Opinion 1/15, para. 150.

[196] Brkan (2019), pp. 877–878.

DRD required that "certain principles of data protection and data security must be respected."[197] The ECJ required EU member states to ensure that "appropriate technical and organisational measures are adopted against accidental or unlawful destruction, accidental loss or alteration of the data."[198] From this, it seems that the ECJ adopted a technological approach to the essence of Article 8 CFR. The absence of any data security measures certainly constitutes a violation of the GDPR but it is difficult to imagine that this would also adversely affect the essence of the right to data protection or even interfere with the right to data protection at all.[199] Orla Lynskey observes that data security is not even a constituent part of Article 8 CFR.[200] The simple absence of data security measures do not call the whole right to data protection with its constituents into question.

The ECJ changed course in *Tele2/Watson* and seemed to suggest that Article 7 and Article 8 CFR share a common essence. The ECJ found that the data retention legislation in Sweden and the UK "does not permit retention of the content of a communication and is not, therefore, such as to affect adversely the essence of those *rights*."[201] It is unclear if the use of the plural concerning rights was actually intended. The ECJ again distinguished between the essence of Articles 7 and 8 CFR in Opinion 1/15. The Court found that the draft PNR agreement does not adversely affect the essence of Article 8 CFR because the purposes for which PNR data may be processed are limited and because rules exist to ensure, *inter alia,* the security, confidentiality and integrity of that data, and to protect it against unlawful access and processing.[202] The ECJ continued in Opinion 1/15 to reduce the essence of the right to data protection to security measures.[203] At the same time, the ECJ also introduced the principle of purpose limitation from Article 6(1)(b) Directive 95/46/EC to the essence of Article 8 CFR. Contrary to data security, purpose limitation is partly reflected in the constituent part focused on purpose specification in Article 8(2) CFR. It is questionable that any limitations to the constituent part on purpose specification would automatically affect the core of data protection. It would also be contrary to the wording of Article 52(1) CFR that allows lawful limitations on purpose specification in Article 8(2) CFR. Maria Tzanou thus suggests that the purpose limitation principle found in the constituent part on purpose specification needs to be understood as itself having a core which

[197] ECJ, *Digital Rights Ireland*, para. 40.

[198] Ibid.

[199] See Articles 5(1)(f), 32–34 GDPR. Similarly, Brkan (2019) 880.

[200] She submits that the ECJ might be suggesting that the essence of the right to data protection is not an objective (or value) of Article 8 CFR (such as privacy, informational self-determination, transparency or democracy) but rather it is the means of achieving data protection that constitutes the essence of Article 8 CFR. See Lynskey (2015), p. 172.

[201] The ECJ referred by analogy to the analysis of Article 7 CFR in *Digital Rights Ireland*. See ECJ, *Tele2/Watson*, para. 101 [emphasis added].

[202] ECJ, Opinion 1/15, para. 150.

[203] Brkan (2019), p. 880.

cannot be limited.[204] This also applies to the other constituent parts of Article 8 CFR.

The essence of the right to data protection should be interpreted in such a way that the underlying values of data protection are not made obsolete. Damian Clifford and Jef Ausloos agree that data protection's underlying rationales should be used to interpret the essence of Article 8 CFR.[205] They submit that a "robust architecture of control" aimed at individual autonomy should be the essence of the right to data protection.[206] Such an understanding resonates well with the ECJ's finding that an interference with the essence of a fundamental right would call into question the fundamental right as such. If informational self-determination or any other value of data protection is undermined to the point of becoming obsolete, the right to data protection loses its value for the right holder and for society as a whole.

2.2.4.4 Lawful Limitations

According to Article 52(1) CFR, any limitation on fundamental rights must be provided for by law (Sect. 2.2.4.4.1), genuinely meet objectives of general interest recognized by the EU or the need to protect the rights and freedoms of others (Sect. 2.2.4.4.2) and satisfy the requirement of proportionality (Sect. 2.2.4.4.3).

2.2.4.4.1 Legal Basis

The requirement that any limitation on the exercise of fundamental rights must be provided for by law implies that the legal basis which permits a limitation must itself already define the scope of the limitation.[207] The legal basis must indicate in what circumstances and under which conditions data processing operations take place and impose minimum safeguards providing sufficient guarantees for individuals to effectively protect their personal data against the risk of abuse.[208] These safeguards are particularly important where personal data is subject to automated processing and involves sensitive data.[209]

---

[204] Tzanou (2017a), p. 44.

[205] Clifford and Ausloos (2018), pp. 144–145.

[206] Orla Lynskey seems to agree with the proposition that the foundational values of data protection are important to interpret the essence of Article 8 CFR. She argues, however, that privacy should constitute the essence of Article 8 CFR and not individual control over personal data. Although she does propagate a broader understanding of an architecture of control, she does not refer to such an understanding here. See Lynskey (2015), p. 271.

[207] ECJ, Opinion 1/15, para. 139; ECJ, *WebMindLicenses*, para. 81.

[208] ECJ, Opinion 1/15, para. 141; ECJ, *Tele2/Watson*, para. 109; ECJ, *Schrems*, para. 91; ECJ, *Digital Rights Ireland*, para. 54.

[209] ECJ, Opinion 1/15, para. 141; ECJ, *Schrems*, para. 91; ECJ, *Digital Rights Ireland*, para. 55.

2.2.4.4.2 Objectives of General Interest and Protection of the Rights of Others

Any limitation on the exercise of fundamental rights must genuinely meet objectives of general interest recognized by the Union or the need to protect the rights and freedoms of others.

The reference to general interests recognized by the Union covers primarily the objectives mentioned in Article 3 TEU.[210] The jurisprudence of the ECJ is quite generous in this regard and has acknowledged a wide range of interests as being recognized by the EU so far.[211] For example, the fight against international terrorism[212] and serious crime,[213] transparency,[214] and public health[215] to name but a few. However, purely economic objectives are not accepted as general interests for introducing a limitation to a fundamental right.[216] The ECJ determined with regard to the processing of personal data carried out in the context of an online search engine that an interference with Article 8 CFR "cannot be justified by merely the economic interest which the operator of such an engine has in that processing."[217]

The reference to the rights and freedoms of others covers the rights and freedoms guaranteed in the Charter. Recital (4) GDPR underlines that the right to data protection is not absolute and must be balanced against other fundamental rights. It mentions specifically the freedom of thought, conscience, and religion in Article 10 CFR, the freedom of expression and information in Article 11 CFR, and the freedom to conduct a business in Article 16 CFR.

2.2.4.4.3 Proportionality

The right to data protection must be considered in relation to its function in society.[218] The ECJ never clarified what the function of the right to data protection in society exactly is. Its function thus must be interpreted on the basis of its underlying values.[219] The right to data protection recognizes the inevitability and benefits of data processing operations, but also seeks to prevent disproportionate negative impacts on the individual and society.[220] This is the balance that

[210] Explanations relating to the Charter of Fundamental Rights, 32.

[211] Lenaerts (2012), pp. 391–392.

[212] ECJ, *Kadi,* para. 363.

[213] ECJ, *Tsakouridis*, paras 46–47.

[214] ECJ, *Schecke*, para. 67.

[215] ECJ, *Standley*, para. 56.

[216] Koukiadaki (2019), p. 125.

[217] ECJ, *Google Spain*, para. 81.

[218] ECJ, Opinion 1/15, para. 136; ECJ, *Schwarz v. Stadt Bochum*, para. 33; ECJ, *Schecke*, para. 48.

[219] Mifsud Bonnici (2014), p. 134.

[220] Ferretti (2014), p. 7.

proportionality for limitations on the right to data protection must achieve. Measures must be appropriate in light of the objective pursued and limited to what is strictly necessary.[221] The ECJ examines if there are other measures which affect less adversely the fundamental rights in question and still contribute effectively to the objectives of general interest recognized by the EU or the protection of the rights and freedoms of others.

In 2005, AG Philippe Léger limited the scope of judicial control for the proportionality assessment of the PNR regime with the US based on the wide discretion of the European Commission and the Council in the field of public security.[222] In contrast, in 2017, the ECJ almost acquired the role of legislator itself due to its precise analysis and instructions in the proportionality assessment of the PNR regime with Canada.[223] Detailed safeguards have become very important for limitations on the exercise of the right to data protection in Article 8 CFR.

2.2.5 Summary

The right to data protection in Article 8 CFR protects individuals by structuring and limiting the legal use of their personal data. The right to data protection in Article 8 CFR exists alongside and in addition to the right to private life in Article 7 CFR. The two rights are distinct but share significant overlaps. Each right should be independently applied based on their underlying values. However, the ECJ continues to struggle to apply the right to data protection independently and prefers a combined reading of the two rights. The scope of Article 8 CFR extends to all data processing operation involving personal data of individuals located in the EU. The scope should not be confused with the question of whether the right to data protection has been interfered with. The right to data protection is enshrined in Article 8 CFR taken as a whole including all three paragraphs. The six written constituent parts of the right to data protection are fairness, purpose specification, legitimate basis, the right of access to personal data, the right to rectify personal data, and independent supervision. An interference with Article 8 CFR is an interference with one or more of its constituent parts. Whether such an interference is lawful needs to be examined according to Article 52 CFR. The development of the right to data protection is focused on technological progress and the associated new powers of the state and does not relate to trade concerns.[224] The foundational values of data protection are privacy, informational self-determination, transparency, and

---

221 ECJ, Opinion 1/15, para. 140; ECJ, *Tele2/Watson*, paras 96, 103; ECJ, *Schrems*, para. 92; ECJ, *Digital Rights Ireland*, paras 51–52.

222 ECJ, AG Opinion, *Parliament v. Council and Commission*, para. 246.

223 ECJ, Opinion 1/15, paras 133–231; Kuner (2018), pp. 880–881; Kuner (2017a); Hijmans (2017), p. 410.

224 See Brkan (2016), p. 815.

democracy. The origin of the right to data protection and these values are useful both for the interpretation of the right itself and the determination of its lawful limitations.

2.3 The Extraterritorial Dimension of the Right to Data Protection

The extraterritorial dimension of the right to data protection describes the influence of the fundamental right outside the EU. The jurisprudence of the ECJ on transfers of personal data to third countries reveals an unwritten constituent part of the right to data protection. I argue that the right to data protection, in addition to the six written constituent parts outlined before, contains a right to continuous protection of personal data that is transferred to a third country, which is essentially equivalent to the protection guaranteed within the EU (Sect. 2.3.1). The literature suggests that the assertion of extraterritorial jurisdiction can be categorized either as extraterritoriality (as such) or as territorial extension. The distinction of these two categories is important because extraterritorial jurisdiction has a potential to clash with the prohibition of interfering with the internal affairs of another state or of violating the right to territorial integrity and political independence of another state and must therefore be considered a matter of international law. The right to continuous protection of personal data in Article 8 CFR is a form of territorial extension of Union law because data transfers have a strong territorial connection with the EU (Sect. 2.3.2). Justification of the territorial extension can be found in the EU Treaties, in the Charter and the values of data protection (Sect. 2.3.3). The extraterritorial dimension of the right to data protection operates with the standard of protection that is essential equivalent to the level of protection that is guaranteed within the EU. In order to apply the standard of essential equivalence, it must be clear what its comparison, meaning, level of protection, and limitations are (Sect. 2.3.4).

2.3.1 The Right to Continuous Protection of Personal Data

The jurisprudence of the ECJ on the transfer of personal data to third countries reveals an unwritten constituent of the right to data protection. The judgment *Schrems* (Sect. 2.3.1.1), Opinion 1/15 (Sect. 2.3.1.2), the opinion of AG Henrik Saugmandsgaard Øe on *Schrems 2* (Sect. 2.3.1.3), and the judgment *Schrems 2* (Sect. 2.3.1.4) highlight the development of the right to continuous protection of personal data that is transferred to a third country.

2.3.1.1 Continuous Protection of Personal Data in Schrems

The *Schrems* case involved a dispute between a private citizen and Facebook user Maximilian Schrems and the Irish Data Protection Commissioner (DPC). Decision 2000/520, the Safe Harbor adequacy decision, allowed transfers of personal data from the EU to companies in the US if the companies in the US subscribed to the Safe Harbor framework. The Safe Harbor framework entailed data protection principles for US companies. Schrems made a complaint to the DPC in which he asked the DPC to prohibit Facebook Ireland Ldt. to transfer his personal data to Facebook Inc. in the US. Schrems was of the opinion that the law and practice in the US did not ensure adequate protection for his personal data against the surveillance practices of US public authorities.[225] The DPC saw no evidence that Schrems' personal data had been accessed by US public authorities and rejected his complaint. The DPC explained that the European Commission had found in Decision 2000/520 that the US ensures an adequate level of protection for personal data.[226] Schrems challenged the rejection of his complaint before the Irish High Court (IHC) who considered that there are serious doubts as to whether the US really ensures an adequate level of protection for personal data and that the DPC should have investigated the complaint.[227] The IHC stated that Decision 2000/520 did not satisfy the requirements of Articles 7 and 8 CFR and referred the case to the ECJ. The Grand Chamber of the ECJ decided in 2015 that the issue demanded an examination of the validity of Decision 2000/520 in light of the Charter.[228] The legal basis of the contested Decision 2000/520 was Article 25(6) Directive 46/95/EC. The ECJ noted that Article 25(6) Directive 46/95/EC required that a third country ensures an adequate level of protection for personal data.[229]

> [It] implements the express obligation laid down in Article 8(1) of the Charter to protect personal data and [. . .] is intended to ensure that the high level of that protection continues where personal data is transferred to a third country.[230]

The ECJ also defined the term adequate level of protection in Article 25(6) Directive 46/95/EC.

> [It] must be understood as requiring the third country in fact to ensure [. . .] a level of protection of fundamental rights and freedoms that is essentially equivalent to that guaranteed within the [EU] by virtue of Directive 95/46 read in the light of the Charter.[231]

The ECJ noted that Decision 2000/520 did not require US public authorities to comply with the data protection principles set out therein and that US national

---

[225] ECJ, *Schrems*, para. 28.

[226] Ibid., para. 29.

[227] Ibid., para. 33.

[228] Ibid., paras 36, 67.

[229] Ibid., para. 71.

[230] Ibid., para. 72.

[231] Ibid., para. 73.

security, public interest or law enforcement requirements had primacy over those principles.[232] Decision 2000/520 thus enabled interference with EU fundamental rights by US public authorities based on US interests or on US legislation.[233] The ECJ also addressed limitations on fundamental rights, although without explicitly referring to US legislation. The ECJ explained in which instances legislation concerning the storage of and access to personal data is not limited to what is strictly necessary and specified that legislation permitting public authorities to have access on a generalized basis to the content of electronic communications must be regarded as compromising the essence of the right to private life.[234] The ECJ formally invalidated Decision 2000/520 because the Commission did not state that the US in fact ensures an adequate level of data protection.[235]

Several points highlight how the ECJ started to develop the extraterritorial dimension of the right to data protection as an unwritten constituent part of the right to data protection in *Schrems*:

- The ECJ underlined that the legal mechanism for data transfers in Article 25(6) DPD implements the express obligation laid down in Article 8(1) CFR to protect personal data.
- The ECJ clarified that adequate protection for personal data in a third country in Article 25(6) DPD means protection that is essentially equivalent to the protection guaranteed in Directive 95/46/EC in light of the Charter. The ECJ thus created a standard of protection in a third country, which is essentially equivalent to that guaranteed within the EU.
- The ECJ stressed that the content of the standard of essential equivalence in Article 25(6) DPD is apparent in *Schrems* itself and referred to the explanations regarding the limitations on fundamental rights in the preceding paragraphs of the judgment.[236] The standard of essential equivalence entails the same limitations on fundamental rights as are in force in the EU.[237]
- Even though the ECJ did not invalidate Decision 2000/520 based on concrete interferences of US legislation with EU fundamental rights, the *Schrems* judgment indicates that data transfers based on Decision 2000/520 enable

232 Ibid., paras 82–86.

233 Ibid., para. 87.

234 Ibid., para. 94.

235 Ibid., para. 97. It is a common misconception that the ECJ found in *Schrems* that US legislation did not meet EU fundamental rights standards. Koen Lenaerts, former president of the ECJ, noted in an interview that "[w]e are not judging the U.S. system here, we are judging the requirements of EU law in terms of the conditions to transfer data to third countries, whatever they be." Popp (2015); Kuner (2017b), p. 890.

236 ECJ, *Schrems*, para. 96; Vermeulen (2017), p. 69.

237 Maria Tzanou suggested that the ECJ opted to limit the application of the right to private life outside the EU territorial boundaries to the essence of the fundamental right. She does not, however, take into account para. 96 of the *Schrems* judgement where the ECJ refers to the level of protection apparent in the judgment itself, which includes more than just the essence of fundamental rights. See Tzanou (2017b), p. 559, with reference to Kuner (2015), pp. 243–244.

interferences with EU fundamental rights by US public authorities for purposes of US national security and public interest requirements or on US legislation.[238] This shows that the ECJ is willing to assess interferences of non-EU public authorities outside the EU with EU fundamental rights.

The ECJ started to develop a right to continuous protection for personal data in *Schrems* based on secondary EU law on transfers of personal data to third countries. This is similar to the written constituent parts of the right to data protection. The written constituent parts were also secondary EU law before their integration into the right to data protection.

2.3.1.2 Continuous Protection of Personal Data in Opinion 1/15

Opinion 1/15 was requested by the European Parliament in order to clarify *inter alia* whether or not the draft agreement between Canada and the EU on the transfer of passenger name record data (draft PNR agreement) is compatible with the Charter.[239] Air carriers are under an obligation in Canada to provide the Canada Border Services Agency with access to certain PNR data to the extent it is collected and contained in the air carrier's automated reservation and departure control systems.[240] The PNR data includes the name of an air passenger, information necessary to the reservation such as the dates of intended travel and the travel itinerary, information relating to tickets, groups of persons checked-in under the same reservation number, passenger contact information, information relating to the means of payment or billing, information concerning baggage, and other general remarks regarding a passenger. This information constitutes personal data.[241] Data protection rules in the EU do not allow European and other carriers operating flights from the EU to transmit the PNR data of their passengers to third countries which do not ensure an adequate level of protection of personal data without adding appropriate safeguards for such transfers.[242] Article 5 of the draft PNR agreement noted that subject to compliance with the draft PNR agreement, the Canadian authority responsible for receiving and processing the PNR data was deemed to provide an adequate level of protection.[243] This is why the draft PNR agreement mainly contained provisions regulating and limiting the processing of PNR data from the EU in Canada.

The ECJ found in Opinion 1/15 from 2016 that the transfer of PNR data from the EU to Canadian authorities and the framework negotiated by the EU with Canada for the conditions concerning the retention of that data, its use, and its subsequent

[238] ECJ, *Schrems*, para. 87.
[239] ECJ, Opinion 1/15, para. 1.
[240] Ibid., para. 21.
[241] Ibid., para. 121.
[242] Ibid., para. 21.
[243] Ibid., para. 30.

transfer from Canadian authorities to other Canadian authorities, Europol, Eurojust, judicial or police authorities of the EU member states or authorities of third countries constitute interferences with Article 7 and Article 8 CFR.[244] The ECJ went on to examine the justification for the interferences and found that the aim of the draft PNR agreement—namely, the fight against terrorist offences and serious transnational crime—constitutes an objective of general interest of the EU that is capable of justifying even serious interferences with the fundamental rights enshrined in Article 7 and Article 8 CFR.[245] The ECJ also found that the transfer of PNR data to Canada and the subsequent processing is appropriate for the purpose of ensuring public security.[246] However, some provisions in the draft PNR agreement regulating and restricting the processing of PNR data from the EU by Canadian authorities were not limited to what is strictly necessary.[247] The ECJ thus concluded that the draft PNR agreement was not compatible with Article 7 and Article 8 CFR.[248]

The ECJ continued to develop the extraterritorial dimension of the right to data protection as an unwritten constituent of the right to data protection in Opinion 1/15. Previously, the ECJ found that Article 25(6) Directive 95/46/EC implements the express obligation laid down in Article 8(1) CFR to protect personal data and that the provision is intended to ensure that the high level of that protection continues whenever personal data is transferred to a third country.[249] In Opinion 1/15, however, the ECJ clarified that it is the express obligation laid down in Article 8(1) CFR itself that contains the requirement that the high level of protection of fundamental rights and freedoms conferred by EU law continues when personal data is transferred from the EU to a third country:

> That right to the protection of personal data requires, inter alia, that the high level of protection of fundamental rights and freedoms conferred by EU law continues where personal data is transferred from the European Union to a non-member country.[250]

The ECJ did not stop there. In the same paragraph, the ECJ also included the standard of essential equivalence in Article 8(1) CFR:

> Even though the means intended to ensure such a level of protection may differ from those employed within the European Union in order to ensure that the requirements stemming from EU law are complied with, those means must nevertheless prove, in practice, effective in order to ensure protection essentially equivalent to that guaranteed within the European Union.[251]

244 Ibid., paras 125–126.

245 Ibid., para. 149.

246 Ibid., paras 152–153.

247 Ibid., paras 181, 203, 206, 211, 215, 217.

248 Ibid., para. 232(2) and (3).

249 ECJ, *Schrems*, para. 72.

250 ECJ, Opinion 1/15, para. 134.

251 Ibid.

The ECJ elevated the requirement of continuous protection and the standard of essential equivalence that it previously found in Article 25(6) Directive 95/46/EC to the level of the Charter. In *Schrems*, the ECJ interpreted EU secondary law on transfers of personal data in light of the Charter, while in Opinion 1/15, the ECJ used this interpretation as a standard of the Charter itself. The ECJ explained this elevation with a reference to the Preamble of the Charter, which underlines the necessity to strengthen the protection of fundamental rights in light of changes in society, social progress, and scientific and technological developments.[252]

The ECJ found therefore, that there is a right to continuous protection of personal data that is transferred to a third country, and that this right requires protection in the third country that is essentially equivalent to the protection guaranteed within the EU. The right to continuous protection of personal data is an unwritten constituent part of the right to data protection in Article 8(1) CFR. This right thus manifests the extraterritorial dimension of the right to data protection.

2.3.1.3 Continuous Protection of Personal Data in the AG Opinion on Schrems 2

Following the *Schrems* judgment, the IHC annulled the decision whereby the Irish DPC had rejected the complaint of Maximilian Schrems and referred the case back to the DPC for assessment.[253] The DPC opened a new investigation and requested Schrems to reformulate his complaint with regard to the invalidation of Decision 2000/520, the Safe Harbor adequacy decision.[254]

In his reformulated complaint, Schrems claimed that the standard data protection clauses, on which Facebook relied after the *Schrems* judgment for their data transfers, could not justify such transfers to the US because of the ongoing interference with the exercise of his rights guaranteed in Article 8 CFR.[255] Schrems requested the DPC to issue a prohibition notice suspending all transfers of personal data from Facebook Ireland Ldt. to Facebook Inc. in the US.[256] The DPC concluded that it was impossible to adjudicate Schrems' complaint unless the IHC examined the validity of Decision 2010/87 approving the standard data protection clauses in question.[257] In accordance with the *Schrems* judgment, the DPC brought proceedings before the IHC so that it could request the ECJ to make a preliminary ruling on the validity of Decision 2010/87.[258] The IHC found that the US carries out mass and indiscriminate processing of personal data that might potentially expose data subjects to violations

[252] Ibid., para. 135.
[253] ECJ, AG Opinion, *Schrems 2*, para. 45.
[254] Ibid.
[255] Ibid., para. 47.
[256] Ibid.
[257] Ibid., para. 51.
[258] Ibid.; ECJ, *Schrems*, para. 65.

of the rights which they derive from Article 7 and Article 8 CFR.[259] Accordingly, the IHC questioned whether the standard data protection clauses provided for in Decision 2010/87 ensured the protection of the data subjects' fundamental rights.[260] The IHC shared the doubts as to the validity of Decision 2010/87.[261] The IHC thus decided to refer the issue to the ECJ for a preliminary ruling.[262]

AG Henrik Saugmandsgaard Øe stated in his opinion on *Schrems 2* that in the absence of common personal data protection safeguards at the global level, cross-border flows of personal data entail a risk of a breach in the protection guaranteed in the EU.[263] He agreed with Schrems and the Irish DPC that standard data protection clauses must also guarantee that the individuals whose personal data is transferred to a third country benefit from a level of protection of their personal data which is essentially equivalent to that guaranteed within the EU.[264] He underlined that the requirements for the protection of fundamental rights guaranteed by the Charter do not differ according to the legal mechanisms for a specific transfer in the GDPR.[265] He further explained that the legal mechanisms for data transfers are aimed at ensuring the continuity of the high level of protection for personal data even outside the EU.[266] He stressed that the continuity of the level of protection is designed to avoid circumvention of the standards applicable within the Union.[267]

With regard to Decision 2010/87, AG Saugmandsgaard Øe found that the standard data protection clauses are valid even though they represent a legal mechanism applicable to data transfers irrespective of the third country and the level of protection guaranteed there.[268] He suggested that the compatibility of Decision 2010/87 with the Charter depends on whether there are sufficiently sound mechanisms in place to ensure that data transfers based on the standard contractual clauses are suspended or prohibited in the event that those clauses are breached or impossible to honor.[269] He thus argued that the burden of responsibility lies with the data exporter and insisted that supervisory authorities must examine whether the laws of the third country constitute an obstacle to the implementation of the standard data protection clauses and, therefore, a violation of fundamental rights.[270]

---

[259] ECJ, AG Opinion, *Schrems 2*, para. 65.

[260] Ibid., para. 74.

[261] Ibid.

[262] Ibid., para. 76.

[263] Ibid., para. 1.

[264] Ibid., para. 115.

[265] Ibid., 117. He added in fn. 46 that this is so without prejudice to the possibility of transferring personal data subject to the derogations provided for in Article 49(1) GDPR.

[266] Ibid.

[267] Ibid., para. 204.

[268] Ibid., paras 120, 160.

[269] Ibid., para. 127.

[270] Ibid., para. 126.

Ultimately, AG Saugmandsgaard Øe continued the implementation the extraterritorial dimension of the right to data protection as an unwritten constituent part of the right to data protection in his opinion on *Schrems 2*. He did not however explicitly state that the right to data protection requires that the high level of protection of fundamental rights and freedoms conferred by Union law continues where personal data is transferred from the EU to a third country.[271] Instead, he referred to the second sentence of Article 44 GDPR that requires legal mechanisms be in place for data transfers to third countries to ensure that the level of protection guaranteed by the GDPR is not undermined.[272] This second sentence was added to Article 44 GDPR during the trilogue negotiations and refers to the extraterritorial dimension of the right to data protection.[273] It implies that the "requirements of protection of fundamental rights guaranteed by the Charter do not differ according to the legal basis for a specific transfer."[274] This is why standard data protection clauses must also guarantee that the rights of individuals whose personal data is transferred to a third country benefit from a level of protection essentially equivalent to that which follows from the GDPR read in the light of the Charter.[275] The opinion of AG Saugmandsgaard Øe on *Schrems 2* confirms that individuals have a right to continuous protection for personal data.

2.3.1.4 Continuous Protection of Personal Data in Schrems 2

The ECJ largely followed the opinion of AG Henrik Saugmandsgaard Øe in *Schrems 2*. The ECJ explicitly referred to the AG's opinion and confirmed that all the provisions in Chapter V of the GDPR are intended to ensure the continuity of the high level of protection for personal data in the EU.[276] The Court held that data subjects must be afforded a level of protection essentially equivalent to that which is guaranteed within the EU whenever their personal data is transferred to a third country.[277]

Similarly to the AG, the ECJ did not explicitly state that the right to data protection in Article 8 CFR requires that the high level of protection of fundamental rights and freedoms conferred by Union law continues where personal data is transferred from the EU to a third country.[278] Rather, the Court underlined that Article 44 GDPR requires that the level of protection for personal data, essentially equivalent to that guaranteed within the EU, must be guaranteed irrespective of the

[271] Cp. ECJ, Opinion 1/15, para. 134.

[272] ECJ, AG Opinion, *Schrems 2*, para. 117.

[273] Schantz (2019), p. 970; see Sect. 3.1.1.4.

[274] ECJ, AG Opinion, *Schrems 2*, para. 117.

[275] Ibid., para. 115.

[276] ECJ, *Schrems 2*, para. 93.

[277] Ibid., para. 96.

[278] Cp. ECJ, Opinion 1/15, para. 134.

legal mechanism on which a transfer of personal data to a third country is carried out.[279] The ECJ added that Article 44 GDPR must be interpreted in light of the Charter to guarantee that the protection of personal data is not undermined.[280] Article 44 GDPR is the vehicle that carries the necessary level of protection for personal data that is transferred from the EU to a third country from the Charter into the GDPR. In the end, the ECJ confirmed that individuals have a right to continuous protection for personal data by subjecting data transfers based on standard data protection clauses to the same standard of protection like data transfers based on adequacy decisions.[281]

2.3.2 *Theory of Territorial Extension of Union Law*

Extraterritorial jurisdiction can be described as "the exercise of jurisdiction by a State over activities occurring outside its borders."[282] Joanne Scott distinguishes between extraterritoriality (as such) and the territorial extension of Union law.[283] She argues that in the case of extraterritoriality (as such) the application of a measure to activities outside the EU is triggered by something other than a territorial connection with the EU, whereas, in the case of territorial extension, the application of a measure to activities outside the EU is triggered by a territorial connection, but in applying the measure the EU is required, as a matter of law, to take into account circumstances abroad.[284] Distinguishing between extraterritoriality (as such) and territorial extension thus requires an analysis of the triggers.

The right to continuous protection for personal data is an unwritten constituent part of the right to data protection. It applies to the transfer of personal data from the EU to third countries. An interference with the right to continuous protection for personal data takes place if the transferred data is not subject to protection which is essentially equivalent to that guaranteed within the EU. The application of the right to continuous protection for personal data depends on the transfer of personal data. This application does not constitute an instance of extraterritoriality (as such) but an

[279] ECJ, *Schrems 2*, para. 93.

[280] Ibid., para. 132.

[281] Jeffery Atik and Xavier Groussot argue that while the ECJ decided *Schrems 2* correctly as a matter of EU law, the Court need not have acted as it did in reaching its judgment in *Schrems 2* and that there was ample discretionary space for the Court to have reached a differing result. The authors propose that the judgment of the CJEU in *Schrems 2* constitutes a belligerent use of law. See Groussot and Atik (2021), pp. 11–18.

[282] Senz and Charlesworth (2001), p. 69, 72. The considerations here are mostly concerned with the exercise of prescriptive or legislative jurisdiction by the EU. Prescriptive or legislative jurisdiction relates to the power to make law in relation to a specific subject matter.

[283] Scott (2014), p. 90.

[284] She discusses the application of her theory in many fields of EU law but, surprisingly, not with respect to data protection. See ibid.

instance of territorial extension. The concept of data transfers has a strong territorial connection with the EU because data transfers work with a geographical element that involves the EU.[285]

This observation is important from the perspective of international law. Any form of extraterritorial jurisdiction has the potential to clash with the prohibition on interfering with the internal affairs of another state or the right to territorial integrity and political independence of another state and must therefore be considered as a matter of international law.[286] The Permanent Court of International Justice held in *S.S. Lotus (France v. Turkey)* that the exercise of extraterritorial enforcement jurisdiction is forbidden but that "[i]t does not, however, follow that international law prohibits a State from exercising jurisdiction in its own territory, in respect of any case which relates to acts which have taken place abroad."[287] It is a matter of debate whether this finding in *S.S. Lotus (France v. Turkey)* allows the exercise of legislative or prescriptive extraterritorial jurisdiction. The International Court of Justice (ICJ) stated in *Barcelona Traction (Belgium v. Spain)* that international law

> involve[s] for every State an obligation to exercise moderation and restraint as to the extent of the jurisdiction assumed by its courts in cases having a foreign element, and to avoid undue encroachment on a jurisdiction more properly appertaining to, or more appropriately exercisable by, another State.[288]

I argue that the territorial extension of EU law with a strong territorial nexus such as the transfer of personal data from the EU to a third country respects the principle in *S.S. Lotus* and the statement in *Barcelona Traction*.[289]

2.3.3 *Justification*

The right to continuous protection of personal data has an impact on third countries. Their ability to import personal data from the EU depends on the level of protection they afford to that personal data. The impact of the right to continuous protection for personal data on third countries can be justified in EU law. Article 16(2) TFEU offers

[285] In contrast, Maja Brkan argues that the application of fundamental rights in *Schrems* constitutes an instance of extraterritoriality (as such) and not of territorial extension because the link with the EU is established through transfer of data of EU citizens to the US and not through a direct link with the EU territory. This argument has to be rejected because EU data protection rules do not only apply to EU citizens. Everyone has the right to the protection of personal data concerning him or her based on Article 16 TFEU and Article 8(1) CFR. Similarly, the ECJ did not refer to transfers of personal data of EU citizens to the US but used the geographical element of data transfers: "personal data that is or could be transferred from the European Union to the United States." ECJ, *Schrems*, para. 87. See Brkan (2016), p. 839. Of the same opinion, Taylor (2015), p. 247.

[286] Kamminga (2020), p. 6.

[287] PCIJ, *S.S.* Lotus, para. 46.

[288] ICJ, *Barcelona Traction*, para. 70.

[289] See also Hijmans (2016), pp. 475–476.

a legal basis for the territorial extension of Union law in the field of data protection (Sect. 2.3.3.1), Article 8 CFR requires effective protection that does not end at the borders of the EU member states (Sect. 2.3.3.2), and the foundational values of the right to data protection are also relevant in transborder contexts (Sect. 2.3.3.3). However, the suggestion of Marko Milanovich that states have a territorially unlimited negative obligation to refrain from conduct that would assist third parties in violating the right to data protection in analogy with the ECtHR's judgment in *Soering v. United Kingdom* is not convincing (Sect. 2.3.3.4).

2.3.3.1 Legal Basis in the Treaties

The field of application of the Charter in Article 51 CFR must be interpreted on the basis of EU competences (Sect. 2.3.3.1.1). Article 16 TFEU empowers the EU to define standards for the protection of individuals in the EU with regard to the processing of their personal data in third countries when it is transferred from the EU (Sect. 2.3.3.1.2). This argument finds support from other provisions on external relations in the EU Treaties (Sect. 2.3.3.1.3).

2.3.3.1.1 Field of Application of the Charter

It is necessary to address the field of application of the Charter in order to justify the extraterritorial dimension of the right to data protection. The Charter does not have a territorial jurisdiction clause to determine (and limit) its field of application, in contrast to human rights treaties like the ECHR (in Article 1) or the International Covenant on Civil and Political Rights (ICCPR)[290] (in Article 2).[291] The Charter follows a different approach to determine its field of application.[292] Article 51(1) CFR states that the provisions of the Charter are addressed to the institutions and bodies of the EU (and to the EU member states when they are implementing EU law). The addressees have to respect the rights, observe the principles, and promote the application of the provisions in the Charter in accordance with their respective powers and the limits of these powers conferred on them in the EU Treaties. The Charter seems to apply to a particular situation once EU law governs it. In the words of the ECJ: "The applicability of European Union law entails applicability of the fundamental rights guaranteed by the Charter."[293] In that regard, the General Court

[290] International Covenant on Civil and Political Rights of 16 December 1966, 999 UNTS 171.

[291] The jurisdiction of a state within the meaning of Article 1 ECHR is primarily territorial. It is deemed to be exercised normally throughout the state's territory. ECtHR, *Assanidze v. Georgia*, para. 137.

[292] Violeta Moreno-Lax and Cathryn Costello underline that the Charter's field of application is regulated independent of international human rights jurisdiction. Moreno-Lax and Costello (2014), p. 1679.

[293] ECJ, *Åkerberg Fransson*, para. 21.

of the EU (EGC) found in the *Front Polisario* case that implications for fundamental rights in third countries must be examined when the EU concludes international agreements.[294]

Article 51(2) CFR further clarifies that the Charter does not extend the field of application of EU law beyond the powers of the EU, establish any new power or task for the EU, or modify powers and tasks as defined in the EU Treaties. Violeta Moreno-Lax and Cathryn Costello have observed that the language used in Article 51 CFR is that of competence, allocation of powers, and their application within the realm of the EU legal order, irrespective of the geographical space within which these powers are exercised.[295] They emphasize the need to rid the discussion on the extraterritorial jurisdiction of the Charter from the debate on borders and territory and bring it to the less-static space of EU competences and legality.[296] They submit that fundamental rights apply as a matter of EU constitutional obligation.[297] Based on the principle of conferral in Article 5(2) TEU, the EU can only act within the limits of the competences conferred upon it by the EU member states in the EU Treaties for the purpose of attaining the objectives set out therein. Within these limits, the EU can act and must, at the same time, respect, observe, and promote the fundamental rights in the Charter.

This interpretation of the field of application of the Charter in Article 51 CFR based on EU competences is convincing and compatible with the jurisprudence of the ECJ. It is the basis for the assertion of EU extraterritorial jurisdiction regarding the fundamental rights in the Charter within the limits of EU competences. The Charter's field of application and its extraterritorial dimension must be explored based on EU competences.

The alternative, more static, and border-oriented interpretation of the Charter's field of application follows the territorial scope of the EU Treaties as laid down in Article 52 TEU and Article 355 TFEU.[298] This interpretation ignores the language of competence and allocation of powers in Article 51 CFR and uses the territorial jurisdiction clauses of the EU Treaties as the jurisdictional basis of the Charter. Even such an interpretation would not, however, exclude the possibility of the assertion of extraterritorial jurisdiction regarding the fundamental rights in the Charter. While

---

[294] EGC, *Front Polisario*, paras 227–228. The ECJ annulled the EGC's judgment, but the ECJ did not comment on the obligation to examine the fundamental rights implications of the agreement in the third country. ECJ, *Front Polisario,* para. 132.

[295] Moreno-Lax and Costello (2014), p. 1679.

[296] Ibid., 1682. Mistale Taylor criticizes that territorial sovereignty and the authority to legislate cannot possibly be divorced from political concerns. She argues that the EU's obligations under public international law and the basic premise of public international law are founded on territorial sovereignty, and that they are needed to discuss the extraterritoriality of the Charter. Taylor (2015), p. 250.

[297] Moreno-Lax and Costello (2014), p. 1678.

[298] Article 52 TEU refers to all EU member states by their official name and is supplemented with Article 355 TFEU that also refers to various territories and overseas countries related to EU member states.

Article 52 TEU and Article 355 TFEU determine (and limit) the application of the EU Treaties (and thus of the Charter) based on territory, the ECJ specifically pointed out in *Boukhalfa*, a case involving the prohibition of discrimination based on nationality, that "[t]he geographical application of the Treaty defined in Article 227 [. . .] does not, however, preclude Community rules from having effects outside the territory of the Community."[299]

2.3.3.1.2 The Right to Data Protection in the EU Treaties

In order to establish the Charter's field of application with respect to the right to data protection, it is necessary to look at the EU competences in the area of data protection. The Lisbon Treaty introduced a provision on data protection into the EU Treaties. Article 16(1) TFEU guarantees that everyone has the right to the protection of personal data concerning them. The first paragraph of Article 16 TFEU almost exactly mirrors the wording of the first paragraph of Article 8 CFR. Article 16(2) TFEU empowers the European Parliament and the Council to establish rules relating to the protection of individuals with regard to the processing of personal data by EU institutions, bodies, offices and agencies, and the member states when they carry out activities which fall within the scope of EU law. Based on Article 16 TFEU, the EU has an explicit mandate and positive obligation to regulate the field of data protection, which is rather unique in comparison to other fundamental rights.[300] The second paragraph of Article 16 TFEU, however, contains ambiguities with regard to the addressees for whom the data protection rules should be laid down.[301] It is generally accepted that Article 16(2) TFEU also empowers the EU to lay down data protection rules with regard to the processing of personal data by the private sector.[302]

I would argue that Article 16(2) TFEU also empowers the EU to define standards for the protection of individuals in the EU with regard to the processing of their personal data in third countries when it is transferred from the EU. There are two indications to support this argument. First, Article 16 TFEU was the legal basis in the EU Treaties for adequacy decisions such as Decision (EU) 2016/1250, the Privacy Shield adequacy decision. Decision (EU) 2016/1250 contained the so-called "privacy principles" that US companies had to comply with in the US as part of their self-certification under the EU-US Privacy Shield to import personal data from the

[299] ECJ, *Boukhalfa*, para. 14. Article 227 of the Treaty Establishing the European Community corresponds to Article 52 TEU and Article 355 TFEU.

[300] van der Sloot (2017), p. 11.

[301] Hijmans (2016), p. 268.

[302] AG Paolo Mengozzi elaborated that a strictly literal interpretation of Article 16(2) TFEU would "run counter to the intention of the High Contracting Parties" and "have the consequence of depriving that provision of a large part of its practical effect". ECJ, AG Opinion, Opinion 1/15, para. 119.

EU.[303] Second, the ECJ decided in Opinion 1/15 that Article 16 TFEU is the correct legal basis for the draft agreement on the transfer and processing of PNR data between the EU and Canada.[304] The draft PNR agreement consisted of detailed rules relating to the protection of individuals in the EU with regard to the processing of their PNR data by Canadian authorities when it is transferred from EU to Canada.[305]

Article 16 TFEU empowers the EU to define standards for the protection of individuals in the EU with regard to the processing of their personal data in third countries when it is transferred from the EU. The standard of essential equivalence is an example.[306] Article 16 TFEU also constitutes the basis for the extraterritorial dimension of the right to data protection because the Charter applies based on EU competences and Article 51(1) CFR requires the EU to promote the application of fundamental rights within the powers conferred on it in the Treaties.

2.3.3.1.3 External Relations of the European Union

Article 3(5) TEU states that "[i]n its relations with the wider world, the Union shall uphold and promote its values and interests and contribute to the protection of its citizens."[307] This implies that the values of the EU defined in Article 2 TEU such as respect for human dignity, freedom, democracy, equality, the rule of law, and human rights are not confined to the geographical application of the Treaties, but that the EU has to actively pursue them abroad to protect its citizens. The requirements for external action of the EU in Article 21(1) TEU are formulated in the same spirit:

> The Union's action on the international scene shall be guided by the principles which have inspired its own creation, development and enlargement, and which it seeks to advance in the wider world: democracy, the rule of law, the universality and indivisibility of human rights and fundamental freedoms, respect for human dignity, the principles of equality and solidarity, and respect for the principles of the United Nations Charter and international law.

Human dignity and democracy are of particular importance for the right to data protection as guiding principles of the EU's action on the international scene. Human dignity is enshrined in Article 1 CFR and constitutes "the real basis of fundamental rights" according to the explanations relating to the Charter.[308] Human dignity is

---

[303] These principles were not a subject of the ECJ's *Schrems 2* judgment that invalidated Decision (EU) 2016/1250.

[304] ECJ, Opinion 1/15, paras 95–97.

[305] Ibid., paras 83–92.

[306] See Sect. 2.3.4.

[307] Lorand Bartels argues with reference to the ECJ case *Air Transport Association of America* that "these phrases are not devoid of normative force". Bartels (2015), p. 1074; ECJ, *Air Transport Association of America*, para. 101.

[308] The Explanations also state that "the dignity of the human person is part of the substance of the rights laid down in this Charter." Explanations relating to the Charter of Fundamental Rights, 17.

also often considered the ultimate foundation of data protection.[309] Similarly, democracy is one of the underlying values of data protection.[310]

Article 21(3)(1) TEU supplements the requirements for the EU's external action. The EU shall respect the guiding principles, such as human dignity and democracy, not only in the different areas of its external action, but also in the development and implementation "of the external aspects of its other policies." Lorand Bartels observes that this addition in Article 21(3)(1) TEU carries normative force "insofar as it requires the EU to 'respect' the principles previously described."[311] Data protection must be considered a domestic policy with external aspects because of the legal mechanisms for the transfer of personal data in Chapter V GDPR. Article 21 TEU thus supports the extraterritorial dimension of the right to data protection.

2.3.3.2 Effective Protection of Fundamental Rights

It is also necessary to address effective protection of fundamental rights in the digital sphere to justify the extraterritorial dimension of the right to data protection. The internet is a worldwide network of networks.[312] An individual's presence as data subject in the physical world is often separated from the interferences with his or her right to data protection in the digital sphere.[313] Every action of a data importer located outside the EU on personal data transferred from the EU may have an impact on individuals inside the EU.

It is generally accepted that individuals are entitled to the protection of their personal data on the internet.[314] Effective protection of personal data on the internet can only be guaranteed, however, if the protection of personal data does not end when personal data crosses territorial borders. It would be easy to bypass data protection if this were not the case. Hielke Hijmans notes that protection is thus needed whenever personal data moves outside the EU even if the individuals do not actively move outside the EU.[315] He also argues that the extraterritorial dimension of Article 8 CFR is apparent from the fact that in an internet environment "data are ubiquitously available and not only present in one jurisdiction."[316] Effective protection of personal data in an internet environment necessarily involves protection from acts in third countries whenever personal data is transferred abroad. Such a technological justification of the extraterritorial dimension of the right to data protection is

[309] Tzanou (2017a), p. 29; Lynskey (2015), p. 94.

[310] See Sect. 2.2.1.4.

[311] Bartels (2015), p. 1074.

[312] Kuner (2017c), pp. 3–4.

[313] Taylor (2015), p. 250; Milanovic (2015), p. 124; Nyst (2013).

[314] ECJ, *Lindqvist*, paras 25–27.

[315] Hijmans (2016), p. 34.

[316] Ibid., 452.

also reflected in the Charter. The Preamble of the Charter acknowledges that it is necessary "to strengthen the protection of fundamental rights in the light of changes in society, social progress and scientific and technological developments."[317]

2.3.3.3 Foundational Values of the Right to Data Protection

Furthermore, it is necessary to address the foundational values of the right to data protection to justify the extraterritorial dimension of the right to data protection. These values are just as relevant in a transborder context as they are within the EU.

The value of privacy limits the ways that personal data can be processed legally. Conceptions of privacy such as the right to be let alone or limited accessibility to a person illustrate the need to limit the ways that personal data can be processed legally. These conceptions do not differentiate between privacy intrusions that take place within the EU or abroad. Privacy-intrusive practices harm the individual's right to be let alone and the inaccessibility of persons irrespective of the location where personal data is processed. The same is true for informational self-determination. The value of informational self-determination requires that individuals are able to determine for themselves the disclosure and use of their personal data. This applies regardless of the place where personal data is disclosed or used. The value of transparency addresses power imbalances between data controllers and data subjects and requires that the latter are in a position to learn of the existence of data processing operations that concern them. Such power imbalances do not stop at territorial borders either, especially not in the digital sphere.

The value of democracy may seem less relevant in a transborder context. The value of democracy expresses the need to safeguard the ability of individuals to freely participate in society and its political discourse. The absence of rules on data protection can hamper the ability of individuals to do so. There can be chilling effects on the behavior of individuals when they are aware of excessive data processing, especially in the form of surveillance.[318] This may cause individuals to suppress their autonomy in order to appear less obtrusive to government surveillance.[319] These chilling effects can affect individuals in their exercise of rights that are of the utmost importance for democracy such as freedom of speech and association.[320] This is particularly relevant in the domestic context.[321] However, it can also be relevant in a transborder context in light of intelligence sharing networks such as the Five Eyes. There are also more specific situations where the lack of rules on data protection and excessive data processing abroad, especially in the form of

[317] Cp. ECJ, Opinion 1/15, para. 135.

[318] Solove (2008), p. 109.

[319] Cohen (2000), p. 1426.

[320] Parsons (2015), pp. 5–9; Solove (2007), pp. 121–123.

[321] For empirical evidence of the chilling effects caused by internet surveillance practices see Stoycheff (2016); Penney (2016); Townend (2014).

surveillance, is relevant for the value of democracy in the EU. For example, political refugees seeking asylum in an EU member state may stop communicating for their cause via the internet because they fear reprisals for their loved ones back home when they know that the data they generate is transferred to and accessed in their home country.

2.3.3.4 No Analogy with Soering v. United Kingdom

Marko Milanovic offers an additional justification for the extraterritorial dimension of the right to data protection.[322] He suggests that "states [could] have a territorially unlimited negative obligation to refrain from conduct that would assist third parties in violating the right to privacy, e.g. by analogy to the nonrefoulement rule in cases such as *Soering v. United Kingdom*."[323] In this particular case, the ECtHR decided that the extradition of Mr. Soering to the US, where he potentially faced the death penalty, incurred the liability of the extraditing state. The ECtHR based the decision on the absolute nature of the prohibition of torture in Article 3 ECHR, the existence of a specific prohibition in Article 3 Convention Against Torture and Other Cruel, Inhuman or Degrading Treatment or Punishment[324] to extradite a person to another state where there are substantial grounds for believing that he or she would be in danger of being subjected to torture, and the irreparable nature of the suffering caused by the inhumane and degrading treatment prohibited in Article 3 ECHR.[325] The ECtHR established that the extraditing state has a territorially unlimited negative obligation to refrain from conduct that would assist third parties in violating the prohibition of torture in Article 3 ECHR.

The suggestion of a territorially unlimited negative obligation to refrain from conduct that would assist third parties in violating the right to data protection by analogy to *Soering v. United Kingdom* is not convincing. The right to data protection in Article 8 CFR is not absolute, there is no international agreement prohibiting transfers of personal data of an individual to countries where there are substantial grounds for believing that the individual would be in danger of being subjected to data processing operations with adverse consequences, and such consequences cannot be compared to the irreparable nature of the suffering caused by the inhumane and degrading treatment prohibited in Article 3 ECHR.

---

[322] Milanovic (2015), p. 124.

[323] Ibid., fn. 176. See also Taylor (2015), p. 252. ECtHR, *Soering v. the United Kingdom.*

[324] Convention Against Torture and Other Cruel, Inhuman or Degrading Treatment or Punishment of 10 December 1984, 1465 UNTS 85.

[325] It was not the death penalty but the "death row phenomen" that amounted to inhumane and degrading treatment under Article 3 ECHR. See ECtHR, *Soering v. the United Kingdom,* paras 90–91, 111.

2.3.4 *Essential Equivalence*

The extraterritorial dimension of the right to data protection entails a standard for the protection of personal data that is transferred to a third country. The protection must be essentially equivalent to that guaranteed within the EU. The standard of essential equivalence uses the protection within the EU as a comparison (Sect. 2.3.4.1). Moreover, the meaning of essential equivalence is not entirely clear. The ECJ only stated that the standard of essential equivalence does not require that the level of protection in a third country must be identical to that in the Union (Sect. 2.3.4.2). The ECJ indicated that the level of protection in the Union itself must be assessed with recourse to the lawful limitations on Article 7 and Article 8 CFR (Sect. 2.3.4.3). However, the right to continuous protection of personal data is not absolute. Limitations on the basis of Article 52(1) CFR are possible (Sect. 2.3.4.4).

2.3.4.1 Comparison

The right to continuous protection of personal data uses the standard of protection that is essentially equivalent to that guaranteed within the EU. Essential equivalence requires a comparison between the rules and practices prevailing in a third country, on the one hand, and the standards of protection in the EU, on the other hand.[326] The comparison is also a question of competence and coverage under Union law. The EU has a competence in the domain of data protection based on Article 16 TFEU. However, there is a reservation of competence in relation to the protection of national security for EU member states in Article 4(2) TEU. The reservation in Article 4(2) TEU states that national security remains the sole responsibility of each member state.[327]

At first sight, it seems that there cannot be any comparison with the level of protection of personal data in the EU for measures protecting national security because the EU has no competence in that field. This would imply that measures for the protection of national security in third countries would be excluded from the standard of essential equivalence. However, AG Yves Bot found in his opinion in *Schrems* that the processing by US authorities for national security purposes of personal data that was transferred from the EU to the US was not excluded from the standard of essential equivalence.[328] The ECJ confirmed this finding.[329] More

[326] See also Recital (104) GDPR.

[327] The European Council clarified its interpretation of Article 4(2) TEU in a draft decision concerning a pre-Brexit settlement for the UK within the EU: "Article 4(2) of the Treaty on European Union confirms that national security remains the sole responsibility of each Member State. This does not constitute a derogation from Union law and should therefore not be interpreted restrictively." European Council (2016), Section C, Point 5.

[328] ECJ, AG Opinion, *Schrems*, para. 170.

[329] ECJ, *Schrems*, para. 87.

specifically, AG Henrik Saugmandsgaard Øe stated in his opinion in *Schrems 2* that an assessment of the level of protection of personal data in a third country

> cannot ignore any interference with the exercise of the fundamental rights of the persons concerned that would result from State measures, notably in the field of national security, which, if they were adopted by a Member State, would fall outside the scope of EU law.[330]

The Article 29 WP explained that Article 4(2) TEU defines the competence of the Union *vis-à-vis* the EU member states, and that the reservation of national security must be understood in light of this relationship.[331]

> From a legal perspective, a distinction needs to be made between surveillance programmes run by intelligence services of the Member States and those carried out by intelligence services of third countries making use of data of EU citizens. [. . .] In fact, the national security exemption [in Article 4(2) TEU] only applies to the national security of an EU Member State, and not to the national security of a third country.[332]

Furthermore, Article 45(2)(a) GDPR explicitly requires that the rules on national security in force in a third country need to be taken into account for an adequacy assessment without any restriction whatsoever.[333] Thus, the rules and measures of third countries in the field of national security cannot fall outside of the assessment of essential equivalence. This is even true when surveillance practices take place outside the territory of the state in question and during the stage in which the respective data is in transit from the EU to the third country.[334]

However, should the rules and measures of third countries in the field of national security fall outside the scope of EU law, if they were adopted by EU member states, they need other standards for comparison. I would argue that this should be the level of protection required within the Union under the law of the EU member states, including their commitments under the ECHR, which constitute a common denominator among all the EU member states.[335] The ECHR is a privileged source of legal interpretation and inspiration of Union law. This status has been codified in Article 6(3) TEU. Including the requirements of the ECHR in the assessment of essential equivalence is not an extraordinary exercise. The ECJ regularly refers to the jurisprudence of the ECtHR in surveillance cases.

The ECHR does not contain an exemption for national security measures.[336] Instead, national security is mentioned as the first legitimate aim for derogations from the right to private life in Article 8(2) ECHR. Any national security measure that encroaches on the right to private life must be in accordance with law and necessary in a democratic society. Nevertheless, the contracting states of the ECHR

---

[330] ECJ, AG Opinion, *Schrems 2*, para. 206.

[331] Article 29 WP (2015), p. 25.

[332] Article 29 WP (2014), p. 6.

[333] ECJ, *Schrems 2*, para. 87.

[334] ECJ, AG Opinion, *Schrems 2*, para. 236.

[335] Ibid., para. 207.

[336] Lidberg and Muller (2018), p. 201; Christakis (2017), p. 331.

have a certain—arguably even a large—margin of appreciation when evaluating threats to national security and when deciding how to combat these.[337] The ECtHR applies a deferential approach *vis-à-vis* national security measures. The ECtHR has even found that "the judgment by the national authorities in any particular case in which national security considerations are involved is one which [the Court] is not well equipped to challenge."[338]

2.3.4.2 Meaning

The standard of essential equivalence was invented by AG Yves Bot and the ECJ in *Schrems* as a way to interpret the term adequate protection in Article 25(6) Directive 95/46/EC.[339] However, they did not define what essential equivalence exactly means. The ECJ only indicated that the standard of essential equivalence does not require that the level of protection in a third country is identical to that in the EU.[340]

The GDPR also uses the term "equivalent." According to Recital (10) GDPR, an objective of the GDPR is that "the level of protection of the rights and freedoms of natural persons with regard to the processing of [personal] data should be equivalent in all Member States."[341] The GDPR aims at establishing equivalent protection for personal data in all EU member states. The right to continuous protection of personal data does not require that the protection for the transferred data in the third country is equivalent to the level of protection guaranteed within the EU, but that the protection is *essentially* equivalent to that guaranteed within the EU.

The Oxford English Dictionary (OED) defines the term essentially as "in respect of the essential points, materially, substantially."[342] The OED further defines materially as "to a material or important extent" and substantially as "to a great extent."[343] A literal interpretation thus suggests that the level of protection for personal data in a third country must, to an important or great extent, be the same as that guaranteed within the EU. Consequently, any discrepancies between the protection for personal data in the EU and a third country must not be significant enough to result in a different level of protection. AG Henrik Saugmandsgaard Øe explained in his opinion in *Schrems 2* that a third country may still reflect its own scale of values according to which the respective weight of the various interests involved may diverge from that attributed to them in the EU legal order.[344] The standard of essential equivalence should therefore "be applied in such a way as to preserve a

[337] ECtHR, *Weber and Saravia v. Germany*, para. 106; ECtHR (2013), p. 41.

[338] ECtHR, *Janowiec and Others v. Russia*, para. 213.

[339] ECJ, AG Opinion *Schrems*, paras 141–142; ECJ, *Schrems*, para. 73.

[340] ECJ, *Schrems*, para. 74.

[341] See also Recital (170) GDPR.

[342] OED, entry for essentially (adv.).

[343] Ibid., entries for materially (adv.) and substantially (adv.).

[344] ECJ, AG Opinion, *Schrems 2*, para. 249.

certain flexibility in order to take the various legal and cultural traditions into account."[345] AG Saugmandsgaard Øe underlined, however, that the standard of essential equivalence requires that the minimum safeguards and general requirements for the protection of fundamental rights that follow from the Charter and the ECHR must have an equivalent in the legal order of the third state.[346] The Article 29 WP also emphasizes that the "objective is not to mirror point by point the European legislation, but to establish the essential – core requirements of that legislation."[347]

2.3.4.3 Level of Protection

The ECJ stressed in *Schrems* that a level of protection, which is essentially equivalent to that guaranteed in the EU, can partly be found in the judgment itself.[348]

> [A] level of protection of fundamental rights essentially equivalent to that guaranteed in the EU legal order, [is] a level that is apparent in particular from the preceding paragraphs of the present judgment.[349]

The preceding paragraphs referred to in this excerpt contain the following:

> Legislation is not limited to what is strictly necessary where it authorises, on a generalised basis, storage of all the personal data of all the persons whose data has been transferred from the European Union to the United States without any differentiation, limitation or exception being made in the light of the objective pursued and without an objective criterion being laid down by which to determine the limits of the access of the public authorities to the data, and of its subsequent use, for purposes which are specific, strictly restricted and capable of justifying the interference which both access to that data and its use entail.[350]
>
> In particular, legislation permitting the public authorities to have access on a generalised basis to the content of electronic communications must be regarded as compromising the essence of the fundamental right to respect for private life, as guaranteed by Article 7 of the Charter.[351]

These paragraphs generalize the previous findings of unlawful limitations on Article 7 and Article 8 CFR in the jurisprudence of the ECJ on specific surveillance issues.[352] The ECJ underlined that a level of protection, which is essentially equivalent to that guaranteed in the EU, is apparent in particular from these findings. There will undoubtedly be more findings on unlawful limitations on Article 7 and Article 8 CFR and Article 8 ECHR that can be generalized as the jurisprudence of

[345] Ibid.

[346] Ibid.

[347] Article 29 WP (2018), p. 2.

[348] Vermeulen (2017), p. 69.

[349] ECJ, *Schrems*, para. 96.

[350] Ibid., para. 93.

[351] Ibid., para. 94.

[352] See ibid., paras 91–92.

the ECJ and the ECtHR on specific surveillance issues advances.[353] These findings are relevant to define the level of protection sought with the standard of essential equivalence.

2.3.4.4 Limitations

An interference with Article 8 CFR is an interference with one or more of its constituent parts. Only the essence of a fundamental right cannot be limited, diminished, restricted, or interfered with. The standard of essential equivalence is embedded in the right to continuous protection of personal data that is transferred to a third country, which is an unwritten constituent part of Article 8 CFR. This extraterritorial dimension of the right to data protection is not part of its essence. Limitations on the right to continuous protection for personal data are possible if they satisfy the requirements of Article 52(1) CFR. However, the right to continuous protection of personal data already embraces the lawful limitations on Article 8 CFR because it operates with the standard of essential equivalence. Any additional limitations on the right to continuous protection for personal data would lead to more generous limitations on Article 8 CFR for third countries than would be allowed in the EU. These limitations must therefore be subject to a strict proportionality assessment.

2.3.5 *Summary*

I argue that the right to data protection in Article 8 CFR has an extraterritorial dimension. The jurisprudence of the ECJ has revealed an unwritten constituent of the right to data protection in relation to transfers of personal data to third countries. This right to continuous protection of personal data requires that the protection for personal data that is transferred to a third country is essentially equivalent to that guaranteed within the EU. It can be categorized as a territorial extension of Union law because data transfers have a strong territorial connection with the EU. This extraterritorial dimension of the right to data protection can be justified. It is necessary to effectively protect fundamental rights in the digital sphere. Effective protection on the internet cannot be guaranteed if the protection ends at the borders of the EU member states. It would be easy to bypass the protection of personal data in the EU if that were the case. The Preamble of the Charter underlines the necessity of strengthening the protection of fundamental rights in the light of changes in society, social progress, and scientific and technological developments. The foundational values of the right to data protection are also relevant in a transborder context. They support the extraterritorial dimension of the right to data protection.

[353] See Sect. 2.4.2.

Article 16(2) TFEU offers a legal basis in the Treaties. However, the right to data protection is not absolute. As an unwritten constituent part of Article 8 CFR, the right to continuous protection for personal data and the standard of essential equivalence are both open to lawful limitations according to Article 52(1) CFR.

2.4 The Extraterritorial Dimension of the Right to Data Protection and Foreign Surveillance

This section is dedicated to foreign surveillance as a focal point of the extraterritorial dimension of the right to data protection. There is a triangular interface between data protection, surveillance, and trade.[354] Personal data that is transferred from the EU to a third country can become subject to foreign internet surveillance practices. If the protection for personal data from these practices is not essentially equivalent to that guaranteed within the EU, then the necessary restrictions imposed on these cross-border flows of personal data will influence trade relations. Two internet surveillance practices are particularly important: government access to personal data held by private companies and government interception of data flows from the internet (Sect. 2.4.1). The extraterritorial dimension of the right to data protection can easily come into conflict with these practices. The right to continuous protection of personal data implies that personal data cannot be exported from the EU to a third state that does not guarantee a level of protection for personal data that satisfies the standard of essential equivalence with regard to internet surveillance practices. The requirements for essential equivalence of protection from foreign internet surveillance practices can be found in the jurisprudence of the ECJ and the ECtHR (Sect. 2.4.2). Contrary to what some scholars argue, the EU does not maintain double standards for foreign internet surveillance practices (Sect. 2.4.3). Furthermore, the extraterritorial dimension of the right to data protection is complementary to the obligations of states in the field of internet surveillance under international human rights law such as the ICCPR (Sect. 2.4.4).

2.4.1 Foreign Internet Surveillance

Foreign internet surveillance has an impact on the activities of individuals in the EU on the internet. Police, secret services, immigration control, and intelligence agencies around the world are increasingly using personal data generated by individuals for their work. When the personal data of individuals in the EU is transferred to a third country, that data can become subject to foreign internet surveillance practices.

[354] Cp. Yakovleva and Irion (2020), p. 17.

These institutions either access personal data held by private companies (Sect. 2.4.1.1) or they directly intercept data flows from the internet (Sect. 2.4.1.2).

2.4.1.1 Access to Personal Data Held by Private Companies

After introducing the surveillance practice of access to personal data held by private companies (Sect. 2.4.1.1.1), the standards for the comparison of essential equivalence with the protection of personal data guaranteed within the EU are analyzed (Sect. 2.4.1.1.2).

2.4.1.1.1 Surveillance Practice

Servers of private companies often store the personal data of their users, clients, and employees. This data is of interest to governments, the police, and intelligence agencies. Consequently, these institutions seek access to personal data held by private companies. Access to this personal data is sometimes mediated by the entity holding the data and sometimes direct. Access to personal data held by private companies in third countries also concerns individuals in the EU whose personal data has been transferred to a third country and stored on the servers of a private company.

The most famous example for systematic access to personal data held by private companies is the PRISM program in the US. It was revealed through the leaks of classified information by former NSA contractor Edward Snowden in 2013.[355] Through the PRISM program, the NSA claimed to have direct access to the servers of nine of the big online business operators: Microsoft, Yahoo, Google, Facebook, PalTalk, AOL, Skype, YouTube, and Apple. Access to these servers enabled US officials to collect information about individuals including their search histories, the content of their e-mails, file transfers, live chats, etc.[356] The PRISM program operated under the scope of Section 702 Foreign Intelligence Surveillance Act (FISA) which only allows the surveillance of persons who are not US citizens and who are reasonably believed to be located outside the US.[357] The PRISM program also targeted individuals in the EU. All the companies involved in the PRISM program were certified under the Safe Harbor scheme of Decision 2000/520, the Safe Harbor adequacy decision.[358] This made Decision 2000/520 one of the conduits through which US intelligence agencies were able to access and collect personal data that has been transferred from the EU to the US.[359]

---

[355] Greenwald and MacAskill (2013); Gellman and Poitras (2013).

[356] Ibid.

[357] PCLOB (2014), pp. 20–21.

[358] European Commission (2013), p. 16.

[359] Ibid.

The US is not the only state where the government, the police, and intelligence agencies have systematic access to personal data held by private companies. Ira S. Rubinstein, Gregory T. Nojeim, and Ronald D. Lee found in their comparative analysis of different states in Asia, Australia, Europe, and the Americas that governments are increasingly turning to the private sector for information that they see as critical in countering criminal activity, terrorism, and threats to national security.[360] These scholars go on to identify common themes regarding systematic access to personal data held by private companies in different states. They found that systematic access is often not foreseeable from the text of the law.[361] In many states, the law appears to say something different from what governments are reportedly doing. This calls into question whether those states afford protection that is essentially equivalent to that guaranteed within the EU for individuals whose personal data is transferred from the EU to a third country. Rubinstein, Nojeim, and Lee write that oversight mechanisms are either absent or limited in scope and that they generally do not include voluntary data sharing arrangements between private companies and intelligence agencies, which, again, is troublesome in the light of the right to continuous protection of personal data.[362] They also underline that in many states, even in those with otherwise comprehensive data protection laws, access to personal data for law enforcement and/or national security purposes are often excluded, or treated as accepted purposes for which access is authorized under separate laws that may or may not provide safeguards against possible abuses.[363] China and India stand out when it comes to access to personal data held by (private) companies because of an almost total lack of protection and oversight concerning access for law enforcement and/or national security purposes.[364]

2.4.1.1.2 Standards for Comparison of Essential Equivalence

The determination of the applicable standards for the comparison of essential equivalence for government access to personal data held by private companies depends on whether the surveillance practice would—if it emanated from an EU member state—fall within the limitations placed on the scope of Union law in the field of national security. Should the surveillance practice fall within the limitations placed on the scope of Union law, the applicable standards for the comparison of essential equivalence can be found under the law of the EU member states, including

[360] In a six-year research project, different scholars produced country reports on bulk collection of personal data and the respective laws regarding government access to private-sector data (France, Germany, Israel, Italy, Brazil, Canada, the US, Australia, China, India, Japan and South Korea). Rubinstein et al. (2017), p. 12.

[361] Ibid., 7, 19.

[362] Ibid., 17.

[363] Ibid., 20.

[364] With regard to China see Wang (2017), pp. 244, 250–255; Fry (2015), pp. 479–481. With regard to India see Abraham (2017), pp. 264–267.

their commitments under the ECHR. Should the surveillance practice be covered under Union law, the applicable standards for the comparison of essential equivalence can be found in the Charter, the GDPR, and other relevant instruments of EU secondary law.

The ECJ stated multiple times that the exclusion from EU data protection law for activities of EU member states protecting national security only concerns activities of the state or of state authorities that are unrelated to fields in which individuals are active. For example, the ECJ decided in *Tele2/Watson* that national provisions requiring providers of electronic communications services to retain traffic and location data as well as to grant public authorities access to the data for law enforcement and national security purposes are *not* excluded from the scope of Directive 2002/58/EC because they concern the processing of personal data by those providers and thus relate to fields in which individuals are active.[365] The ECJ confirmed this in *Ministerio Fiscal* and found that national provisions that require providers of electronic communications services to make personal data available to the police are *not* excluded from the scope of Directive 2002/58/EC because they concern the processing of personal data by those providers and thus relate to fields in which individuals are active.[366] The ECJ also followed this practice in *Privacy International* and in *La Quadrature du Net* concerning national legislative measures on the basis of which competent authorities may give the providers of electronic communications services a direction to disclose bulk data to security and intelligence agencies.[367] The ECJ stressed that according to settled case law, the allocation of competence in Article 4(2) TEU cannot invalidate this conclusion.

> [A]lthough it is for the Member States to define their essential security interests and to adopt appropriate measures to ensure their internal and external security, the mere fact that a national measure has been taken for the purpose of protecting national security cannot render EU law inapplicable and exempt the Members States from their obligation to comply with that law.[368]

However, the ECJ also specifically mentioned that in cases in which national provisions derogate from the rule guaranteeing the confidentiality of electronic communications without imposing processing obligations on providers, the protection of the data of the persons concerned is not covered by Directive 2002/58, but only by national law subject to the application of Directive (EU) 2016/680 on the protection of natural persons with regard to the processing of personal data by competent authorities for the purposes of the prevention, investigation, detection or prosecution

[365] ECJ, *Tele2/Watson*, para. 78.

[366] ECJ, *Ministerio Fiscal*, para. 34.

[367] ECJ, *Privacy International*, para. 49; ECJ, *La Quadrature du Net*, para. 104.

[368] ECJ, *Privacy International*, para. 44 and ECJ, *La Quadrature du Net*, para. 99, with reference to ECJ, *ZZ v. Secretary of State for the Home Department*, para. 38; ECJ, *Commission v. Austria (State printing office)*, paras 75–76; ECJ, *Commission v Poland, Hungary and Czech Republic*, paras 143, 170.

of criminal offences or the execution of criminal penalties.[369] Consequently, the measures in question must comply with, *inter alia*, national constitutional law and the requirements of the ECHR.[370]

As long as government access to personal data held by private companies requires the processing of personal data by the respective companies, it is covered by EU data protection law. Accordingly, the standard for comparison of essential equivalence for such surveillance practices must be found in the Charter, the GDPR, and other relevant instruments of EU secondary law. However, once the data are in the possession of state authorities, the retention and subsequent use of those data by those authorities for national security purposes fall within the limitations placed on the scope of Union law in the light of Article 4(2) TEU and the applicable standards for the comparison of essential equivalence must here be found under the law of the EU member states, including their commitments under the ECHR.[371] The same is true when governmental access to personal data held by private companies does not require the processing of personal data by the respective companies.

2.4.1.2 Interception of Data Flows from the Internet

After introducing the surveillance practice of interception of data flows from the internet (Sect. 2.4.1.2.1), the standards for the comparison of essential equivalence with the protection of personal data guaranteed within the EU are analyzed (Sect. 2.4.1.2.2).

2.4.1.2.1 Surveillance Practice

The internet is a worldwide network of networks.[372] Large submarine and overland fiber-optic cables connect these networks (internet backbone). Data travels in tiny packages separately and possibly on different routes (packet switching) through multiple internet exchange points (peering) to its destination. Some of that data can be interesting for governments, the police, and intelligence agencies. Some of these institutions tap directly into the infrastructure of the internet. Data is copied from interceptors placed on the submarine and overland fiber-optic cables connecting the different networks at landing points where the submarine cables make landfall and

[369] Directive (EU) 2016/680 of the European Parliament and of the Council of 27 April 2016 on the protection of natural persons with regard to the processing of personal data by competent authorities for the purposes of the prevention, investigation, detection or prosecution of criminal offences or the execution of criminal penalties, and on the free movement of such data, and repealing Council Framework Decision 2008/977/JHA [2016] OJ L 119/89.

[370] ECJ, *Privacy International*, para. 48; ECJ, *La Quadrature du Net*, para. 101.

[371] ECJ, AG Opinion, *Schrems 2*, para. 226.

[372] Kuner (2017c), pp. 3–4.

from central exchanges which switch internet traffic between the major carriers.[373] This practice is also called "upstreaming" because the collection of data does not occur at a local private company but in real-time in the flow of data.[374] Access to data flows is either secret, negotiated with the operating companies, or enforced with a legal order served on the operating companies. It can take place either inside or outside the territory of the state accessing the data flows, for example in the open sea. This surveillance practice may also concern personal data that has been transferred from the EU to a third country. Once gathered, the data is usually retained for a certain period of time and organized through platforms of integration to make it intelligible.[375]

2.4.1.2.2 Standards for Comparison of Essential Equivalence

The determination of the applicable standards for the comparison of essential equivalence for the interception of data flows from the internet depends on whether the internet surveillance practice would—if it emanated from an EU member state—fall within the limitations placed on the scope of Union law in the field of national security. Should the surveillance practice fall within the limitations placed on the scope of Union law, the applicable standards for the comparison of essential equivalence can be found under the law of the EU member states, including their commitments under the ECHR. Should the surveillance practice be covered under Union law, the applicable standards for the comparison of essential equivalence can be found in the Charter, the GDPR, and other relevant instruments of EU secondary law.

The ECJ stated multiple times that the exclusion from EU data protection law for the national security activities of EU member states only applies to activities of the state or of state authorities that are unrelated to fields in which individuals are active.[376] Government interception of data flows from the internet may, but does not necessarily have to, relate to fields in which individuals are active. The surveillance practice does not relate to fields in which individuals are active if a national measure authorizes direct interception of data flows from the internet infrastructure by its intelligence agencies without any cooperation of the companies operating the internet infrastructure.[377] Such a measure falls within the limitations placed on the scope of Union law in the light of Article 4(2) TEU. The applicable standards for the comparison of essential equivalence can be found under the law of the EU

[373] Bauman et al. (2014), p. 122; Roberts and Palfrey (2010), p. 37; Bowden (2013), p. 13.

[374] See explanation in PCLOB (2014), pp. 36–39.

[375] The US National Research Council published a conceptual model illustrating the different stages of the process with the example. See National Research Council (2015), p. 28–32.

[376] ECJ, *Tele2/Watson*, para. 78; ECJ, *Ministerio Fiscal*, para. 34; ECJ, *Privacy International*, para. 49; ECJ, *La Quadrature du Net*, para. 104; see Sect. 2.4.1.1.2.

[377] ECJ, AG Opinion, *Schrems 2*, para. 225.

member states, including their commitments under the ECHR. The surveillance practice relates to fields in which individuals are active only if a national measure requires companies operating the internet infrastructure to grant the authorities responsible for national security access to the data flows on the infrastructure they operate.[378] Such a measure does not fall within the limitations placed on the scope of Union law in the light of Article 4(2) TEU. Accordingly, the standards for comparison of essential equivalence must be found in the level of protection accorded by Union law defined in the Charter, the GDPR, and other relevant instruments of secondary legislation.

2.4.2 *Requirements for Essential Equivalence of Protection from Internet Surveillance*

Foreign internet surveillance is a focal point of the extraterritorial dimension of the right to data protection. The requirements for essential equivalence of protection of personal data from internet surveillance practices can be found in the Charter, the GDPR, and other relevant instruments of secondary Union law, on the one hand, and in the law of the EU member states, including their commitments under the ECHR, on the other hand. In 2016, after the ECJ handed down the *Schrems* judgment, the Article 29 WP screened the jurisprudence of the ECJ and the ECtHR and defined four "European Essential Guarantees" in order to group the requirements for essential equivalence of protection from internet surveillance practices.[379] The EDPB updated the European Essential Guarantees in 2020 after the ECJ handed down the *Schrems 2* judgment.[380] These requirements have to be seriously taken into account for all transfers of personal data to third countries.[381] They prescribe data processing based on clear, precise and accessible rules (Sect. 2.4.2.1), necessity and proportionality of data processing with regard to a legitimate objective (Sect. 2.4.2.2), the existence of an independent oversight mechanism (Sect. 2.4.2.3), and the availability of effective remedies (Sect. 2.4.2.4).

[378] Ibid., para. 211.

[379] It is the conclusion of work undertaken by the Article 29 WP in the aftermath of the ECJ's judgment in *Schrems*. See the Article 29 WP (2016).

[380] EDPB (2020), p. 5.

[381] The Article 29 WP also underlines that individuals could call upon their DPA for help investigating and protecting fundamental rights "should a third country allow for interferences that go beyond what should be regarded as strictly necessary in a democratic society." Article 29 WP (2016), p. 6, 12.

2.4.2.1 Clear, Precise and Accessible Rules

Guarantee A requires that the processing of personal data for surveillance purposes should be based on clear, precise and accessible rules.[382] This guarantee corresponds to the requirements in Article 52 CFR that any limitation on the exercise of fundamental rights must be provided for by law, and in Article 8(2) ECHR that any interference with the right to private life must be in accordance with the law. Limitations must be foreseeable as to their effect for the individual in order to give him or her adequate protection against arbitrary interferences.[383] The reference to foreseeability in the surveillance context cannot be the same as in many other fields.[384] Nonetheless, domestic law must be sufficiently clear to give individuals an adequate indication as to the circumstances and conditions which empower public authorities to resort to such measures.[385] It would be against the rule of law for the discretion of the implementation of surveillance legislation to be expressed in terms of unfettered power because that implementation is not open to public scrutiny.[386]

The two internet surveillance practices discussed above can be used for targeted and untargeted surveillance. Mireille Delmas-Marty has summarized the distinction between targeted and untargeted surveillance: "*Au lieu de partir de la cible pour trouver les données, on part des données pour trouver la cible.*"[387] The Dutch Review Committee for Intelligence and Security Services (CTIVD) provides a useful definition for targeted and untargeted surveillance regarding the interception of data flows from the internet.[388] Targeted interception is a form of interception where the person, organization or technical characteristic at whom/which the data collection is targeted can be specified in advance. Untargeted interception is a form of interception where the person, organization or technical characteristic at whom/ which the data collection is targeted cannot be specified in advance. The two types of surveillance are often treated differently when it comes to the requirements for protection of human rights and fundamental rights from surveillance practices. This is also the case for requirement of clear, precise and accessible rules:

Regarding targeted surveillance, the ECtHR developed minimum safeguards that should be set out in law in order to avoid abuses of power:[389]

382 EDPB (2020), p. 8–10; Article 29 WP (2016), p. 7.

383 Ibid.

384 ECtHR, *Big Brother Watch and others v. United Kingdom,* para. 333; ECtHR, *Zakharov v. Russia*, paras 228–229.

385 ECtHR, *Zakharov v. Russia*, paras 228–229.

386 Ibid., para. 230.

387 The English translation of this summary: "Instead of starting with the target to find the data, you start with the data to find the target." Delmas-Marty (2015).

388 CTIVD (2014), pp. 45–46.

389 ECtHR, *Weber and Saravia v. Germany*, para. 95 with further references to the case-law; EDPB (2020), p. 9; Article 29 WP (2016), p. 3.

- the nature of the offences which may give rise to an interception or surveillance order;
- a definition of the categories of people that might be subject to surveillance;
- a limit on the duration of the measure;
- the procedure to be followed for examining, using and storing the data obtained;
- the precautions to be taken when communicating the data to other parties;
- the circumstances in which the data must be destroyed.

Regarding untargeted surveillance, the ECtHR held in *Big Brother Watch and others v. United Kingdom* and *Centrum för rättvisa v. Sweden* that these safeguards for targeted surveillance have to be adapted to reflect the specific features of a bulk interception regime.[390] The ECtHR found that the first two of the six minimum safeguards are not readily applicable to a bulk interception regime but that the other safeguards are still relevant.[391] Nevertheless, the ECtHR suggested a new set of criteria that domestic legal frameworks need to define when it comes to untargeted surveillance:[392]

- the grounds on which bulk interception may be authorised;
- the circumstances in which an individual's communications may be intercepted;
- the procedure to be followed for granting authorisation;
- the procedures to be followed for selecting, examining and using intercept material;
- the precautions to be taken when communicating the material to other parties;
- the limits on the duration of interception, the storage of intercept material and the circumstances in which such material must be erased and destroyed;
- the procedures and modalities for supervision by an independent authority of compliance with the above safeguards and its powers to address non-compliance;
- the procedures for independent ex post facto review of such compliance and the powers vested in the competent body in addressing instances of non-compliance.

2.4.2.2 Necessity and Proportionality

Guarantee B requires that any interference with fundamental rights must be necessary and proportional with regard to the legitimate objectives pursued.[393] This

[390] ECtHR, *Big Brother Watch and others v. United Kingdom*, para. 348; ECtHR, *Centrum för rättvisa v. Sweden*, para. 261. This stands in contrast to the ECtHR's position in *Liberty and others v. United Kingdom* where the Court there saw no reason to apply different principles concerning the clarity and accessibility of the rules governing more general programs of surveillance. See ECtHR, *Liberty and others v. United Kingdom*, para. 63.

[391] ECtHR, *Big Brother Watch and others v. United Kingdom*, para. 348; ECtHR, *Centrum för rättvisa v. Sweden*, para. 261.

[392] ECtHR, *Big Brother Watch and others v. United Kingdom*, para. 361; ECtHR, *Centrum för rättvisa v. Sweden*, para. 275.

[393] EDPB (2020), pp. 10–12; Article 29 WP (2016), pp. 7–9.

guarantee corresponds to the requirement in Article 52 CFR that subject to the principle of proportionality, limitations on the exercise of fundamental rights are possible if they are necessary and genuinely meet objectives of general interest recognized by the EU, and the requirement in Article 8(2) ECHR that an interference with the right to private life must be necessary in a democratic society. It is settled case law of the ECJ that "derogations and limitations in relation to the protection of personal data must apply only in so far as is strictly necessary."[394] Targeted surveillance and untargeted surveillance are again treated differently when it comes to necessity and proportionality:

Regarding targeted surveillance, the ECtHR held in *Zakharov v. Russia* that there must be a "reasonable suspicion" against a person for surveillance measures to be authorized.[395] The authorization for the interception of telephone communication must clearly identify a specific person or premises to be placed under surveillance. The identification may be made by name, address, telephone number, or other relevant information.[396]

The ECJ used the standard of reasonable suspicion developed in *Zakharov v. Russia* to address government access to personal data retained by providers of electronic communications services in *Tele2/Watson*:

> In that regard, access can, as a general rule, be granted, in relation to the objective of fighting crime, only to the data of individuals suspected of planning, committing or having committed a serious crime or of being implicated in one way or another in such a crime.[397]

The ECJ showed that access to the retained data must be targeted for the objective of fighting crime. The ECJ relaxed the standard of reasonable suspicion in *Tele2/Watson* when the retained data is accessed for the objective of national security:

> However, in particular situations, where for example vital national security, defence or public security interests are threatened by terrorist activities, access to the data of other persons might also be granted where there is objective evidence from which it can be deduced that that data might, in a specific case, make an effective contribution to combating such activities.[398]

It seems that in order to comply with this standard, access to retained data must still be targeted, but there does not have to be a "reasonable suspicion" against the person whose data is accessed.[399]

Regarding untargeted surveillance, the Article 29 WP elaborated in 2016 that the standards of reasonable suspicion and identification suggest that only targeted surveillance is justifiable because untargeted surveillance would, by definition, not

[394] ECJ, *Digital Rights Ireland*, para. 52; ECJ, *Schrems*, para. 92; ECJ, *Tele2/Watson*, para. 96; ECJ, Opinion 1/15, para. 140.

[395] ECtHR, *Zakharov v. Russia*, para. 262.

[396] Ibid., para. 264.

[397] ECJ, *Tele2/Watson*, para. 119.

[398] Ibid.

[399] See also ECJ, *Privacy International*, para. 78.

comply with these requirements.[400] The EDPB did not specifically address the issue of reasonable suspicion and untargeted surveillance in the update of the European Essential Guarantees in 2020. The ECtHR clarified in *Big Brother Watch and others v. United Kingdom* and *Centrum för rättvisa v. Sweden* that the requirement of reasonable suspicion is less germane in the bulk interception context, the purpose of which is in principle preventive, rather than for the investigation of a specific target and/or an identifiable criminal offence.[401] The Accordingly, ECtHR did not use the standard of reasonable suspicion from its case-law on targeted surveillance in these two cases on bulk interception.

Furthermore, the ECJ ruled on a series of untargeted data retention cases. The ECJ decided in *Tele2/Watson* that national legislation providing for the untargeted retention of traffic and location data for the purpose of combating serious crime *exceeds* the limits of what is strictly necessary and cannot be considered justified within a democratic society.[402] The ECJ already explained in *Digital Rights Ireland* that this is because such legislation is not restricted to retention of data pertaining to a time period and/or geographical area and/or a group of persons likely to be involved in a serious crime, or to persons who could contribute, through their data being retained, to the combating of a serious crime.[403] Nevertheless, the ECJ underlined in *La Quadrature du Net* that the objective of safeguarding national security is capable of justifying measures that entail more serious interferences with fundamental rights than those which might be justified by other objectives.[404] Accordingly, the ECJ decided that even the untargeted, general, and indiscriminate retention of traffic and location data of all persons using electronic communications systems can be justified, as long as there are sufficiently solid grounds for considering that the member state concerned is confronted with a serious threat to national security that is both genuine and present or foreseeable.[405] This retention must be limited in time to what is strictly necessary, but it can be renewed.[406]

In contrast, and with regard to transmission and not retention, the ECJ decided in *Privacy International* that the untargeted, general, and indiscriminate transmission of traffic data and location data of all persons using electronic communications services to security and intelligence agencies for the purpose of safeguarding national security cannot be justified.[407] The ECJ explained that legislation which permits the untargeted, general, and indiscriminate transmission of data to public

[400] The Article 29 WP (2016), p. 8.

[401] ECtHR, *Big Brother Watch and others v. United Kingdom*, para. 348; ECtHR, *Centrum för rättvisa v. Sweden*, para. 262.

[402] ECJ, *Tele2/Watson*, para. 107.

[403] ECJ, *Digital Rights Ireland*, para. 59.

[404] ECJ, *La Quadrature du Net*, para. 136; ECJ, *Privacy International*, para. 75; EDPB (2020), p. 10.

[405] Ibid., para. 137.

[406] Ibid., para. 138.

[407] ECJ, *Privacy International*, para. 81.

authorities also entails general access and is prohibited.[408] In accordance, the ECJ held that general access to all retained data, regardless of whether there is any link, at least indirect, with the aim pursued, cannot be regarded as limited to what is strictly necessary.[409]

2.4.2.3 Independent Oversight Mechanism

Guarantee C requires an independent oversight mechanism for surveillance activities of the state.[410] This guarantee is reflected in Article 8(3) CFR. Independent oversight is also relevant for the assessment of lawful limitations of surveillance measures according to Article 52 CFR and Article 8(2) ECHR.

The ECtHR found it essential that the oversight mechanisms should themselves provide adequate and effective safeguards to keep the interference to what is necessary in a democratic society.[411] The ECtHR stressed that in a field such as secret surveillance, where abuse in individual cases is easy and could have harmful consequences for a democratic society as a whole, it is desirable to entrust supervisory control to a judge because judicial control offers the best guarantees of independence, impartiality, and proper procedure.[412] A non-judicial authority may be compatible with the Convention provided that the authority is sufficiently independent from the executive.[413]

An interference with the right to private life and the right to data protection can occur at different states of the surveillance process; for example, at the time of collection of the personal data and at the time the data is accessed by intelligence agencies for further processing.[414] Consequently, the ECtHR considers that independent oversight should also take place at different stages: when the surveillance is first ordered, while it is being carried out, and/or after it has been terminated.[415]

For a long time, the ECtHR did not find prior authorization of secret surveillance measures to be an absolute requirement. Only with regard to targeted surveillance measures concerning the media, has the ECtHR ruled that prior authorization is indispensable.[416] In *Zakharov v. Russia*, the ECtHR hinted that prior judicial

---

[408] Ibid., para. 80.

[409] Ibid., para. 78.

[410] EDPB (2020), pp. 12–13; Article 29 WP (2016), p. 9.

[411] ECtHR, *Zakharov v. Russia*, para. 233.

[412] Ibid.

[413] ECtHR, *Szabó and Vissy v. Hungary*, para. 77. Cp. also ECtHR, *Big Brother Watch and others v. United Kingdom*, para. 351.

[414] ECtHR, *Big Brother Watch and others v. United Kingdom*, para. 356; ECtHR, *Centrum för rättvisa v. Sweden*, para. 244; ECtHR, *Szabó and Vissy v. Hungary*, para. 77.

[415] Ibid.; ECtHR, *Klass and others v. Germany*, paras 55–56.

[416] The ECtHR underlined that an *ex post* review cannot restore the confidentiality of journalistic sources once it is destroyed. ECtHR, *Telegraaf Media Nederland Landelijke Media B.V. and Others v. the Netherlands*, para. 101.

authorization of secret surveillance measures is an important safeguard against arbitrariness of secret surveillance and serves to limit the authorities' discretion in interpreting the scope of mandating and performing surveillance.[417] In *Big Brother Watch and others v. United Kingdom* and *Centrum för rättvisa v. Sweden*, the ECtHR underlined that in the context of untargeted surveillance (bulk interception), the importance of supervision and review will be amplified because of the risk of abuse and because the legitimate need for secrecy will mean that, for national security reasons, states will often not be able to disclose information concerning their surveillance operations.[418] The ECtHR then held that in order to minimize the risk of the bulk interception being abused, the process must be subject to "end-to-end safeguards", meaning that an assessment should be made at each stage of the process of the necessity and proportionality of the measures being taken; that bulk interception should be subject to independent authorization at the outset, when the object and scope of the bulk operation are being defined; and that the operation should be subject to supervision and independent *ex post facto* review.[419] Prior authorization has therefore become a new standard in the jurisprudence of the ECtHR. Regarding the objective and the scope of the bulk operation that needs to be subject to independent authorization, the ECtHR further clarified that the information—next to the purpose of the interception and the bearers or communication routes—must include at the very least the types or categories of selectors to be used.[420] In case of hard selectors such as e-mail addresses or names, every such selector must be justified—with regard to the principles of necessity and proportionality—by the intelligence services and that justification should be scrupulously recorded and be subject to a process of prior internal authorization providing for separate and objective verification of whether the justification meets these principles.[421]

The ECJ made it clear in its jurisprudence on data retention that prior authorization is necessary. The ECJ held that access to retained personal data should be made dependent on a prior review carried out by a court or by an independent administrative body, whose decision seeks to limit access to the data and their use to what is strictly necessary for the purpose of attaining the objective pursued.[422]

---

[417] ECtHR, *Zakharov v. Russia*, para. 249.

[418] ECtHR, *Big Brother Watch and others v. United Kingdom*, para. 349; ECtHR, *Centrum för rättvisa v. Sweden*, para. 263.

[419] ECtHR, *Big Brother Watch and others v. United Kingdom*, para. 350; ECtHR, *Centrum för rättvisa v. Sweden*, para. 264.

[420] ECtHR, *Big Brother Watch and others v. United Kingdom*, paras 352, 354; ECtHR, *Centrum för rättvisa v. Sweden*, paras 266, 268.

[421] ECtHR, *Big Brother Watch and others v. United Kingdom*, para. 353; ECtHR, *Centrum för rättvisa v. Sweden*, para. 269.

[422] ECJ, *Digital Rights Ireland*, para. 62; see also ECJ, *Tele2/Watson*, para. 120.

2.4.2.4 Effective Remedies

Guarantee D requires that effective remedies are available to individuals who are (or suspect to be) subject to surveillance activities.[423] This guarantee is reflected in Article 47 CFR but it is also relevant under Article 8(2) ECHR. The first paragraph of Article 47 CFR states that everyone, whose rights guaranteed by EU law are violated, needs to have an effective remedy before a tribunal.[424]

The ECtHR recalled in *Zahkarov v. Russia* that there are two ways of addressing the issue of remedies: either by notifying concerned individuals of the surveillance measures taken and, thus, enabling a challenge to their legality retrospectively, or, by enabling individuals who suspect to be subject to surveillance measures to apply to a court or tribunal whose jurisdiction does not depend on any notification.[425] Such a court must be independent and impartial, adopt its own rules of procedure, consist of members that hold or have held high judicial office or be experienced lawyers, and, in undertaking its examination of complaints, the court should have access to all relevant information, including closed materials, and it should have the powers to remedy non-compliance.[426]

The ECJ relied heavily on notification of concerned individuals in *Tele2/Watson* for the targeted access to retained data as soon as notification would no longer jeopardize the surveillance measure.[427] The ECJ found that the "notification is, in fact, necessary to enable the persons affected to exercise, *inter alia*, their right to a legal remedy."[428] With regard to the notification required for an automated and untargeted analysis of traffic and location data of all persons using electronic communications systems, the ECJ found that the competent national authority is obliged to publish information of a general nature relating to that analysis without having to notify the persons concerned individually. However, if the data matches the parameters specified in the measure authorizing the automated analysis and that authority identifies the person concerned in order to further analyze the data concerning him or her, it is necessary to notify that person individually, as soon as notification would no longer jeopardize the surveillance measure.[429]

In contrast, the ECtHR did say in *Big Brother Watch and others v. United Kingdom* and *Centrum för rättvisa v. Sweden* that it has repeatedly found the subsequent notification of surveillance measures to be a relevant factor in assessing the effectiveness of remedies before the courts, but it acknowledges that notification is not necessary if the system of domestic remedies permits any person who suspects that his or her communications are being or have been intercepted to apply to the

[423] EDPB (2020) 13–15; Article 29 WP (2016), p. 11.

[424] ECJ, *Schrems*, para. 95.

[425] ECtHR, *Zakharov v. Russia*, paras 286–288.

[426] ECtHR, *Kennedy v. the United Kingdom*, para. 167.

[427] ECJ, *Tele2/Watson*, para. 121.

[428] Ibid.

[429] ECJ, *La Quadrature du Net*, para. 191.

courts.[430] In the absence of a notification requirement, the ECtHR found it imperative that the remedy should be before a body which, while not necessarily judicial, is independent of the executive and ensures the fairness of the proceedings, offering, in so far as possible, an adversarial process.[431] The decisions of such authority shall be reasoned and legally binding with regard, inter alia, to the cessation of unlawful interception and the destruction of unlawfully obtained and/or stored intercept material.[432]

2.4.3 No Double Standards for Foreign Internet Surveillance

Some commentators alleged that it is hypocritical for EU policymakers and the ECJ to concern themselves with foreign surveillance practices when the EU does not seem to discipline surveillance practices at home.[433] They criticize that the EU maintains double standards between EU member states and third states when it comes to data protection. These allegations are nurtured by the fact that many EU member states (continue to) employ large-scale surveillance programs. Scholars inform that

> [i]n the UK, the GCHQ's Tempora program is reported to have placed 200 interceptors on cables running from the British Isles to Western Europe and the United States. The French DGSE has allegedly placed similar interceptors on underwater cables out of its military base in Djibouti. Among other activities, the German BND has been said to tap directly into the largest Internet Hub in Europe, the Frankfurt-based DE-CIX. Sweden's FRA taps the underwater cables that connect to the Baltic countries and Russia. The different intelligence services work more or less together in networks to gather information and extend a global reach, covering the Internet.[434]

Six EU member states have detailed legislation on surveillance of data flows: France, Germany, the Netherlands, Sweden, the UK and Finland.[435] Other EU member

[430] ECtHR, *Big Brother Watch and others v. United Kingdom*, paras 357–358; ECtHR, *Centrum för rättvisa v. Sweden*, paras 271–272. The ECtHR also explains why a system not based on notification might be better for the protection of individuals.

[431] ECtHR, *Big Brother Watch and others v. United Kingdom*, para. 359; ECtHR, *Centrum för rättvisa v. Sweden*, para. 273.

[432] Ibid.

[433] Chander (2020), pp. 8–11; Baker (2016); Robertson (2016); Bourgeois et al. (2016), pp. 118–119; Moerel (2016), p. 2; Wolf and Winston (2015); Heumann and Scott (2013), p. 2; Kuner (2013), pp. 115–116; Kuner (2017c), p. 35.

[434] Bauman et al. (2014), p. 122.

[435] FRA (2017), p. 40; Bigo et al. (2013), pp. 39–60. For a comprehensive overview of the statutory and constitutional legal framework governing the bulk collection of communication data by the German Federal Intelligence Service (*Bundesnachrichtendienst*, BND) see Schaller (2018), pp. 955–958; Broy (2017), pp. 226–228.

states allow for general surveillance of data flows, but do not regulate it in detail. Italy is an example.[436]

The allegations of double standards do not prove true. The determination of the applicable standards for the comparison of essential equivalence for foreign surveillance practices depends on whether a surveillance practice would, if it emanated from an EU member state, fall within the limitations placed on the scope of Union law in the light of Article 4(2) TEU. Should a surveillance practice be covered under Union law, the applicable standards for the comparison of essential equivalence can be found in the Charter, the GDPR, and other relevant instruments of EU secondary law. Should a surveillance practice fall within the limitations placed on the scope of Union law, the applicable standards for the comparison of essential equivalence can be found under the law of the EU member states, including their commitments under the ECHR. Either way, the same standards apply for EU member states and third states.

The Article 29 WP noted that the European Essential Guarantees are based on what is required by the law and not necessarily on what is the current practice in EU member states.[437] The current practice in EU member states might not live-up to the requirements of Union law or to their commitments under the ECHR. However, that practice can always be challenged before the respective judicial authorities.

2.4.4 International Human Rights Law and Internet Surveillance

The right to continuous protection of personal data has an impact on third countries. Their ability to import personal data from the EU depends on the level of protection they afford to personal data that is transferred from the EU. The extraterritorial dimension of the right to data protection requires protection of personal data that is essentially equivalent to that guaranteed within the EU. This also includes protection from internet surveillance. The right to continuous protection of personal data therefore restrains the ability of states to apply surveillance practices if they want to import personal data from the EU. However, international human rights law also restrains the ability of states to apply surveillance practices. Article 17 ICCPR contains a right to privacy that covers data protection issues (Sect. 2.4.4.1). That right applies regardless of nationality (Sect. 2.4.4.2), and it also protects individuals located outside the territory of the surveilling state (Sect. 2.4.4.3). The standard of protection from internet surveillance of the right to privacy in Article 17 ICCPR is similar to the extraterritorial dimension of the right to data protection (Sect. 2.4.4.4).

---

[436] FRA (2017), p. 42.

[437] The Article 29 WP also underlined that it does not maintain a double standard and that the EU member states were also called upon to ensure that their surveillance legislation is in line with the jurisprudence of the ECJ and the ECtHR. Article 29 WP (2016), p. 12.

2.4.4.1 Data Protection in the ICCPR

Privacy is widely recognized as a fundamental human right.[438] Article 17 ICCPR determines that no one shall be subjected to arbitrary or unlawful interference with his privacy, family, home or correspondence, nor to unlawful attacks on his honor and reputation, and that everyone has the right to the protection of the law against such interference or attacks. The Human Rights Committee (HRC) already concluded in its General Comment No. 16 of 1988 that data protection is part of Article 17 ICCPR:

> The gathering and holding of personal information on computers, data banks and other devices, whether by public authorities or private individuals or bodies, must be regulated by law. Effective measures have to be taken by States to ensure that information concerning a person's private life does not reach the hands of persons who are not authorized by law to receive, process and use it, and is never used for purposes incompatible with the Covenant. In order to have the most effective protection of his private life, every individual should have the right to ascertain in an intelligible form, Whether, and if so, What personal data is stored in automatic data files, and for What purposes. Every individual should also be able to, ascertain which public authorizes or private individuals or bodies control or may control their files. If such files contain incorrect personal data or have been collected or processed contrary to the provisions of the law, every individual should have the right to request rectification or elimination.[439]

The HRC was willing to adapt Article 17 ICCPR to the potential dangers that new or uncontrolled forms of data processing create for the liberties of individuals and the life of democratic societies. The words used in General Comment No. 16 were inspired by the body of legal instruments on data protection found nationally and internationally at the time.[440] Developments at the UN confirm that data protection can be anchored in international human rights law.[441] The UN General Assembly and the Human Rights Council both underlined that Article 17 ICCPR is implicated by the online gathering and processing of personal data.[442] The UN General Assembly specifically called upon states to review their surveillance practices "with a view to upholding the right to privacy by ensuring the full and effective implementation of all their obligations under international human rights law."[443]

---

[438] Joseph et al. (2004), pp. 476–477; Bygrave (2010), p. 45.

[439] HRC (1988), para. 10.

[440] Bygrave (1998), pp. 252, 283–284.

[441] Kittichaisaree and Kuner (2015).

[442] See, e.g., UN GA (2018); Human Rights Council (2015).

[443] UN GA (2018), para. 6(c).

2.4.4.2 Application of the ICCPR

2.4.4.2.1 Nationality

Laws regulating surveillance practices in many states have traditionally distinguished between insiders (citizens and permanent residents) and outsiders (all others) and have protected the privacy and data protection rights of the insiders far more assiduously than those of the outsiders.[444] The threshold question of whether individuals enjoy human rights should in principle not depend on whether they have a state's nationality.[445] The distinction between insiders and outsiders can be criticized. The rights under the ICCPR (and the ECHR) apply to everyone within a state's jurisdiction. The UN Special Rapporteur on the promotion and protection of human rights and fundamental freedoms while countering terrorism remarked that asymmetrical protection regimes for nationals and non-nationals are incompatible with the principle of non-discrimination in Article 26 ICCPR.[446] The High Commissioner for Human Rights stated that Article 17 ICCPR has to be read together with Article 26 ICCPR.[447] No one shall be subjected to arbitrary interference with his privacy and everyone has the right to the protection of the law against such interference or attacks. The Venice Commission similarly concluded that all individuals have privacy rights *vis-à-vis* states party to the ICCPR.[448]

2.4.4.2.2 Territory

If citizenship is normatively irrelevant for the threshold question of whether the ICCPR applies to a particular surveillance practice, the truly critical question becomes the territorial scope of the ICCPR on the basis of the location of the individual and/or the interference with his or her rights.[449] Article 2(1) ICCPR defines the territorial scope the Covenant and obliges every state party to ensure the rights recognized in the Covenant to all individuals within its territory *and* subject to its jurisdiction. The provision is somewhat awkwardly formulated.[450] It is disputed whether the provision's seemingly conjunctive reference to territory admits of any extraterritorial application, i.e. whether an individual who is subject

[444] Bignami and Resta (2018), p. 358. The most prominent example is the US. The Five Eyes network member states Australia, New Zealand, Canada and the UK similarly distinguish between citizens (and permanent residents) and non-citizens. Milanovic (2015), fn. 25.

[445] Milanovic (2015), p. 99. In the words of Ronald Dworkin, "[t]he domain of human rights has no place for passports." Dworkin (2006), p. 48.

[446] UN GA (2014a), para. 42.

[447] UN GA (2014b), para. 36.

[448] European Commission for Democracy Through Law (2015), para. 72.

[449] Milanovic (2015), p. 101.

[450] Nowak (2005), p. 43.

to the jurisdiction but not within the territory of the (surveilling) state is protected by Article 17 ICCPR.[451] The US minority position is that the ICCPR applies only to individuals who are both within the state's territory and subject to the state's jurisdiction.[452] This interpretation does not cover communications involving individuals abroad under Article 17 ICCPR. The US position has been criticized by other states, human rights experts, and treaty bodies as fundamentally flawed.[453]

According to the general rule of interpretation in Article 31(1) VCLT, the ICCPR must be interpreted in good faith in accordance with the ordinary meaning to be given to the terms of the Covenant in their context and in the light of its object and purpose. This means, at the very least, that when there are several plausible readings of the territorial scope in Article 2(1) ICCPR, the one that more accords with the treaty's object and purpose should be preferred. The HRC determined in General Comment No. 31 that the object and purpose of the ICCPR is to extend human rights comprehensively around the globe and leave as few gaps as possible in that protection.[454] The HRC concluded that "a State party must respect and ensure the rights laid down in the Covenant to anyone within the power or effective control of that State Party, even if not situated within the territory of the State Party."[455] According to the supplementary means of interpretation in Article 32(a) VCLT, recourse may be had to the preparatory work of the ICCPR to determine the meaning of a provision when the interpretation according to Article 31 VCLT leaves the meaning ambiguous. The ICJ confirmed the conclusion of the HRC in the *Wall* case:

> The *travaux préparatoires* of the Covenant confirm the Committee's interpretation of Article 2 of that instrument. These show that, in adopting the wording chosen, the drafters of the Covenant did not intend to allow States to escape from their obligations when they exercise jurisdiction outside their national territory. They only intended to prevent persons residing abroad from asserting, vis-à-vis their State of origin, rights that do not fall within the competence of that State, but of that of the State of residence.[456]

[451] Milanovic (2015), p. 102.

[452] Bignami and Resta (2018), p. 360. However, the US position on the extraterritorial application of the ICCPR is not as clear, long-standing and principled as it is often suggested. Milanovic (2015), pp. 102–108.

[453] Georgieva (2015), p. 110.

[454] HRC (2004), pp. 3–4. Peter Marguilles critically noted that "[w]hile some have argued that the rights promoting nature of a multilateral treaty like the ICCPR justifies less regard for the agreement's text, an inappropriately expansive reading of the text sacrifices essential virtues of a treaty: predictability, legitimacy, and connection to state consent." Nevertheless, he concluded that the ICCPR applies to foreign internet surveillance practices. Margulies (2014), p. 2147. Similarly, Thomas Buergenthal, a former ICJ judge, noted that Article 2(1) ICCPR could have been drafted more clearly, but that failure of drafting does not license interpreters to import their own policy preferences without regard to the text. Nevertheless, he also finds that other provisions of the ICCPR make no sense if they do not protect individuals outside of a state's territory. Buergenthal (1981), p. 74.

[455] HRC (2004), para. 10. See also HRC, *Lopez v. Uruguay*, para. 12.1–12.3; HRC, *Montero v. Uruguay*, para. 5.

[456] ICJ, *Wall*, para. 179.

It is now widely held that Article 2(1) ICCPR guarantees the Covenant rights to all individuals within a state's territory and, equally, to all individuals subject to its jurisdiction.[457] Even Harold Koh, former legal advisor to the US State Department, agreed in an internal memorandum on the extraterritorial application of the ICCPR (leaked in 2014 and published by the New York Times) with the critics of the US minority position that the language of the ICCPR is not clear and that reading Article 2(1) ICCPR to categorically disallow extraterritorial application would be contrary to the Covenant's object and purpose.[458]

It is therefore necessary to consider whether a state exercises effective control regarding internet surveillance practices in order to establish the jurisdiction of the ICCPR. It is clear that a state exercises effective control in the case of government access to personal data held by private companies in the territory of that state.[459] However, on the basis of a narrow interpretation of the effective control test, it is unclear whether the application of the ICCPR can be triggered by practices of a purely incorporeal character, such as the interception of data flows from the internet outside the territory of a state.[460] Many scholars argue that the effective control test should be applied flexibly in order to cope with the challenges arising from technological advances.[461] Conventional modes of exercising control such as police searches of physical premises are rarely employed in the realm of the internet and online communications. Technology enables massive intrusions into the privacy of individuals abroad. The effective control test must also be tailored to the specific character of the right at issue.[462] The test of effective control could be interpreted as meaning that either the right of an individual outside state territory[463] or his or her correspondence and communication[464] is under the effective control of the supervising state.[465] Whenever a state collects personal data, it is indirectly exercising control over those individuals that generated the data.[466]

Human rights bodies have confirmed an expansive interpretation of the effective control test in the area of internet surveillance. The HRC urged the US to take "all

457 Rodley (2012), p. 110.

458 US Department of State (2010), pp. 12–13.

459 The territorial model of jurisdiction applies. Milanovic (2015), pp. 122–123.

460 Daskal (2014); Bellinger (2014), p. 3. The Tallinn Manual on the International Law Applicable to Cyber Warfare argues that the effective control test should apply to cyber warfare. See Schmitt (2013), pp. 32–33.

461 Bignami and Resta (2018), pp. 362–363; Langer (2019), pp. 17–20; Milanovic (2015), pp. 126–129; Margulies (2014), pp. 2150–2152; Georgieva (2015), p. 113; Nowak (2014).

462 Milanovic (2015), p. 120; Scheinin (2014).

463 Scheinin (2014).

464 Nowak (2005).

465 Some scholars call for a virtual control test in this regard. See Margulies (2014), pp. 2150–2152; Peters (2013); Watt (2017), p. 14. Jordan J. Paust criticizes the virtual control test for being "without support in patterns of generally shared legal expectations about personal jurisdiction". Paust (2015), p. 625.

466 Bignami and Resta (2018), p. 363.

necessary measures to ensure that its surveillance activities, both within and outside the United States, conform to its obligations under the Covenant, including article 17."[467] The UN High Commissioner for Human Rights similarly took the position that internet surveillance

> may engage a State's human rights obligations if that surveillance involves the State's exercise of power or effective control in relation to digital communications infrastructure, wherever found, for example, through direct tapping or penetration of that infrastructure. Equally, where the State exercises regulatory jurisdiction over a third party that physically controls the data, that State also would have obligations under the Covenant.[468]

And the UN Rapporteur on the Right to Privacy underlined the universal nature of privacy in the digital age:

> Surveillance activities, regardless of whether they are directed towards foreigners or citizens, must only be carried out in compliance with fundamental human rights such as privacy. Any national laws or international agreements disregarding this fact, must be considered outdated and incompatible with the universal nature of privacy and fundamental rights in the digital age.[469]

I thus conclude that internet surveillance practices, including those applied abroad, fall within the scope of the ICCPR and individuals subject to such practices should be entitled to the protection of their privacy according to Article 17 ICCPR.[470] This includes individuals in the EU whose personal data is transferred from the EU to a third country.

2.4.4.3 Standards of the Right to Privacy

Article 17 ICCPR prohibits unlawful or arbitrary interferences with privacy.[471] The HRC has cautioned a number of states that their legal arrangements on surveillance were insufficiently clear and precise in order to satisfy the standard in Article 17 ICCPR.[472]

The HRC explained that the standard of non-arbitrariness is intended to guarantee that even interference provided for by law should be in accordance with the provisions, aims and objectives of the Covenant and should be, in any event, reasonable for the particular circumstances.[473] The standard of non-arbitrariness in the ICCPR

---

[467] HRC (2014a), para. 22.

[468] UN GA (2014b), para. 34.

[469] UN GA (2017), para. 31.

[470] Marko Milanovic adds that even if the interception of data flows from the infrastructure of the internet would not be under the effective control of the surveilling state, its subsequent storage, processing and use may well take place within such control and constitute fresh interferences with the right to privacy in Article 17 ICCPR. Milanovic (2015), pp. 126–127.

[471] HRC (1988), para. 2.

[472] See, e.g., HRC (1997), para. 20; HRC (1995), para. 19.

[473] HRC (1988), para. 4.

appears to be more lenient than the standard of necessity in a democratic society in the ECHR. However, the HRC has never read the term arbitrary in Article 17 ICCPR, or in other provisions of the Covenant, by its literal meaning, as referring to unrestrained decisions made purely by discretion or on whim without any rational reason behind it—which would be a standard so low that it could be easily satisfied by almost any rule allowing for the interference.[474] The HRC observed in *Canepa v. Canada* that the standard of non-arbitrariness includes "compatibility [of an interference] with the purpose, aim and objectives of the Covenant."[475] The HRC defined the term arbitrary (albeit in a different context, with relation to arbitrary detention) in the following manner:

> "The notion of "arbitrariness" is not to be equated with "against the law", but must be interpreted more broadly to include elements of inappropriateness, injustice, lack of predictability and due process of law, as well as elements of reasonableness, necessity and proportionality."[476]

The HRC used proportionality in *Canepa v. Canada* to assess the relationship between the legitimate objective of an interference and its impact on the individual.[477] The HRC has considered in its concluding observations regarding (internet) surveillance practices in states subject to periodic human rights review that independent, especially judicial, supervision of surveillance practices and effective remedies are crucial safeguards for preventing arbitrary interferences with the right to privacy.[478]

2.4.4.4 Violation of the ICCPR

Whether or not internet surveillance practices violate the right to privacy in Article 17 ICCPR has been subject to scholarly debate. Ilina Georgieva raises serious doubts about the legality of mass surveillance practices. She argues that the bulk collection of personal data and the indiscriminate interception of data flows constitute a disproportionate restriction of the right to privacy under Article 17 ICCPR.[479] Anne Peters observes that "dragnet searches and stock data retention of the entire population or large groups without concrete indications founding a suspicion that terrorist or criminal acts are being planned seems prima facie disproportionate."[480]

[474] Milanovic (2015), p. 133.

[475] HRC, *Canepa v. Canada*, para. 11.4.

[476] HRC (2014b), para. 12.

[477] Ibid.

[478] Shany (2017). See e.g. HRC (2017), para. 36; HRC (2016a), 37; HRC (2016b), para. 15; HRC (2015a), para. 42; HRC (2015b), para. 12; HRC (2015c), para. 24; HRC (2014a), para. 22; HRC (2009a), para. 14; HRC (2009b), para. 18; HRC (1998), para. 25.

[479] Georgieva (2015), p. 124.

[480] She added that it is difficult to assess the proportionality of a governmental measure in the absence of thorough knowledge of the facts. Peters (2013).

Marko Milanovich does not offer a definitive position on the compatibility of internet surveillance practices with the ICCPR.[481] He contends instead that a more restrictive position on domestic internet surveillance practices than on practices outside the territory of the surveilling state is justified. He argues that the state has alternative tools at its disposal in the domestic context. This would need to be considered in a proportionality analysis for internet surveillance practices outside the territory of the surveilling state.

In contrast, Jordan J. Paust argues that these practices cannot be considered unlawful according to Article 17 ICCPR.[482] He interprets the term unlawful so as to give primacy to international law, and especially to competences of states under the law of self-defense and the laws of war when they are applicable. According to him, war and state surveillance for the purposes of self-defense can "buttress claims that particular forms of privacy intrusion are rational, reasonable, and not arbitrary under the circumstances, and that should inform the legal meaning of the word unlawful in the ICCPR."[483] Peter Margulies is of the opinion that most surveillance programs carried out by the NSA outside the US cannot be considered arbitrary under Article 17 ICCPR because they target "terrorists, national security threats, and espionage in a tailored fashion."[484] He reads Article 17 ICCPR in tandem with the law of armed conflict and UN Security Council resolutions on counterterrorism and advances a "model of procedural pluralism that gives states flexibility in creating protections if they honor core principles such as notice, oversight, and minimization."[485] However, the arguments of Paust and Margulies are not as convincing considering that the EU, its member states, or militant groups in the EU are not engaging in military actions against a surveilling state and/or when they are not actively harboring terrorists planning attacks against a surveilling state.

It is neither necessary nor possible within this context to make a definitive judgment on the violation of Article 17 ICCPR as a result of foreign internet surveillance practices. However, I would argue that the standards for internet surveillance, including outside the territory of the surveilling state, under Article 17 ICCPR are similar to the standards of the EU.[486] There is a high probability that internet surveillance practices also interfere with Article 17 ICCPR if they interfere with the right to continuous protection of personal data that is transferred from the EU to third countries in Article 8 CFR. The obligations of states under the ICCPR are complementary to the extraterritorial dimension of the right to data protection.

[481] Milanovic (2015), pp. 138–139.

[482] Paust (2015), p. 647.

[483] Ibid., 647–648 [fn. omitted].

[484] Margulies (2014), p. 2152.

[485] Ibid., 2153.

[486] Cp. Shany (2017). Contrarily, Peter Margulies argues that Article 17 ICCPR does not mandate the same itemized menu of safeguards required in the jurisprudence of the ECJ and the ECtHR. See Margulies (2014), p. 2153.

2.4.5 *Summary*

The extraterritorial dimension of the right to data protection requires continuous protection of personal data that is transferred from the EU to third countries. This protection must be essentially equivalent to that guaranteed within the EU. Foreign internet surveillance is a focal point of the right to continuous protection of personal data. Foreign internet surveillance is an obstacle to trade if the protection of personal data is not essentially equivalent to that guaranteed within the EU. Four Essential European Guarantees entail the relevant requirements for essential equivalence of protection from internet surveillance. However, there are still uncertainties as to what kind of surveillance measures are lawful under the Charter and the ECHR because the jurisprudence in the field is still developing. This is problematic because the EU cannot communicate in sufficient details what kind of internet surveillance practices would be compatible with the right to continuous protection of personal data. Nevertheless, allegations of double standards for third states regarding the required standards for surveillance practices cannot be substantiated. This is important for the analysis in international trade law. In addition, the obligations of states under international human rights law regarding the standards for surveillance practices are complementary to the extraterritorial dimension of the right to data protection.

2.5 Conclusion

From the very beginning, the development of data protection was focused on technological progress and the associated new powers of the state. Connections with the protection of privacy emerged in European constitutions and connections with the protection of trade emerged through international instruments. The inclusion in the Charter of a right to data protection, in addition to the right to private life, expressed the necessity of strengthening protections for fundamental rights in light of changes in society, social progress, and scientific and technological developments enshrined in the Preamble of the Charter. The right to data protection in Article 8 CFR consists of six written constituent parts. The jurisprudence of the ECJ reveals an unwritten constituent part of Article 8 CFR, which is connected to cross-border flows of personal data. The right to continuous protection of personal data that is transferred from the EU to a third country represents the extraterritorial dimension of the right to data protection. Individuals in the EU are entitled to receive protection that is essentially equivalent to that guaranteed within the EU, when their personal data is transferred from the EU to a third country. This protection has a strong legal basis in the Treaties and is supported by the foundational values of the right to data protection. Effective protection for fundamental rights in the digital sphere cannot be guaranteed if the protection ends at the borders of the EU member states. The extraterritorial dimension of the right to data protection also mirrors the necessity of strengthening protections for fundamental rights in light of changes in society, social progress, and scientific and technological developments enshrined in the Preamble of the Charter.

Since the development of data protection is focused on technological progress and the associated new powers of the state, it is evident that foreign internet surveillance practices are the focal point of the extraterritorial dimension of the right to data protection. The internet has not only revolutionized communication, it has also enabled new forms of trade. Digital trade often involves personal data. Information about individuals now travels around the world on an unprecedented and rapidly growing scale. This information is valuable for governments and their intelligence agencies. They seek access to personal data held by private companies or directly intercept data flows from the internet. When personal data is exported from the EU to a third country, the right to continuous protection of personal data demands that the protection for the exported data in the third country must be essentially equivalent to that guaranteed within the EU. Any third country that wants to import personal data from the EU must align their internet surveillance practices with the standards of the Charter and the ECHR. This is how the right to data protection has unfolded its reach globally.

References

Bibliography

Abraham S (2017) Systematic government access to private-sector data in India. In: Cate FH, Dempsey JX (eds) Bulk collection. Systematic government access to private-sector data. Oxford University Press, Oxford, pp 257–286

Allen A (1988) Uneasy access: privacy for women in a free society. Rowman & Littlefield, Totowa

Baker J (2016) A clash of EU privacy standards. European countries could face charges of hypocrisy over data protection. Politico, 13 February 2016. https://www.politico.eu/article/chash-over-data-protection-standards-privacy-safe-harbor-europe/. Accessed 3 January 2021

Bartels L (2015) The EU's human rights obligations in relation to policies with extraterritorial effects. Eur J Int Law 25(4):1071–1091

Bauman Z, Bigo D, Esteves P, Guild E, Jabri V, Lyon D, Walker RBJ (2014) After Snowden: rethinking the impact of surveillance. Int Political Sociol 8(2):121–144

Bellinger JB (2014) Testimony Before the Privacy & Civil Liberties Oversight Board of 19 March 2014. https://www.pclob.gov/library/20140319-Testimony-8Bellinger.pdf. Accessed 3 January 2021

Bennet CJ (1997) Convergence revisited: toward a global policy for the protection of personal data? In: Agre PE, Rotenberg M (eds) Technology and privacy: the new landscape. MIT Press, Cambridge, pp 99–123

Bergemann B (2018) The consent paradox: accounting for the prominent role of consent in data protection. In: Hansen M et al (eds) Privacy and identity management. The smart revolution. Springer, Heidelberg, pp 111–131

Bignami F, Resta G (2018) Human rights extraterritoriality: the right to privacy and National Security Surveillance. In: Benvenisti E, Nolte G (eds) Community interests across international law. Oxford University Press, Oxford, pp 357–380

Bigo D, Carrera S, Hernanz N, Jeandesboz J, Parkin J, Ragazzi F, Scherrer A (2013) Mass Surveillance of Personal Data by EU Member States and its Compatibility with EU Law, CEPTS Paper in Liberty and Security in Europe, November 2013
Boehme-Neßler V (2016) Privacy: a matter of democracy. Why democracy needs privacy and data protection. Int Data Priv Law 6(3):222–229
Bok S (1982) Secrets: on the ethics of concealment and revelation. Pantheon Books, New York
Bourgeois J, Kerry CF, Long WRM, Maarten M, Charles RA (2016) Essentially Equivalent A comparison of the legal orders for privacy and data protection in the European Union and United States. Report prepared by Sidley Austin LLP, January 2016. https://www.sidley.com/~/media/publications/essentially-equivalent%2D%2D-final.pdf. Accessed 3 January 2021
Bowden C (2013) The US surveillance programmes and their impact on EU citizens' fundamental rights. Note requested by the European Parliaments Committee on Civil Liberties, Justice and Home Affairs. September 2013
Braibant G (2001) La Charte des Droits fondamentaux de l'Union européenne Seuil, Paris
Brkan M (2016) The unstoppable expansion of the EU fundamental right to data protection. Little shop of horrors? Maastricht J Eur Comp Law 23(5):812–841
Brkan M (2018) The concept of essence of fundamental rights in the EU legal order: peeling the onion to its Core. Eur Const Law Rev 14(2):332–368
Brkan M (2019) The essence of the fundamental rights to privacy and data protection: finding the way through the maze of the CJEU's constitutional reasoning. German Law J 20(6):864–883
Brouwer E (2008) Digital Borders and real rights. Effective remedies for third-country nationals in the Schengen information system. Martinus Nijhoff Publishers, Leiden/Boston
Brouwer E (2011) Legality and data protection law: the forgotten purpose of purpose limitation. In: Besselink L, Pennings F, Prechal S (eds) The eclipse of the legality principle in the European Union. Wolters Kluwer, Alphen aan den Rijn, pp 273–294
Broy D (2017) Extended rights for the German foreign secret service concerning data recovery from the internet infrastructure. Eur Data Protect Law Rev 3(1):226–228
Buergenthal T (1981) To respect and to ensure: state obligations and permissible derogations. In: Henkin L (ed) The international bill of rights: the covenant on civil and political rights. Columbia University Press, New York, pp 72–91
Burkert H (2009) Towards a new generation of data protection legislation. In: Gutwirth S, Poullet Y, de Hert P et al (eds) Reinventing data protection? Springer, Heidelberg, pp 335–342
Bygrave L (1998) Data protection pursuant to the right to privacy in human rights treaties. Int J Law Inf Technol 6(3):247–284
Bygrave L (2002) Data protection law. Approaching its rationale, logic and limits. Kluwer, The Hague
Bygrave L (2010) International agreements to protect personal data. In: Rule JB, Greenleaf G (eds) Global privacy protection. The First Generation, Cheltenham, Northampton, pp 15–49
Carolan E (2016) The continuing problems with online consent under the EU's emerging data protection principles. Comput Law Secur Rev 32(3):462–473
Chander A (2020) Is data localization a solution for Schrems II? J Int Econ Law 23:1–14
Christakis T (2017) National security, terrorism and the legality of secret surveillance: the case of France. In: Conway M, Jarvis L, Lehane O, Macdonald S, Nouri L (eds) Terrorists' Use of the Internet, Amsterdam/Berlin/Washington D.C. pp 327–337
Clifford D, Ausloos J (2018) Data protection and the role of fairness. Yearb Eur Law 37(1):130–187
Cockfield AJ (2007) Protecting the social value of privacy in the context of state investigations using new technologies. Univ Br Columbia Law Rev 40(1):41–67
Cohen JE (2000) Examined lives: informational privacy and the subject as object. Stanford Law Rev 52(5):1373–1438
Cole D (2014) 'We kill People Based on Metadata'. The New York Review of Books, 10 May 2014. www.nybooks.com/daily/2014/05/10/we-kill-people-based-metadata/. Accessed 3 January 2021

Coudray L (2010) La protection des données personnelles dans l'Union européenne: Naissance et consécration d'un droit fundamental. Editions universitaires europeennes, Berlin
Daskal J (2014) Extraterritorial Surveillance Under the ICCPR... The Treaty Allows It! Just Security, 7 March 2014. https://www.justsecurity.org/7966/extraterritorial-surveillance-iccpr-its-allowed/. Accessed 3 January 2021
De Hert P, Gutwirth S (2006) Privacy, data protection and law enforcement. Opacity of the individual and transparency of power. In: Claes E, Duff A, Gutwirth S (eds) Privacy and the criminal law. Antwerp/Oxford, Intersentia, pp 61–104
De Hert P, Gutwirth S (2009) Data protection in the case law of Strasbourg and Luxembourg: constitutionalisation in action. In: Gutwirth S, Poullet Y, de Hert P et al (eds) Reinventing data protection? Springer, Heidelberg, pp 3–44
De Hert P, Papakonstantinou V (2012) The proposed data protection regulation replacing Directive95/46/EC: a sound system for the protection of individuals. Comput Law Secur Rev 28(2): 130–142
De Hert P, Papakonstantinou V (2016) The new general data protection regulation: still a sound system for the protection of individuals? Comput Law Secur Rev 32(2):179–194
Delmas Marty M (2015) La démocratie dans les bras de Big Brother, Interview by Franck Johannès, Le Monde, 4 June 2015
Dias Venâncio P (2008) A previsão constitucional da utilização da informática. Revista de Estudos Politécnicos 5(8):243–264
Dworkin R (2006) Is democracy possible here? Princeton University Press, Princeton
ECtHR (2013) National security and European case-law. Strasbourg
Eger JM (1978) Emerging restrictions on transnational data flows: privacy protection or non-tariff trade barriers. Law Policy Int Bus 10(4):1055–1104
Ferretti F (2014) Data protection and the legitimate interest of data controllers: much ado about nothing or the winter of rights? Common Mark Law Rev 51(3):1–26
Flemming JE (1995) Securing deliberative autonomy. Stanford Law Rev 48(1):1–71
Flemming JE (2004) Securing deliberative democracy. Fordham Law Rev 72(5):1435–1476
Floridi L (2006) Four challenges for a theory of informational privacy. Ethics Inf Technol 8(3): 109–119
Forgó N, Hänold S, Schütze B (2017) The principle of purpose limitation and big data. In: Corrales M, Fenwick M, Forgó N (eds) New technology, big data and the law. Springer, Heidelberg, pp 17–42
FRA (2017) Surveillance by intelligence services: fundamental rights safeguards and remedies in the EU. Volume II: field perspectives and legal update, Vienna
Fry JD (2015) Privacy, predictability and internet surveillance in the U.S. and China: better the devil you know? Univ Pennsylvania J Int Law 37(2):419–502
Gavison R (1980) Privacy and the limits of law. Yale Law J 89(3):421–471
Gellman B, Poitras L (2013) U.S., British intelligence mining data from nine U.S. Internet companies in broad secret program. The Washington Post, 7 June 2013. https://www.washingtonpost.com/investigations/us-intelligence-mining-data-from-nine-us-internet-companies-in-broad-secret-program/2013/06/06/3a0c0da8-cebf-11e2-8845-d970ccb04497_story.html. Accessed 3 January 2021
Georgieva I (2015) The right to privacy under fire – foreign surveillance under the NSA and the GCHQ and its compatibility with Art. 17 ICCPR and Art. 8 ECHR. Utrecht J Int Eur Law 31(8): 104–130
González Fuster G (2014a) The emergence of personal data protection as a fundamental right of the EU. Springer, Heidelberg
González Fuster G (2014b) How uninformed is the average data subject? A quest for benchmarks in EU personal data protection. Revista de Internet, Derecho y Política 19:92–104
González Fuster G, Gellert R (2012) The fundamental right of data protection in the European Union: in search of an uncharted right. Int Rev Law Comput Technol 26(1):73–82

Granger M-P, Irion K (2014) The court of justice and the data retention directive in *digital rights Ireland*: telling off the EU legislator and teaching a lesson in privacy and data protection. Eur Law Rev 39(6):834–850
Greenwald G, MacAskill E (2013) NSA Prism program taps into user data of Apple, Google and others. The Guardian, 7 June 2013. https://www.theguardian.com/world/2013/jun/06/us-tech-giants-nsa-data. Accessed 3 January 2021
Groussot X, Atik J (2021) A Weaponized court of justice in schrems ii. Nordic J Eur Law 2:1–21
Heumann S, Scott B (2013) Law and Policy in Internet Surveillance Programs: United States, Great Britain and Germany. Stiftung Neue Verantwortung Impulse 25/13, September 2013. https://www.stiftung-nv.de/sites/default/files/impulse.pdf. Accessed 3 January 2021
Hijmans H (2016) The European Union as a constitutional Guardian of internet privacy and data protection: the story of Article 16 TFEU. Springer, Heidelberg
Hijmans H (2017) PNR agreement EU-Canada scrutinised: CJEU gives very precise guidance to negotiators. Eur Data Protect Law Rev 3(3):406–412
Hinchman L (1996) Autonomy, individuality, and self-determination. In: Schmidt J (ed) What is enlightenment? Eighteenth-Century answers and twentieth-century questions. University of California Press, Berkley, pp 488–515
Hondius FW (1975) Emerging data protection in Europe. Elsevier, Amsterdam
Hornung G, Schnabel C (2009) Data protection in Germany I: the population census decision and the right to informational self-determination. Comput Law Secur Rev 25(1):84–88
Hustinx P (2017) EU data protection law: the review of directive 95/46/EC and the general data protection regulation. In: Cremona M (ed) New technologies and EU law. Oxford University Press, Oxford, pp 123–173
Joseph S, Schultz J, Castan M (2004) The international covenant on civil and political rights, 2nd edn. Oxford University Press, Oxford
Kamminga MT (2020) Extraterritoriality. In: Wolfrum R, Sólveigardóttir M (eds) Max Planck Encyclopedia of Public International Law. https://opil.ouplaw.com/view/10.1093/law:epil/9780199231690/law-9780199231690-e1040?prd=EPIL&q=extraterritoriality. Accessed 3 January 2021
Kirby M (1980) Transborder data flows and the basic rules of data privacy. Stanford J Int Law 16: 27–66
Kirby M (2011) The history, achievement and future of the 1980 OECD guidelines on privacy. Int Data Priv Law 1(1):6–15
Kittichaisaree K, Kuner C (2015) The Growing Importance of Data Protection in Public International Law. EJIL:Talk! 14. October 2015
Klosek J (2000) Data privacy in the information age. Praeger, Westport
Kokott J, Sobotta C (2013) The distinction between privacy and data protection in the jurisprudence of the CJEU and the ECtHR. Int Data Priv Law 3(4):222–228
Kosta E (2013) Consent in European data protection law. Nijhoff, Leiden/Boston
Koukiadaki A (2019) Application (Article 51) and limitations (article 52(1)). In: Dorssemont F, Lörcher K, Clauwaert S, Schmitt M (eds) The charter of fundamental rights of the European Union and the employment relation. Hart Publishing, Oxford, pp 101–134
Krotoszynski RJ Jr (2016) Privacy revisited: a global perspective on the right to be left alone. Oxford University Press, Oxford
Kuner C (2013) Transborder data flows. Oxford University Press, Oxford
Kuner C (2015) Extraterritoriality and regulation of international data transfers in EU data protection law. Int Data Priv Law 5(4):235–245
Kuner C (2017a) Data Protection, Data Transfers, and International Agreements: the CJEU's Opinion 1/15. Verfassungsblog, 26 July 2017. https://verfassungsblog.de/data-protection-data-transfers-and-international-agreements-the-cjeus-opinion-115/. Accessed 3 April 2022
Kuner C (2017b) Reality and illusion in EU data transfer regulation Post Schrems. German Law J 18(4):881–918

Kuner C (2017c) The Internet and the Global Reach of EU Law. University of Cambridge Faculty of Law Research Paper No. 24/2017
Kuner C (2018) International agreements, data protection, and EU fundamental rights on the international stage: opinion 1/15 (EU-Canada PNR). Common Mark Law Rev 55(3):857–882
Langer L (2019) "Cyberspace does not lie with your borders" - Jurisdiktion und Menschenrechte im digitalen Raum. Swiss Rev Int Eur Law 29(1):3–22
Lazaro C, Le Métayer D (2015) Control over personal data: Ture remedy or Fary tale? SCRIPTed 12(1):3–34
Lenaerts K (2012) Exploring the limits of the EU charter of fundamental rights. Eur Const Law Rev 8(3):375–403
Lidberg J, Muller D (2018) Journalism and National Security in the European Union. In: Lidberg J, Muller D (eds) In the name of security – secrecy, surveillance and journalism. Anthem Press, London/New York, pp 195–208
Lynskey O (2014) Deconstructing data protection: the 'added-value' of a right to data protection in the EU legal order. Int Comp Law Q 63(3):569–597
Lynskey O (2015) The foundations of EU data protection law. Oxford University Press, Oxford
Lyon D (2014) Surveillance, Snowden, and big data: capacities, consequences, critique. Big Data Soc 1(2):1–13
Margulies P (2014) The NSA in global perspective: surveillance, human rights, and international counterterrorism. Fordham Law Rev 82(5):2137–2167
McDermott Y (2017) Conceptualising the right to data protection in an era of big data. Big Data Soc 4(1):1–7
Michael J (1994) Privacy and human rights: an international and comparative study, with special reference to developments in information technology. Dartmouth Publishing Company, London
Mifsud Bonnici JP (2014) Exploring the non-absolute nature of the right to data protection. Int Rev Law Comput Technol 28(2):131–143
Milanovic M (2015) Human rights treaties and foreign surveillance. Privacy in the digital age. Harv Int Law J 56(1):82–146
Moerel L (2016) Prohibition on data transfers to the U.S. turns into protectionism. World Data Protect Rep 16(6):1–2
Moreno-Lax V, Costello C (2014) The extraterritorial application of the EU charter of fundamental rights: from territoriality to facticity, the effectiveness model. In: Peers S, Hervey T, Kenner J, Ward A (eds) The EU charter of fundamental rights. A commentary. Nomos, Baden-Baden, pp 1700–1727
National Research Council (2015) Bulk Collection of Signals Intelligence: Technical Options. Washington DC
Nissenbaum H (1998) Protecting privacy in an information age: the problem of privacy in public. Law Philos 17(5):559–596
Nowak M (2005) U.N. Covenant on Civil and Political Rights. CCPR-Commentary, 2nd edn. Engel, Kehl am Rhein
Nowak M (2014) Letter to the Editor from Manfred Nowak, What does extraterritorial application of human rights treaties mean in practice? Just Security, 11 March 2014. https://www.justsecurity.org/8087/letter-editor-manfred-nowak-extraterritorial-application-human-rights-treaties-practice/. Accessed 3 January 2021
Nyst C (2013) Interference-Based Jurisdiction Over Violations of the Right to Privacy. EJIL:Talk! 21 November 2013
Ohm P (2010) Broken promises of privacy responding to the surprising failure of anonymization. UCLA Law Rev 57(6):1701–1777
Ojanen T (2016) Making the essence of fundamental rights real. The court of justice of the European Union clarifies the structure of fundamental rights under the charter. Eur Const Law Rev 12(2):318–329
Parsons C (2015) Beyond privacy: articulating the broader harms of pervasive mass surveillance. Media Commun 3(3):1–11

Paust JJ (2015) Can you hear me now?: private communication, National Security, and the human rights disconnect. Chic J Int Law 15(2):612–651
Penney JW (2016) Chilling effects: online surveillance and Wikipedia use. Berkley Technol Law J 31(1):117–182
Peters A (2013) Surveillance without Borders: The Unlawfulness of the NSA Panopticon, Part II. EJIL:Talk! 4 November 2013
Petersen N (2012) Human dignity, international protection. In: Wolfrum R (ed) Max Planck Encyclopedia of public international law. Oxford University Press, Oxford, pp 1013–1020
Popp V (2015) ECJ President on EU Integration, Public Opinion, Safe Harbor, Antitrust. Wall Street Journal, 14 October 2015. http://blogs.wsj.com/brussels/2015/10/14/ecj-president-on-eu-integration-public-opinion-safe-harbor-antitrust/tab/print/. Accessed 3 January 2021
Post RC (2001) Three concepts of privacy. Georgetown Law J 89(6):2087–2098
Poullet Y (2006) EU data protection policy: the directive 95/46/EC: ten years after. Comput Law Secur Rev 22(3):206–217
Prakke L (2004) The republic of Austria. In: Prakke L, Kortmann C (eds) Constitutional law of 15 EU member states. Kluwer, The Hague, pp 3–74
Purtova N (2018) The law of everything. Broad concept of personal data and future of EU data protection law. Law Innov Technol 10(1):40–81
Reding V (2012) The European data protection framework for the twenty-first century. Int Data Priv Law 2(3):119–129
Regan PM (1995) Legislating privacy. Technology, social values, and public policy. University of North Carolina Press, Chapel Hill
Roberts H, Palfrey J (2010) The EU data retention directive in an era of internet surveillance. In: Deibert R, Palfrey J, Rohozinski R, Zittrain J (eds) Access controlled. The shaping of power, rights, and rule in cyberspace. MIT Press, Cambridge MA, pp 35–54
Robertson G (2016) Opinion of Geoffrey Robertson QC for Facebook. Financial Times, 14 January 2016. http://blogs.ft.com/brusselsblog/files/2016/01/Geoffrey-Robertson-QC.docx. Accessed 3 January 2021
Rodley N (2012) Civil and political rights. In: Kraus C, Scheinin M (eds) International protection of human rights: a textbook, 2nd edn. Åbo Akademi University Institute for Human Rights, Turku, pp 105–129
Rodotà S (2009) Data protection as a fundamental right. In: Gutwirth S, Poullet Y, de Hert P et al (eds) Reinventing data protection? Springer, Heidelberg, pp 77–82
Rothmann R (2017) Video surveillance and the right of access: the empirical proof of panoptical asymmetries. Surveil Soc 15(2):222–238
Rouvroy A, Poullet Y (2009) The right to informational self-determination and the value of self-development: reassessing the importance of privacy for democracy. In: Gutwirth S, Poullet Y, de Hert P et al (eds) Reinventing data protection? Springer, Heidelberg, pp 45–76
Rubinstein IS, Nojeim GT, Lee RD (2017) Systematic government access to personal data: a comparative analysis. In: Cate FH, Dempsey JX (eds) Bulk collection. Systematic government access to private-sector data. Oxford University Press, Oxford, pp 5–46
Schaller C (2018) Strategic surveillance and extraterritorial basic rights protection. German intelligence law after Snowden. German Law J 19(4):941–980
Schantz P (2019) Artikel 44-49. In: Simitis S, Hornung G, Spiecker I (eds) Datenschutzrecht. DSGVO mit BDSG. Nomos, Baden-Baden, pp 962–1032
Scheinin M (2014) Letter to the Editor from Former Member of the Human Rights Committee, Martin Scheinin. Just Security, 10 March 2014. https://www.justsecurity.org/8049/letter-editor-martin-scheinin/. Accessed 3 January 2021
Schermer BW, Custers B, van der Hof S (2014) The crisis of consent: how stronger legal protection may lead to weaker consent in data protection. Ethics Inf Technol 16(2):171–182
Schmitt MN (ed) (2013) Tallinn manual on the international law applicable to cyber warfare. Cambridge University Press, Cambridge

Schwartz PM (1994) Constitutional change and constitutional legitimation: the example of German unification. Houston Law Rev 31(4):1027–1104
Schwartz PM (1995) Privacy and participation: personal information and public sector regulation in the United States. Iowa Law Rev 80(3):471–496
Schwartz PM, Solove DJ (2011) The PII problem. Privacy and a new concept of personally identifiable information. N Y Univ Law Rev 86(6):1814–1894
Scott J (2014) Extraterritoriality and territorial extension in EU law. Am J Comp Law 62(1):87–126
Senz D, Charlesworth H (2001) Building blocks: Australia's response to foreign extraterritorial legislation. Melbourne J Int Law 2(1):68–121
Shany Y (2017) On-Line Surveillance in the case-law of the UN Human Rights Committee. The Federmann Cyber Security Center Blog, 13 July 2017. https://csrcl.huji.ac.il/people/line-surveillance-case-law-un-human-rights-committee#_ftn1. Accessed 3 January 2021
Simitis S (1990) Datenschutz und Europäische Gemeinschaft. Recht der Datenverarbeitung 6(1): 3–23
Simitis S (2010) Privacy–an endless debate? Calif Law Rev 98(6):1989–2005
Solove DJ (2007) The first amendment as criminal procedure. N Y Univ Law Rev 82(1):112–176
Solove DJ (2008) Understanding privacy. Harvard University Press, Cambridge MA
Stoycheff E (2016) Under surveillance: examining Facebook's spiral of silence effects in the wake of NSA internet monitoring. J Mass Commun Q 93(2):296–311
Strömholm S (1967) Right of Privacy and Rights of the Personality. A comparative survey. Working paper prepared for the Nordic Conference on Privacy organized by the International Commission of Jurists, Stockholm May 1967
Tadros V (2006) Power and the value of privacy. In: Claes E, Duff A, Gutwirth S (eds) Privacy and the criminal law. Intersentia, Antwerp/Oxford, pp 105–120
Taylor M (2015) The EU's human rights obligations in relation to its data protection laws with extraterritorial effect. Int Data Priv Law 5(4):246–256
Tene O, Polonetsky J (2013) Big data for all: privacy and user control in the age of analytics. Northwest J Technol Intellect Prop 11(5):239–273
Townend J (2014) Online chilling effects in England and Waltes. Intern Policy Rev 3(2):1–12
Tzanou M (2013) Data protection as a fundamental right next to privacy. Reconstructing a not so new right. Int Data Priv Law 3(2):88–99
Tzanou M (2017a) The fundamental right to data protection. Normative value in the context of counter-terrorism surveillance. Hart Publishing, Oxford/Portland
Tzanou M (2017b) European Union regulation of transatlantic data transfers and online surveillance. Hum Rights Law Rev 17(3):545–565
van der Sloot B (2017) Legal fundamentalism: is data protection really a fundamental right. In: Leenes R, van Brakel R, Gutwirth S, de Hert P (eds) Data protection and privacy. (In)visibilities and Infrastructure. Springer, Dordrecht, pp 3–30
Vermeulen G (2017) Eyes wide shut. The privacy Shield's blunt denial of continued bulk, mass or indiscriminate collection or processing and unnecessary or disproportionate access and use by US intelligence and law enforcement authorities. In: Vermeulen G, Lievens E (eds) Data protection and privacy under pressure transatlantic tensions, EU surveillance, and big data. Maklu, Antwerp, pp 49–75
Wagner DeCew J (1997) In pursuit of privacy: law, ethics, and the rise of technology. Cornell University Press, Ithaca
Wang Z (2017) Systematic government access to private-sector data in China. In: Cate FH, Dempsey JX (eds) Bulk collection. Systematic government access to private-sector data. Oxford University Press, Oxford, pp 241–258
Warren SD, Brandeis LD (1890) The right to privacy. Harv Law Rev 4(5):193–220
Watt E (2017) The Role of International Human Rights Law in the Protection of Online Privacy in the Age of Surveillance, 9th International Conference on Cyber Conflict: Defending the Core
Westin AF (1967) Privacy and freedom. Atheneum Press, New York

Whitley EA (2009) Informational privacy, consent and the "control" of personal data. Inf Secur Tech Rep 14(3):154–159

Wolf C, Winston M (2015) Why the U.S. Is Held to a Higher Data Protection Standard Than France. IAPP Privacy Perspectives, 2 November 2015. https://iapp.org/news/a/why-the-u-s-is-held-to-a-higher-data-protection-standard-than-france/#. Accessed 3 January 2021

Yakovleva S, Irion K (2020) Pitching trade against privacy- reconciling EU governance of personal data flows with external trade. Int Data Priv Law 10(3):1–21

Zanfir G (2014) Forgetting about consent. Why the focus should be on "suitable safeguards" in data protection law. In: Gutwirth S, Leenes R, De Hert P (eds) Reloading data protection. Multidisciplinary insights and contemporary challenges. Springer, Heidelberg, pp 237–258

Zuiderveen FJ, Arnbak A (2015) New data security requirements and the proceduralization of mass surveillance law after the European data retention case. IvIR Research Paper, Amsterdam

Jurisprudence

BVerfGE, *Volkzählung:* BVerfGE 65, 1, *Volkzählung,* Urteil vom 15 December 1983, 1 BvR 209/83

Conseil d'État, *Les Pages Jaunes:* Conseil d'État, Arrêt du 12 mars 2014, *Les Pages Jaunes,* n° 353193

ECJ, AG Opinion, *Digital Rights Ireland:* ECJ, Opinion of AG Cruz Villalón delivered on 12 December 2013, *Digital Rights Ireland*, C-293/12, EU:C:2013:845

ECJ, AG Opinion, Opinion 1/15, ECJ, Opinion of AG Mengozzi delivered on 8 September 2016, Opinion 1/15, *Draft agreement between Canada and the European Union*, EU:C:2016:656

ECJ, AG Opinion, *Parliament v. Council and Commission:* ECJ, Opinion of AG Léger delivered on 22 November 2005, *Parliament v. Council and Commission*, C-317/04 and C-318/04, EU: C:2005:710

ECJ, AG Opinion, *The Queen v. Minister of Agriculture, Fisheries and Food*: ECJ, Opinion of AG Alber delivered on 10 February 2000, *The Queen v. Minister of Agriculture, Fisheries and Food*, C-369/98, EU:C:2000:79

ECJ, AG Opinion, *Schrems:* ECJ, Opinion of AG Yves Bot delivered on 23 September 2015, *Schrems*, C-362/14, EU:C:2015:627

ECJ, AG Opinion, *Schrems 2:* ECJ, Opinion of AG Saugmandsgaard Øe delivered on 19 December 2019, *Schrems 2*, C-311/18, EU:C:2019:1145

ECJ, *Air Transport Association of America:* ECJ, Judgment of 21 December 2011, *Air Transport Association of America*, C-366/10, EU:C:2011:864

ECJ, *Åkerberg Fransson*: ECJ, Judgment of 26 February 2013, *Åkerberg Fransson*, C-617/10, EU: C:2013:105

ECJ, *Breyer:* ECJ, Judgement of 19 October 2016, *Breyer,* C-582/14, EU:C:2016:779

ECJ, *Boukhalfa*: ECJ, Judgment of 30 April 1996, *Boukhalfa*, C-214/94, EU:C:1996:174

ECJ, *Commission v. Austria:* ECJ, Judgment of 16 October 2012, *Commission v. Austria,* C-614/10, EU:C:2012:631

ECJ, *Commission v. Austria (State printing office):* ECJ, Judgment of 20 March 2018, *Commission v. Austria (State printing office),* C-187/16, EU:C:2018:194

ECJ, *Commission v. Germany:* ECJ, Judgment of 9 March 2010, *Commission v. Germany,* C-518/07, EU:C:2010:125

ECJ, *Commission v. Hungary:* ECJ, Judgment of 8 April 2014, *Commission v. Hungary,* C-288/12, EU:C:2014:237

ECJ, *Commission v. Poland, Hungary and Czech Republic:* ECJ, Judgment of 2 April 2020, *Commission v. Poland, Hungary and Czech Republic (Temporary mechanism for the relocation of applicants for international protection),* C-715/17, C-718/17 and C-719/17, EU:C:2020:257

ECJ, *Deutsche Telekom*: ECJ, Judgement of 5 May 2011, *Deutsche Telekom*, C-543/ 09, EU: C:2011:279

ECJ, *Digital Rights Ireland:* ECJ, Judgment of 8 April 2014, *Digital Rights Ireland*, C-293/12 and C-594/12, EU:C:2014:238

ECJ, *Florescu:* ECJ, Judgement of 13 June 2017, *Florescu*, C-258/14, EU:C:2017:448

ECJ, *Front Polisario:* ECJ, Judgment of 21 December 2016, *Front Polisario,* C-104/16 P, EU: C:2016:97

ECJ, *Google Spain:* ECJ, Judgment of 13 May 2004, *Google Spain*, C-131/12, EU:C:2014:317

ECJ, *Kadi:* ECJ, Judgment of 3 September 2008, *Kadi,* C-402/05 P and C-415/05, EU:C:2008:461

ECJ, *La Quadrature du Net:* ECJ, Judgment of 6 October 2020, *La Quadrature du Net*, C-511/18, C-512/18 and C-520/18, EU:C:2020:791

ECJ, *Lindqvist:* ECJ, Judgment of 6 November 2003, *Lindqvist*, C-101/01, EU:C:2003:596

ECJ, *Ministerio Fiscal:* ECJ, Judgment of 2 October 2018, *Ministerio Fiscal*, C-207/ 16, EU: C:2018:788

ECJ, Opinion 1/15*:* ECJ, Opinion 1/15 of 26 July 2017, *Draft agreement between Canada and the European Union*, EU:C:2017:592

ECJ, *Österreichischer Rundfunk*, ECJ, Judgment of 20 May 2003, *Österreichischer Rundfunk*, C-465/00, C-138/01 and C-139/01, EU:C:2003:294

ECJ, *Politi s.a.s. v Ministry for Finance of the Italian Republic:* ECJ, Judgment of 14 December 1971, *Politi s.a.s. v Ministry for Finance of the Italian Republic*, C-43/71, EU:C:1971:122

ECJ, *Promusicae:* ECJ, Judgment of 29 January 2008, *Promusicae*, C-275/06, EU:C:2008:54

ECJ, *Privacy International:* ECJ, Judgment of 6 October 2020, *Privacy international*, C-623/ 17, EU:C:2020:790

ECJ, *Puškár*: ECJ, Judgment of 27 September 2017, *Puškár*, C-73/16, EU:C:2017:725

ECJ, *Rijkeboer*: ECJ, Judgment of 7 May 2009, *Rijkeboer*, C-553/07, EU:C:2009:293

ECJ, *Satamedia*: ECJ, Judgment of 16 December 2008, *Satamedia*, C-73/0756, EU:C:2008:727

ECJ, *Scarlet Extended*: ECJ, Judgment of 24 November 2011, *Scarlet Extended*, C-70/10, EU: C:2011:771

ECJ, *Schecke*: ECJ, Judgment of 9 November 2010, *Schecke*, C-92/09 and C-93/09, EU:C:2010: 662

ECJ, *Schrems:* ECJ, Judgment of 6 October 2015, *Schrems*, C-362/14, EU:C:2015:650

ECJ, *Schwarz v. Stadt Bochum:* ECJ, Judgment of 17 October 2013, *Schwarz v. Stadt Bochum,* C-291/12, EU:C:2013:670

ECJ, *Spasic:* ECJ, Judgment of 27 May 2014, *Spasic*, C-129/14, EU:C:2014:586

ECJ, *Standley*: ECJ, Judgment of 29 April 1999, *Standley*, C-293/97, EU:C:1999:215

ECJ, *Tele2/Watson*: ECJ, Judgment of 21 December 2016, *Tele2/Watson*, C-203/15 and C-698/ 15, EU:C:2016:970

ECJ, *Tsakouridis:* ECJ, Judgment of 23 November 2010, *Tsakouridis*, C-145/09, EU:C:2010:708

ECJ, *WebMindLicenses:* ECJ, Judgment of 17 December 2015, *WebMindLicenses*, C-419/14, EU: C:2015:832

ECJ, *ZZ v. Secretary of State for the Home Department*: ECJ, Judgment of 4 June 2013, *ZZ v. Secretary of State for the Home Department*, C-300/11, EU:C:2013:363

ECtHR, *Amann v. Switzerland:* ECtHR, Judgment of 16 February 2000, *Amann v. Switzerland*, App no. 27798/95

ECtHR, *Assanidze v. Georgia*: ECtHR, Judgment of 8 April 2014, *Assanidze v. Georgia*, App no. 71503/01

ECtHR, *Big Brother Watch and Others v. the United Kingdom:* ECtHR, Judgment of 25 May 2021, *Big Brother Watch and Others v. the United Kingdom*, App nos. 58170/13, 62322/14 and 24960/15

ECtHR, *Centrum för rättvisa v. Sweden*: ECtHR, Judgement of 25 May 2021, *Centrum för rättvisa v. Sweden*, App no. 35252/08

ECtHR, *Janowiec and Others v. Russia*: ECtHR, Judgment of 21 October 2013, *Janowiec and Others v. Russia*, App nos. 55508/07 and 29520/09

ECtHR, *Kennedy v. the United Kingdom*: ECtHR, Judgment of 18 May 2010, *Kennedy v. the United Kingdom*, App no. 26839/05
ECtHR, *Klass and others v. Germany:* ECtHR, Judgment of 6 September 1978, *Klass and others v. Germany*, App no. 5029/71
ECtHR, *Liberty and others v. the United Kingdom*: ECtHR, Judgment of 1 July 2008, *Liberty and others v. the United Kingdom*, App no. 58243/00
ECtHR, *Marckx v. Belgium:* ECtHR, Judgment of 13 June 1979, *Marckx v. Belgium*, App no. 6833/74
ECtHR, *M. K. v. France*: ECtHR, Judgment of 18 April 2013, *M.K. v. France*, App no. 19522/09
ECtHR, *Mürsel Eren v. Turkey:* ECtHR, Judgement of 7 February 2006, *Mürsel Eren v. Turkey*, App. No. 60856/00
ECtHR, *Prince Hans-Adam II of Liechtenstein v. Germany:* ECtHR, Judgment of 12 July 2001, *Prince Hans-Adam II of Liechtenstein v. Germany*, App. No. 42527/98
ECtHR, *Rotaru v. Romania*: ECtHR, Judgment of 4 May 2000, *Rotaru v. Romania*, App no 28341/95
ECtHR, *S. and Marper v. the United Kingdom:* ECtHR, Judgment of 4 December 2008, *S. and Marper v. the United Kingdom,* App nos. 30562/04 and 30566/04
ECtHR, *S.W. v. the United Kingdom:* ECtHR, Judgment of 22 November 1995, *S.W. v. the United Kingdom*, App no. 20166/92
ECtHR, *Soering v. the United Kingdom:* ECtHR, Judgement of 7 July 1989, *Soering v. the United Kingdom,* App no. 14038/88
ECtHR, *Szabó and Vissy v. Hungary*: ECtHR, Judgment of 12 January 2016, *Szabó and Vissy v. Hungary*, App no. 37138/14
ECtHR, *Weber and Saravia v. Germany*: ECtHR, Judgement of 29 June 2006, *Weber and Saravia v. Germany*, App no. 54934/00
ECtHR, *Zakharov v. Russia*: ECtHR, Judgment of 4 December 2015, *Zakharov v. Russia*, App no. 47143/06
EGC, *Front Polisario:* EGC, Judgment of 10 December 2015, *Front Polisario*, T-512/12, EU:T:2015:953
HRC, *Lopez v. Uruguay*: HRC, Decision of 29 July 1981, *Lopez v. Uruguay,* Comm. No. R.12/52, A/36/40
HRC, *Montero v. Uruguay*: HRC, Decision of 29 August 1981, Comm. No. 106/1981, CCPR/C/OP/2
ICJ, *Barcelona Traction:* ICJ, Judgment of 5 February 1970, BarcelonaTraction (Belgium v. Spain), I.C.J. 3
ICJ, *Wall:* ICJ, Advisory Opinion of 9 July 2004, *Legal Consequences of the Construction of a Wall in the Occupied Palestinian Territory*, I.C.J. 136
PCIJ, *S.S, Lotus:* PCIJ, Judgment of 7 September 1927, *S.S. Lotus (France v. Turkey)*, P.C.I.J. ser A No. 10

Documents

Article 29 WP (1999) Recommendation 4/99 on the inclusion of the fundamental right to data protection in the European catalogue of fundamental rights. WP 26. 7 September 1999
Article 29 WP (2007) Opinion 04/2007 on the concept of personal data. WP 136. 20 June 2007
Article 29 WP (2011) Opinion 15/2011 on the definition of consent. WP 187. 13 July 2011
Article 29 WP (2014) Opinion 04/2014 on surveillance of electronic communications for intelligence and national security purposes. WP 215. 10 April 2014
Article 29 WP (2015) Working Document on surveillance of electronic communications for intelligence and national security purposes. WP 228. 5 December 2015

Article 29 WP (2016) Working Document 01/2016 on the justification of interferences with the fundamental rights to privacy and data protection through surveillance measures when transferring personal data (European Essential Guarantees). WP 237. 13 April 2016

Article 29 WP (2017) Guidelines on transparency under Regulation 2016/679. WP260. 29 November 2017

Article 29 WP (2018) Adequacy Referential. WP 254 rev.01. 6 February 2018

Comité des Sages (1996) For a Europe of civic and social rights. Brussels

Commission of the European Communities (1973) Community policy on data processing. SEC (73) 4300 final. 21 November 1973

Commission of the European Communities (1981) Recommendation relating to the Council of Europe Convention for the protection of individuals with regard to automatic processing of personal data. [1981] OJ L246/31. 29 July 1981

Council of Europe (1973) Committee of Ministers, Resolution (73) 22 on the protection of the privacy of individuals vis-à-vis electronic data banks in the private sector, adopted by the Committee of Ministers on 26 September 1973 (224th Meeting)

Council of Europe (1974) Committee of Ministers, Resolution (74) 29 on the protection of the privacy of individuals vis-à-vis electronic data banks in the public sector, adopted by the Committee of Ministers on 20 September 1974 (236th Meeting)

Council of Europe (1980) Parliamentary Assembly, Recommendation 890 (1980) on the protection of personal data, adopted on 1 February 1980

Council of Europe (1981) Meeting of the Ministers' Deputies, Conclusions of the 336th meeting of the Ministers' Deputies held in Strasbourg from 9 to 11 September 1981. CM/Del/ Concl/(81) 336

Council of Europe, Recommendation 509 (1968): Council of Europe, Parliamentary Assembly, Recommendation 509 (1968) on Human rights and modern scientific and technological developments, adopted on 31 January 1968

CTIVD (2014) Annual Report 2013–2014 of the Review Committee for the Intelligence and Security Services. 31 March 2014

ECtHR (2019) Grand Chamber Panel's decisions, Press Release of 5 February 2019, ECHR 053 (2019)

EDPB (2020) Recommendations 02/2020 on the European Essential Guarantees for surveillance measures. 10 November 2020

European Commission (1990a) Communication, The protection of individuals in relation to the processing of personal data in the Community and information security. COM(90) 314 final. 13 September 1990

European Commission (1990b) Proposal for a Council Directive concerning the protection of individuals in relation to the processing of personal data. [1990] OJ C277/3. 27 July 1990

European Commission (2011) A comprehensive approach on personal data protection in the European Union. COM(2010) 609 final. 4 November 2011

European Commission (2012) Proposal for a Regulation of the European Parliament and of the Council on the protection of individuals with regard to the processing of personal data and on the free movement of such data (General Data Protection Regulation). COM(2012) 11 final. 27 July 1990

European Commission (2013) Communication, Functioning of the Safe Harbour from the Perspective of EU Citizens and Companies Established in the EU. COM(2013) 847 final. 27 November 2013

European Commission for Democracy Through Law (2015) Report on the democratic oversight of signal intelligence agencies. Study No. 719/2013, CDL-AD(2015)011. 15 December 2015

European Council(1999) Decision on the drawing up of a Charter of Fundamental Rights of the European Union, Annex IV to the Presidency Conclusions, Cologne European Council 3 and 4 June 1999. 150/99 REV 1 ANNEXES

European Council (2000) Presidency Conclusions, Nice European Council Meeting 7, 8 and 9 December 2000

European Council (2016) Draft Decision of the European Council concerning a New Settlement for the United Kingdom within the European Union. EUCO 4/16. 2 February 2016
European Parliament (1979) Resolution on the protection of the rights of the individual in the face of technical developments in data processing [1979] OJ C140/34. 8 May 1979
Expert Group on Fundamental Rights (1999) Affirming Fundamental Rights in the European Union: Time to Act, Brussels
HRC (1988) General Comment No. 16: Article 17 (Right to Privacy) The Right to Respect of Privacy, Family, Home and Correspondence, and Protection of Honour and Reputation, 8 April 1988
HRC (1995) Concluding Observations on the Russian Federation. CCPR/C/79/Add.54. 26 July 1995
HRC (1997) Concluding Observations on Jamaica. CCPR/C/79/Add.83. 19 November 1997
HRC (1998) Concluding Observations on Zimbabwe. CCPR/C/79/Add.89. 6 April 1998
HRC (2004) General Comment No. 31: The Nature of the General Legal Obligation Imposed on States Parties to the Covenant. CCPR/C/21/Rev.1/Add. 13. 26 May 2004
HRC (2009a) Concluding Observations on the Netherlands. CCPR/C/NLD/CO/4. 25 August 2009
HRC (2009b) Concluding Observations on Sweden. CCPR/C/SWE/CO/6. 2 April 2009
HRC (2014a) Concluding observations on the fourth periodic report of the United States of America. CCPR/C/USA/CO/4. 23 April 2014
HRC (2014b) General Comment No. 34: Article 9 (Liberty and security of person). CCPR/C/GC/35. 16 December 2014
HRC (2015a) Concluding Observations on the Republic of Korea. CCPR/C/KOR/CO/4. 3 December 2015
HRC (2015b) Concluding Observations on France. CCPR/C/FRA/CO/5. 17 August 2015
HRC (2015c) Concluding Observations on the United Kingdom of Great Britain and Northern Ireland. CCPR/C/GBR/CO/7. 17 August 2015
HRC (2016a) Concluding Observations on Namibia. CCPR/C/NAM/CO/2. 22 April 2016
HRC (2016b) Concluding Observations on New Zealand. CCPR/C/NZL/CO/6. 28 April 2016
HRC (2017) Concluding Observations on Italy. CCPR/C/ITA/CO/6. 1 May 2017
Human Rights Council (2015) Resolution 28/16, The right to privacy in the digital age, 24 March 2015
OECD (1980) Explanatory Memorandum, Guidelines governing the protection of privacy and transborder flows of personal data, Annex to the recommendation of the Council of 23 September 1980
PCLOB (2014) Report on the Surveillance Program Operated Pursuant to Section 702 of the Foreign Intelligence Surveillance Act. 2 July 2014
Praesidium (2000a) Draft Charter of Fundamental Rights of the European Union – Proposed Articles (Articles 10–19). CHARTE 4137/00 CONVENT 8. 24 February 2000
Praesidium (2000b) Draft Charter of Fundamental Rights of the European Union – Amendments submitted by the members of the Convention regarding civil and political rights and citizens' rights (Reference document: CHARTE 4284/00 CONVENT 28 (REV 1 in French only). CHARTE 4332/00 CONVENT 35. 25 June 2000
Praesidium (2000c) Draft Charter of Fundamental Rights of the European Union. CHARTE 4487/00 CONVENT 50. 28. September 2000
Presidency Note (2000) Draft list of fundamental rights. CHARTE 4112/2/00 REV 2, BODY 4. 27 January 2000
UN GA (2014a) Report of the Special Rapporteur on the promotion and protection of human rights and fundamental freedoms while countering terrorism. A/69/397. 23 September 2014

UN GA (2014b) The right to privacy in the digital age. Report of the Office of the United Nations High Commissioner for Human Rights. A/HRC/27/37. 30 June 2014
UN GA (2017) Report of the Special Rapporteur on the right to privacy. A/HRC/34/60. 6 September 2017
UN GA (2018) Resolution 73/179, The right to privacy in the digital age. 17 December 2018
US Department of State (2010) Office of the Legal Advisor, Memorandum Opinion on the Geographic Scope of the International Covenant on Civil and Political Rights, 19 October 2010

Chapter 3
The Restrictive Effect of the Legal Mechanisms for Data Transfers in the European Union

The right to data protection in Article 8 CFR has an extraterritorial dimension, which requires continuous protection for personal data that is essentially equivalent to the protection guaranteed within the EU. This right to continuous protection of personal data is an unwritten constituent part of the right to data protection in Article 8 CFR. Primary Union law in Article 16(2) TFEU instructs the European Parliament and the Council to establish rules relating to the protection of individuals regarding the processing of their personal data. This mandate also extends to the extraterritorial dimension of the right to data protection. Accordingly, Chapter V GDPR sets out the system for the transfer of personal data from the EU to third countries. The first section of this chapter defines the legal concept of "data transfers" and introduces the three legal mechanisms for the transfer of personal data in Chapter V GDPR (Sect. 3.1). The following sections address the three legal mechanism and their role in guaranteeing the right to continuous protection for personal data. Each section entails a fundamental rights analysis for the transfer of personal data on the basis of a legal mechanism in Chapter V GDPR. The second section is dedicated to data transfers based on adequacy decisions for third countries following Article 45 GDPR (Sect. 3.2). The third section is dedicated to data transfers based on the instruments providing appropriate safeguards in Article 46 GDPR such as standard data protection clauses and binding corporate rules (BCRs) (Sect. 3.3). Finally, the fourth section is dedicated to data transfers subject to contract-based and consent-based derogations in Article 49 GDPR (Sect. 3.4).

3.1 The System of Data Transfers

The first section of this chapter is dedicated to introducing the EU's system for the transfer of personal data from the EU to third countries. Rules on data transfers have been a part of data protection legislation since the beginning (Sect. 3.1.1). The EU system for data transfers has two major policy objectives: first, anticircumvention and

T. Naef, *Data Protection without Data Protectionism*, EYIEL Monographs - Studies in European and International Economic Law 28,
https://doi.org/10.1007/978-3-031-19893-9_3

the protection of fundamental rights, and second, enhancing trust in the information society (Sect. 3.1.2). There are different ways to describe the journey of personal data from one place to another following the GDPR. It thus has to be clear which data processing operations constitute data transfers and which do not (Sect. 3.1.3). Chapter V GDPR entails three legal mechanisms that enable the transfer of personal data from the EU to third countries: adequacy decisions, instruments providing appropriate safeguards, and derogations for specific situations (Sect. 3.1.4).

3.1.1 Development of the Rules on Data Transfers

Rules on the transfer of personal data have been a part of data protection legislation since the early data protection laws in Europe beginning from the 1970s (Sect. 3.1.1.1). The first international instruments for data protection were articulated in the 1980s and suggested the introduction of systems to facilitate cross-border flows of personal data (Sect. 3.1.1.2). In the EC, diverging rules on data transfers created problems on the common market. The EC thus sought to harmonize rules on data transfers with Directive 95/46/EC in the 1990s (Sect. 3.1.1.3). Ultimately, the EU consolidated those rules on an EU-wide level with the GDPR in 2016 (Sect. 3.1.1.4).

3.1.1.1 Early Data Protection Laws in Europe

Continental European countries were the first to adopt rules on the processing of personal data.[1] Computers and telecommunications were already facilitating transborder data flows when the first data protection laws were passed in Europe.[2] Legislators in Sweden, France, and Germany realized that it was pointless to establish a framework for the protection of personal data if that protection could be circumvented by simply sending the data of individuals it was designed to protect to another jurisdiction. In recognition of this transborder character of data processing, the laws in Sweden (Sect. 3.1.1.1.1), France (Sect. 3.1.1.1.2), and Germany (Sect. 3.1.1.1.3) all contained rules designed to protect personal data when it is transferred abroad.[3]

3.1.1.1.1 Sweden

Section 11 of the Swedish *Datalag* of 1973 contained the first data transfer rule:

---

[1] See Sect. 2.1.1.

[2] Wochner (1981), pp. 51–54.

[3] Bignami and Resta (2018), p. 370; Kuner (2013), p. 26.

> If there is reason to assume that an item will be used for data processing abroad, it may be released only after permission by the Data Inspection Board. Such permission may be granted only in cases where it can be assumed that the disclosure will not entail undue encroachment on privacy.[4]

The Swedish data transfer system relied on obtaining permissions from the Data Inspection Board.[5] Without such permission, personal data was not allowed to be sent abroad. However, the government reserved the right to overturn decisions made by the Data Inspection Board. The Swedish data transfer system also had a direct link to the protection of fundamental rights. The Data Inspection Board was tasked with assessing data transfers according to their risk for privacy. An important guideline for this risk assessment was that data transfers should be permitted if it was ensured, to a relative degree of certainty, that there were rules for the processing of personal data in place in the country of destination, which corresponded to the principles of protection established in the Swedish *Datalag*.[6] This is the first legal manifestation of the idea of continuous protection for personal data across borders.

There were other important issues for the Swedish data transfer system, too. Sweden wanted to preserve national independence. For instance, Sweden feared that its centralized personal identification number system could be misused by foreign powers.[7] Nevertheless, the main focus of the law was the protection of personal data. In one case, the Swedish *Datalag* was used to deny the German company Siemens the ability to send Swedish employee records to Germany for storage because Germany did not have a reciprocal data protection law in effect at the time.[8]

3.1.1.1.2 Germany

The data transfer rules in the German *Datenschutzgesetz* of 1977 must be interpreted with recourse to the general provisions of the law.[9] These rules were different for the public and private sector. Article 11 of the *Datenschutzgesetz* entailed the rules for the public sector:

> The transmission of personal data [. . .] is permissible where it is necessary for the lawful fulfilment of the tasks within the competence of the transmitting authority or where the recipient can demonstrate convincingly a legitimate interest in the knowledge of the data to be transmitted and if protection-worthy interests of the data subject are not harmed as a result.

There was wide consensus that data transfers from public authorities to third countries in which the protection of personal data was not guaranteed impaired the

---

[4]For the original Swedish text of Section 11 of the Swedish *Datalag* see Svantesson (2011), p. 180.

[5]González Fuster (2014), p. 77.

[6]Wochner (1981), p. 193.

[7]Burkert (2000), p. 48; Wochner (1981), pp. 194–195; SARK (1979), p. 9, 18.

[8]McGuire (1979), p. 5; Walsh (1978), p. 29.

[9]Günther (1991), p. 1096; Baumeister (1990), p. 23.

interests of the data subjects and were thus not permitted.[10] This is also a manifestation of the idea of continuous protection for personal data.

The rules for the private sector distinguished between data transfers for internal purposes and commercial purposes. Article 24(1) of the *Datenschutzgesetz* entailed the rules for internal purposes. The transfer of personal data for internal purposes was permitted

> within the scope of the purpose of a contractual relationship or a relationship of trust similar to a contract with the data subject or insofar as it is necessary to safeguard the legitimate interests of the transferring body or a third party or the general public and the protection-worthy interests of the data subject are not impaired as a result.

It was disputed whether a contractual arrangement had to impose data protection rules on the recipient and whether this was sufficient to safeguard the legitimate interests of the data subject when a third country did not have a data protection law comparable to the German *Datenschutzgesetz*.[11] It was undisputed, however, that the consent of the data subject was required for the transfer of personal data if the third country did not have a comparable data protection law. Article 32 of the *Datenschutzgesetz* entailed the rules for commercial purposes. The transfer of personal data for commercial purposes was permitted

> if the recipient has shown a legitimate interest in their knowledge in a credible manner. The reasons for the existence of a legitimate interest and the means used to establish credibility shall be recorded.

The transfer of personal data for commercial use required less safeguards than the transfer of personal data for internal use. The recipient only needed to assert his or her legitimate interest in a credible manner. Such an assertion did not require much detail.[12] The German *Datenschutzgesetz* did not give any reason for providing individuals with less protection when companies used their personal data commercially. Spiros Simits reported that this difference in treatment was a concession to business at the expense of data protection.[13] Moreover, the German *Datenschutzgesetz* was not associated with fundamental or human rights.[14] This could explain why, unlike the Swedish data transfer system, the German data transfer system did not require express licensing of data transfers and mostly relied on a liberal approach of self-regulation.[15] A protectionist application of the German data transfer system was simply not in the DNA of the *Datenschutzgesetz*.

---

[10] Wochner (1981), p. 146; Ordemann and Schomerus (1988), Sect. 11 N. 3; Günther (1991), p. 1096.

[11] Günther (1991), p. 1097. Of the opinion that a contractual arrangement is enough are Ordemann and Schomerus (1988), Sect. 24 N. 5; Baumeister (1990), pp. 23–24. Contra Simitis et al. (1981), Sect. 24 N. 46.

[12] Ordemann and Schomerus (1988), p. 241.

[13] Simitis (1977), pp. 732–733.

[14] Lee Bygrave describes the German *Datenschutzgesetz* as particularly elusive to the interests or values it aimed to substantiate. Bygrave (2002), p. 8; see Sect. 2.1.1.

[15] Additionally, the data protection authorities were only able to act based on a complaint from a data subject according to Article 30(1) of the *Datenschutzgesetz*. Coombe Jr. and Kirk (1983), p. 40.

The rules for the private sector in the German *Datenschutzgesetz* introduced a new dimension to the idea of continuous protection for personal data. The liberal approach in the German *Datenschutzgesetz* allowed for the creation of a new mechanism for lawful data transfers. While contractual relationships were used to extend protection for personal data obligations to recipients in the third countries, the consent of the data subject was used to justify situations in which the third country did not have a data protection law comparable to the German *Datenschutzgesetz*.

3.1.1.1.3 France

Article 19 of the French *loi relative à l'informatique, aux fichiers et aux libertés* of 1979 addressed data transfers for the private sector:

> [T]he transmissions between France and third countries of personal information subject to automated processing [. . .] may be subject to prior authorization or regulated in accordance with procedures laid down by decree in the Council of State, in order to ensure compliance with the principles laid down by this law.

The transfer of personal data from France to another country had to be registered with the French National Data Processing and Freedom Commission (*Commission nationale de l'informatique et des libertés*, CNIL). The CNIL had discretionary power to prohibit data transfers abroad in order to ensure adherence to the standards of the French *loi relative à l'informatique, aux fichiers et aux libertés.* [16] This licensing model in France was similar to the Swedish data transfer system. The CNIL also drew on its powers to negotiate contractual solutions concerning data transfers by private organizations.

It has been argued that the French were specifically concerned that personal data might be transferred from France to "data havens" (*paradis de données*) with lower standards for protection.[17] There are (scholarly transmitted) rumors that this concern was also related to the realization that dating service records might be sent overseas.[18] Consequently, a protectionist application of the French data transfer system cannot be completely ruled out. In any case, Article 1 of the French *loi relative à l'informatique, aux fichiers et aux libertés* specifically stated that information technology must not infringe human identity, human rights, private life, and individual or public freedoms. This was not simply a pretext. The CNIL blocked the transfer of employee data between the Fiat corporate offices in France and Italy in 1989 because Italy did not have adequate data protection regulations.[19] The CNIL required the company's main office in Italy to sign a contract with its French offices obligating Fiat Italy to provide the standards of the French *loi relative à l'informatique, aux fichiers et aux libertés* to the data once it had been transferred to Italy.

---

[16] Schwartz (1995), pp. 491–492; Reidenberg (1992), p. 162; Coombe Jr. and Kirk (1983), p. 39.

[17] Jacqué (1980), p. 774.

[18] Reidenberg (1992), p. 162; Lucas (1987), pp. 173–175.

[19] CNIL (1989), pp. 32–34; Schwartz (1995), pp. 491–492.

3.1.1.2 Materialization in International Instruments

The early rules on data transfers in Europe created tensions. There were strong sentiments against restricting cross-border flows of personal data because of their importance for communication, commerce, science, and many other human endeavors.[20] These tensions occasioned the creation of international instruments specifically intended to address the restrictions of data flows. The OECD drafted the Privacy Guidelines (Sect. 3.1.1.2.1) and the Council of Europe passed the Convention 108 (Sect. 3.1.1.2.2) both of which were supplemented with a model contract (Sect. 3.1.1.2.3).

3.1.1.2.1 OECD Privacy Guidelines

The rapid proliferation of national data protection laws as well as their different rules on transfers of personal data worried international economic organizations such as the OECD. The OECD focused their work in the field of data protection on retaining the ability to exchange personal data between member states in their Privacy Guidelines of 1980.[21] The OECD's approach was based on the creation of minimum standards for the protection of personal data and an approximation of national data protection laws in order to guarantee frictionless transborder data flows. Part three of the OECD Privacy Guidelines specifically addresses transborder data flows. OECD member states should:

- consider the implication of their policies on processing and re-export of personal data for other member countries (Paragraph 15 OECD Privacy Guidelines);
- take all reasonable and appropriate steps to ensure that transborder flows of personal data, including transit through member countries, are uninterrupted and secure (Paragraph 16 OECD Privacy Guidelines);
- refrain from restricting transborder flows of personal data to other member countries except where a member country does not yet substantially observe the OECD Privacy Guidelines or where the re-export of such data would circumvent a country's own domestic privacy legislation (Paragraph 17 OECD Privacy Guidelines); and
- avoid developing laws, policies, and practices for the protection of privacy and individual liberties, which would create obstacles to transborder flows of personal data exceeding requirements for such protection (Paragraph 18 OECD Privacy Guidelines).

These paragraphs establish a system in which implementing the privacy principles of the OECD Privacy Guidelines enables the unhindered exchange of personal data between OECD member states. The explanatory memorandum describes the system

[20] Phillips (2018), p. 575; Ploman (1982), pp. 143, 228–232.

[21] Tzanou (2017), pp. 15–16; Nouwt (2009), p. 278; Kirby (2011), p. 8; see Sect. 2.1.2.

(in relation with Paragraph 17 OECD Privacy Guidelines) as establishing "a standard of equivalent protection, by which is meant protection which is substantially similar in effect to that of the exporting country, but which need not be identical in form or in all respects."[22] This was the first occurrence of a concept similar to the standard of "essential equivalence." The principles contained in the OECD Privacy Guidelines were intended to be the benchmark for the safe exportation of personal data. The OECD warned that lax data protection laws that do not respect the principles contained in the OECD Privacy Guidelines affect the ability of other member states to allow transborder data flows (Paragraph 15 OECD Privacy Guidelines). The OECD Privacy Guidelines also called upon member countries to avoid creating obstacles to transborder data flows exceeding the requirements for the protection of personal data (Paragraph 18 OECD Privacy Guidelines). It was the first international instrument to formulate an international policy for data protection. The OECD realized that fighting against data protectionism meant fighting for data protection.

3.1.1.2.2 Council of Europe Convention 108

The Council of Europe was primarily concerned with the protection of human rights in Convention 108.[23] The preamble of Convention 108 aims to reconcile the values of privacy and free flow of information between peoples. Chapter three of Convention 108 addresses transborder data flows. It stipulates that members to Convention 108:

- should not, for the sole purpose of the protection of privacy, prohibit or subject to special authorization transborder flows of personal data going to the territory of another member state (Article 12(2) Convention 108);
- should be able to prohibit or otherwise regulate transborder flows of personal data when certain categories of personal data are specifically protected, except where the other member state provides equivalent protection (Article 12(3)(a) Convention 108); and
- should be able to prohibit or otherwise regulate transborder flows of personal data when personal data is re-exported in order to circumvent the protection afforded to personal data in domestic legislation (Article 12(3)(b) Convention 108).

Just as in the OECD Privacy Guidelines, these articles established a system in which the implementation of the rules of Convention 108 actually facilitated the exchange of personal data between member countries.[24] Once again, a concept similar to the standard of "essential equivalence" appears.[25] The explanatory report maintains

[22] OECD (1980), para. 67.

[23] See Sect. 2.2.2.

[24] Council of Europe (2001), pp. 5–6.

[25] This is not entirely surprising since the drafters of these two international instruments coordinated their efforts. Dove and Philipps (2015), p. 650.

(with regard to Article 12(2) Convention 108) that a contracting state may not deny transborder data flows on the ground of protecting privacy if the recipient country provides equivalent protection.[26] The principles contained in Convention 108 were also intended to be the benchmark for safe exports of personal data.[27] Convention 108 makes clear that if the processing of personal data is subject to the same fundamental rules, then transborder data flows should not be subject to restrictions. Convention 108 was the first *legally binding* international instrument that formulated an international policy for data protection.

3.1.1.2.3 Council of Europe Model Contract

A study made jointly by the Council of Europe, the European Commission, and the International Chamber of Commerce (ICC) in 1992 found that "Article 12 [Convention 108] in itself may, at this stage, not be sufficient to ensure adequate protection of personal data which are transferred from one country to another."[28] The study noted that by 1992 only 12 states had ratified Convention 108.[29] It was thus important, the study concluded, to find alternative legal solutions to balance effective protection of personal data and allow for the free flow of personal data across borders. The study went on to underline that "the personal data protection principles laid down in Convention 108 are not yet enshrined in the legislation, common law and social practices of the great majority of third countries" and "potential risks to the rights of data subjects of the countries that are Party to Convention 108 may arise when the processing of personal data of those individuals is carried out in such third countries."[30]

Contractual techniques were seen as the best legal solution to manage cross-border flows of personal data. The 1992 study highlighted that some European countries already had experience with the use of contractual techniques for ensuring data protection beyond their borders and noted that several sectoral recommendations on data protection adopted by the Council of Europe Committee of Ministers referred to such contractual techniques.[31] A conference organized jointly by the Council of Europe and the EC two years before had also cautiously concluded that contractual techniques could promote equivalent protection in the context of trans-border data flows:

[26] Council of Europe (2001), pp. 12–13.

[27] Ibid., 5.

[28] Council of Europe/European Commission/ICC (1992), para. 3.

[29] Ibid., para. 4.

[30] Council of Europe Consultative Committee of Convention 108 (2002), para. 4.

[31] Council of Europe/European Commission/ICC (1992), paras 8–11.

> While emphasising that the law of contract could never replace the need to legislate for data protection, contractual techniques could nevertheless be used as a sort of palliative or complement to the legal framework for data protection and transborder data flow.[32]

Erik Harremoes, Director of Legal Affairs at the Council of Europe and Rapporteur General of the Conference of Data Protection Commissioners, summarized the conclusion of the 13th Conference of Data Protection Commissioners in 1991:

> The debate has shown that as long as legal lacunae subsist, such contracts may contribute to improving the protection of personal data which are communicated from one country to the other with different regulations. It has, however, also been underlined that such contracts do not provide a waterproof guarantee; questions remain as to the possibilities of controlling their implementation, or enforcing their clauses.[33]

The 1992 study offered a model contract containing a number of clauses designed to ensure equivalent protection in the context of transborder data flows. The model was based on the guarantees in Convention 108 and also adhered to the provisions in the OECD Privacy Guidelines.[34] The objectives of the model contract were:

- to provide an example of one way of resolving the complex problems which arise following the transfer of personal data subjected to different protection regimes;
- to facilitate the free circulation of personal data in the respect of privacy;
- to allow the transfer of data in the interest of international commerce;
- to promote a climate of security and certainty of international transactions involving the transfer of personal data.[35]

According to the model contract, the party sending personal data should affirm that the data was obtained and handled in accordance with domestic laws. The party receiving the personal data should commit to abiding by the same principles that bind the sending party domestically. The receiving party should also agree to use the data only for the purposes set out in the contract, to protect sensitive data in the manner required by the domestic law of the sending party, to refrain from communicating the data to a third party unless specifically authorized in the contract, and to rectify, delete and update the data as required by the sending party.

This joint venture of the Council of Europe, the European Commission, and the ICC provided a comprehensive foundation for the application of contractual techniques as a way to protect transborder data flows.[36] Nevertheless, the Consultative Committee of Convention 108 reiterated in 2002 that while contractual techniques provide a valid alternative legal solution to manage transborder data flows, "the use of contractual clauses should not be seen as a long-term substitute for domestic law protecting personal data."[37] This is especially true in the public sector.

---

[32] Ibid., para. 12.

[33] Ibid., para. 13.

[34] OECD (2000), p. 14.

[35] Council of Europe/European Commission/ICC (1992), para. 23.

[36] OECD (2000), p. 15.

[37] Council of Europe Consultative Committee of Convention 108 (2002), para. 5.

3.1.1.3 Harmonization in Union Law

The differing data protection laws in EC member states and their rules on data transfers created problems on the common market. The hopes of the European Commission that Convention 108 would solve these problems were left unfulfilled. This is why in 1990 the Commission proposed a draft for Community wide legislation.[38] The legislation also established common rules on transfers of personal data to non-Community states.[39] The EC system of data transfers in the first draft of Directive 95/46/EC (Sect. 3.1.1.3.1) was reviewed in the amended draft of Directive 95/46/EC (Sect. 3.1.1.3.2) and slightly changed in the final draft of Directive 95/46/EC (Sect. 3.1.1.3.3).

3.1.1.3.1 First Draft of Directive 95/46/EC

The first draft of Directive 95/46/EC from 1990 established a system for data transfers that was similar to the one found in Convention 108.[40] Article 24 of the 1990 draft established, as a principle, that the transfer of personal data from an EC member state to a third country may take place only if that third country ensures an adequate level of protection. The European Economic and Social Committee (EESC) noted in its opinion on the 1990 draft that instead of the term "adequate protection," the principle of "equivalent protection," which was used in Convention 108, should be adopted.[41] This was the first time that a predecessor of the right to continuous protection for personal data appeared in the legislative process of the EC. While these suggestions of the EESC were not ultimately implemented, the ECJ found in the *Schrems* judgment of 2015 that the term "adequate protection" should be interpreted as "protection essentially equivalent to that guaranteed within the European Union."[42]

Article 24 of the 1990 draft charged the EC member states and, subsidiarily, the European Commission, with determining whether a third country ensured an adequate level of protection. To make this determination they had to consider the international commitments the third country had entered into and/or its domestic law. This reference to "international commitments" was clearly an invocation of Convention 108 as the international benchmark for data protection.[43]

If a country did not ensure an adequate level of protection, a derogation allowing the transfer of personal data according to Article 25 of the 1990 draft was available. The EC member state in which the data was located could authorize such a transfer if

[38] European Commission (1990).

[39] European Commission (1992), p. 34.

[40] European Commission (1990), p. 41; Kong (2010), p. 443.

[41] EESC (1991), para. 2.2.19.1.

[42] ECJ, *Schrems*, para. 74; see Sect. 2.3.4.

[43] European Commission (1990), p. 41.

the controller of the data was able to guarantee an adequate level of protection for the transfer, and if neither the other EC member states nor the Commission had objections. Article 25 of the 1990 draft established a framework including a ten-day waiting period in which notice of opposition could be given. In cases where notice of opposition was given, the Commission could take all appropriate measures to prohibit the transfer. The whole data transfer system of the 1990 draft, including the derogation, was built around the objective of adequate protection for personal data when transferred to a third country. In retrospect, this data transfer system was quite restrictive, but it was able to guarantee fundamental rights. The explanatory memorandum of the draft considered the draft as a global approach and underlined that "the European Community must promote among its partners the introduction of adequate protection measures and support the efforts of the Council of Europe in this field."[44] According to Recital (21) of the draft, in the absence of adequate protection in a third country, the Community should enter into negotiations with a view to promoting membership to Convention 108.[45] Overall, the data transfer system of the 1990 draft heavily relied on Convention 108 and aimed at expanding its membership.

3.1.1.3.2 Amended Draft of Directive 95/46/EC

In the course of draft consultations, some interest groups expressed concerns that the adequacy-based data transfer system might be too restrictive.[46] One of the main concerns raised by business associations during the consultation was the "impossibility of conducting international trade with third countries not guaranteeing an adequate level of protection."[47] The amended draft of 1992 tried to accommodate this concern. The derogations in the 1990 draft were replaced with alternative legal mechanisms for data transfer to third countries.

The amended draft of 1992 included contractual techniques for data transfers co-developed by the European Commission within the framework of the Council of Europe.[48] Article 27 of the amended draft allowed the transfer of personal data to third countries that do not ensure an adequate level of protection when the data exporter can show "sufficient justification" in the form of contractual provisions. This mechanism explicitly referred to guarantees that the effective exercise of data subjects' rights would not be jeopardized when deviating from the adequacy-based data transfer mechanism. The explanatory memorandum of the amended draft

---

[44] Ibid., 6.

[45] European Commission (1992), p. 35.

[46] Ibid.

[47] Ibid., 129.

[48] Article 29 WP (1998a), p. 2.

specifically mentions that these exceptions must also be compatible with the protection of individuals.[49]

Article 26(1) of the amended also draft allowed the transfer of personal data to third countries that do not ensure an adequate level of protection if the data subject has given consent, or if the transfers are necessary for the performance of a contract between the data subject and the data controller. In the last case, the data subject must be informed that personal data may be transferred to a third country. The data subject may then decide whether he or she wishes to take such a risk.

3.1.1.3.3 Final Draft and Directive 95/46/EC

The final draft of Directive 95/46/EC adopted by the Council in 1995 contained only minor changes regarding the system of data transfers.[50] Article 25 Directive 95/46/EC established adequacy decisions as the main pillar of the data transfer system. A decision on the adequacy for transfers of personal data was generally made at the EC member state level and on a case-by-case basis for individual data transfers. The European Commission was also entitled to find that third countries did not ensure an adequate level of protection and thus enter into negotiations with these countries with a view to remedying the situation.[51]

Just like the amended draft, the final Article 26 Directive 95/46/EC contained two types of derogations from the adequacy system. Article 26(1) Directive 95/46/EC entailed a list of derogations for data transfers in specific situations (such as the consent of the data subject or the necessity of performing a contract between the data subject and the data controller) and Article 26(2) Directive 95/46/EC outlined appropriate safeguards for data transfers. The Commission had the power to decide that certain standard contractual clauses offered appropriate safeguards according to Article 26(4) Directive 95/46/EC. Contrary to the amended draft, the second derogation in Article 26(2) Directive 95/46/EC did not use the words "sufficient justification" but "adequate safeguards" instead. Article 26(2) Directive 95/46/EC also added that "adequate safeguards" must be oriented toward the protection of the privacy and the fundamental rights and freedoms of individuals.[52] This explicit and strong reference to fundamental rights and freedoms clarified that the derogation must comply with them. The final draft of Directive 95/46/EC was clearly intended to close remaining loopholes in the language of the amended draft. The system for data transfers was thus presented as a fundamental rights-based regulation.

---

[49] European Commission (1992), p. 35.

[50] European Council (1995).

[51] Schwartz (2013), p. 1973.

[52] The Common Position (EC) No 1/95 adopted by the Council on 20 February 1995 referred here to a mechanism of "sufficient guarantees" which was changed to "adequate safeguards" in the final draft.

Soon after the adoption of Directive 95/46/EC in 1995, it became clear that the adequacy system with decisions on a case-by-case basis for individual data transfers was reaching its functional limits. Given the huge number of personal data leaving the EC on a daily basis and the multitude of actors involved, no EC member state could ensure that each case was examined thoroughly.[53] The Article 29 WP claimed that "mechanisms are to be developed to rationalize the decision-making process for a large number of cases, allowing decisions to be made timely and efficiently."[54] Accordingly, the Article 29 WP suggested that the Commission should determine at a general level whether certain third countries ensured an adequate level of protection.[55] This more general approach avoided differences between national assessments and increased the stability and predictability for data exporters.[56] Subsequently, the Commission initiated procedures to make a series of adequacy decisions under Article 25(6) Directive 95/46/EC.

3.1.1.4 Consolidation in Union Law

The GDPR was adopted in 2016 and consolidated the EU rules on data transfers. EU member states no longer have any room left to implement individual rules in their national laws. Jan Albrecht, the GDPR rapporteur of the European Parliament, writes that the new regulation was designed from the beginning to follow the rules for data transfers in Directive 95/46/EC.[57] This is why the legal mechanisms for data transfers to third countries under the GDPR are basically the same as in Directive 95/46/EC although they are set out in more detail.[58] Some of these details concern adequacy decisions. Article 45 GDPR centralizes the adequacy assessment procedure by designating the European Commission as the sole body competent to execute this task. The deferral to the Commission aimed at eliminating problematic divergences that derived from the member state-based assessment in Directive 95/46/EC.[59] For example, under Directive 95/46/EC some member states required a determination of adequacy by a national supervisory authority, whereas others referred the responsibility for the adequacy assessment to the data controller.[60] There were also divergences in the standards set by EU member states for the adequacy assessment.[61] In that regard, the European Parliament demanded generally that more attention be paid to the laws

[53] Kong (2010), pp. 444–445.

[54] Article 29 WP (1998b), p. 26.

[55] Ibid.

[56] Kong (2010), p. 445.

[57] Albrecht (2016), p. 94.

[58] Ibid., 95.

[59] Mouzakiti (2015), p. 47.

[60] European Commission (2010a), para. 77.

[61] European Commission (2003a), pp. 18–19.

surrounding data protection in the area of national security.[62] Article 45(2)(a) GDPR now requires the Commission to take into account the rule of law, respect for human rights and fundamental freedoms, relevant legislation, bot general and sectoral, including concerning public security, defense, national security and criminal law, and the access of public authorities to personal data, as well as the implementation of such legislation when assessing the adequacy of the level of protection in a third country. Article 45 GDPR also entails the possibility of an adequacy decision in respect to a territory or one or more specified sectors within a third country.

Even though the legal mechanisms for data transfers to third countries in the GDPR are basically the same as in Directive 95/46/EC, there are two important changes from Directive 95/46/EC to the GDPR. The first change relates to the derogations. According to Article 26(2) Directive 95/46/EC, data transfers based on adequate safeguards, for example in the form of appropriate contractual clauses, were treated as derogations. According to Article 46 GDPR, such data transfers are *not* treated as derogations anymore. This change is important for the interpretation of data transfers based on instruments providing appropriate safeguards with regard to the right to continuous protection of personal data in Article 8 CFR. The second change relates to Article 44 GDPR on the general principle for data transfers, which is the opening provision of Chapter V GDPR on transfers of personal data to third countries. The change is connected to the *Schrems* judgment of the ECJ. The Court decided *Schrems* before the conclusion of the trilogue negotiations that would culminate in the GDPR. The *Schrems* judgment pushed the trilogue negotiations toward a focus on data transfers and led to the introduction of a new sentence into Article 44 GDPR:

> All provisions in this Chapter shall be applied in order to ensure that the level of protection of natural persons guaranteed by this Regulation is not undermined.

This sentence was introduced in order to ensure that the obligation to protect personal data transferred to a third country is taken seriously.[63] It is the implementation in the GDPR of the right to continuous protection for personal data in Article 8 CFR.[64] There was not enough time during the trilogue negotiations to adapt all legal mechanisms for the transfer of personal data in the GDPR to the findings of the ECJ in *Schrems*. Consequently, the second sentence of Article 44 GDPR now serves as a general interpretative rule for the EU system for data transfers.[65]

To conclude the development of the rules on transfers: The early rules on data transfers in Europe created tensions. The protection of personal data and privacy was certainly their main focus and not just a pretext, even though a protectionist application of these rules cannot be completely ruled out in some instances. There have always been strong reservations against restricting international data flows

[62] Ibid.

[63] Albrecht and Jotzo (2016), pp. 102–103.

[64] Schantz (2019), p. 970.

[65] Kuner (2020), p. 757.

because of their importance for communication, commerce, science, and many other human endeavors. This is why international organizations such as the OECD and the Council of Europe sought to address the issue. The OECD realized that fighting against data protectionism meant fighting for data protection. Its approach was based on the creation of minimum standards for the protection of personal data and the approximation of national data protection laws in order to guarantee frictionless transborder data flows. The Council of Europe followed a similar approach. In Europe, however, these instruments failed to enable free movement of personal data between the EC member states. This is why the EC then sought to harmonize the protection of personal data on the common market, including the rules on data transfers abroad. All legal mechanisms for data transfers in Directive 95/46/EC had a prototype in the early data protection laws in Europe: decisions regarding the level of data protection in a third countries (in Sweden and France), contractual models for cross-border flows of personal data (in Germany and France), and consent-based constructions (in Germany). Importantly, the EC data transfer system in Directive 95/46/EC was already a fundamental rights-based system. The GDPR's legal mechanisms for data transfers were modeled after Directive 95/46/EC, but compliance with fundamental rights was further strengthened. Article 44 GDPR provides—as a general interpretative rule for all legal mechanisms—that they must be applied in order to ensure that the level of protection of natural persons guaranteed by the GDPR is not undermined. It is the implementation in the GDPR of the right to continuous protection of personal data in Article 8 CFR.

3.1.2 Policy Objectives of the Rules on Data Transfers

Laws often have different kinds of policy objectives. Some of those objectives are explicitly stated, some are unexpressed or implicit.[66] It is important to clarify the objectives of the EU rules on data transfers to understand their restrictive effects. Anticircumvention (Sect. 3.1.2.1) and enhancing trust in the information society (Sect. 3.1.2.2) are the two main objectives of the EU rules on data transfers. In contrast, there is nothing to suggest that public security (Sect. 3.1.2.3) or economic protectionism (Sect. 3.1.2.4) must also be seen as objectives of the EU rules on data transfers.

3.1.2.1 Anticircumvention

The early data protection laws in Europe mainly regulated the export of personal data because they wanted to avoid that their rules are being circumvented.[67] The

[66]Cp. Kuner (2013), p. 107.

[67]Hon (2017), p. 29, 149; González Fuster (2014), p. 77; Hondius (1975), p. 248.

pioneering countries feared the erosion of their chosen level of data protection through the sending of personal data to third countries where the protection offered was lower. The problem at the root of the anticircumvention objective was the re-importation of personal data processed abroad in violation of certain provisions of the law of the country of origin. Third countries with less stringent data protection legislation were dubbed "data havens" to express this role.[68] Consequently, the first international instruments for data protection also addressed the issue of anticircumvention. The explanatory report to Convention 108 states that

> [c]oncern has been expressed that data users might seek to avoid data protection controls by moving their operations, in whole or in part, to "data havens", i.e. countries which have less strict data protection laws, or none at all.[69]

Similarly, the explanatory memorandum to the OECD Privacy Guidelines refers to "attempts to circumvent national legislation by processing data in a Member country which does not yet substantially observe the Guidelines."[70]

It is no surprise that anticircumvention then was one of the original policy objectives of EU rules on data transfers. After all, they originated in the early data protection laws in Europe and the international instruments of the OECD and the Council of Europe. This is apparent from the commentary regarding the amended draft of Directive 95/46/EC:

> The rule intended to prevent the Community rules from being circumvented in the course of transfers of data to non-community countries takes the form of a ban on the transfer of data to countries which do not provide an adequate level of protection; this has now been clarified in order to remove any ambiguity as to the purpose pursued.[71]

The Council highlighted in its Common Position that the rules on data transfers are "merely a corollary to the other Articles of the Directive of which they formed an integral part, in that they were designed to make the system 'water-tight'."[72] It is also evident from the fact that the Article 29 WP suggested early on that also the possibilities to transfer personal data from the destination third country to other third countries had to be part of the adequacy assessment.[73] In the same spirit, AG Henrik Saugmandsgaard Øe explained in his opinion in *Schrems 2* with regard to Article 44 GDPR that

> it should be borne in mind that the *raison d'être* of the restrictions that EU law places on international transfers of personal data, by requiring that the continuity of the level of protection of the fundamental rights of the data subjects be guaranteed, is designed to avoid the risk that the standards applicable within the Union will be circumvented.[74]

---

[68] Kirby (1980), p. 2; Wochner (1981), pp. 33–45.

[69] Council of Europe (1981), para. 9.

[70] OECD (1980), para. 64.

[71] European Commission (1992), p. 4.

[72] European Council (1995), Sect. III.A.

[73] Article 29 WP (1997), para. 3(i)(6); see also ECJ, Opinion 1/15, para. 214.

[74] ECJ, AG Opinion, *Schrems 2*, para. 204.

The policy objective of anticircumvention is closely connected with the protection of fundamental rights, including the right to continuous protection for personal data.

3.1.2.2 Enhancing Trust in the Information Society

Before the adoption of Directive 95/46/EC, a high-level group that reported to the Corfu European Council in 1994 on issues concerning the information society (the Bangemann Group) concluded that the lack of consumer confidence will undermine the rapid development of the information society.[75] This is why the Bangemann Group found that "a fast decision from Member States is required on the Commission's proposed Directive setting out general principles of data protection."[76] Similarly, the European Commission underlined in the explanations to the first draft of Directive 95/46/EC from 1990 that "[e]ffective protection of personal data and privacy is developing into an essential precondition for social acceptance of the new digital networks and services."[77] Enhancing trust in the information society was thus a policy objective of EU data protection law from early on.

Trust in the information society is especially important regarding rules on data transfers. Dara Hallinan, Michael Friedewald, and Paul McCarthy submitted a meta-analysis of various public opinion surveys in 2012 demonstrating that there is a lack of clarity among Europeans when it comes to cross-border flows of personal data and that this lack of clarity feeds uncertainty with regard to digital trade.[78] They underlined that Europeans displayed significant fear regarding data processing and the potential consequences for the individual and society. That was before the revelations on mass surveillance by Edward Snowden in 2013, which certainly did not help public opinion in Europe. The need to enhance trust in data processing has been cited again and again as a motivation for EU data protection law.[79] The OECD recently stressed that "[t]he benefits of digital trade for both business and consumers are contingent on the degree of trust that is placed on the activities of different players operating in the digital space."[80]

The European Commission underlined in the runup to the GDPR that the lack of trust makes consumers in the EU hesitant to buy online and accept new digital services and that, therefore, a high level of data protection is crucial to enhance trust in digital services and fulfil the potential of the digital economy.[81] Recital (6) GDPR describes how technology has transformed both the economy and social life, and outlines how it could further facilitate the free flow of personal data within the Union

---

[75] Bangemann Group (1994), p. 22.

[76] Ibid.

[77] European Commission (1990), pp. 77–78.

[78] Hallinan et al. (2012), p. 271.

[79] Kuner (2013), p. 118.

[80] OECD (2018), para. 60.

[81] European Commission (2012b), p. 2.

and the transfer of personal data to third countries, while ensuring a high level of protection for personal data. Recital (7) GDPR underlines that

> [t]hose developments require a strong and more coherent data protection framework in the Union, backed by strong enforcement, given the importance of creating the trust that will allow the digital economy to develop.

The EU also started to recognize the necessity of ensuring the trust and confidence of users in the information society in free trade agreements (FTAs).[82] In Article 7.48(2) EU-South Korea FTA,

> [t]he Parties agree that the development of electronic commerce must be fully compatible with the international standards of data protection, in order to ensure the confidence of users of electronic commerce.[83]

Rules on data transfers enable trust in the information society, which is of fundamental importance for digital trade to flourish.[84] Enhancing trust in the information society is a major policy objective of rules on data transfers.

3.1.2.3 Security

The 2017 Chinese Draft Administrative Measures on Evaluating the Security of Transmitting Personal Information and Important Data Overseas foresaw very restrictive data transfer rules based on national security concerns.[85] Yanquing Hong showed that many private businesses control vast amount of data resources and that this data may influence national and public interests.[86] He used Alibaba as an example to show how the scale and "granularity" of data on consumers can match the public security organs' basic national population database and even surpass it in accuracy. He explained how a leak or exportation of this data could create a serious threat to national security. Similar considerations were already present in the early data protection laws in Europe. Sweden introduced rules on data transfers in 1973 because it feared that its centralized personal identification number system could be misused by foreign powers.[87]

Access to sensitive information about the population of a state by foreign governments (or other institutions, groups, etc.) can pose a threat to security.[88] When Directive 95/46/EC was drafted, different scholars reflected on the nexus

[82] Mishra (2019), p. 503.

[83] Free Trade Agreement between the European Union and its Member States, of the one part, and the Republic of Korea, of the other part [2011] OJ L 127/6.

[84] Kuner (2013), p. 118.

[85] The 2017 Chinese Draft Administrative Measures were never adopted. A new version of the Draft Administrative Measures was published on 13 June 2019. Delval (2019).

[86] Hong (2017), p. 8.

[87] Burkert (2000), p. 48; Wochner (1981), pp. 194–195; SARK (1979), p. 9, 18.

[88] IIF (2019), p. 4.

between data transfers and the loss of national sovereignty. Cees Hamelink argued in 1994 that cross-border flows of personal data "imply a threat to national sovereignty since they facilitate the control over critical national decisions by foreign actors" and that "[c]ontrol over locations where vital data are processed and stored is an important factor in national and world politics."[89] Eli Cohen argued in 1992 that a country is vulnerable when its data is in the hands of others.[90] He used the example of the US restricting access of Dresser Industry France to its US database during the 1982–1983 Siberian pipeline dispute to support his argument.

However, the preparatory materials of Directive 95/46/EC and the GDPR do not reveal any link between rules on data transfers and the protection of public security, national security, sovereignty, or data sovereignty. To the contrary, the communication of the European Commission on the first draft of Directive 95/46/EC underlined that it is essential that national information security policies do not become an obstacle to relations with third countries.[91] While states could—and some do—make a case for national security as a policy objective of (restrictive) rules on data transfers, it does not seem that national security is a policy objective of the EU rules on data transfers.

3.1.2.4 Economic Protectionism

A restrictive system for data transfers could suggest the existence of a protectionist policy objective. A restrictive system for data transfers requires companies to locally store and process data. Companies would need to invest in local servers and data centers. This generates economic activity, employment opportunities, and other spillovers associated with high-tech sectors.[92] Mishra Neha argues that many states with a highly restrictive system for data transfers explicitly state that their intentions are to protect fundamental rights and/or national security, while they are implicitly using them as a policy tool to promote economic protectionism.[93] The EU system for data transfers is often accused of serving a protectionist objective, especially in US literature and political discourse.[94] The US criticized the first draft of Directive 95/46/EC on the grounds that it imposes unfair non-tariff barriers to trade.[95] In 2015, President Barack Obama said in an interview that privacy challenges against US internet companies from European countries as well as EU roadblocks for data

---

[89] Hamelink (1994), p. 230.

[90] Cohen (1992), p. 263.

[91] European Commission (1990), p. 3.

[92] IIF (2019), p. 6.

[93] Mishra (2016), p. 147.

[94] Chander (2020), p. 784; Aaronson (2019), pp. 557–562; Schwartz and Peifer (2017), p. 118; Farrell and Newman (2016); Aaronson (2015), p. 674; USITC (2013), pp. 5-1, 5-2; Bennett and Raab (2006), p. 87; Eger (1979), p. 1066.

[95] Madsen (1992), p. 26.

transfers to the US are not always entirely sincere because European countries want to displace US companies.[96] However, this criticism goes beyond the US. Hosuk Lee-Makiyama, director of the European Centre for International Political Economy, referred to the GDPR and stressed that "while it is no doubt a worthwhile endeavor to protect European citizens from illicit online surveillance, the landmark bill comes at a cost: it is a form of digital protectionism." [97]

Nevertheless, the legislative documents concerning EU data protection do not show any protectionist intentions behind the EU system for data transfers. The general comments in the EU Council's Common Position in the preparation of the final draft of Directive 95/46/EC is one of the first legislative documents on data protection in the EC that mentions trade:

> The Council felt that Articles 25 and 26 of the Directive, which dealt with the transfer of personal data to third countries, did not pursue a trade policy objective as such; they were merely a corollary to the other Articles of the Directive of which they formed an integral part, in that they were designed to make the system 'water-tight' by avoiding any 'laxity' as regards the transfer of data to third countries.[98]

This statement emphasizes that anticircumvention is the policy objective of EU rules on data transfers and denies that economic protectionism is one at all. Recital (56) Directive 95/46/EC even stressed that "cross-border flows of personal data are necessary to the expansion of international trade." The EU is cognizant of the relationship between data transfers and trade. When the European Commission passed the first standard contractual clauses, which were considered to offer adequate safeguards for data transfers as required by Article 26(2) Directive 95/46/EC, it underlined in Recital (4) Decision 2001/497/EC that a flexible instrument for data transfer is "essential for maintaining the necessary flow of personal data between the Community and third countries without unnecessary burdens for economic operators," particularly "in view of the fact that the Commission is unlikely to adopt adequacy findings under Article 25(6) for more than a limited number of countries in the short or even medium term." The proactive role of the Commission regarding adequate safeguards under Article 26(2) Directive 95/46/EC shows that the EU is committed to reconcile data transfers and trade.

When the Commission started to review Directive 95/46/EC for an update in 2010, it identified "a general need to improve the current mechanisms allowing for international transfers of personal data."[99] The European Data Protection Commissioner (EDPS) agreed in his corresponding opinion that the review of the data protection framework in the EU requires "consideration of how personal data protection can be ensured effectively in the globalised world without substantially

[96] Kara Swisher Interviews President Barack Obama on Cyber Security, Privacy and His Relationship With Silicon Valley, Re/code, 13 February 2015.

[97] Lee-Makiyama (2018).

[98] European Council (1995), Sect. III.A.

[99] European Commission (2011), p. 16.

hampering international processing activities."[100] The Commission recognized in its comments on the first proposal of the GDPR that

> [t]he complexity of the rules on international transfers of personal data is considered as constituting a substantial impediment to [operations of economic stakeholders] as they regularly need to transfer personal data from the EU to other parts of the world.[101]

In reaction, the EDPS again underlined that "EU rules on international data transfer should ensure that there is adequate protection of personal data without an unnecessary restriction of international trade and cooperation."[102] The entire process that led to the adoption of the GDPR emphasizes the importance of trade concerns. This is also why Recital (101) GDPR contains a strong reference to trade: "Flows of personal data to and from countries outside the Union [. . .] are necessary for the expansion of international trade." While the legislative documents concerning data protection in the EU do not reveal any protectionist intentions behind the EU rules on data transfers, it is necessary to keep in mind that "policies that may appear protectionist may not have been designed to achieve trade-distorting effects."[103]

3.1.3 *The Concept of Data Transfers*

The legal concept of data transfers is the centerpiece of the EU's fundamental rights-based regulation of data transfers. The GDPR uses several terms to describe the transfer of personal data from one place to another including: the free movement of data, data flows, and data transfers. These terms must be distinguished from each other (Sect. 3.1.3.1). The GDPR uses the notion of data transfers without defining further what kind of data processing operations it entails (Sect. 3.1.3.2). However, it seems to be clear that the so-called data transits are excluded from the concept of data transfers (Sect. 3.1.3.3) and that the data flows to the special territories of the EU may not be considered data transfers (Sect. 3.1.3.4).

3.1.3.1 Terminology

The GDPR uses different terms to describe the transfer of personal data from one place to another: free movement of data (Sect. 3.1.3.1.1), data flows (Sect. 3.1.3.1.2), and data transfers (Sect. 3.1.3.1.3).

---

[100] EDPS (2011), para. 15.

[101] European Commission (2012a), p. 4.

[102] EDPS (2011), para. 12.

[103] Aaronson (2019), p. 6.

3.1.3.1.1 Free Movement of Data

The first term that refers to the journey of personal data from one place to another in EU data protection law is the "free movement of data." The title of Directive 95/46/EC defined two goals. It set out to protect individuals with regard to the processing of personal data, and to enable the free movement of this data. The legal basis for Directive 95/46/EC was Article 100a TEC on the approximation of laws for measures which have as their object the establishment and functioning of the EU common market. It was thus the goal of free movement of personal data within the EU that justified data protection legislation on the level of the Community. Article 1(2) Directive 95/46/EC forbade member states to restrict or prohibit the free flow of personal data between member states for reasons connected with the protection of personal data. Article 1(2) Directive 95/46/EC employed the notion of "free flow" of personal data instead of "free movement" of personal data, which appears to have been an editorial mistake, when considered alongside the title of Directive 95/46/EC. Article 1(3) GDPR now refers to the "free movement" of personal data within the Union. Recital (13) GDPR explicitly mentions that the proper functioning of the common market requires the free movement of personal data within the EU.

The term free movement of data therefore refers to data processing operations across the borders of EU member states.[104] It is a key element of EU data protection law and policy. There are obvious similarities between the free movement of data and the four freedoms of the common market.[105]

3.1.3.1.2 Data Flows

The second term that refers to the journey of personal data from one place to another in EU data protection law is "data flows." This term has already been used in the OECD Privacy Guidelines and Convention 108. The definition in these instruments reveals a data location centric understanding of cross-border data flows. The state of technology at the time of drafting only allowed straightforward point-to-point transactions and it was, compared with today, fairly easy to identify in which country data was actually located.

The GDPR also at times uses the notion of data flows to describe the journey of data across borders of EU member states[106] and sometimes to describe the journey of

[104] The use of the word "move" in Recital (116) GDPR describing data flows to and from countries outside the EU does not change the interpretation of "free movement of personal data." The French and the German versions are not consistent with the English version. They use other notions (*franchissent* and *übermittelt*) which do not correspond to the notion of free movement of personal data.

[105] Cp. Krzysztofek (2017), p. 166; Gunnarsdótir (2016), p. 89.

[106] See Recitals (3), (9), (10), (53), (123), (170) and Articles 4(24) and 51(1) GDPR.

data outside the EU to third countries.[107] The notion of data flows should thus be understood neutrally as referring to any cross-border journey of personal data. It is a descriptive term and does not constitute a legal concept like data transfers. Such an interpretation is consistent with Recital (101) GDPR:

> Flows of personal data to and from countries outside the Union and international organisations are necessary for the expansion of international trade and international cooperation. The increase in such flows has raised new challenges and concerns with regard to the protection of personal data. However, when personal data are *transferred* from the Union to [. . .] third countries or to international organisations, the level of protection of natural persons ensured in the Union by this Regulation should not be undermined, including in cases of onward transfers of personal data from the third country or international organization.[108]

Recital (101) GDPR indicates that out of all flows of personal data to third countries there is a special category of transfers of personal data from the EU to third countries.[109] The EDPB shares this interpretation, although in a different context.[110]

3.1.3.1.3 Data Transfers

The third term that refers to the journey of personal data from one place to another in EU data protection law is "data transfers." The term is remarkably prominent in EU data protection law.[111] It signals a type of data processing operation endowed with legal implications. Directive 95/46/EC already used the term "data transfers" in Article 25 and Article 26. It did not further define the kind of data processing operation described by the term "data transfers". Kuan Hon has suggested that the drafters of Directive 95/46/EC thought that the term was self-explanatory, although this is not necessarily the case.[112] This is why the EDPS called for a clear definition of data transfers in his opinion on the data protection reform package in 2012. An early draft of the GDPR actually contained an amendment that defined data transfers

---

[107] See Recital (101) and Articles 58(2)(j) and 83(5)(e) GDPR. While the French version uses the same notion in these articles (*flux de données*), the German version uses the notion of data transfers (*Datenübermittlung*) which is better suited according to the differentiation suggested below because these articles refer to the legal concept in Chapter V GDPR. Article 8.81 of the Economic Partnership Agreement between the EU and Japan also contains a *rendez-vous* clause according to which the two parties "shall reassess within three years of the date of entry into force of this Agreement the need for inclusion of provisions on the free flow of data into this Agreement." See Bartl and Irion (2017), p. 4.

[108] The French and German version of Recital (101) GDPR are consistent with the English version in differentiating these notions (*flux de données/transfert de données* and *Datenströme/ Datenübermittlung*).

[109] Cp. ECJ, *Lindqvist*, para. 71.

[110] See EDPB (2021), p. 4.

[111] Despite the undisputable relevance for the understanding of EU data protection law and policy, the term "data transfers" has rarely been questioned, and is often simply quoted and plainly embraced even by critical literature. González Fuster (2016), p. 160, fn. 1; Hon (2017), p. 55.

[112] Hon (2017), p. 71.

as "any communication of personal data, actively made available to a limited number of identified parties, with the knowledge or intention of the sender to give the recipient access to the personal data."[113] This definition was omitted from the final version of the GDPR. The data processing operation of data transfers therefore requires further clarification.

3.1.3.2 The Data Processing Operation of Data Transfers

The transfer of personal data from the EU to a third country constitutes a data processing operation.[114] The transmission of personal data to a location in a third country is a suitable description of the term "data transfers" (Sect. 3.1.3.2.1). Equating the term transfer with disclosure could jeopardize fundamental rights protection where data flows do not involve intelligible access to personal data, such as cloud computing (Sect. 3.1.3.2.2). In addition, there is a reasonability test that limits the scope of data transfers (Sect. 3.1.3.2.3). Finally, the meaning of the term "third countries" has to be assessed in relation with the data processing operation of data transfers (Sect. 3.1.3.2.4).

3.1.3.2.1 Transmission of Personal Data

Conceptually, a data transfer denotes personal data traveling from the EU to a third country where something happens to that data. According to the OED, "transfer" means to convey or take from one place to another.[115] The European Commission has informally provided a basic definition for the data processing operation of data transfers:

> The term 'transfer of personal data' is often associated with the act of sending or transmitting personal data from one country to another, for instance by sending paper or electronic documents containing personal data by post or e-mail.[116]

The sending of personal data is not the best description for data transfers. This is because—in the digital sphere— it usually only covers push technology, which is a style of internet-based communication in which the request for a given transaction is initiated by the publisher or central server. It does not include pull technology, or requests for the transmission of information initiated by the receiver. Consequently, the transmission of personal data describes data transfers better than sending.

[113] European Parliament (2013), Amendment 86, 65.

[114] ECJ, *Parliament v. Council and Commission*, para. 56.

[115] OED online, entry for transfer (v.).

[116] European Commission (2009), p. 18.

The location of servers to which data is transmitted plays an important role in determining whether a data transfer to a third country took place.[117] The Article 29 WP found that SWIFT, a worldwide financial messaging service that facilitates international money flows, transferred personal data to third countries when it mirrored personal data from servers in datacenters in the EU to servers in datacenters in the US.[118] With regard to cloud computing, the Article 29 WP found that the rules on data transfers have limitations because "cloud computing is most frequently based on a complete lack of any stable location of data within the cloud provider's network."[119] Nevertheless, the Article 29 WP insisted that cloud computing data flows to servers outside the EU also constitute data transfers to a third country. Cloud related decisions of supervisory authorities in EU member states confirm this finding. For example, the Swedish supervisory authority highlighted that Google Apps' personal data flows to datacenters located in the US constituted data transfers and so found a list of subproviders for data storage inadequate without knowledge of their location.[120]

3.1.3.2.2 Disclosure of Personal Data

Kwan Hon has argued that a location centric approach in determining data transfers is not appropriate for cloud computing because there is no disclosure or making available of personal data when it is simply transmitted to servers in a third country. In such cases, persons have no intelligible access to the data because of strong encryption.[121] She thus concluded that the concept of data transfers should be understood in terms of disclosure and the making available of personal data across borders. The European Commission's definition of data transfers considers similar situations:

> Other situations also fall under this definition: all the cases where a controller takes action in order to make personal data available to a third party located in a third country.[122]

The possibility of access to personal data in a third country is an essential part of making data available across borders. The EDPS argued in a position paper that absent a formal definition of data transfer, controllers should consider that the term implies: "communication, disclosure or otherwise making available of personal data, conducted with the knowledge or intention of a sender subject to the Regulation that the recipient(s) will have access to it."[123] The EDPS thus added the element of

[117] Article 29 WP (2010), p. 21.

[118] Article 29 WP (2006), p. 21.

[119] Article 29 WP (2012a), p. 17. See also Tene (2013), p. 1229.

[120] Datainspektionen, *Salems*, para. 3.3; Hon (2017), p. 96.

[121] Hon (2017), p. 138.

[122] European Commission (2009), p. 18.

[123] EDPS (2014), p. 7.

knowledge or intentionality to its definition of data transfers. According to the OED, to "disclose" means "to uncover and expose to view."[124] The uncovering and exposing of something usually involves intention. To disclose personal data therefore means that a recipient or recipients must intentionally be afforded intelligible access to that data. The disclosure of personal data in a cross-border context certainly constitutes a data transfer. However, the concept of data transfers is broader than this.

The title of Article 48 GDPR—Transfers or disclosures not authorized by Union law—is an indication that transfers must mean something in addition to disclosures. According to Article 48 GDPR, data transfers can also be something different than intentionally afforded intelligible access to personal data in a cross-border context. Such an interpretation is consistent with the history of the GDPR. The definition of transfer in the draft of the GDPR—which was ultimately omitted—would have effectively equated the term transfer with the meaning of disclosure.[125] The omission of this definition in the GDPR indicates that the drafters wanted to have a broad understanding of the term transfer. Data transfers can also take place if personal data is not disclosed, i.e., if there is no recipient that is afforded intelligible access to the data in the third country. This is especially important for cloud computing where there is often no recipient afforded intelligible access to the data stored in the third country. Simply equating the term transfer with disclosure could jeopardize the fundamental right protection for cross-border flows of personal data that do not involve intelligible access to the data. Even Hon accepts that the location of personal data in a third country is important for the protection of fundamental rights to the extent that it gives that country jurisdiction over the data.[126] Foreign internet surveillance practices can threaten fundamental rights, even in a cloud computing context.[127] The three cumulative criteria defined by the EDPB in 2021 to qualify a processing as a transfer also seem to fall short of recognizing that a transfer is more than a disclosure or making available, or at least they do not describe what making available exactly means.[128]

3.1.3.2.3 Reasonableness Test

The ECJ had to deal with the concept of data transfers in the *Lindqvist* case. An elderly woman, Ms. Lindqvist, was uploading the personal data of her colleagues to an internet site hosted in the European Economic Area (EEA) that could also be accessed from any third country. The ECJ was confronted with the question of

---

[124] OED online, entry for disclose (v.).

[125] European Parliament (2013), Amendment 86, 65.

[126] Nonetheless, she argues then that even if that country has jurisdiction, cloud supply chains' complexity may prevent it from having effective jurisdiction. Hon (2017), p. 123, 321.

[127] Ibid., 305; see Sect. 2.4.1.

[128] Cp. EDPB (2021), p. 4.

whether the activities of Ms. Lindqvist constituted data transfers. The ECJ decided that

> in circumstances such as those in the case in the main proceedings, personal data which appear on the computer of a person in a third country, coming from a person who has loaded them onto an internet site, were not directly transferred between those two people but through the computer infrastructure of the hosting provider where the page is stored.[129]

The ECJ stressed that there must be a *direct* transfer of personal data. The ECJ found that in the case at hand the direct transfer of personal data was not between Ms. Lindqvist and a person in a third country but between the hosting provider of Ms. Lindqvist's internet site and a person in a third country. The uploading of personal data onto an internet site by Ms. Lindqvist did not therefore constitute a transfer of personal data, even though Ms. Lindqvist disclosed and transmitted personal data to one or more third parties located in one or more third countries. The ECJ emphasized that the referring court only asked about the activities of Ms. Lindqvist and not about the activities carried out by the hosting provider.[130] The ECJ did not elaborate whether the activities of the provider on the behalf of Ms. Lindqvist—namely, the storing of the uploaded personal data on its servers and the disclosure and transmission of that data from its servers—actually constituted data transfers. The ECJ provided an important determination regarding data transfers in *Lindqvist.* If the concept of data transfers

> were interpreted to mean that there is 'transfer [of data] to a third country' every time that personal data are loaded onto an internet page, that transfer would necessarily be a transfer to all the third countries where there are the technical means needed to access the internet. The special regime provided for by Chapter IV of the directive would thus necessarily become a regime of general application, as regards operations on the internet.[131]

The ECJ applied here what Dan Svantesson has called a reasonableness test.[132] The consequences of finding that the activities of Ms. Lindqvist constituted data transfers would have led to a massive coverage by EU law of activities on the internet. The ECJ explained that

> if the Commission found, pursuant to Article 25(4) of Directive 95/46, that even one third country did not ensure adequate protection, the Member States would be obliged to prevent any personal data being placed on the internet.[133]

Such a result would have been devastating for the use of the internet and unreasonable, if not impossible, to enforce.[134] The ECJ's reasonableness test has been described by Christopher Kuner as "praiseworthy, even visionary, in its willingness

---

[129] ECJ, *Lindqvist*, para. 61.

[130] Ibid., para. 62.

[131] Ibid., para. 69.

[132] Svantesson (2010), p. 16.

[133] ECJ, *Lindqvist*, para. 69.

[134] Hon argues that data controllers would have simply ignored a contrary finding in *Lindqvist*. Hon (2017), p. 81.

to consider the international implications."[135] On the basis of this reasonableness test it can also be argued that even hosting providers of internet sites in the EU do not "transfer" personal data to third countries when they make the uploaded data from their servers available to everyone on an internet site. This would also lead to a massive coverage of activities on the internet. In conclusion, in cases where the application of the concept of data transfers would lead to unreasonable results, the cross-border flow of personal data should not constitute data transfers.

3.1.3.2.4 Third Countries

The data processing operation of data transfers is connected to the notion of "third countries." Generally, all countries that are not EU member states are considered third countries for the purpose of the GDPR. The only exceptions are the three members to the Agreement on the EEA: Iceland, Liechtenstein, and Norway.[136] Together with the EU member states, the EEA member states form a common market. In light of the importance of data protection and the free movement of data for the functioning of the common market, Directive 95/46/EC has been considered EEA-relevant and was incorporated into Annex XI of the Agreement on the EEA in 1999.[137] On 6 July 2018, the EEA Joint Committee decided to update Annex XI and incorporate the GDPR into the Agreement on the EEA as the successor to Directive 95/46/EC.[138] With the incorporation of Directive 95/46/EC, as well as the GDPR, into the Agreement on the EEA, personal data can move freely within the EEA just as in the EU. Iceland, Liechtenstein, and Norway are therefore not considered third countries within the meaning of Articles 44-49 GDPR.[139]

Decisions by the European Commission regarding the adequacy of data protection laws of third countries made according to Article 25 Directive 95/46/EC include several locations which are not independent countries but have a kind of home rule that includes data protection law. One of the examples are the Faeroe Islands.[140] It has been argued that these decisions are based on the fact that the aforementioned locations exercise sovereignty with respect to data protection law.[141] The possibility in the GDPR for adequacy decisions of a "territory" covers these locations without stretching the concept of a third country.

[135] Kuner (2013), p. 13; Svantesson (2010), p. 16.

[136] Agreement on the European Economic Area of 2 May 1992 [1994] OJ L 1/3.

[137] EEA Joint Committee (1999).

[138] EEA Joint Committee (2018).

[139] Krzysztofek (2017), p. 167.

[140] According to the European Commission, the Faeroe Islands are a self-governing community within the Kingdom of Denmark that did not join the EU when Denmark did. Cp. European Commission (2003b), Recital (5).

[141] Blume (2015), p. 36.

3.1.3.3 Data Transits

The routing of internet traffic often involves data flows passing through other countries before reaching their final destination in a third country. This passing through other countries is called data transits. The GDPR does not mention data transits. Directive 95/46/EC only referred to data transits through EU member states in Article 4(1)(c) as exceptions from the application of national data protection provisions. The UK Information Commissioner's Office published a guidance paper on data transfers in 2017 and stressed that "transfer does not mean the same as mere transit" because the ordinary meaning of transfer is transmission from one place to another.[142] Scholars also distinguish data transfers from data transits. Hon argues that data transits should not be considered when determining whether a data transfer occurs because neither the OECD Privacy Guidelines nor Convention 108 consider data transits to be relevant and Directive 95/46/EC (and the GDPR) largely adopted the legal mechanisms for the transfer of personal data from these international instruments.[143] Lianne Colonna maintained that routing data through a network is something different from its delivery to a final destination.[144] She suggested that the network can be thought of as a bridge and the activities that occur while the data travels across are thus unimportant. According to Colonna, what matters is what happens at the beginning and the end of the transaction. Christopher Kuner explained that the policy behind the exemption of data transits from data transfers is rooted in the fact that in mere transits the rights and freedoms of individuals in the EU are not affected.[145]

The problem with this perception is that surveillance practices of third country can capture the personal data in transit between the EU and another third country. Contrary to what Colonna and Kuner have argued, the surveillance activities that occur while the data travels across the network bridge does affect the rights and freedoms of individuals in the EU. Already in 1989, a study prepared by the Committee of Experts on Data Protection under the authority of the Council of Europe considered that "[p]roblems of data security and confidentiality are heightened when data are piped through communication lines which traverse countries where little or no attention is accorded to issues of data protection."[146] The current infrastructure of the internet makes it very difficult to determine the actual route of data flows.[147] The internet is structured to route data flows based on technical parameters (such as latency, velocity, thermal control) rather than on geography.[148]

---

[142] ICO (2017), para. 18.

[143] Hon (2017), p. 75.

[144] Colonna (2014), p. 217.

[145] Kuner (2013), p. 16; Simitis and Dammann (1997), p. 130.

[146] Council of Europe (1989), para. 9.

[147] "Internet protocols have no notion of national borders, and interdomain paths depend in large part on existing interconnection business relationships (or lack thereof)." Edmundson et al. (2016), p. 1.

[148] Kuner (2013), p. 6.

A huge part of global internet traffic crosses the US, which has the highest developed international cable network worldwide.[149] The end-user cannot dictate the data's routing (such as e.g. to avoid cables passing through the US or to use only the cable from Portugal to Brazil). Internet service providers could potentially do this if they had to, but such efforts would be technically difficult, very costly, and certainly require new cable infrastructure.[150] A group of scholars from Princeton found empirical evidence in 2016 that at the time some countries were completely avoidable, but that many of the most prominent surveillance states were the least avoidable.[151] For example, they showed that over 50% of the paths from the Netherlands to top domains transit the US.[152]

If the concept of data transfers were to include every time that personal data passes through a third country on its way to its destination, the special regime provided for by Chapter V GDPR would become a regime that demands practically impossible solutions for internet routing. If an "unavoidable" country (for internet routing) does not ensure adequate protection, a huge part of internet traffic from the EU would not be allowed. For example, if the US was found to ensure inadequate protection of personal data *and* the US could not be avoided for data flows to other destinations, internet traffic from the EU containing personal data would be severely restricted. The inclusion of data transits in the legal concept of data transfers would then have a huge impact on the internet as we know it today. The ECJ underlined in *Lindqvist* that it is necessary to take into account the technical nature of internet transactions in order to apply the concept of data transfers.[153] The ECJ demonstrated a willingness to apply data protection law based on technical realities rather than enforce unreasonable demands that would, in fact, disable the internet. I thus argue that data transits should not constitute data transfers based on the same reasoning. It would be unreasonable to prohibit a huge part of internet traffic from the EU that including data transits in the legal concept of data transfers would entail. It should be added that internet surveillance practices that affect personal data in transit are relevant under international human rights law and raise possibilities of international action in order to safeguard not only the right to data protection in Article 8 CFR but also Article 17 ICCPR.[154]

---

[149] It is possible that up to 80% of global internet traffic crosses the US. Hon (2017), p. 310 with reference to Ball (2013).

[150] Bennett and Oduro-Marfo (2018), p. 887; Hon et al. (2016), p. 254; Hon (2017), p. 311.

[151] Edmundson et al. (2016), p. 11.

[152] Ibid., 2.

[153] ECJ, *Lindqvist*, para. 57.

[154] Hon (2017), p. 311; see Sect. 2.4.4.

3.1.3.4 Special Territories of the EU

The special territories of the EU are territories of EU member states, which, for historical, geographical, or political reasons, enjoy special status in the EU. There are nine outermost regions (OMR) that form part of the EU including the Azores, French Guiana, La Réunion, and the Canary Islands.[155] There are 13 overseas countries and territories (OCT) that do not form part of the EU, though they cooperate with the EU via the overseas countries and territories association including Greenland, French Polynesia, and Aruba.[156] Lastly, there are several special cases. For example, the Faroe Islands where the EU Treaties do not apply, and which are considered a third country for the sake of the GDPR, have their own adequacy decision.[157] In contrast, the OMR and OCT are usually not considered third countries for the sake of the GDPR. In France, for example, the national adaption of the French law to the GDPR entails extensions of the GDPR to the French OCT such as French Polynesia and the Wallis and Futuna Islands.[158]

Data flows to the OMR and the OCT do not constitute data transfers to third countries and fall instead within the free movement of personal data according to Article 1(1) GDPR. The free movement of personal data to the OMR and the OCT may involve data transits, i.e. the routing of internet traffic through other (non-EU) countries before reaching their destination. It was explained above how data transits can be subject to surveillance practices while it travels across the network bridge. These surveillance practices affect the rights and freedoms of individuals in the EU. The GDPR allows the free movement of personal data, including to the OMR and the OCT, even if the respective data transits affect the rights and freedoms of individuals in the EU. This is clearly stated in Article 1(3) GDPR:

> The free movement of personal data within the Union shall be neither restricted nor prohibited for reasons connected with the protection of natural persons with regard to the processing of personal data.

Article 1(3) GDPR entails potential limitations on the right to continuous protection of personal data in Article 8 CFR when data transits to the OMR and the OCT are subject to surveillance measures of third countries. AG Henrik Saugmandsgaard Øe accepted the risk that a third country other than the destination country may secretly intercept data flows from the internet infrastructure while the data are in transit in his opinion in *Schrems 2*.[159]

---

[155] Article 355(1) TFEU.

[156] Article 198 TFEU and Annex II TFEU.

[157] Article 355(5)(a) TFEU; see Sect. 3.1.3.2.4.

[158] Titre V Loi n° 78-17 du 6 janvier 1978 relative à l'informatique, aux fichiers et aux libertés; CNIL (2019); Tambou (2019), p. 53.

[159] ECJ, AG Opinion, *Schrems 2*, para. 237.

3.1.4 Legal Mechanisms for Data Transfers

Chapter V GDPR from Article 44 to Article 49 GDPR is dedicated to the transfer of personal data from the EU to third countries. Article 44 GDPR maintains that data transfers may only take place according to the conditions laid down in Chapter V GDPR, which is the default position of the EU system for data transfers (Sect. 3.1.4.1). There are three legal mechanisms for data transfers: adequacy decisions according to Article 45 GDPR (Sect. 3.1.4.2), instruments providing appropriate safeguards in Article 46 GDPR (Sect. 3.1.4.3), and derogations for specific situations in Article 49 GDPR (Sect. 3.1.4.4).

3.1.4.1 Default Position

The default position for the cross-border flow of personal data is the principal rule underlying the system for data transfers. It describes the regulatory choice of a jurisdiction about cross-border flows of personal data.[160] There are two different options: Either cross-border flows of personal data are generally allowed, and regulators retain possibilities to block or limit them in certain instances, or cross-border flows of personal data are not allowed and should not take place unless a legal basis is present.

Christopher Kuner argues that the first option (allowing cross-border flows of personal das unless specific risks are present) may prove to be too reactive and allow enforcement only after personal data has already been misused abroad, whereas the second option (requiring a legal basis before cross-border flows of personal data take place) may be unduly restrictive and prove to be increasingly futile in light of technological developments such as cloud computing.[161] Which default position a jurisdiction chooses will largely depend on its own culture, history, and legal tradition. Article 44 GDPR maintains the regulatory choice of the EU. It follows the approach of the early data protection laws in Europe:

> Any transfer of personal data which are undergoing processing or are intended for processing after transfer to a third country [...] shall take place only if, subject to the other provisions of this Regulation, the conditions laid down in this Chapter are complied with.

Recital (107) GDPR specifies that in cases where the conditions of the three legal mechanisms for data transfers in the GDRP are not met, the transfer of personal data should be prohibited. Article 44 GDPR itself does not explicitly mention such a prohibition but it is clear from the wording of the provision that data transfers may not take place outside of the three legal mechanisms in Chapter V GDPR. The EU

[160] Weber (2013), p. 123.

[161] Kuner (2011), p. 27.

system for data transfers in the GDPR thus operates on the default position that data transfers should not take place unless a legal basis allows them.[162]

3.1.4.2 Adequacy Decisions

The first legal mechanism for data transfers is an adequacy decision for a third country according to Article 45 GDPR. The European Commission adopts adequacy decisions to enable data transfers from the EU to third countries without any further specific authorization. There are no limitations for data exporters who transfer personal data to third countries with an adequacy decision except for compliance with the other provisions of the GDPR. Article 45 GDPR sets out the elements that ought to be considered by the Commission when making an adequacy decision for a third country:[163]

Article 45(2)(a) GDPR specifically mentions that the Commission shall consider relevant legislation—both general and sectoral—concerning public security, defense, national security, and criminal law as well as the access of public authorities to personal data. This element covers internet surveillance practices in third countries and is extremely relevant for the right to continuous protection of personal data in Article 8 CFR.[164] Article 45(2)(a) GDPR also mentions effective and enforceable data subject rights in combination with effective administrative and judicial redress for data subjects whose personal data are being transferred. Furthermore, Article 45(2)(a) GDPR includes rules for the onward transfer of personal data to another third country. Article 45(2)(b) GDPR requires the existence and effective functioning of an independent supervisory authority in the third country with the responsibility and power to ensure and enforce compliance with data protection rules. An independent supervisory authority in the third country must also assist and advise the data subjects in exercising their rights and cooperate with the supervisory authorities of the EU member states. This element refers to the constituent requirement of independent supervision enshrined in Article 8(3) CFR, which is also relevant for the right to continuous protection of personal data. Finally, Article 45(2)(c) GDPR refers to the international commitments a third country has undertaken as well as to participation in multilateral or regional systems in relation to the protection of personal data such as Convention 108.

At the moment, the Commission recognizes the following countries and territories as providing adequate protection for personal data: Andorra, Argentina, Canada (only commercial organizations), Faroe Islands, Guernsey, Israel, Isle of Man, Japan, Jersey, New Zealand, Republic of Korea, Switzerland, the United

[162] New Zealand, for example, operates on the default position that presumes that data transfers are generally allowed unless the regulator exercises its authority to limit or forbid them in certain circumstances. Article 29 WP (2011), pp. 9–10; Greenleaf and Bygrave (2011), p. 9.

[163] Mouzakiti (2015), p. 47.

[164] See Sect. 2.4.1.

Kingdom and Uruguay.[165] Two adequacy decisions for special frameworks in the US—Safe Harbor and Privacy Shield—were invalidated by the ECJ.[166] A third country that is not found to provide adequate protection, like the majority of third countries, is neither implicitly nor explicitly "black-listed." According to the Article 29 WP, "[t]he public message would rather be that no general guidance regarding that particular country is yet available."[167] The GDPR foresees that the other legal mechanisms in Chapter V GDPR should be used for data transfer in the absence of an adequacy decision. Up through present, the Commission has never issued a negative decision regarding the adequacy of data protection in a third country.

3.1.4.3 Instruments Providing Appropriate Safeguards

The second legal mechanism for data transfers is the provision of appropriate safeguards according to Article 46 GDPR. In the absence of an adequacy decision, a data exporter may transfer personal data to a third country if appropriate safeguards are provided and under the condition that enforceable data subject rights and effective legal remedies for data subjects are available. The EDPS noted, with respect to the notion of adequate safeguards in Article 26(2) Directive 95/46/EC, that these safeguards should be understood as data protection guarantees which are created for the specific situation and which do not already exist in the recipient's legal system.[168] These safeguards are necessary because data subjects are not subject to an enforceable set of data protection rules providing an adequate level of protection in the third country.[169] It can be inferred from the right to continuous protection of personal data in Article 8 CFR that a legal mechanism for data transfers faces problems if it focuses solely on data protection obligations for the recipient of the personal data in the third country and ignores the shortcomings of the legal framework to which the recipient is subject in the third country.[170]

Article 46 GDPR contains different instruments that provide appropriate safeguards for the transfer of personal data. These instruments must contain the full set of basic data protection principles in Article 5 GDPR.[171] Lingjie Kong correctly described the instruments providing appropriate safeguards as "contractualized versions of Directive 95/46/EC" (or of the GDPR).[172] They have to guarantee the

[165] With the exception of the United Kingdom, these adequacy decisions do not cover data exchanges in the law enforcement sector which are governed by the Law Enforcement Directive. See Article 36 Directive (EU) 2016/680.

[166] ECJ, *Schrems*, para. 106; ECJ, *Schrems 2*, para. 201.

[167] Article 29 WP (1998b), p. 27.

[168] EDPS (2014), p. 18.

[169] Article 29 WP (1998a), p. 3.

[170] Recital (114) GDPR; see also Kuner (2020), p. 802; Schantz (2019), p. 993.

[171] Article 29 WP (1998a), p. 4.

[172] Taking the example of standard data protection clauses. Kong (2010), pp. 447–448.

data subject rights in Articles 15-22 GDPR[173] and they must provide effective legal remedies according to Articles 77-84 GDRP. The Article 29 WP explains that the effectiveness of instruments providing appropriate safeguards for the transfer of personal data must be judged on the grounds of three criteria:[174]

- They must deliver a good level of compliance. A good system is characterized by a high degree of awareness among data controllers of their obligations; the existence of oversight mechanisms; and effective and dissuasive sanctions for ensuring respect for rules.
- They must provide support and help to data subjects in the exercise of their rights. Individuals must be able to enforce their rights rapidly and effectively without prohibitive cost.
- They must provide appropriate redress to injured parties where rules are broken. This must involve impartial judgments.

The Article 29 WP further underlined that detail is imperative in cases where data transfers are based on a contractual instrument because they have to replace the substantive data protection rules of EU data protection legislation in the third country.[175]

Article 46 GDPR divides the instruments providing appropriate safeguards into two categories: those in Article 46(3) GDPR requiring further authorization from a supervisory authority and those in Article 46(2) GDPR not requiring further involvement of a supervisory authority once the safeguard has been approved by the competent authority.[176] The latter category entails standard data protection clauses that have been adopted by the European Commission and which were already recognized under Directive 95/46/EC (Article 46(2)(c) GDPR) as well as standard data protection clauses that have been adopted by a supervisory authority and approved by the Commission (Article 46(2)(d) GDPR). It explicitly recognizes two instruments that have been developed through practice under Directive 95/46/EC: legally binding and enforceable instruments between public authorities or bodies (Article 46(2)(a) GDPR) and BCRs (Article 46(2)(b) and Article 47 GDPR). In addition, it introduces new instruments: codes of conduct (Article 46(2)(e) GDPR) and certification mechanisms (Article 46(2)(f) GDPR). According to the European Commission, the new instruments are intended to allow for the development of more tailor-made solutions for the transfer of personal data, reflecting, for instance, the specific features and needs of a given sector or industry.[177] The first category of safeguards requires further authorization from a supervisory authority and so entails "*ad hoc*" contractual clauses between the data controller or processor and the controller, the processor or the recipient of the personal data in the third country (Article 46(3)(a) GDPR), and specific

---

[173] See Article 12(2) GDPR.

[174] Article 29 WP (1998a), p. 6.

[175] Ibid., 5.

[176] Slokenberga et al. (2019), p. 37.

[177] European Commission (2017), p. 5.

provisions to be inserted into administrative arrangements between public authorities or bodies (Article 46(3)(b) GDPR).

This research focuses on standard data protection clauses according to Article 46(2)(c) GDPR and on BCRs according to Article 46(2)(b) and 47 GDPR. The selection of instruments mirrors their usage. According to the Commission, standard data protection clauses based on Article 46(2)(c) GDPR are the main instrument on which companies rely for their data export.[178] BCRs are commonly used for data transfers within the same group of enterprises that are engaged in a joint economic activity. The selection covers an instrument that is approved for unspecified data transfers to unspecified third countries such as the standard data protection clauses (Sect. 3.1.4.3.1), and an instrument that is approved for specified data transfers to specified third countries such as the BCRs (Sect. 3.1.4.3.2).

3.1.4.3.1 Standard Data Protection Clauses

To date, the European Commission has issued four sets of standard data protection clauses for the transfer of personal data from the EU to third countries. Three sets were adopted under Directive 95/46/EC and repealed with effect from 27 September 2021 but still deemed to provide appropriate safeguards under the GDPR until 27 December 2022 (provided the processing operations that are the subject matter of the contract remain unchanged and that reliance on those clauses ensures that the transfer of personal data is subject to appropriate safeguards).[179] A new set of clauses was adopted under the GDPR.[180] Standard data protection clauses based on Article 46(2)(c) GDPR simplify data transfers. Rather than use attorneys to draft contractual solutions to provide appropriate safeguards from scratch and then have them authorized by a supervisory authority according to Article 46(3)(a) GDPR, a company can use the model standard data protection clauses and their "off-the-rack" language without further engaging a supervisory authority.[181]

Standard data protection clauses based on Article 46(2)(c) GDPR are approved without referring to specified data transfers and specified third countries. The decision of the Commission provides a blueprint of contractual clauses that can be inserted in contracts for different types of data transfers to different third countries. However, the liberal approach of approving standard data protection clauses based on Article 46(2)(c) GDPR for unspecified data transfers to unspecified third countries is mostly blind to the inadequacies of data protection in third countries.[182]

---

[178] European Commission (2019), p. 10.

[179] European Commission (2001); European Commission (2004); European Commission (2010b). European Commission, Draft Decision on standard contractual clauses for the transfer of personal data to third countries pursuant to Regulation (EU) 2016/679 of the European Parliament and of the Council.

[180] European Commission (2021).

[181] Cp. Schwartz (2013), p. 1982.

[182] Kuner (2020), p. 802; Schantz (2019), p. 993; see Sect. 3.3.3.1.

3.1.4.3.2 BCRs

Many companies use BCRs based on Article 46(2)(b) GDPR for data transfers within their group of enterprises. Article 47(1) GDPR requires that BCRs be approved by the competent supervisory authority in accordance with the consistency mechanism set out in Article 63 GDPR. Article 47(2) GDPR contains different requirements for BCRs. They must specify, among others,

- the structure and contact details of the group of undertakings, or group of enterprises engaged in the joint economic activity as well as the structure and contact details of each of its members (Article 47(a) GDPR);
- the data transfers or set of transfers, including the categories of personal data, the type of processing and its purposes, the type of data subjects affected and the identification of the third country or countries in question (Article 47(b) GDPR);
- their legally binding nature, both internally and externally (Article 47(c) GDPR);
- the application of the general data protection principles and in particular purpose limitation, data minimization, limited storage periods, data quality, data protection by design and by default, legal basis for processing, processing of special categories of personal data, measures to ensure data security, and the requirements in respect of onward transfers to bodies not bound by the BCRs (Article 47(d) GDPR);
- the rights of data subjects in regard to processing and their means to exercise those rights (Article 47(e) GDPR);
- the complaint procedures (Article 47(i) GDPR);
- the cooperation mechanism with the relevant supervisory authority to ensure compliance by all members of the group of undertakings (Article 47(l) GDPR); and
- the mechanisms for reporting to the relevant supervisory authority any legal requirements to which a member of the group of undertakings is subject to in a third country and which is likely to have a substantial adverse effect on the guarantees provided by the BCRs (Article 47(m) GDPR).

A company has a claim on the approval of their BCR if they fulfill the requirements in Article 47 GDPR. The rules in Article 47 GDPR only cover an examination of the BCRs and their application by the companies involved, and not relevant legislation concerning public security, defense, national security and criminal law in third countries nor the access of public authorities to personal data that is transferred to third countries. However, unlike the approval of standard data protection clauses based on Article 46(2)(c) GDPR, the approval of BCRs is for specified data transfers to specified third countries and this information thus allows supervisory authorities to take risks for fundamental rights into account when assessing whether to approve BCRs.[183]

---

[183] See Sect. 3.3.3.2.

3.1.4.4 Derogations for Specific Situations

The third legal mechanism for data transfers is a derogation for specific situations according to Article 49 GDPR. As the wording in the title of Article 49 GDPR suggests, derogations are exceptions from the general principle that personal data may only be transferred to third countries if an adequate level of protection is provided for in the third country or if appropriate safeguards have been adduced.[184] The derogations in Article 49 GDPR must respect the principle inherent in EU law that any clauses making exceptions must be interpreted narrowly so that the exception does not become the rule.[185]

There are different types of derogations according to Article 49(1) GDPR. This research focuses on two derogations that are especially relevant for companies that use data transfers for the conduct of their business: the consent-based derogation in Article 49(1)(a) GDPR, which requires that the data subject has explicitly consented to the proposed transfer, after having been informed of the possible risks of such transfers for the data subject (Sect. 3.1.4.4.1); and the contract-based derogation in Article 49(1)(b) GDPR, which requires that the transfer is necessary for the performance of a contract between the data subject and the controller or the implementation of pre-contractual measures taken at the data subject's request (Sect. 3.1.4.4.2).

3.1.4.4.1 Contract-based Derogation

Article 49(1)(b) GDPR contains the contract-based derogation for data transfers. This derogation refers to data transfers that are necessary for the performance of a contract between the data subject and the controller.[186] The use of the contract-based derogation is restricted. Recital (111) GDPR states that the contract-based derogation in Article 49(1)(b) GDPR shall be limited to occasional transfers. The EDPB underlined that "[d]ata transfers regularly occurring within a stable relationship would be deemed as systematic and repeated, hence exceeding an 'occasional' character."[187] Furthermore, Article 49(1)(b) GDPR itself requires that data transfers must be necessary for the performance of a contract. At least one of the central contractual services must therefore be impossible if the data is not transferred to the third country in question. There must be a close and direct or substantial link between the data transfer and the performance of the contract.[188] Such a close and direct link does not exist, for example, simply for data storage in the third country or

---

[184] EDPB (2018), pp. 3–4; Article 29 WP (2005), p. 9.

[185] Article 29 WP (2005), p. 7; Council of Europe (2001), para. 31.

[186] The derogation in Article 49(1)(b) GDPR also covers data transfers that are necessary for the implementation of pre-contractual measures taken at the data subject's request. This part of the derogation in Article 49(1)(b) GDPR is of lesser interest here.

[187] EDPB (2018), p. 9; contra Chander (2020), pp. 776–777.

[188] Article 29 WP (2005), p. 13.

for additional direct marketing purposes.[189] It is not enough if the data transfer is only useful or allows cost savings. These conditions restrict the room for data exporters to lawfully use the contract-based derogation in Article 49(1)(b) GDPR. They prevent the contract-based derogation in Article 49(1)(b) GDPR from being used to undermine the extraterritorial dimension of the right to data protection.

This liberal approach of allowing unspecified data transfers to unspecified third countries within the limits of the contract-based derogation is not entirely blind to the inadequacies of data protection in third countries. The contract referred to in Article 49(1)(b) GDPR must outline the risks of the data transfer in the third country. Even if Article 49(1)(b) GDPR does not contain any specific duty for the data controller concerning the risks of the data transfer, such a duty results from the transparency requirement in Article 5(1)(a) GDPR and the general information duty for data transfers in Article 13(1)(f) GDPR.[190]

3.1.4.4.2 Consent-based Derogation

Article 49(1)(a) GDPR contains the consent-based derogation for data transfers. This derogation refers to data transfers in which the data subject has explicitly consented to the proposed transfer, after having been informed of the possible risks of such transfers. The use of the consent-based derogation is restricted. Article 4(11) GDPR states that all consent must be freely given and Recital (42) GDPR holds that consent should not be regarded as freely given if the data subject has no genuine choice or is unable to refuse or withdraw consent without detriment. Recital (43) GDPR adds that consent is presumed not to be freely given if the performance of a contract, including the provision of a service, is dependent on the consent despite such consent not being necessary for such performance. Article 4(11) GDPR further states that any consent must be unambiguous. The Article 29 WP underlined that the GDPR is clear that unambiguous consent "requires a statement from the data subject or a clear affirmative act which means that it must always be given through an active motion or declaration."[191] Similarly, the ECJ found that "[o]nly active behaviour on the part of the data subject with a view to giving his or her consent may fulfil that requirement."[192] Recital (32) GDPR specifies that this could include ticking a box when visiting an internet website, choosing technical settings for information society services or some other statement or conduct which clearly indicates in context the data subject's acceptance of the proposed processing of his or her personal data. Silence, pre-ticked boxes, or inactivity cannot therefore constitute consent.

[189] Article 29 WP (2006), p. 23.

[190] Schantz (2019), pp. 1025–1026.

[191] Article 29 WP (2018), p. 15.

[192] ECJ, *Planet49 GmbH*, para. 54.

Article 49(1)(a) GDPR is even stricter as it requires "explicit" consent. The GDPR requires explicit consent in situations in which particular data protection risks may emerge, and so, a high individual level of control over personal data is required.[193] Such risks appear in the context of cross-border flows of personal data. The term "explicit" refers to the way consent is expressed by the data subject. It requires that the data subject must give an express statement of consent.[194] Article 4(11) GDPR also states that consent must be specific. Article 49(1)(a) GDPR therefore holds that the data subject must explicitly consent to the proposed data transfer.

The consent-based derogation in Article 49(1)(a) GDPR is not entirely blind to the inadequacies of data protection in third countries, even though it allows unspecified data transfers to unspecified third countries. That is because Article 4(11) GDPR also requires that all consent must be informed. Article 29 WP found that "[f]or consent to be informed, it is necessary to inform the data subject of certain elements that are crucial to make a choice."[195] This includes, among other things, the data controller's identity, the purpose of the transfer, the type of data, the existence of the right to withdraw consent, and the identity or the categories of recipients.[196] Article 49(1)(a) GDPR specifically requires that the data subject may only consent to data transfers after having been informed of the possible risks of such transfers due to the absence of an adequacy decision and appropriate safeguards. An abstract reference to the absence of an adequacy decision and appropriate safeguards is not enough.[197] It is necessary to list the typical risks associated with a transfer to a third country lacking an adequate level of data protection such as difficult enforcement of data subject rights, lack of control over further processing and onward transfer of personal data, lack of a supervisory authority, and access to personal data by government agencies, i.e. surveillance activities.[198]

The recitals to the GDPR do not provide for a limitation to occasional data transfers for the consent-based derogation in Article 49(1)(b) GDPR. Nonetheless, the EDPS has highlighted that even though some of the derogations in Article 49 GDPR are not expressly limited to occasional or not repetitive transfers, they still have to be interpreted in a way that does not contradict the very nature of derogations as exceptions from a rule.[199]

---

[193] EDPB (2018), p. 6.

[194] Article 29 WP (2018), p. 18.

[195] Article 29 WP (2018), p. 13.

[196] Ibid.; EDPB (2018), p. 7.

[197] That information must already be included on the basis of Article 13(1)(f) and Article 14(1)(f) GDPR.

[198] EDPB (2018), p. 8; Schantz (2019), p. 1023.

[199] EDPB (2018), p. 5; contra Chander (2020), p. 776.

3.1.5 Summary

The EU system for data transfers is the result of over fifty years of development. It has two major policy objectives. First, anticircumvention and the protection of fundamental rights, and second, enhancing trust in the information society. In contrast, there is no evidence that national security or economic protectionism is also a policy objective of the EU system for data transfers. The legal concept of data transfers is the heart of the EU system for data transfers. Out of all cross-border flows of personal data, there is a special category of transfers of personal data from the EU to third countries. The transmission of personal data to a (server) location in a third country is a suitable description for data transfers. Generally equating the term transfer with disclosure jeopardizes fundamental right protection for data flows that do not involve intelligible access to personal data in the third country. Where the application of the concept of data transfers leads to unreasonable results, cross-border data flows should not be interpreted to constitute data transfers. This is one reason why data transits do not constitute data transfers. The EU system for data transfers in the GDPR operates on the default position that transfers of personal data to third countries should not take place unless a legal mechanism in Chapter V GDPR allows the transfer of personal data to a third country. There are three legal mechanisms for data transfers. Adequacy decisions according to Article 45 GDPR; instruments providing appropriate safeguards in Article 46 GDPR; and derogations for specific situations in Article 49 GDPR.

3.2 Continuous Protection of Personal Data and Adequacy Decisions

The second section of this chapter is dedicated to the interplay of the right to continuous protection of personal data in Article 8 CFR and adequacy decisions as a legal mechanism to transfer personal data from the EU to third countries according to Article 45 GDPR. The analysis of the politics of adequacy decisions shows that their adoption is not always focused on fundamental rights (Sect. 3.2.1). This is problematic because adequacy decisions have to fully comply with the right to continuous protection of personal data in Article 8 CFR (Sect. 3.2.2). Nonetheless, the regulatory framework validates adequacy decisions as a legal mechanism for data transfers (Sect. 3.2.3). The European Commission carries the primary responsibility for the transfer mechanism in Article 45 GDPR to comply with fundamental rights (Sect. 3.2.4).

3.2.1 The Politics of Adequacy Decisions

An adequacy decision for a third country is the easiest legal mechanism for data exporters to use because it does not require any further specific authorization for the transfer of personal data. Many third countries want to be recognized as providing adequate protection for personal data under EU law. However, only a small number of countries and territories are currently recognized to provide such protection. Importantly, there is no right to an adequacy finding in EU law (Sect. 3.2.1.1). Furthermore, an analysis of the politics of adequacy decisions reveals shortcomings: arbitrary procedures (Sect. 3.2.1.2), content-related inconsistencies (Sect. 3.2.1.3), and indications of preferential treatment (Sect. 3.2.1.4).

3.2.1.1 No Right to an Adequacy Finding

The European Commission has so far only recognized a small number of countries and territories as providing an adequate level of data protection. Not everyone is happy with the small number of adequacy findings so far. After all, adequacy decisions are the least complicated legal mechanism for data exporters. The Article 29 WP recognized early on the potential for diplomatic tensions surrounding adequacy decisions and noted that

> [a] risk is that some third countries might come to see the absence of a finding that they provided adequate protection as politically provocative or at least discriminatory, in that the absence of a finding is as likely to be the result of their case not having been examined as of a judgement on their data protection system.[200]

Peter Blume has argued that not placing a country on the white list is similar to blacklisting it.[201] He has also claimed that blacklisting a country can cause diplomatic problems. However, the Article 29 WP suggested that in cases in which a country is not (yet) found to have adequate protection, "this need not imply that the country is implicitly or explicitly 'black-listed'" but rather only that "no general guidance regarding that particular country is yet available."[202] Alex Boniface Makulilo has suggested that mitigating the possibilities of diplomatic tensions with third countries is the main reason why the EU has mostly awaited requests from third countries to initiate adequacy determinations instead of actively selecting third countries for adequacy assessments.[203] Theoretically, all countries can ask to be assessed.

---

[200] Article 29 WP (1998b), p. 27.

[201] Blume (2000), p. 70.

[202] Article 29 WP (1998b), p. 27.

[203] Makulilo (2013), p. 49.

The Commission has the power to determine, based on Article 45 GDPR, whether a country outside the EU offers an adequate level of data protection.[204] The Commission is not obliged to use that power. Matthias Oesch has argued that "[t]here is a common understanding in the EU that there is no right for a third country to receive a positive adequacy decision from the European Commission, even where the third country is convinced that the requirements are met."[205] Stewart Room, the data protection lead partner at PwC UK, has also stated with regard to Brexit that "an adequacy decision is not an automatic right".[206] In accordance with the ECJ's settled case law, "there is in the FEU Treaty no general principle obliging the Union, in its external relations, to accord in all respects equal treatment to different third countries and traders do not in any event have the right to rely on the existence of such a principle."[207] Indeed, there is nothing in the GDPR, or in EU law in general, indicating that a third country has a right to an adequacy finding, even if the conditions are met.

3.2.1.2 Arbitrary Procedures

The European Commission is responsible for adequacy decisions. The EDPB provides the Commission with opinions on the level of data protection in third countries according to Article 70(1)(s) GDPR.[208] In order to do that, the Commission provides the EDPB with all necessary documentation, including correspondence with the government of the third country. Makulilo has observed that the Commission sometimes engages in a bilateral dialogue with a third country to try to facilitate improvement of data protection until the required level of protection is achieved.[209] This happens before the Commission even consults the EDPS for an opinion. There were also instances where the Article 29 WP itself tried to facilitate improvements. The proactive role of the Commission and of the Article 29 WP in facilitating adequacy decisions is positive, but it seems to be arbitrary in application at times because it has not been equally applied to third countries.

---

[204] Statement on the website of the European Commission on adequacy decisions from 5 March 2020.

[205] Oesch (2018), p. 147.

[206] Room (2018). There are also substantial reasons not to be optimistic that a positive outcome will be achieved, especially because of the UK's surveillance practices. Patel and Lea (2019), pp. 9–10.

[207] ECJ, *Swiss International Air Lines AG*, paras 26–35 with respect to the surrender of greenhouse gas emission allowances for flights between EU member states and third countries; ECJ, *Balkan-Import Export GmbH*, para. 14 with respect to the exemption from payment of compensatory amounts granted to certain varieties of cheese from third countries; ECJ, *T. Port GmbH*, para. 76 with respect to the allocation of country quotas for bananas to certain third countries.

[208] The Article 29 WP was responsible for opinions on the level of data protection in third countries under Article 30(1)(b) Directive 95/46/EC.

[209] Makulilo (2013), p. 49.

A good example is the adequacy decision for Monaco. The supervisory authority tasked by the Article 29 WP with producing a preliminary report on the adequacy of Monaco's data protection regime—the French *Commission nationale de l'informatique et des libertés* (CNIL)—called for a mediation meeting between the data protection authoritiy of Monaco, the *Commission de contrôle des informations nominatives* (CCIN), and the Monegasque government to discuss deficiencies regarding the effective independence of the CCIN.[210] This meeting led to an agreement clarifying the competences and the relationships between both parties in terms of human resources and budget management. This example stands in contrast with the case of Québec during which the CNIL made no attempt to contact the federal privacy commissioner in order to discuss deficiencies resulting from the relationship between federal and provincial data protection law.[211]

Another example concerns the four African countries—Burkina Faso, Mauritius, Tunisia, and Morocco—which sought adequacy assessments from the EU. In these cases, the Commission mandated the Research Centre on IT and Law (CRID) at the University of Namur in Belgium in 2010 to research the level of data protection in the four African countries. None of these jurisdictions were considered to provide adequate protection for personal data in the confidential report of the CRID.[212] Yet there has been no official opinion of the Article 29 WP or the EDPB on the adequacy of these countries and it is not clear if and how the Commission (or the EDPB) is engaging with these countries to remedy their deficiencies. Jennifer Stoddart, Benny Chan, and Yann Joly have highlighted the *ad hoc* and discretionary manner in which the Article 29 WP, the EDPB, and the Commission seek clarifications and broker deals.[213]

3.2.1.3 Content-related Inconsistencies

There are also some content-related inconsistencies between adequacy assessments that have been made. The adequacy assessments for Monaco and Argentina are good examples. The Article 29 WP determined that Monaco and Argentina both ensure an adequate level of protection for personal data transferred from the EU.[214] In the case of Monaco however, the Article 29 WP noted that the Monegasque supervisory authority did not in practice enjoy a sufficient degree of financial independence and then referred to an agreement clarifying the competences and the relationships in

[210] The Article 29 WP noted that even on a wide interpretation of complete independence, as put forward by the ECJ, the CCIN would not be considered independent as expenditure control opens up the CCIN to the government's influence on the recruitment and promotion of CCIN staff, thus potentially impacting the independence of the CCIN. Article 29 WP (2012b), pp. 2, 15–16.

[211] Stoddart et al. (2016), p. 147; Article 29 WP (2014), pp. 2, 17–18.

[212] Makulilo (2013), p. 49.

[213] Stoddart et al. (2016), p. 147.

[214] Article 29 WP (2012b), pp. 15–17; Article 29 WP (2002), p. 17.

terms of human resources and budget management. In the case of Argentina, the Article 29 WP considered that the power to nominate and dismiss the head of the Argentinian supervisory authority by the Minister of Justice and Human Rights, who also decides on the staffing of the authority, does not guarantee that the supervisory authority can act in complete independence, and did not even mention the issue of independent budget management.[215] In addition, Monaco received an adequacy decision because the deal between the Monegasque supervisory authority and the Monegasque government covered the deficiency regarding the independence of the supervisory authority, whereas Argentina received an adequacy decision without having to significantly safeguard the independence of their supervisory authority.[216] It is important to highlight that independent supervision is one of the constituent parts of the right to data protection enshrined in Article 8(3) CFR, which aggravates the content-related inconsistency of the adequacy decision for Argentina.

Another content-related inconsistency can be found in the adequacy assessments for New Zealand and Québec. The Article 29 WP found seven instances in which New Zealand's data protection legislation and practices were not fully adequate, but they were neither singly nor jointly sufficient to prevent a finding of overall adequacy.[217] One of the seven instances referred to onward transfers of personal data to another third country. The Article 29 WP noted that

> [a]lthough the Working Party does not consider that New Zealand law complies fully with the onward transfer principle, it does not believe that there is a major shortfall or that this needs to stand in the way of an 'adequacy' finding.[218]

In the adequacy assessment for Québec, which did not result in finding that Québec ensures an adequate level of protection for data transferred from the EU, the Article 29 WP heavily criticized that

> the onward transfer principle needs to be clarified in Quebec's law. In fact, any onward transfer should require the use of contractual or other binding provisions in order to provide a comparable level of protection with the protection awarded by EU law. A comparable level of protection refers to all data protection principles, and is not limited to the purposes of processing and the requirement of consent for further communication of the personal data. Consent should not be promoted as the general legal basis for onward transfers as the recipient then does not commit to take any action to ensure an adequate level of protection; this situation should thus remain an exception.[219]

It is important to note that the regulation of onward data transfers is important for the right to continuous protection of personal data in Article 8 CFR, which aggravates the content-related inconsistency of the adequacy decision for New Zealand. Furthermore, New Zealand is a member of the Five Eyes intelligence sharing network

---

215 Stoddart et al. (2016), p. 147; Article 29 WP (2012b), 16, 20; Article 29 WP (2002), 14–15.

216 Stoddart et al. (2016), p. 147; Wolf (2014), p. 241.

217 Greenleaf and Bygrave (2011), p. 8; Article 29 WP (2011), p. 15.

218 Article 29 WP (2011), p. 10.

219 Article 29 WP (2014), p. 17.

and also maintains internet surveillance practices.[220] The examples reveal content-related inconsistencies in the assessment of adequacy. Adequacy findings cannot thus always be said to focus on fundamental rights.

Finally, it is worth mentioning that the politics of adequacy decisions is not immune from ulterior considerations. An example, although ultimately of no effect, was Ireland's objection to the adequacy decision for Israel. After Israel received a favorable adequacy assessment from the Article 29 WP,[221] Ireland officially objected and delayed the European Commission's adequacy decision. Ireland made an objection for reasons wholly unrelated to data protection, as it was outraged by the use of fake Irish passports by alleged Israeli agents in a targeted killing.[222] Christopher Wolf rightly points out that the use of the adequacy mechanism to achieve unrelated political ends could threaten the legitimacy and coherence of the EU system for data transfers.[223]

3.2.1.4 Indications of Preferential Treatment

The examples of Monaco and Québec show that the French CNIL went to extra lengths to broker a deal with Monaco. The Article 29 WP opinion also mentions that the French CNIL was appointed as rapporteur on the adequacy study for Monaco "due to its historical relationship with Monaco."[224] One may thus think that European countries will find it easier to obtain a positive adequacy finding than non-European countries. However, geography may not be a central factor when it comes to the politics of adequacy decisions. The examples of Argentina and New Zealand show that distant countries were able to profit from lax adequacy assessments. With respect to New Zealand, the Article 29 WP opinion even stated that

> given the geographical isolation of New Zealand from Europe, its size and the nature of its economy, it is unlikely that New Zealand agencies will have any business interest in sending significant volumes of EU-sourced data to third countries.[225]

In the case of New Zealand, geographical isolation from Europe was a factor that enabled a lax adequacy assessment with regard to onward data transfers.[226] The Article 29 WP opinion did not only consider the geographical isolation of New Zealand from Europe, but also the nature of its economy and the likelihood that significant volumes of EU-sourced personal data will be transferred onwards.

---

[220] See Sect. 2.4.1.2.1.

[221] Article 29 WP (2009).

[222] Peter (2010).

[223] Wolf (2014), p. 242.

[224] Article 29 WP (2012b), p. 2.

[225] Article 29 WP (2011), p. 10.

[226] Wolf (2014), pp. 239–240; Greenleaf and Bygrave (2011), p. 9.

This is why Christopher Wolf has argued that there is "a different standard for large- versus small-scale data processing countries when seeking adequacy determinations."[227] Graham Greenleaf and Lee Bygrave argue that

> [i]n a country like India, where outsourcing of the processing of European data is of large scale, as are other forms of business and travel involving personal data, different considerations are likely to apply.[228]

However, this position is put into perspective when one looks at the invalidated special framework adequacy decisions for the US or the most recent adequacy decision for Japan which followed an FTA between Japan and the EU. Nevertheless, apart from Argentina and Uruguay, all countries deemed to provide adequate protection for personal data transferred from the EU are members of the OECD. This selection of countries is not without strategy. The Commission explicitly stated that

> [u]nder its framework on adequacy findings, the Commission considers that the following criteria should be taken into account when assessing with which third countries a dialogue on adequacy should be pursued: (i) the extent of the EU's (actual or potential) commercial relations with a given third country, including the existence of a free trade agreement or ongoing negotiations; (ii) the extent of personal data flows from the EU, reflecting geographical and/or cultural ties; (iii) the pioneering role the third country plays in the field of privacy and data protection that could serve as a model for other countries in its region; and (iv) the overall political relationship with the third country in question, in particular with respect to the promotion of common values and shared objectives at international level.[229]

This strategy potentially puts third countries at a disadvantage if they are not negotiating an FTA with the EU, are potentially dangerous as a destination country for outsourcing of data processing operations, and are neither geographically nor culturally close to the EU. Despite this, the strategy also allows the consideration of countries informally at a disadvantage if they are data protection champions and serve as a role model for other third countries.

3.2.2 Limitations on Continuous Protection of Personal Data Using Adequacy Decisions

The right to continuous protection of personal data requires that the level of protection for personal data that is transferred from the EU to a third country is essentially equivalent to that guaranteed within the EU. This right is not absolute. Limitations on the exercise of the right to continuous protection of personal data can be lawful according to Article 52(1) CFR. Yet this interference must be found in the EU rather than in the third country (Sect. 3.2.2.1). The legal basis for the interference

---

[227] Wolf (2014), p. 240.

[228] Greenleaf and Bygrave (2011), p. 9.

[229] European Commission (2017), p. 8.

must indicate under what circumstances and conditions the interference takes place and impose minimum safeguards providing sufficient guarantees for individuals to effectively protect their personal data against the risk of abuse (Sect. 3.2.2.2). The material objectives of the interference must either qualify as a general interest recognized by the EU or be protected by another right or freedom in the Charter (Sect. 3.2.2.3). The principle of proportionality demands that there cannot be another measure, which would affect less adversely the right to continuous protection of personal data and still contribute effectively to the material objectives being pursued (Sect. 3.2.2.4).

3.2.2.1 Interference

The European Commission adopts adequacy decisions as the means of acknowledging that a third country provides an adequate level of protection for personal data. An interference with the right to data protection takes place when the processing of personal data does not respect one or more of the constituent parts enshrined in Article 8 CFR.[230] The right to continuous protection of personal data is an unwritten constituent part of the right to data protection in Article 8 CFR. Any processing of personal data that does not respect that right constitutes an interference with Article 8 CFR.

AG Yves Bot found in his opinion in *Schrems* that "the access enjoyed by the United States intelligence services to the transferred data [...] constitutes an interference with the fundamental right to protection of personal data guaranteed in Article 8 of the Charter."[231] His finding indicated that the processing of personal data by US intelligence services interferes with Article 8 CFR. He added, however, that this interference is permitted by derogations in Decision 2000/520, i.e. the Safe Harbor adequacy decision.[232] According to the fourth paragraph of Annex I Decision 2000/520, the applicability of the Safe Harbor principles in the adequacy decision may be limited by US authorities "to the extent necessary to meet national security, public interest, or law enforcement requirements." The ECJ similarly explained in *Schrems* that

> [i]n the light of the general nature of the derogation set out in the fourth paragraph of Annex I to Decision 2000/520, that decision thus enables interference, founded on national security and public interest requirements or on domestic legislation of the United States, with the fundamental rights of the persons whose personal data is or could be transferred from the European Union to the United States.[233]

The ECJ elaborated that while an interference with fundamental rights may take place in the third country, the legal basis that enables that interference in the third

[230] See Sect. 2.2.4.1.

[231] ECJ, AG Opinion, *Schrems*, para. 170.

[232] Ibid., para. 174.

[233] ECJ, *Schrems*, para. 87.

country must lie in the EU. With regard to Decision 2000/520, the ECJ recognized the fourth paragraph of Annex I Decision 2000/520 as the basis that enabled the interference in the US. Similarly, the ECJ held in *Schrems 2* that the derogations set out in paragraph I.5 of Annex II Decision (EU) 2016/1250, the Privacy Shield adequacy decision, enable interference with the fundamental rights of the persons whose personal data is transferred to the US based on national security and public interest requirements or the domestic legislation of the US.[234]

Nevertheless, this seems to fall short of a comprehensive understanding of an interference with fundamental rights caused by data transfers on the basis of adequacy decisions. Apart from Decision 2000/520 and Decision (EU) 2016/1250, no other adequacy decision contains a similar derogation that explicitly enables public authorities of a third country to limit the protection of personal data for national security and law enforcement purposes. However, an interference with fundamental rights in the third country can also take place if an adequacy decision does not entail an explicit derogation for public authorities of the third country. In such a case, the ECJ would have to look elsewhere to find the legal basis that enables the interference in the third country.

Article 1 Decision (EU) 2019/419, i.e., the adequacy decision for Japan, which was also the first adequacy decision made under the GDPR, provides that

> Japan ensures an adequate level of protection for personal data transferred from the European Union to personal information handling business operators in Japan subject to the Act on the Protection of Personal Information as complemented by the Supplementary Rules set out in Annex I, together with the official representations, assurances and commitments contained in Annex II.

Annex II Decision (EU) 2019/419 covers the legal framework in Japan concerning access to information by the government of Japan for criminal law enforcement and national security purposes. The Commission's adequacy finding in Article 1 Decision (EU) 2019/419 is connected to the official representations, assurances and commitments contained in Annex II Decision (EU) 2019/419. Recital (173) Decision (EU) 2019/419 provides that

> on the basis of the available information about the Japanese legal order, including the representations, assurances and commitments from the Japanese government contained in Annex II, the Commission considers that any interference with the fundamental rights of the individuals whose personal data are transferred from the European Union to Japan by Japanese public authorities for public interest purposes, in particular criminal law enforcement and national security purposes, will be limited to what is strictly necessary to achieve the legitimate objective in question, and that effective legal protection against such interference exists.

Article 1 Decision (EU) 2019/419 is the legal basis that enables possible interferences with fundamental rights in Japan because it connects the possibility to transfer personal data to Japan with an acknowledgment of the legal framework described in Annex II Decision (EU) 2019/419.

[234] ECJ, *Schrems 2*, para. 165.

Older adequacy decisions under Directive 95/46/EC, such as the Decision 2000/518/EC, i.e. the adequacy decision for Switzerland, do not contain any specific reference to the legal frameworks of the third countries concerning access to information by public authorities of the third country for criminal law enforcement and national security purposes. Article 1 Decision 2000/518/EC only provides that "Switzerland is considered as providing an adequate level of protection for personal data transferred from the Community."

Even if there is no explicit acknowledgment of the legal framework in the third country concerning access to information by public authorities of the third country for criminal law enforcement and national security purposes, the Commission's adequacy finding still implies that it implicitly approves the legal framework of the third country. Accordingly, Article 1 Decision 2000/518/EC is the legal basis that enables possible interferences in Switzerland because it entails the possibility to transfer personal data to Switzerland.

All adequacy decisions approve, albeit in different ways, the legal framework concerning access to information in the third country for criminal law enforcement and national security purposes. Their common denominator in providing the legal basis for a potential interference is that they enable the transfer of personal data to a third country. Without the actual transfers of personal data there is no possibility of interference in the third country.

The ECJ had to determine the validity of a draft PNR agreement that would have enabled the transfer of PNR data from the EU to Canada in Opinion 1/15. The opinion required the ECJ to identify possible interferences with fundamental rights. The ECJ found that

> both the transfer of PNR data from the European Union to the Canadian Competent Authority and the framework negotiated by the European Union with Canada of the conditions concerning the retention of that data, its use and its subsequent transfer [...] constitute interferences with the right guaranteed in Article 7 of the Charter.[235]

The ECJ added that "[t]hose operations also constitute an interference with the fundamental right to the protection of personal data guaranteed in Article 8 of the Charter."[236]

The ECJ underlined in Opinion 1/15 that not only the negotiated framework constitutes an interference but also the actual transfer of PNR data. If that finding is applied to adequacy decisions, both the transfer of personal data from the EU and the adequacy finding that approves the legal framework in the third country concerning access to information in the third country for criminal law enforcement and national security purposes constitute interferences with Article 8 CFR should they not respect the right to continuous protection of personal data.

The interference with the right to continuous protection of personal data in Article 8 CFR should be found in the EU. Ultimately, the rules, measures, and actions of third states also entail intrusions, which, if they were attributable to the

[235] ECJ, Opinion 1/15, para. 125.

[236] Ibid., para. 126.

authorities of an EU member state, would be regarded as interferences with the exercise of the right to data protection in Article 8 CFR.[237] Those intrusions should, however, be assessed with regard to the standard of essential equivalence that is part of the right to continuous protection of personal data. If intrusions caused by the rules, measures, and actions of third states do not respect the standard of essential equivalence, then the transfer of personal data based on the adequacy decision and the adequacy finding itself constitute interferences with the right to continuous protection for personal data enshrined in Article 8(1) CFR.

3.2.2.2 Legal Basis

The limitation of the exercise of fundamental rights must be provided for by law. The legal basis that permits an interference with Article 8 CFR must itself already define the scope of the limitation on the exercise of fundamental rights.[238] The legal basis for interferences with Article 8 CFR must indicate under what circumstances and conditions the interference will take place and impose minimum safeguards providing sufficient guarantees for individuals to effectively protect their personal data against the risk of abuse.[239] These safeguards are particularly important in cases in which personal data is subject to automated processing and involves sensitive data.[240]

The transfer of personal data based on an adequacy decision as well as the adequacy finding are both interferences with Article 8 CFR if the level of protection for personal data in the third country is not essentially equivalent to that guaranteed within the EU. The adequacy finding is usually elaborated in the first article of an adequacy decision. The adequacy decision of the Commission constitutes the legal basis for the transfer of personal data as it enables data transfers without any further authorization, implementation, or application of the decision. The question is whether adequacy decisions fulfill the conditions regarding the scope of the limitations on the exercise of fundamental rights and minimum safeguards.

Some adequacy decisions refer (or referred) to the scope of the limitations on the exercise of fundamental rights permitted for the respective third state, which, if they were attributable to the authorities of an EU member state, would be regarded as interferences with the exercise of the right to data protection in Article 8 CFR:

– Decision (EU) 2019/419, i.e., the adequacy decision for Japan, contains representations, assurances, and commitments of the Japanese government regarding their legal framework for the collection and use of personal data by public authorities for criminal law enforcement and national security purposes. Annex II

---

[237] Cp. ECJ, AG Opinion, *Schrems 2*, para. 256.

[238] ECJ, Opinion 1/15, para. 139; ECJ, *WebMindLicenses*, para. 81; see 2.2.4.4.

[239] ECJ, Opinion 1/15, para. 141; ECJ, *Tele2/Watson*, para. 109; ECJ, *Schrems*, para. 91; ECJ, *Digital Rights Ireland*, para. 54.

[240] ECJ, Opinion 1/15, para. 141; ECJ, *Schrems*, para. 91; ECJ, *Digital Rights Ireland*, para. 55.

of Decision (EU) 2019/419 refers in particular to available legal bases for surveillance measures, applicable conditions (limitations) and safeguards, including independent oversight and individual redress possibilities. Article 3(5)(b) Decision (EU) 2019/419 holds that the Commission may suspend, amend or repeal the decision, if there are indications that the Japanese public authorities do not comply with the representations, assurances, and commitments contained in Annex II of Decision (EU) 2019/419, including as regards the conditions and limitations for the collection of and access to personal data transferred under Decision (EU) 2019/419 by Japanese public authorities for criminal law enforcement or national security purposes.
- Decision (EU) 2016/1250, the Privacy Shield adequacy decision, maintained in Article 1(2) that the EU-US Privacy Shield is constituted by the principles issued by the US Department of Commerce as set out in Annex II of Decision (EU) 2016/1250 and the official representations and commitments contained in the documents listed in Annexes I, III to VI of Decision (EU) 2016/1250. Section I(5) Annex II Decision (EU) 2016/1250 held that the privacy principles in Annex II may be limited to the extent necessary to meet national security, public interest, or law enforcement requirement. Annex VI of Decision (EU) 2016/1250 contained two letters from the US General Counsel of the Office of the Director of National Intelligence that were sent to the US Department of Commerce which "extensively discuss, among other things, the policies, safeguards, and limitations that apply to signals intelligence activities conducted by the US"[241] Annex III of Decision (EU) 2016/1250 contained representations regarding the rules for the new EU-US Privacy Shield Ombudsperson mechanism for signals intelligence activities.
- Older adequacy decisions under Directive 95/46/EC such as Decision 2000/518/EC, the adequacy decision for Switzerland, also refer to the scope of the limitations on the exercise of fundamental rights and minimum safeguards regarding the rules, measures and actions of the respective third state, which, if they were attributable to the authorities of an EU member state, would be regarded as interferences with the exercise of the right to data protection in Article 8 CFR, but in a less comprehensive way.[242]

With regard to minimum safeguards, independent oversight and remedies are important. According to Article 45(3) and (4) GDPR, the Commission has to monitor the application of the legal framework in the third country, upon which an adequacy decision is based, and, at least once every four years, evaluate the adequacy finding for the third country in question.[243] In cases where the Commission has indications that an adequate level of protection for personal data is no longer ensured, it may decide to suspend, amend, limit, or repeal an adequacy decision according to Article 45(5) GDPR.[244] In addition, supervisory authorities also have the

[241] Annex I of Decision (EU) 2016/1250.

[242] See Recitals (5)–(10) Decision 2000/518/EC.

[243] See also Article 3(1) and (4) Decision (EU) 2019/419.

[244] See also Article 3(5) Decision (EU) 2019/419.

investigative powers in Article 58(1) GDPR at their disposal, which should protect individuals against the risk of abuse of their personal data. Supervisory authorities are entitled to consider the validity of adequacy decisions, but the ECJ alone has jurisdiction to declare adequacy decisions invalid. Individuals have the right to lodge a complaint with a supervisory authority according to Article 77(1) GDPR. Supervisory authorities must handle complaints lodged with them, investigate the subject matter of the complaint, and inform the complainant of the progress and outcome of the investigation within a reasonable period of time based on Article 57(1)(f) GDPR. Adequacy decisions therefore provide a valid legal basis for an interference with the right to continuous protection for personal data in Article 8 CFR.

3.2.2.3 Objectives of General Interest and Protection of the Freedoms of Others

According to Article 52 CFR, justification for an interference that limits the exercise of fundamental rights further requires that the limitations genuinely meet objectives of general interest recognized by the EU or the need to protect the rights and freedoms of others. The public security in third countries qualifies as a general interest recognized by the EU (Sect. 3.2.2.3.1) and, both the freedom of expression and information in Article 11 CFR (Sect. 3.2.2.3.2) and the freedom to conduct a business in Article 16 CFR (Sect. 3.2.2.3.3) qualify as rights of others which must be protected.

3.2.2.3.1 Public Security in a Third Country

The protection of public security is an objective of general interest recognized by the EU.[245] The question is whether this objective also covers public security in third countries. In this regard it must be observed that the EU should contribute to peace and security in its relations with the wider world according to Article 3(5) TEU. The EU should also define and pursue common policies in all fields of international relations, to preserve peace, prevent conflicts, and strengthen international security based on Article 21(2)(c) TEU. The protection of international security is thus clearly an objective of general interest recognized in the EU Treaties. The ECJ elaborated in Opinion 1/15 that

> the transfer of PNR data by air carriers to Canada and the use of that data by the Canadian Competent Authority are justified [. . .] only by the objective of ensuring public security in that non-member country and in the European Union.[246]

[245] ECJ, *Digital Rights Ireland*, para. 41.

[246] Ibid., para. 91.

It seems, therefore, that the protection of public security in a third country can be an objective of general interest recognized by the EU. In order to justify an interference with the right to continuous protection of personal data based on the protection of public security in a third country, that protection must be one of the material objectives of the data transfers and the adequacy finding.[247] However, data transfers on the basis of an adequacy decision are normally part of a commercial activity.[248] They do not typically relate to the protection of public security in a third country. Nevertheless, the adequacy findings must be interpreted in light of the whole adequacy decision.

Decision 2000/520, the Safe Harbor adequacy decision, allowed limitations on the privacy principles contained in the adequacy decision in the fourth paragraph of Annex I of Decision 2000/520:

> (a) to the extent necessary to meet national security, public interest, or law enforcement requirements;
> (b) by statute, government regulation, or case law that create conflicting obligations or explicit authorizations, provided that, in exercising any such authorization, an organization can demonstrate that its non-compliance with the Principles is limited to the extent necessary to meet the overriding legitimate interests furthered by such authorization.

AG Yves Bot found that point (a) is "sufficiently precise to be regarded as an objective of general interest recognised by the European Union within the meaning of Article 52(1) of the Charter" and that point (b) does "not pursue an objective of general interest defined with sufficient precision."[249]

Decision (EU) 2016/1250, the Privacy Shield adequacy decision, maintained in Section I(5) of Annex II that adherence to the privacy principles contained in the adequacy decision may be limited to the extent necessary to meet national security, public interest, or law enforcement requirements. Section I(b) of Annex VI added six specific purposes for signal intelligence:

> detecting and countering certain activities of foreign powers; counterterrorism; counter-proliferation; cybersecurity; detecting and countering threats to US or allied armed forces; and combating transnational criminal threats, including sanctions evasion.

Decision (EU) 2019/419, the adequacy decision for Japan, also contains a series of representations of the Japanese government regarding the legal framework for the collection and use of personal data by Japanese public authorities for criminal law enforcement and national security purposes in Annex 2 of Decision (EU) 2019/419. In these adequacy decisions, the protection of public security in a third country was or—in the case of Japan—is one of the material objectives.

In contrast, older adequacy decision such as Decision 2000/518/EC, the adequacy decision for Switzerland, do not refer to security concerns of the third state at all.

[247] ECJ, *Digital Rights Ireland*, para. 41.

[248] ECJ, AG Opinion, *Schrems 2*, paras 106–107.

[249] ECJ, AG Opinion, *Schrems*, paras 181, 184.

Accordingly, the public security of the third country cannot be considered a material objective of these older adequacy decisions.

3.2.2.3.2 Freedom of Expression and Information

The right to freedom of expression and information in Article 11 CFR includes the freedom to hold opinions and to receive and impart information and ideas without interference by public authorities and regardless of frontiers. AG Juliane Kokott suggested in her opinion in *Satamedia* that the freedom of expression in Article 11 CFR should be understood "in the sense of freedom of communication."[250] AG Verica Trstenjak agreed with AG Kokott in her opinion in *MSD Sharp* and summarized that Article 11 CFR "includes the freedom to communicate information without interference by public authority" and that "not only is the communication of one's own ideas but also the transmission of third-party ideas and information protected."[251] It must be acknowledged at this point that data transfers enable the communication of information involving personal data.

The freedom of expression and information in Article 11 CFR corresponds to Article 10 ECHR.[252] The freedom to communicate information and ideas under Article 10 ECHR includes many types of information: political speech, cultural speech, and artistic speech, but it also includes economic communication, the so-called commercial speech.[253] The same is true for Article 11 CFR.[254] A private legal entity can invoke the protection of the right to freedom of expression and information even for purely commercial activities, that is, activities that are conducted for purposes of monetary gain.[255] Data transfers enable different types of speech that involve personal data.

The wording of Article 11 CFR implies that the freedom of communication is not confined to the borders of the EU.[256] The wording is similar to the freedom of expression enshrined in Article 19(2) ICCPR. Molly Land described Article 19(2) ICCPR as providing "an important countervailing force to the rise of borders on-line by creating an explicit right to seek, receive, and impart information across borders."[257] Data

---

[250] ECJ, AG Opinion, *Satamedia*, para. 39.

[251] ECJ, AG Opinion, *MSD Sharp*, para. 81.

[252] EU (2007), p. 21.

[253] ECtHR, *Casado Coca v. Spain*, para. 50; ECtHR, *Markt intern Verlag GmbH and Klaus Beermann v. Germany*, para. 26.

[254] ECJ, *Germany v Parliament and Council*, para. 142; Thiele (2017), p. 1161; Frenz (2009), p. 545.

[255] ECtHR, *Autronic AG v. Switzerland*, para. 47.

[256] See Thiele (2017), p. 1162.

[257] Land (2013), p. 438.

transfers are a key tool for the exercise of the freedom of expression and information enshrined in Article 11 CFR. [258]

In order to justify an interference with the right to continuous protection of personal data in Article 8 CFR based on the protection of the freedom of expression and information, the protection of this freedom must be one of the material objectives of the data transfers and the adequacy finding.[259] No adequacy decision to date refers to the protection of Article 11 CFR, but this does not preclude an argument using Article 11 CFR as a justification. Recital (4) GDPR states that the GDPR respects all fundamental rights and mentions, in particular, the freedom of expression and information. Furthermore, Article 85(1) GDPR specifically requires the EU member states to reconcile the right to data protection with the freedom of expression and information. The protection of freedom of expression and information is one of the material objectives of the GDPR and, therefore, also of Chapter V GDPR on the transfer of personal data to third countries.

3.2.2.3.3 Freedom to Conduct a Business

The freedom to conduct a business is a fundamental right enshrined in Article 16 CFR.[260] Article 16 CFR recognizes the freedom to conduct a business in accordance with Union law and national laws and practices. According to the explanations relating to the Charter, Article 16 CFR constitutes a bundle of rights: the freedom to exercise an economic or commercial activity, the freedom of contract, and the right to free competition.[261] AG Pedro Cruz Villalón maintained in his opinion in *Alemo-Herron* that "the case-law has not, in fact, provided a full and useful definition of this freedom."[262] He then provided a useful description based on the explanations relating to the Charter:

> In effect, the freedom to conduct a business, as stated in that article, acts to protect economic initiative and economic activity, obviously within limits but nevertheless ensuring that there are certain minimum conditions for economic activity in the internal market. Thus, the freedom to conduct a business acts as a limit on the actions of the Union in its legislative and executive role as well as on the actions of the Member States in their application of European Union law.[263]

---

[258] Anupam Chander and Uyên Lê also maintain that measures prohibiting data flows (data localization) interfere with the freedom of expression. Chander and Le (2015), p. 739.

[259] ECJ, *Digital Rights Ireland*, para. 41.

[260] Xavier Groussot, Gunnar Thor Pétursson and Justin Pierce submit that even if Article 16 CFR bears signs of a principle in the sense of Article 52(5) CFR, it is more akin to a right. Groussot et al. (2017), pp. 332–333.

[261] See EU (2007), p. 23.

[262] ECJ, AG Opinion, *Alemo-Herron*, para. 49.

[263] Ibid., para. 50.

AG Cruz Villalón added that "the freedom to conduct a business protects economic initiative and the ability to participate in a market, rather than the actual profit, seen in financial terms, that is earned in that market."[264] The free movement of personal data protects the freedom to conduct a business on the internal market. It is, however, not clear whether data transfers and the freedom to conduct business across borders are also covered.

The ECJ dealt with questions regarding cross-border economic activities and Article 16 CFR on multiple occasions. In *Affish BV*, the ECJ had to assess the validity of Decision 95/119/EC concerning certain protective measures on fishery products originating in Japan.[265] Affish BV, a private company established in the Netherlands, imports deep-frozen fish products from Japan and distributes them in the EU. Affish BV argued that Decision 95/119/EC is a disproportional restriction on its business activity and a danger to its viability since a significant part of its revenue comes from the importation of fishery products from Japan.[266] The ECJ found that the freedom to pursue a trade or business is not absolute and that the contested decision cannot be regarded as constituting a disproportionate interference.[267] Even though the ECJ did not side with Affish BV, it did apply the freedom to conduct a business in a cross-border context. The ECJ also had to assess the quota arrangements for importing bananas imposed by Regulation (EEC) 1442/93 in *Germany v Council.*[268] The ECJ found that the restrictions imposed by Regulation (EEC) 1442/93 on the freedom of traditional third country banana traders correspond to objectives of general Community interest and thus do not impair the very substance of that right.[269] Again, the ECJ did not find a violation of Article 16 CFR, but it applied the freedom to conduct a business in cross-border context. The freedom to conduct a business in Article 16 CFR therefore also covers cross-border economic activities.[270] Data transfers to third countries may be used—and have to be used, at times—for cross-border economic activities. In this sense, they can be viewed as a tool for exercising the freedom to conduct a business that is enshrined in Article 16 CFR.

In order to justify an interference with the right to continuous protection of personal data in Article 8 CFR based on the protection of the freedom to conduct a business, that protection must be one of the material objectives of the data transfers and the adequacy finding objectives.[271] No adequacy decision to date refers to the protection of Article 16 CFR but that does not generally preclude an argument using

---

[264] Ibid., para. 51.

[265] ECJ, *Affish BV*, para. 15.

[266] Ibid., para. 41.

[267] Ibid., paras 42–43. The case was handed down before the entry into force of the Charter and decided on the basis of a general principle of EU law that was replaced by Article 16 CFR. See Oliver (2013), p. 283.

[268] ECJ, *Germany v Council (Bananas)*, paras 14–26.

[269] Ibid., para. 87.

[270] Kühling (2017), p. 1228; Frenz (2009), p. 799, Grabenwarter (2014), p. 517.

[271] ECJ, *Digital Rights Ireland*, para. 41.

Article 16 CFR as a justification. Recital (4) GDPR states that the GDPR respects all fundamental rights and also specifically mentions the freedom to conduct a business. Recital (101) GDPR states that flows of personal data to and from countries outside the Union are necessary for the expansion of international trade. Adequacy decisions also refer to the importance of data transfers for international trade. For example, Recital (1) Decision (EU) 2019/419, the adequacy decision for Japan, maintains that

> [t]he flow of personal data to and from countries outside the European Union is necessary for the expansion of international cooperation and international trade while guaranteeing that the level of protection afforded to personal data in the European Union is not undermined.

This is also reflected in the submission of the Irish DPC in *Schrems 2* before the IHC (but with a view to standard data protection clauses). The DPC argued that there is a crucial distinction between the data transfers in a PNR agreement and Facebook's data transfers. The DPC maintained that PNR agreements have "no other, independent commercial reason for the transfer of the data" and that the data transfers of Facebook in *Schrems 2* "are for commercial purposes by definition."[272] The IHC also stated that "[t]he free transfer of data around the world is now central to economic and social life in the Union and elsewhere."[273] The protection of the freedom to conduct a business in Article 16 CFR is one of the material objectives of the GDPR and, therefore, also of Chapter V GDPR on the transfer of personal data to third countries.

3.2.2.4 Proportionality

The principle of proportionality requires that limitations on fundamental rights must be appropriate in light of the objective pursued and limited to what is strictly necessary.[274] It is also necessary to examine if there are other measures which affect the right to continuous protection of personal data less adversely and still contribute effectively to the objectives of general interest recognized by the EU or the need to protect the fundamental rights and freedoms of others. It has to be seen if the interference with the right to continuous protection of personal data is proportional to the objective of public security in a third country (Sect. 3.2.2.4.1), to the protection of the freedom of expression and information in Article 11 CFR (Sect. 3.2.2.4.2), and to the protection of the freedom to conduct a business in Article 16 CFR (Sect. 3.2.2.4.3).

---

[272] IHC, *Schrems 2*, paras 59, 61(4).

[273] Ibid., para. 45.

[274] ECJ, Opinion 1/15, para. 140; ECJ, *Tele2/Watson*, paras 96, 103; ECJ, *Schrems*, para. 92; ECJ, *Digital Rights Ireland*, paras 51–52; see Sect. 2.2.4.4.

3.2.2.4.1 Public Security in a Third Country

The ECJ found in *Digital Rights Ireland* that—with regard to the growing importance of means of electronic communication—the retention of personal data from such communications may help criminal investigations shed light on serious crime and is, therefore, appropriate for the purposes of ensuring public security.[275] Similarly, the ECJ found in Opinion 1/15 that the transfer of PNR data from the EU to Canada and the subsequent processing of that data in Canada is appropriate for the purpose of ensuring public security.[276]

Adequacy findings may be considered appropriate for protecting public security in a third country because they allow systematic, structural, and continuous transfers of personal data to a third country. Normally, data transfers are part of a commercial activity. However, transfers of personal data can be used by third countries to extract information about individuals in the EU if they employ surveillance measures to analyze the transmitted information. Intelligence agencies of third countries can use the abundance of transmitted information to protect public security.

The ECJ held in *Digital Rights Ireland* that a proportionality assessment must take into account the extent and seriousness of the interference.[277] The extent of the interference depends on the amount of personal data and the number of individuals that are subject to intrusions in the third country. Because adequacy findings enable systematic, structural, and continuous data transfers to a third country without further authorization they potentially entail interference with the fundamental rights of a significant part of the European population.[278] The interference therefore requires a strict proportionality assessment. I argue that under such an assessment, the interference with the right to continuous protection of personal data in Article 8 CFR *exceeds* the limits of what is necessary to protect public security in a third country. There are measures that affect the right to data protection less adversely and could still effectively contribute to public security in third countries. For example, targeted international cooperation between intelligence agencies of EU member states and third countries could protect public security in a third country without subjecting a significant part of the European population to interferences with fundamental rights. Adequacy findings that do not respect the right to continuous protection for personal data cannot be justified based on the protection of public security in the third country.

[275] ECJ, *Digital Rights Ireland*, para. 49.

[276] ECJ, Opinion 1/15, para. 152.

[277] ECJ, *Digital Rights Ireland*, para. 48.

[278] Ibid., para. 56.

3.2.2.4.2 Freedom of Expression and Information

Data transfers based on an adequacy finding enable individuals and companies to impart information and ideas without interference by public authorities and regardless of borders. Adequacy findings allow systematic, structural, and continuous data transfers to third countries and may, therefore, be considered appropriate to protect the freedom of expression and information enshrined in Article 11 CFR.

There must be a fair balance between the interference with the right to data protection and the protection of the freedom of expression and information. In this context, it is important to emphasize that some cross-border flows of personal data do not fall under the concept of data transfers. The ECJ held in *Lindqvist* that the uploading of personal data onto an internet site hosted in the EEA does not constitute a transfer of personal data.[279] I also underlined that even hosting providers of internet sites in the EEA do not transfer personal data to third countries when they make the uploaded data available to everyone on an internet site.[280] Consequently, these cross-border flows of personal data do *not* require an adequacy decision or another legal mechanism to legitimate them. This type of cross-border flows of personal data covers an important part of the freedom to impart information and ideas without interference by public authorities and regardless of borders. In order to address proportionality, it necessary to distinguish between cross-border flows of personal data for commercial speech and other forms of expression. The level of protection and the margin of appreciation are important considerations for balancing between two or more fundamental rights and freedoms.[281]

Commercial speech typically attracts a lower level of protection than other forms of expression and there is a greater margin of appreciation in determining limits to it.[282] The ECJ found multiple times that derogations from and limitations on the protection of personal data must apply only in so far as is strictly necessary.[283] Accordingly, it would not be proportional to justify limitations on the right to continuous protection of personal data using protection of commercial speech because the right to data protection attracts a higher level of protection than commercial speech.

Other forms of expression, however, are explicitly mentioned in Article 85(2) GDPR. Article 85(2) GDPR requires EU member states to provide exemptions or derogations from the rules in the GDPR, such as the legal mechanisms for the transfer of personal data in Chapter V GDPR, for journalistic purposes or the purpose of

---

[279] ECJ, *Lindqvist*, para. 69.

[280] See Sect. 3.1.3.2.3.

[281] Rosas (2014), p. 356.

[282] ECJ, *Germany v Parliament and Council*, para. 155; ECtHR, *Casado Coca v. Spain*, para. 50; ECtHR, *Markt intern Verlag GmbH and Klaus Beermann v. Germany*, paras 32–33; Woods (2014), p. 322; Walter (2014), p. 497.

[283] ECJ, *Satamedia*, para. 56; ECJ, *Schecke*, para. 77; ECJ, *Digital Rights Ireland*, para. 52; ECJ, *Schrems*, para. 92; ECJ, *Tele2/Watson*, para. 96; see Sect. 2.2.3.4.

academic, artistic, and literary expression if they are necessary to reconcile the right to data protection with the freedom of expression and information.[284] The EU legislator clearly indicated in Article 85(2) GDPR that the right to data protection and journalistic, academic, artistic, and literary speech must be reconciled and that the freedom of expression and information may justify data transfers even if they interfere with the right to continuous protection for personal data. The EU legislator determined in Article 85(2) GDPR that this reconciliation should take place outside the regular legal mechanisms for the transfer of personal data in Chapter V GDPR and on the level of EU member states. In Sweden, for example, the Data Protection Act with supplementing provisions to the EU Data Protection Regulation of 18 April 2018 entails in Chapter 1 Section 7 that neither the GDPR nor this Act shall apply so far that they will infringe upon the Freedom of the Press Act or the Freedom of Expression Act and that the articles of the GDPR, which include the data transfer system, shall not apply to the processing of personal data for journalistic purposes and the purposes of academic, artistic or literary expression.[285]

It would therefore not be proportional to justify limitations on the right to continuous protection of personal data with the protection of journalistic, academic, artistic and literary speech because Article 85(2) GDPR explicitly requires EU member states to adopt rules that affect less adversely the right to data protection and still contribute effectively to the protection of journalistic, academic, artistic, and literary speech.

3.2.2.4.3 Freedom to Conduct a Business

Data transfers based on adequacy findings enable individuals and companies to operate business models that require transfers of personal data to third countries and must, therefore, be considered appropriate to protect the freedom to conduct a business enshrined in Article 16 CFR.

In these cases, there must be a fair balance between the interference of data transfers on the basis of an adequacy decision with the right to data protection and the protection of the freedom to conduct a business. AG Cruz Villa pointed out in his opinion in *Alemo-Herron* that the ECJ often used the freedom to conduct a business in its case law as a counterweight to other fundamental rights.[286] For example, the ECJ found in *Achbita* that an employer's wish to project an image of religious neutrality towards customers falls under the freedom to conduct a business and that this wish allows the employer to restrict, within certain limits, the freedom of

---

[284] Albrecht and Janson (2016), p. 502.

[285] Jonason (2019), p. 46.

[286] ECJ, AG Opinion, *Alemo-Herron*, para. 52 with reference to, for example, ECJ, *Scarlet Extended*, para. 49 and ECJ, *SABAM*, para. 47 where the injunction to install a filtering system did not struck a fair balance between the protection of the intellectual-property right enjoyed by copyright holders, and that of the freedom to conduct business enjoyed by operators such as hosting service providers. Cp. Oliver (2013), p. 299.

religion enshrined in Article 10 CFR.[287] ECJ Judge Allan Rosas suggested that one consideration for the balancing of different rights or freedoms is related to the wording and context of the rights or freedoms in question.[288] If the wording provides that someone has a right "in accordance with national laws and practices," then this would suggest a wider margin of appreciation for limitations.[289] This is true for the freedom to conduct a business. In light of the wording of Article 16 CFR, the ECJ found that "the freedom to conduct a business may be subject to a broad range of interventions on the part of public authorities which may limit the exercise of economic activity in the public interest."[290] It seems that the right to data protection in Article 8 CFR attracts a higher level of protection than the freedom to conduct a business in Article 16 CFR. The ECJ found multiple times that derogations from and limitations on the protection of personal data must apply only in so far as is strictly necessary.[291] Furthermore, in the absence of an adequacy decision for a third country, individuals and companies may still rely on other legal mechanisms for data transfers such as the derogations in Article 49 GDPR.

It would not be proportional to justify the limitations on the right to continuous protection of personal data with the freedom to conduct a business because the right to data protection attracts a higher level of protection and there are measures that affect the right to data protection less adversely and still effectively contribute to the protection of the freedom to conduct a business.

3.2.3 The Validity of Adequacy Decisions as a Legal Mechanism

Adequacy decisions must fully comply with the right to continuous protection of personal data. The validity of an adequacy decision depends on the level of protection in the third country being essentially equivalent to that guaranteed within the EU.[292] The validity of adequacy decisions as a legal mechanism for data transfers depends on the regulatory framework surrounding the transfer mechanism that guarantees the right to continuous protection of personal data. First, the Commission must be able to assess, review, and monitor the level of protection in a third country. Second, the transfer of personal data based on adequacy decisions must be subject to independent supervision. Third, data subjects must be able to enforce their right to continuous protection for personal data.

---

[287] ECJ, *Achbita*, C-157/15, paras 38–39.

[288] Rosas (2014), p. 356.

[289] Ibid.

[290] ECJ, *Sky Österreich*, para. 46.

[291] ECJ, *Satamedia*, para. 56; ECJ, *Schecke*, para. 77; ECJ, *Digital Rights Ireland*, para. 52; ECJ, *Schrems*, para. 92; ECJ, *Tele2/Watson*, para. 96; see Sect. 2.2.3.4.

[292] ECJ, *Schrems 2*, para. 129; see Sect. 2.3.4.

The assessment of the level of protection for personal data in the third country for an adequacy decision is regulated in Article 45(2) GDPR. The Commission is required to assess relevant legislation, both general and sectoral, concerning public security, defense, national security, and criminal law as well as the access of public authorities in the third country to personal data. The review of the level of protection for personal data in the third country is regulated in Article 45(3) GDPR.[293] The Commission must review every adequacy decision at least once every four years in order to take into account any relevant developments in the third country. The monitoring of the level of protection for personal data in third countries for an adequacy decision is regulated in Article 45(4) GDPR. The Commission must also monitor developments in the third country on an ongoing basis. If the review or the monitoring reveals that a third country no longer ensures an adequate level of protection for personal data, then the Commission must repeal, amend, or suspend an adequacy decision according to Article 45(5) GDPR.

Supervisory authorities are responsible for ensuring compliance with the legal mechanisms for data transfers in accordance with Article 8(3) CFR. They are vested with the power to check whether the transfer of personal data from the EU member state to the third country complies with the requirements laid down in the GDPR.[294] The ECJ made it clear that adequacy decisions can be subject to judicial review.[295] Data subjects have a right to lodge a complaint with a supervisory authority in order to protect their fundamental rights with regard to data transfers.[296] In cases in which a supervisory authority considers that there are well-founded objections as to the compliance of an adequacy decision with the GDPR and the Charter, the national legislature must provide for legal remedies enabling the supervisory authority to advance these objections before the national courts to allow them to make a reference to the ECJ for a preliminary ruling regarding the validity of the respective adequacy decision.[297] The same is true in cases in which a supervisory authority comes to the conclusion that the complaint of an individual against an adequacy decision is unfounded and therefore rejects it.[298] The data subject who lodged the complaint must have access to judicial remedies enabling him or her to challenge such a decision before national courts.[299] Finally, the ECJ has jurisdiction to declare an adequacy decision invalid.[300] The regulatory framework surrounding adequacy decisions validates them as a legal mechanism for data transfers.

---

[293] The ECJ found in *Schrems* that the Commission must "check periodically whether the finding relating to the adequacy of the level of protection ensured by the third country in question is still factually and legally justified." ECJ, *Schrems*, para. 76.

[294] Ibid., para. 47; see also Article 58 GDPR.

[295] ECJ, *Schrems*, para. 59; ECJ, *Schrems 2*, paras 156–157.

[296] ECJ, *Schrems*, para. 58; see also Article 77(1) GDPR.

[297] Ibid., para. 65.

[298] Ibid., para. 64.

[299] Ibid.; see also Article 47 CFR and Article 78 GDPR.

[300] Ibid., para. 61.

3.2.4 *The European Commission as Guardian of Fundamental Rights*

Control over continuous protection for personal data in relation with adequacy decisions lies primarily with the European Commission. The Commission assesses the level of protection for personal data in third countries, decides whether that level is essentially equivalent to that guaranteed within the EU, reviews and monitors developments in third countries that could affect the validity of a previously made adequacy decision, and repeals, amends, or suspends an adequacy decision in cases in which available information reveals that a third country no longer ensures a level of protection for personal data that is essentially equivalent to that guaranteed within the EU. In this way, the European Commission acts as the guardian of fundamental rights with regard to the transfer of personal data based on an adequacy decision.

The primary responsibility for ensuring continuous protection for personal data in relation with the adequacy decisions of the Commission is complemented by the tasks of supervisory authorities and the judicial system. Supervisory authorities are responsible for monitoring compliance with rules concerning the protection of individuals regarding the processing of their personal data in accordance with Article 57 GDPR. Each of the supervisory authorities in the EU member states is vested with the power to examine whether the transfer of personal data complies with the requirements laid down in the GDPR.[301] This is also required by Article 8(3) CFR. The supervisory authorities and national judicial systems are entitled to consider the validity of adequacy decisions, but the ECJ alone has jurisdiction to declare adequacy decisions invalid.[302]

3.2.5 *Summary*

Adequacy decisions must fully comply with the right to continuous protection for personal data and the standard of essential equivalence. No limitations on the exercise of the right to continuous protection for personal data are possible for data transfers based on adequacy decisions. The right to continuous protection for personal data in Article 8 CFR has a restrictive effect on data transfers based on adequacy decisions. Only countries that guarantee a level of protection that is essentially equivalent to that guaranteed within the EU qualify for an adequacy decision. The justification of this restrictive effect is firmly rooted in the protection of fundamental rights. However, there are some problems when it comes to a consistent fundamental rights-based application of adequacy decisions. My analysis has revealed discriminatory procedures, content-related inconsistencies, geographic

---

[301] ECJ, *Schrems*, para. 47.

[302] Ibid., paras 61–62.

and economic biases, and other unconnected considerations. The European Commission is the guardian of fundamental rights with regard to adequacy decisions. It must follow a fundamental rights-based approach regarding the adoption of adequacy decisions.

3.3 Continuous Protection of Personal Data and Appropriate Safeguards

The third section of this chapter is dedicated to the interplay of the right to continuous protection of personal data in Article 8 CFR and the instruments providing appropriate safeguards according to Article 46 GDPR. The analysis of the politics behind appropriate safeguards reveals a *laissez-faire* attitude towards fundamental rights protection (Sect. 3.3.1). This is problematic because the instruments providing appropriate safeguards must fully comply with the right to continuous protection for personal data (Sect. 3.3.2). Nonetheless, the regulatory framework around the instruments in Article 46 GDPR validates appropriate safeguards as a legal mechanism for data transfers (Sect. 3.3.3). The supervisory authorities in the EU member states carry the primary responsibility for the instruments providing appropriate safeguards to comply with fundamental rights (Sect. 3.3.4).

3.3.1 The Politics of Appropriate Safeguards

The instruments providing appropriate safeguards in Article 46 GDPR allow systematic, structural, and continuous data transfers just like adequacy decisions. For a long time, the politics of appropriate safeguards could best be described with the term "*laissez faire*" because it tolerated the functional limits of the instruments providing appropriate safeguards and the associated violations of the right to continuous protection for personal data for many data transfers (Sect. 3.3.1.1). This kind of *laissez-faire* politics was especially evident after the ECJ invalidated Decision 2000/520, the Safe Harbor adequacy decision, in the *Schrems* judgment (Sect. 3.3.1.2). By now, it has become clear that the assumption of layered levels of protection among the different data transfer mechanisms cannot be maintained in light of the right to continuous protection for personal data (Sect. 3.3.1.3). The ECJ clarified that the data exporter is responsible to act on the functional limits of the instruments providing appropriate safeguards (Sect. 3.3.1.4).

3.3.1.1 Laissez-Faire Politics

Many of the instruments deemed to provide appropriate safeguards for the transfer of personal data in Article 46 GDPR are somewhat "blind" to the inadequacy of data protection in third countries.[303] For example, the European Commission generally approves standard data protection clauses in Article 46(2)(c) GDPR without specifying which data transfers to which third countries they can be used for. The standard data protection clauses adopted by the Commission are solely intended to provide contractual guarantees that apply uniformly in all third countries to controllers and processors established in the EU.[304] However, the standard data protection clauses do not offer all-encompassing guarantees for the protection of personal data. Due to their contractual nature, the standard data protection clauses cannot bind the public authorities of third countries, since they are not party to the contract.[305] This makes the data transfers vulnerable to surveillance practices in third countries. Even if this is not a recent realization, the standard data protection clauses, and other instruments providing appropriate safeguards, have long been used with little attention to the continuous protection of personal data.[306] According to the Commission, the standard data protection clauses in Article 46(2)(c) GDPR are still the main legal mechanism companies rely on for the export of personal data.[307] In practice, they are often being used for data transfers to third countries with a terrible track record when it comes to surveillance, data protection, and fundamental rights such as China, Russia, and also the US.[308] Before the ECJ handed down the judgment in *Schrems 2* the politics of appropriate safeguards was one of a *laissez-faire* attitude that tolerated the functional limits of the instruments and the associated potential violations of the right to continuous protection for personal data in Article 8 CFR.

3.3.1.2 The Effect of Repealed or Invalidated Adequacy Decisions

The kind of *laissez-faire* politics described above is also apparent when it comes to the effect of repealed or invalidated adequacy decisions. The European Commission has to repeal, amend, or suspend an adequacy decision where available information reveals that a third country, a territory, or one or more specified sectors within a third country no longer ensures an adequate level of protection according to Article 45(5) GDPR.

---

303 Kuner (2020), p. 802; Schantz (2019), p. 993.

304 EDPB (2020), p. 5.

305 ECJ, *Schrems 2*, para. 125.

306 The criticism that instruments such as the standard data protection clauses do not offer all-encompassing guarantees for the protection of personal data dates back to the discussions around the Council of Europe Model Contract in the early 1990s. See Sect. 3.1.1.2.3.

307 European Commission (2019), p. 10.

308 Rotenberg (2020), pp. 10–12; Swire (2019).

The ECJ invalidates adequacy decisions for the same reasons.[309] The legal vacuum left in the wake of an adequacy decision being repealed or invalidated creates a special situation for the instruments providing appropriate safeguards in Article 46 GDPR. In these cases, it has become clear that the third country does not provide a level of protection for personal data that is essentially equivalent to that guaranteed within the EU.

After the ECJ invalidated Decision 2000/520, the Safe Harbor adequacy decision, in the *Schrems* judgment, the Commission argued that instruments providing appropriate safeguards may be used as an alternative data transfer mechanism.[310] However, the Commission was careful to stress that their decision should not prejudice the powers and duties of supervisory authorities in the examination of the lawfulness of such transfers.[311] The Commission also pointed out that the availability of standard contractual clauses after the invalidation of Decision 2000/520 is without prejudice to additional measures that the data exporter may have to take.[312] The Commission thus acknowledged that the invalidation of Decision 2000/520 may have consequences for other data transfer mechanisms. The Article 29 WP also released a statement asserting that even if Decision 2000/520 cannot be relied on for data transfers to the US, other legal mechanisms for data transfers like the standard data protection clauses can still be used in the meantime as a legal basis for such transfers.[313] At the same time the Article 29 WP stressed that they will continue to analyze the impact of the *Schrems* judgment on these alternative legal mechanisms.[314] Some national supervisory authorities went further than that. For example, the Conference of the German Data Protection Authorities at the Federal and State Level stressed that they will no longer grant new authorizations for the use of alternative data transfer mechanisms for data transfers to the US.[315] Overall, however, there was no comprehensive reaction limiting data transfers to the US on the basis of instruments providing appropriate safeguards.

Similarly, after the ECJ invalidated Decision (EU) 2016/1250, the Privacy Shield adequacy decision, in the *Schrems 2* judgment, the Commission underlined that even in the absence of the Privacy Shield, transatlantic data transfers can continue using other mechanisms for international transfers of personal data available under the GDPR.[316] Two commissioners even stressed that standard contractual clauses remain a valid tool for such transfers.[317]

---

[309] ECJ, *Schrems*, para. 97; ECJ, *Schrems 2*, para. 198.

[310] European Commission (2015), p. 4.

[311] Ibid.

[312] Ibid., 7.

[313] Article 29 WP (2015), p. 1.

[314] Ibid.

[315] DSK (2015), para. 7.

[316] European Commission (2020).

[317] Ibid.

An isolated reading of the GDPR would support such a conclusion. Article 45(7) GDPR states that a decision to repeal, amend, or suspend an adequacy decision pursuant to Article 45(5) GDPR is without prejudice to the other legal mechanisms for data transfers. In the same spirit, Article 46(1) GDPR maintains that data transfers with instruments providing appropriate safeguards are possible in the absence of an adequacy decision. This covers not only situations where the adequacy of data protection has not (yet) been officially assessed, but also situations where an adequacy decision has been repealed or invalidated. This is also confirmed in Recital (107) GDPR:

> The Commission may recognise that a third country, a territory or a specified sector within a third country, or an international organisation no longer ensures an adequate level of data protection. Consequently the transfer of personal data to that third country [...] should be prohibited, unless the requirements in this Regulation relating to transfers subject to appropriate safeguards [...] and derogations for specific situations are fulfilled.

Such an isolated reading of the GDPR thus creates the impression that the repeal or invalidation of an adequacy decision has no influence on the other legal mechanisms for data transfers. This is problematic from a fundamental rights perspective.

3.3.1.3 Layered Levels of Protection Versus Same Levels of Protection

One of the reasons for this *laissez-faire* politics is the assumption that the different legal mechanisms for the transfer of personal data should provide different levels of protection for personal data. For example, Christopher Kuner has suggested—based on Directive 95/46/EC—that the legal mechanism of adequate safeguards in Article 26(2) Directive 96/46/EC "can be seen as the middle level of protection."[318] He also argued that the different standards of protection of the legal mechanisms for data transfers can help explain how one legal mechanism can be invalid without affecting the other.[319] He maintained that "the fact that an adequacy decision is invalid for not providing essential equivalence (the highest standard) does not mean that a transfer may not be possible based on adequate safeguards (the middle standard)."[320]

Facebook, Digital Europe, and the Business Software Alliance argued similarly in the proceedings of *Schrems 2* before the IHC. They pointed out that Article 26 Directive 95/46/EC—the legal basis of the standard contractual clauses— is a derogation from Article 25 Directive 95/46/EC—the legal basis of the adequacy decisions—and that "[b]y definition, transfers of data to third countries pursuant to Article 26 are on the basis that the third country does not afford the data an 'adequate level of protection'."[321] In contrast, the DPC relied on Recital (10) Directive 95/46/EC, which

[318] Kuner (2017), p. 905.

[319] Ibid.

[320] Ibid.

[321] IHC, *Schrems 2*, para. 137.

maintains that the objective of laws on data processing is to protect fundamental rights and freedoms, to argue that

> whether the Directive refers to adequate protection (Article 25), adequate safeguards (Article 26 (2)) or sufficient safeguards (Article 26 (4)), data processing is entitled to the same high level of protection whether or not the processing occurs within the EU or is transferred for processing to a third country and regardless of the method employed to effect a lawful transfer of personal data to a third country.[322]

The IHC accepted that Article 26 Directive 95/46/EC is a derogation from Article 25 Directive 95/46/EC and that data transfers pursuant to Article 26 Directive 95/46/EC are not premised upon the existence of an adequate level of protection in the third country.[323] At the same time, the IHC also maintained that even if Article 26 Directive 95/46/EC is a derogation, "the data is still entitled to a high level of protection" and that "[i]t follows therefore that transfers of personal data to a third country cannot simply step outside the protection guaranteed by the Directive entirely."[324] The IHC found "that data exporters cannot rely solely upon the [standard contractual clauses] as complying with the requirements of the Directive regardless of the legal regime in the third country to which the data is exported."[325] According to the IHC, the high level of protection accorded personal data is mandatory for the instruments providing adequate safeguards for data transfers in Article 26 Directive 95/46/EC.

AG Henrik Saugmandsgaard Øe supported this argument in his opinion in *Schrems 2*. He maintained—based on the GDPR—that both "Articles 45 and 46 of the GDPR are aimed at ensuring the continuity of the high level of protection of personal data."[326] He referred to Article 44 GDPR and explained that the "rule is designed to ensure that the standards of protection resulting from EU law are not circumvented by transfers of personal data to a third country" and that "it is immaterial that the transfer is based on an adequacy decision or on guarantees provided by the controller or processor, in particular by means of contractual clauses."[327] The ECJ followed the opinion of the AG in *Schrems 2* and held that the instruments providing appropriate safeguards in Article 46 GDPR must be capable of ensuring that data subjects whose personal data are transferred to a third country are afforded, as in the context of a transfer based on an adequacy decision, a level of protection essentially equivalent to that which is guaranteed within the EU.[328] This is consistent with the finding of the ECJ in Opinion 1/15 in which the Court decided that the draft PNR agreement between the EU and Canada must provide continuous protection of personal data that is essentially equivalent to

[322] Ibid., para. 134.

[323] Ibid., para. 153.

[324] Ibid.

[325] Ibid.

[326] ECJ, AG Opinion, *Schrems 2*, para. 117.

[327] Ibid.

[328] ECJ, *Schrems 2*, para. 96.

that guaranteed within the EU.[329] The PNR agreement is an instrument providing appropriate safeguards according to Article 46(2)(a) GDPR—a legally binding and enforceable instrument between public authorities or bodies.

The jurisprudence of the ECJ clarified that the assumption that the different legal mechanisms for the transfer of personal data should provide different levels of protection for personal data cannot be maintained with regard to adequacy decisions and instruments providing appropriate safeguards. AG Saugmandsgaard Øe summarized that only the way in which the continuity of the high level of protection is provided differs according to the legal basis of the transfer.[330] This finding is important as the instruments providing appropriate safeguards in Article 46 GDPR allow systematic, structural, and continuous data transfers just like Article 45 GDPR.

3.3.1.4 Responsibility for the Data Exporter

The findings of the ECJ that instruments providing appropriate safeguards in Article 46 GDPR must provide the same level of protection as adequacy decisions in Article 45 GDPR did not change the fact that many of those instruments cannot bind the public authorities of third countries, since they are not party to the contract between the data exporter and the data importer.[331] This is why the ECJ added in *Schrems 2* that it is for the data exporter to verify whether the law of the third country of destination ensures adequate protection, under EU law, of personal data transferred pursuant to the instruments providing appropriate safeguards.[332] Should the data exporter not be able to ensure such protection, the transfer of personal data to the third country concerned must be suspended or ended.[333] It is thus the responsibility of the data exporter to guarantee that the instruments providing appropriate safeguards are not being used when they cannot guarantee a level of protection for personal data that is essentially equivalent to that guaranteed within the EU.[334] This seems to be a continuation of the *laissez-faire* politics of appropriate safeguards but with a clear allocation of the responsibility and a clear indication of the level of protection for personal data. Accordingly, the European Commission adopted a new set of standard data protection clauses on 4 June 2021—the old sets of standard data protection clauses were repealed with effect from 27 September 2021 but still deemed to provide appropriate safeguards under the GDPR until 27 December 2022 (provided the processing operations that are the subject matter of the contract remain unchanged and that reliance on those clauses ensures that the transfer of personal data is subject to appropriate safeguards) according to Article 4

[329] ECJ, Opinion 1/15, para. 134.

[330] ECJ, AG Opinion, *Schrems 2*, para. 117.

[331] ECJ, *Schrems 2*, para. 125.

[332] Ibid., para. 134.

[333] Ibid., para. 135.

[334] Corrales Compagnucci et al. (2021), p. 40.

Decision (EU) 2021/914. This new set of standard data protection clauses adds specific duties for the data exporter and the data importer such as data protection impact assessments that should include a data transfer impact assessment, which has to be provided to the competent supervisory authority upon request,[335] as well as a description of security and organizational measures that are taken to ensure the protection of the data.[336]

3.3.2 *Limitations on Continuous Protection of Personal Data Using Appropriate Safeguards*

The right to continuous protection for personal data requires that the level of protection for personal data that is transferred from the EU to a third country is essentially equivalent to that guaranteed within the EU. That right is not absolute. Limitations on the exercise of the right to continuous protection of personal data can be lawful according to Article 52(1) CFR. This section analyzes the contract-based derogation in Article 49(1)(b) GDPR. Just as described with regard to the other legal mechanisms for the transfer of personal data, the interference must be found in the EU rather than in the third country (Sect. 3.3.2.1). The legal basis for the interference must indicate under what circumstances and conditions the interference will take place and impose minimum safeguards providing sufficient guarantees for individuals to effectively protect their personal data against the risk of abuse (Sect. 3.3.2.2). The material objectives of the interference must either qualify as a general interest recognized by the EU or be protected by another right or freedom in the Charter (Sect. 3.3.2.3). Finally, the principle of proportionality must be observed (Sect. 3.3.2.4).

3.3.2.1 Interference

Any interference with the right to continuous protection of personal data must be found in the EU.[337] Ultimately though, the rules, measures, and actions of third states also entail intrusions, which, if they were attributed to the authorities of an EU member state, would be regarded as interferences with the exercise of the right to data protection in Article 8 CFR.[338] Those intrusions should, however, be assessed with regard to the standard of essential equivalence. If the intrusions caused by the rules, measures, and actions of third states do not respect the standard of essential equivalence, then the transfer of personal data based on instruments providing

---

[335] Cp. Recital (22) Decision (EU) 2021/914.

[336] Cp. Annex II Decision (EU) 2021/914.

[337] ECJ, *Schrems*, para. 87; see Sect. 3.2.2.1.

[338] Cp. ECJ, AG Opinion, *Schrems 2*, para. 256.

appropriate safeguards constitutes an interference with the right to continuous protection of personal data enshrined in Article 8 CFR.

Unlike adequacy decisions, the approval of the instruments in Article 46 GDPR does not acknowledge the conditions for the processing of personal data in the third country but rather the provision of appropriate safeguards by the instruments themselves. Many of the instruments in Article 46 GDPR are "blind" to the inadequacies of data protection in third countries. This is why the actual transfer of personal data based on these instruments constitutes an interference with Article 8 CFR if it does not respect the right to continuous protection of personal data.

3.3.2.2 Legal Basis

The limitation on the exercise of a fundamental right must be provided for by law. The legal basis that permits the interference with Article 8 CFR must itself already define the scope of the limitation.[339] The legal basis for interferences with Article 8 CFR must indicate under what circumstances and conditions this interference can legally take place and impose minimum safeguards to provide sufficient guarantees that individuals' rights will not be abused.[340] These safeguards are particularly important in cases in which personal data is subject to automated processing and involves sensitive data.[341]

The transfer of personal data based on instruments providing appropriate safeguards constitutes an interference with Article 8 CFR if the level of protection for personal data in the third country is not essentially equivalent to that guaranteed within the EU. The legal basis for transfers of personal data is different for each instrument. The two most important instruments in Article 46 GDPR will be analyzed here: standard data protection clauses based on Article 46(2)(c) GDPR (Sect. 3.3.2.2.1) and BCRs based on Article 46(2)(b) GDPR (Sect. 3.3.2.2.2).

3.3.2.2.1 Standard Data Protection Clauses Based on Article 46(2)(c) GDPR

Standard data protection clauses indicate under what circumstances and conditions a data processing operation may be said to interfere with the right to continuous protection for personal data, i.e., the transfer of personal data to a third country. This research covers both an old set of standard data protection clauses provided by Decision 2010/87/EU that was subject to the judgment in *Schrems 2* and the new set of standard data protection clauses provided by Decision (EU) 2021/914.

---

[339] ECJ, Opinion 1/15, para. 139; ECJ, *WebMindLicenses*, para. 81; see Sect. 2.2.4.4.

[340] ECJ, Opinion 1/15, para. 141; ECJ, *Tele2/Watson*, para. 109; ECJ, *Schrems*, para. 91; ECJ, *Digital Rights Ireland*, para. 54.

[341] ECJ, Opinion 1/15, para. 141; ECJ, *Schrems*, para. 91; ECJ, *Digital Rights Ireland*, para. 55.

Appendix 1 of the standard data protection clauses provided by Decision 2010/87/EU required the contracting parties to specify the data exporter, the data importer, the data subjects, the categories of data, and the processing operations that the transferred data will be subject to. Appendix 2 of the standard data protection clauses provided by Decision 2010/87/EU required the contracting parties to outline the technical and organizational security measures that the data importer will implement. Decision 2010/87/EU also described the circumstances which were compatible with these clauses regarding access to the transferred personal data by public authorities in the third country.[342]

As regards minimum safeguards, Clause 5(a) of the standard data protection clauses provided by Decision 2010/87/EU required the data importer to process the personal data in compliance with the standard data protection clauses. If the importer could not comply with those clauses, then the importer had to promptly inform the exporter. Under Clause 5(b) the data importer had to certify that there was no reason to believe that applicable legislation prevented it from fulfilling its obligations under the standard data protection clauses. In the event of a change in that legislation which was likely to have a substantial adverse effect on the warranties and obligations provided by the standard data protection clauses, the importer further had to promptly notify the data exporter about the change. In both cases, the data exporter was entitled to suspend the transfer and/or terminate the contract under the standard data protection clauses and was even required to do so.[343] Unless the controller terminated the contract, it was in breach of its obligations under Clause 4(a) as interpreted in the light of the GDPR and of the Charter.[344]

In accordance with Clause 4(g) of the standard data protection clauses provided by Decision 2010/87/EU, the data exporter had to forward all notifications received from the data importer to the competent supervisory authority if the exporter decided to continue the transfer. The forwarding of this notification to the supervisory authority as well as the supervisory authority's right to conduct an audit of the

---

[342] See Footnote 2 relating to Clause 5 of the standard data protection clauses provided by Decision 2010/87/EU:

> Mandatory requirements of the national legislation applicable to the data importer which do not go beyond what is necessary in a democratic society on the basis of one of the interests listed in Article 13(1) of Directive 95/46/EC, that is, if they constitute a necessary measure to safeguard national security, defence, public security, the prevention, investigation, detection and prosecution of criminal offences or of breaches of ethics for the regulated professions, an important economic or financial interest of the State or the protection of the data subject or the rights and freedoms of others, are not in contradiction with the standard contractual clauses.

[343] ECJ, *Schrems 2*, para. 140. AG Saugmandsgaard Øe stressed that "[t]he fact that the exporter is given a right, *in its bilateral relations with the importer*, to suspend the transfer or terminate the contract where the importer is unable to honour the standard clauses is without prejudice to the obligation placed on the exporter to do so *in the light of the requirements to protect the rights of the persons concerned arising under the GDPR*." ECJ, AG Opinion, *Schrems 2*, para. 132.

[344] ECJ, *Schrems 2*, para. 140.

recipient of personal data pursuant to Clause 8(2) enabled the supervisory authority to ascertain whether the proposed transfer should have been suspended or prohibited in order to ensure an adequate level of protection.[345] The current Article 4 Decision 2010/87/EU refered to the powers of supervisory authorities set out in Article 28(3) Directive 95/46/EC, which were replaced by Article 58 GDPR. The supervisory authorities were invested with investigative and corrective powers to protect individuals against the risk of abuse of their personal data. Data subjects may—when they consider that there has been a breach of the standard data protection clauses—request the relevant supervisory authorities to exercise their corrective powers according to Article 77(1) GDPR.

The standard data protection clauses provided by Decision 2010/87/EU also established, in favor of data subjects, enforceable rights and remedies against the exporter and against the importer. Clause 3(1) entailed a remedy for the data subject against the exporter in the event of a breach of standard data protection clauses. Clause 3(2) included the same remedy for the data subject against the data importer in cases in which the exporter has factually disappeared or had ceased to exist in law. These minimum safeguards guaranteed that individuals could effectively protect their personal data against the risk of abuse. Because of these safeguards, standard data protection clauses could provide a valid legal basis for interferences with Article 8 CFR.

This conclusion is also true for the new set of standard data protection clauses provided by Decision (EU) 2021/914. Annex 1 also requires the contracting parties to specify the data exporter, the data importer, the categories of data subjects whose personal data is transferred, the categories of personal data that is transferred, the frequency of the transfer (one-off or continuing), nature of the processing, purposes of the transfer and further processing, the period for which the personal data will be retained, or, if that is not possible, the criteria used to determine that period and the competent supervisory authority. Annex 2 also requires the contracting parties to outline the technical and organizational measures to ensure the security of the data. It provides a more detailed list of the possible technical and organizational measures necessary to ensure an appropriate level of protection, including measures to ensure the security of the data.[346] In addition, Clause 5 clearly stipulates that the new standard data protection clauses take precedence and supersede, for example, contradictory contractual or general terms and conditions clauses.

As regards minimum safeguards, the parties warrant in Clause 14(a) that they have no reason to believe that the laws and practices in the third country of destination applicable to the processing of the personal data by the data importer, including any requirements to disclose personal data or measures authorizing access by public authorities, prevent the data importer from fulfilling its obligations under the standard data protection clauses. Again, this is based on the understanding—which is explicitly stated in Clause 14(a)—that laws and practices that respect the

[345] Ibid., para. 145.

[346] Corrales Compagnucci et al. (2021), p. 44.

essence of the EU fundamental rights and freedoms and do not exceed what is necessary and proportionate in a democratic society to safeguard one of the objectives listed in Article 23(1) GDPR, are not in contradiction with standard data protection clauses. The warranty in Clause 14(a) has to rely on an assessment of different elements surrounding the data transfers in Clause 14(b). This 'data transfer impact assessment'[347] must be documented and made available to the competent supervisory authority upon request according to Clause 14(d).

There are different notification requirements for the data importer in different situation: In Clause 14(e) notification must be given when the data importer has *reason to believe* that it is or has become subject to laws or practices that prevent it from fulfilling its obligations under the standard data protection clauses (such as protection from unauthorized disclosure or access). In Clause 15(a) the data importer has to notify the data exporter if it *actually receives a legally binding request* from a public authority for the disclosure of data transferred pursuant to the standard data protection clauses or if it *becomes aware of any direct access* by public authorities to personal data transferred pursuant to the standard data protection clauses. In Clause 16(a) the data importer generally needs to inform the data exporter if it is *unable to comply—for whatever reason*—with the standard data protection clauses.

When the data exporter receives a notification that the data importer has reason to believe that it is or has become subject to laws or practices that prevent it from fulfilling its obligations under the standard data protection clauses Clause 14(f) requires that it has to identify appropriate measures (e.g. technical or organizational measures to ensure security and confidentiality) to address the situation or suspend the data transfers if it considers that no appropriate safeguards for such transfer can be ensured. The data exporter *immediately* has to suspend the data transfer according to Clause 16(b) in the event that the data importer is in breach of or unable to comply with the standard data protection clauses. Clause 16(c) then regulates the grounds for the data exporter to terminate the contract with the data importer.

The data subjects are entitled to challenge compliance with the standard data protection clauses according to Clause 11. They can invoke third-party beneficiary rights in Clause 3 and lodge complaints with a supervisory authority and they can also be represented by not-for-profit body, organization or association.

Finally, according to Clause 8 the data exporter warrants that it has used reasonable efforts to determine that the data importer is able, through the implementation of appropriate technical and organisational measures, to satisfy its obligations under the standard data protection clauses. This might imply that the data exporter has to make sure that the data importer has an active monitoring policy for any internet surveillance practice that it might be subject to.

[347] Ibid.

3.3.2.2.2 BCRs Based on Article 46(2)(b) GDPR

BCRs also indicate under what circumstances and conditions the data processing operations can be said to interfere with the right to continuous protection for personal data, i.e., the transfer of personal data to a third country. According to Article 46(1) GDPR, a data exporter in the EU may only transfer personal data if appropriate safeguards are provided and under the condition that enforceable data subject rights and effective legal remedies are available. BCRs provide these appropriate safeguards. The circumstances of the data processing operations can be found in the BCRs themselves. Article 47(2) GDPR contains a list of requirements for BCRs to be approved by the relevant supervisory authority. For example, BCRs must specify the group of enterprises engaged in a joint economic activity that export and import the personal data; the data transfers or set of transfers, including the categories of personal data, the type of processing and its purposes, the type of data subjects affected, and the identification of the third country or countries in question; and the application of the general data protection principles. Additionally, some BCRs also provide general descriptions of the circumstances that are compatible with the BCRs regarding data processing operations carried out by public authorities in third countries.[348]

Regarding the minimum safeguards, the list in Article 47(2) GDPR entails further requirements: BCRs must specify the complaint procedures; the cooperation mechanism with the supervisory authority to ensure compliance by any member of the group of enterprises engaged in the joint economic activity; and the mechanisms for reporting to the competent supervisory authority any legal requirements which a member of the group of enterprises is subject to in a third country and which is likely to have a substantial adverse effect on the guarantees provided by the BCRs. Additionally, the GDPR framework for supervision as well as the complaint and appellate mechanisms concerning supervisory authorities also apply to BCRs. These minimum safeguards guarantee that individuals can effectively protect their personal data against the risk of abuse. BCRs therefore provide a valid legal basis for the interference with Article 8 CFR.

3.3.2.3 Objectives of General Interest and Protection of Freedoms of Others

The justification of an interference that limits the exercise of fundamental rights according to Article 52 CFR further requires that the limitations genuinely meet objectives of general interest recognized by the EU or are necessary to protect the

[348] See Article IX BCRs of Mastercard Europe SA from December 2018:

> Mandatory requirements of local law applicable to a Mastercard BCRs Entity, which are not massive, disproportionate, indiscriminate and do not go beyond what is necessary in a democratic society on the basis of one of the interests listed in Article 23 of the GDPR are in principle not in contradiction with Mastercard BCRs.

rights and freedoms of others. Public security in a third country qualifies as a general interest recognized by the EU (Sect. 3.3.2.3.1) and both the freedom of expression and information (Sect. 3.3.2.3.2) and the freedom to conduct a business (Sect. 3.3.2.3.3) are rights of others which need to be protected.

3.3.2.3.1 Public Security in a Third Country

The public security in a third country can be an objective of general interest recognized by the EU.[349] In order to justify limitations to the right to continuous protection of personal data on the basis of public security in a third country, the public security of the third country must be one of the material objectives of the data transfers.[350] The data transfers in question are usually part of a commercial activity.[351] They thus do not relate to the protection of public security in a third country

3.3.2.3.2 Freedom of Expression and Information

Data transfers are a tool for the exercise of the freedom of expression and information enshrined in Article 11 CFR.[352] In order to justify an interference with the right to continuous protection of personal data based on the protection of the freedom of expression and information, the freedom of expression and information must be one of the material objectives of the data transfers.[353]

To date, instruments providing appropriate safeguards for data transfers have not specifically referred to the protection of Article 11 CFR, but this does not generally preclude an argument using Article 11 CFR as a justification. The protection of the freedom of expression and information and its reconciliation with the right to data protection is one of the material objectives of the GDPR and, therefore, of Chapter V GDPR as well, which includes the instruments providing appropriate safeguards.[354]

3.3.2.3.3 Freedom to Conduct a Business

Data transfers to third countries may be used for transborder economic activities protected by the freedom to conduct a business enshrined in Article 16 CFR.[355] In order to justify an interference with the right to continuous protection of personal

---

[349] See Sect. 3.2.2.3.1.

[350] ECJ, *Digital Rights Ireland*, para. 41.

[351] ECJ, AG Opinion, *Schrems 2*, paras 106–107.

[352] See Sect. 3.2.2.3.2.

[353] ECJ, *Digital Rights Ireland*, para. 41.

[354] See Recital (4) and Article 85(1) GDPR; see also Sect. 3.2.2.3.2.

[355] See Sect. 3.2.2.3.3.

data based on the freedom to conduct a business, that freedom's practice must be one of the material objectives of the data transfers.[356]

To date, instruments providing appropriate safeguards for data transfers have not specifically referred to the protection of Article 16 CFR, but that does not generally preclude an argument using Article 16 CFR as a justification. The IHC stated that the "free transfer of data around the world is now central to economic and social life in the Union and elsewhere."[357] The protection of the freedom to conduct a business in Article 16 CFR is one of the material objectives of the GDPR and, therefore, of Chapter V GDPR as well.[358]

3.3.2.4 Proportionality

The principle of proportionality requires that limitations on fundamental rights must be appropriate in light of the objective pursued and limited to what is strictly necessary.[359] It is also necessary to examine if there are other measures which affect the right to continuous protection of personal data less adversely and still contribute effectively to the objectives of general interest recognized by the EU or the need to protect the fundamental rights and freedoms of others. It has to be seen if the interference with the right to continuous protection of personal data is proportional to the protection of the freedom of expression and information (Sect. 3.3.2.4.1), and to the protection of the freedom to conduct a business (Sect. 3.3.2.4.2).

3.3.2.4.1 Freedom of Expression and Information

Data transfers based on the instruments providing appropriate safeguards enable companies to distribute information and ideas without interference by public authorities and regardless of borders. Instruments providing appropriate safeguards allow systematic, structural, and continuous data transfers to a third country just like adequacy decisions and may thus be considered appropriate to protect the freedom of expression and information enshrined in Article 11 CFR.

It would, however, be disproportionate to justify limitations on the right to continuous protection of personal data with the protection of commercial speech, because the right to data protection attracts a higher level of protection than commercial speech.[360] It would also be disproportionate to justify the limitations on the right to continuous protection for personal data with the protection of journalistic,

---

[356] ECJ, *Digital Rights Ireland*, para. 41.

[357] IHC, *Schrems 2*, para. 45.

[358] See Recitals (4) and (101) GDPR; see also Sect. 3.2.2.3.3.

[359] ECJ, Opinion 1/15, para. 140; ECJ, *Tele2/Watson*, paras 96, 103; ECJ, *Schrems*, para. 92; ECJ, *Digital Rights Ireland*, paras 51–52; see Sect. 2.2.4.4.

[360] See Sect. 3.2.2.4.2.

academic, artistic, and literary speech, because Article 85(2) GDPR contains a derogation for EU member states which affects less adversely the right to data protection and still contributes effectively to the protection of Article 11 CFR.[361]

3.3.2.4.2 Freedom to Conduct a Business

Data transfers based on instruments providing appropriate safeguard enable individuals and companies to operate business models that depend on transfers of personal data to third countries and must, therefore, be considered appropriate to protect the freedom to conduct a business enshrined in Article 16 CFR.

It would, however, be disproportionate to limit the right to continuous protection of personal data with the freedom to conduct a business because the right to data protection attracts a higher level of protection and the derogations for data transfers in specific situations according to Article 49 GDPR contain measures that affect the right to data protection less adversely while still effectively contributing to the protection of the freedom to conduct a business.[362]

3.3.3 The Validity of Appropriate Safeguards as a Legal Mechanism

Instrument providing appropriate safeguards must fully comply with the right to continuous protection for personal data. AG Henrik Saugmandsgaard Øe found in his opinion in *Schrems 2* that the validity of the instruments providing appropriate safeguards depends on the soundness of the safeguards which those instruments provide to compensate for any inadequacy of protection created in the third country of destination.[363] In the following, the validity of the standard data protection clauses based on Article 46(2)(c) GDPR (Sect. 3.3.3.1) and of the BCRs based on Article 46(2)(b) GDPR should be analyzed (Sect. 3.3.3.2).

3.3.3.1 Standard Data Protection Clauses Based on Article 46(2)(c) GDPR

Article 46(1) GDPR states that in the absence of an adequacy decision, it is for the data controller or data processor to provide appropriate safeguards for the transfer of

[361] Albrecht and Janson (2016), p. 502.

[362] See Sect. 3.2.2.4.3.

[363] That finding specifically refers to standard data protection clauses, but it may also be extended to other instruments providing appropriate safeguards in Article 46 GDPR. See ECJ, AG Opinion, *Schrems 2*, para. 124.

personal data to third countries.[364] The standard data protection clauses adopted by the European Commission on the basis of Article 46(2)(c) GDPR are intended to provide contractual guarantees independently of the level of protection for personal data in any given third country.[365] AG Henrik Saugmandsgaard Øe underlined in his opinion in *Schrems 2* that the validity of the standard data protection clauses "cannot depend on the level of protection guaranteed in each of the individual third countries to which data might be transferred."[366] Due to their contractual nature, the standard data protection clauses cannot provide guarantees beyond contractual obligations to ensure compliance with the level of protection for personal data required under EU law. They are not binding on the authorities of third countries to which the personal data is transferred and they cannot prevent the authorities in a third country from accessing personal data.[367] The ECJ held that the mere fact that standard data protection clauses "do not bind the authorities of third countries to which personal data may be transferred cannot affect the validity" of these clauses.[368]

The standard data protection clauses have to incorporate effective mechanisms that make it possible to ensure compliance with the level of protection required by EU law and to suspend or prohibit data transfers in the event of the breach of the clauses or it being impossible to honor them.[369] I argue that standard data protection clauses, such as those that were provided by Decision 2010/87/EU and are newly provided by Decision (EU) 2021/914 are valid as a legal mechanism to transfer personal data because they can be supplemented with additional safeguards (Sect. 3.3.3.1.1), they provide adequate compliance mechanisms (Sect. 3.3.3.1.2), the supervisory authorities have sufficient investigative and corrective powers (Sect. 3.3.3.1.3), individuals have rights and remedies at hand (Sect. 3.3.3.1.4), and there is a system for consistent enforcement of the right to continuous protection for personal data among the different EU member states (Sect. 3.3.3.1.5).

3.3.3.1.1 Additional Safeguards

The ECJ explicitly stated in *Schrems 2* that insofar as the standard data protection clauses cannot by their very nature provide guarantees beyond a contractual obligation to ensure compliance with the level of protection required under EU law, it may prove necessary to supplement the guarantees contained in the standard data protection clauses with additional safeguards.[370] Recital (109) GDPR also mentions that data exporters should be encouraged to use additional safeguards via contractual

---

[364] ECJ, *Schrems 2*, para. 131.

[365] Ibid., para. 133.

[366] Ibid.

[367] Ibid., para. 125.

[368] ECJ, *Schrems 2*, para. 136.

[369] Ibid., para. 137.

[370] ECJ, *Schrems 2*, paras 132–133.

commitments to supplement standard protection clauses. However, neither the GDPR nor the ECJ have defined or specified what such additional safeguards to the standard data protection clauses could be. Consequently, the EDPB has adopted a recommendation on measures that supplement transfer instruments to ensure compliance with EU law.[371]

Based on the principle of accountability in Article 5(2) and Article 28(3)(h) GDPR, the EDPB argued that data exporters "must seek to comply with the right to data protection in an active and continuous manner by implementing legal, technical and organisational measures that ensure its effectiveness."[372] Annex II of those recommendations provides examples.[373] Annex 2 of Decision (EU) 2021/914 also entails examples for possible technical and organizational measures to ensure the security of the data.

Nevertheless, the EDPB also stated that there are scenarios in which no effective additional safeguards can be implemented. This is the case, for example, when personal data is transferred to cloud services providers or other processors which require access to the data in the clear.[374] This is consistent with the finding of the ECJ in *Schrems* 2 that additional safeguards may not be enough to provide the required protection, especially

> where the law of [a] third country imposes on the recipient of personal data from the European Union obligations which are contrary to those clauses and are, therefore, capable of impinging on the contractual guarantee of an adequate level of protection against access by the public authorities of that third country to that data.[375]

This particularly concerns internet surveillance practices by third states not compatible with the European Essential Guarantees, and which cannot be addressed simply with additional safeguards.[376] However, these clauses entail compliance mechanisms for the data exporter and the data importer that can mitigate the risks of the personal data becoming subject to illegal practices.

3.3.3.1.2 Compliance Mechanisms

Should a third country not provide a level of protection for personal data transferred from the EU that is essentially equivalent to that guaranteed within the EU, the standard data protection clauses provided by Decision 2010/87/EU and by Decision (EU) 2021/914 entailed and entail compliance mechanism with obligations for the data exporter and the data importer leading to the suspension of the concerned data transfers.

---

[371] EDPB (2020), p. 6.

[372] Ibid., 7.

[373] Ibid., 21–37.

[374] Ibid., 26–27.

[375] ECJ, *Schrems 2*, para. 135.

[376] See EDPB (2020), pp. 4–6; see also Sect. 2.4.2.

Regarding Decision 2010/87/EU, the data exporter warranted in Clause 4(a) that the processing of personal data, including the transfer itself, has been and will continue to be carried out in accordance with the relevant provisions of the applicable data protection law. The data exporter had to guarantee the right to continuous protection of personal data in Article 8 CFR and suspend the transfer and/or terminate the contract with the data importer if it was not able to guarantee the full exercise of that right. Under Clause 5(a), the data importer undertook to process the personal data in compliance with the standard data protection clauses. If the importer was not able comply with these clauses, the importer had to promptly inform the exporter. According to Clause 5(b), the data importer also had to certify that it had no reason to believe that the legislation applicable to it prevents it from fulfilling its obligations under the standard data protection clauses. In the event of a change in legislation that was likely to have a substantial adverse effect on the warranties and obligations provided by the standard data protection clauses, the importer had to promptly notify the data exporter about the change.[377] The data exporter was then entitled to suspend the transfer and/or to terminate the contract under the standard data protection clauses and indeed was required to do so in light of the right to continuous protection of personal data in Article 8 CFR.[378] Unless the controller did so, it was in breach of its obligations under Clause 4(a) as interpreted in the light of the GDPR and the Charter.[379]

The same logic applies under the new set of standard data protection clauses provided by Decision (EU) 2021/914. When the data exporter receives a notification from the data importer that it has reason to believe that it can no longer fulfil its obligations under the standard data protection clauses according to Clause 14(e), the data exporter has to promptly identify appropriate measures, such as technical or organizational measures to ensure security and confidentiality, to be adopted by the data exporter and/or data importer to address the situation as required by Clause 14(f). The same clause also demands that the data exporter suspends the data transfer if it considers that no appropriate safeguards for such transfer can be ensured. Clause 16(b) also demands that the data exporter suspends the data transfer to the data importer if the data importer is in breach of the standard data protection clauses until compliance is again ensured or the contract is terminated. There are obligations on the data importer to notify the data exporter but also on the data exporter to monitor compliance with the right to continuous protection of personal data in Article 8 CFR.[380] If the data transfers are subject to laws and practices that do not

[377] This includes surveillance practices that are not compatible with fundamental rights in the EU. See Schantz (2019), p. 1003.

[378] ECJ, *Schrems 2*, para. 140. AG Saugmandsgaard Øe stressed that "[t]he fact that the exporter is given a right, *in its bilateral relations with the importer*, to suspend the transfer or terminate the contract where the importer is unable to honour the standard clauses is without prejudice to the obligation placed on the exporter to do so *in the light of the requirements to protect the rights of the persons concerned arising under the GDPR*." ECJ, AG Opinion, *Schrems 2*, para. 132.

[379] ECJ, *Schrems 2*, para. 140.

[380] Flint (2021), p. 252.

respect the essence of the fundamental rights and freedoms or exceed what is necessary and proportionate in a democratic society to safeguard one of the objectives listed in Article 23(1) GDPR they must be suspended.

3.3.3.1.3 Powers of Supervisory Authorities

In accordance with Article 8(3) CFR and Article 57 GDPR, the supervisory authorities are responsible for monitoring compliance with EU rules concerning the protection of individuals regarding the processing of their personal data. Each supervisory authority is vested with the power to examine whether data transfers from its home EU member state to a third country comply with the requirements laid down in the GDPR.[381] If these data transfers do not comply with the requirements laid down in the GDPR, then the supervisory authorities must use their corrective powers to remedy the problem. These corrective powers include: the imposition of a temporary or definitive limitation including a ban on the processing of personal data according to Article 58(2)(f) GDPR and the suspension of data flows to a recipient in a third country according to Article 58(2)(j) GDPR.

Supervisory authorities have different ways in which they can become active in protecting the right to continuous protection of personal data.

Clause 4(g) of the standard data protection clauses provided by Decision 2010/87/EU asked the data exporter to forward all notifications received from the data importer to the relevant supervisory authority based on Clause 5(b) if the exporter decided to continue the transfer of personal data. This enabled the supervisory authority to ascertain whether the data transfers in question should have been suspended or prohibited in order to ensure an adequate level of protection.[382] Article 4 Decision 2010/87/EU also referred to the corrective powers of supervisory authorities.[383] The IHC expressed concerns in its referral of *Schrems 2* to the ECJ that the corrective powers of supervisory authorities have to be interpreted narrowly in light of Recital (11) Decision 2010/87/EU:[384]

> The supervisory authorities should have the power to prohibit or suspend a data transfer or a set of transfers based on the standard contractual clauses in those exceptional cases where it is established that a transfer on contractual basis is likely to have a substantial adverse effect on the warranties and obligations providing adequate protection for the data subject.

---

[381] ECJ, *Schrems*, para. 47.

[382] Ibid., para. 145.

[383] An older version of Article 4 Decision 2010/87/EU entailed a mechanism that allowed supervisory authorities to prohibit or suspend data transfers to a third country in *specific* situations. It was amended in 2016 because the ECJ clarified in *Schrems* that the Commission has no competence to restrict the powers of supervisory authorities under Article 28 Directive 95/46/EC. See ECJ, *Schrems*, paras 47, 101–103; Recital (6), Article 1 and 2 Decision (EU) 2016/2297 amending Decisions 2001/497/EC and 2010/87/EU on standard contractual clauses for the transfer of personal data to third countries and to processors established in such countries.

[384] IHC, *Schrems 2*, para. 306.

The IHC adduced from the fact that Recital (11) Decision 2010/87/EU described the power of supervisory authorities to prohibit or suspend data transfers in "exceptional cases" that the standard data protection clauses only envisage the use of the corrective powers in particular circumstances, rather than a systemic use of those powers.[385] AG Henrik Saugmandsgaard Øe stated that "the Commission failed to remove or amend that recital in order to adapt its content to the requirements of the new Article 4."[386] Article 8(3) CFR demands that supervisory authorities are independent. A recital of a Commission decision cannot therefore bind them. Furthermore, Recital (5) Decision 2016/2297, the decision amending Article 4 Decision 2010/87/EU, reasserted the power of supervisory authorities to suspend or prohibit any transfer which they consider to be contrary to EU law.[387] The ECJ also confirmed that Article 4 Decision 2016/2297 did not confine the exercise of corrective powers to exceptional circumstances.[388]

In addition, the IHC expressed concerns that the corrective powers of the supervisory authorities are discretionary powers only.[389] The IHC argued that if the standard data protection clauses are valid because the supervisory authorities have the power to suspend or ban data transfers, then this can only be on the basis that supervisory authorities are obligated to so in circumstances in which it is established that a transfer of personal data on the basis of standard data protection clauses is likely to violate fundamental rights of individuals in the EU.[390] The IHC thus submitted that such an obligation would be incompatible with the independence of the supervisory authorities. AG Saugmandsgaard Øe rejected this claim and concluded that "the exercise of the powers to suspend and prohibit transfers set out in Article 58(2)(f) and (j) of the GDPR is no longer merely an option left to the supervisory authorities' discretion."[391] The ECJ confirmed this and stated that the relevant supervisory authority is required to use its corrective powers in cases in which the data controller or data processor has not itself suspended or put an end to the transfer of personal data.[392]

In order to *use* these corrective powers, Article 58(1) GDPR confers on the supervisory authorities significant investigative powers as well.[393] Supervisory authorities may order data exporters to provide any and all information they require for the performance of their tasks, carry out investigations in the form of data protection audits, obtain access to the personal data, and even to the premises of the data exporter.

[385] Ibid., para. 308.

[386] ECJ, AG Opinion, *Schrems 2*, para. 143.

[387] ECJ, *Schrems 2*, para. 146.

[388] Ibid., para. 114.

[389] IHC, *Schrems 2*, para. 316.

[390] Ibid.

[391] ECJ, AG Opinion, *Schrems 2*, para. 144.

[392] ECJ, *Schrems 2*, para. 121.

[393] Ibid., para. 146.

The new standard data protection clauses provided by Decision (EU) 2021/914 explicitly refer in Article 2 of the decision to the corrective powers of supervisory authorities in Article 58 GDPR to suspend or ban data transfers to third countries when the data importer is or becomes subject to laws or practices in the third country that prevent it from complying it with the standard data protection clauses. This is repeated in Clause 14(f). The responsibility of the competent supervisory authority to ensure compliance by the data exporter with the GDPR is laid down in Clause 13(a). Furthermore, the data importer has to agree to submit itself to the jurisdiction of and cooperate with the competent supervisory authority in any procedures aimed at ensuring compliance with the standard data protection clauses in Clause 13(b). The supervisory authority may demand access to the data transfer impact assessment carried out according to Clause 14 based on Clause 14(d). This and other information that the supervisory authority may request based on Clauses 15.1(d) or 15.2(b) help it to assess the situation at hand.[394]

3.3.3.1.4 Rights of Individuals

Supervisory authorities are also responsible for complaints of individuals concerning the transfer of their personal data. Article 57(1)(f) GDPR requires supervisory authorities to handle complaints lodged with them, to investigate the subject matter of the complaint, and to inform the complainant of the progress and outcome of the investigation within a reasonable period of time. Data subjects may also request the supervisory authorities to exercise their corrective powers according to Article 77(1) GDPR. In such cases, the supervisory authorities must make a legally binding decision. Article 78(1) GDPR sets out the right of the concerned data subjects to an effective judicial remedy against the decision of a supervisory authority. This guarantees that individuals have the possibility to enforce their right to continuous protection of personal data in Article 8 CFR against a data exporter. The standard data protection clauses provided by Decision (EU) 2021/914 explicitly state that the data subjects have third-party beneficiary rights in Clause 3 and that they may lodge complaints with supervisory authorities or refer the dispute to the competent courts according to Clause 11.

3.3.3.1.5 Consistent Enforcement Among Member States

The decentralized system of supervisory authorities in each EU member state faces challenges when it comes to the consistent enforcement of the right to data protection in Article 8 CFR among the EU member states. The IHC expressed concerns in its referral of *Schrems 2* to the ECJ that the transfer of personal data to a specific third

[394] Flint (2021), p. 252.

country on the basis of standard data protection clauses could be permitted in some EU member states but suspended or banned in others.[395]

AG Saugmandsgaard Øe did not deny the difficulties linked to the legislative choice to make the supervisory authorities in the EU member states responsible for ensuring that the fundamental rights of data subjects are observed in the context of data transfers.[396] The risk that such a choice takes is that the different supervisory authorities will be fragmented. But this is inherent in the decentralized structure intended by the EU legislator.[397] AG Saugmandsgaard Øe thus argued that "EU law does not require that a general and preventive solution be applied for all transfers to a given third country that might entail the same risks of a violation of fundamental rights."[398] He referred to the consistency mechanism entailed in the GDPR that offers a procedure for cooperation between the supervisory authorities.[399] The consistency mechanism requires that the EDPB issues an opinion in cases in which a supervisory authority intends to adopt any of the measures listed in Article 64(1) GDPR. Three of the six measures listed in Article 64(1) GDPR relate to data transfers, but the decision of a supervisory authority to suspend or ban data transfers according to Article 58(2)(j) GDPR is not among the measures that obligate a supervisory authority to obtain an opinion from the EDPB.

The ECJ correctly referred to the possibility to use the voluntary alternative consistency mechanism in Article 64(2) GDPR.[400] The voluntary consistency mechanism allows any supervisory authority, the Chair of the EDPB, or the Commission to request that any matter having effects in more than one EU member state be examined by the EDPB with a view to obtaining an opinion from the EDPB. The decision of a supervisory authority to suspend or ban data transfers to a third country based on fundamental rights concerns should fall into this category. If a supervisory authority decides to suspend or ban certain data transfers to a third country, many data transfers from other EU member states to that third country must also be presumed to be incompatible with fundamental rights. In such cases, supervisory authorities have an interest that their practice is consistent with the practice of supervisory authorities in other EU member states. Supervisory authorities should therefore be inclined to use the voluntary consistency mechanism according to Article 64(2) GDPR and request an opinion from the EDPB when deciding to suspend or ban data transfers to a third country. The use of the voluntary consistency mechanism facilitates a unionwide enforcement of the right to continuous protection of personal data in Article 8 CFR.

Regular opinions of the EDPB are not legally binding, but they carry considerable weight. It is expectable that supervisory authorities will follow an EDPB opinion. They

---

[395] IHC, *Schrems 2*, para. 315.

[396] ECJ, AG Opinion, *Schrems 2*, para. 153.

[397] ECJ, *Wirtschaftsakademie Schleswig-Holstein*, paras 69–73.

[398] ECJ, AG Opinion, *Schrems 2*, para. 154.

[399] Ibid., para. 155.

[400] ECJ, *Schrems 2*, para. 147.

could be faced with many complaints of individuals concerned with the protection of their personal data if they do not. However, the ECJ also referred to the possibility of the EDPB adopting a legally binding decision under Article 65(1)(c) GDPR, should a supervisory authority not follow an opinion of the EDPB.[401]

Article 4 Decision 2010/87/EU already provided an instrument for the consistency of enforcement and Article 2 Decision (EU) 2021/914 entails the same instrument:

> Where the competent Member State authorities exercise corrective powers pursuant to Article 58 of Regulation (EU) 2016/679 in response to the data importer being or becoming subject to laws or practices in the third country of destination that prevent it from complying with the standard contractual clauses set out in the Annex, leading to the suspension or ban of data transfers to third countries, the Member State concerned shall, without delay, inform the Commission, which will forward the information to the other Member States.

This mechanism guarantees that all EU member states are informed about any suspensions or bans on data transfers to third countries.

3.3.3.2 BCRs Based on Article 46(2)(b) GDPR

The mechanism to approve BCRs provides the possibility for the responsible supervisory authority to prohibit data transfers to a third country that interferes with the right to continuous protection of personal data in Article 8 CFR. In order to be approved, BCRs must specify a number of requirements listed in Article 47(2) GDPR. For example, BCRs must specify the types of data transfers, the categories of personal data, and the third country or countries to which the personal data will be transferred.[402] This information allows supervisory authorities to assess the risks of BCRs for the specific data transfers and to apply the right to continuous protection of personal data in Article 8 CFR. The approval of BCRs is subject to the mandatory consistency mechanism in Article 63 GDPR.[403] This mechanism supports the consistent application of the right to continuous protection for personal data in Article 8 CFR.

Once BCRs are approved, the supervisory authorities are still responsible for monitoring and enforcing the application of the GDPR in light of the Charter according to Article 57(1)(a) GDPR and Article 8(3) CFR. They thus retain their investigative and corrective powers enumerated in Article 58(1) and (2) GDPR. In order to be approved, BCRs must also specify the mechanisms for ensuring the verification of compliance with the BCRs. These mechanisms include data protection audits and methods for ensuring corrective actions to protect the rights of data subject. The results of such audits must be made available to the responsible supervisory authority upon request.[404] Data subjects have the right to lodge a

---

[401] Ibid.

[402] Article 47(2)(b) GDPR.

[403] Articles 47(1) and 64(1)(f) GDPR.

[404] Article 47(2)(j) GDPR.

complaint with the relevant supervisory authority against data transfers on the basis of BCRs according to Article 77(1) GDPR and to appeal a decision of the responsible supervisory authority according to Article 78(2) GDPR. Data subjects also have the right to a judicial remedy against the data exporter according to Article 79(1) GDPR. In order to be approved, BCRs must thus specify the means for the exercise of these rights.[405]

The validity of BCRs does not depend on the level of protection for personal data that exists in the given third country to which data might be transferred. Instead, the validity depends only on the soundness of the safeguards which those instruments provide in order to compensate for any inadequacy that results in the third country of destination. The information required for the approval of BCRs allows the responsible supervisory authority to assess the risks of BCRs for the data transfers in question and to apply the right to continuous protection of personal data. Just as in the case of the standard data protection clauses, the BCRs might have to include additional safeguards for the transfer of personal data to third countries where the protection of personal data is not essentially equivalent to that guaranteed within the EU.[406] If BCRs are used for data transfers that do not comply with the right to continuous protection for personal data, then there are compliance mechanisms in place.[407] The regulatory framework surrounding BCRs validates this instrument as a legal mechanism for data transfers.

3.3.4 *Supervisory Authorities as Guardians of Fundamental Rights*

Control over continuous protection of personal data in relation to the instruments providing appropriate safeguards often lies with the supervisory authorities. They are the bodies responsible for approving many of the instruments providing appropriate safeguards for data transfers. This includes BCRs according to Article 46(2)(b) GDPR and certifications according to Article 46(2)(f) GDPR.[408] Supervisory authorities are also responsible for authorizing specific (*ad hoc*) contractual clauses according to Article 46(3)(a) GDPR. Moreover, they adopt standard data protection clauses according to Article 46(2)(d) GDPR and submit them for approval to the Commission.[409] Lastly, the EDPD, which consists of all the supervisory authorities in the EU member states, is responsible for providing opinions to the Commission on whether a

[405] Article 47(2)(e) GDPR.

[406] EDPB (2020), p. 18.

[407] See Sect. 3.3.2.2.2.

[408] Articles 47(1) and 42(5) GDPR.

[409] Subject to the examination procedure in Article 5 of Regulation (EU) 182/2011.

code of conduct according to Article 46(2)(e) GDPR provides appropriate safeguards.[410]

In accordance with Article 8(3) CFR and Article 57 GDPR, the supervisory authorities are responsible for monitoring compliance with EU rules concerning the protection of individuals regarding the processing of their personal data. Each supervisory authority is vested with the power to examine whether data transfers from its home EU member state to a third country comply with the requirements laid down in the GDPR and the right to continuous protection of personal data in Article 8 CFR.[411] If the data transfers do not comply with these requirements, then the supervisory authorities must use their corrective powers to fix the problem. The responsibility of the supervisory authorities is of a subsidiary nature. First of all, it is for the data exporter

> to verify, on a case-by-case basis and, where appropriate, in collaboration with the recipient of the data whether the law of the third country of destination ensures adequate protection, under EU law, of personal data transferred pursuant to standard data protection clauses.[412]

Only in cases in which the data exporter does not suspend or end the transfer, if protection that is essentially equivalent to that guaranteed within the EU cannot be guaranteed, is the competent supervisory authority required to act.[413] Accordingly, the data exports are primarily responsible for safeguarding the right to continuous protection of personal data in Article 8 CFR. This architecture of self-regulation is not perfect. Due to the economic nature of many data transfers, a data exporting company will often have to decide between its economic goals and compliance with fundamental rights protection. Furthermore, this sort of private enforcement is underpinned by the threat of legal action by data subject. "It assumes data subjects have the energy and the resources to take action – a real weakness in this approach, despite the possibility for class actions."[414] Lastly, the assessment of the level of protection for the personal data transferred to third countries is complicated and requires far-reaching information about government access to personal data in third countries. A diligent exercise of the responsibility of data exporters to comply with the right to continuous protection of personal data in Article 8 CFR is quite an effort and it is questionable if data exporters are ready to make this effort. Given the shortcomings of this self-regulation model, the supervisory authorities will in practice play an important role as guardians of fundamental rights.

---

[410] Article 40(7) GDPR.

[411] ECJ, *Schrems*, para. 47.

[412] ECJ, *Schrems 2*, para. 134.

[413] Ibid., para. 135.

[414] Woods (2019).

3.3.5 Summary

The instruments providing appropriate safeguards must fully comply with the right to continuous protection of personal data and the standard of essential equivalence. No limitations on the exercise of that right are possible for data transfers on the basis of this legal mechanism. The right to continuous protection of personal data has a restrictive effect on data transfers based on instruments providing appropriate safeguards. The instruments in Article 46 GDPR do not acknowledge the conditions for the processing of personal data in third countries but rather the provision of appropriate safeguards through the instruments themselves. Nevertheless, the prevailing legal context in a third country of destination may, depending on the actual circumstances of the data transfer, make it impossible to comply with the right to continuous protection of personal data and the standard of essential equivalence. In such cases, data transfers may *not* take place. The justification of this restrictive effect is firmly rooted in the protection of fundamental rights. However, the politics behind appropriate safeguards are problematic when it comes to a consistent fundamental rights-based application of the instruments in Article 46 GDPR. The analysis of this section has revealed a *laissez-faire* attitude towards fundamental rights protection that has been grounded in an outdated understanding of the level of protection required for data transfers. The *Schrems 2* judgment made it clear that the data exporter using the instruments in Article 46 GDPR for the transfer of personal data must ensure that the right to continuous protection of personal data is respected. However, based on the shortcomings of his architecture of self-regulation, the supervisory authorities in the EU member states have to act as the guardians of fundamental rights regarding the instruments in Article 46 GDPR. They must therefore take their responsibility seriously and make sure that the application of those instruments in practice respects the right to continuous protection of personal data in Article 8 CFR.

3.4 Continuous Protection of Personal Data and Derogations

The fourth section of this chapter is dedicated to the interplay of the right to continuous protection for personal data and the derogations for specific situations as a legal mechanism for data transfers according to Article 49 GDPR. An analysis of the politics of the derogations pursuant to Article 49 GDPR reveals a contradiction. While Article 49 GDPR allows derogations from the right to continuous protection of personal data, those derogations may not cause additional exemptions from the rule that fundamental rights should be respected nor lead to a situation in which fundamental rights might be breached (Sect. 3.4.1). There are two options for settling this contradiction: lawful limitations on the right to continuous protection for personal data with the contract-based derogation in Article 49(1)(b) GDPR

(Sect. 3.4.2), or a waiver of the right to continuous protection for personal data with the consent-based derogation in Article 49(1)(a) GDPR (Sect. 3.4.3). In both cases, data subjects must be attentive because they are responsible for ensuring that their fundamental rights are respected (Sect. 3.4.4).

3.4.1 The Politics of Derogations

3.4.1.1 Contradiction

The derogations in Article 49 GDPR allow data transfers in the absence of an adequacy decision and the possibility of using instruments providing appropriate safeguards. However, the politics behind these derogations for specific situations is contradictory.

Adequacy decisions as much as instruments providing appropriate safeguards must fully comply with the right to continuous protection of personal data in Article 8 CFR. Limitations on the exercise of that right cannot be justified for data transfers based on these two legal mechanisms. The title of Article 49 GDPR indicates that it entails derogations from these other legal mechanisms. The title implies that the legal mechanism for data transfers in Article 49 GDPR does not have to comply fully with the right to continuous protection of personal data. Christopher Kuner has written that "derogations, by definition, may apply when there is no essential equivalence."[415] However, Article 44 GDPR states that all provisions in Chapter V GDPR on transfers of personal data to third countries shall be applied in order to ensure that the level of protection of natural persons guaranteed by the GDPR is not undermined. Additionally, Recital (114) GDPR indicates that in cases in which the Commission has not made an adequacy decision, data exporters must use solutions for data transfers in which data subjects continue to benefit from their fundamental rights and safeguards. From its position among the other recitals, Recital (114) GDPR seems to apply to data transfers based on the derogations in Article 49 GDPR. This would imply that the derogations must still comply with the right to continuous protection of personal data.

The Article 29 WP has added to this contradiction by claiming with regard to the same derogations in Article 26(1) Directive 95/46/EC that

> while the cases listed in Article 26(1) may constitute a derogation to the principle that the third country should guarantee an adequate protection, they do not provide additional exemptions from the rule that fundamental rights should be respected.[416]

On the one hand, the Article 29 WP states that the derogations in Article 26(1) Directive 95/46/EC are derogations from the principle that the third country should guarantee adequate protection. The ECJ defined adequate protection as protection

---

[415] Kuner (2017), p. 905.

[416] Article 29 WP (2005), p. 9.

that is essentially equivalent to that guaranteed within the EU.[417] Essential equivalence for protection of personal data in a third country entails the same limitations on fundamental rights in the third country as are permitted in the EU.[418] Article 26(1) Directive 95/46/EC would therefore allow data transfers that do not respect the right to continuous protection for personal data, which is essentially equivalent to that guaranteed within the EU. On the other hand, the Article 29 WP also states that the derogations in Article 26(1) Directive 95/46/EC do not provide additional exemptions from the rule that fundamental rights should be respected.

The EDPB similarly found with regard to the derogations under Article 49 GDPR that

> derogations under Article 49 are exemptions from the general principle that personal data may only be transferred to third countries if an adequate level of protection is provided for in the third country" and that "recourse to the derogations of Article 49 should never lead to a situation where fundamental rights might be breached.[419]

So, while Article 49 GDPR seems to allow for derogations from the right of continuous protection of personal data, they may nonetheless *not* provide additional exemptions from the rule that fundamental rights should be respected nor lead to a situation in which fundamental rights can be breached.

3.4.1.2 Resolution

How is it possible to settle this contradiction? How can derogations from the right to continuous protection of personal data not provide additional exemptions from the rule that fundamental rights should be respected? There are two solutions to settle this contradiction.

The first solution is a lawful limitation on the right to continuous protection of personal data. The right to continuous protection for personal data is an unwritten constituent part of the right to data protection enshrined in Article 8 CFR.[420] An interference with Article 8 CFR is an interference with one or more of its constituent parts. Only the essence of a fundamental right cannot be touched, limited, diminished, restricted, or interfered with. The right to continuous protection of personal data and the standard of essential equivalence, however, have not been defined as part of the essence of Article 8 CFR. Limitations on the right to continuous protection of personal data are thus theoretically possible.[421] Such limitations would not provide additional exemptions from the rule that fundamental rights

[417] ECJ, *Schrems*, para. 73.

[418] Ibid., para. 96.

[419] EDPB (2018), pp. 3–4. The EDPS wrongly refers to Recital (114) GDPR, which also seems to apply to data transfers based on the derogations in Article 49 GDPR from its position among the other recitals.

[420] See Sect. 2.3.1.

[421] See Sect. 2.3.4.4.

should be respected nor lead to a situation in which fundamental rights might be breached if the limitations are justified according to Article 52(1) CFR.

The second solution is a waiver on the right to continuous protection of personal data in Article 8 CFR. There is no obligation to exercise fundamental rights. It is thus possible to waive fundamental rights. Problems arise, in particular, in cases in which the decision to waive a fundamental right does not take place freely.[422] Moreover the waiver of a fundamental right should not be read as equivalent with the loss of that fundamental right.[423] If individuals lawfully waive their right to continuous protection of personal data, then this does not provide additional exemptions from the rule that fundamental rights should be respected nor lead to a situation in which fundamental rights can be breached.

3.4.2 *Limitations on Continuous Protection of Personal Data with the Derogations*

The right to continuous protection for personal data requires that the level of protection for personal data that is transferred from the EU to a third country is essentially equivalent to that guaranteed within the EU. That right is not absolute. Limitations on the exercise of the right to continuous protection of personal data can be lawful according to Article 52(1) CFR. This section analyzes the contract-based derogation in Article 49(1)(b) GDPR. Just as described with regard to the other legal mechanisms for the transfer of personal data, the interference must be found in the EU rather than in the third country (Sect. 3.4.2.1). The legal basis for the interference must indicate under what circumstances and conditions the interference will take place and impose minimum safeguards providing sufficient guarantees for individuals to effectively protect their personal data against the risk of abuse (Sect. 3.4.2.2). The material objectives of the interference must either qualify as a general interest recognized by the EU or be protected by another right or freedom in the Charter (Sect. 3.4.2.3). Finally, the principle of proportionality must be observed (Sect. 3.4.2.4).

3.4.2.1 Interference

Any interference with the right to continuous protection of personal data must be found in the EU.[424] Ultimately, the rules, measures, and actions of third states also entail intrusions, which, if they were attributed to the authorities of an EU member state, would be regarded as interferences with the exercise of the right to data

[422] Winkler (2006), p. 112.

[423] Ibid.

[424] ECJ, *Schrems*, para. 87; see Sect. 3.2.2.1.

protection in Article 8 CFR.[425] Those intrusions should, however, be assessed with regard to the standard of essential equivalence. If the intrusions caused by the rules, measures, and actions of third states do not respect the standard of essential equivalence, then the transfer of personal data subject to the contract-based derogation in Article 49(1)(b) GDPR itself constitutes an interference with the right to continuous protection of personal data enshrined in Article 8 CFR.

The contract-based derogation in Article 49(1)(b) GDPR cannot make up for the inadequacies of data protection in third countries. This is why the actual transfer of personal data subject to the contract-based derogation in Article 49(1)(b) GDPR constitutes an interference with Article 8 CFR to the extent that it does not respect the right to continuous protection of personal data.

3.4.2.2 Legal Basis

The limitation of the exercise of fundamental rights must be provided for by law. The legal basis that permits an interference with Article 8 CFR must itself define the scope of the limitation.[426] Moreover, the legal basis for interferences with Article 8 CFR must indicate under what circumstances and conditions the data processing operations will take place and impose minimum safeguards providing sufficient guarantees for individuals to effectively protect their personal data against the risk of abuse.[427] These safeguards are particularly important in cases in which personal data is subject to automated processing and involves sensitive data.[428] The transfer of personal data subject to the contract-based derogation in Article 49(1)(b) GDPR constitutes an interference with Article 8 CFR if, for the specific transfer of personal data, the level of protection for personal data in the third country is not essentially equivalent to that guaranteed within the EU.

The derogation in Article 49(1)(b) GDPR must be applied in a contract between the data exporter in the EU and the data importer in the third country if the transfer of personal data is to legally occur.[429] Article 49(1)(b) GDPR constitutes the legal basis for an interference with Article 8 CFR because it enables the transfer of personal data to a third country. The question is whether the legal basis fulfills the conditions regarding the scope of the limitations to the concerned fundamental rights and the presence of minimum safeguards.

The derogations in Article 49 GDPR are faced with functional limits regarding the definition of the scope of the limitations on the right to data protection in Article 8 CFR. The derogations in Article 49 GDPR ignore the conditions for the

---

[425] Cp. ECJ, AG Opinion, *Schrems 2*, para. 256.

[426] ECJ, Opinion 1/15, para. 139; ECJ, *WebMindLicenses*, para. 81; see Sect. 2.2.4.4.

[427] ECJ, Opinion 1/15, para. 141; ECJ, *Tele2/Watson*, para. 109; ECJ, *Schrems*, para. 91; ECJ, *Digital Rights Ireland*, para. 54.

[428] ECJ, Opinion 1/15, para. 141; ECJ, *Schrems*, para. 91; ECJ, *Digital Rights Ireland*, para. 55.

[429] Not unlike BCRs. See Sect. 3.3.2.2.2.

processing of personal data in the third country. They cannot refer to the scope of the limitations on the exercise of fundamental rights regarding the intrusions with rules, measures, and actions of the respective third state, which, if they were attributed to the authorities of an EU member state, would be regarded as interferences with the exercise of the right to data protection. Nonetheless, the contract-based derogation still indicates under what circumstances and conditions the data processing operations will take place that interfere with the right to continuous protection of personal data, i.e., the transfer of personal data to the third country.

According to Article 49(1)(b) GDPR, a data exporter may only transfer personal data to a third country if the transfer is necessary for the performance of a contract between a data subject and the controller. At least one of the central contractual services must therefore be impossible if the data is not transferred to the third country in question. This means there must be a close, direct or substantial link between the data transfer and the performance of the contract.[430] For example, such a close and direct link does not exist for additional direct marketing purposes or simply for data storage in the third country.[431] It is not enough if the data transfer is simply useful or allows cost savings. Additionally, Recital (111) GDPR states that the use of the contract-based derogation in Article 49(1)(b) GDPR shall be limited to occasional transfers. The EDPB has underlined that "[d]ata transfers regularly occurring within a stable relationship would be deemed as systematic and repeated, hence exceeding an "occasional" character."[432]

Regarding the minimum safeguards required to provide sufficient guarantees for individuals to effectively protect their personal data against the risk of abuse, independent oversight and remedies are important. It is important to underline that the contract referred to in Article 49(1)(b) GDPR must outline the risks for individuals whose personal data will be transferred to a third country. Article 49(1)(b) GDPR itself does not contain any specific information duties for the data controller concerning the risks of the data transfer. The duty results from the transparency requirement in Article 5(1)(a) GDPR and the general information duty for data transfers in Article 13(1)(f) GDPR.[433] Supervisory authorities must monitor and enforce the application of the GDPR according to Article 57(1)(a) GDPR. Their investigative and corrective powers outlined in Article 58 GDPR should protect individuals against the risk of abuse of their personal data. Furthermore, data subjects may, according to Article 77(1) GDPR, request the relevant supervisory authorities to exercise their powers in cases in which they consider that the contract-based derogation has not been used properly. Data subjects also have the right to an effective judicial remedy against the data exporter according to Article 79(1) GDPR, in cases in which they consider that their rights under the GDPR have been infringed as a result of the transfer of their personal data. These

---

[430] Article 29 WP (2005), p. 13.

[431] Article 29 WP (2006), p. 23.

[432] EDPB (2018), p. 9.

[433] Schantz (2019), pp. 1025–1026.

minimum safeguards guarantee that individuals can effectively protect their personal data against the risk of abuse. The contract-based derogation in Article 49(1)(b) GDPR therefore provides a valid legal basis for interferences with Article 8 CFR.

3.4.2.3 Objectives of General Interest and Protection of the Freedoms of Others

The justification of an interference that limits the exercise of fundamental rights according to Article 52 CFR further requires that the limitations genuinely meet either objectives of general interest recognized by the EU or the need to protect the rights and freedoms of others. The public security in a third country (Sect. 3.4.2.3.1) qualifies as a general interest recognized by the EU and the freedom of expression and information (Sect. 3.4.2.3.2) and the freedom to conduct a business (Sect. 3.4.2.3.3) as rights of others which validate limitations on the right to continuous protection of personal data.

3.4.2.3.1 Public Security in a Third Country

The public security in a third country can be an objective of general interest recognized by the EU.[434] In order to justify the limitation on the right to continuous protection of personal data, the protection of public security in a third country must be one of the material objectives of the data transfers.[435] Because the data transfers in question are usually part of a commercial activity,[436] they rarely relate to the protection of public security in a third country.

3.4.2.3.2 Freedom of Expression and Information

Data transfers are a tool for the exercise of the freedom of expression and information enshrined in Article 11 CFR.[437] In order to justify an interference with the right to continuous protection of personal data based on the protection of the freedom of expression and information, the protection of that freedom must be one of the material objectives of the data transfers.[438]

The contract-based derogation in Article 49(1)(b) GDPR does not refer to the protection of Article 11 CFR but this does not generally preclude an argument using Article 11 CFR as a justification. The protection of the freedom of expression and

---

[434] See Sect. 3.2.2.3.1.

[435] ECJ, *Digital Rights Ireland*, para. 41.

[436] ECJ, AG Opinion, *Schrems 2*, paras 106–107.

[437] See Sect. 3.2.2.3.2.

[438] Cp. ECJ, *Digital Rights Ireland*, para. 41.

information and its reconciliation with the right to data protection is one of the material objectives of the GDPR and, therefore, also of Chapter V GDPR.[439] In addition, the contract itself can refer to the freedom of expression and information in Article 11 CFR.

3.4.2.3.3 Freedom to Conduct a Business

Data transfers to third countries may be used for cross-border economic activities and therefore to protect the freedom to conduct a business enshrined in Article 16 CFR.[440] In order to justify an interference with the right to continuous protection of personal data based on the protection of the freedom to conduct a business, then the protection of that freedom must be one of the material objectives of the data transfers.[441]

The contract-based derogation in Article 49(1)(b) GDPR does not refer to the protection of Article 16 CFR but this does not generally preclude an argument using Article 16 CFR as a justification. The protection of the freedom to conduct a business is one of the material objectives of the GDPR and, therefore, also of Chapter V GDPR.[442] In addition, the contract itself can refer to the freedom to conduct a business in Article 16 CFR.

3.4.2.4 Proportionality

The principle of proportionality requires that limitations on fundamental rights must be appropriate in light of the objective pursued and limited to what is strictly necessary.[443] It is also necessary to examine if there are other measures which affect the right to continuous protection of personal data less adversely and still contribute effectively to the objectives of general interest recognized by the EU or the need to protect the fundamental rights and freedoms of others. It has to be seen if the interference with the right to continuous protection of personal data is proportional to the protection of the freedom of expression and information (Sect. 3.2.2.4.1), and to the protection of the freedom to conduct a business (Sect. 3.2.2.4.2).

---

[439] See Recital (4) and Article 85(1) GDPR; see also Sect. 3.2.2.3.2.

[440] See Sect. 3.2.2.3.3.

[441] ECJ, *Digital Rights Ireland*, para. 41.

[442] See Recitals (4) and (101) GDPR; see also Sect. 3.2.2.3.3.

[443] ECJ, Opinion 1/15, para. 140; ECJ, *Tele2/Watson*, paras 96, 103; ECJ, *Schrems*, para. 92; ECJ, *Digital Rights Ireland*, paras 51–52; see Sect. 2.2.4.4.

3.4.2.4.1 Freedom of Expression and Information

Data transfers based on the derogation in Article 49(1)(b) GDPR enable companies to distribute information and ideas without interference by public authorities and regardless of borders. The contract-based derogation does *not* allow data transfers to third countries that are systematic, structural, and continuous. It allows data transfers that are occasional and necessary for the performance of a contract between a data subject and the data controller.

In theory, the contract-based derogation enables data transfers that protect journalistic, academic, artistic, and literary speech. However, the requirements of Article 49(1)(b) GDPR are strict and often pose an obstacle for such cross-border expression. The obligation in Article 85(2) GDPR for EU member states to provide exemptions or derogations from Chapter V GDPR on transfers of personal data to third countries for journalistic purposes or the purpose of academic, artistic or literary expression seems to be more appropriate for such data flows.

In theory, the contract-based derogation also enables data transfers that protect commercial speech. Again, the requirements of Article 49(1)(b) GDPR are strict and often pose an obstacle for such transfers. AG Nial Fennelly defined commercial speech as "the provision of information, expression of ideas or communication of images as part of the promotion of a commercial activity and the concomitant right to receive such communication."[444] According to that definition, commercial speech encompasses statements strictly linked to the commercial promotion of products and services.[445] Article 49(1)(b) GDPR enables data transfers necessary for the facilitation of e-commerce services, but it does not allow additional follow-up transfers for marketing measures.[446] Such measures would not satisfy the requirement of a close and direct or substantial link between the data transfer and the performance of the contract. It is thus questionable whether the contract-based derogation is of much use to a data exporter with regard to commercial speech. The consent-based derogation in Article 49(1)(a) GDPR seems to be a more appropriate avenue for such purposes.[447]

3.4.2.4.2 Freedom to Conduct a Business

Data transfers subject to the contract-based derogation in Article 49(1)(b) GDPR enable companies to distribute information and ideas without interference from public authorities and regardless of borders. Even though the contract-based derogation does not allow for data transfers to third countries that are systematic, structural, and continuous, it is an appropriate tool for protecting the freedom to

---

[444] ECJ, AG Opinion, *Germany v. Parliament and Council*, para. 153.

[445] Krzemińska-Vamvaka (2008), p. 116.

[446] Article 29 WP (2005), p. 13.

[447] See Sect. 3.4.2.

conduct a business enshrined in Article 16 CFR. While cloud computing applications such as Facebook or Google would not be able to rely on the contract-based derogation to outsource their data processing operations, e-commerce services for hotels, airlines, credit cards etc. could do so based on Article 49(1)(b) GDPR.

I thus argue that limitations on the right to continuous protection of personal data with data transfers subject to the contract-based derogation in Article 49(1)(b) GDPR can be justified under the freedom to conduct a business enshrined in Article 16 CFR. The derogation in Article 49(1)(b) GDPR is limited to occasional data transfers necessary for the performance of a contract between a data subject and the data controller. As it stands, it therefore already constitutes a measure that affects the right to data protection less adversely than data transfers based on adequacy decisions or data transfers based on instruments providing appropriate safeguards.

Normally, the right to data protection attracts a higher level of protection than the freedom to conduct a business. However, the contract-based derogation in Article 49(1)(b) GDPR reflects and protects the written constituent parts of the right to data protection enshrined in Article 8 CFR. The constituent part on purpose specification reflects the idea that data processing operations should be foreseeable for the data subject and should not go beyond the reasonable expectations of the individuals concerned.[448] The contract-based derogation requires the data exporter to specify the purposes of the data transfers. The constituent part on fairness demands that the data subject is in a position to learn of the existence of intended and possible data processing operations.[449] The contract-based derogation also requires the data exporter to outline the risks of the data transfers. The constituent part on consent as a legitimate basis for the processing of personal data is an expression of informational self-determination.[450] The contract-based derogation requires the data subject to consent to the data transfers by agreeing to the data transfers in question. The constituent part on independent supervision addresses the power asymmetries between data controllers and data subjects.[451] Independent supervision by the supervisory authorities of the EU member states is part of the minimum safeguards available for data transfers subject to the contract-based derogation. Only the right of access and the right to rectify data would have to be specifically included in the contract in order for the derogation in Article 49(1)(b) GDPR to reflect these two constituent parts in the second sentence of Article 8(2) CFR.[452]

Overall, the contract-based derogation in Article 49(1)(b) GDPR takes the written constituent parts of the right to data protection into account while protecting the freedom to conduct a business. This is why limitations on the right to continuous protection of personal data by data transfers subject to the contract-based derogation in Article 49(1)(b) GDPR can be justified using the freedom to conduct a business

[448] See Sect 2.2.2.2.

[449] See ibid.

[450] See ibid.

[451] See Sect. 2.2.2.4.

[452] See Sect. 2.2.2.3.

enshrined in Article 16 CFR even if the right to data protection attracts a higher level of protection than the freedom to conduct a business.

3.4.3 Waiver on Continuous Protection for Personal Data

This section analyzes the consent-based derogation in Article 49(1)(a) GDPR. The right to continuous protection of personal data requires that the level of protection for personal data that is transferred from the EU to a third country is essentially equivalent to that guaranteed within the EU. That right can be waived by the data subject (Sect. 3.4.3.1). The ECtHR has developed a standard test for determining the legality of a waiver of human rights under the ECHR. The ECJ has copied that test with regard to the fundamental rights in the Charter (Sect. 3.4.3.2). The test requires that six conditions are met: unforcedness, full knowledge of the surrounding circumstances, unequivocalness, minimum safeguards, respect for important public interests, and the condition that the waiver should not be connected with the loss of the respective fundamental right (Sect. 3.4.3.3). The consent-based derogation in Article 49(1)(a) GDPR complies with these requirements and therefore constitutes a lawful waiver of the right to continuous protection of personal data (Sect. 3.4.3.4).

3.4.3.1 Availability of the Waiver

The derogation in Article 49(1)(a) GDPR refers to data transfers in which the data subject has explicitly consented to the proposed transfer after having been informed of the possible risks of such transfers due to the absence of an adequacy decision and appropriate safeguards. The consent could amount to a waiver on the right to continuous protection of personal data if the level of protection in the third country is not essentially equivalent to that guaranteed within the EU. However, not every fundamental right can be waived. Some core elements of substantive rights cannot be waived since they reach beyond the individual right holder's sphere. It must thus first be established that the text and spirit of the right to be waived does not prevent a waiver.

It is necessary to look at some of the foundational values of the right to data protection to determine whether the right to continuous protection of personal data can be waived with regard to data transfers subject to the consent-based derogation in Article 49(1)(a) GDPR.[453]

- Privacy can be conceptualized as either the right to be let alone or limited accessibility to a person. It is possible to forgo one's privacy. For example, individuals may voluntarily subject themselves to permanent video surveillance.

[453] See Sect. 2.2.1.

- Informational self-determination guarantees the ability of individuals to determine for themselves the disclosure and use of their personal data. The consent of an individual to allow occasional data transfers to third countries in which personal data is at risk of becoming subject to government surveillance can be seen as an act of informational self-determination as long as the consent is informed.
- Transparency addresses the power imbalances between a data controller and the data subjects. The consent of an individual to allow occasional data transfers to third countries is only possible after having been informed of the possible risks of such transfers due to the absence of an adequacy decision and appropriate safeguards. This information provides the necessary transparency.

The right to data protection can thus be waived pursuant to the consent-based derogation in Article 49(1)(a) GDPR. Consent allows individuals to decide for themselves if they want to accept the opportunities and the corresponding risks of data processing operations.

3.4.3.2 Test for the Waiver

The ECJ has previously ruled on the legitimacy of waivers. The case law of the ECJ so far covers waivers of the right to an effective judicial remedy and a fair trial provided for in Article 47 CFR and the rights of the defense guaranteed by Article 48(2) CFR.[454] In this context, the ECJ normally referred to the jurisprudence of the ECtHR.[455] Much of the ECtHR's case law on waivers also relates to matters of fair trial based on Article 6 ECHR.[456] Nonetheless, there have been some cases that concerned waivers on substantive rights such as the right to damages under Article 41 ECHR or the right to education under Article 2 of Protocol No. 1 to the ECHR combined with the prohibition of racial discrimination in educational matters under Article 14 ECHR.[457]

The ECtHR has developed a standard test for determining the legality of a waiver of human rights under the ECHR, which the ECJ copied in *Melloni* with regard to the Charter. The ECJ stated, with respect to Articles 47 and 48(2) CFR, that an accused person may waive these rights of his or her own free will, provided that the waiver is established in an unequivocal manner, is attended by minimum safeguards commensurate to its importance, and does not run counter to any important public

[454] See ECJ, *Melloni,* para. 49.

[455] The ECJ explicitly acknowledged that the interpretation of Articles 47 and 48(2) CFR "is in keeping with the scope that has been recognised for the rights guaranteed by Article 6(1) and (3) of the ECHR by the case-law of the European Court of Human Rights". Ibid., para. 50.

[456] Caflisch (2011), p. 422, 426.

[457] See ECtHR, *Neumeister v. Austria*; ECtHR, *Perez v. France*; ECtHR, *D.H. v. Czech Republic.*

interest.[458] The lawfulness of the consent-based derogation in Article 49(1)(a) GDPR primarily depends on the lawfulness of the waiver.

3.4.3.3 Conditions of the Waiver

The test for the lawfulness of a waiver requires that certain conditions be met. The waiver for the right to continuous protection of personal data based on the derogation in Article 49(1)(a) GDPR is lawful because it is unforced (Sect. 3.4.3.3.1), made in full knowledge of the surrounding circumstances (Sect. 3.4.3.3.2), unequivocal (Sect. 3.4.3.3.3), attended by minimum safeguards (Sect. 3.4.3.3.4), does not run counter any important public interest (Sect. 3.4.3.3.5), and is not connected with the loss of the right to data protection (Sect. 3.4.3.3.6).

3.4.3.3.1 Unforcedness

The waiver for a fundamental right must be unforced. Waivers made under duress are invalid.[459] Article 4(11) GDPR requires that any and all consent must be freely given. Recital (42) GDPR states that consent should not be regarded as freely given if the data subject has no genuine choice or is unable to refuse or withdraw consent without detriment. Recital (43) GDPR adds that consent is presumed not to be freely given if the performance of a contract, including the provision of a service, is made dependent on the giving of consent despite such consent not being necessary for the performance. If a service is provided across borders, then the transfer of personal data is usually appropriate and necessary for the provision of that service. If a service could also be delivered without the transfer of personal data *and* consent for that data transfer is still required, then that consent cannot be presumed to be freely given. The requirement that consent must be freely given guarantees that the waiver for the right to continuous protection of personal data based on Article 49(1)(a) GDPR is unforced.

3.4.3.3.2 Full Knowledge of the Surrounding Circumstances

The waiver for a fundamental right must be made in full knowledge of the surrounding circumstances.[460] Article 4(11) GDPR requires that any consent must be informed. The Article 29 WP found that "[f]or consent to be informed, it is necessary to inform the data subject of certain elements that are crucial to make a choice."[461]

---

[458] ECJ, *Melloni*, para. 49.

[459] ECtHR, *D.H. v. Czech Republic*, para. 202.

[460] Ibid; ECtHR, *Thompson v. United Kingdom*, para. 44.

[461] Article 29 WP (2018), p. 13.

Those elements include the data controller's identity, the purpose of the transfer, the type of data, the existence of the right to withdraw consent, and the identity or the categories of recipients.[462] Article 49(1)(a) GDPR specifically requires that the data subject may only consent to data transfers after having been informed of the possible risks of such transfers due to the absence of an adequacy decision and appropriate safeguards. An abstract reference to the absence of an adequacy decision and appropriate safeguards is not enough to comply with this requirement.[463] It is necessary to list the typical risks associated with a transfer to a third country in which the level of protection for personal data is not essentially equivalent to that guaranteed within the EU. Those risks include difficult enforcement of data subject rights, lack of control over further processing and onward transfer of personal data, lack of a supervisory authority, and access to personal data by government agencies including surveillance practices.[464] The requirements that consent must be informed and that a data subject may only consent to data transfers after having been informed of the possible risks of such transfers guarantee that the waiver for the right to continuous protection of personal data based on Article 49(1)(a) GDPR is made in full knowledge of the surrounding circumstances.

3.4.3.3.3 Unequivocalness

The waiver for a fundamental right must be unequivocal. Article 4(11) GDPR requires that any consent must be unambiguous. The Article 29 WP emphasized that it is clear in the GDPR that unambiguous consent "requires a statement from the data subject or a clear affirmative act which means that it must always be given through an active motion or declaration."[465] Similarly, the ECJ found that "[o]nly active behaviour on the part of the data subject with a view to giving his or her consent may fulfil that requirement."[466] Recital (32) GDPR specifies that this could include ticking a box when visiting an internet website, choosing technical settings for information society services, or another statement or conduct which clearly indicates in context the data subject's acceptance of the proposed processing of his or her personal data. Silence, pre-ticked boxes or inactivity cannot constitute unequivocal consent. Article 49(1)(a) GDPR is even stricter as it requires "explicit" consent. The GDPR demands explicit consent in situations in which particular data protection risks emerge and a high individual level of control over personal data is mandated.[467] Such risks emerge in the context of cross-border flows of personal data. The term "explicit" refers to the way consent is expressed by the data subject. It

---

[462] Ibid.; EDPB (2018), p. 7.

[463] That information must already be included on the basis of Articles 13(1)(f) and 14(1)(f) GDPR.

[464] EDPB (2018), p. 8; Schantz (2019), p. 1023.

[465] Article 29 WP (2018), p. 15.

[466] ECJ, *Planet49 GmbH*, para. 54.

[467] EDPB (2018), p. 6.

means that the data subject must give an express statement of consent.[468] Furthermore, Article 4(11) GDPR also requires that consent must be specific. Article 49(1)(a) GDPR implements that requirement by specifying that the data subject must explicitly consent to the proposed data transfer. All these requirements guarantee that the waiver for the right to continuous protection of personal data based on Article 49(1)(a) GDPR is unequivocal.

3.4.3.3.4 Minimum Safeguards

The waiver for a fundamental right must be attended by minimum safeguards.[469] The Article 29 WP explains that obtaining consent does not negate or in any way diminish the data controller's obligations to observe the principles of data processing enshrined in the GDPR, especially Article 5 GDPR regarding the fairness, necessity, proportionality, and quality of the data.[470] Furthermore, Article 7(3) GDPR mandates that the data controller must ensure that consent can be withdrawn by the data subject at any time and that withdrawing consent be as easy as giving consent. The principles of data processing and the possibility to withdraw consent at any time guarantee that the waiver for the right to continuous protection of personal data based on Article 49(1)(a) GDPR is attended by minimum safeguards.

3.4.3.3.5 Respect for Important Public Interests

The waiver for a fundamental right may not run counter to any important public interest.[471] Recital (111) GDPR states that data transfers subject to the contract-based derogation in Article 49(1)(b) GDPR may only be occasional. The EDPB noted that although such a limitation is absent from the consent-based derogation in Article 49(1)(a) GDPR, the consent-based derogation must still be interpreted in a way which does not contradict the very nature of the derogation as being an exception.[472] Following this opinion, the consent-based derogation does not allow systematic, structural, and continuous data transfers like adequacy decisions or the instruments providing appropriate safeguards. Matthias Christoph Schwenke has argued that consent to data processing must be restricted when the related processing of personal data poses a threat to democracy which relies on individual self-determination and the free formulation of opinions.[473] He does not discern a threat like this in the context of individualized and personalized services. Similarly, such a

[468] Article 29 WP (2018), p. 18.

[469] Caflisch (2011), pp. 427–429.

[470] EDPB (2018), p. 3.

[471] Caflisch (2011), pp. 427–429.

[472] EDPB (2018), p. 5.

[473] Schwenke (2006), p. 226.

threat should not arise in the context of occasional data transfers. Article 49(1)(a) GDPR does not allow data controllers to rely on the consent of individuals for systematic, structural, and continuous data transfers that would create a problematic aggregation of personal data that could pose a threat to democracy. The limitation for such data transfers guarantees that the waiver for the right to continuous protection of personal data based on Article 49(1)(a) GDPR does not run counter any important public interest.

3.4.3.3.6 Maintaining the Right

The waiver for the exercise of a fundamental right should not be connected with the *loss* of that fundamental right.[474] It must be repeated that consent for data transfers subject to the derogation in Article 49(1)(a) GDPR is only valid for the proposed data transfers and *not* for any other transfer. The waiver for the right to continuous protection of personal data subject to the derogation in Article 49(1)(a) GDPR only concerns the proposed data transfers. Furthermore, the consent can be withdrawn at any time. The waiver for the right to continuous protection of personal data based on Article 49(1)(a) GDPR is not connected with the loss of the right to data protection enshrined in Article 8 CFR.

3.4.3.4 Lawfulness of the Waiver

The waiver for the right to continuous protection for personal data pursuant to the consent-based derogation in Article 49(1)(a) GDPR is lawful. The EU legislator has anchored the requirements for a lawful waiver in Article 49(1)(a) GDPR. It is the responsibility of the data controller to adhere to these requirements when requesting the consent of individuals for data transfers based on Article 49(1)(a) GDPR. For the enforcement of the lawful waiver, it is however, indispensable that the concerned individuals are also responsible. This sensitivity to fundamental rights protection must and indeed may be assumed.

3.4.4 *The Data Subjects as Guardians of Fundamental Rights*

Control over the lawfulness of limitations on continuous protection for personal data in relation to derogations for specific situations lies primarily with the data subjects themselves. In cases in which data transfers take place subject to the consent-based derogation in Article 49(1)(a) GDPR, the data subjects must make sure that the conditions of the waiver for the right to continuous protection of personal data are

[474] Winkler (2006), p. 112.

met. In cases in which data transfers take place subject to the contract-based derogation in Article 49(1)(b) GDPR, the data subjects must make sure that there is a close, direct or substantial link between the data transfer and the performance of the contract and that the contract outlines the risks of the data transfer in the third country. Article 8(2) CFR explicitly allows consent as a legal basis for the processing of personal data. The Charter therefore accepts that some degree of control over compliance with the right to data protection stays with the individuals themselves. In these cases, the data subjects must act as their own guardian of fundamental rights with regard to data transfers subject to the derogations in Article 49 GDPR.

However, individual data subjects are not always in a position to control whether the derogations for specific situations are used for data transfers to third countries that are systematic, structural, and continuous. Consequently, the primary responsibility for control over the lawfulness of limitations on continuous protection for personal data in relation to derogations for specific situations is complemented with the tasks of the supervisory authorities. In accordance with Article 8(3) CFR and Article 57 GDPR, the supervisory authorities of EU member states are responsible for monitoring compliance with EU rules concerning the protection of individuals regarding the processing of their personal data. Each supervisory authority is therefore vested with the power to examine whether data transfers from its home member state to a third country comply with the requirements laid down in the GDPR.[475] While the control over individual data transfers rests with the data subjects, the supervisory authorities must ensure that data transfers based on the two derogations are only used for occasional transfers and *not* abused for data transfers to third countries that are systematic, structural, and continuous. This does not, however, release the data exporters from their own responsibility in complying with the derogation in Article 49 GDPR.

3.4.5 Summary

The right to continuous protection of personal data leaves two doors open for data transfers to third countries even if the transferred personal data will not be subject to a level of protection that is essentially equivalent to that guaranteed within the EU. The first door is for data transfers subject to the contract-based derogation in Article 49(1)(b) GDPR. The contract-based derogation allows lawful limitations on the right to continuous protection of personal data in Article 8 CFR. The second door is for data transfers subject to the consent-based derogation in Article 49(1)(a) GDPR. The consent-based derogation constitutes a lawful waiver for the right to continuous protection of personal data in Article 8 CFR. These two derogations, however, do not allow data transfers to third countries that are systematic, structural,

---

[475] ECJ, *Schrems*, para. 47.

and continuous. Cloud computing applications such as Facebook or Google are thus not able to rely on these legal mechanisms to outsource their data processing operations. However, there are many service providers that may still rely on these legal mechanisms for data transfers that are occasional. In these cases, the data subjects must be attentive and insist that the requirements of the derogations are complied with. The supervisory authorities are responsible for ensuring that the exceptions in Article 49 GDPR are not abused.

3.5 Conclusion

The right to continuous protection of personal data is an unwritten constituent part of the right to data protection enshrined in Article 8 CFR. This right is not absolute. Limitations on the exercise of the right to continuous protection for personal data are lawful according to the conditions in Article 52(1) CFR. This chapter shows that an interference with the right to continuous protection of personal data must first be found in the EU. Intrusions in the third country—which, if they were attributed to the authorities of an EU member state would be regarded as interferences with Article 8 CFR—should be assessed with regard to the standard of essential equivalence. It is the transfer of personal data to a third country itself that constitutes an interference with the right to continuous protection of personal data in cases in which the personal data is not subject to protection essentially equivalent to that guaranteed within the EU after it has been transferred to a third country.

The restrictive effect of the EU system for data transfers materializes in cases in which systemic, structural, and continuous data transfers to third countries take place. Adequacy decisions based on Article 45 GDPR and instruments providing appropriate safeguards based on Article 46 GDPR allow such transfers of personal data. Even though these mechanisms would constitute valid legal bases for an interference with the right to continuous protection of personal data, data transfers fail the proportionality test in cases in which a third country does not provide a level of protection for personal data that is essentially equivalent to that guaranteed within the EU. The objectives of general interest and the rights and freedoms of other identified cannot justify the interference with the right to continuous protection of personal data. The legal mechanisms for data transfers in Articles 45 and 46 GDPR cannot thus be used for systematic, structural, and continuous data transfers in these circumstances.

In contrast, the derogations in Article 49 GDPR, which do not allow for systematic, structural, and continuous transfers of personal data, can be used to limit the right to continuous protection of personal data. If the level of protection for the transferred data is not essentially equivalent to that guaranteed within the EU, occasional transfers of personal data are still possible based on the derogations in Article 49 GDPR. The contract-based derogation in Article 49(1)(b) GDPR provides for a lawful limitation on the right to continuous protection for personal data. This derogation allows occasional data transfers that are necessary for the performance of a contract between the data subject and the controller. Nevertheless, the contract must outline the risks for the personal data of the individual in the third country. In these cases, the limitation on the right to continuous protection for personal data can be justified based on the protection of the freedom to conduct a business in Article 16 CFR. In addition, the consent-based derogation in Article 49(1)(a) GDPR provides for a lawful waiver for the right to continuous protection of personal data. This derogation allows occasional data transfers in cases in which the data subject has explicitly consented to the proposed transfer after having been informed of the possible risks it entails. The waiver set out in Article 49(1)(a) GDPR is lawful because it does not force an individual to waive the right to continuous protection of personal data, allows for a decision made in full knowledge of the surrounding circumstances, requires an unequivocal statement of consent, is attended by minimum safeguards, does not run counter any important public interest, and is not connected with the loss of the right to data protection in Article 8 CFR. Nevertheless—without some sort of agreement of the data subject to the data transfer and the risk it entails—even occasional transfers of personal data are not possible when the level of protection for the transferred personal data is not essentially equivalent to that guaranteed within the EU. The restrictive effects of the EU system for data transfers are firmly rooted in the protection of fundamental rights.

References

Bibliography

Aaronson SA (2015) Why Trade Agreements are not setting information free: the lost history and reinvigorated debate over cross-border data flows, human rights, and national security. World Trade Rev 14(4):671–700

Aaronson SA (2019) What are we talking about when we talk about digital protectionism? World Trade Rev 18(4):541–577

Albrecht J (2016) Das neue EU-Datenschutzrecht – von der Richtlinie zur Verordnung. Überblick und Hintergründe zum finalen Text für die Datenschutz-Grundverordnung der EU nach der Einigung im Trilog. Computer und Recht 32(2):88–98

Albrecht J, Janson N (2016) Datenschutz und Meinungsfreiheit nach der Datenschutzgrundverordnung. Computer und Recht 32(8):500–509

Albrecht J, Jotzo F (2016) Das neue Datenschutzrecht der EU. Nomos, Baden-Baden

Ball J (2013) NSA stores metadata of millions of web users for up to a year, secret files show. Guardian. 30 September 2013. https://www.theguardian.com/world/2013/sep/30/nsa-americans-metadata-year-documents. Accessed 3 Jan 2021

Bartl M, Irion K (2017) The Japan EU Economic Partnership Agreement: Flows of Personal Data to the Land of the Rising Sun. Institute for Information Law University of Amsterdam Commissioned Research Paper

Baumeister D (1990) Grenzüberschreitender Datentransfer und Datenschutz im nicht-öffentlichen Bereich aus der Sicht der Bundesrepublik Deutschland. Recht der Datenverarbeitung 24(1): 23–25

Bennett CJ, Oduro-Marfo S (2018) Global privacy protection: adequate laws, accountable organizations and/or data localization? Proceedings of the UbiComp 18. New York, pp 880–890

Bennett CJ, Raab CD (2006) The governance of privacy: policy instruments in global perspectives. MIT Press, Cambridge

Bignami F, Resta G (2018) Human rights extraterritoriality: the right to privacy and national security surveillance. In: Benvenisti E, Nolte G (eds) Community interests across international law. Oxford University Press, Oxford, pp 357–380

Blume P (2000) Transborder data flow. Is there a solution in sight? Int J Law Inf Technol 1(8): 65–86

Blume P (2015) EU adequacy decisions: the proposed new possibilities. Int Data Priv Law 5(1): 34–39

Burkert H (2000) Privacy - data protection. A German/European perspective. In: Engel C, Keller KH (eds) Governance of global networks in the light of differing local values. Baden-Baden, Nomos, pp 44–69

Bygrave L (2002) Data protection law. Approaching its rationale, logic and limits. Kluwer, The Hague

Caflisch L (2011) Waivers in international and European Human Rights Law. In: Arsanjani MH, Cogan J, Sloane R, Wiessner S (eds) Looking to the future. Essays on international law in Honor of W. Michael Reisman. Martinus Nijhoff, Leiden, pp 407–431

Chander A (2020) Is data localization a solution for Schrems II? J Int Econ Law 23:1–14

Chander A, Le UP (2015) Data nationalism. Emory Law J 64(3):677–739

Cohen E (1992) Metanational information technology, national sovereignty, and social responsibility. In: Khosrowpourj M, Travers J (eds) Emerging information technologies for competitive advantage and economic development. Proceedings of 1992 Information Resources Management Association International Conference, Charleston, 1992, pp 262–268

Colonna L (2014) Article 4 of the EU Data Protection Directive and the irrelevance of the EU – US Safe Harbor Program? Int Data Priv Law 4(3):203–221

Coombe GW Jr, Kirk SL (1983) Privacy, data protection, and transborder data flow: a corporate response to international expectations. Bus Lawyer 39(1):33–66

Corrales Compagnucci M, Aboy M, Minssen T (2021) Cross-border transfers of personal data after Schrems II: supplementary measures and new standard contractual clauses (SCCs). Nordic J Eur Law 4(2):37–47

Delval G (2019) China pushes for approval-based cross-border transfer of personal information overseas. IAPP. 25 June 2019. https://iapp.org/news/a/china-pushes-for-an-approval-based-cross-border-transfer-of-personal-information-overseas/. Accessed 3 Jan 2021

Dove ES, Philipps M (2015) Privacy law, data sharing policies, and medical data: a comparative perspective. In: Gkoulalas-Divanis A, Loukides G (eds) Medical data privacy handbook. Springer, Heidelberg, pp 639–678

Edmundson A, Ensafi R, Feamster N, Rexford J (2016) Characterizing and avoiding routing detours through surveillance states. Princeton University

EDPB (2021) Guidelines 05/2021 on the Interplay between the application of Article 3 and the provisions on international transfers as per Chapter V of the GDPR. 18 November 2021

Eger JM (1979) Emerging restrictions on transnational data flows: privacy protection or non-tariff trade barriers. Law Policy Int Bus 10(4):1055–1104

Farrell H, Newman A (2016) The Transatlantic Data War. Europe Fights Back Against the NSA. Foreign Affairs January/February 2016. https://www.foreignaffairs.com/articles/united-states/2015-12-14/transatlantic-data-war. Accessed 3 Jan 2021

Flint D (2021) Raising the standard. Bus Law Rev 42(5):252–255

Frenz W (2009) Handbuch Europarecht, Band 4 Europäische Grundrechte. Springer, Heidelberg

González Fuster G (2014) The emergence of personal data protection as a fundamental right of the EU. Springer, Heidelberg

González Fuster G (2016) Un-mapping personal data transfers. Eur Data Protect Law Rev 2(2): 160–168

Grabenwarter C (2014) Wirtschaftliche Grundrechte. In: Hatje A, Müller-Graf P-C (eds) Enzyklopädie Europarecht. Band 2: Europäischer Grundrechteschutz. Nomos, Baden-Baden, pp 507–526
Greenleaf G, Bygrave L (2011) Not entirely adequate but far away. Lessons from how Europe sees New Zealand data protection. Priv Law Bus Int Rep 111:8–9
Groussot X, Péturson GT, Pierce J (2017) Weak right, strong Court – the freedom to conduct business and the EU Charter of Fundamental Rights. In: Douglas-Scott S, Hatzis N (eds) Research handbook on EU human rights law. Edward Elgar, Cheltenham, pp 326–344
Gunnarsdótir K (2016) The fifth freedom and the burden of executive power. In: Delgado A (ed) Technoscience and citizenship: ethics and governance of emerging technologies. Springer, Heidelberg, pp 80–98
Günther A (1991) Datenschutzrechtliche Spaltung in Europa? - Teil 1. jur-pc 1991 5:1094–1098
Hallinan D, Friedewald M, McCarthy P (2012) Citizens' perceptions of data protection and privacy in Europe. Comput Law Secur Rev 28(3):263–272
Hamelink C (1994) The politics of world communication. A human rights perspective. Sage Publications, London
Hon WK (2017) Data localization laws and policy. The EU data protection international transfers restriction through a cloud computing lens. Edward Elgar, Cheltenham
Hon WK, Millard C, Jatinder S, Walden I, Crowcroft J (2016) Policy, legal and regulatory implications of a Europe-only cloud. Int J Law Inf Technol 24(3):251–278
Hondius FW (1975) Emerging data protection in Europe. Elsevier, Amsterdam
Hong Y (2017) The cross-border data flows security assessment: an important part of protecting China's basic strategic resources. Yale Law School Paul Tsai China Center Working Paper. 20 June 2017
Jacqué J-P (1980) La Convention pour la protection des personnes à l'égard du traitement automatisé des données à caractère personnel. Annuaire français de droit international 26: 773–789
Jonason P (2019) The Swedish measures accompanying the GDPR. In: McCullagh K, Tambou O, Bourton S (eds) National adaptations of the GDPR. Blogdroiteuropeen, Luxembourg, pp 42–51
Kirby M (1980) International guidelines to protect privacy in transborder data flows. Australian & New Zealand Association for the Advancement of Science Jubilee Congress
Kirby M (2011) The history, achievement and future of the 1980 OECD guidelines on privacy. Int Data Priv Law 1(1):6–15
Kong L (2010) Data protection and transborder data flow in the European and global context. Eur J Int Law 2(21):441–456
Krzemińska-Vamvaka J (2008) Freedom of commercial speech in Europe. Kovač, Hamburg
Krzysztofek M (2017) Post-Reform Personal Data Protection in the European Union. General Data Protection Regulation (EU) 2016/679. Kluwer, Alphen aan den Rijn
Kühling J (2017) Artikel 16 Unternehmerische Freiheit. In: Pechstein M/Nowak C/Häde C (eds) Frankfurter Kommentar zu EUV, GRC und AEUV. Mohr Siebeck, Tübingen, pp 1221–1233
Kuner C (2011) Regulation of Transborder Data Flows under Data Protection and Privacy Law: Past, Present and Future, OECD Digital Economy Papers No. 187. Paris
Kuner C (2013) Transborder data flows. Oxford University Press, Oxford
Kuner C (2017) Reality and illusion in EU data transfer regulation post schrems. German Law J 18(4):881–918
Kuner C (2020) Chapter V transfers of personal data to third countries or international organisations (Articles 44-50). In: Kuner C, Bygrave L, Docksey C (eds) The EU general data protection regulation (GDPR). Oxford University Press, Oxford, pp 755–862
Land M (2013) Toward an international law of the internet. Harv Int Law J 54(2):393–458
Lee-Makiyama H (2018) Japan, not Europe, is now the leader of free trade. The World Post. 10 August 2018. https://www.washingtonpost.com/news/theworldpost/wp/2018/08/10/japan-free-trade/. Accessed 3 Jan 2021
Lucas A (1987) Le droit de l'informatique. Presses Universitaires de France, Paris

Madsen W (1992) Handbook of personal data protection. Stockton Press, New York
Makulilo AB (2013) Data protection regimes in Africa: too far from the European 'adequacy' standard? Int Data Priv Law 3(1).42–50
McGuire RP (1979) The information age. An introduction to transborder data flow. Jurimetrics 20(1):1–7
Mishra N (2016) Data localization laws in a digital world. Data protection or data protectionism? The Public Sphere 2016: 135–158
Mishra N (2019) Building bridges: international trade law, internet governance, and the regulation of data flows. Vanderbilt J Transnatl Law 52(2):464–509
Mouzakiti F (2015) Transborder data flows 2.0: mending the holes of the data protection directive. Eur Data Protect Law Rev 1(1):9–51
Nouwt S (2009) Towards a common European approach to data protection: a critical analysis of data protection perspectives of the Council of Europe and the European Union. In: Gutwirth S, Poullet Y, de Hert P et al (eds) Reinventing data protection? Springer, Heidelberg, pp 275–292
Oesch M (2018) Switzerland and the European Union. Schulthess, Zurich
Oliver P (2013) What purpose does Article 16 of the Charter Serve? In: Bernitz U, Groussot X, Schulyok F (eds) General principles of EU law and European private law. Kluwer, Alphen aan den Rijn, pp 281–300
Ordemann HJ, Schomerus R (1988) Bundesdatenschutzgesetz mit Erläuterungen, 4th edn. Beck, Munich
Patel O, Lea N (2019) EU-UK data flows, Brexit and No-Deal: Adequacy or Disarray? UCL European Institute Brexit Insights Series, London
Peter L (2010) Ireland Delays EU Deal with Israel on Data Transfers. BBC News. 3 September 2010. http://www.bbc.co.uk/news/world-europe-11176926. Accessed 3 Jan 2021
Phillips M (2018) International data-sharing norms: from the OECD to the general data protection regulation (GDPR). Hum Genet 137(8):575–582
Ploman EW (1982) International law governing communications and information. Greenwood Press, Westport
Reidenberg JR (1992) The privacy obstacle course. Hurding barriers to transnational financial services. Fordham Law Rev 60(6):137–177
Room S (2018) No adequacy decision, no panic - PwC comments on the latest European Commission statement on Brexit and EU Data Protection Law. PwC UK. 10 January 2018. https://www.pwc.co.uk/press-room/press-releases/european-commission-data-protection-notice-brexit-adequacy.html. Accessed 3 Jan 2021
Rosas A (2014) Balancing fundamental rights in EU law. Cambridge Yearb Eur Legal Stud 16:347–360
Rotenberg M (2020) *Schrems II*, from Snowden to China: toward a new alignment on transatlantic data protection. Eur Law J 26(1):1–12
Schantz P (2019) Artikel 44-49. In: Simitis S, Hornung G, Spiecker I (eds) Datenschutzrecht. DSGVO mit BDSG. Nomos, Baden-Baden, pp 962–1032
Schwartz PM (1995) Privacy and participation: personal information and public sector regulation in the United States. Iowa Law Rev 80(3):471–496
Schwartz PM (2013) The EU U.S. privacy collision: a turn to institutions and procedures. Harv Law Rev 126(7):1966–2009
Schwartz PM, Peifer K-N (2017) Transatlantic data privacy law. Georgetown Law J 106(1): 115–179
Schwenke MC (2006) Individualisierung und Datenschutz. Rechtskonformer Umgang mit personenbezogenen Daten im Kontext der Individualisierung. Deutscher Universitätsverlag, Wiesbaden
Simitis S (1977) Bundesdatenschutzgesetz – Ende der Diskussion oder Neubeginn? Neue Juristische Wochenschrift 30(17):729–737
Simitis S, Dammann U (1997) EU-Datenschutzrichtlinie Nomos, Baden-Baden

Simitis S, Dammann U, Mallmann O, Reh HJ (1981) Kommentar zum Bundesdatenschutzgesetz, 3rd edn. Nomos, Baden-Baden
Slokenberga S, Reichel J, Niringiye R, Croxton T, Swanepoel C, Okal J (2019) EU data transfer rules and African legal realities: is data exchange for biobank research realistic? Int Data Priv Law 9(1):30–48
Stoddart J, Chan B, Joly Y (2016) The European Union's adequacy approach to privacy and international data sharing in health research. J Law Med Ethics 44(1):143–155
Svantesson DJB (2010) Privacy, internet and transborder data flows. Masaryk Univ J Law Technol 4(1):1–20
Svantesson DJB (2011) The regulation of cross-border data flow. Int Data Priv Law 1(3):180–198
Swire PP (2019) The US, China, and Case 311/18 on Standard Contractual Clauses. European Law Blog. 15 July 2019. https://europeanlawblog.eu/2019/07/15/the-us-china-and-case-311-18-on-standard-contractual-clauses/. Accessed 3 Jan 2021
Tambou O (2019) The French adaptation of the GDPR. In: McCullagh K, Tambou O, Bourton S (eds) National adaptations of the GDPR. Blogdroiteuropéen, Luxembourg, pp 52–60
Tene O (2013) Privacy laws midlife crisis. A critical assessment of the second wave of global privacy laws. Ohio State Law J 74(6):1217–1261
Thiele C (2017) Artikel 11 Freiheit der Meinungsäußerung und Informationsfreiheit. In: Pechstein M, Nowak C, Häde U (eds) Frankfurter Kommentar zu EUV, GRC und AEUV. Mohr Siebeck, Tübingen, pp 1157–1172
Tzanou M (2017) The fundamental right to data protection. Normative value in the context of counter-terrorism surveillance. Hart, Oxford
Walsh J (1978) There's trouble in the air over transborder data flow. Science 202(4363):29–32
Walter C (2014) Kommunikationsfreiheiten. In: Hatje A, Müller-Graf P-C (eds) Enzyklopädie Europarecht. Band 2: Europäischer Grundrechteschutz. Nomos, Baden-Baden, pp 475–506
Weber R (2013) Transborder data transfers: concepts, regulatory approaches and new legislative initiatives. Int Data Priv Law 3(2):117–130
Winkler R (2006) Die Grundrechte der Europäischen Union. Springer, Wien
Wochner LN (1981) Der Persönlichkeitsschutz im grenzüberschreitenden Datenverkehr. Schulthess, Zürich
Wolf C (2014) Delusions of adequacy? Examining the case for finding the United States adequate for cross-border EU-U.S. Data transfers. Wash Univ J Law Policy 43(1):227–257
Woods L (2014) Article 11 – freedom of expression and information. In: Peers S, Hervey R, Kenner J, Ward A (eds) The EU Charter of fundamental rights. A Commentary. Oxford University Press, Oxford, pp 354–383
Woods L (2019) The AG Opinion in Schrems II: Facebook, national security and data protection law. EU Law Analysis, 21 December 2019. http://eulawanalysis.blogspot.com/2019/12/the-ag-opinion-in-schrems-ii-facebook.html. Accessed 3 Jan 2021

Jurisprudence

Datainspektionen, *Salems:* Datainspektionen, Decision of 31 May 2013, *Salems 2013*, 263-2011, 1351-2012
ECJ, AG Opinion, *Alemo-Herron:* ECJ, Opinion of AG Cruz Villalón delivered on 19 February 2013, *Alemo-Herron,* C-426/11, ECLI:EU:C:2013:82
ECJ, AG Opinion, *Germany v. Parliament and Council:* ECJ, Opinion of AG Fennelly delivered on 15 June 2000, *Germany v. Parliament and Council*, C-376/98, EU:C:2000:324
ECJ, AG Opinion, *MSD Sharp:* ECJ, Opinion of AG Trstenjk delivered on 24 November 2010, *MSD Sharp,* C-316/09, EU:C:2010:712

ECJ, AG Opinion, *Satamedia:* ECJ, Opinion of AG Kokott delivered on 8 May 2008, *Satamedia*, C-73/07, EU:C:2008:266

ECJ, AG Opinion, *Schrems:* ECJ, Opinion of AG Bot delivered on 23 September 2015, *Schrems*, C-362/14, EU:C:2015:627

ECJ, AG Opinion, *Schrems 2:* ECJ, Opinion of AG Saugmandsgaard Øe delivered on 19 December 2019, *Schrems 2*, C-311/18, EU:C:2019:1145

ECJ, *Achbita:* ECJ, Judgment of 14 March 2017, *Achbita*, C-157/15, EU:C:2017:203

ECJ, *Affish BV:* ECJ, Judgment of 17 July 1997, *Affish BV,* C-183/95, EU:C:1997:373

ECJ, *Balkan-Import Export GmbH*, ECJ, Judgment of 22 January 1976, *Balkan-Import Export GmbH*, C-55/75, EU:C:1976:8

ECJ, *Digital Rights Ireland:* ECJ, Judgment of 8 April 2014, *Digital Rights Ireland*, C-293/12 and C-594/12, EU:C:2014:238

ECJ, *Germany v. Council (Bananas)*: ECJ, Judgment of 10 March 1998, *Germany v. Council*, C-122/95, EU:C:1998:94

ECJ, *Germany v. Parliament and Council*: ECJ, Judgment of 12 December 2006, *Germany v. Parliament and Council*, C-380/03, EU:C:2006:772.

ECJ, *Lindqvist:* ECJ, Judgment of 6 November 2003, *Lindqvist*, C-101/01, EU:C:2003:596

ECJ, *Melloni:* ECJ, Judgment of 26 February 2013, *Melloni*, C-399/11, EU:C:2013:107

ECJ, Opinion 1/15*:* ECJ, Opinion 1/15 of 26 July 2017, *Draft agreement between Canada and the European Union*, EU:C:2017:592

ECJ, *Parliament v. Council and Commission*: ECJ, Judgment of 30 May 2006, *Parliament v. Council and Commission*, Joined Cases C-317/04 and C-318/04, EU:C:2006:346

ECJ, *Planet 49 GmbH:* ECJ, Judgment of 1 October 2019, *Planet49 GmbH*, C-673/17, EU:C:2019: 801

ECJ, *SABAM:* ECJ, Judgment of 24 November 2011, *SABAM,* C-70/10, EU:C:2011:771

ECJ, *Satamedia*: ECJ, Judgment of 16 December 2008, *Satamedia*, C-73/0756, EU:C:2008:727

ECJ, *Scarlet Extended*: ECJ, Judgment of 24 November 2011, *Scarlet Extended*, C-70/10, EU: C:2011:771

ECJ, *Schecke*: ECJ, Judgment of 9 November 2010, *Schecke*, C-92/09 and C-93/09, EU:C:2010: 662

ECJ, *Schrems:* ECJ, Judgment of 6 October 2015, *Schrems*, C-362/14, EU:C:2015:650

ECJ, *Schrems 2:* ECJ, Judgment of 16 July 2020, *Facebook Ireland and Schrems*, C-311/18, EU: C:2020:559

ECJ, *Sky Österreich:* ECJ, Judgment of 22 January 2013, *Sky Österreich*, C-283/11, EU:C:2013:28

ECJ, *Swiss International Air Lines AG*: ECJ, Judgment of 21 December 2016, *Swiss International Air Lines AG*, C-272/15, EU:C:2016:993

ECJ, *T. Port GmbH*: ECJ, Judgment of 10 March 1998, *T. Port GmbH*, C-364/95 and C-365/ 95, EU:C:1998:95

ECJ, *Tele2/Watson*: ECJ, Judgment of 21 December 2016, *Tele2/Watson*, C-203/15 and C-698/ 15, EU:C:2016:970

ECJ, *WebMindLicenses:* ECJ, Judgment of 17 December 2015, *WebMindLicenses*, C-419/14, EU: C:2015:832

ECJ, *Wirtschaftsakademie Schleswig-Holstein:* ECJ, Judgment of 5 June 2018, *Wirtschaftsakademie Schleswig-Holstein,* C-210/16, EU:C:2018:388

ECtHR, *Autronic AG v. Switzerland:* ECtHR, Judgment of 22 May 1990, *Autronic AG v. Switzerland*, App no. 12726/87

ECtHR, *Casado Coca v. Spain:* ECtHR, Judgment of 24 February 1994, *Casado Coca v. Spain*, App no. 15450/89

ECtHR, *D.H. v. Czech Republic*: ECtHR, Judgment of 13 November 2007, *D.H. v. Czech Republic*, App No. 57325/00

ECtHR, *Markt intern Verlag GmbH and Klaus Beermann v. Germany:* ECtHR, Judgement of 20 November 1989, *Markt intern Verlag GmbH and Klaus Beermann v. Germany*, App no. 10572/83

ECtHR, Neumeister v. *Austria:* ECtHR, Judgment of 7 May 1974, *Neumeister v. Austria*, App no. 1936/63
ECtHR, *Perez v. France*: ECtHR, Judgment of 12 February 2004a, *Perez v. France*, App no. 47287/99
ECtHR, *Thompson v. United Kingdom:* ECtHR, Judgment of 15 June 2004b, *Thompson v. United Kingdom*, App no. 36256/97
IHC, *Schrems 2:* IHC, Judgment of 3 October 2017, *Data Protection Commissioner v. Facebook Ireland and Schrems*, 2016 No. 4809 P 8

Documents

Article 29 WP (1997) First orientations on Transfers of Personal Data to Third Countries - Possible Ways Forward in Assessing Adequacy. WP 4. 26 June 1997
Article 29 WP (1998a) Preliminary views on the use of contractual provisions in the context of transfers of personal data to third countries. WP 9. 22 April 1998
Article 29 WP (1998b) Transfers of personal data to third countries: Applying Articles 25 and 26 of the EU data protection directive. WP 12. 24 July 1998
Article 29 WP (2002) Opinion 04/2002 on the level of protection of personal data in Argentina. WP 63. 3 October 2002
Article 29 WP (2005) Working Document on a common interpretation of Article 26(1) of Directive 95/46/EC of 24 October 1995. WP 114. 25 November 2005
Article 29 WP (2006) Opinion 10/2006 on the processing of personal data by the Society for Worldwide Interbank Financial Telecommunication (SWIFT). WP 128. 22 November 2006
Article 29 WP (2009) Opinion 6/2009 on the level of protection of personal data in Israel. WP 165. 1 December 2009
Article 29 WP (2010) Opinion 02/2010 on online behavioural advertising. WP 171. 22 June 2010
Article 29 WP (2011) Opinion 11/2011 on the level of protection of personal data in New Zealand. WP 182. 4 April 2011
Article 29 WP (2012a) Opinion 05/2012 on Cloud Computing. WP 196. 1 July 2012
Article 29 WP (2012b) Opinion 07/2012 on the level of protection of personal data in the Principality of Monaco. WP 198. 19 July 2012
Article 29 WP (2014) Opinion 7/2014 on the protection of personal data in Quebec. WP 219. 4 June 2014
Article 29 WP (2015) Statement of the Article 29 Working Party. 16 October 2015
Article 29 WP (2018) Guidelines on consent under Regulation 2016/679. WP 259 rev.01. 28 November 2017 as last revised and adopted on 10 April 2018
Bangemann Group (1994) Europe and the global information society. Recommendations of the high-level group on the information society to the Corfu European Council. Luxembourg
CNIL (1989) Délibiration No. 89-78. 10e Rapport. 11 juillet 1989
CNIL (2019) Loi «Informatique et Libertés» et RGPD: ce qui change pour l'outre-mer. 4 juillet 2019
Council of Europe (1981) Explanatory Report to Convention 108: Council of Europe, Explanatory Report to the Convention for the Protection of Individuals with regard to Automatic Processing of Personal Data. 28 January 1981.
Council of Europe (1989) New technologies: a challenge to privacy protection? Study prepared by the Committee of experts on data protection (CJ-PD) under the authority of the European Committee on Legal Co-operation (CDCJ). Strasbourg 1989
Council of Europe (2001) Explanatory Report to the Additional Protocol to the Convention for the Protection of Individuals with regard to Automatic Processing of Personal Data, regarding supervisory authorities and transborder data flows. 8 November 2001

Council of Europe Consultative Committee of Convention 108 (2002) Guide to the preparation of contractual clauses governing data protection during the transfer of personal data to third parties not bound by an adequate level of data protection

Council of Europe/European Commission/ICC (1992) Model contract to ensure equivalent protection in the context of transborder data flows. 2 November 1992

DSK (2015) Positionspapier Safe-Harbor – Update. 26 October 2015

EDPB (2018) Guidelines 2/2018 on derogations of Article 49 under Regulation 2016/6793. 25 May 2018

EDPB (2020) Recommendations 02/2020 on the European Essential Guarantees for surveillance measures. 10 November 2020

EDPS (2011) Opinion on the Communication from the Commission on "A comprehensive approach on personal data protection in the European Union". 14 January 2011

EDPS (2014) The transfer of personal data to third countries and international organisations by EU institutions and bodies. 14 July 2014

EEA Joint Committee (1999) Decision No 83/1999 of 25 June 1999 amending Protocol 37 and Annex XI (Telecommunication services) to the EEA Agreement, [2000] OJ L 296/41

EEA Joint Committee (2018) Decision No 154/2018 of 6 July 2018 amending Annex XI (Electronic communication, audiovisual services and information society) and Protocol 37 (containing the list provided for in Article 101) to the EEA Agreement, [2018] OJ L 183/23

EESC (1991) Opinion on the proposal for a Council Directive concerning the protection of individuals in relation to the processing of personal data [1991] OJ C 159/38. 24 April 1991

EU (2007) Explanations relating to the Charter of Fundamental Rights [2007] OJ C303/17. 14 December 2007

European Commission (1990) Proposal for a Council Directive concerning the protection of individuals in relation to the processing of personal data. [1990] OJ C277/3. 27 July 1990

European Commission (1992) Amended proposal for a Council Directive on the protection of individuals with regard to the processing of personal data and on the free movement of such data. COM(92) 422 final. 15 October 1992

European Commission (2001) Decision 2001/497/EC on standard contractual clauses for the transfer of personal data to third countries, under Directive 95/46/EC [2001] OJ L 181/19. 15 June 2001

European Commission (2003a) First report on the implementation of the Data Protection Directive (95/46/EC). COM(2003) 265 final. 15 May 2003

European Commission (2003b) Decision 2003/821/EC on the adequate protection of personal data in Guernsey [2003] OJ L 308/27. 21 November 2003

European Commission (2004) Decision 2004/915/EC amending Decision 2001/497/EC as regards the introduction of an alternative set of standard contractual clauses for the transfer of personal data to third countries [2004] OJ L 385/74. 27 December 2004

European Commission (2009) Frequently asked questions relating to transfers of personal data from the EU/EEA to third countries. 13 March 2009

European Commission (2010a) Comparative Study on Different Approaches to New Privacy Challenges, in Particular in the Light of Technological Developments. LS/2008/C4/ 011 – 30-CE-0219363/00-28. 20 January 2010

European Commission (2010b) Decision 2010/87/EU on standard contractual clauses for the transfer of personal data to processors established in third countries under Directive 95/46/EC of the European Parliament and of the Council [2010] OJ L 39/5. 5 February 2010

European Commission (2011) A comprehensive approach on personal data protection in the European Union. COM(2010) 609 final. 4 November 2011

European Commission (2012a) Proposal for a Regulation of the European Parliament and of the Council on the protection of individuals with regard to the processing of personal data and on the free movement of such data (General Data Protection Regulation). COM(2012) 11 final. 27 July 1990

European Commission (2012b) Safeguarding Privacy in a Connected World. A European Data Protection Framework for the 21st Century. COM(2012) 9/3. 25 January 2012
European Commission (2015) Communication regarding the Transfer of Personal Data from the EU to the United States of America under Directive 95/46/EC following the Judgment by the Court of Justice in Case C-362/14 (Schrems). COM(2015) 566 final. 6 November 2015
European Commission (2017) Communication on Exchanging and Protecting Personal Data in a Globalised World. COM(2017) 7 final. 10 January 2017
European Commission (2019) Data protection rules as a trust-enabler in the EU and beyond – taking stock. COM(2019) 374 final. 24 July 2019
European Commission (2020) Opening remarks by Vice-President Jourová and Commissioner Reynders at the press point following the judgment in case C-311/18 Facebook Ireland and Schrems. STATEMENT/20/1366. 16 July 2020
European Commission (2021) Implementing Decision (EU) 2021/914 on standard contractual clauses for the transfer of personal data to third countries pursuant to Regulation (EU) 2016/679 of the European Parliament and of the Council [2021] OJ L 199/31. 4 June 2021
European Council (1995) Common Position (EC) No 1/95 with a view to adopting Directive 95/.../EC of the European Parliament and of the Council of... on the protection of individuals with regard to the processing of personal data and on the free movement of such data (95/C 93/01) [1994] OJ C 93/1. 20 February 1995
European Parliament (2013) LIBE, Draft Report on the proposal for a regulation of the European Parliament and of the Council on the protection of individual with regard to the processing of personal data and on the free movement of such data (General Data Protection Regulation). (COM(2012)0011 – C7-0025/2012 – 2012/ 0011(COD)), PE501.927v04-00. 21 November 2013
ICO (2017) The eighth data protection principle and international data transfers. Version 4.1. 30 June 2017
IIF (2019) Data Flows Across Borders. Overcoming Data Localization Restrictions. March 2019
OECD (1980) Explanatory Memorandum. Guidelines governing the protection of privacy and transborder flows of personal data. Annex to the recommendation of the Council of 23 September 1980
OECD (2000) Transborder Data Flow Contracts in the Wider Framework of Mechanisms for Privacy Protection on Global Networks. OECD Digital Economy Papers No. 66. DSTI/ICCP/REG(99)15/FINAL. 21 September 2000
OECD (2018) Trade and cross-border data flows. TAD/TC/WP(2018)19. 21 December 2018
SARK (1979) The Vulnerability of the Computerized Society: Considerations and Proposals. TDRS Doc. No. SW01.01. December 1979
USITC (2013) Digital Trade in the U.S. and Global Economies, Part 1. Investigation No. 332-531. USITC Publication 4415

Part II
International Trade Law

Chapter 4
Restrictions on Data Transfers and the WTO

The WTO is not well-known for being an institution that regulates the free flow of personal data across borders. The trade agreements under the auspices of the WTO either predate or coincide with the invention and early development of the internet. When the WTO was created in 1994, its members agreed to create rules for trade in services. Tim Wu observed that as a consequence, and almost by accident, "the WTO has put itself in an oversight position for most of the national laws and practices that regulate the Internet." Wu (2006). Over a quarter century later, the internet has become indispensable for trade in services, facilitating not only communication and payment between parties involved in any transaction, but also as a platform for the transmission of the services themselves, and the driving technology for the creation of new services. The first section of this chapter shows how cross-border flows of personal data (on the internet) have become intertwined with the supply of many digital services (Sect. 4.1). The second section describes how the rules of the WTO on trade in services are relevant for the regulation of cross-border flows of personal data (Sect. 4.2). These multilateral trade rules can be used as proxies to distinguish between legitimate regulatory concerns and protectionism. Regarding the regulation of cross-border flows of personal data, these rules allow for the legal assessment of the line between data protection and data protectionism. The third section of this chapter analyzes whether the EU's fundamental rights-based regulation of data transfers interferes with the rules of the WTO on trade in services (Sect. 4.3). The fourth section assesses whether the interferences that have been identified can be justified under the relevant exceptions to the rules of the WTO on trade in services (Sect. 4.4).

4.1 Data Flows and Trade in Digital Services

Internet connectivity is rising around the world. The flow of information across the internet's electronic highways has replaced physical proximity for trade in services. Economists estimate that already 50% of the world's traded services are digitized

T. Naef, *Data Protection without Data Protectionism*, EYIEL Monographs - Studies in European and International Economic Law 28,
https://doi.org/10.1007/978-3-031-19893-9_4

(Sect. 4.1.1). A consequence of this development are data localization policies. They require that data is locally stored, processed, and/or accessed. Governments offer a variety of arguments for data localization policies; from avoiding foreign surveillance and promoting users' security and privacy to bolstering domestic law enforcement and securing domestic economic development. The common denominator of these policies is that they affect trade in digital services. In this regard, the EU's fundamental rights-based regulation of data transfers may also have the effect of a data localization policy (Sect. 4.1.2). Many digital services rely on cross-border flows of personal data. Some services require systematic, structural, and continuous flows of personal data (Sect. 4.1.3), other services require only occasional flows of personal data (Sect. 4.1.4).

4.1.1 Trade in Digital Services

The internet is growing fast and has brought both disruption and innovation.[1] It has become indispensable for trade, facilitating not only communication and payment between parties involved in any transaction, but also acting as a platform for the transmission of goods and services, and the driving technological force for the creation of new products. This research focuses on digital services because they are usually associated with cross-border flows of personal data. For a long time, many services were considered to be non-tradable because it is in their nature that the provision coincides with the consumption and thus requires physical proximity and the interaction of the seller and the buyer.[2] When services were first considered as trade, it was usually the movements of individuals or organizations across borders that brought sellers and buyers into physical and temporal proximity. The internet has created new means of supply: electronic highways that allow sellers and buyers to remain apart while exchanging digital services.[3] The flow of information across the network bridge replaces physical proximity. Economists estimate that already 50% of the world's traded services are digitized.[4] In short, the once non-tradable became hyper-tradable.[5]

[1] ITU (2019), p. 1; Cisco (2019), pp. 1, 4–5.

[2] Burri (2019), p. 86.

[3] For early predictions of the importance of these electronic highways for trade in services see Drake and Nicolaidis (1992), p. 48 with further references in fn. 19.

[4] A pilot survey of the UNCTAD included Costa Rica (39%), India (57%), the US (over 50%), and the EU (52% or 56% when excluding intra-EU trade). UNCTAD (2015), pp. 4–5.

[5] See WTO (2019a), pp. 14–15.

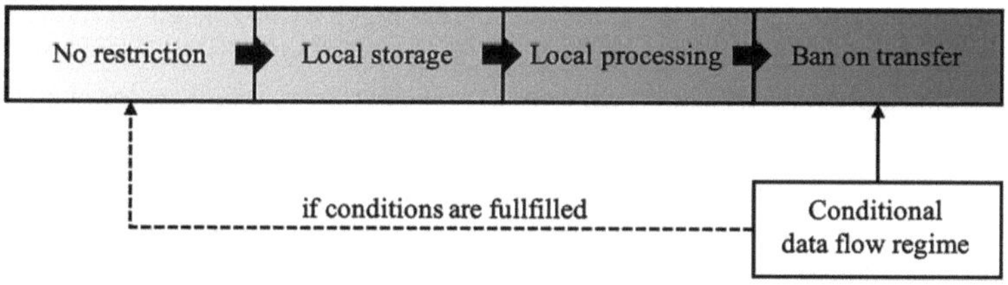

Fig. 4.1 Taxonomy for restrictions on transborder data flows

4.1.2 Data Localization

A consequence of the growth of the internet are data localization policies. There is no settled definition for data localization, but it is widely understood that such policies limit the free flow of data across borders.[6] Data localization policies take different forms. They may include rules preventing information from being sent outside a country, requirements to obtain prior consent of data subjects before information about them is transmitted across borders, obligations to store copies of information domestically, and even taxes on the export of data.[7] Governments offer a variety of arguments for data localization policies; from avoiding foreign surveillance and promoting users' security and privacy, to bolstering domestic law enforcement and securing economic development. Martina Ferracane created a taxonomy for data localization policies based on restrictions on cross-border data flows:[8]

A. Strict restrictions on cross-border data flows:

    I. Local storage requirement
    II. Local storage and processing requirement
    III. Ban on data transfer (local storage, processing, and access requirement)

B. Conditional restrictions on cross-border data flows:

    IV. Conditional flow regime in which conditions apply to the recipient country
    V. Conditional flow regime in which conditions apply to the controller/processor

Ferracane distinguishes between strict restrictions on cross-border data flows and conditional restrictions on cross-border data flows:

- Strict restrictions apply without conditions for the recipient country or the controller/processor. Local storage means that data cannot be transferred unless

[6]Brehmer (2018), p. 930; Sen (2018), p. 326; Saluzzo (2017), p. 808; Sargsyan (2016), p. 2222; Chander and Le (2015), p. 680.

[7]Chander and Le (2015), p. 680.

[8]See Ferracane (2017), p. 3.

a copy of the data is stored domestically. As long as a copy is saved in the territory of the country where it is produced, data storage and processing can also take place outside the country and companies can operate as usual. A local storage and processing requirement requires companies to use data centers located in the country for the main processing of the data. Companies must either build data centers or switch to local providers for data processing solutions (or leave the market altogether). A ban on data transfers also requires companies to access the data only locally.

– Conditional data flow regimes apply conditions to the recipient country and/or to the data controller or data processor (see Fig. 4.1). The cross-border flow of personal data is prohibited unless these conditions are fulfilled. If the conditions are not satisfied, then such a data flow regime constitutes a ban on data transfers (i.e. a requirement for local storage, processing, and access).

The regulation of data transfers in the EU constitutes a conditional data flow regime. It entails legal mechanisms for the transfer of personal data with conditions that apply to the recipient country (adequacy decisions according to Article 45 GDPR), legal mechanisms with conditions that apply to the data exporter and data importer in which conditions for the recipient country also play a role (instruments providing appropriate safeguards according to Article 46 GDPR), and legal mechanisms with conditions that apply only to the data exporter (derogations for specific situations according to Article 49 GDPR). Should the respective conditions not be fulfilled, the transfer of personal data is prohibited.[9]

The regulation of data transfers in the EU has the effect of a data localization policy.[10] Exporters of personal data may be subject to data localization in the EU if they require systematic, structural, and continuous transfers of personal data for the supply of their services and the recipient country lacks an adequacy decision or the data exporter cannot ensure a level of protection that is essentially equivalent to that guaranteed within the EU for the respective data transfers with the instruments providing appropriate safeguards. In addition, data exporter may be subject to data localization in the EU if they require occasional transfers of personal data for the supply of their services and the data transfers are not necessary for the performance of a contract and data subjects do not consent to the respective transfers of personal data.

[9] See Sect. 3.1.4.1.

[10] Chander (2020), pp. 777–778; Sen (2018), p. 325; Mishra (2016), p. 140. Anecdotal evidence shows that several foreign service providers have had to relocate or build new data centers in the EU because of the EU regulation of data transfers. Korolov (2018).

4.1.3 Services with Systematic Flows of Personal Data

Personal data is increasingly intertwined with trade in digital services. Personal data can be an input factor to customize or make a service better, but it can also be a factor of production because some services are impossible to provide without it. In addition, personal data can be a form of payment for the delivery of services in so far as companies monetize the free delivery of their services by using consumers' personal data to better target advertising. Finally, personal data can also be a service itself because it contains valuable information that is sold to companies for different purposes.[11] Digital services therefore often require cross-border flows of personal data. Research on the interface of personal data and international trade law so far has not distinguished between different types of services.[12] These distinctions are necessary for a detailed analysis of international trade law.[13] The most important distinction that has to be made is between services that require systematic, structural, and continuous cross-border flows of personal data and those that do not. The following list entails examples for services that require systematic, structural, and continuous cross-border flows of personal data: cloud computing services (Sect. 4.1.3.1), search engine services (Sect. 4.1.3.2), social network services (Sect. 4.1.3.3), internet of things services (Sect. 4.1.3.4), and sharing economy platform services (Sect. 4.1.3.5).

4.1.3.1 Cloud Computing Services

Cloud computing is a term used to refer to the delivery of computing services over the internet. It allows for tapping into data and software from the internet, rather than accessing it offline via a personal device or a local server.[14] Cloud computing has a hybrid nature as a service. It can be a service itself and, at the same time, it enables many other digital services. Three forms of cloud computing must be distinguished:

- Software as a service (SaaS): The cloud provider offers software applications on its computing infrastructure and the consumer uses the provider's application on various client devices.

[11] So-called data brokers collect and sell information about individuals. Yakovleva and Irion (2018), p. 17.

[12] Velli (2019), p. 887; Saluzzo (2017), pp. 823–824; Yakovleva and Irion (2016), p. 202; Reyes (2011), p. 22; but see Shaffer (2000), p. 48.

[13] See Sect. 4.3.3.

[14] Urs Gasser and John Palfrey also provide a more specific definition for cloud computing: "A model for enabling ubiquitous, convenient, on-demand network access to a shared pool of configurable computing resources (for example networks, servers, storage, applications, and services) that can be rapidly provisioned and released with minimal management effort or service provider interaction." Gasser and Palfrey (2012), p. 142.

- Platform as a service (PaaS): The cloud provider offers tools and programming languages on its computing infrastructure and the consumer-producers can create or acquire applications with them.
- Infrastructure as a service (IaaS): The cloud provider only offers the computing infrastructure and the consumer can rent it for processing, storage, and other computing activities.

Cloud computing services may involve cross-border flows of personal data when servers are (also) located outside of the EU.

4.1.3.2 Search Engine Services

Search engines crawl the internet and index the results for search queries.[15] Consumers get access to databases containing a plethora of websites and the information contained therein. Search engines are usually cloud-based. Alphabet is a well-known example of a company that operates a search engine (Google) and exports large amounts of personal data from individuals using their search engine in the EU to the US. However, this cross-border flow of personal data is not directly linked to the supply of search engine services. In the ECJ case *Google Spain and Google*, the referring *Audiencia Nacional* (Spanish National High Court) established that Google does not merely give access with its search engine to content hosted on the indexed websites, but takes advantage of the users' search activity and includes, in return for payment, advertising associated with the users' search terms.[16] Alphabet has recourse to its subsidiaries in EU member states, such as Google Spain, for promoting the sale of its advertising space. Even though the ECJ held that Alphabet's "advertising activity [. . .] is separate from its search engine service," the Court also found that the activities "are inextricably linked since the activities relating to the advertising space constitute the means of rendering the search engine at issue economically profitable and that engine is, at the same time, the means enabling those activities to be performed."[17] Accordingly, search engines do not necessarily require cross-border flows of personal data for the supply search engine services, but for the corresponding *targeted* advertising services.

4.1.3.3 Social Network Services

Social networks are online platforms encompassing digital relationships between individuals, groups, organizations, or even entire societies. The structure of a social network is determined by interactions between persons or entities. Users share

[15] Chen (2018), p. 298; Brin and Page (1998), p. 108.

[16] See ECJ, *Google Spain and Google*, para. 43.

[17] Ibid., paras 51, 56. See also ECJ, *Google v. CNIL*, para. 50.

values and beliefs among the community and form social links with other users of the network.[18] Facebook is a well-known example of a company that operates a social network and exports a large amount of personal data of users residing in the EU to its parent company Meta in the US.[19] Although the cross-border flows of personal data are also used for targeted advertising services, social networks still require those data flows for the supply of their main services. Social networks use the information that users upload to connect them with other users of the network.

4.1.3.4 Internet of Things Services

The term "internet of things" (IoT) refers to the interconnection of computing devices embedded in everyday objects, enabling them to send and receive data. The IoT allows companies to create large sets of data generated by sensors on the respective objects, analyze it, train algorithms with it, and find patterns that can be used either in the supply of services or in the creation of new services. Companies using IoT sensor data often store and process the collected data in servers located outside of the EU.[20] Two examples can illustrate how IoT services require cross-border flows of personal data:

- The first example of IoT services relates to vehicles. Vehicles such as automobiles are increasingly connected to the internet and transmit information to the manufacturer and other service providers. This information may include client data, the vehicle serial number or any other unique identifier of the vehicle such as the license plate number, geolocation data, technical data relating to the state of the vehicle and its parts, the driver's biometric data and data relating to the use of the vehicle by the driver or the occupants.[21] This information includes personal data and allows the manufacturer and other service providers to supply specific services across borders such as maintenance services or services relating to improvements of the driving experience. These services may involve cross-border flows of personal data.

The second example of IoT services relates to fridges. Smart fridges take care of food management by assessing the contents of the refrigerator with the help of sensors. They can track food preferences as well as search and even order groceries from online stores. Various traits of the smart fridge owners' eating behaviors can be inferred based on the collected data. Smart fridges also use client data and credit card information. This information includes personal data and allows the manufacturer or other service providers to supply specific services across borders such as restocking services. Those services may involve cross-border flows of personal data.

---

[18] Weber and Burri (2012), p. 115.

[19] See IHC, *Schrems 2*, para. 35.

[20] Urquhart et al. (2019), p. 6.

[21] CNIL (2017), p. 6.

4.1.3.5 Sharing Economy Platform Services

The term "sharing economy" refers to a "peer-to-peer-based activity of obtaining, giving, or sharing access to goods and services, coordinated through community-based online services."[22] Companies usually provide a web-based or mobile application, which suppliers and customers use to buy and sell goods or services. These companies offer a platform service. In offering that platform, the companies themselves also supply a service. Two examples can illustrate how sharing economy platform services require cross-border flows of personal data:

- The first example relates to lodging. Companies provide a platform for arranging lodging, primarily homestays, or tourism experiences. The companies do not own any of the real estate listings, nor do they host events, they only act as a broker, receiving commission from each booking over their platform. Airbnb is a well-known example of such a company. The application coordinating the bookings involves cross-border flows of personal data.

The second example relates to passenger transportation. Companies provide a platform for arranging ride-hailing or transportation services. Again, the companies do not own any of the cars used for the services nor do they usually employ the drivers of the cars. The companies only act as a broker, receiving commission from each booking over their platform. Uber is a well-known example of such a company. The application coordinating the bookings involves cross-border flows of personal data.

4.1.4 Services with Occasional Flows of Personal Data

Not all digital services require systematic, structural, and continuous cross-border flows of personal data for their performance. The following list entails examples of services that only require occasional cross-border flows of personal data: travel agency services (Sect. 4.1.4.1), digital medical services (Sect. 4.1.4.2), and legal services (Sect. 4.1.4.3).

4.1.4.1 Travel Agency Services

Travel agencies organize voyages, holidays, and other international activities for their clients. They often must transfer personal data of their clients in their communication with hotels or other commercial partners for the organization of their clients'

[22] Hamari et al. (2016), p. 2047.

stay abroad. These cross-border flows of personal data are occasional and tailored to the specific wishes of the clients.[23]

4.1.4.2 Digital Medical Services

Digital medical services supplied across borders include e-health applications for online diagnosis and medical transcription.[24] The handling of personal data concerning the health of an individual is subject to the strict rules on processing of special categories of personal data in Article 9 GDPR. Where data is aggregated for the supply of digital medical services, it is possible to anonymize the personal data of an individual or a number of individuals.[25] This is difficult for personalized services. In that case, there will be occasional flows of personal data that are tailored to the specific wishes or needs of the patient.[26]

4.1.4.3 Legal Services

The legal industry is an industry founded upon the exchange of information. Lawyers often face transactions involving multiple countries and are required to provide services and advice in more than one jurisdiction. Legal services supplied across borders include document review, due diligence in large-scale litigation or corporate transactions, basic contract drafting, and legal research.[27] The information necessary for the supply of digital legal services may involve personal data.[28] The supply of digital legal services is on demand and personalized to individuals, and thus cross-border flows of personal data are usually only occasional.

4.1.5 Summary

The EU's fundamental rights-based regulation of data transfers is a conditional data flow regime that has the effect of a data localization policy. Different digital services require different types of cross-border flows of personal data. Data exporters may be

[23] Article 29 WP (2018c), p. 8.

[24] Blouin et al. (2006), pp. 203–207.

[25] The principles of data protection should not apply to anonymous information according to Recital (26) GDPR, namely information which does not relate to an identified or identifiable natural person or to personal data rendered anonymous in such a manner that the data subject is not or no longer identifiable.

[26] If these services are not used sporadically when health issues arise but regularly or on an ongoing way, such data flows will be systematic as well.

[27] Susskind (2013), p. 26.

[28] Collins (2019), p. 89.

subject to data localization in the EU if they require systematic, structural, and continuous flows of personal data across borders for the supply of their services and the destination country lacks an adequacy decision or a data exporter cannot ensure a level of protection that is essentially equivalent to that guaranteed within the EU. Data exporters may also be subject to data localization in the EU if they require occasional flows of personal data across borders for the supply of their digital services and the transfer of personal data is not necessary for the performance of a contract and the data subject does not consent to the transfer of personal data.

4.2 Data Flows and the Law on Trade in Services

Multilateral trade rules can be used as proxies to distinguish legitimate regulatory concerns and protectionism. The rules for trade in services in WTO law are codified in the GATS (Sect. 4.2.1). In addition, the GATS Annex on Telecommunications specifically requires WTO members to grant access to their internet network. The use of foreign internet networks is quintessential for cross-border flows of personal data (Sect. 4.2.2). When the GATS was drafted, many digital services that now rely on the free flow of personal data were not yet invented. Nevertheless, I show that most digital services are covered by the commitments in the schedules of WTO members (Sect. 4.2.3). Current negotiations at the WTO also turn to personal data as an important asset for the global economy. The conclusion of the e-commerce negotiations might see the inclusion of a provision on the free flow of personal data across borders in WTO law (Sect. 4.2.4).

4.2.1 General Agreement on Trade in Services

The GATS aims at protecting the equality of competitive opportunities for companies in domestic markets, irrespective of their origin or the origin of their services, all while recognizing the right of WTO members to regulate in order to meet domestic public policy objectives. The GATS applies to measures that affect trade in services (Sect. 4.2.1.1). It entails general obligations for WTO members (Sect. 4.2.1.2) and obligations subject to the specific commitments in their schedules (Sect. 4.2.1.3). Different exceptions can justify GATS-inconsistent measures (Sect. 4.2.1.4).

4.2.1.1 Scope

The GATS does not offer a definition of services (Sect. 4.2.1.1.1). It rather encompasses four modes by which services can be traded (Sect. 4.2.1.1.2). The liberalization of trade in services follows a positive list approach. A WTO member is required to open its markets to foreign services and service suppliers when it commits to do so in its schedule of specific commitments (Sect. 4.2.1.1.3). The rules in the GATS apply when measures of WTO members affect trade in services (Sect. 4.2.1.1.4).

4.2.1.1.1 Services

The GATS does not offer a definition of services.[29] Article I:3(b) GATS describes services as "any services in any sector except supplied in the exercise of governmental authority." In the context of the GATS, services need to be classified along different sectors. The GATT Secretariat provided a list of classifications to the negotiating parties in 1991.[30] The Service Sectoral Classification List (W/120) consists of 11 broad service sectors and a residual category "Other Services Not Included Elsewhere." The W/120 is intended to be comprehensive.[31] It is further divided into over 150 subsectors. Each sector and various subsectors also include a residual category "Other Services." The subsectors are normally annotated with the relevant numbers of the 1991 Provisional Central Product Classification (CPCprov), which was prepared by the UN for the purpose of trade statistics.[32] The CPCprov numbers in the W/120 classification also point to the corresponding explanatory notes in the CPCprov that describe what is covered by the listed services. Although the W/120 is not a mandatory classification system, almost all WTO members follow the structure of the W/120 for the classification of services when scheduling their commitments under the GATS.

4.2.1.1.2 Supply of Services

The supply of services is defined in Article XXVIII(b) GATS and includes the production, distribution, marketing, sale, and delivery of a service. The GATS encompasses four modes by which services can be supplied:

- Mode 1, cross-border supply: The service provider is domiciled in its own country and delivers the services to a customer domiciled in another WTO member (Article I:2(a) GATS).
- Mode 2, consumption abroad: The service is used by a customer in the country of origin of the service supplier, but the customer using the service comes from a different WTO member (Article I:2(b) GATS).
- Mode 3, commercial presence: The service provider establishes a domicile within the territory of another WTO member, and the service is delivered by this

[29] Van den Bossche and Zdouc (2017), p. 329; Matsushita et al. (2015), p. 560; Munin (2010), p. 21; Zacharias (2008), p. 38; WTO AB Report, *Argentina – Financial* Services, para. 6.27.

[30] GATT Secretariat (1991).

[31] Van den Bossche and Zdouc (2017), pp. 526–527; Matsushita et al. (2015), p. 561; Munin (2010), p. 140; Molinuevo (2008), pp. 450–451.

[32] UN (1991).

commercial presence to a customer within the same territory (Article I:2(c) GATS).
- Mode 4, presence of natural persons: The service provider is present with natural persons within the territory of another WTO member and the service is delivered by the natural persons to a customer within the same territory (Article I:2(d) GATS).

The four modes are not only of definitional value for trade in services, they are also used as a pattern to schedule the specific commitments of WTO members.[33]

4.2.1.1.3 Schedules

The GATS regulates trade in services with a positive list approach.[34] A WTO member is only bound to open its markets to foreign services and service suppliers when it commits to do so in its schedule of specific commitments. Article XX:1 GATS requires each WTO member to submit such a schedule that specifies:

(a) the terms, limitations, and conditions on market access;
(b) conditions and qualifications on national treatment;
(c) undertakings relating to additional commitments;
(d) where appropriate the time-frame for implementation of such commitments; and
(e) the day of entry into force of such commitments.

Most WTO members base their schedule on the Service Sectoral Classification List (W/120) provided by the GATT Secretariat. In practice, the schedules of WTO members represent a codification of the conditions in their market upon which a foreign service provider can rely and which can be enforced in WTO dispute settlement. A WTO member can modify or withdraw a commitment only according to the rules in Article XXI GATS, usually by making concessions in the form of compensatory adjustments in other areas.[35] The schedules of specific commitments of the WTO members are appended to the GATS and form an integral part of the Agreement according to Article XX:3 GATS. They are legally binding and subject to WTO dispute settlement as explicitly stated in Article XXIII:1 GATS.

4.2.1.1.4 Measures Affecting Trade in Services

The GATS applies to measures affecting trade in services according to Article I:1 GATS. The AB explained in *Canada – Autos* that the "determination of whether a

[33] Van den Bossche and Zdouc (2017), p. 527; Matsushita et al. (2015), pp. 590–591; Munin (2010), p. 131; Molinuevo (2008), pp. 454–455.

[34] Matsushita et al. (2015), p. 586; Munin (2010), p. 126; Molinuevo (2008), p. 451.

[35] See generally Van den Bossche and Zdouc (2017), pp. 532–534; Matsushita et al. (2015), p. 593; Nartova (2008), pp. 467–471.

measure is, in fact, covered by the GATS must be made before the consistency of that measure with any substantive obligation of the GATS can be assessed."[36] The threshold examination involves two elements.[37] There must be trade in services and there must be a measure of a WTO member state that affects this trade in services. The AB concluded in *EC – Bananas III* that "the use of the term 'affecting' reflects the intent of the drafters to give a broad reach to the GATS."[38] Importantly, for a measure to be considered to affect trade in services it is not necessary that the measure directly addresses such trade.[39] The panel underlined in *EC – Bananas III* that the "GATS encompasses any measure of a Member to the extent it affects the supply of a service regardless of whether such measure directly governs the supply of a service or whether it regulates other matters but nevertheless affects trade in services."[40] Many services require cross-border flows of personal data.[41] Any restriction on such data flows would affect trade in those services. Even if the EU system for data transfers does not directly govern the supply of services, it falls within the scope of the GATS.

4.2.1.2 General Obligations

The GATS entails general obligations that apply to all measures affecting trade in services, irrespective of the specific commitments undertaken by WTO members in their schedules. Two general obligations in the GATS are especially important for cross-border flows of personal data: The most-favored nation (MFN) treatment obligation in Article II GATS (Sect. 4.2.1.2.1) and the domestic regulation obligation in Article VI GATS (Sect. 4.2.1.2.2).

4.2.1.2.1 MFN Treatment

The core general obligation of the GATS is the MFN treatment obligation in Article II GATS. It requires each WTO member to accord immediately and unconditionally to services and service suppliers of any other WTO member treatment no less favorable than that it accords to like services and service suppliers of any other country. The MFN treatment obligation prohibits discrimination between different foreign services and services suppliers. It captures both *de jure* and *de facto*

---

[36] WTO AB Report, *Canada – Autos*, para. 151.

[37] Ibid., para. 155; cp. Van den Bossche and Zdouc (2017), pp. 328–329; see generally Matsushita et al. (2015), pp. 565–567; Munin (2010), pp. 60–85; Zacharias (2008), p. 37.

[38] WTO AB Report, *EC – Bananas III*, para. 220.

[39] Saluzzo (2017), p. 818.

[40] WTO Panel Report, *EC – Bananas III*, para. 7.285.

[41] See Sects. 4.1.3 and 4.1.4.

discrimination.[42] The MFN treatment obligation applies to any measure affecting trade in services irrespective of whether specific commitments have been undertaken.[43] WTO members were allowed to list exemptions from the MFN treatment obligation in the Annex on Article II Exemptions until the date of entry into force of the WTO Agreement on 1 January 1995. Paragraph 6 Annex on Article II Exemptions states that, in principle, the exemptions should not exceed ten years.[44] The EU did not list any exemption from the MFN treatment obligation relating to cross-border flows of personal data, or data protection in general.[45]

Article II:1 GATS identifies a mode for comparison and establishes that there shall be no discrimination against services and service suppliers of any WTO member compared to like services and services suppliers of any other country. The basis of comparison is the likeness of services and service suppliers. The AB clarified in *Argentina – Financial Services* that the phrase "like services and service suppliers" should be seen as "an integrated element for the likeness analysis."[46] It serves to assess the competitive relationship of the services and service suppliers at issue.[47] The criteria traditionally employed as analytical tools for assessing likeness in the context of trade in goods may also be employed in assessing likeness in the context of trade in services, provided that they are adapted as appropriate to account for the specific characteristics of trade in services.[48] The four criteria are properties, nature, and quality of the products; the end-uses of the products; consumers' tastes and habits or consumers' perceptions and behavior in respect of the products; and the tariff classification of the products.[49] The AB implied in *Argentina – Financial Services* that a consideration of the nature and characteristics of a service transaction may be seen as an appropriate adaptation of the original criterion of properties.[50] Similarly, the AB stated with respect to the original criterion of tariff classification that the classification under the CPCprov will be relevant for trade in services.[51]

---

[42] WTO AB Report, *Argentina – Financial Services*, para. 6.105; WTO AB Report, *EC – Bananas III*, para. 233; see generally Van den Bossche and Zdouc (2017), pp. 326–327; Matsushita et al. (2015), pp. 570–571; Munin (2010), pp. 117–118; Wolfrum (2008), p. 88.

[43] WTO Panel Report, *EC – Bananas III*, para. 7.298.

[44] Many WTO members continue to apply the exemptions they listed. They argue that Paragraph 6 Annex on Article II Exemptions does not explicitly forbid their continuous application. The reviews of the Council for Trade in Services did not result in any finding that a listed exemption was no longer justified.

[45] See Yakovleva and Irion (2016), p. 197 fn. 46.

[46] WTO AB Report, *Argentina – Financial Services*, para. 6.29.

[47] Ibid.

[48] Ibid., para. 6.31; see generally Van den Bossche and Zdouc (2017), pp. 332–335; Matsushita et al. (2015), pp. 568–570; Munin (2010), pp. 122–124; Wolfrum (2008), pp. 82–85.

[49] GATT (1970), para. 18.

[50] WTO AB Report, *Argentina – Financial Services*, para. 6.32; WTO Panel Report, *EC – Bananas III*, para. 7.322.

[51] Ibid.

It could be asserted that a high level of data protection influences the likeness analysis in so far as it affects the nature and characteristics of a service transaction as well as consumers' perceptions and behavior in respect of a service and service supplier. Such an assertion stands on shaky ground. It would require a very specific example to prove that a high level of data protection can alter the very nature or important characteristics of a service transaction. For example, the level of data protection in a state does not affect the nature and the characteristics of search engine services. The search engine services might be more customized to an individual when supplied by a state with a low level of data protection. Nevertheless, the very nature or important characteristics of search engine services are not altered. Even consumers' perceptions and behavior in respect to a service and service supplier are not different based on the level of data protection. Individual consumers clearly value data protection and privacy, but often act irrationally so that the result that their preferences do not manifest in their choices.[52] End use and classification under the CPCprov are the same regardless of the level of data protection. A high level of data protection cannot (yet) be held to have distinctively altered the competitive relationship between services and service suppliers for the purposes of the GATS.[53]

Article II:1 GATS requires treatment no less favorable between like services and service suppliers of any country. The concept of "treatment no less favorable" focuses on a measure's modification of the conditions of competition.[54] This legal standard is met in cases in which a WTO member intrudes into the competitive relationship between service suppliers or services. It is not sufficient under Article II GATS to accord a WTO member similar treatment to that accorded to another country. By virtue of the MFN treatment obligation, the WTO member is rather to be given exactly the same treatment as the other country.[55] That treatment must be afforded immediately and unconditionally.

4.2.1.2.2 Domestic Regulation

A second important general obligation is the domestic regulation obligation in Article VI GATS. The preamble of the GATS entails two potentially antagonizing objectives.[56] First, the preamble expresses the wish to expand trade in services as a means of promoting the economic growth of all trading partners. Second, the preamble also recognizes the right of WTO members to regulate and introduce

52 The so-called privacy paradox. See Yakovleva and Irion (2016), p. 204; Barth and de Jong (2017), p. 1038.

53 Cp. Yakovleva and Irion (2016), p. 204; Velli (2019), p. 885.

54 WTO AB Report, *Argentina – Financial* Services, para. 6.105; WTO AB Report, *EC – Bananas III*, paras 244, 246, 248; see generally Van den Bossche and Zdouc (2017), pp. 570–571; Matsushita et al. (2015), p. 571; Munin (2010), pp. 118–120; Wolfrum (2008), p. 87.

55 Wolfrum (2008), p. 88.

56 Krajewski (2003), p. 59.

new regulations on the supply of services within their territories in order to meet national policy objectives. The panel in *US – Gambling* underlined that "regulatory sovereignty is an essential pillar of the progressive liberalization of trade in services, but this sovereignty ends whenever rights of other Members under the GATS are impaired."[57] The panel also stressed that "Members maintain the sovereign right to regulate within the parameters of Article VI of the GATS."[58]

Four paragraphs of Article VI GATS relate to the application, administration, and review of regulatory measures and therefore provide procedural standards (Article VI:1-3 and 6 GATS). Two paragraphs relate to the content of regulatory measures and therefore provide substantive guidance (Article VI:4 and 5 GATS).[59] Article VI:1 and 2 GATS are particularly important for cross-border flows of personal data and the supply of services.[60]

Article VI:1 GATS obligates WTO members to administer measures of general application affecting trade in services in sectors where specific commitments are undertaken in "a reasonable, objective, and impartial manner."[61] A measure of general application covers a range of cases and situations and thus affects an unidentified number of economic operators.[62] The EU system for data transfers is a measure of general application.

There is little guidance as to what makes something "reasonable, objective and impartial." Joel Trachtman has argued that Article VI:1 GATS might imply a proportionality requirement, meaning that the regulatory burden imposed on foreign services and service suppliers must not be disproportionate in relation to the policy objective pursued.[63] It seems that this would produce an overlap with the requirements for the application of general exceptions in Article XIV GATS.[64] Furthermore, the negotiation history of the GATS does not support this argument. The

[57] WTO Panel Report, *US – Gambling*, para. 6.316.

[58] Ibid.

[59] See ibid., para. 6.432; Krajewski (2008), p. 167.

[60] First, Article VI:3 GATS does not apply to the EU' system for data transfers because it not an authorization requirement for the supply of services. See Yakovleva and Irion (2016), p. 205. Contra Reyes (2011), p. 20. Second, Article VI:4 and 5 GATS do not apply to the EU regulation of data transfers either because it is not a technical standard in the sense of a measure that lays down the characteristics of a service or the manner in which it is supplied. Contra Weber (2012), p. 37.

[61] Even though Article VI GATS is a general obligation, its first paragraph is applicable only for sectors in which a WTO member has undertaken specific commitments. It is not clear whether this requires commitments in both market access and national treatment columns, but the general wording seems to suggest that specific commitments in one domain are sufficient. Wouters and Coppens (2008), p. 217; see generally Van den Bossche and Zdouc (2017), p. 535; Munin (2010), pp. 272–275; Krajewski (2008), pp. 168–172.

[62] Cp. WTO Panel Report, *EC – Selected Custom Matters*, para. 7.116 (on Article X:1 GATT); WTO Panel Report, *US – Underwear*, para. 7.65 (on Article X:1 GATT). See Munin (2010), pp. 272–273; Krajewski (2008), pp. 169–170.

[63] Trachtman (2003), p. 66.

[64] Saluzzo (2017), p. 825 fn. 84.

negotiators explicitly refused to impose a general necessity test on domestic regulation.[65]

The ordinary meaning of the terms and previous panel reports on Article X:3(a) GATT—which is the equivalent provision for trade in goods—give indications regarding the applicable standards.[66] The administration of a measure is "reasonable" if it is in accordance with generally accepted standards of rationality and of sound judgment.[67] There must be a rational reason for the conduct in question.[68] For the administration of a measure to be "objective," its application should not be arbitrary.[69] Lastly, the administration of a measure is "impartial" if the application of the relevant laws and regulations is fair, unbiased, and unprejudiced.[70] Giving special consideration or privileges to one party or commercial interest without giving the same consideration or privileges to other parties or commercial interests is not impartial.[71] Even though the three standards in Article VI:1 GATS are closely linked and serve similar functions, they are separate legal obligations.[72] All three must be satisfied if Article VI:1 GATS is not to be interfered with. However, to constitute an interference with Article VI:1 GATS, there must be "a significant impact on the overall administration of the law, and not simply on the outcome in the single case in question."[73]

Article VI:2(a) GATS requires WTO members to maintain practicable, judicial, arbitral or administrative tribunals or procedures that provide for the prompt review of administrative decisions affecting trade in services, and where justified, appropriate remedies[74] The requirement of providing review and appeal procedures leave considerable discretion to WTO members.[75] In cases in which the procedures are not independent from the institution entrusted with the relevant administrative decision, WTO members must at least ensure that the procedures are objective and impartial.[76] An appropriate remedy involves either the possibility of replacing an incorrect

65 GATT Secretariat (1971), Article VII; Pauwelyn (2005), 138 fn. 24.

66 Article VI:1 GATS is modelled on Article X:3(a) GATT. The case law relating to Article X:3(a) GATT can be used to guide the interpretation of Article VI:1 GATS. See Van den Bossche and Zdouc (2017), p. 535; Munin (2010), pp. 273–274; Krajewski (2008), p. 168.

67 WTO Panel Report, *Dominican Republic – Import and Sale of Cigarettes*, para 7.385 (on Article X:3(a) GATT).

68 Krajewski (2008), p. 171.

69 Ibid.

70 WTO Panel Report, *Thailand – Cigarettes (Philippines)*, para. 7.898 (on Article X(3)(a) GATT).

71 Krajewski (2008), p. 172.

72 Ibid.; Munin (2010), p. 277.

73 WTO Panel Report, *US – Hot Rolled Steel*, para. 7.268 (on Article X:3(a) GATT).

74 See generally Van den Bossche and Zdouc (2017), pp. 535–536; Munin (2010), pp. 277–281; Krajewski (2008), pp. 173–176.

75 Munin (2010), p. 278.

76 Ibid., 280; Van den Bossche and Zdouc (2017), p. 535.

administrative decision, or the awarding of compensation for suffered economic loss of the service supplier.[77]

4.2.1.3 Obligations Subject to Specific Commitments

The GATS also entails obligations subject to the specific commitments undertaken by WTO members in their schedules. Two obligations are important for cross-border flows of personal data: The market access obligation in Article XVI GATS (Sect. 4.2.1.3.1) and the national treatment obligation in Article XVII GATS (Sect. 4.2.1.3.2).[78]

4.2.1.3.1 Market Access

The market access obligation in Article XVI GATS requires WTO members to accord services and service suppliers of other WTO members treatment no less favorable than that provided for under the terms, limitations, and conditions agreed and specified in their schedules.[79] Market access is not a general concept under GATS.[80] The obligation to grant market access cannot be equated with common terms (such as entry or admission) that imply the general ability to perform business activities in a given market. Article XVI:2 GATS provides a list with a well-defined set of quantitative restrictions that may hamper the ability to supply a service and are thus forbidden.[81] The list with forbidden market access restrictions is exhaustive.[82] Other measures are not covered under Article XVI GATS.[83] Importantly, the list does not relate to the quality of the supplied service.[84]

In *US – Gambling*, the WTO adjudicative bodies dealt with the question of whether a complete ban on the cross-border supply of a service should be regarded as a market access limitation falling within the ambit of Article XVI:2(a) and

---

[77] Krajewski (2008), p. 174.

[78] The panel in *China – Electronic Payment Services* clarified that the scope of Article XVI GATS and the scope of Article XVII GATS are not mutually exclusive. Both provisions can apply to a single measure. WTO Panel Report *China – Electronic Payment Services*, para. 7.658.

[79] See generally Van den Bossche and Zdouc (2017), pp. 517–521; Matsushita et al. (2015), pp. 593–603; Munin (2010), pp. 183–206; Delimatsis and Molinuevo (2008), pp. 369–386.

[80] Van den Bossche and Zdouc (2017), p. 518; Munin (2010), p. 183; Delimatsis and Molinuevo (2008), p. 369.

[81] Article XVI:2(e) is an exception because it does not constitute a quantitative restriction. It refers to the form of legal entity.

[82] WTO Panel Report, *US – Gambling*, para. 6.298.

[83] Ibid., para. 6.318; WTO AB Report, *US – Gambling*, para. 215.

[84] WTO (2001), para. 8; Van den Bossche and Zdouc (2017), p. 519; Matsushita et al. (2015), p. 594; Munin (2010), p. 214; Delimatsis and Molinuevo (2008), pp. 370–371.

(c) GATS. According to the two provisions, WTO members may not maintain or adopt:

(a) limitations on the number of service suppliers whether in the form of numerical quotas, monopolies, exclusive service suppliers or the requirements of an economic needs test.
(c) limitations on the total number of service operations or on the total quantity of service output expressed in terms of designated numerical units in the form of quotas or the requirement of an economic needs test.

The AB stated "that the thrust of sub-paragraph (a) is not on the *form* of limitations, but on their *numerical*, or *quantitative*, nature."[85] Consequently, the AB found that a measure that totally prohibits the supply of certain services effectively limits to zero the number of service suppliers. The AB explained that such a prohibition results in a zero quota and hence constitutes a market access limitation that takes the form of a numerical quota, as zero is quantitative in nature, and, thus, numerical.[86]

With regard to subparagraph (c), the panel defined service output as the result of the production of the service.[87] The panel found, and the AB confirmed, that the measure in question "imposes a 'limitation on the total number of service operations... expressed... in the form of quotas' contrary to Article XVI:2(c) of the GATS."[88]

The underlying rationale of this jurisprudence is that WTO members should not be allowed to circumvent their market access commitments by prohibiting the entry into their markets of services and service suppliers either overall and directly, or indirectly with regard to essential characteristics of a service (e.g. the electronic supply).[89] Article XVI GATS has a wide scope in order to guarantee the access to the market as committed by WTO members in their schedules. The market access obligations cover regulatory measures that make it factually impossible to supply a service.

4.2.1.3.2 National Treatment

The national treatment obligation in Article XVII GATS requires WTO members to accord to services and service suppliers of other WTO members treatment no less favorable than that it accords to its own like services and service suppliers in respect

[85] WTO AB Report, *US – Gambling*, para. 232; WTO Panel Report, *US – Gambling*, paras 6.330–6.332; Delimatsis and Molinuevo (2008), p. 378.

[86] WTO AB Report, *US – Gambling*, para. 227; WTO Panel Report, *US – Gambling*, para. 6.355.

[87] WTO Panel Report, *US – Gambling*, para. 6.349.

[88] Ibid., para. 6.347; WTO AB Report, *US – Gambling*, para. 252.

[89] Cp. Van den Bossche and Zdouc (2017), pp. 601–603; Delimatsis and Molinuevo (2008), p. 381.

of all measures affecting the supply of services.[90] The national treatment obligation also uses the concept of "likeness" and establishes that there shall be no negative discrimination against foreign services and service suppliers compared to like services and services suppliers located in the EU.

Formally identical and formally different treatment can amount to less favorable treatment according to Article XVII:2 GATS. The national treatment obligation captures both *de jure* and *de facto* discrimination.[91] It prohibits measures which openly link a difference in treatment to the origin of a service or service supplier. It also prohibits measures that do not distinguish between services and service suppliers on the basis of their origin but with respect to a neutral criterion that still modifies the conditions of competition in favor of domestic services and service suppliers. The decisive aspect of less favorable treatment is the modification of the competition to the detriment of foreign services or service suppliers according to Article XVII:3 GATS.[92]

The interpretative Footnote 10 to Article XVII GATS stresses that specific commitments assumed under the national treatment obligation should not be construed to require any WTO member to compensate for any inherent competitive disadvantages, which result from the foreign character of the relevant services or service suppliers.[93] An inherent disadvantage due to the foreign nature of a service or service supplier must be distinguished from a disadvantage caused by *de facto* discrimination.[94]

4.2.1.4 Exceptions

The GATS entails different exceptions to justify interferences with the obligations under GATS. Article V GATS allows exceptions from the MFN treatment obligation for economic integration (Sect. 4.2.1.4.1); Article XIV GATS provides general exceptions for public policy objectives that apply to all provisions and existing commitments under the GATS (Sect. 4.2.1.4.2); and Article XIV *bis* GATS foresees

---

[90] The national treatment obligation applies to measures affecting the supply of services and is hence narrower than the general scope of the GATS, which covers measures affecting trade in services. The supply of services is defined in Article XXVIII(b) GATS and includes the production, distribution, marketing, sale, and delivery of a service whereas trade in services also includes the purchase, payment or use of a service according to Article XXVIII(b)(i) GATS. The national treatment obligation therefore does not extend to measures affecting only the consumption of services. Krajewski and Engelke (2008), p. 399.

[91] Van den Bossche and Zdouc (2017), p. 401; Matsushita et al. (2015), p. 609; Munin (2010), pp. 160–162; Krajewski and Engelke (2008), pp. 410–411.

[92] Van den Bossche and Zdouc (2017), pp. 408–411; Matsushita et al. (2015), p. 609; Munin (2010), pp. 162–163; Krajewski and Engelke (2008), p. 409.

[93] See generally Van den Bossche and Zdouc (2017), pp. 411–412; Munin (2010), pp. 157–158.

[94] Krajewski and Engelke (2008), p. 411.

the security exceptions that are also applicable to all provisions and existing commitments under the GATS (Sect. 4.2.1.4.3).

4.2.1.4.1 Economic Integration

The economic integration exception in Article V GATS allows WTO members to deviate from the MFN treatment obligation as a consequence of having entered into an economic integration agreement liberalizing trade in services.[95] It is in the very nature of economic integration agreements to accord preferential treatment to the contracting parties.[96] As a deviation from the MFN treatment obligation, economic integration agreements have to comply with the following three conditions in Article V GATS:

- Article V:1(a) GATS requires that an economic integration agreement liberalizing trade in services must have substantial sectoral coverage.[97] The interpretative Footnote 1 to Article V GATS explains that this condition is understood in terms of number of sectors, volume of trade affected, and modes of supply. It clarifies that the condition entails both qualitative and quantitative requirements.[98] With regard to the economic integration exception in the GATT, the AB held that substantially all the trade (the wording used in Article XXIV:8(b) GATT) "is not the same as *all* the trade," and that it is "something considerably more than merely *some* of the trade."[99] The same reasoning also applies to trade in services. Article V GATS does not require all sectors to be covered but rather that an economic integration agreement excludes no more than a very limited number of sectors.[100] The panel in *Canada – Autos* noted that "the purpose of Article V is to allow for ambitious liberalization to take place at a regional level, while at the same time guarding against undermining the MFN obligation by engaging in minor preferential arrangements."[101]
- Article V:1(b) GATS requires the elimination of substantially all discrimination in the sectors covered, by granting national treatment to the contracting parties.[102] Economic integration agreements liberalizing trade in services need to bring

---

[95] WTO Panel Report, *Canada – Autos,* para. 10.271; Van den Bossche and Zdouc (2017), p. 689; Munin (2010), p. 222; Cottier and Molinuevo (2008), p. 129.

[96] Ibid., para. 10.271.

[97] See generally Van den Bossche and Zdouc (2017), pp. 689–690; Matsushita et al. (2015), p. 574; Munin (2010), pp. 226–230; Cottier and Molinuevo (2008), pp. 130–133.

[98] Cottier and Molinuevo (2008), p. 130.

[99] WTO AB Report, *Turkey – Textiles*, para. 48.

[100] Van den Bossche and Zdouc (2017), p. 690; Cottier and Molinuevo (2008), p. 131.

[101] WTO Panel Report, *Canada – Autos,* para. 10.271.

[102] See generally Van den Bossche and Zdouc (2017), pp. 690–691; Matsushita et al. (2015), pp. 574–575; Munin (2010), pp. 230-235; Cottier and Molinuevo (2008), pp. 135–137.

about a level playing field between domestic and foreign services and service suppliers on the markets of the contracting parties.

Article V:4 GATS prohibits so-called fortress integration.[103] Economic integration agreements liberalizing trade in services should be designed to facilitate trade between the contracting parties and not raise the overall level of barriers to trade in services for other WTO members compared to the level prior to the conclusion of the agreement.[104]

4.2.1.4.2 General Exceptions

The preamble of the GATS not only expresses the intention to expand trade in services as a means of promoting the economic growth of all trading partners, but also the right of WTO members to regulate in order to meet national policy objectives. This right is guaranteed with the general exceptions of Article XIV GATS. The general exceptions require a two-tier analysis of a measure that interferes with a GATS obligation.[105] First, a measure must fall within the scope of the paragraphs of Article XIV GATS. Second, a measure must also satisfy the requirements of the *chapeau* of Article XIV GATS. The analysis under the paragraphs of Article XIV GATS focuses on the content of a measure whereas the analysis under the *chapeau* is directed toward the application of a measure.[106] The design of the general exceptions in Article XIV GATS is basically the same as the design of the general exceptions in Article XX GATT. This is why the adjudicative bodies of the WTO frequently refer to the interpretation of the general exceptions in Article XX GATT when they apply the general exceptions in Article XIV GATS.[107]

4.2.1.4.2.1 Privacy Exception

The subparagraphs of Article XIV GATS entail a list of pre-defined public policy objectives. The most important one for restrictions on cross-border flows of personal data is the privacy exception in Article XIV(c)(ii) GATS:

---

[103] Cottier and Molinuevo (2008), p. 143.

[104] See generally Van den Bossche and Zdouc (2017), p. 691; Munin (2010), pp. 238–242; Cottier and Molinuevo (2008), pp. 143–145.

[105] WTO AB Report, *US – Gambling*, para. 292 with reference to WTO AB Report, *US – Shrimp*, para. 147 (on Article XX GATT) and WTO AB Report, *US – Gasoline*, 20 (on Article XX GATT); Van den Bossche and Zdouc (2017), pp. 606–607; Matsushita et al. (2015), p. 614; Munin (2010), pp. 340–341; Cottier et al. (2008), pp. 294–296.

[106] WTO AB Report, *US – Shrimp*, paras 115–116 (on Article XX GATT); Van den Bossche and Zdouc (2017), p. 616; Munin (2010), p. 372; Cottier et al. (2008), p. 296, 321.

[107] For example, WTO AB Report, *US – Gambling*, para. 292. See Van den Bossche and Zdouc (2017), p. 616; Matsushita et al. (2015), p. 620; Cottier et al. (2008), pp. 292–293.

> nothing in this Agreement shall be construed to prevent the adoption or enforcement by any Member of measures necessary:
>
> (c) to secure compliance with laws or regulations which are not inconsistent with the provisions of this Agreement including those relating to
>
> (ii) the protection of the privacy of individuals in relation to the processing and dissemination of personal data and the protection of confidentiality of individual records and accounts.

The privacy exception in Article XIV(c)(ii) GATS requires that a GATS-inconsistent measure is necessary to secure compliance with GATS-consistent laws or regulations.[108] The reference to "secure compliance" means that the measures for which justification is sought must enforce the relevant laws and regulations.[109] The privacy exception also requires a necessity test. The AB explained in *US – Gambling* that necessity should be determined through a process of weighing and balancing a series of factors.[110] The AB characterized this process as a determination of whether a WTO-consistent alternative measure is available, which a WTO member could reasonably be expected to employ, or whether a less WTO-inconsistent measure is reasonably available.[111] The relevant considerations are the relative importance of the interest at issue, the contribution of the measure to the realization of the ends pursued by it, and the restrictive impact of the measure on international commerce.[112]

The negotiation history of the privacy exception reveals a close relationship between the privacy exception and the EU's fundamental rights-based regulation of data transfers. A former official of the European Commission told Abraham Newman in an interview that the EC went into the negotiations of the GATS with the goal of exempting rules for the protection of data privacy.[113] The records of the Group of Negotiations on Services (GNS) show that the EC stressed at a meeting from 5-9 June 1989 that domestic regulation of data privacy "might mean that personal data could not be transmitted across borders without guarantees of equivalent protection for that data in a foreign country."[114] This was before the Commission proposed the first draft for Directive 95/46/EC on 13 September 1990.[115]

---

[108] See generally Van den Bossche and Zdouc (2017), p. 613; Matsushita et al. (2015), pp. 615–617; Munin (2010), pp. 343–356.

[109] WTO Panel Report, *US – Gambling*, para. 6.538; Munin (2010), pp. 366–367; Cottier et al. (2008), pp. 307–308.

[110] WTO AB Report, *US – Gambling*, para. 305 with reference to WTO AB Report, *Korea – Various Measures on Beef*, para. 164 (on Article XX GATT).

[111] Ibid. with reference to WTO AB Report, *Korea – Various Measures on Beef*, para. 166 (on Article XX GATT).

[112] Ibid., para. 306.

[113] Newman (2009), p. 117, 188 fn. 69.

[114] GATT (1989), para. 93.

[115] See Sect. 2.1.3.

The EC circulated its first draft framework proposal for the GATS in the beginning of June 1990.[116] This draft included an exception for the protection of personal data and individual privacy in Article XV(c).[117] At the first meeting of the sectoral *ad hoc* Working Group on Telecommunications Services from 5-6 June 1990, the EC stressed with regard to a possible annex for telecommunications services that "annex provisions might also need to be considered in regard to the protection of data transmitted over networks as well as the need to protect information of a personal and private nature."[118] At the second meeting of this working group from 9-11 July 1990, the US stated that "[t]he issue of privacy was not specific to the telecommunications sector and should be addressed in the framework."[119] At that point, the first draft of Directive 95/46/EC was still not published and the negotiation parties could not have been aware of its impact on trade.

Shortly after, the so-called July Text from 1990—essentially the first official draft of the GATS—was prepared and circulated.[120] It did not contain any reference to privacy or data protection. There were intense discussions at the following third meeting of the sectoral *ad hoc* Working Group on Telecommunications Services. The representative from Canada, supported by the US representative, "wondered whether there was truly a need for a privacy exception in either the framework or a telecommunications annex."[121] The representative from Canada stated that

> [w]hile the issue of privacy was becoming increasingly important, his delegation's view was that the protection of personal information could be adequately covered through existing contractual arrangements between individuals and legal entities rather than through legislative solutions.[122]

This was tricky for the EC as the contractual approach was not included in the first draft of Directive 95/46/EC (which was still not published at the time of these discussions). The representative of the EC recalled that the July Text foresaw the need for exceptions to protect public morals, order, safety, health, etc. "The need to specify the nature of such exceptions was to minimize the scope for disputes among parties. He saw no reason not to apply a similar logic with regard to privacy-related matters in a telecommunications annex."[123] During the discussions, the US seemed to turn around and support the inclusion of a privacy exception into the framework text of the GATS as "[t]he issues of privacy and data/information protection were viewed in the United States as content issues which were not specific to the

---

[116] GATT (1990a).

[117] Ibid., 13.

[118] GATT (1990b), para. 22. This was also supported by the representative of Switzerland. Ibid., para. 25.

[119] GATT (1990c), para. 70. Other representatives that supported this position were from Sweden and Canada. Ibid., paras 138 and 141.

[120] GATT (1990d).

[121] GATT (1990e), para. 99.

[122] Ibid.

[123] Ibid.

telecommunications sector only." Nevertheless, the US insisted that the EC had to explain its reasons for a privacy exception:

> The representative of the United States recalled that her country did not legislate prospectively and sought concrete examples from the EC delegation to better understand the problems it foresaw in the area of privacy protection. She emphasized that her delegation believed that the issue under discussion was one of private contractual relations between a customer and an information vendor. It was not apparent to her why an international agreement should enter into this area.[124]

The representative from Canada also started to speculate and stated that "the EC seemed to want to capture the activities of private operators through their provisions on information-related matters."[125] The EC successfully avoided this topic and did not mention its intention to legislate in the field of data protection and its plans for an adequacy-based system for cross-border flows of personal data. The discussions ended without a clear result and the chairman concluded that "[t]he outcome of the GNS discussions would be conditioning the group's approach to privacy-related matters."[126] However, the privacy exception was not on the agenda of the fourth meeting of the sectoral *ad hoc* Working Group on Telecommunications Services on 15-17 October 1990. In her complaint that the current text did not include many of the points considered important by her delegation, the representative from the US nevertheless mentioned again that "[m]atters related to privacy should be dealt with under the framework [of the GATS]."[127] She reiterated this position, even though the first draft of Directive 95/46/EC was published a month before. It seems that the US was not aware of its impact on trade.[128]

The so-called Brussels Text from December 1990—the draft of the GATS for the Ministerial Conference in Brussels—was the first official draft that contained a reference to privacy.[129] The reference to privacy was not included in the draft framework of the GATS, but in Paragraph 15 of the draft Annex on Telecommunications. An important footnote was attached:

> The privacy-related aspects of this sentence may need to be reviewed in light of the final text of the provisions of the Agreement related to protection of personal privacy.[130]

The question of including a privacy exception in the framework text of the GATS was still open after the Ministerial Conference in Brussels in 1990. Only a year later, in the so-called Dunkel Draft of December 1991—named after Arthur Dunkel, the Director General of the GATT—it was decided that the privacy exception should be

---

[124] Ibid., para. 105.

[125] Ibid., para. 107.

[126] Ibid., para. 112.

[127] GATT (1990f), para. 39.

[128] Cp. Newman (2009), p. 117, 188 fn. 69.

[129] GATT (1990g).

[130] Ibid., 373.

included into the framework text of the GATS.[131] In the absence of consensus on a particular provision, Dunkel requested the chairs of the negotiation groups to include their personal views regarding the negotiations of that provision when submitting their part to the Dunkel Draft.[132] In the case of services, it was in fact the view of two chairs, because, since April 1991, Ambassador Felipe Jaramillo from Colombia had been assisted in his tasks by Ambassador David Hawes form Australia, who became a sort of co-chair of the GNS, and succeeded Ambassador Jaramillo when he left Geneva.[133] It seems that the inclusion of the privacy exception into the framework of the GATS was dealt with as an issue without consensus and it was the two chairs who decided to integrate the privacy exception into the framework of the GATS.[134]

Even though the GATS negotiations started before the first draft of Directive 95/46/EC was proposed, the European Commission realized that in order to safeguard the EC's future data protection framework, it required a privacy exception in the framework of the GATS to justify potential infringements of the WTO rules on trade in services. The EC clearly intended to and were successful in pushing the privacy exception through the negotiations. The arrangement in the Dunkel Draft was adopted in the final text.[135]

4.2.1.4.2.2 Chapeau

According to the two-tier analysis, GATS-inconsistent measures that are provisionally justified under one of the paragraphs of Article XIV GATS must also satisfy the *chapeau* of Article XIV GATS. The *chapeau* requires that measures are not applied in a manner which would constitute a means of arbitrary or unjustifiable discrimination between countries where like conditions prevail, or a disguised restriction on trade in services.[136] WTO members must act in a consistent manner across comparable situations.[137] The jurisprudence of the WTO's adjudicating bodies shows that the *chapeau* presents a stumbling block for the justification of measures with legitimate policy objectives. Out of all cases that reached the adjudicative stage of WTO dispute settlement, eight cases entailed a measure that was provisionally justified under a paragraph of the general exceptions in Article XX GATT or

---

[131] GATT (1991).

[132] Marchetti and Mavroidis (2011), p. 712.

[133] Ibid., 712–713.

[134] Notably, a representative of Australia stressed during the negotiations "the need to keep any exceptions article very tightly circumscribed and considered the list in the [. . .] draft framework to be sufficiently broad. That statement concerned the July Text that did not include a privacy exception. It seems therefore that the support of the US to include the privacy exception into the framework text of the GATS—instead of the Annex on Telecommunications—was a decisive element of the inclusion of the privacy exception into the Dunkel Draft. GATT (1990h), para. 27.

[135] GATT (1991), p. 18.

[136] See generally Van den Bossche and Zdouc (2017), pp. 615–616; Matsushita et al. (2015), pp. 620–621; Munin (2010), pp. 372–379; Cottier et al. (2008), pp. 321–326.

[137] Matsushita et al. (2015), p. 620.

Article XIV GATS, but only in one case could the measure successfully pass analysis under the *chapeau*.[138]

The AB has portrayed the *chapeau* as an expression of the principle of good faith.[139] Its function is to prevent the general exceptions from being abused.[140] The interpretation of the *chapeau* focuses on the equilibrium between the right of WTO members to invoke the general exceptions and the obligation not to misuse that right and thereby frustrate the rights of other WTO members under WTO law.[141] The first requirement for the application of a measure under the *chapeau* is due process. The AB stressed in *US – Shrimp* that rigorous compliance with the fundamental requirements of due process should be required in the application and administration of a measure which purports to be an exception to the treaty obligations of the Member imposing the measure and which effectively results in a suspension *pro hac vice* of the treaty rights of other Members.[142]

The *chapeau* entails three written standards to assess a measure: arbitrary discrimination, unjustifiable discrimination, and disguised restriction on trade. The AB has chosen a conceptual and holistic approach to interpret the *chapeau* without emphasizing the individual meaning of the three standards because they involve overlapping concepts that are not easy to separate.[143] In general, the WTO adjudicating bodies do not distinguish between the standards of arbitrary and unjustifiable discrimination.[144]

The words arbitrary and unjustifiable qualify the word discrimination. A certain degree of discrimination is allowed under the *chapeau*.[145] In order to determine arbitrary or unjustifiable discrimination, the adjudicating bodies often use a proxy:

---

[138] The case that successfully passed the analysis under the *chapeau* was *EC – Asbestos*. The panel decided that the standards of the *chapeau* are not violated, and the appellant did not bring forward any claims of error. The AB did not address the *chapeau*. WTO Panel Report, *EC – Asbestos*, para. 8.240 (on Article XX GATT). Cp. Public Citizen (2015), p. 5.

[139] WTO AB Report, *US – Shrimp*, para. 158 (on Article XX GATT); Panizzon (2006), pp. 89–90; Munin (2010), p. 372; Cottier et al. (2008), p. 322.

[140] WTO AB Report, *Indonesia – Import Licensing Regimes*, para. 595 (on Article XX GATT) with reference to WTO AB Report, *EC – Seal Products*, para. 5.297 (on Article XX GATT); WTO AB Report, *US – Shrimp*, para. 156 (on Article XX GATT) and WTO AB Report, *US – Gasoline*, 22 (on Article XX GATT); Cottier et al. (2008), p. 321.

[141] "The location of the line of equilibrium, as expressed in the chapeau, is not fixed and unchanging; the line moves as the kind and the shape of the measures at stake vary and as the facts making up specific cases differ." WTO AB Report, *US – Shrimp*, para. 159 (on Article XX GATT).

[142] WTO AB Report, *US – Shrimp*, para. 182 (on Article XX GATT).

[143] WTO AB Report, *US – Gasoline*, 24–25 (on Article XX GATT); Conrad (2011), p. 350; Munin (2010), p. 372; Cottier et al. (2008), p. 323.

[144] WTO AB Report, *EC – Seal Products*, paras 5.328, 5.337 (on Article XX GATT); WTO AB Report, *Brazil – Retreaded Tyres*, paras 228, 233, 246 (on Article XX GATT); WTO AB Report, *US – Gasoline*, 25 (on Article XX GATT).

[145] WTO AB Report, *US – Shrimp*, para. 150 (on Article XX GATT); WTO Panel Report, *EC – Asbestos*, para. 8.226 (on Article XX GATT); Lang (2011), pp. 264–265; Munin (2010), p. 375; Cottier et al. (2008), p. 322.

> [W]hether a measure was applied in a manner which would constitute a means of arbitrary or unjustifiable discrimination depends on if the measure has been applied reasonably.[146]

The fact that discrimination could have been reasonably avoided with another application of a measure renders the measure arbitrary and unjustifiable.[147] It is also important that the discrimination can be reconciled with, or is rationally related to, the policy objective under which the measure has been provisionally justified.[148]

With regard to disguised restrictions on international trade, the scope of the standard remains rather unclear.[149] GATT panels seem mainly concerned with transparency.[150] The AB has underlined that "concealed or unannounced restriction or discrimination in international trade does not exhaust the meaning of disguised restriction."[151] A measure need not be formally hidden in order to constitute a disguised restriction on international trade within the meaning of the *chapeau*.[152]

The application of the general exceptions follows the standard patterns of WTO law. It is incumbent upon the responding party to prove that a measure is justified under Article XIV GATS. After a complaining party has established a *prima facie* case of inconsistency with a provision in the GATS, the burden of proof shifts to the responding party if the latter claims an affirmative defense.[153]

4.2.1.4.3 Security Exceptions

The *raison d'être* of the security exceptions in Article XIV *bis* GATS is to preserve WTO members' freedom of action in areas relating to national defense and security.[154] The security exceptions are the widest among the exceptions listed in the WTO texts and have only rarely been invoked by WTO members.[155] Recently,

---

[146] WTO Panel Report, *EC – Asbestos*, para. 8.226 (on Article XX GATT) with reference to WTO AB Report, *US – Gasoline*, 22 (on Article XX GATT).

[147] WTO AB Report, *US – Shrimp*, para. 171 (on Article XX GATT); WTO AB Report, *US – Gasoline*, 26–27 (on Article XX GATT).

[148] WTO AB Report, *EC – Seal Products*, para. 5.306 (on Article XX GATT); WTO AB Report *US – Shrimp*, para. 165 (on Article XX GATT); WTO AB Report *Brazil – Retreaded Tyres*, paras 227, 228, 232 (on Article XX GATT); Bartels (2015), pp. 117–118.

[149] Lo (2013), p. 112; Munin (2010), p. 378; Nadakavukaren Schefer (2009), p. 435; Cottier et al. (2008), p. 325; cp. WTO Panel Report, *EC – Asbestos*, para. 8.233 (on Article XX GATT).

[150] GATT Panel Report, *US – Tuna (Canada)*, para. 4.8 (on Article XX GATT); GATT Panel Report, *US – Spring Assemblies*, para. 56 (on Article XX GATT).

[151] WTO AB Report, *US – Gasoline*, 25 (on Article XX GATT).

[152] WTO Panel Report, *Brazil – Retreaded Tyres*, para. 7.319 (on Article XX GATT).

[153] WTO AB Report, *US – Gambling*, paras 282, 309; Matsushita et al. (2015), pp. 616–617; Munin (2010), pp. 344–345, 373; Cottier et al. (2008), pp. 291–292.

[154] See generally Van den Bossche and Zdouc (2017), p. 623; Munin (2010), pp. 379–386; Cottier and Delimatsis (2008), p. 331.

[155] There is a trend to use the security exceptions more often. See Mantilla and Pehl (2020), pp. 12–15; Voon (2019), p. 45.

national security has been cited more often as a rationale to restrict digital trade.[156] The most important paragraph of the security exception for the EU system for data transfers can be found in Article XIV *bis*:(1)(b)(iii) GATS:

> 1. Nothing in this Agreement shall be construed:
>
> (b) to prevent any Member from taking any action which it considers necessary for the protection of its essential security interests:
>
> (iii) taken in time of war or other emergency in international relations;

The panel in *Russia – Traffic in Transit* provided some guidance regarding the application of the security exception in Article XXI GATT.[157] The design of the security exception in Article XIV *bis* GATS is basically the same as the design of the security exceptions in Article XXI GATT. This is why the interpretation of the security exception in Article XXI GATT serves as a guideline for the interpretation of Article XIV *bis* GATS.[158] The panel in *Russia – Traffic in Transit* clarified that the term "essential security interests" may generally be understood to refer to those interests relating to the quintessential functions of the state, namely, the protection of its territory and its population from external threats, and the maintenance of law and public order internally.[159] The final determination is left in the hands of WTO members and will depend on the particular situation and the perception of the state in question.[160] A WTO member only needs to consider that its essential security interests are endangered, which amounts to a subjective standard. That determination is nevertheless subject to good faith.[161]

The panel also clarified that the subparagraphs in Article XIV *bis*:1(b) GATS operate as limitative qualifying clauses, implying that they limit the discretion granted to WTO members when invoking the security exceptions.[162] This prevents the security exceptions from becoming a catch-all provision for unverified unilateral determinations and a circumvention of the GATS.[163] For example, the term emergency in international relations is amenable to an objective determination.[164] The term is not firmly entrenched in international law and must be construed by the WTO adjudicative bodies.[165] The panel in *Russia – Traffic in Transit* pointed out that "political or economic differences between Members are not sufficient, of

[156] Ferracane (2018), p. 2.

[157] WTO Panel Report, *Russia – Traffic in Transit* (on Article XXI GATT); see generally Oesch et al. (2020), pp. 282–293; Wang (2019), pp. 699–710.

[158] Van den Bossche and Zdouc (2017), p. 623; Munin (2010), p. 380; Cottier and Delimatsis (2008), p. 331

[159] WTO Panel Report, *Russia – Traffic in Transit*, para. 7.130 (on Article XXI GATT).

[160] Ibid., para. 7.131 (on Article XXI GATT).

[161] Ibid., paras 7.132–7.134 (on Article XXI GATT); Cottier and Delimatsis (2008), pp. 335–336.

[162] WTO Panel Report, *Russia – Traffic in Transit*, para. 7.65 (on Article XXI GATT); Bogdanova (2019).

[163] Bogdanova (2019).

[164] WTO Panel Report, *Russia – Traffic in Transit*, paras 7.70–7.71 (on Article XXI GATT).

[165] Cottier and Delimatsis (2008), pp. 344–345.

themselves, to constitute an emergency in international relations."[166] It defined an emergency in international relations as a "situation of armed conflict, or of latent armed conflict, or of heightened tension or crisis, or of general instability engulfing or surrounding a state."[167] This limits the application of the security exception to restrictions on cross-border flows of personal data to very specific circumstances.

4.2.2 Annex on Telecommunications

The telecommunications sector was one of the sectors that required additional rules to the GATS because it is essential for the supply of other services (Sect. 4.2.2.1). The GATS Annex on Telecommunications entails substantive obligations on access to and use of public telecommunications transport networks and services (Sect. 4.2.2.2). The internet can be qualified as a public telecommunications transport network (Sect. 4.2.2.3). In addition to the substantive obligations, the Annex on Telecommunications also foresees exceptions for the confidentiality of messages (Sect. 4.2.2.4).

4.2.2.1 Enabling Function

During the negotiations of the GATS, WTO members recognized that the telecommunications sector played an important role as the underlying means for other economic activities.[168] The GATS Annex on Telecommunications thus aimed to ensure that commitments of WTO members in sectors other than telecommunications were not frustrated through the lack of access to and use of foreign telecommunications services.[169] The Annex on Telecommunications only comes into effect once a WTO member has offered a specific commitment in a given sector.[170] Despite being an act on telecommunications, the Annex on Telecommunications mostly liberalized trade in non-telecommunications services whose effective performance require access to and use of communications networks and services in the destination country.[171] The Annex on Telecommunications is a general insurance policy for service suppliers to have access to telecommunications networks and services abroad.[172]

---

[166] WTO Panel Report, *Russia – Traffic in Transit*, para. 7.75 (on Article XXI GATT).

[167] Ibid., para. 7.76 (on Article XXI GATT).

[168] See generally Matsushita et al. (2015), pp. 621–622; Munin (2010), pp. 407–410; Gao (2008), pp. 687–690.

[169] Matsushita et al. (2015), p. 621; Munin (2010), p. 407; Krajewski (2003), p. 167; Roseman (2003), p. 86.

[170] WTO Panel Report, *Mexico – Telecoms*, paras 7.292–7.293; Luff (2012), p. 87.

[171] Burri (2015), p. 32.

[172] Bronckers and Larouche (2008), p. 326.

4.2.2.2 Substantive Obligations

The main substantive obligation of the Annex on Telecommunications can be found in Paragraph 5. The Annex on Telecommunications requires in Paragraph 5(a) that WTO members grant access to and use of public telecommunications transport networks and services on reasonable and non-discriminatory terms and conditions for the supply of services included in their schedules.[173] The Annex on Telecommunications specifically requires in Paragraph 5(c) that other WTO members may use public telecommunications transport networks and services for the movement of information within and across borders, including for intra-corporate communications, and for access to information contained in data bases or otherwise stored in machine-readable form on the territory of any WTO member.[174]

4.2.2.3 Coverage of the Internet

A "public telecommunications transport network" is defined in Paragraph 3(c) Annex on Telecommunications as "the public telecommunications infrastructure which permits telecommunications between and among defined network termination points."[175] The exact scope of this obligation is not entirely clear, especially when it comes to the internet.

The GATS was drafted with a narrow idea of telecommunications in mind. Tim Wu explains that the drafters "had no idea that nearly every type of service under the GATS might eventually be offered over the TCP/IP protocol. In trade lingo, the framers thought of the Internet as a service sector, when, instead, it is usually a service mode."[176] Cross-border flows of personal data on the internet are relevant for the supply of many services.[177] Access to and use of the internet in the territory of another WTO member is of the utmost importance for trade in services. The Council for Trade in Services noted regarding the application of the Annex on Telecommunications to the internet that

> [t]he general view was that the Annex on Telecommunications applies to access to and use of the Internet network when it is defined in a Member's regulatory system as a public telecommunications transport service and/or network in terms of that Annex.[178]

This view is widely shared by scholars.[179] The aim of the Annex on Telecommunications was to prevent access to communication networks becoming a barrier to

---

[173] Munin (2010), pp. 408-409; Gao (2008), pp. 697–701.

[174] Munin (2010), p. 409; Gao (2008), p. 703.

[175] Gao (2008), p. 694.

[176] Wu (2006), p. 266.

[177] See Sects. 4.1.3 and 4.1.4.

[178] WTO (1999a), para. 19.

[179] Willemyns (2018), pp. 9–10; Batura (2013), p. 228; Kariyawasam (2007), p. 81; Luff (2012), p. 88; Luff (2004), p. 44.

trade.[180] This is why the WTO adjudicative bodies applied the GATS to internet-based service transactions.[181] Article 2(2) Regulation (EU) 2015/2120 defines an "internet access service" as a "publicly available electronic communications service that provides access to the internet, and thereby connectivity to virtually all end points of the internet, irrespective of the network technology and terminal equipment used."[182] The EU is therefore obligated to grant access to and use of the internet for the services it has scheduled in order for service suppliers to move information within the EU, for their cross-border data flows, including intra-corporate communications, and for access to information contained in data bases or otherwise stored in the EU.

The regulation of data transfers in the EU does not forbid access to and use of the internet for foreign service suppliers and services. Rather it regulates the cross-border flow of personal data from the EU to a third country. Even in cases in which the EU does not allow cross-border flows of personal data to a service supplier in the territory of a WTO member, this does not violate Paragraph 5(c) Annex on Telecommunications. The reason for the restriction on the cross-border flows of personal data is not a prohibition to access and use the internet for the movement of information within and across borders *but related to the protection for personal data*. The fact that the based regulation of data transfers in the EU also applies to the manual transportation of personal data to third countries underlines this.

Nevertheless, it must be acknowledged that Paragraph 5(c) Annex on Telecommunications has never been subject to dispute settlement and its exact scope is still unclear. During the negotiations, the US stated that "the cross-border movement of information was an intrinsic part of access to and use of the services of the public telecommunications transport network."[183] The EC, in reaction, said that "the issue of data protection and privacy bore a strong link to that of the movement of information."[184] There is a possibility that a restriction on cross-border flows of personal data could amount to a restriction on access to and use of a public telecommunications transport network because the movement of (personal) information is intrinsically linked with the access and use.

---

[180] WTO (2000), para. 5; Mathew (2003), p. 77.

[181] WTO Panel Report, *US – Gambling*, paras 6.362–6.363 upheld by WTO AB Report, *US – Gambling*, para. 265; WTO Panel Report, *China – Audiovisual Products*, para. 7.1265 upheld by WTO AB Report, *China – Audiovisual Products*, para. 412; Burri (2015), pp. 39–40; Wunsch-Vincent (2006), p. 323; see Sect. 4.2.3.

[182] Regulation (EU) 2015/2120 of the European Parliament and of the Council of 25 November 2015 laying down measures concerning open internet access and amending Directive 2002/22/EC on universal service and users' rights relating to electronic communications networks and services and Regulation (EU) No 531/2012 on roaming on public mobile communications networks within the Union [2015] OJ L 310/1.

[183] GATT (1990c), para. 154.

[184] Ibid., para. 155.

4.2.2.4 Confidentiality Exception

Paragraph 5(d) Annex on Telecommunications allows WTO members to take measures that are necessary to ensure the security and confidentiality of messages, notwithstanding the obligation to open public telecommunications transport networks and services for the movement of information within and across borders, including the intra-corporate communications of such service suppliers, and for access to information contained in data bases or otherwise stored in machine-readable form in their territory.[185] These measures may not be applied in a manner which would constitute a means of arbitrary or unjustifiable discrimination or a disguised restriction on trade in services.

Some scholars have argued that this exception covers privacy and data protection considerations.[186] The OED explains that confidential means "characterized by the communication of secrets or private matters."[187] Nevertheless, context suggests that this exception does *not* cover privacy and data protection considerations. It must be observed from a systematic perspective that Paragraph 8 GATS Understanding on Commitments in Financial Services and the privacy exception in Article XIV(c)(ii) GATS distinguish the concepts of privacy and data protection from the concept of confidentiality by naming them separately. The negotiation history of the Annex on Telecommunications as supplementary means of interpretation according to Article 32 VCLT helps to clarify the interpretation of Paragraph 5(d). It was unclear during the GATS negotiations where a privacy exception should be inserted (if at all).[188] At the end, it was decided that the privacy-related aspects in the Annex on Telecommunications of the Brussels Text from December 1990 should be deleted and included in the framework text of the GATS in the Dunkel Draft from December 1991.[189] It seems to be clear from the preparatory work of the Annex on Telecommunications and the circumstances of the conclusion of the GATS that the concepts of privacy and data protection should not be part of Paragraph 5(d) Annex on Telecommunications.[190]

Accordingly, the exception in Paragraph 5(d) Annex on Telecommunications must be construed narrowly and privacy as well as data protection considerations are only relevant where they overlap with considerations relating to the confidentiality of messages.

[185] Gao (2008), p. 703.

[186] Mitchell and Neha (2018), p. 1091; Tuthill (2016), p. 367. But see Irion et al. (2016), p. 43.

[187] OED online, entry for confidential (adj.).

[188] See Sect. 4.2.1.4.2.

[189] Cp. GATT (1990g) and GATT (1991), p. 18.

[190] Similarly, Yakovleva and Irion (2020a), p. 12.

4.2.3 Treatment of Digital Services

Since the negotiation of the GATS coincided with the early development of the internet, the parties did not necessarily think of digital services when they drafted the GATS. This raises legal questions that are highly relevant for restrictions on cross-border flows of personal data, which affect trade in digital services: Are digital services part of the scope of the commitments in the schedule of WTO members (Sect. 4.2.3.1)? Which mode of supply covers the supply of digital services (Sect. 4.2.3.2)? How should digital services be classified in the Service Sectoral Classification List (W/120) (Sect. 4.2.3.3)? The classification of digital services is important for the commitments of WTO members in their respective schedules. A list with examples illustrates the classification of different digital services (Sect. 4.2.3.4).

4.2.3.1 Commitments

There was an early understanding among WTO members that the electronic supply of a service is covered by the commitments under GATS. The WTO Council for Trade in Services underlined in 1999 that

> [t]he electronic delivery of services falls within the scope of the GATS, since the Agreement applies to all services regardless of the means by which they are delivered, and electronic delivery can take place under any of the four modes of supply. Measures affecting the electronic delivery of services are measures affecting trade in services and would therefore be covered by GATS obligations.[191]

The Council for Trade in Services stressed that according to the technological neutrality of the GATS, the electronic supply of a service is covered by specific commitments unless the schedule of a WTO member states otherwise.[192] All GATS provisions would be applicable to the supply of services through electronic means.[193] The WTO adjudicative bodies followed this interpretation. They found in *US – Gambling* that by limiting the electronic supply of gambling services, the US failed to accord services and service suppliers in Antigua treatment no less favorable than that provided for under the terms, limitations, and conditions agreed and specified in the market access column of its schedule.[194] The modes of supply in the GATS cover the "supply [of] a service through all means of delivery, whether by mail, telephone, Internet etc., unless otherwise specified in a Member's Schedule."[195] The panel added that this was "in line with the principle of 'technological neutrality',

[191] WTO (1999b), para. 4.

[192] Ibid.

[193] Ibid.

[194] WTO Panel Report, *US – Gambling*, paras 6.285–6.286; WTO AB Report, *US – Gambling*, para. 265; Burri (2015), pp. 39–40; Weber and Burri (2012), p. 75.

[195] WTO Panel Report, *US – Gambling*, para. 6.285; Wunsch-Vincent (2006), pp. 332–333.

which seems to be largely shared among WTO Members" and also referred to the above mentioned report of the Council on Trade in Services.[196]

In the subsequent case *China – Audiovisual Products*, the panel found that the electronic distribution of sound recordings was technically feasible and a commercial reality as early as 1998, and in any case before China's accession to the WTO in December 2001.[197] It found, and the AB confirmed, that sound recording distribution services in China's schedule of specific commitments extend to the distribution of sound recordings in non-physical form through technologies such as the internet.[198] The panel added that there was no need to invoke the principle of technological neutrality because it has already found that the core meaning of China's commitment on these services includes the distribution of audio content on non-physical media.[199] The WTO adjudicative bodies confirmed that the GATS applies to digital services.

4.2.3.2 Mode of Supply

The supply of digital services could either fall within mode 1 (cross-border) or mode 2 (consumption abroad).[200] With regard to mode 1, it can be argued that a digital service is sent to a recipient in another country via the internet. The panel in *Mexico – Telecoms* confirmed that the cross-border supply of services can encompass services which begin on one country's telecommunication network and terminate on another's.[201] With regard to mode 2, it can be argued that the consumer abroad actually visits the website of a service provider in another country.[202] The distinction is of some interest as, generally, concessions under mode 2 are more liberal than under mode 1.[203]

The panel in *US – Gambling* addressed the question with regard to digital gambling services. The panel first established that cross-border supply must be distinguished from remote supply.[204] It used the term "remote supply" to refer to "any situation where the supplier, *whether domestic or foreign*, and the consumer of gambling and betting services are not physically together."[205] The logic behind the panel's reasoning is that the GATS does not distinguish between remote or on-site supply but between four modes of supply out of which only mode 1 can be

[196] WTO Panel Report, *US – Gambling*, para. 6.285.
[197] WTO Panel Report, *China – Audiovisual Products*, paras 7.1220, 7.1247.
[198] Ibid.; WTO AB Report, *China – Audiovisual Products*, para. 398; Hodson (2019), p. 587.
[199] WTO Panel Report, *China – Audiovisual Products*, para. 7.1258.
[200] WTO (1999a), para. 5; Weber and Burri (2012), p. 51.
[201] WTO Panel Report, *Mexico – Telecoms*, para. 7.45.
[202] WTO (1999c), para. 4.
[203] Tinawi and Berkey (2000), pp. 5–6, 8.
[204] WTO Panel Report, *US – Gambling*, para. 6.32.
[205] Ibid.

remote.[206] The panel therefore limited its analysis to mode 1. It clearly stated that "[t]his dispute concerns one of the four modes of supply under the GATS, that is, the so-called 'cross-border supply' of gambling and betting services."[207] The AB followed this line of reasoning and only assessed mode 1 in its review of the dispute.[208] The WTO adjudicative bodies therefore confirmed that digital services are supplied through mode 1.[209]

4.2.3.3 Classification

The Service Sectoral Classification List (W/120) has remained unchanged since 1991.[210] The W/120 is somewhat outdated when it comes to the classification of digital services. Nevertheless, it has proven to be flexible enough to cover most current digital services (Sect. 4.2.3.3.1). The allocation of a digital service to a service sector and subsector is an interpretative exercise of the WTO members' schedules (Sect. 4.2.3.3.2). Three elements should be given due consideration when classifying digital services:[211] First, the ordinary meaning of the terms in a schedule of commitments might change with the development of technology (Sect. 4.2.3.3.3). Second, the classification is based upon the output of services (Sect. 4.2.3.3.4). Third, integrated or composite services should be classified as if they consisted of the service that gives them their essential character (Sect. 4.2.3.3.5). Finally, a functional approach is suggested for the classification of digital services (Sect. 4.2.3.3.6).

4.2.3.3.1 Coverage of the Service Sectoral Classification List

The GATS is molded by a comprehensive approach. It should be applicable in principle to any service in any sector as laid down in Article I:I(3)(b) GATS.[212] Given that the W/120 and the CPC are intended to be exhaustive, presumably any service should automatically fall under some category on the list.[213] The GATS

[206] Wunsch-Vincent (2006), p. 326.

[207] WTO Panel Report, *US – Gambling*, paras 6.29, 6.280.

[208] WTO AB Report, *US – Gambling*, para. 215.

[209] Hodson (2019), p. 586; Crosby (2016), pp. 2–3; Tuthill and Roy (2012), p. 159. Sacha Wunsch-Vincent suggested that WTO members should use the opportunity of *US – Gambling* to enter into an agreement declaring mode 1 as fully applicable to all cross-border electronic transactions. That has not yet happened. Wunsch-Vincent (2006), p. 327.

[210] In contrast, the CPCprov—the source and annotation of the W/120—has been revised and updated several times to reflect technological changes.

[211] Willemyns (2019), p. 67.

[212] Weber and Burri (2012), p. 32; Zacharias (2008), p. 43; Zhang (2015), p. 11; AB Report, *US – Gambling*, para. 172.

[213] Zhang (2015), p. 11. Ines Willemyns points out that, strictly speaking, the AB only confirmed that the CPC classification is exhaustive, not whether this consideration also applies to the W/120. Willemyns (2019), p. 67 fn. 39.

liberalized trade in services with a positive list approach, in which WTO members actively commit to open their markets for a specific service sector or subsector. The result of this approach is that potentially not all current tradable services are encompassed. The question here is whether a WTO member could be assumed to have undertaken commitments on a service that was not foreseen at the time of submitting the commitments. New services might only be covered if they can be clearly identified under an existing sectoral classification that has been committed by a WTO member.[214]

The concept of new services must be approached cautiously. There is no definition of new services in the GATS.[215] During discussions in the WTO Committee on Specific Commitments in 2014, it was underlined that in considering new services, WTO members should be mindful of the distinction between new means of delivery and genuinely new services.[216] Many WTO members shared the opinion that genuinely new services are rare, if they exist at all, and that the rest could be accommodated in the W/120.[217] The same opinion is also expressed by scholars. Ines Willemyns has argued that "very limited genuinely new services exist and that many allegedly new digital services can be classified within the W/120."[218] The question is how an activity can be allocated to a service sector and subsector.

4.2.3.3.2 Interpretation of the Schedules

The W/120 is based on a taxonomy of distinct and mutually exclusive services. The sectors and subsectors in a WTO member's schedule must be mutually exclusive. If that were not the case, and a WTO member scheduled the same service in two different sectors, then the scope of the commitment would not be clear if the WTO member made a full commitment in one of those sectors and a limited commitment in the other.[219] The allocation of digital services to a service sector and subsector is an interpretative exercise of WTO members' schedules. The general rules of interpretation of public international law in Articles 31 and 32 VCLT apply.[220] First, the ordinary meaning of the relevant terms in a schedule must be determined based on

---

214 Weber and Burri (2012), p. 51.

215 The Understanding on Commitments in Financial Services contains a particular provision devoted to "New financial services" where *new* depends on the availability of such service in a particular territory and not to the innovative character of a service. Zhang (2015), p. 15.

216 WTO (2014a), para. 1.2.

217 For example, Canada, the US, the EU, Australia and South Africa. Ibid., paras 1.3, 1.5, 1.6, 1.8 and 1.11.

218 Willemyns (2019), p. 67.

219 WTO Panel Report, *US – Gambling*, paras 6.63, 6.101, 6.119; AB Report, *US – Gambling*, para. 180 fn. 219.

220 In accordance with Article 3.2 DSU. See Sorel and Boré Eveno (2011), pp. 820–821.

the dictionary meaning.[221] The AB cautioned that panels should acknowledge when multiple interpretations are possible and not just focus solely on the preferred interpretation.[222] Second, the meaning of the terms can be informed by the relevant context, namely:

> (i) the remainder of the [...] Schedule of specific commitments; (ii) the substantive provisions of the GATS; (iii) the provisions of covered agreements other than the GATS; and (iv) the GATS Schedules of *other* Members.[223]

Context does not include the W/120 or the Scheduling Guidelines of 1993 because they do not constitute agreements between the parties.[224] The object and purpose of the GATS can offer further guidance for the interpretation.[225] Finally, Article 31 VCLT also refers to subsequent practice as a tool for interpretation.[226]

Where the ordinary meaning of the terms, interpreted together with the context and relevant subsequent practice, leaves the meaning of the terms ambiguous, recourse should be made to the supplementary means of interpretation as provided in Article 32 VCLT.[227] The AB confirmed that both the W/120 and the Scheduling Guidelines of 1993 constitute supplementary means of interpretation.[228]

4.2.3.3.3 Evolution of Technology

When classifying digital services it is important to take into consideration that the ordinary meaning of the terms in a schedule of commitments can change with the development of technology. Exactly how this works has been an issue in dispute settlement before:

In *EC – IT Products*, a dispute concerning the Information Technology Agreement (ITA) that entails concessions to provide zero tariffs for selected IT products, the panel was asked to elaborate to what extent the state of technology that existed at the time of the negotiations is relevant to determining the scope of the concessions. The panel stated that "it is neither desirable nor possible to answer such questions in

---

[221] The AB reminded panels not to equate the ordinary meaning of a term with the definition provided by dictionaries and reiterated that "interpretation pursuant to the customary rule codified in Article 31 of the *Vienna Convention* is ultimately a holistic exercise that should not be mechanically subdivided into rigid components." WTO AB Report, *China – Publications and Audiovisual Products*, para. 348. See generally Dörr (2018a), pp. 580–582; Villiger (2009), pp. 426–427.

[222] WTO AB Report, *US – Gambling*, para. 167; Willemyns (2019), p. 67.

[223] Ibid., para. 178; Dörr (2018a), pp. 582–584; Sorel and Boré Eveno (2011), pp. 823–825; Villiger (2009), p. 427.

[224] Ibid., paras 175–176.

[225] Ibid., para. 187; Dörr (2018a), pp. 584–587; Villiger (2009), pp. 427–428.

[226] Ibid., paras 190–194; Dörr (2018a), pp. 592–603; Villiger (2009), pp. 431–432.

[227] See generally Dörr (2018b), pp. 617–618; le Bouthillier (2011), pp. 842–843; Villiger (2009), pp. 444–449.

[228] WTO AB Report, *US – Gambling*, paras 196–197.

the abstract and without reference to the terms of the concessions that are being interpreted."[229] In responding to the EC's argument that multifunctional monitors were new products that had not existed at the time of negotiations, the panel explained that the notion of multifunctional monitors was not unknown to the negotiators at the time. The panel continued to explain that even if the EC's argument were accepted, it was of limited relevance to the question of whether the product in question was covered by the concessions, because "this must be determined by interpreting the terms of the concession in accordance with the Vienna Convention."[230] The panel decided that the products in question were covered by the ITA on the basis of a strict textual interpretation.[231]

In *China – Publications and Audiovisual Products*, the panel had to assess China's argument that its commitment on sound recording distribution services should not be considered to cover the electronic distribution of sound recordings because the latter had emerged as an established business only after the negotiation of its schedule of commitments and its accession to the WTO.[232] The panel admitted that evidence on the technical feasibility or commercial reality of a service at the time of the commitments might constitute circumstances that are relevant to the interpretation of the commitment under Article 32 VCLT:

> We consider therefore that any evidence that sound recordings delivered in non-physical form were not, unlike today, technically possible or commercially practiced at the time China's Schedule was negotiated might, in principle, be relevant as a supplementary means of interpretation with respect to the scope of that commitment.[233]

The panel assessed the technical feasibility and commercial practice with respect to the electronic distribution of sound recordings before and at the time of China's Protocol of Accession and found that it was technically feasible and a commercial reality before China's accession to the WTO and therefore confirmed its finding under Article 31 VCLT.[234] The AB upheld the panel's finding but added a nuance as to how schedules should be interpreted:

> We further note that interpreting the terms of GATS specific commitments based on the notion that the ordinary meaning to be attributed to those terms can only be the meaning that they had at the time the Schedule was concluded would mean that very similar or identically worded commitments could be given different meanings, content, and coverage depending on the date of their adoption or the date of a Member's accession to the treaty.[235]

---

[229] WTO Panel Report, *EC – IT Products*, paras 7.596, 7.952.

[230] Ibid., paras 7.599–7.601.

[231] Luff (2012), pp. 70–71. In contrast, Rolf H. Weber and Mira Burri submitted that "[t]he Panel decided in favor of the complainants with the argument that lists of IT products would soon be outdated and that the liberalization objective of WTO Members would embody new products having a similar function." They concluded that the panel in *EC – IT Products* applied a teleological interpretation of the concessions in the ITA. Weber and Burri (2012), pp. 14–15.

[232] WTO Panel Report, *China – Publications and Audiovisual Products*, para. 7.1235.

[233] Ibid., para. 7.1237.

[234] Ibid., para. 7.1247.

[235] WTO AB Report, *China – Publications and Audiovisual Products*, para. 397.

Without explicitly referring to the state of technology, the AB argued that a historic interpretation "would undermine the predictability, security, and clarity of GATS specific commitments."[236] Especially because GATS schedules, like the GATS itself and all WTO agreements, constitute multilateral treaties with continuing obligations entered into for an indefinite period of time—regardless of whether they were original WTO members or acceded after 1995.[237] The AB also argued that "the terms used in China's GATS Schedule ('sound recording' and 'distribution') are sufficiently generic that what they apply to may change over time."[238] The AB therefore indicated that the ordinary meaning of the terms of specific commitments could not be limited to the meaning that they had at the time the schedule had been concluded. They rather must be interpreted based on their contemporary meaning if the terms are sufficiently generic.[239]

4.2.3.3.4 Service Output

Another element that should be given due consideration when classifying digital services is that the classification of services in the W/120 and the CPC is based on the service output provided by service suppliers.[240] Service output means the result of the production of the service.[241] Footnote 9 to the GATS excludes input services from the market access obligation in Article XVI:2(c) GATS. This qualification in Footnote 9 to the GATS provides a safeguard against unwanted liberalization.[242] It allows WTO members to limit trade in input services that have not been committed to themselves. The Scheduling Guidelines of 2001 clarify that market access and national treatment commitments "do not imply a right for the service supplier of a committed service to supply uncommitted services which are inputs to the committed service."[243] It is ultimately the service output (i.e. the product), and not the activity that generates the output, which enters trade and is subject to the commitments in the schedules of WTO members.[244] The classification of a service must focus on the output.

---

[236] Ibid.

[237] Ibid., para. 396.

[238] WTO AB Report, *China – Publications and Audiovisual Products*, para. 396 with reference to the approach taken in *US – Shrimp*, where the AB interpreted the term "exhaustible natural resources" in Article XX(g) GATT. WTO AB Report, *US – Shrimp*, paras 129–130.

[239] Willemyns (2019), p. 69; Zhang (2015), pp. 28–29.

[240] Willemyns (2019), p. 67; Zhang (2015), p. 8; Weber and Burri (2012), p. 18.

[241] WTO Panel Report, *US – Gambling*, para. 6.349.

[242] Delimatsis and Molinuevo (2008), p. 381; Lapid (2006), p. 341, 355; Mattoo and Wunsch-Vincent (2004), p. 779.

[243] WTO (2001), para. 25.

[244] Cp. the definition of services in European Commission/IMF/OECD/United Nations/ World Bank (2009), para. 6.17: "Services are the result of a production activity that changes the conditions of the consuming units, or facilitates the exchange of products or financial assets."

4.2.3.3.5 Integrated Services

A third element that should be given due consideration when classifying digital services is that integrated or composite services should be classified as if they consisted of the service that gives them their essential character. WTO members have already acknowledged that due to the evolution of technology, increasingly complex and combined services are entering the market.[245] This is especially true for digital services.

The notion of integrated services was introduced in *China – Electronic Payment Services*. In identifying the nature of electronic payment services, the panel noted that two issues arise: One was whether the services at issue could be considered as an integrated service, which was supplied as such. The other was whether the services at issue should be classified under a single subsector or under more than one subsector in the classification system.[246] The panel first underlined that electronic payment services are composed of several elements, which are services in their own right.[247] In spite of this, the panel found that while these elements might be individually identifiable services, all of them together, were necessary for a payment card transaction to materialize and are thus integrated into a whole.[248] Thus the different services *combined together* result in a distinct service that is supplied and consumed as such.[249] The panel therefore concluded that electronic payment services for payment card transactions constitute an integrated service.[250] Furthermore, the panel found that electronic payment services, as an integrated service, were covered by China's commitments under a single subsector.[251]

These findings are compatible with the focus on service output and the fact that input services are not automatically committed.[252] The panel focused on the service output and found that the final service, as supplied to the consumer (considering the transaction from start to end), is a distinct service (without input services) and can therefore be classified within a single subsector. This is also compatible with Article

[245] WTO (2011), para. 5.

[246] WTO Panel Report, *China – Electronic Payment Services*, para. 7.57.

[247] Such as the process and coordination of approving or declining a transaction; the delivery of transaction information among participating entities; the calculation, determination, and reporting of the net financial position of relevant institutions for all transactions that have been authorized; and the facilitation, management and/or other participation in the transfer of net payments owed among participating institutions. Ibid., para. 7.58.

[248] Ibid., para. 7.59.

[249] Ibid., para. 7.188.

[250] Ibid.

[251] Ibid., paras 7.180, 7.188. The US raised a valid point that was not further discussed by the panel. The US submitted that if China's position were accepted—that a service must first be disaggregated into subcomponents and each subcomponent separately classified—it would render WTO members' concessions meaningless for a wide range of services. Ibid., para. 7.173.

[252] Willemyns (2019), p. 70; but see Zhang (2015), p. 23.

XXVIII(b) GATS that defines the supply of a service as including production, distribution, marketing, sale, and delivery of a service.

The CPC also addresses integrated services. The introductory part of the CPC suggests some general rules to guide statisticians in their use of the classification system.[253] These include: Composite services shall be classified as if they consisted of the service which gives them their essential character.[254] Services that cannot be classified in accordance with the general rules shall be classified under the category appropriate to the services to which they are most akin.[255]

4.2.3.3.6 Functional Approach

The functional approach to classification of digital services focuses on service output and considers integrated services where applicable. The functional approach to classification is based on the determination of a service's end-use.[256] The question is what function is achieved by the service?[257] Based on this determination, the service sector and subsector that has the closest relation to the function can be considered the correct classification.[258] The panel in *China – Publications and Audiovisual Products* made an important finding in this regard:

> A description of a service sector in a GATS schedule does not need to enumerate every activity that is included within the scope of that service, and is not meant to do so. A service sector or subsector in a GATS schedule thus includes not only every service activity specifically named within it, but also any service activity that falls within the scope of the definition of that sector or subsector referred to in the schedule.[259]

The determination of a service's function can be tricky when it comes to services that may serve multiple end-uses.[260] For example, advertising online games, which are either specifically designed for advertising purposes or simply entail advertisements.[261] The determination will depend on the perspective taken. This could be the perspective of the producers, consumers, or regulators and each might yield a different result. In *China – Electronic Payment Services*, the panel referred to the consumers' perspective when determining the correct classification.[262] The functional approach is also supported by the principle of technological neutrality, as the

[253] While designed to guide statisticians, these rules may also be helpful for the scheduling of commitments.

[254] UN (2015a), para. 56(b).

[255] Ibid., para. 57.

[256] Sen (2018), p. 334; Zhang (2015), p. 9.

[257] Willemyns (2019), p. 71.

[258] Weber and Burri (2012), p. 127.

[259] WTO Panel Report, *China – Publications and Audiovisual Products*, para. 7.1014.

[260] Zhang (2015), pp. 10–11.

[261] Ibid.

[262] WTO Panel Report, *China – Electronic Payment Services*, paras 7.61, 7.180.

focus on the end-use of the service does not take account of, or is at least not determined by, the means through which the service is being supplied.[263]

The components-based approach to classification stands in contrast to the functional approach. The components-based approach relies on identifying the separate components a service consists of, after which the main component (or the one most easily classified) determines the classification of the service. Ines Willemyns explains that a components-based classification approach can lead to converging classification of widely different digital services, because it is based on the main constituting elements (that may even be inputs) of the service rather than the final service being provided.[264] If the components-based approach would prevail, a majority of digital services might be classified as data transmission services, since data transmission is the major component in how these services are supplied. This would not allow for a differentiated classification of different digital services. Consequently, I argue that the components-based approach to classification is not suitable and the functional approach should be used.[265]

4.2.3.4 Examples

The functional approach to classification is best illustrated with examples. The following examples have already been introduced as examples of services that require cross-border flows of personal data.[266] The classifications suggested here for these examples will be used in the legal analysis of the regulation of data transfers in the EU and the market access obligation in Article XVI GATS.[267]

4.2.3.4.1 Cloud Computing Services

The use of cloud computing should not automatically be considered as a single final service output for trade in services. It also offers ways in which other services can be supplied.[268] Services using cloud computing do not necessarily amount to computer services based on the functional approach to service classification. They often constitute integrated services, which can be classified elsewhere. Nevertheless, cloud computing services are also traded independently. In order to produce a

---

[263] Willemyns (2019), p. 71.

[264] Ibid., 72.

[265] An illustrative example can be found in *Canada – Periodicals*, where the two services components of periodicals were identified (editorial content and advertising content), but the AB concluded that the services combined into a final good, which is why the GATT (and not the GATS) was applicable to the measure at issue. WTO AB Report, *Canada – Periodicals*, para. 17.

[266] See Sects.. 4.1.3 and 4.1.4.

[267] See Sect. 4.3.3.

[268] See Sect. 4.1.3.1.

service that relies on cloud computing, the supplier of that service might have recourse to foreign suppliers and import cloud computing services.

4.2.3.4.1.1 Cloud Computing Without Distinction by Type

In 2007, a group of 19 WTO members, including the EC (not counting its member states) and the US, circulated the Understanding on the scope of coverage of CPCprov 84 in which they submitted that CPCprov 84 covers *all* computer and related services.[269] Division 84 of the CPCprov includes the following groups:

841 - Consultancy services related to the installation of computer hardware
842 - Software implementation services
843 - Data processing services
844 - Data base services
845 - Maintenance and repair services of office machinery and equipment including computers
849 - Other computer services

The US and the EU later argued that according to this understanding, CPCprov 84 also includes cloud computing services.[270] They did not maintain a distinction between the different types of cloud computing services. In 2015, the WTO Secretariat provided the United Nations Expert Group on International Statistical Classifications with an illustrative list of services that did not have explicit references in W/120 and included on it cloud computing services.[271] The experts also concluded that cloud computing services would fall under CPCprov 84.[272] They also did not push for a distinction between the different types of cloud computing services either.

It was mainly China that objected and stated that cloud computing clearly overlapped with both computer and related services and telecommunications services.[273] China argued that cloud computing could not simply be classified as falling either under computer-related services or telecommunications services.[274] The EU disagreed with China that cloud computing is a new service and that it should (also) be considered as a (value-added) telecommunication service.[275] The EU pointed out that telecommunications are only the means of delivery, and not the core of the service provided (just as cloud computing itself could be an enabling service).[276] In

[269] WTO (2007).

[270] WTO (2015a), para. 1.8; WTO (2014b), para. 5; Kelsey (2019), p. 47.

[271] UN (2015b), paras 1.2–1.3.

[272] Kelsey (2019), p. 38.

[273] WTO (2015a), para. 1.3; WTO (2015b), para. 4.21; WTO (2016), para. 2.2; Anuradha (2018), p. 29.

[274] WTO (2012), para. 66.

[275] WTO (2015b), para. 4.33.

[276] Ibid.

2016, the WTO Secretariat noted that the discussions on the classification of cloud computing services in the WTO had not resulted in any consensus.[277]

I argue that cloud computing services themselves also should be seen as integrated services.[278] They are composed of several elements, each of which are services in their own right. Even though there are elements that are individually identifiable services, such as computer and related services and telecommunications services, all of them *together*, are necessary to supply could computing services. Only the elements *combined* result in a distinct service that is supplied and consumed as such. With a focus on the output, it seems that cloud computing services should be classified in the sector "Business Services" and the subsector "Computer and Related Services" (W/120-1.B), which corresponds to CPCprov 84.

Nevertheless, China made a valid point that there are three different types of cloud computing services that should be individually classified because they satisfy different consumer needs: IaaS, PaaS, and SaaS.[279]

4.2.3.4.1.2 IaaS

IaaS may be classified in the category "Data processing services" (W/120-1.B.c), which corresponds to CPCprov 843.[280] The OED defines processing as "the subjection of something to a special process."[281] Cloud computing as IaaS allows a consumer to rent cloud computing infrastructure from the provider. The consumer can rely on the provider for processing, storage, networks, and other fundamental computing resources located in the cloud. The provider therefore subjects the data of the consumer to special processing operations. The CPC as a supplementary means of interpretation supports that conclusion. CPCprov 843 entails a sub-class 84320 with the title "Data-processing and tabulation services." The sub-class is defined as services such as data processing tabulation services, computer calculating services, and rental services of computer time. The rental of computer time fits the IaaS model.

4.2.3.4.1.3 PaaS

PaaS may be classified in the category "Software implementation services" (W/120-1.B.b), which corresponds to CPCprov 842. The OED defines software as the "collection of programs essential to the operation of a particular computer system" or as "programs designed to enable a computer to perform a particular task or series of tasks."[282] Implementation refers to an action and also means

[277] WTO (2016), para. 2.9.

[278] Cp. WTO Panel Report, *China – Electronic Payment Services*, paras 7.58–7.59, 7.188.

[279] WTO (2016), para. 2.2.

[280] Cp. Anuradha (2018), p. 76.

[281] OED online, entry for processing (n.).

[282] Ibid., entry for software (n.).

fulfillment.[283] Cloud computing as PaaS allows a consumer to work with tools supported by the cloud provider. A consumer can create web or mobile applications on an existing cloud computing platform. The interpretation based on the ordinary meaning of the terms "software implementation services" is not conclusive. It is not clear how the action of implementing something should be associated with PaaS. The CPC as a supplementary means of interpretation clarifies the classification. The description of software implementation services in CPCprov 842 explains that all services involving consultancy services for *development* and implementation of software are covered. Sub-class 84230 with the title "Systems design services" includes technical solutions, with respect to methodology or new technologies.[284] PaaS offers technical solutions for consumers.

4.2.3.4.1.4 SaaS

SaaS may also be classified in the category "Software implementation services" (W/120-1.B.b). SaaS allows a consumer to use a software application of a cloud provider on various client devices. The provider manages the application and handles maintenance. The interpretation based on the ordinary meaning of the terms software implementation services is not conclusive, but the CPC as a supplementary means of interpretation clarifies the classification. Sub-classes 84240 with the title "Programming services" and 84250 with the title "System maintenance services" suggest that the writing of programs and the maintenance of software products in use are covered by software implementation services.

4.2.3.4.2 Search Engine Services

Search engines crawl the internet and index the results for search queries.[285] They use cloud computing and algorithms to grant users access to databases containing a plethora of websites and the information therein. The use of cloud computing should not be considered the final service output for trade in search engine services. The use of cloud computing is an element of the integrated service of a search engine.

Before classifying search engine services, it is necessary to address an important element of the operation of a search engine. The services offered by search engines are usually free of charge to the consumers. Additional targeted advertising services usually cover the financial needs of the search engine. Virtual space is sold to businesses which are interested in reaching a wide, but targeted audience. Advertising is the main revenue source for search engines. The ECJ found that the search engine functions and advertising activities

---

[283] Ibid., entry for implementation (n.).

[284] Cp. Anuradha (2018), p. 237.

[285] Chen (2018), p. 298; Brin and Page (1998), p. 108.

> are inextricably linked since the activities relating to the advertising space constitute the means of rendering the search engine economically profitable and that the search engine is, at the same time, the means enabling those advertising activities to be performed.[286]

The reasoning of the ECJ does not translate easily into WTO law. The panel found in *China – Electronic Payment Services* that electronic payment services are composed of several elements, which are services in their own right but that all of them, together, are necessary for a payment card transaction to materialize and are thus integrated into a whole.[287] The panel's jurisprudence on integrated services is based on functional and not economic considerations. From a functional perspective, the advertising services are not necessary for the supply of search engine services. In addition, there could be other business models for search engine services than advertising.[288] This indicates that search engine services do not necessarily have to be linked with advertising services. I thus conclude that search engine services should not be seen as an integrated service that includes advertising services.[289] Rather the advertising services should be classified separately.

Search engine services may be classified under the sector "Business Services" and the subsector "Computer and Related Services" as "Data base services" (W/120-1.B.c), which correspond to CPCprov 844. The OED defines "database" as a "structured set of data held in computer storage and typically accessed or manipulated by means of specialized software."[290] Search engines consist of a database and an interface that makes the database accessible.[291] They fit the ordinary meaning of W/120-1.B.c perfectly. The CPCprov as a supplementary means of interpretation supports this classification. The description of database services in CPCprov 844 includes all services provided from primarily structured databases through a communication network. Search engines satisfy both conditions of that description.[292]

---

[286] ECJ, *Google Spain and Google*, paras 51, 56; ECJ, *Google v. CNIL*, para. 50.

[287] WTO Panel Report, *China – Electronic Payment Services*, paras 7.58–7.59.

[288] DuckDuckGo is an example for a search engine that allows its users to turn off advertisements.

[289] Henry Gao similarly distinguishes between Google's search engine and advertising services. Tim Wu does not mention the corresponding advertisement services at all. Fred Erixon, Brian Hindley and Hosuk Lee-Makiyama argue that the whole service provided by a search engine could be classified as advertisement services. Ines Willemyns argues that a classification as advertisement services follows a components-based approach, after which the main component (or the one most easily classified) determines the classification. The components-based approach does not harmonize well with the focus on output of services inherent in W/120. Gao (2011), p. 359; Wu (2006), pp. 282–283; Erixon et al. (2009), p. 12; Willemyns (2019), p. 72.

[290] OED online, entry for database (n.).

[291] Gao (2012), p. 256.

[292] Cp. Willemyns (2019), p. 76 (but with recourse to CPC2.1); Gao (2012), pp. 256–257.

4.2.3.4.3 Social Network Services

Social networks are cloud-based platforms encompassing digital relationships between individuals, groups, organizations, or even entire societies. The use of cloud computing should not be considered the final service output for trade in social network services. The use of cloud computing rather is an element of the integrated service of a social network.

Just as in the case of search engines, it is necessary to address advertising services before classifying social network services. The services offered by a social network are usually free of charge to the consumers. Additional targeted advertising services often cover the financial needs of a social network. It is the main revenue source for social networks. The jurisprudence of the WTO adjudicative bodies on integrated services is based on functional and not economic considerations. From a functional perspective, the advertising services are not necessary for the supply of social network services. Social network services cannot be seen as an integrated service that includes advertising services.[293] The advertising services must be classified separately.

Social networks may be classified under the sector "Business Services" and the subsector "Computer and Related Services" as "Data base services" (W/120-1.B.c), which correspond to CPCprov 844.[294] Social network services enable electronic interaction and allow access to and manipulation of information in databases because whatever is posted or shared by the users is included in the online database of the social network.[295] The CPCprov as a supplementary means of interpretation supports this classification. The description of database services in CPCprov 844 includes all services provided from primarily structured databases through a communication network. Social networks satisfy both conditions of this description.[296]

---

[293] Rolf Weber and Mira Burri similarly distinguish advertisement services from social network services. They argue that an "easy" classification as advertisement services puts this element of social networks at the forefront, which is not in the main interest of the users. Ines Willemyns does not mention the corresponding advertisement services. Weber and Burri (2012), p. 116; Willemyns (2019), p. 76.

[294] Ines Willemyns argues that social networks may be classified as packet-switched data transmission services (W/120-2.C.b), which correspond to CPCprov 7523. Henry Gao explains that CPCprov 7523 covers network services but not the actual contents carried over such networks. Rolf Weber and Mira Burri argue that, as far as telecommunications are concerned, the underlying purpose of that classification does not really comply with the functions of a social network, since the transmission services are not at the forefront and the availability of data in the databases is more important. Willemyns (2019), p. 76; Gao (2011), p. 364; Weber and Burri (2012), p. 117.

[295] Willemyns (2019), p. 76.

[296] Ines Willemyns argues that this classification seems to focus on a components-based approach, considering not the output of the service, but rather its technical components. She disregards the fact that the database is not only a technical component of a social network, but, arguably, also its function from the perspective of its users. Willemyns (2019), p. 76. Cp. Weber and Burri (2012), p. 118.

4.2.3.4.4 Online Advertising Services

Online advertising services may be classified under the sector "Business Services" and the subsector "Other Business Services" as "Advertising services" (W/120-1.F.a), which correspond to CPCprov 871.[297] The ordinary meaning of the term advertising services in W/120-1.F.a matches online advertisement services, especially when taking account of the evolution of technology. It is not necessary to consult the CPCprov as a supplementary means of interpretation as the result of the interpretation according to Article 31 VCLT does not leave the meaning of the terms ambiguous.

4.2.3.4.5 IoT Services

One of the examples given above for IoT services was related to internet-connected automobiles. Maintenance and the improvement of the driving experience are important services with regard to internet-connected vehicles. IoT maintenance services for internet-connected vehicles can be classified in the sector "Transport Services" and the subsector "Road Transport Services" as "Maintenance and repair of road transport equipment" (W/120-11.F.d), which corresponds to CPCprov 6112. The ordinary meaning of the terms "maintenance" and "repair of road transport equipment" matches the IoT maintenance services for internet-connected vehicles, especially when taking account of the evolution of the ordinary meaning of the term due to technological development. The CPCprov as a supplementary means of interpretation supports this classification. Sub-class 611120 with the title "Maintenance and repair services of motor vehicles" includes a detailed list of maintenance services. The terms are sufficiently generic that what they apply to may change over time.[298]

The second example for IoT service given above was related to smart fridges. Restocking groceries is an important service provided by smart fridges. IoT restocking services for smart fridges cannot be classified in any sector and subsector of W/120. I am of the opinion that IoT restocking services for smart fridges is one of the rare examples of a new service that is not covered by the W/120. The subsector "Retailing services" is not pertinent (W/120-4.C). The OED defines "retail" as the "action or business of selling goods in relatively small quantities for use or consumption rather than for resale."[299] IoT restocking services of smart fridges involve the buying of goods and not their sale. The subsector "Computer and Related Services" is not pertinent either (W/120-1.B). Even though data processing services

[297] UN (1991), p. 253. Cp. Weber and Burri (2012), p. 116.

[298] Cp. WTO AB Report, *China – Publications and Audiovisual Products*, para. 396 with reference to the approach taken in *US – Shrimp*, where the AB interpreted the term "exhaustible natural resources" in Article XX(g) GATT. WTO AB Report, *US – Shrimps*, paras 129–130.

[299] OED online, entry for retail (n.).

are a component of IoT restocking services, the classification must focus on the service output, which is ordering groceries and filling up the fridge. Furthermore, none of the "Other" subsectors are pertinent. IoT restocking services are essentially personal shopping services from a technologically neutral perspective. Someone (or something) is going to the stores (or contacting the stores) for you (or maybe with you) to select and/or buy the things you need. There is no classification for personal shopping in the W/120.

4.2.3.4.6 Sharing Economy Platform Services

The treatment of sharing economy platform services is tricky, not only with regard to the GATS. Countries have historically struggled to find sensible regulatory solutions for the sharing economy. Should the respective companies be treated as tech-companies or the same as their analogue counterparts?[300] Similarly, in the GATS context, their services can be classified either as computer and related services, or as the services that they facilitate.

The first example for sharing economy platform services discussed above was related to the arrangement of lodging. I would classify digital lodging arrangement platform services under the sector "Tourism and Travel Related Services" and the subsector "Hotels and restaurants" (W/120-9.A), which corresponds to CPCprov 641-643. The interpretation, however, based on the ordinary meaning of the terms hotels and restaurants leaves the classification ambiguous. The CPCprov as a supplementary means of interpretation offers further guidance. Sub-class 64193 with the title "Letting services of furnished accommodation" includes lodging and related services provided by cabins, private apartments, and homes. There is no requirement as to who owns the subject property. The mere fact that a company like Airbnb does not own the property does not preclude them from providing such services.[301] The classification in the subsector hotels and restaurants focuses on service output from the perspective of the consumer/user that travels. Data processing and database services are certainly elements of digital lodging arrangement platform services, and constitute services in their own right, but all of them, together, are necessary for digital lodging arrangement platform services to materialize. The different services are thus combined and result in a distinct integrated service that is supplied and consumed as such.[302]

[300] The ECJ decided in *Airbnb Ireland* that even if Airbnb's intermediary service is aimed at the rental of accommodation, it can be separated from the actual real estate business. It acted as an "information society service" rather than a real estate agency. ECJ, *Airbnb Ireland*, paras 49, 52. In contrast, the ECJ found that the intermediary service of Uber must be regarded as forming an integral part of an overall service whose main component is a transport service and, accordingly, must not be classified as an "information society service." ECJ, *Uber France*, para. 21; ECJ, *Asociación Profesional Élite Taxi*, paras 39–40.

[301] Anuradha (2018), p. 73.

[302] Cp. WTO Panel Report, *China – Electronic Payment Services*, paras 7.58–7.59, 7.188.

The second example for sharing economy platform services was related to the arrangement of transportation. I would classify digital transportation arrangement platform services under the sector "Transportation Services" and the subsector "Road Transport Services" as "Passenger transportation" (W/120-11.F.a), which corresponds to CPCprov 7121+7122. The interpretation based on the ordinary meaning provides a clear classification. The CPCprov as a supplementary means of interpretation supports this classification. Sub-class 71221 with the title "Taxi services" includes services that are generally rendered on a distance-traveled basis, for a limited duration of time, and to a specific destination. The classification as passenger transportation focuses on service output from the perspective of the consumer/user that travels. Data processing and database services are certainly elements of digital transportation arrangement platform services, and constitute services in their own right, but all of them, together, are necessary for digital transportation arrangement platform services to materialize. The different services are combined together and result in a distinct integrated service that is supplied and consumed as such.[303]

4.2.3.4.7 Travel Agencies

Travel agencies supply services that can be classified under the sector "Tourism and Travel Related Services" and the subsector "Travel agencies and tour operator services" (W/120-9.B), which corresponds to CPCprov 7471. The services offered by travel agencies fit the ordinary meaning of W/120-1.B.c perfectly.

4.2.3.4.8 Digital Medical Services

Digital medical services as described above may be classified under the sector "Business Services" and the subsector "Professional Services" as "Medical and dental services" (W/120-1.A.h), which correspond to CPCprov 9312. The ordinary meaning of the term "medical services" matches digital medical services, especially when taking into account the evolution of technology. The CPCprov as a supplementary means of interpretation supports this classification.

4.2.3.4.9 Legal Services

Legal services as described above may be classified under the sector "Business Services" and the subsector "Professional Services" as "Legal Services" (W/120-1.A.a), which correspond to CPCprov 861. The interpretation according to the ordinary meaning of the terms suffices for the classification.

---

[303] Cp. ibid.

4.2.4 Electronic Commerce Negotiations

The cross-border flow of personal data is not directly regulated by the law of the WTO yet, but it is part of the electronic commerce negotiations held at the WTO since 1998. These negotiations can be divided into four stages: the preparatory work until 2015 (Sect. 4.2.4.1), the emancipation from the Doha structure from 2015 to 2017 (Sect. 4.2.4.2), the Joint Statement Initiative from 2017 to 2019 (Sect. 4.2.4.3), and the current negotiations that started in 2019 (Sect. 4.2.4.4).

4.2.4.1 Preparatory Work

At the second Ministerial Conference of the WTO in May 1998, the delegations recognized that growing global electronic commerce was creating new opportunities for trade. They thus adopted the Declaration on Global Electronic Commerce.[304] The declaration directed the WTO General Council to establish a comprehensive work program to address trade-related issues concerning electronic commerce. In September 1998, the General Council established the "Work Programme on Electronic Commerce," instructing each of its councils to look at specific issues under their respective responsibilities.[305]

The Work Programme on Electronic Commerce has an exploratory and informative nature. It was mainly designed to build understanding around the trade-related aspects of electronic commerce without the pre-set objective to negotiate new rules.[306] Discussions did not see significant progress until the Nairobi Ministerial Conference in 2015.[307] The International Centre for Trade and Sustainable Development noted that the topic was completely absent in some of the councils for years.[308] In spite of this and in spite of the Doha agenda deadlock, some pertinent trade-related aspects of electronic commerce were identified.[309] With regard to trade in services, such aspects included the technological neutrality of the GATS, the fact that specific commitments for market access and national treatment also cover the supply of services through electronic means (unless otherwise specified), and the application of the Annex on Telecommunications to access and use of the internet when it is defined in a WTO member's regulatory system as a public telecommunications transport service.[310]

---

[304] WTO (1998a).

[305] The term "electronic commerce" is understood to mean the production, distribution, marketing, sale or delivery of goods and services by electronic means. WTO (1998b), para. 1.3.

[306] Ismail (2020), p. 9.

[307] Ibid., 10.

[308] ICTSD (2017).

[309] Ismail (2020), p. 10.

[310] WTO (1999d), paras 4, 15, 17, 19.

4.2.4.2 Emancipation from the Doha Structure

At the Nairobi Ministerial Conference in 2015, it was recognized that many WTO members desired to carry out the work on the basis of the Doha structure, while some wanted to explore new negotiation architectures.[311] Given the rapid growth of electronic commerce and the absence of global rules, some WTO members called for electronic commerce to be prioritized among the new issues for consideration.[312]

In the runup to the Buenos Aires Ministerial Conference in 2017, the discussions of the Work Programme on Electronic Commerce intensified and several WTO members, or groups of WTO members, issued statements and proposals on potential issues for discussion. These issues also included data flows and data protection. Developing countries, especially WTO members in Africa, argued against negotiating new rules at the WTO, concerned that this would detract attention from the outstanding issues of the Doha agenda, along with imposing constraints on policy space.[313]

4.2.4.3 Joint Statement Initiative

The Buenos Aires Ministerial Conference in 2017 witnessed the launch of a Joint Statement Initiative for exploratory talks on potential negotiations of trade rules on electronic commerce by 71 WTO members.[314] The WTO members involved in this Joint Statement Initiative met on an almost monthly basis. A total of nine meetings were held, in which proposals and submissions were discussed with the aim of setting and agreeing on the agenda for the negotiations.[315] That phase was concluded by the signing of a second Joint Statement Initiative in Davos in January 2019, announcing the intention of 76 WTO members to begin plurilateral negotiations on electronic commerce.[316]

4.2.4.4 Current Negotiations

By the end of February 2020, seven negotiating rounds had been completed, with more than 80 WTO members participating. Big differences have been reported between three influential WTO members—China, the EU and the US—but also

---

311 WTO, Nairobi Ministerial Declaration of 19 December 2015, WT/MIN(15)/DEC, para. 32.

312 Ismail (2020), p. 11.

313 Ibid., 12.

314 WTO (2017).

315 Garcia-Israel and Grollier (2019), pp. 5–14.

316 WTO (2019a).

between developed and developing countries when it comes to subjects like data protection and cross-border flows of personal data.[317]

The EU's first proposal was circulated on 26 April 2019 and entailed safeguards for WTO members to regulate the protection of personal data and privacy:[318]

> **2.8 Protection of Personal Data and Privacy**
>
> 1. Members recognize that the protection of personal data and privacy is a fundamental right and that high standards in this regard contribute to trust in the digital economy and to the development of trade.
> 2. Members may adopt and maintain the safeguards they deem appropriate to ensure the protection of personal data and privacy, including through the adoption and application of rules for the cross-border transfer of personal data. Nothing in the agreed disciplines and commitments shall affect the protection of personal data and privacy afforded by the Members' respective safeguards.
> 3. Personal data means any information relating to an identified or identifiable natural person.

The wording of the EU's proposal is very similar to the Model Data Flow Clauses for their future trade agreements.[319] It entails a deferential approach allowing WTO members to choose the safeguards they deem appropriate for the protection of personal data and privacy including rules on cross-border flows of personal data. It does not mention any qualifying requirement such as necessity or standards similar to the *chapeau* of Article XIV GATS. The EU's proposal tries to safeguard the right to continuous protection of personal data in Article 8 CFR and the legal mechanisms for the transfer of personal data in the GDPR.

China's first proposal was circulated on 23 April 2019 and only briefly addressed the protection of personal information:[320]

> 3.9. *Personal Information Protection*: Members should adopt measures that they consider appropriate and necessary to protect the personal information of electronic commerce users.

The wording of China's proposal, while less detailed, is similarly deferential as regards the protection of personal data. China explicitly stated that WTO members "should respect each other's design of the electronic commerce development paths, and the legitimate right to adopt regulatory measures in order to achieve reasonable public policy objectives."[321] China seems to side with the EU on privacy issues in its proposal, arguing that appropriate and necessary measures can be implemented to

[317] Fefer (2020), p. 22; Hufbauer and Lu (2019), p. 1.

[318] WTO (2019b).

[319] A detailed analysis is provided in Sect. 5.4.

[320] WTO (2019c).

[321] Ibid., para. 4.1.

protect privacy.[322] However, while the EU's focus is on fundamental rights, China's focus is on security:

> 4.1. [. . .] However, more importantly, the data flow should be subject to the precondition of security, which concerns each and every Member's core interests. To this end, it is necessary that the data flow orderly in compliance with Members' respective laws and regulations.

This might be explained by the fact that China's Cybersecurity Law states that operators of critical information infrastructure must pass a security assessment by government agencies before cross-border flows of personal data are possible.[323]

The US proposal was circulated on 26 April 2019 and entailed detailed rules on protection of personal information and cross-border transfers of information:[324]

Article 7: Personal Information Protection

1. Each Party shall adopt or maintain a legal framework that provides for the protection of the personal information of the users of digital trade.[325]
2. Each Party shall publish information on the personal information protections it provides to users of digital trade, including how:
   (a) individuals can pursue remedies; and
   (b) an enterprise can comply with legal requirements.
3. Recognizing that the Parties may take different legal approaches to protecting personal information, each Party should encourage the development of mechanisms to promote interoperability between these different regimes.
4. The Parties recognize the importance of ensuring compliance with measures to protect personal information and ensuring that any restrictions on cross-border flows of personal information are necessary and proportionate to the risks presented.

Article 8: Cross-Border Transfer of Information by Electronic Means

1. No Party shall prohibit or restrict the cross-border transfer of information, including personal information, by electronic means, if this activity is for the conduct of the business of a covered person.
2. This Article does not prevent a Party from adopting or maintaining a measure inconsistent with paragraph 1 that is necessary to achieve a legitimate public policy objective, provided that the measure:
   (a) is not applied in a manner which would constitute a means of arbitrary or unjustifiable discrimination or a disguised restriction on trade; and

[322] Hufbauer and Lu (2019), p. 6.

[323] The definition of CII has a very broad scope. Ibid., 4.

[324] WTO (2019d).

[325] For greater certainty, a Party may comply with the obligation in this paragraph by adopting or maintaining measures such as comprehensive privacy, personal information, or personal data protection laws, sector-specific laws covering privacy, or laws that provide for the enforcement of voluntary undertakings by enterprises relating to privacy.

(b) does not impose restrictions on transfers of information greater than are necessary to achieve the objective.[326]

The US proposal is characterized by a commitment to recognize different legal approaches to protect personal data and the interoperability of these approaches.[327] The US suggested in a follow-up communication from 17 June 2019 that so-called "interoperability regimes" can be instituted between economies where national standards on data protection diverge.[328] It explicitly mentioned the Privacy Shield as an example for the use of such an interoperability regime.[329] The invalidation of Decision (EU) 2016/1250, the Privacy Shield adequacy decision, by the ECJ in *Schrems 2* shows the limits of such regimes from the perspective of the EU.[330] At the same time, the US proposal also significantly limits domestic regulatory space for rules on cross-border flows of personal data with qualifying requirements. First, parties must generally ensure that restrictions on cross-border flows of personal data are necessary and proportionate to the risks presented. This requires an explanation of the risks of cross-border flows of personal data and a test of necessity and proportionality of the restrictions. Second, and somewhat overlapping, the proposal forbids prohibitions and restrictions of cross-border flows of personal data for the conduct of businesses, except where a measure is necessary to achieve a legitimate public policy objective and is not applied in a manner which would constitute a means of arbitrary or unjustifiable discrimination or a disguised restriction on trade; and does not impose restrictions on transfers of information greater than are necessary to achieve the objective. Contrary to the EU's and China's proposal, the US proposal entails many legal tests for data flow regimes.

An agreement that reconciles differing national approaches to personal privacy seems elusive.[331] Nevertheless, the parties had hoped to publish a consolidated text at the Nur-Sultan Ministerial Conference of the WTO in June 2020.[332] The conference was postponed due to the COVID-19 pandemic, which has given the negotiations more time. On 14 December 2021 the co-convenors of the WTO e-commerce negotiations—Australia, Japan and Singapore—issued a joint statement welcoming the substantial progress in the negotiations and setting the goal for members to secure convergence on the majority of issues by the end of 2022.[333] The negotiations seem to have produced a number of clean articles such as on spam, electronic signatures, online consumer protection and open government data but privacy

---

[326] A measure does not meet the conditions of this paragraph if it accords different treatment to data transfers solely on the basis that they are cross-border in a manner that modifies the conditions of competition to the detriment of a covered person of another Party.

[327] Hufbauer and Lu (2019), p. 6; Stelly (2019).

[328] WTO (2019e), para. 33.

[329] Ibid.

[330] ECJ, *Schrems 2*, para. 201.

[331] Burri (2021), p. 97; Hufbauer and Lu (2019), p. 6.

[332] Cimino-Isaacs et al. (2020), p. 1.

[333] WTO (2021a), p. 1.

and data flows remain two of the significant open issues.[334] The co-convenors stated on 15 September 2022 that a finalisation of the negotiations in 2023 is within reach.[335]

4.2.5 Summary

Digital services often require cross-border flows of personal data. When the GATS was drafted, many digital services that now rely on the free flow of personal data were not yet invented. Nevertheless, I argue that most digital services are covered by the commitments in the schedules of WTO members. They fall under mode 1 (cross-border supply of services). Since the GATS applies to measures affecting trade in services, the EU's fundamental rights-based regulation of data transfers is subject to the obligations in the GATS because any restriction on the free flow of personal data across borders affects trade in services. The MFN treatment obligation in Article II GATS prohibits discrimination between foreign services and service suppliers from different third countries. The domestic regulation obligation in Article VI GATS requires "reasonable, objective, and impartial" administration of measures and practicable, judicial, arbitral, or administrative tribunals or procedures that provide for the prompt review of measures and appropriate remedies. Subject to the specific commitments undertaken by the EU, the market access obligation in Article XVI (a) and (c) GATS does not allow limitations on the number of service suppliers and operations, and the national treatment obligation in Article XVII GATS prohibits discrimination between foreign and domestic services and service suppliers. Exceptions pertaining to economic integration in Article V GATS, privacy in Article XIV(c)(ii) GATS, and security in Article XIV *bis* GATS can justify violations of the obligations in the GATS. The GATS Annex on Telecommunications aims to ensure that the specific commitments are not frustrated through lack of access to foreign telecommunications services. In addition, the ongoing electronic commerce negotiations at the WTO involve rules on cross-border flows of personal data. However, it still seems rather difficult to reconcile the differing national approaches to privacy protection at the level of the WTO.

[334] WTO (2022a); WTO (2021b). The ongoing difficulties finding agreement on data flows are also evident from leaked negotiation texts from December 2020. See WTO (2020), pp. 27–29, 45–47.

[335] WTO (2022b).

4.3 The Regulation of Data Transfers as Trade Barrier

The multilateral framework of the WTO allows its members to challenge the EU's fundamental rights-based regulation of data transfers as a trade barrier. The analysis of the obligations under the GATS highlights how the regulation of data transfers in the EU interferes with the rules of the WTO on trade in services. The analysis focuses on the MFN treatment obligation in Article II GATS (Sect. 4.3.1), the domestic regulation obligation in Article VI GATS (Sect. 4.3.2), the market access obligation in Article XVI:2(a) and (c) GATS (Sect. 4.3.3), and the national treatment obligation in Article XVII GATS (Sect. 4.3.4).

4.3.1 MFN Treatment

The MFN treatment obligation in Article II:1 GATS applies to any measure affecting trade in services irrespective of whether specific commitments have been undertaken.[336] The EU is required to accord to services and services suppliers of any WTO member treatment no less favorable than that it accords to like services and service suppliers of any other country immediately and unconditionally. The analysis of the EU's regulation of data transfers under the MFN treatment obligation focuses on regular adequacy decisions (Sect. 4.3.1.1), special framework adequacy decisions (Sect. 4.3.1.2), the management of the adequacy assessment (Sect. 4.3.1.3), and instruments providing appropriate safeguards (Sect. 4.3.1.4).

4.3.1.1 Adequacy Decisions

The EU system for data transfers interferes with the MFN treatment obligation in so far as adequacy decisions by the European Commission lead to situations in which services and service suppliers in some WTO members are treated less favorably than services and service suppliers in other states. Where the Commission decides that a third country provides an adequate level of protection for personal data according to Article 45 GDP, services and services suppliers from that third country benefit from the possibility to transfer personal data without any specific authorization. Services and service suppliers in WTO members without an adequacy decision must have recourse to other legal mechanisms for their data transfers. An interference with the MFN treatment obligation may occur with regard to services and service suppliers that require systematic, structural, and continuous cross-border flows of personal

[336] See Sect. 4.2.1.2.1.

data (Sect. 4.3.1.1.1) but also with regard to services and service suppliers that only require occasional cross-border flows of personal data (Sect. 4.3.1.1.2).[337]

4.3.1.1.1 Services with Systematic Flows of Personal Data

Service suppliers in a WTO member without an adequacy decision that require systematic, structural, and continuous cross-border flows of personal data for their services have to rely on instruments providing appropriate safeguards according to Article 46 GDPR to transfer personal data from the EU to their home country. In such cases, services and service suppliers are treated less favorably than like services and service suppliers from third countries with an adequacy decision. It is not sufficient under Article II:1 GATS to accord a WTO member similar treatment to that accorded to another state.[338] By virtue of the MFN treatment obligation, any WTO member must be given exactly the same treatment as any other state.[339] The use of instruments providing appropriate safeguards is more burdensome than transferring personal data on the basis of an adequacy decision.[340] The concept of treatment no less favorable in Article II:1 GATS focuses on a measure's modification of the conditions of competition.[341] Any evidence that the EU intruded into the competitive relationship between services or service suppliers satisfies that legal standard and establishes treatment less favorable under Article II:1 GATS. It is more costly for services and service suppliers to use instruments providing appropriate safeguards than relying on an adequacy decision. The instruments in Article 46 GDPR are less flexible, they entail additional obligations, and require ongoing legal management. The requirement to use those instruments creates a competitive disadvantage for services and service suppliers in WTO members without an adequacy decision. This constitutes treatment less favorable. The EU does not immediately and unconditionally accord to those services and service suppliers treatment no less favorable than that it accords to like services and service suppliers in states with an adequacy decision. This constitutes an interference with the MFN treatment obligation in Article II:1 GATS.[342]

Carla Reyes argues that there is less favorable treatment for services and service suppliers in the specific situation where a WTO member's claim of adequacy has

[337] Gregory Shaffer submitted that "the EU Directive applies equally to transfers to all countries and thus should not violate the GATS most-favored-nations clause." However, he did not consider that the MFN treatment obligation in Article II:1 GATS also covers *de facto* discrimination. See Shaffer (2000), pp. 49–50.

[338] See Sect. 4.2.1.2.1.

[339] Wolfrum (2008), p. 88.

[340] See generally Wojtan (2011), pp. 76–80.

[341] WTO AB Report, *Argentina – Financial* Services, para. 6.105; WTO AB Report, *EC – Bananas III*, paras 244, 246, 248; see generally Van den Bossche and Zdouc (2017), pp. 570–571; Matsushita et al. (2015), p. 571; Munin (2010), pp. 118–120; Wolfrum (2008), p. 87.

[342] Saluzzo (2017), p. 821.

been rejected compared to like services and service suppliers from those states for which adequacy remains undetermined.[343] Svetlana Yakovleva and Kristina Irion disagree because the available legal mechanisms for the transfer of personal data in the GDPR for a country with a negative adequacy decision by the Commission and for countries whose data protection regime have never been assessed are the same, i.e. the instruments providing appropriate safeguards according to Article 46 GDPR.[344] Yakovleva and Irion also add that this is a highly hypothetical scenario because the Commission has never issued a single negative adequacy decision so far.[345] It must be added that there might in fact be consequences for the available data transfer mechanisms should the Commission, or a supervisory authority, or the ECJ, find that the level of protection for personal data that is transferred from the EU to a third country, is not essentially equivalent to that guaranteed within the EU. The instruments providing appropriate safeguards in Article 46 GDPR can only be used if they comply with the right to continuous protection of personal data. They are not available for the transfer of personal data to third countries in which they cannot ensure a level of protection for personal data that is essentially equivalent to that guaranteed within the EU.

4.3.1.1.2 Services with Occasional Flows of Personal Data

Without an adequacy decision, services and service suppliers that only require occasional cross-border flows of personal data from the EU will usually rely on the derogations in Article 49 GDPR. In such cases, services and service suppliers are treated less favorably than like services and service suppliers from states with an adequacy decision. The use of the derogations creates a competitive disadvantage for services and service suppliers in WTO members without an adequacy decision because of the additional burden to comply with the conditions of the derogations.[346] Services and service suppliers from a state with an adequacy decision may transfer personal data without any further requirements. This amounts to treatment less favorable and constitutes an interference with the MFN treatment obligation in Article II:1 GATS.

[343] Reyes (2011), pp. 14–15.

[344] Yakovleva and Irion (2016), p. 203.

[345] Ibid. They also explain that the argument made by Reyes that Australia was granted an inadequacy finding is not valid. Australia received a refusal to grant an adequacy finding from the Article 29 WP. The opinion of the Article 29 WP is not legally binding and does not give a final conclusion on the inadequacy of data protection in Australia. See Article 29 WP (2001), p. 6.

[346] See Sect. 3.1.4.4.

4.3.1.2 Special Framework Adequacy Decisions

The EU adopted some adequacy decisions for special frameworks with third countries such as the invalidated Decision 2000/520, the Safe Harbor adequacy decision, or Decision (EU) 2016/1250, the Privacy Shield adequacy decision. The EU already has plans to adopt a new special framework adequacy decision regarding the US called the Transatlantic Data Privacy Framework.[347] Special framework adequacy decisions must be assessed separately under WTO law. Although these adequacy decisions have the same effect as regular adequacy decisions with regard to the modification of the conditions of competition for services and service suppliers from third countries without an adequacy decision, the justification for the interference with the MFN treatment obligation under the general exceptions in Article XIV GATS will be different. This is because special framework adequacy decisions are often tailor-made decisions for countries that otherwise would not necessarily qualify for a regular adequacy decision.

Perry Keller has argued that that the more lenient treatment for an adequacy finding with such special framework adequacy decisions—a privilege only so far given to the US—in effect afforded the US more favorable treatment compared to other third countries.[348] This argument focuses on the management of the adequacy procedure by the Commission and not on the competitive advantages that the enactment of an adequacy decision can produce for certain countries and not for others. This argument is relevant under Article VI:1 GATS on domestic regulation.

4.3.1.3 Adequacy Assessment

Some scholars have focused on the adequacy assessment in their analyses of the MFN treatment obligation in Article II:1 GATS. First, Stefano Saluzzo argues that the EU would be able to claim that there is no interference with the MFN treatment obligation because all WTO members are on equal footing concerning the access to an adequacy assessment (Sect. 4.3.1.3.1). Second, Eric Shapiro and Carla Reyes claim that irregularities in the management of the adequacy assessment may amount to an infringement of the MFN treatment obligation (Sect. 4.3.1.3.2).

4.3.1.3.1 Access

The panel in *EC – Bananas III (Article 21.5 – Ecuador)* maintained that the EC had treated Ecuador less favorably than other WTO members because Ecuador's service suppliers did "not have opportunities to obtain access to import licences on terms

[347] European Commission (2022a); European Commission (2022b).

[348] Keller (2011), pp. 352–353; Yakovleva and Irion (2016), p. 203.

equal to those enjoyed by service suppliers of EC/ACP origin."[349] Stefano Saluzzo used this finding to show that the EU could rebut a *prima facie* case that the EU's handling of adequacy decisions constitutes a *de facto* interference with the MFN treatment obligation.[350] He argued that "the EU would be able to claim that no violation of the MFN clause occurred in relation to data transfer restrictions, since every country is on an equal footing as far as the adequacy assessment is concerned."[351]

I am of the opinion that the situation in *EC – Bananas III (Article 21.5 – Ecuador)* cannot be applied to adequacy decisions. Saluzzo is right to point out that any country is on equal footing to (informally) ask for an adequacy decision. In that regard, any country has the opportunity to obtain access to an adequacy *assessment* on terms equal to those enjoyed by other countries. However, in *EC – Bananas III (Article 21.5 – Ecuador)*, access to import licenses on equal terms would automatically have created equal competitive opportunities and erased the less favorable treatment. This is different with respect to adequacy decisions. Access to an adequacy assessment does not automatically create equal competitive opportunities. Access to an adequacy assessment does not erase the less favorable treatment because it does not guarantee a favorable outcome in the form of an adequacy decision.

The argument brought forward by Saluzzo would imply that there is an aims-and-effect test in Article II:1 GATS. Only considering the aim of the EU's fundamental rights-based regulation of data transfers under Article II:1 GATS would justify that some countries receive a positive adequacy decision, while others do not. According to the aims-and-effect test, a measure will not be considered as discriminating if the aim of the measure is not discriminatory, even if the result is discriminatory.[352] This is basically what Saluzzo noted when he wrote that "the EU would be able to claim that no violation of the MFN clause occurred in relation to data transfer restrictions, since every country is on an equal footing as far as the adequacy assessment is concerned."[353] The AB stated clearly in *EC – Bananas III* that there is no authority in Article II:1 GATS for the proposition that the aims and effects of a measure are in any way relevant in determining whether that measure is inconsistent with the MFN treatment obligation.[354] In *Argentina – Financial Services*, the AB underlined that the legal standard for the concept of treatment no less favorable in Article II:1 GATS focuses on the modification of the conditions of competition and that this legal standard does not include a separate and additional inquiry into the regulatory objective of, or the regulatory concerns underlying, the contested measure.[355]

[349] WTO Panel Report, *EC – Bananas III (Article 21.5 – Ecuador)*, para. 6.133.

[350] Saluzzo (2017), p. 821.

[351] Ibid.

[352] See generally Van den Bossche and Zdouc (2017), p. 336; Munin (2010), p. 121.

[353] Saluzzo (2017), p. 821.

[354] WTO AB Report, *EC – Bananas III*, para. 241.

[355] WTO AB Report, *Argentina – Financial Services*, para. 6.106.

4.3.1.3.2 Management

Some scholars have claimed that there is less favorable treatment between services and service suppliers in different WTO members because the management of the adequacy assessments lacks consistency.[356] For example, Eric Shapiro argued that there is an interference with the MFN treatment obligation because the EU offered the US much less rigorous terms and that the (invalidated) Safe Harbor adequacy decision required much less of the US than the EU required of Hungary or Australia.[357] Similarly, Carla Reyes argued that services and service suppliers from Australia have been afforded less favorable treatment than like services and service suppliers from other countries where the Article 29 WP also made determinations of inadequate data protection standards, such as for the US and Canada.[358]

These arguments are based on the fact that the application of the adequacy mechanism may amount to an interference with the MFN treatment obligation.[359] They primarily focus on the management of the adequacy assessment by the Commission and not on the advantages that the enactment of an adequacy decision can produce for certain countries and not for others. These arguments are rather relevant under Article VI:1 GATS on domestic regulation, which concerns the administration of a measure, than under Article II:1 GATS, which focuses on the conditions of competition.

4.3.1.4 Appropriate Safeguards

Where no adequacy decision is in place and where the instruments providing appropriate safeguards in Article 46 GDPR are not available either, service suppliers that require systematic, structural, and continuous cross-border flows of personal data for their services cannot rely on any other legal mechanism in the GDPR. Such situations may arise in cases in which a supervisory authority in an EU member state uses its corrective powers and imposes a temporary or definitive limitation including a ban on processing of personal data in the form of data transfers to a third country according to Article 58(2)(f) GDPR or suspends data flows to a recipient in a third country according to Article 58(2)(j) GDPR.[360] In such cases, services and service suppliers are treated less favorably than like services and service suppliers from countries in which the use of the instruments in Article 46 GDPR are generally possible. This modifies the conditions of competition in favor of services and service suppliers from these countries. The EU does not immediately and unconditionally

356 Yakovleva and Irion (2016), p. 203.

357 Shapiro (2003), p. 2819.

358 Reyes (2011), p. 14.

359 Cp. Saluzzo (2017), p. 821.

360 See Sect. 3.3.4.

accord treatment no less favorable. This interferes with the MFN treatment obligation in Article II:1 GATS.

4.3.2 Domestic Regulation

Article VI GATS on domestic regulation balances trade liberalization with the right of WTO members to regulate. Some of the requirements for domestic regulation in Article VI GATS are relevant for the EU system for data transfers. This concerns the procedural requirements in Paragraph 1 that relate to the administration of a measure (Sect. 4.3.2.1) and the requirements in Paragraph 2 that relate to judicial, arbitral or administrative mechanisms for the review of measures at the request of an affected service supplier (Sect. 4.3.2.2). Contrary to the claims of some scholars, the other requirements in Article VI GATS are not relevant for the EU system for data transfers. This concerns Paragraph 3 relating to authorization requirements (Sect. 4.3.2.3) and Paragraphs 4 and 5 relating to qualification procedures, technical standards, and licensing requirements (Sect. 4.3.2.4).

4.3.2.1 Administration of Measures

Article VI:1 GATS relates to the administration of measures.[361] The requirements for domestic regulation in Article VI:1 GATS oblige WTO members to administer measures of general application affecting trade in services in sectors where specific commitments are undertaken in a reasonable, objective, and impartial manner. A measure of general application covers a range of cases and situations and thus affects an unidentified number of economic operators.[362] The GDPR in general, and the regulation of data transfers specifically, can be considered a measure of general application as they cover all transfers of personal data from the EU to third countries and thus affect an unidentified number of economic operators.[363] The aim of Article VI:1 GATS is to promote the principles of consistency and predictability in the application of domestic measures, so as to avoid adverse effects on the business performance of foreign service suppliers. The regulation of data transfers in the EU should be dealt with according to the different ways and procedures it is applied rather than the degree of the restrictions imposed.[364] Potential problems with

---

[361] See generally Van den Bossche and Zdouc (2017), p. 535; Munin (2010), pp. 272–275; Krajewski (2008), pp. 168–172.

[362] Cp. WTO Panel Report, *EC – Selected Custom Matters*, para. 7.116 (on Article X:1 GATT); WTO Panel Report, *US – Underwear*, para. 7.65 (on Article X:1 GATT).

[363] Yakovleva and Irion (2016), p. 205; Irion et al. (2016), p. 31; Reyes (2011), p. 18.

[364] Cp. Saluzzo (2017), p. 825. In contrast, Carla Reyes assumes that under one of two competing standards, Article VI:1 GATS imposes a substantive proportionality requirement. Reyes argues that the prohibition to transfer personal data to countries without an adequate level of protection for

the administration may occur with regard to regular adequacy decisions (Sect. 4.3.2.1.1), special framework adequacy decisions (Sect. 4.3.2.1.2), standard data protection clauses (Sect. 4.3.2.1.3), BCRs (Sect. 4.3.2.1.4), derogations (Sect. 4.3.2.1.5), and overlapping requirements due to the geographical scope of application of the GDPR (Sect. 4.3.2.1.6).

4.3.2.1.1 Adequacy Decisions

The administration of the regulation for data transfers in the EU potentially faces four problems regarding adequacy decisions and Article VI:1 GATS. The number of adequacy decisions (Sect. 4.3.2.1.1.1), the selection of countries for adequacy decisions (Sect. 4.3.2.1.1.2), the consistency of the adequacy assessment (Sect. 4.3.2.1.1.3), and the procedures of the adequacy assessment (Sect. 4.3.2.1.1.4).

4.3.2.1.1.1 Number of Adequacy Decisions

A first problem relates to the number of countries that receive an adequacy decision. Carla Reyes has argued that the EU has had difficulties in explaining why the current selection of countries with an adequacy decision—14 in total under the GDPR—is reasonable given the more than 140 other countries that continue to import personal data from the EU in the absence of an adequacy decision.[365]

The administration of a measure is reasonable if it is in accordance with generally accepted standards of rationality and sound judgment.[366] There must be a rational reason for the conduct in question.[367] Apart from the fact that adequacy decisions are only available for countries that provide a level of protection of personal data that is essentially equivalent to that guaranteed within the EU, it would require a huge amount of effort on the part of the European Commission to maintain 100 or more adequacy decisions. The GDPR entails extensive obligations regarding their monitoring and review.[368] These obligations are necessary to comply with the right to continuous protection of personal data. It is reasonable that the Commission has

personal data is the most restrictive means available for a data transfer system to achieve its objectives. According to Reyes, this violates Article VI:1 GATS. While the assumption cannot be maintained that Article VI:1 GATS imposes a substantive proportionality requirement, Reyes also ignores that the derogations in Article 49 GDPR still allow data transfers to countries in which the protection for personal data is not essentially equivalent to that guaranteed within the EU. See Reyes (2011), p. 19. This was also criticized by Svetlana Yakovleva and Kristina Irion. See Yakovleva and Irion (2016), p. 205.

[365] Reyes (2011), pp. 19–20; Velli (2019), p. 886.

[366] WTO Panel Report, *Dominican Republic – Import and Sale of Cigarettes*, para. 7.385 (on Article X:3(a) GATT).

[367] Krajewski (2008), p. 171.

[368] Article 45(3)–(6) GDPR. See also Sect. 3.2.3.

been slow to extend the number of adequacy decisions as the necessary assessments and negotiations for an adequacy decision are complicated and lengthy.

This is supported by the fact that the GDPR provides alternative legal mechanisms for the transfer of personal data for WTO members that do not yet have an adequacy decision yet provide a level of protection of personal data that is essentially equivalent to that guaranteed within the EU. The instruments providing appropriate safeguards in Article 46 GDPR allow the same kind of data transfers as adequacy decisions. The lack of an adequacy decision thus has no impact on the kind of transfers of personal data from the EU to a third country, *but* it is more burdensome to use the instruments in Article 46 GDPR. A *prima facie* case of compliance with Article VI:1 GATS could be rebutted when a complainant shows that there are many WTO members without an adequacy decision that provide a level of protection for personal data that is essentially equivalent to that guaranteed within the EU and that the EU consciously avoids granting them an adequacy decision or even enter into the procedures to adopt one. I do not find that this is currently the case, but I submit that such a situation would amount to an unreasonable administration of the EU regulation of data transfers and as such would interfere with the standards of Article VI:1 GATS.

4.3.2.1.1.2 Selection of Countries for Adequacy Decisions

A second problem relates to the selection of countries that receive adequacy decisions. Svetlana Yakovleva and Kristina Irion have submitted that the country-by-country adequacy assessment falls short of the impartiality and objectivity standard in Article VI:1 GATS.[369] They argue that there are no formal criteria on when and how third countries' data protection regimes are to be assessed for their adequacy. They underline that adequacy decisions do not seem to rely on a legal-only assessment and may not be considered even-handed.

The administration of a measure is not impartial if the application is unfair, biased or prejudiced.[370] For the administration of a measure to be objective, it may not be arbitrary.[371] According to the OED, "arbitrary" means "derived from mere opinion or preference" and "not based on the nature of things."[372] While it is true that there are certain indications for preferential treatment of countries with regard to adequacy decisions, none of these indications amount to a biased application of the EU's regulation of data transfers in general, and adequacy decisions specifically. I have shown that neither geographical nor economic factors seem to be coherently applied for preferential treatment with regard to adequacy decisions.[373] Yakovleva and Irion

[369] Yakovleva and Irion (2016), p. 205; see also Reyes (2011), pp. 19–20.

[370] Cp. WTO Panel Report, *Thailand – Cigarettes (Philippines)*, para. 7.898 (on Article X(3)(a) GATT).

[371] See Krajewski (2008), p. 171.

[372] OED online, entry for arbitrary (adj.).

[373] See Sect. 3.2.1.4.

point out that there are no formal criteria on when and how third countries' data protection regimes are to be assessed for their adequacy, but the Commission has a strategy for adequacy decisions with informal criteria.[374] The strategy puts third countries at a disadvantage if they are not negotiating a trade agreement with the EU, could be dangerous for the outsourcing of data processing operations, and are neither geographically nor culturally close to the EU.[375] But even this strategy allows the consideration of countries that are potentially at a disadvantage if they are data protection champions and serve as a role model for other third countries. This would underline that the country-by-country adequacy assessment is not unfair nor prejudiced, but actually based on the nature of things, i.e., the protection for personal data that is essentially equivalent to that guaranteed within the EU.

I thus argue that the administration of the EU regulation of data transfers regarding the selection of countries that receive an adequacy decision does not interfere with the standards in Article VI:1 GATS. An exception to that submission would concern a country that is constantly denied an adequacy decision even when it is widely acknowledged—over a substantial period of time—that it provides a level of protection for personal data that is essentially equivalent to that guaranteed within the EU. There does not, however, seem to be a WTO member to which this description applies.

4.3.2.1.1.3 Consistency of Adequacy Assessments

A third problem relates to the consistency of adequacy assessments. Some content-related inconsistencies have been mentioned above.[376] Yakovleva and Irion have specifically highlighted that not all of the Commission's adequacy decisions require that the third country restricts the onward transfer of personal data to countries without adequate protection.[377] Even though the GDPR now entails more detailed requirements for adequacy decisions, including rules for the onward transfer of personal data, such inconsistencies in the adequacy assessment under Directive 95/46/EC may put into question the impartiality of the administration of the EU system for data transfers with regard to adequacy decisions.[378] In spite of this, it has to be noted that in order to constitute a violation of Article VI:1 GATS, there must be "a significant impact on the overall administration of the law, and not simply on the outcome in the single case in question."[379] The EU's more recent adequacy decisions have been much more carefully drafted and the new detailed requirements in the GDPR leave less room for such inconsistencies, if any at all. It would thus be difficult to argue that the mentioned content-related inconsistencies have a

[374] European Commission (2017), p. 8.

[375] See Sect. 3.2.1.4.

[376] See Sect. 3.2.1.3.

[377] Yakovleva and Irion (2016), p. 205.

[378] Yakovleva and Irion refer to the standard of reasonableness instead. Ibid.

[379] Cp. WTO Panel Report, *US – Hot Rolled Steel*, para. 7.268 (on Article X:3(a) GATT).

significant impact on the overall administration of the EU system for data transfers with regard to adequacy decisions and not just on the single case in question. This is especially true when considering that under the GDPR all adequacy decisions must be reviewed every four years, which includes the adequacy decisions taken under Directive 95/46/EC.[380] I thus conclude that the administration of the EU regulation of data transfers with regard to the consistency of adequacy assessments does not interfere with the high standards in Article VI:1 GATS.

4.3.2.1.1.4 Procedures of the Adequacy Assessment

A fourth problem relates to the procedures of adequacy assessments. The Commission oversees all adequacy decisions. There are no formal procedures third countries can pursue to apply for an adequacy decision. Consequently, the informal ways in which the EU deals with inquires for an adequacy decision may be susceptible to interferences with Article VI:1 GATS.

The Commission has never issued a negative adequacy decision. However, Australia received a negative adequacy assessment from the Article 29 WP and the four African countries Burkina Faso, Mauritius, Tunisia, and Morocco all received negative adequacy assessments from an academic institution in the EU tasked to research the level of data protection in these countries.[381] The administration of a measure is not impartial if the application is unfair, biased or prejudiced.[382] The mentioned example do not show prejudice because there is some form of assessment even if it is not by the same institution for all inquiring countries, and even if it is not followed by a final administrative decision when the preliminary results of the assessment are negative. Article VI:1 GATS does not require the EU to issue negative administrative decisions in order for the EU system for data transfers to be fair with regard to adequacy decisions.[383]

Jennifer Stoddart, Benny Chan, and Yann Joly underline that the *ad hoc* and discretionary manner in which the Article 29 WP, the EDPB and the Commission seek clarifications and broker deals for adequacy decisions "speaks volumes about the consistency and predictability of adequacy assessments" and therefore seems to be arbitrary at times.[384] It has also been mentioned above that some countries receive

[380] Article 45(3)–(6) and (9) GDPR.

[381] Makulilo (2013), p. 49.

[382] Cp. WTO Panel Report, *Thailand – Cigarettes (Philippines)*, para. 7.898 (on Article X(3)(a) GATT).

[383] Article VI:2(a) GATS only obliges WTO members to maintain practicable, judicial, arbitral or administrative tribunals or procedures that provide, at the request of an affected service supplier, for the prompt review of, and where justified, appropriate remedies for, *administrative decisions* affecting trade in services. It cannot be adduced from Article VI:2(a) GATS that Article VI:1 GATS requires an administrative decision when a WTO member extends an advantage to a third country, but not to another.

[384] Stoddart et al. (2016), p. 147.

more active support in order to reach an adequacy decision.[385] Nevertheless, any claim about impartiality here is highly unlikely to succeed because this extra support does not have a significant impact on the overall administration of the EU's regulation of data transfers with regard to adequacy decisions, but rather on the outcome of the single case in question.[386] In consequence, I argue that the administration of the EU system for data transfers with regard to the procedures of the adequacy assessment does not interfere with the standards in Article VI:1 GATS.

4.3.2.1.2 Special Framework Adequacy Decisions

The administration of the EU's regulation for data transfers also faces a problem with special framework adequacy decisions such as the invalidated Decision 2000/520, the Safe Harbor adequacy decision, or the invalidated Decision (EU) 2016/1250, the Privacy Shield adequacy decision, and Article VI:1 GATS. Special framework adequacy decisions are tailor-made decisions for countries that otherwise would not necessarily qualify for a regular adequacy decision. After the invalidation of the Privacy Shield adequacy decision by the ECJ in *Schrems 2*, there are no special framework adequacy decisions in force anymore. However, the European Commission already negotiated a new special framework for an adequacy decision with the US and initiated the process to adopt the corresponding adequacy decision.[387] If this adequacy decision is adopted, then other WTO members that may not necessarily qualify for an adequacy decision either—and have not been able to negotiate such a special framework—could claim that the administration of the EU system for data transfers with regard to special framework adequacy decisions is not compatible with Article VI:1 GATS because it is not impartial. These countries could also claim that there is a significant impact on the overall administration of the EU system for data transfers because the special framework adequacy decisions are an additional mechanism for data transfers which is not available to them.[388] Accordingly, the administration of the EU's regulation of data transfers with regard to special framework adequacy decisions would not comply with Article VI:1 GATS.

4.3.2.1.3 Standard Data Protection Clauses

The administration of the EU's regulation of data transfers could also have a problem with regard to the standard data protection clauses and Article VI:1 GATS. Control over continuous protection for personal data in relation with standard data protection

---

[385] See Sect. 3.2.1.2.

[386] Cp. WTO Panel Report, *US – Hot Rolled Steel*, para. 7.268 (on Article X:3(a) GATT).

[387] European Commission (2022a); European Commission (2022b).

[388] Cp. ibid.

clauses lies primarily with the supervisory authorities of the EU member states.[389] Each of them is vested with the power to examine whether data transfers from its home EU member state to a third country on the basis of standard data protection clauses comply with the requirements laid down in the GDPR and the right to continuous protection of personal data in Article 8 CFR. If data transfers do not comply with these requirements, the supervisory authorities must use their corrective powers such as the imposition of a temporary or definitive limitation according to Article 58(2)(f) GDPR or the suspension of data flows to a recipient in a third country according to Article 58(2)(j) GDPR.

There is a risk that some transfers of personal data to a third country on the basis of standard data protection clauses could be permitted in one EU member state but suspended or banned in another depending on whether the responsible supervisory authority had investigated issues surrounding the transfer of personal data to that third country, or had reached a different conclusions regarding the violation of the requirements in the GDPR and Article 8 CFR.[390] The risk that the approaches taken by the different supervisory authorities can be fragmented is inherent in the decentralized structure for supervision intended by the EU legislator.[391] That risk is somewhat mediated with the voluntary consistency mechanism in Article 64(2) GDPR, which enables supervisory authorities to request an opinion from the EDPB when deciding to suspend or ban data transfers to a third country. Regular opinions of the EDPB are not legally binding, but they carry considerable weight. It can be expected that supervisory authorities will follow an EDPB opinion regarding the suspension or ban of data transfers to a third country. The EDPB also has the option to adopt a legally binding decision under Article 65(1)(c) GDPR, should a supervisory authority not follow an opinion of the EDPB.[392] Even though this voluntary mechanism is in place, the risk remains that some transfers of personal data to a third country on the basis of standard data protection clauses could be permitted in one EU member state but suspended or banned in another.

I therefore argue that a fragmented application of the corrective powers of supervisory authorities with regard to data transfers on the basis of standard data protection clauses would allow for a successful claim under the objective and/or impartial standard of Article VI:1 GATS. This is especially true since the assessment of an interference with Article VI:1 GATS may also involve an examination of the impact on the competitive situation due to alleged partiality in the application of a law or regulation.[393] The voluntary consistency mechanism in Article 64(2) GDPR and the power of the EDPB to adopt a legally binding decision in Article 65(1)(c) GDPR should be used in order to prevent any incompatibility with Article VI:1 GATS.

---

[389] See Sect. 3.3.4.

[390] See Sect. 3.3.3.1.5.

[391] ECJ, *Wirtschaftsakademie Schleswig-Holstein*, paras 69–73.

[392] Ibid.

[393] Cp. WTO Panel Report, *Argentina – Hides and Leather*, para. 11.77 (on Article X(3)(a) GATT).

4.3.2.1.4 BCRs

The administration of the EU's regulation of data transfers regarding BCRs and Article VI:1 GATS is not as problematic compared to standard data protection clauses. Control over continuous protection for personal data through BCRs also primarily lies with the supervisory authorities of the EU member states.[394] The mechanism to approve BCRs allows the responsible supervisory authority the possibility to prohibit data transfers to third countries where interferences with the right to continuous protection for personal data might occur. The approval of BCRs is subject to the mandatory consistency mechanism in Article 63 GDPR.[395] This mechanism supports a consistent administration of the EU system for data transfers with regard to BCRs that is compatible with Article VI:1 GATS.

4.3.2.1.5 Derogations

The administration of the EU's regulation of data transfers regarding derogations under Article 49 GDPR and Article VI:1 GATS is also unproblematic. Andrew D. Mitchell and Jarrod Hepburn have submitted that there is a likelihood that the requirement to obtain consent before transmitting personal information across borders violates the domestic regulation obligation in Article VI GATS.[396] In their argument they refer to Usman Ahmed and Anupam Chander who in turn have argued that there are difficulties in obtaining consent when it comes to devices that capture information about more than one person.[397] While it may be a valid point that a framework that requires consent for systematic, structural, and continuous data transfer is unreasonable, the derogations under Article 49 GDPR can only be used for *occasional* data transfers anyway. Even though Usman and Chander also stated that "[w]e do not typically require a special consent before a consumer purchases a good, or even food, from a foreign source," a consent requirement is reasonable with regard to occasional data transfers because, contrary to the mentioned examples, the purchase of a service such as supplied by travel agencies, or digital medical diagnosis services, or legal services requires processing of personal data.[398] The requirement of an agreement from the data subject for occasional data transfers based either on consent according to Article 49(1)(a) GDPR or on a contract according to Article 49(1)(b) GDPR is not unreasonable and therefore compatible with Article VI:1 GATS.

---

[394] See Sect. 3.3.4.

[395] Articles 47(1) and 64(1)(f) GDPR.

[396] Mitchell and Hepburn (2017), p. 200.

[397] Usman and Chander (2015), pp. 6–7.

[398] Ibid.

4.3.2.1.6 Overlapping Requirements

There is an additional element that must be considered when analyzing the administration of the EU's regulation of data transfers according to Article VI:1 GATS. Svetlana Yakovleva and Kristina Irion have stressed that the regulation of data transfers and the provisions on the geographical scope of application in the GDPR create two sets of overlapping requirements that are not coordinated with each other.[399] According to Article 3(2)(a) GDPR, the regulation also applies to the processing of personal data of data subjects who are in the EU by a controller or processor not established in the EU in cases in which the processing activities are related to the offering of services to data subjects in the EU irrespective of whether a payment of the data subject is required.[400] A service supplier in a WTO member without an adequacy decision whose services require data transfers from the EU must thus potentially comply with the regulation of data transfers *and* the other rules of the GDPR at the same time. I therefore conclude that the overlapping requirements are reasonable with regard to Article VI:1 GATS.[401] The safeguards for personal data provided by the EU's regulation of data transfers are necessary to prevent the circumvention of EU law.[402] I thus argue that the administration of the EU regulation of data transfers as a measure to prevent the circumvention of EU law taken together with the provisions on the geographical scope of application in the GDPR, does not interfere with accepted standards of rationality and sound judgment.[403] It is consistent with Article VI:1 GATS.

4.3.2.2 Judicial, Arbitral or Administrative Mechanisms

Article VI:2(a) GATS relates to the administration of justice.[404] The requirements for domestic regulation in Article VI:2(a) GATS oblige WTO members to maintain practicable, judicial, arbitral or administrative tribunals or procedures that provide, at the request of an affected service supplier—and where justified—appropriate remedies for administrative decisions affecting trade in services. Potential problems with the administration of justice regarding the EU's fundamental rights-based regulation

[399] Yakovleva and Irion (2016), p. 205; Kuner (2015), p. 244.

[400] See generally Svantesson (2020), pp. 88–91; Ruotolo (2018), pp. 22–24.

[401] Yakovleva and Irion (2016), p. 205.

[402] See Sect. 3.1.2.1.

[403] Cp. WTO Panel Report, *Dominican Republic – Import and Sale of Cigarettes*, para. 7.385 (on Article X:1 GATT). See also Yakovleva and Irion (2016), p. 205.

[404] See generally Van den Bossche and Zdouc (2017), pp. 535–536; Munin (2010), pp. 277–281; Krajewski (2008), pp. 173–176.

of data transfers may occur with regard to adequacy decisions (Sect. 4.3.2.2.1), standard data protection clauses (Sect. 4.3.2.2.2), and BCRs (Sect. 4.3.2.2.3).[405]

4.3.2.2.1 Adequacy Decisions

Adequacy decisions face a potential problem with Article VI:2(a) GATS. Stefano Saluzzo has submitted that a rejection of an adequacy assessment may not easily be subject to judicial scrutiny in the EU.[406] Saluzzo has argued that a positive adequacy assessment is adopted in the form of an "implementing act," the legitimacy of which can be verified by the ECJ, whereas in case of a negative adequacy assessment no formal act is actually made.[407] There is no right to an adequacy assessment under EU law.[408] Consequently, there is no obligation for the European Commission to issue a negative adequacy decision under EU law when a third country does not provide an adequate level of protection for personal data. Negative adequacy assessments were/are either issued by the Article 29 WP, the EDPB or an academic institution tasked to research the level of protection for personal data in a third country.[409] The reports that contain negative adequacy assessments are not legally binding and do not constitute administrative decisions according to Article VI:2(a) GATS. In the absence of an administrative decision, ArticleVI:2(a) GATS does not oblige the EU to maintain review procedures and remedies. There is no interference with Article VI:2(a) GATS.

4.3.2.2.2 Standard Data Protection Clauses

The procedures surrounding standard data protection clauses satisfy the requirements in Article VI:2(a) GATS. Every natural and legal person has the right to an effective judicial remedy against a legally binding decision of a supervisory authority concerning them based on Article 78(1) GDPR. This also covers a decision of a supervisory authority to impose a temporary or definitive limitation or ban on

---

[405] Kristina Irion, Svetlana Yakovleva and Marija Bartl suggested that the EU's fundamental rights-based regulation does not trigger Article VI:2 GATS because it does not mount authorization, qualification or licensing requirements, nor can it be considered a technical standard. That is not important because Article VI:2 GATS relates to administrative decisions without referring to authorization, qualification or licensing requirements, or technical standards. Irion et al. (2016), p. 31.

[406] Saluzzo (2017), p. 826.

[407] Ibid.

[408] See Sect. 3.2.1.1.

[409] Australia is an example of a country that received a negative adequacy assessment from the Article 29 WP and the four African countries Burkina Faso, Mauritius, Tunisia, and Morocco are examples of countries that received a negative adequacy assessment from an academic institution in the EU tasked to research the level of data protection in these countries.

processing of personal data according to Article 58(2)(f) GDPR or the suspension of data flows to a recipient in a third country according to Article 58(2)(j) GDPR. The proceedings against a supervisory authority must be brought before the courts of the EU member state in which the supervisory authority is established according to Article 78(3) GDPR. There is no interference with Article VI:2(a) GATS.

4.3.2.2.3 BCRs

The procedures surrounding BCRs satisfy the requirements in Article VI:2(a) GATS. The right of every legal person to an effective judicial remedy against a legally binding decision of a supervisory authority in Article 78(1) GDPR also covers the decisions of a supervisory authority not to approve BCRs. The proceedings against the supervisory authority must be brought before the courts of the EU member state in which the supervisory authority is established according to Article 78(3) GDPR. Where the proceedings are brought against a decision of a supervisory authority which was preceded by an opinion of the EDPB according to the consistency mechanism, such as in the case of the approval of BCRs, the opinion must be forwarded to the responsible court based on Article 78(4) GDPR. In these cases, there is no interference with Article VI:2(a) GATS.

4.3.2.3 Authorization Requirements

Article VI:3 GATS relates to authorization requirements for the supply of a service on which a specific commitment has been made. Where such authorization requirements are in place, Article VI:3 GATS obliges WTO members to inform applicants of the decision concerning the status of their application. Carla Reyes claims that the regulation of data transfers in the EU interferes with this provision to the extent that countries initially determined to provide inadequate data protection standards remain uninformed of opportunities to rectify their status, and countries for which no determination has been made remain uninformed of the investigation timeline.[410] This claim is wrong because the regulation of data transfers in the EU does *not* constitute an authorization requirement for the supply of services.[411] Article VI:3 GATS does not apply to the EU system for data transfers.

---

[410] Reyes (2011), p. 20.

[411] Cp. Yakovleva and Irion (2016), p. 205.

4.3.2.4 Qualification Procedures, Technical Standards and Licensing Requirements

Article VI:4 and Article VI:5 GATS relate to qualification procedures, technical standards, and licensing requirements. Shin-Yi Peng claims that these paragraphs apply to the rules on the protection of personal data because they constitute technical standards within the meaning of Article VI GATS.[412] Peng argues that according to WTO negotiating papers, technical standards are measures that lay down the characteristics of a service or the manner in which it is supplied.[413] The regulation of data transfers in the EU, however, determines how personal data can be transferred from the EU to a third country. While it affects the supply of services, it does *not* lay down the characteristics of a service or the manner in which it is supplied.[414] Paragraphs 4 and 5 of Article VI GATS therefore do not apply to the EU system for data transfers.

4.3.3 Market Access

The market access obligation in Article XVI GATS applies only to the commitments, conditions, and qualifications in the schedule of a WTO member.[415] In sectors in which the EU has undertaken market access commitments, it need not maintain—unless specified in the schedule—limitations on the number of service suppliers according to Article XVI:2(a) GATS and limitations on the total number of service operations or on the total quantity of service output according to Article XVI:2(c) GATS. The analysis of the EU's fundamental rights-based regulation of data transfers under the market access obligation requires clarifications regarding the relationship of data localization and market access (Sect. 4.3.3.1). It is only possible to determine an interference with Article XVI:2(a) and (c) GATS when looking at specific examples of services that require systematic, structural, and continuous cross-border flows of personal data (Sect. 4.3.3.2) and specific examples of services that require occasional cross-border flows of personal data (Sect. 4.3.3.3). To complete the picture, it is necessary to mention two options to prevent interference with the market access obligation in Article XVI:2(a) and (c) GATS: the EU could either modify its schedule of commitments or the WTO members could conclude the electronic commerce negotiations with a horizontal provision on the protection of personal data and privacy (Sect. 4.3.3.4).

---

[412] Peng (2011), p. 764. See also Weber (2012), p. 37.

[413] Ibid. See for example WTO (2009), para. 9 accessible in South Centre (2009), Annex 1.

[414] Cp. Yakovleva and Irion (2016), p. 205; Irion et al. (2016), p. 31.

[415] See generally Van den Bossche and Zdouc (2017), pp. 517–521; Matsushita et al. (2015), pp. 593–603; Munin (2010), pp. 183–206; Delimatsis and Molinuevo (2008), pp. 369–386.

4.3.3.1 The Relationship Between Data Localization and Market Access

The relationship between data localization and market access has to be clarified before the obligation in Article XVI GATS can be assessed. When cross-border flows of personal data are restricted, foreign service suppliers are required to store and process personal data on servers located in the EU. It is necessary to clarify whether the supply of services in mode 1 (cross-border) includes the ability to store and process personal data in the territory of the WTO member where the service supplier is located (Sect. 4.3.3.1.1). Furthermore, it is necessary to clarify whether the market access obligation covers both quantitative and qualitative implications of data localization on trade in services (Sect. 4.3.3.1.2).

4.3.3.1.1 Cross-border Supply of Services and Data Localization

When the regulation of data transfers in the EU leads to a restriction on cross-border flows of personal data to a certain country, foreign service suppliers in that country may not export personal data from the EU and store and process it where they are located. This amounts to a data localization requirement. In that case, foreign service suppliers have to store and process personal data in the EU. Should the supply of services in mode 1 (cross-border) include the ability to store and process personal data in the territory of the WTO member in which the service supplier is located, then the market access obligation in Article XVI:2(a) and (c) GATS is affected by the EU's regulation of data transfers.

The Scheduling Guidelines of 2001 clarify that under mode 1 the "[s]ervice supplier [is] not present within the territory of the Member."[416] The panel in *Mexico – Telecoms* relied on the explanatory note on scheduling of initial commitments in trade in services, which states that the supply of a service through telecommunications is an example of cross-border supply "since the service supplier is not present within the territory of the Member where the service is delivered."[417] This indicates that the cross-border supply of services is not compatible with data localization. Data localization implies a certain presence or operation of the service supplier in the territory of the WTO member where the service is consumed. Daniel Crosby has submitted that where a WTO member makes a full mode 1 commitment, "it may not condition the supply of cross-border services on the services suppliers' presence or operation within its territory."[418]

This submission is supported by the fact that the supply of services includes the production, distribution, marketing, sale, and delivery of a service according to the definition in Article XXVIII(b) GATS. The storage and processing of personal data can be essential to *produce* a service. The supply of services in mode 1 (cross-

---

[416] WTO (2001), para. 26.

[417] WTO Panel Report, *Mexico – Telecoms*, para. 7.43; GATT Secretariat (1993), para. 19(a).

[418] Crosby (2016), p. 3.

border) therefore includes the ability to store and process personal data in the territory of the WTO member where the service supplier is located. Trade in services under mode 1 thus covers cross-border flows of personal data required to produce services. Data localization hinders this cross-border supply of services.

4.3.3.1.2 Quantitative and Qualitative Implications of Data Localization

The implications of data localization for the cross-border supply of services can be either quantitative or qualitative in nature. Market access is a legally defined concept that encompasses a limited set of situations that do not entail qualitative elements.[419] The AB has maintained that a measure that totally prohibits the supply of a service constitutes a market access limitation according to Article XVI:2(a) and (c) GATS because it effectively limits to zero the number of service suppliers, service operations, and service output.[420] The focus lies on the numerical or quantitative nature of a measure. A zero quota constitutes a market access limitation that takes the form of a numerical quota.[421]

The regulation of data transfers in the EU, however, is not numerical or quantitative in regard to the supply of services. It does not directly prohibit the supply of services. Rather it relates to cross-border flows of personal data and not to the supply of specific services. Nevertheless, the regulation of data transfers may amount to an indirect prohibition for the supply of a service when cross-border flows of personal data are restricted.[422] Two types of services that require data transfers need to be distinguished:

- The first type covers services for which the cross-border flow of personal data is an unavoidable element. In this type, the use of personal data, and the corresponding data flows, are a *conditio sine qua non* for the supply of those services. This creates an interference with the market access obligation in Article XVI:2(a) and (c) GATS whenever the regulation of data transfers in the EU prevents the performance of a service for which cross-border flows of personal data are an unavoidable element.[423] In these cases, the data localization amounts to a zero quota because it effectively limits to zero the number of service suppliers, service operations, and service output.
- The second type covers services which can also be supplied without cross-border flows of personal data. In this type, the use of personal data, and the corresponding data flows, are not unavoidable for the services to be supplied. Such services use personal data, and the corresponding data flows, to improve the

[419] Delimatsis and Molinuevo (2008), pp. 376–377.
[420] WTO AB Report, *US – Gambling*, paras 232; 252.
[421] Ibid., para. 227; WTO Panel Report, *US – Gambling*, para. 6.355.
[422] See Sect. 4.1.2.
[423] Cp. Ruotolo (2018), p. 20.

quality of the services or to generate additional income. In these cases, the data localization is a qualitative element not encompassed by Article XVI:2(a) and (c) GATS.[424]

4.3.3.2 Services with Systematic Flows of Personal Data

Some scholars have submitted that the default prohibition on the transfer of personal data from the EU to third countries with inadequate protection effectively constitutes a zero quota violating the market access obligation in Article XVI:2(a) and (c) GATS.[425] Svetlana Yakovleva, Kristina Irion, and Marija Bartl argue that this submission ignores the availability of other legal mechanisms for data transfers.[426] They offer a convincing argument, but it needs further differentiation:

In the absence of an adequacy decision, service suppliers may use instruments that provide appropriate safeguards according to Article 46 GDPR for systematic, structural, and continuous cross-border flows of personal data. Nevertheless, this still leaves open situations in which the data exporter has to stop the transfer of personal data from the EU or supervisory authorities in EU member states use their corrective powers and ban or suspend the data transfers in order to comply with the right to continuous protection for personal data in Article 8 CFR. It has to be stressed that the exercise of the powers of supervisory authorities to suspend and prohibit transfers set out in Article 58(2)(f) and (j) of the GDPR is no longer merely an option left to the supervisory authorities' discretion.[427] The data exporter and the supervisory authorities are obliged to ensure compliance with the GDPR and the right to continuous protection for personal data. This could increasingly lead to the unavailability of the instruments that provide appropriate safeguards under Article 46 GDPR for certain transfers of personal data to certain third countries in the future. Especially in cases in which measures that supplement transfer tools to ensure compliance with the EU level of protection of personal data are not available.[428] In this situation, the fundamental rights-based regulation of data transfers in the EU potentially interferes with the market access obligations in Article XVI:2(a) and (c) GATS with regard to services that require systematic, structural, and continuous cross-border flows of personal data.

In addition, the availability of derogations for data transfers in Article 49 GDPR cannot preclude an interference with the market access obligation in Article XVI:2(a) and (c) GATS when the services require systematic, structural, and continuous cross-border flows of personal data. The consent-based derogation in Article 49(1)(a)

---

[424] But see Meltzer (2019), p. 25.

[425] See Weber (2012), pp. 33–34; Reyes (2011), p. 20; Peng (2011), p. 762.

[426] Yakovleva and Irion (2016), pp. 204–205; Irion et al. (2016), p. 32.

[427] ECJ, *Schrems 2*, para. 135; ECJ, AG Opinion, *Schrems 2*, para. 144.

[428] EDPB (2020), pp. 26–27.

GDPR and the contract-based derogation in Article 49(1)(b) GDPR are not available are only available for services that require occasional cross-border flows of personal data.

I now turn to analyze whether the following services cannot be supplied through mode 1withouth cross-border flows of personal data: cloud computing services (Sect. 4.3.3.2.1), search engine services (Sect. 4.3.3.2.2), social network services (Sect. 4.3.3.2.3), online advertising services (Sect. 4.3.3.2.4), IoT services (Sect. 4.3.3.2.5), and sharing economy platform services (Sect. 4.3.3.2.6).

4.3.3.2.1 Cloud Computing Services

When cloud computing is not part of another integrated service, it may constitute trade in services itself. There are three different types of cloud computing services that should be individually classified. IaaS may be classified as "Data processing services" (W/120-1.B.c) while PaaS as well as SaaS may be classified as "Software implementation services" (W/120-1.B.b).[429] The EU did not schedule any limitations on market access with regard to the cross-border supply of data processing services. Apart from Malta, which remains unbound, the EU member states committed to open their markets to the cross-border supply of data processing services.[430] The same is true for software implementation services.[431]

It is difficult to determine whether restrictions on structural, continuous, and systematic cross-border flows of personal data amounts to a zero quota for cloud computing services (regardless of the type). Answering this question requires in-depth knowledge of the industry, the technology, and current practices. It is not possible to give a definitive answer here. There are examples for IaaS that do not involve cross-border flows of personal data such as IaaS in support of cloud-based numerical weather prediction.[432] Yet, restrictions on the free flow of personal data across borders drastically limits the possibilities of foreign cloud computing providers to supply IaaS. Nevertheless, I would argue that it does not amount to a zero quota and an interference with the market access obligation in Article XVI:2(a) and (c) GATS because IaaS would be available for a certain segment of the market that does not require personal data. The limitations on the possibilities of foreign cloud computing providers to supply IaaS will be relevant with regard to the modification of the conditions of competition under the national treatment obligation in Article XVII GATS.

It is less clear whether there are also examples for PaaS or SaaS that do not involve cross-border flows of personal data.[433] It should be assumed that there is a valid case

[429] See Sect. 4.2.3.4.1.

[430] WTO (2019f), p. 61.

[431] Ibid., 58.

[432] Molthan et al. (2015), p. 1371.

[433] W. Kuan Hon, Christopher Millard, and Ian Walden show that cross-border flows of personal data necessarily occur in cloud computing services that use personal data because excluding the

for a zero quota for PaaS and SaaS when such data flows are prohibited. In these cases, the fundamental rights-based regulation of data transfers in the EU would constitute an interference with the market access obligation in Article XVI:2(a) and (c) GATS.[434]

4.3.3.2.2 Search Engine Services

Search engine services may be classified as "Data base services" (W/120-1.B.c).[435] The EU did not schedule any limitations on market access with regard to the cross-border supply of data processing services. Apart from Malta, which remains unbound, the EU member states committed to open their markets to the cross-border supply of data base services.[436]

Systematic, structural, and continuous cross-border flows of personal data are not necessary for the supply of search engine services. For the delivery of search results, it is not absolutely necessary to process personal data.[437] There are examples of search engines that do not collect any personal data from their users, and accordingly do not depend on personal data flows.[438] Some search engines use personal data and the corresponding cross-border flows of personal data to improve the quality of their services (targeted search results) and for the supply of other services (online advertising) to generate income. The restriction on the free flow of personal data across borders in such cases is not of numerical or quantitative nature with regard to the supply of services, but a qualitative element not encompassed by Article XVI:2(a) and (c) GATS.

4.3.3.2.3 Social Network Services

Social network services may also be classified as "Data base services" (W/120-1.B.c).[439] The EU did not schedule any limitations on market access with regard to the cross-border supply of data processing services. Apart from Malta,

(re-)identification of anonymized data or encrypted data may be impossible. Hon et al. (2011), p. 217, 224.

[434] Gianpaolo Maria Ruotolo arrived at a similar conclusion but he argues that the specific commitment in the case of cloud computing consists in the transfer of (personal) data. Ruotolo (2018), p. 20.

[435] See Sect. 4.2.3.4.2.

[436] WTO (2019f), p. 62. See the commitments of the EU for data base services that was used as an example in Sect. 4.2.1.1.3.

[437] See Sect. 4.1.3.2.

[438] Swisscows is an example of such a search engine that does not collect any personal data from its visitors, including the search requests entered and the IP addresses associated with the request.

[439] See Sect. 4.2.3.4.3.

which remains unbound, the EU member states committed to open their market to the cross-border supply of data base services.[440]

Systematic, structural, and continuous cross-border flows of personal data are necessary for the supply of social network services. Social networks are platforms on which individuals interact. Even in cases in which individuals are not identifiable for other visitors of a social network, the suppliers of the social network services still necessarily handle personal data. The restriction on the free flow of personal data across borders amounts to a zero quota for social network services because it effectively limits to zero the number of service suppliers, service operations, and service outputs. In these cases, the fundamental rights-based regulation of data transfers in the EU interferes with the market access obligation in Article XVI:2 (a) and (c) GATS.

4.3.3.2.4 Online Advertising Services

Online advertising services may be classified as "Advertising services" (W/120-1.F.a).[441] The EU did not schedule any limitations on market access with regard to the cross-border supply of advertising services.[442] All EU member states committed to open their markets to the cross-border supply of advertising services.[443]

Systematic, structural, and continuous cross-border flows of personal data are not necessary for the supply of online advertising services. For the posting of advertisements, it is not absolutely necessary to process personal data.[444] Some suppliers of online advertising services use personal data and the corresponding data flows to improve the quality of their services (targeted advertising).[445] The restrictions on the free flow of personal data in such cases is not of a numerical or quantitative nature with regard to the supply of services, but instead a qualitative element that is not encompassed by Article XVI:2(a) and (c) GATS.

---

[440] WTO (2019f), p. 62. See the EU's commitments for data base services that was used as an example in Sect. 4.2.1.1.3.

[441] See Sect. 4.2.3.4.4.

[442] Only Poland specifically excluded all forms of advertising of tobacco products, alcoholic beverages, and pharmaceuticals.

[443] WTO (2019f), p. 76.

[444] See Sect. 4.1.3.2.

[445] In *Google Spain and Google*, the referring *Audiencia Nacional* (Spanish National High Court) established that Google takes advantage of the users' search activity and includes, in return for payment, advertising associated with the users' search terms, for undertakings which wish to use that information in order to offer their goods or services to the users. ECJ, *Google Spain and Google*, para. 43.

4.3.3.2.5 IoT Services

The first example for IoT services considered above was internet-connected vehicles.[446] IoT maintenance services of connected vehicles may be classified as "Maintenance and repair of road transport equipment" (W/120-11.F.d). Most EU member states did not schedule any limitation on market access regarding the cross-border supply of maintenance and repair services of road transport equipment. With the exceptions of Cyprus, the Czech Republic, Finland, Lithuania, Latvia, Malta, Poland, Sweden, and the Slovak Republic—which each remain unbound—all other EU member states committed to open their markets to the cross-border supply of maintenance and repair services of road transport equipment.[447]

Systematic, structural, and continuous cross-border flows of personal data are necessary for the supply of IoT maintenance services of connected vehicles. This kind of service would not be possible without the processing of personal data and the corresponding data flows it requires. Consequently, in these cases the fundamental rights-based regulation of data transfers in the EU interferes with the market access obligation in Article XVI:2(a) and (c) GATS.

The second example for IoT services considered above was smart fridges.[448] Restocking and ordering food are important services pertaining to smart fridges, but they cannot be classified in any sector and subsector of W/120. IoT restocking services for smart fridges is one of the rare examples of a new service not covered by the W/120. Accordingly, no commitments were scheduled, and the EU member states did not commit to open their markets to the cross-border supply of IoT restocking services for smart fridges. There is thus no interference with the market access obligation in Article XVI:2(a) and (c) GATS.

4.3.3.2.6 Sharing Economy Platform Services

The first example of a sharing economy platform services considered above was the arrangement of lodging.[449] Digital lodging arrangement platform services may be classified as "Hotel and restaurant" services (W/120-9.A). Most EU member states did not schedule any limitation on market access regarding the cross-border supply of hotel and restaurant services. With the exceptions of Estonia, Finland, and Hungary, which remain unbound, the EU member states committed to open their market to the cross-border supply of hotel and restaurant services.[450]

Systematic, structural, and continuous cross-border flows of personal data are necessary for the supply of digital lodging arrangement platform services. This kind

446 See Sect. 4.1.3.4.

447 WTO (2019f), p. 187.

448 See Sect. 4.1.3.4.

449 See Sect. 4.1.3.5.

450 WTO (2019f), p. 164.

of service would not be possible without the processing of personal data and the corresponding data flows. The service supplier has to connect users with the hosts, and this is not possible without cross-border flows of personal data when the service is supplied across borders. The EU system for data transfers thus interferes with the market access obligation in Article XVI:2(a) and (c) GATS with such restrictions.

The second example considered above of sharing economy platform services related to the arrangement of transportation.[451] Digital transportation arrangement platform services may be classified as "Passenger transportation" services (W/120-11.F.a). All EU member states remain unbound regarding the cross-border supply of passenger transportation services.[452] There is no interference with the market access obligation in Article XVI:2(a) and (c) GATS.

4.3.3.3 Services with Occasional Flows of Personal Data

Occasional cross-border flows of personal data are possible based on contract with Article 49(1)(b) GDPR or based on consent with Article 49(1)(a) GDPR even if the level of protection for personal data is not essentially equivalent to that guaranteed within the EU.[453] Both derogations require an agreement by the data subject to the risk of the data transfer. Without the agreement of the data subject, the transfer of personal data may not take place. The examples for services that require occasional cross-border flows of personal data include travel agency services, digital medical diagnosis, and legal services.[454] They are strongly intertwined with the necessary data transfers. In cases in which the data subject rejects the data transfers, they also essentially reject the cross-border supply of such a service.

Gianpaolo Maria Ruotolo has submitted that this cannot be "compatible with the multilateral trading rules, since it leaves to the will of private individuals the possibility for the EU of respecting international trade obligations."[455] Ruotolo does not consider, however, the quantitative nature of the market access obligation in Article XVI:2(a) and (c) GATS. The AB maintained that a measure that totally prohibits the supply of a service constitutes a market access limitation because it effectively limits to zero the number of service suppliers, service operations, and service output.[456] The contract-based and consent-based derogations do not limit to zero the number of service suppliers, service operation, and service output in cases in which the data subject (which is also the consumer of the service in question) agrees to the data transfers. The consumer decides whether they want a service based on the

[451] See Sect. 4.1.3.5.

[452] WTO (2019f), p. 183.

[453] See Sects. 3.4.2 and 3.4.3.

[454] See Sect. 4.1.4. They will usually also satisfy the condition of the derogation in Article 49(1)(b) GDPR that the data transfers must be necessary for the performance of the contract.

[455] Ruotolo (2018), p. 28.

[456] WTO AB Report, *US – Gambling*, paras 232, 252.

conditions of the service. This is *not* a zero quota on the number of service suppliers, service operations, and service output. There is no interference with the market access obligation in Article XVI:2(a) and (c) GATS.

4.3.3.4 Preventing Interferences

There are two options to prevent an interference with the market access obligation in Article XVI:2(a) and (c) GATS. The first option requires the EU to modify its schedule of commitments and include a reservation concerning the EU system for data transfers (Sect. 4.3.3.4.1). The second option requires that the ongoing e-commerce negotiations conclude with an exception for data protection-based restrictions on cross-border flows of personal data (Sect. 4.3.3.4.2).

4.3.3.4.1 Modification of the Schedule

Each WTO member specified the terms, limitations, and conditions on market access according to Article XX:1(a) GATS when it joined the WTO. Even though the EC was well aware of data protection issues relating to trade in services when it negotiated the GATS, it did not specify any terms, limitations, and conditions on market access with regard to data protection when it joined the WTO. Presumably, the EC was satisfied with the inclusion of the privacy exception in Article XIV GATS and convinced that it could justify any potential inconsistencies of the developing data protection directive with the market access obligation in Article XVI GATS.[457]

WTO members can modify or withdraw a commitment according to the rules in Article XXI GATS, usually by making concessions in the form of compensatory adjustments in other areas. The EU could add a horizontal reservation for compliance with the GDPR and the Charter (including the regulation of data transfers) in the market access column of its schedule.[458] Should the EU choose to include such a reservation, it has to notify the Council for Trade in Services three months before the intended date of implementation of the modification.[459] Any WTO member whose benefits under the GATS might be affected by this modification, could then enter into negotiations with the EU regarding necessary compensatory adjustments.[460] These adjustments would have to be made on an MFN basis.[461] Without any agreement between the parties on necessary compensatory adjustments, affected

[457] See Sect. 4.2.1.4.2.1.

[458] Irion et al. (2016), p. 47.

[459] Article XXI:1(b) GATS.

[460] Article XXI:2(a) GATS.

[461] Article XXI:2(b) GATS.

WTO members can refer the matter to arbitration.[462] The findings of the arbitration would be binding for the EU.

Such a modification of the schedule of commitments is nearly unprecedented. The only effort to withdraw a commitment was initiated in 2007 by the US after they lost their case in *US – Gambling*. The process to find compensatory adjustments is still ongoing.[463] As long as the general exceptions in Article XIV GATS can justify an interference with the market access obligation, the modification of commitments seems like an unnecessary and potentially risky undertaking. It is not foreseeable which WTO members might seek compensatory adjustments and what form these adjustments might take or how much it would ultimately cost the EU. There is also the chance that WTO members with a bad track record on data protection issues would use this opportunity to demand further commitments.

4.3.3.4.2 Electronic Commerce Negotiations

It is still unclear if there will be an outcome of the electronic commerce negotiations and what it will look like. Should the position of the EU on cross-border flows of personal data (or a similar one) prevail and WTO members adopt a new provision on the protection of personal data and privacy, this provision could also legitimate interferences with the market access obligation in Article XVI:2(a) and (c) GATS by the EU system for data transfers. Article 2.8(2) of the EU proposal provides that

> Members may adopt and maintain the safeguards they deem appropriate to ensure the protection of personal data and privacy, including through the adoption and application of rules for the cross-border transfer of personal data. Nothing in the agreed disciplines and commitments shall affect the protection of personal data and privacy afforded by the Members' respective safeguards.[464]

According to this provision, the fundamental rights-based regulation of data transfers in the EU would not affect the market access obligation in Article XVI:2(a) and (c) GATS because nothing in the agreed disciplines and commitments shall affect the protection of personal data and privacy. This provision would amount to a *super exception* without any *chapeau* requirements as in Article XIV GATS.

4.3.4 National Treatment

The national treatment obligation in Article XVII GATS also applies only according to the commitments, conditions, and qualifications in the schedule.[465] In sectors in

---

[462] Article XXI:3(a) GATS.

[463] See Rothstein (2008), p. 158, 162, 170, 175–177; European Commission (2020), pp. 53–54.

[464] WTO (2019b).

[465] See generally Van den Bossche and Zdouc (2017), p. 401; Matsushita et al. (2015), p. 609; Munin (2010), pp. 160–162; Krajewski and Engelke (2008), pp. 410–411.

which the EU has undertaken national treatment commitments, it must—unless specified in the schedule—accord to foreign services and service suppliers treatment no less favorable than that it accords to like services and service suppliers located in the EU. The analysis of the compatibility of the EU's regulation of data transfers with the national treatment obligation focuses on adequacy decisions according to Article 45 GDPR (Sect. 4.3.4.1), instruments providing appropriate safeguards in Article 46 GDPR (Sect. 4.3.4.2), and the derogations of Article 49 GDPR (Sect. 4.3.4.3). Just as in the case of interferences with the market access obligation in Article XVI GATS, there are two options to justify an interference with the national treatment obligation in Article XVII GATS. The EU could modify its schedule of commitments or the WTO members could conclude the electronic commerce negotiations with a horizontal provision on the protection of personal data and privacy (Sect. 4.3.4.4).

4.3.4.1 Adequacy Decisions

Adequacy decisions according to Article 45 GDPR apply equally to cross-border flows of personal data of foreign and domestic service suppliers. Although treatment is identical, adequacy decisions are especially relevant for foreign service suppliers because they need cross-border flows of personal data for the cross-border supply of their services in the EU.[466]

Foreign service suppliers located in a third country with an adequacy decision can use this legal mechanism for their data transfers without any specific authorization. There are no restrictions on the free flow of personal data between the EU and third countries with an adequacy decision. The situation is comparable to the free movement of data on the internal market of the EU.[467] Competition between foreign and domestic service suppliers is not affected by the EU system for data transfers when a third country has an adequacy decision. There is no interference with the national treatment obligation in Article XVI GATS.

4.3.4.2 Appropriate Safeguards

The instruments providing appropriate safeguards in Article 46 GDPR also apply equally to foreign and domestic service suppliers for their systematic, structural, and continuous cross-border flows of personal data. Although treatment is identical, the instruments providing appropriate safeguards are especially relevant for foreign

[466] Gregory Shaffer argued that the EU Directive "applies equally to EU-owned and -registered companies and foreign-owned and -registered companies and thus should not violate the GATS national treatment clause" Shaffer does not consider that the national treatment obligation in Article XVII GATS also covers *de facto* discrimination. Shaffer (2000), p. 50.

[467] See Sect. 3.1.3.1.1.

service suppliers because they need cross-border flows of personal data for the cross-border supply of their services in the EU. An interference with the national treatment obligation in Article XVII GATS may obviously occur in cases in which instruments providing appropriate safeguards cannot be used (Sect. 4.3.4.2.1) but an interference may also occur in cases in which they can (Sect. 4.3.4.2.2).

4.3.4.2.1 Appropriate Safeguards Are Not Available

In cases in which foreign service suppliers *cannot* rely on Article 46 GDPR for their systematic, structural, and continuous cross-border flows of personal data, and the EU has made a positive commitment to grant national treatment, foreign service suppliers are treated less favorably than domestic service suppliers because they have no possibility to make the necessary transfers of personal data.

This is especially true for foreign services and service suppliers for whom cross-border flows of personal data are an unavoidable element. In these cases, there is a modification of the competition between foreign and domestic service suppliers to the detriment of foreign service suppliers when the instruments providing appropriate safeguards in Article 46 GDPR are not available. I thus argue that this constitutes less favorable treatment for foreign service suppliers and thus an interference with the national treatment obligation in Article XVII GATS.[468] From the list of examples for services that require systematic, structural. and continuous cross-border flows of personal data, this concerns some cloud computing services,[469] social network services,[470] IoT maintenance services of connected vehicles,[471] and digital lodging arrangement platform services.[472]

In the analysis of the market access obligation, I have argued that only the quantitative implications of data localization may lead to an interference with Article XVI GATS because the qualitative implications do not amount to a zero quota for the supply of services. This is different regarding interferences with the national treatment obligation in Article XVII GATS. Foreign service suppliers whose services can also be supplied without cross-border flows of personal data rely on Article 46 GDPR for systemic, structural, and continuous data flows to improve

---

[468] Cp. WTO Panel Report, *China – Publications and Audiovisual Products*, paras 7.978–7.979.

[469] With the exception of Malta, which remains unbound, the EU member states committed to national treatment for software implementation services in mode 1. WTO (2019f), p. 59.

[470] With the exception of Malta, which remains unbound, the EU member states committed to national treatment for data base services in mode 1. Ibid., 62.

[471] With the exception of Cyprus, the Czech Republic, Finland, Lithuania, Latvia, Malta, Poland, Sweden and the Slovak Republic, which remain unbound, the EU member states committed to national treatment of maintenance and repair services for road transport equipment in mode 1. Ibid., 187.

[472] With the exception of Estonia, Finland, Hungary and Sweden, which remain unbound, the EU member states committed to national treatment for hotel and restaurant services in mode 1. Ibid., 164.

the quality of their services or use them to generate additional income. When the instruments providing appropriate safeguards in Article 46 GDPR are not available, there is consequently a modification of the competition to the detriment of the foreign service suppliers. I thus conclude that this constitutes less favorable treatment and is thus an interference with the national treatment obligation in Article XVII GATS. The relevant examples from the list of services that require systematic, structural, and continuous data transfers highlight how competition is modified to the detriment of the foreign service suppliers. These include: cloud computing service suppliers that cannot offer IaaS to businesses in the EU that require cross-border flows of personal data;[473] search engines that cannot use cross-border flows of personal data to customize search results for the users and thus lose an important feature;[474] and online advertising services that cannot use cross-border flows of personal data to individually target advertisements.[475]

4.3.4.2.2 Appropriate Safeguards Are Available

In cases in which foreign service suppliers can rely on Article 46 GDPR for systematic, structural, and continuous cross-border flows of personal data, and the EU has made a positive commitment to grant national treatment, foreign service suppliers are *still* treated less favorably than domestic service suppliers because they have to bear a regulatory double burden. Foreign service suppliers must comply with the conditions for instruments providing appropriate safeguards in addition to the other rules of the GDPR. I would argue that this double burden modifies the competition to the detriment of the foreign service suppliers.[476] These additional compliance efforts translate into additional costs, which domestic service suppliers do not have to bear. This amounts to an interference with the national treatment obligation in Article XVII GATS for all services that require systematic, structural, and continuous cross-border flows of personal data (in cases in which the EU has committed to national treatment).

4.3.4.3 Derogations

The derogations in Article 49 GDPR also apply equally to foreign and domestic service suppliers. Although treatment is identical, the derogations in Article 49

[473] With the exception of Malta, which remains unbound, the EU member states committed to national treatment for data processing services in mode 1. Ibid., 61.

[474] Apart from Malta, which remains unbound, the EU member states committed to national treatment for data base services in mode 1. Ibid., 62.

[475] All EU member states committed to national treatment for advertising services in mode 1. Ibid., 76.

[476] "[T]he mere existence of cross-border regulatory diversity represents a burden for foreign service suppliers." Muller (2017), p. 472.

GDPR especially affect foreign service suppliers because they depend on cross-border flows of personal data for the cross-border supply of their services in the EU. Many foreign service suppliers thus have to rely on the contract-based derogation in Article 49(1)(b) GDPR or the consent-based derogation in Article 49(1)(a) GDPR for the transfer of personal data, while service suppliers located in the EU can rely on a contract according to Article 6(1)(b) GDPR or on consent according to Article 6(1)(a) GDPR as legal bases for the processing of personal data.

The decisive aspect for less favorable treatment is the modification of the competition to the detriment of the foreign service or service supplier.[477] There is no detrimental modification of the competition for foreign service suppliers with regard to the contract-based derogation. Article 49(1)(b) GDPR simply requires from foreign service suppliers that data transfers must be necessary for the performance of a contract. The principles of purpose limitation in Article 5(1)(b) GDPR and data minimization in Article 5(1)(c) GDPR impose a similar obligation on service suppliers located in the EU. Furthermore, the transparency requirement in Article 5(1)(a) GDPR and the general information duty in Article 13 GDPR—from which the information duty for foreign service suppliers concerning the risks of the data transfers derives—are also applicable to service suppliers located in the EU. I therefore find that the regulation of data transfers in the EU does not distort the existing market conditions and opportunities in favor of domestic service suppliers with regard to the contract-based derogation in Article 49(1)(b) GDPR because both domestic and foreign service suppliers have to comply with essentially the same obligations under the provisions of the GDPR.

However, it is possible to claim that there are detrimental modifications of the competition for foreign service suppliers with regard to the consent-based derogation. Article 49(1)(a) GDPR requires foreign service suppliers to seek *explicit* consent from the data subject for data transfers, while service suppliers located in the EU can use regular consent for the processing of personal data.[478] The GDPR requires explicit consent in situations in which particular data protection risks may emerge, and so, a high individual level of control over personal data is important.[479] The EU legislator has decided that such high risks appear in the context of international data transfers.

This context might suggest the relevance of Footnote 10 to Article XVII:1 GATS. Footnote 10 stipulates that specific commitments assumed under Article XVII:1 GATS shall not be construed to require any WTO member to compensate for any inherent competitive disadvantages which result from the foreign character of the relevant services or service suppliers. The AB stressed in *Argentina – Financial Services* that the inherent competitive disadvantages caused by the foreign character of the relevant services or service suppliers under Footnote 10 "must be distinguished from the measure's impact on the conditions of competition in the

[477] Article XVII:3 GATS.

[478] See Sect. 3.1.4.4.1.

[479] EDPB (2018), p. 6.

marketplace."[480] With regard to the consent-based derogation, the competitive disadvantage is imposed by the EU's regulation of data transfers requiring explicit instead of routine consent for data transfers. This amounts to a *de facto* discrimination not covered by Footnote 10.

In these cases, foreign service suppliers are placed at a disadvantage because of the additional requirement to seek explicit consent. The term "explicit" refers to the way consent is expressed by the data subject. It means that the data subject must give an express statement of consent.[481] It is evidently an additional burden to obtain such an express statement of consent. The Article 29 WP stated that

> [a]n obvious way to make sure consent is explicit would be to expressly confirm consent in a written statement. Where appropriate, the controller could make sure the written statement is signed by the data subject, in order to remove all possible doubt and potential lack of evidence in the future.[482]

It could be argued that this additional burden of seeking explicit consent only has a minimal effect on the conditions of competition. However, the jurisprudence of the WTO adjudicative bodies does not acknowledge such a *de minimis* standard for the national treatment obligation. Two panels rejected arguments suggesting that the minimal effect of less favorable treatment should be taken into account.[483]

Nevertheless, it must be stressed that service suppliers can always rely on the contract-based derogation in Article 49(1)(b) GDPR that complies with the national treatment obligation in Article XVII GATS. From the perspective of examples like travel agencies, digital medical diagnosis, and legal services, the contract-based derogation seems to be an appropriate legal mechanism for the necessary cross-border flows of personal data. Moreover, the whole fundamental rights-based regulation of data transfers in the EU must be seen as the measure affecting trade in service. The availability of a practical alternative within the derogations for occasional data flows thus prevents the distortion of the market conditions in favor of domestic service suppliers. It is unclear whether the WTO adjudicating bodies would follow such an interpretation. The panel in *Canada – Autos* stated that

> The less favourable treatment of imported products which is the result of the denial of the advantage in case of sale or use of imported products is not negated by the fact that the advantage may also be obtained by other means than sale or use of domestic products.[484]

In spite of this, I conclude that there is no interference with the national treatment obligation in Article XVII GATS based on the fact that the EU's regulation of data transfers *as a whole* guarantees equality of opportunities to compete in the EU market for both foreign and domestic service suppliers.

---

[480] WTO AB Report, *Argentina – Financial Services*, para. 6.104.

[481] Article 29 WP (2018b), p. 18.

[482] Ibid.

[483] WTO Panel Report, *Canada – Autos*, para. 10.84 (on Article III:4 GATT); WTO Panel Report, *China – Audiovisual Products*, para. 7.1537.

[484] WTO Panel Report, *Canada – Autos*, para. 10.87 (on Article III:4 GATT).

4.3.4.4 Preventing Interferences

There are also two possible ways to prevent interferences with the national treatment obligation. The first option requires the EU to modify its schedule of commitments and to include a reservation concerning the EU system for data transfers. The second option requires the ongoing e-commerce negotiations to conclude with an exception for data protection-based restrictions on cross-border flows of personal data.[485]

In addition to what has been outlined above, it is necessary in the case of the national treatment obligation to refer to Article XX:2 GATS:

> Measures inconsistent with both Articles XVI and XVII shall be inscribed in the column relating to Article XVI. In this case the inscription will be considered to provide a condition or qualification to Article XVII as well.

It has been shown that the regulation of data transfers in the EU can be inconsistent with both the market access obligation in Article XVI GATS and the national treatment obligation in Article XVII GATS. To remedy this inconsistency, it would be sufficient to add a horizontal reservation for compliance with the GDPR and the Charter (including the regulation of data transfers) in the market access column of the EU's schedule of commitments.[486]

4.3.5 Summary

Two types of interferences with GATS obligations caused by the EU regulation of data transfers can be distinguished. The first type relates to countries without an adequacy decision where the instruments providing appropriate safeguards generally can be used for data transfers. These countries could raise the following three claims:

- Adequacy decisions interfere with the MFN treatment obligation because the EU does not accord treatment no less favorable to services and service suppliers from WTO members without an adequacy decision.
- Special framework adequacy decisions—should one be adopted again (e. g. the Transatlantic Data Privacy Framework between the EU and the US)—interfere with the domestic regulation obligation. Until now, special framework adequacy decisions were negotiated with third countries that would otherwise not qualify for an adequacy decision. This is not impartial and has a significant impact on the overall administration of the EU's regulation of data transfers.
- Instruments providing appropriate safeguards interfere with the national treatment obligation in cases in which the EU has made specific commitments. Foreign services and service suppliers must comply with the conditions of the

---

[485] See Sect. 4.3.3.4.

[486] Panel Report, *China –Publications and Audiovisual Products*, paras 7.920–7.921.

instruments providing appropriate safeguards *in addition* to the other rules of the GDPR.

The second type of interference relates to countries without an adequacy decision where the instruments providing appropriate safeguards generally *cannot* be used for data transfers. These countries could raise the following four claims:

- The restriction on the use of instruments providing appropriate safeguards interferes with the MFN treatment obligation because the EU does not accord treatment no less favorable to services and service suppliers from WTO members which cannot profit from these instruments.
- The use of corrective powers by supervisory authorities may lead to an interference with the domestic regulation obligation when it results in a fragmentation of EU member states' policies regarding data transfers. Such fragmentation contradicts the standard of objective and/or impartial administration of a measure.
- The restriction on the use of instruments providing appropriate safeguards interferes with the market access obligation when a service that is covered by the EU's market access commitments cannot be supplied without systematic, structural, and continuous cross-border flows of personal data. The restriction then amounts to a zero quota because it effectively limits to zero the number of service suppliers, service operations, and service output.
- The restriction on the use of instruments providing appropriate safeguards also interferes with the national treatment obligation because it modifies the conditions of competition to the detriment of foreign services and service suppliers.

4.4 The Regulation of Data Transfers as a Justifiable Trade Barrier

The interferences with GATS obligations caused by the EU fundamental rights-based regulation of data transfers are subject to exceptions in the GATS. These exceptions may justify the trade barriers erected by the EU. The analysis shows, however, that the economic integration exception in Article V GATS (Sect. 4.4.1) and the security exceptions in Article XIV *bis* GATS (Sect. 4.4.2) can only be used in certain circumstances. Moreover, the confidentiality exception in Paragraph 5(d) of the Annex on Telecommunications does not cover interferences of the GATS at all (Sect. 4.4.3). The justification focuses on the privacy exception in Article XIV(c)(ii) GATS (Sect. 4.4.4).

4.4.1 *Economic Integration Exception*

The departure from the MFN treatment obligation may be justified under the economic integration exception in Article V GATS.[487] Interferences with the MFN treatment obligation can be assessed in terms of economic integration based on trade agreements. However, it must be noted that an adequacy decision alone does not qualify as an agreement liberalizing trade in services under Article V GATS (Sect. 4.4.1.1). The first interference with the MFN treatment obligation relates to less favorable treatment for services and service suppliers in a WTO member without an adequacy decision. Only under particular circumstances can such an interference be justified under Article V GATS (Sect. 4.4.1.2). The second interference with the MFN treatment obligation relates to less favorable treatment for services and services suppliers in a WTO member where instruments providing appropriate safeguards cannot be used. Such interferences can be difficult to justify under Article V GATS (Sect. 4.4.1.3). Finally, the EU common market cannot be used to justify interferences with the MFN treatment obligation under Article V GATS (Sect. 4.4.1.4).

4.4.1.1 Adequacy Decisions Are Not Economic Integration Agreement

Adequacy decisions do *not* constitute an agreement liberalizing trade in services. Instead, they are unilateral acts of the EU and while they may have a liberalizing effect, they do not correspond to the logic of Article V GATS that requires the opening of service sectors to the supply of services in the four modes. Adequacy decisions only concern the transfer of personal data and do not specifically cover the supply of services. Adequacy decisions alone therefore do not qualify for the economic integration exception in Article V GATS.

4.4.1.2 Adequacy Decision and Economic Integration Agreements

Adequacy decisions are often adopted for third countries that also have some form of an economic integration agreement with the EU. For example, Andorra is a European microstate and widely integrated into the EU common market through an association agreement. Switzerland is also partly integrated in the common market through an array of bilateral agreements; and Japan, Canada, South Korea, and Israel as well as the UK have all concluded trade agreements with the EU.

The first condition in Article V:1(a) GATS requires that all economic integration agreements liberalizing trade in services must have substantial sectoral coverage. The second condition in Article V:1(b) GATS demands the elimination of substantially all discrimination in the sectors covered by granting national treatment to the

[487] See Sect. 4.2.1.4.1.

contracting parties. Adequacy decisions are a tool for the EU to comply with Article V:1(b) GATS because they eliminate national treatment discrimination among services and service suppliers that require cross-border flows of personal data.[488] Where an adequacy decision was taken for a country that also has an economic integration agreement covering trade in services with the EU, the interference with the MFN treatment obligation could be covered with the requirement to comply Article V:1(b) GATS.

Nevertheless, not all adequacy decisions have been tied to some form of economic integration agreement with the EU. For example, Uruguay and the EU concluded negotiations of a trade agreement at the end of 2019, but the agreement is not yet ratified. Moreover, New Zealand and the EU only started negotiations for a trade agreement in 2018. Furthermore, the partial integration of Switzerland in the common market does not cover trade in services.[489] Consequently, interferences with the MFN treatment obligation involving these states cannot be justified on the basis of the economic integration exception in Article V GATS.

4.4.1.3 Appropriate Safeguards and Economic Integration Agreements

Contrary to adequacy decisions, instruments providing appropriate safeguards do not eliminate national treatment discrimination with regard to services and service suppliers that require cross-border flows of personal data.[490] It is much more difficult to satisfy the second condition in Article V:1(b) GATS concerning the elimination of substantially all discrimination in the sectors covered, by granting national treatment to the contracting parties without an adequacy decision. In addition, there will always be states without an economic integration agreement with the EU. Interferences with the MFN treatment obligation involving these states cannot be justified on the basis of the economic integration exception in Article V GATS.

4.4.1.4 The Common Market of the EU

Some scholars have argued that the EU common market could be used under the economic integration exception in Article V GATS to justify interferences with the MFN treatment obligation in Article II GATS (Sect. 4.4.1.4.1) and the national treatment obligation in Article XVII GATS (Sect. 4.4.1.4.2).

---

[488] See Sect. 4.3.4.1.

[489] There are minor exceptions. See Oesch (2018), pp. 76–83.

[490] See Sect. 4.3.4.2.

4.4.1.4.1 Most-Favored Nations Treatment Violations

Some scholars have implied that the EU common market could be used to justify the interferences with the MFN treatment obligation caused by the EU regulation of data transfers under Article V GATS.[491] However, there seems to be a misunderstanding about the underlying interference with the MFN treatment obligation that needs to be justified. In their explanations, Kristina Irion, Svetlana Yakovleva and Marija Bartl refer to a situation where an EU measure would "accord less favorable treatment to a WTO Member State as compared to an EU Member State."[492] Similarly, Federica Velli refers to an interference of the MFN treatment obligation in cases in which an EU member state accords treatment less favorable to services and service suppliers of a non-EU WTO member than that it accords to like services and service suppliers of another EU member state.

What these scholars fail to consider in their arguments is that such a scenario—an EU member state interferes with the MFN treatment obligation because of its less favorable treatment of a non-EU WTO member compared to another EU member state—is only possible if the measure at issue is attributed to the EU member state and not to the EU itself. From the perspective of EU law, it is clear that Article 16 TFEU is the legal basis of the GDPR and that Chapter V GDPR consolidates the legal mechanisms for the transfer of personal data to third countries on the level of the EU. From the perspective of WTO law however, the international responsibility of the EU *vis-à-vis* that of its member states is decisive. Pursuant to Article 6(1) ARIO complaints that concern the legal acts of EU institutions are regularly attributable to the EU.[493] The GDPR is a legal act of the EU. Consequently, the regulation of data transfers is a measure that is attributable to the EU—and not to the member states—under international law. An EU member state cannot be liable under the MFN treatment obligation for treating other EU member states differently than non-EU WTO members on the basis of the GDPR or the Charter. This also extends to decisions of supervisory authorities in the EU member states to suspend or prohibit data transfers because those powers are based on EU law.[494] The interferences with the MFN treatment obligation concern situations between two

[491] Irion et al. (2016), p. 33; Velli (2019), pp. 887–888. The EU/EEA common market is a regional economic integration agreement in the meaning of Article V GATS and was notified to the WTO Council for Trade in Services. WTO (1998c).

[492] Irion et al. (2016), p. 33.

[493] Marín Durán (2017), pp. 710–711, 720; ILC, Draft Articles on the Responsibility of International Organizations (ARIO), annexed to UN (2012); see for example WTO Panel Report, *EC – Biotech*, paras 2.1–2.5 where the contested measures included national safeguard measures prohibiting the import and/or marketing of specific biotech products, which had been taken by six EU member states relying on the possibility provided for in the relevant EU legislation and where the panel accepted the EU's standing as the single respondent bearing sole responsibility for these measures.

[494] See WTO Panel Report, *EC – Biotech*, paras 2.1–2.5 and WTO Panel Report, *EC – Asbestos*, paras 3.32–3.35, in which the EU was targeted as the sole defendant—and thus potentially, solely responsible for a violation of WTO obligations (*quod non*)—of the challenged French decree

non-EU states.[495] The common market therefore does not provide a justification under the economic integration exception in Article V GATS in these situations.

4.4.1.4.2 National Treatment Violations

It is controversial whether Article V GATS may be used to justify interferences with GATS obligations other than the MFN treatment obligation.[496] Svetlana Yakovleva and Kristina Irion submit that the economic integration exception in Article V GATS also applies to interferences with the national treatment obligation, but they do not substantiate how.[497]

However, interferences with the national treatment obligations based on economic integration agreements should be settled according to the procedures under Article XXI GATS. If the members of an economic integration agreement withdraw or modify specific market access or national treatment commitments they have previously made in the area of services, then the procedures under Article XXI GATS require consultations and negotiations with the affected parties regarding compensation.[498] This implies that interferences with the national treatment obligation cannot find justification under Article V GATS. Such an interpretation is supported by the fact that Article V:5 GATS specifically refers to the procedures of Article XXI GATS *if*, in the conclusion of an economic integration agreement, a WTO member intends to withdraw or modify a specific scheduled commitment. A representative of Japan also stressed this point in a meeting of the Committee on Regional Trade Agreements:

> With regard to paragraph 5 and the chapeau of GATS Article V:1, her delegation considered that the scope of the exemptions granted to EIAS [economic integration agreements] included MFN obligations, but did not include other general obligations of the GATS.[499]

In addition, the panel in *Canada – Autos* stressed that "it is worth recalling that Article V provides legal coverage for measures taken pursuant to economic integration agreements, which would otherwise be inconsistent with the MFN obligation in Article II."[500] Based on these considerations, I argue that the economic integration exception in Article V GATS cannot justify interferences with the national treatment obligation.

---

banning asbestos and asbestos-containing products, even though the link between this national measure and EU legislation was not readily obvious.

495 See Sects. 4.2.1.1 and 4.2.1.4.

496 Cottier and Molinuevo (2008), p. 129.

497 Yakovleva and Irion (2016), p. 204; Irion et al. (2016), p. 34.

498 Stephenson (1999), p. 54.

499 WTO (1999e), para. 18. The representative of New Zealand expressed a similar view in the same meeting. Ibid., para. 17.

500 WTO Panel Report, *Canada – Autos*, para. 10.272.

4.4.2 Security Exceptions

The security exceptions allow for the justification of interferences with obligations in the GATS caused by the EU regulation of data transfers only under very particular circumstances. Article XIV *bis*(1)(b)(iii) GATS requires that the security measure be taken in a time of war or other emergency in international relations. The use of corrective powers by supervisory authorities *might* meet this requirement if it is made in time of an emergency in international relations. The other interferences with obligations in the GATS identified above cannot satisfy the chronological concurrence that is necessary for a security justification under Article XIV *bis*(1)(b)(iii) GATS.[501]

The panel in *Russia – Traffic in Transit* defined an emergency in international relations as "a situation of armed conflict, or of latent armed conflict, or of heightened tension or crisis, or of general instability engulfing or surrounding a state."[502] There would have to be a very specific situation for the EU to be able to invoke this exception. The situation disclosed by Edward Snowden in the US could be an example. If a massive surveillance program is revealed in a WTO member, it could be possible to qualify it as a situation of heightened tension or crisis. Should a supervisory authority react and use its corrective powers to ban or suspend data transfers, it might be interpretable as a measure taken in a time of an emergency in international relations. However, if it is known for a long period of time that there is massive surveillance program in a WTO member, it would not be possible to qualify it as a situation of heightened tension or crisis to justify measures under Article XIV *bis*(1)(b)(iii) GATS.

A measure must also be considered necessary for the protection of essential security interests according to Article XIV *bis*(1)(b)(iii) GATS. It is incumbent on the invoking WTO member to articulate the essential security interests and to demonstrate their veracity.[503] What qualifies as a sufficient level of articulation will depend on the situation.[504] The panel in *Russia – Traffic in Transit* considered that

> the less characteristic is the 'emergency in international relations' invoked by the Member, i.e. the further it is removed from armed conflict, or a situation of breakdown of law and public order (whether in the invoking Member or in its immediate surroundings), the less obvious are the defence or military interests, or maintenance of law and public order interests, that can be generally expected to arise. In such cases, a Member would need to articulate its essential security interests with greater specificity than would be required when the emergency in international relations involved, for example, armed conflict.[505]

---

[501] WTO Panel Report, *Russia – Traffic in Transit*, para. 7.70 (on Article XXI GATT).

[502] Ibid., para. 7.76 (on Article XXI GATT).

[503] Ibid., para. 7.134 (on Article XXI GATT).

[504] Ibid., para. 7.135 (on Article XXI GATT).

[505] Ibid (on Article XXI GATT).

Following the Snowden example, the EU would have to articulate its essential security interests with great specificity because governmental surveillance in a third country is far removed from armed conflict. The panel in *Russia – Traffic in Transit* underlined that "essential security interests" is a narrower concept than security interests and may be understood "to refer to those interests relating to the quintessential functions of the state, namely, the protection of its territory and its population from external threats, and the maintenance of law and public order internally."[506]

Marina Francesca Ferracane has submitted that as long as the surveillance activities do not result in unauthorized access of confidential government, military or critical information that can undermine the sovereignty of third countries, these activities cannot be considered to pose a direct threat to national security.[507] Similarly, Bruce Schneier finds that it is necessary to distinguish between surveillance and espionage.[508] While cyber espionage may be related to national security, cyber surveillance is more likely a law enforcement issue.[509] Only in cases in which governmental surveillance in the respective WTO member also involves cyber espionage would it be possible to claim an essential national security interest.

It must also be underlined that it might not be in the interest of the EU and its member states to use the security exceptions to justify their fundamental rights-based regulation of data transfers in WTO dispute settlement, or in general discourse. Doing so opens the door for other WTO members to do the same for their data transfer regulation, which might not be as deeply rooted in the protection of fundamental rights but rather used as a protectionist tool.

4.4.3 Confidentiality Exception

The confidentiality exception in Paragraph 5(d) of the Annex on Telecommunications only justifies interferences with the provisions in the Annex on Telecommunications. The Annex recognizes that its provisions relate to and build upon the obligations and disciplines contained in the GATS.[510] Paragraph 1 of the Annex on Telecommunications explicitly states that the Annex provides notes and supplementary provisions to the GATS. Consequently, interferences with the GATS cannot be justified with the confidentiality exception in Paragraph 5(d) of the Annex on Telecommunications.

---

[506] Ibid., para. 7.130 (on Article XXI GATT).

[507] Ferracane also argued that conditional data transfer regimes, such as in the GDPR, would hardly be implemented under the national security rationale and that such regimes would normally be justified under the general exceptions of the GATS. Ferracane (2018), pp. 5, 11–12.

[508] Schneier (2014).

[509] Ibid.

[510] WTO Panel Report, *Mexico – Telecoms,* para. 7.332.

Should the EU not be successful with the argument that its regulation of data transfers does not directly restrict the use of the internet but only the movement of certain types of information, it can resort to the confidentiality exception in Paragraph 5(d) of the Annex on Telecommunications for interferences with the annex. The exception, however, must be construed narrowly without referring to privacy or data protection considerations.[511] If the EU is found to restrict the use of the internet for the movement of information across borders because of surveillance practices in a WTO member that compromise the integrity of messages, then the confidentiality exception is available as a justification as long as the restriction is not applied in a manner which would constitute a means of arbitrary or unjustifiable discrimination or a disguised restriction on trade in services.

4.4.4 General Exceptions

The general exceptions in Article XIV GATS are often used to justify interferences with GATS obligations.[512] The interpretation of the general exceptions has become the core mechanism in WTO law to distinguish between domestic measures that are legitimate and those that are protectionist.[513] It is important that the aspect of the measure that gives rise to an interference with a GATS obligation is the same as the one addressed under Article XIV GATS.[514] A respondent may not justify the inconsistency of a measure by basing its defense on aspects of a measure different from those that were found to be inconsistent with the GATS.[515] The different interferences with GATS obligations caused by the EU fundamental rights-based regulation of data transfers must therefore be justified independently from each other.[516] This section analyzes the justification for interferences with the MFN treatment obligation (Sect. 4.4.4.1), the domestic regulation obligation (Sect. 4.4.4.2), the market access obligation (Sect. 4.4.4.3), and the national treatment obligation (Sect. 4.4.4.4).

---

[511] See Sect. 4.2.2.4.

[512] See Sect. 4.2.1.4.2.

[513] Yakovleva (2020), p. 461.

[514] WTO AB Report, *Argentina – Financial Measures*, para. 6.166.

[515] Ibid.

[516] So far, scholars generally address the justification under Article XIV GATS without specifically adapting it to the different interferences with GATS obligations caused by the EU regulation of data transfers. Cp. Velli (2019), pp. 888–889; Mattoo and Meltzer (2018), p. 781; Saluzzo (2017), p. 827; Yakovleva and Irion (2016), p. 206; Weber (2012), p. 39; Reyes (2011), p. 27; Peng (2011), p. 766; Perez Asinari (2003), pp. 3–5.

4.4.4.1 Interference with the MFN Treatment Obligation

The aspects of the EU regulation of data transfers that interfere with the MFN treatment obligation in Article II GATS can be provisionally justified under the privacy exception in Article XIV(c)(ii) GATS (Sect. 4.4.4.1.1),[517] but they encounter challenges under the *chapeau* of Article XIV GATS (Sect. 4.4.4.1.2).

4.4.4.1.1 Privacy Exception

Interferences with the MFN treatment obligation must be justified under the privacy exception in Article XIV(c)(ii) GATS. The first interference considered takes place because service suppliers in WTO members without adequacy decisions must rely on the instruments providing appropriate safeguards for their transfers of personal data (Sect. 4.4.4.1.1.1). The second interference considered takes place because service suppliers in WTO members cannot rely on the instruments providing appropriate safeguards either and thus have to use the derogations for their transfers of personal data (Sect. 4.4.4.1.1.2).

4.4.4.1.1.1 Adequacy Decisions Versus Appropriate Safeguards

The first interference with the MFN treatment obligation in Article II GATS takes place because service suppliers in WTO members without adequacy decisions must use the instruments providing appropriate safeguards for their transfers of personal data. This treats these WTO members unfavorably compared to states with adequacy decisions. The privacy exception requires a demonstration that the respective measure is designed to secure compliance with laws that are not in themselves inconsistent with the GATS.[518] Panels have previously followed a three-step approach, whereby the WTO member invoking such a defense must

> (i) identify the laws and regulations with which the challenged measure is intended to secure compliance, and prove that (ii) those laws and regulations are not in themselves inconsistent with WTO law; and (iii) that the measure challenged is designed to secure compliance with those laws or regulations.[519]

First, adequacy decisions in Article 45 GDPR are intended to secure compliance with the GDPR and the right to continuous protection for personal data in Article 8

[517] Some scholars also find that a justification under the public morals exception in Article XIV(a) GATS would be possible. Cp. Mattoo and Meltzer (2018), p. 781.

[518] WTO Panel Report, *Argentina – Financial Services*, paras 7.592–7.593; WTO AB Report, *Argentina – Financial Services*, para. 6.202.

[519] WTO Panel Report, *Argentina – Financial Services*, paras 7.595–7.5961, referring to WTO Panel Report, *Colombia – Ports of Entry*, para.7.514 (on Article XX GATT), WTO Panel Report, *US – Shrimp (Thailand)*, para. 7.174 (on Article XX GATT) and WTO AB Report, *Korea – Various Measures on Beef*, para.157 (on Article XX GATT).

CFR.[520] Second, the GDPR and the right to continuous protection of personal data in Article 8 CFR are consistent with WTO law. The panel in *Argentina – Financial Services* stated that "a Member's legislation shall be presumed WTO-consistent until proven otherwise."[521] The AB added in its review of *Argentina – Financial Services* that "there may be circumstances in which the GATS-inconsistency of certain provisions of a legal instrument could affect or taint the GATS-consistency of other parts of the same instrument or of the instrument as a whole."[522] I thus argue on this basis that the GDPR and the right to continuous protection of personal data in Article 8 CFR can be presumed to be WTO-consistent and that potential inconsistencies of the GDPR do not affect the GDPR as a whole.[523] Third, it has been shown above that adequacy decisions are designed to comply with the right to data protection in Article 8 CFR.[524]

Furthermore, the privacy exception requires that a measure is *necessary* to secure such compliance.[525] This entails an in-depth and holistic weighing and balancing exercise of the relationship between the inconsistent measure and the relevant laws.

> In particular, this element entails an assessment of whether, in the light of all relevant factors in the 'necessity' analysis, this relationship is sufficiently proximate, such that the measure can be deemed to be 'necessary' to secure compliance with such laws or regulations.[526]

The balancing must take into account the importance of the objective pursued, the measure's contribution to that objective, and the trade restrictiveness of a measure.[527] The AB underlined that the greater a measure's contribution to the end

[520] Yakovleva and Irion (2016), p. 206. But see that Rolf Weber noted that "even if the criterion of the adequate extent to which the enforcement measure contributes to the realization of the end pursued, that is, to the securing of compliance with the rules or regulations to be enforced, can be acknowledged, some doubts still remain whether the international community in the light of the lack of globally harmonized privacy standards would attribute the requested key function to national privacy standards." Weber (2012), pp. 40–41.

[521] WTO Panel Report, *Argentina – Financial Services*, para. 7.625.

[522] WTO AB Report, *Argentina – Financial Services*, para. 6.201.

[523] For example, Aaditya Mattoo and Joshua P. Meltzer have argued that the requirement of local representation in Article 27 GDPR and the failure to extend the so-called "one-stop shop" mechanism in the GDPR to all data processors and controllers requires companies exporting digital services into the EU to interact with and comply with multiple supervisory authorities across the EU, thus creating costs for foreign service suppliers not faced by like domestic suppliers which could amount to a violation of the national treatment obligation. Mattoo and Meltzer (2018), pp. 780–781; Velli (2019), p. 889; Yakovleva and Irion (2016), p. 206.

[524] See Sect. 3.2.3.

[525] WTO Panel Report, *Argentina – Financial Services*, paras 7.592–7.593; WTO AB Report, *Argentina – Financial Services*, para. 6.202.

[526] Ibid., para. 6.204.

[527] WTO Panel Report, *Argentina – Financial Services*, paras 7.659, 7.661 with reference to, among others, WTO AB Report, *EC – Seal Products*, para. 5.169 (on Article XX GATT) and WTO AB Report, *US – Gambling*, paras 306–307.

pursued, the more easily a measure might be considered to be necessary.[528] The assessment of trade restrictiveness is similar.[529] A measure with a relatively small impact on trade might more easily be considered necessary than a measure with intense or broader restrictive effects.[530] But balancing also requires a comparison between the challenged measure and possible alternatives.[531] The AB clarified that a measure can only be necessary "if there were no alternative measure consistent with the General Agreement, *or less inconsistent* with it."[532] It is up to the complaining party to identify reasonably available alternative measures that achieve the same level of protection with respect to the objective pursued.[533] The AB explicitly underlined that a reasonably available alternative measure "must be a measure that would preserve for the responding Member its right to achieve its desired level of protection."[534] In turn, the responding party must demonstrate why it does not consider the proposed alternative measure to be appropriate.[535]

Compliance with the right to continuous protection of personal data is the objective of an adequacy decision. This objective must be considered of the utmost importance because it is a constituent part of the fundamental right to data protection in Article 8 CFR.[536] Adequacy decisions directly contribute to continuous protection for personal data.[537] At the same time, the trade restrictiveness of using instruments

---

[528] WTO AB Report, *Argentina – Financial Services*, para. 6.234 with reference to WTO AB Report, *Korea – Various Measures on Beef*, para. 163 (on Article XX GATT).

[529] Ibid.

[530] WTO AB Report, *Korea – Various Measures on Beef*, para. 163 (on Article XX GATT).

[531] WTO AB Report, *Argentina – Financial Services*, para. 6.201 with reference to WTO Panel Report, *Argentina – Financial Services*, paras 7.658–7.661, WTO AB Report, *EC – Seal Products*, paras 5.169, 5.214 (on Article XX GATT) and WTO AB Report, *US – Gambling*, para. 304.

[532] WTO AB Report, *EC – Asbestos*, para. 171 (on Article XX GATT), with reference to WTO AB Report, *Korea – Various Measures on Beef*, para. 166 (on Article XX GATT), in which the AB expressly affirmed the standard set forth by the panel in GATT Panel Report, *US – Section 337 of the Tariff Act of 1930*, para. 5.26 [emphasis added] (on Article XX GATT).

[533] WTO Panel Report, *Argentina – Financial Services*, para. 7.730 with reference to WTO AB Report, *US – Gambling*, para. 311 and WTO AB Report, *Brazil – Retreaded Tyres*, para. 156 (on Article XX GATT).

[534] WTO AB Report, *US – Gambling*, para. 308. Carla Reyes suggested that the "comparable" rather than "adequate/equivalent" standard will alter the balance under the weighing and balancing test with regard to both the extent to which the "Privacy Directive" secures enforcement and the negative impact on trade. Yet, the EU is free to define its desired level of protection under Article XIV(c)(ii) GATS according to this finding of the AB. The EU is not required to introduce a standard of comparable protection for personal data under WTO law. Reyes (2011), p. 33.

[535] WTO Panel Report, Argentina – Financial Services, para. 7.730 with reference to WTO AB Report, *US – Gambling*, para. 311 and AB Report, *Brazil – Retreaded Tyres*, para. 156 (on Article XX GATT).

[536] Mishra (2019), p. 14.

[537] See Sect. 3.2.4. Christopher Kuner submits that adequacy decisions do not provide a watertight standard of data protection. Kuner (2009), p. 271. While this submission is not wrong, the new rules under the GDPR improve compliance with the right to continuous protection for personal data. The criteria for adequate protection are more detailed and the periodic review mechanism ensures consistency over time.

providing appropriate safeguards instead of an adequacy decision as the legal basis for transfers of personal data is low because instruments providing appropriate safeguards also allow structural, systemic, and continuous cross-border flows of personal data. The interference with the MFN treatment obligation based on adequacy decisions versus appropriate safeguards should therefore satisfy the necessity test in Article XIV(c)(ii) GATS.

Aaditya Mattoo and Joshua P. Meltzer do not share this conclusion. They argue instead that

> the Privacy Shield may be used to show that such flexible negotiated agreements are able to achieve the EU's desired level of privacy protection in a way that is less trade restrictive than the Commission's relatively rigid approach to determining the (lack of) adequacy of India's privacy regime.[538]

This submission cannot be supported. In cases in which the compliance of a measure with its objective is high and the trade restrictiveness is low, necessity can be assumed without resorting to reasonably available alternatives. In addition, Decision (EU) 2016/1250, the Privacy Shield adequacy decision, was invalidated exactly because it did not achieve the EU's desired level of protection.

Should the adjudicative bodies of the WTO nevertheless resort to an assessment of alternative measures and suggest that special framework adequacy decisions, such as the Privacy Shield, constitute a measure that is *less* inconsistent with the GATS, the EU could argue that such special frameworks do not constitute a measure that is reasonably available in all cases.[539] The adoption of special framework adequacy decisions could be impossible in cases in which the WTO members have a level of protection for personal data that is much lower than in the EU.

However, it is possible that the WTO adjudicative bodies would find that special framework adequacy decisions would still be available for other WTO members. The AB held in *China – Publications and Audiovisual Products* that

> an alternative measure should not be found not to be reasonably available merely because it involves some change or administrative costs [...] Rather, in order to establish that an alternative measure is not 'reasonably available', the respondent must establish that the alternative measure would impose undue burden on it, and it must support such an assertion with sufficient evidence.[540]

The EU could argue that negotiating that many special framework adequacy decisions would be an undue burden. Again, it is possible that the WTO adjudicative bodies would find that efforts to adopt special framework adequacy decisions are not an undue burden for the EU, but a legitimate change to the adequacy-based system of data transfers that comes with certain administrative costs. In that case, the interference with the MFN treatment obligation would not satisfy the necessity test in

[538] Mattoo and Meltzer (2018), p. 782.

[539] I showed that special framework adequacy decisions also violate the MFN treatment obligation and the domestic regulation obligation. See Sects. 4.3.1.2 and 4.3.2.1.2.

[540] WTO AB Report, *China – Publications and Audiovisual Products*, paras 326–327, with reference to WTO AB Report, *US – Gambling*, para. 308.

Article XIV(c)(ii) GATS. Nevertheless, it must be underlined one more time that necessity should be assumed here because the compliance of the measure with its objective is high and trade restrictiveness is low.

4.4.4.1.1.2 Appropriate Safeguards Versus Derogations

The second interference with the MFN treatment obligation in Article II GATS occurs when services and service suppliers in WTO members cannot rely on adequacy decisions or the instruments providing appropriate safeguards and have to use the derogations for their transfers of personal data. The first task to justify the interference is demonstrating that the measure in question is designed to secure compliance with laws that are not in themselves inconsistent with the GATS.[541] The instruments providing appropriate safeguards in Article 46 GDPR are intended to secure compliance with the other provisions of the GDPR and the right to continuous protection for personal data in Article 8 CFR.[542] Consequently, the instruments providing appropriate safeguards may be considered as attempting to secure compliance with laws consistent with WTO law. Importantly, the AB underlined in *Argentina – Financial Services* that

> [a] measure can be said 'to secure compliance' with laws or regulations when its design reveals that it secures compliance with specific rules, obligations, or requirements under such laws or regulations, even if the measure cannot be guaranteed to achieve such result with absolute certainty.[543]

This is especially important with regard to the instruments providing appropriate safeguards because the compliance with the right to continuous protection of personal data in Article 8 CFR heavily depends on the awareness of the data exporter and the supervisory authorities' use of their corrective powers and, therefore, cannot be guaranteed to achieve such result with absolute certainty.

The second task to justify the interference is to verify that the measure in question is necessary to secure such compliance.[544] The instruments providing appropriate safeguards must be attributed a lower level of compliance with the right to continuous protection of personal data than adequacy decisions because the responsibility for compliance lies with the data exporter and control over the compliance is decentralized.[545] At the same time, the effect on trade restrictiveness between appropriate safeguards and the derogations is greater than between adequacy decisions and appropriate safeguards because structural, systemic, and continuous cross-border flows of personal data are not possible with the derogations. This may result

[541] WTO Panel Report, *Argentina – Financial Services*, paras 7.592–7.593; WTO AB Report, *Argentina – Financial Services*, para. 6.202.

[542] Yakovleva and Irion (2016), p. 206. But see Weber (2012), pp. 40–41.

[543] WTO AB Report, *Argentina – Financial Services*, para. 6.203 [footnote omitted].

[544] WTO Panel Report, *Argentina – Financial Services*, paras 7.592–7.593; WTO AB Report, *Argentina – Financial Services*, para. 6.202; see Sect. 4.4.4.1.1.

[545] See Sect. 3.3.4.

in a zero quota for certain services.[546] This interference with the MFN treatment obligation therefore requires an additional analysis to determine if there are reasonably available alternative measures that are consistent with the GATS and still achieve the same level of protection for personal data.

Some scholars have submitted—without going into much detail—that the necessity of data transfer rules could be successfully challenged if the complaining party claims that there are less restrictive alternatives, such as the principle of accountability, which has been adopted in Canada and many Asia-Pacific Economic Community (APEC) states.[547] It is important to bear in mind, however, that this interference with the MFN treatment obligation takes place because the instruments providing appropriate safeguards cannot guarantee the right to continuous protection of personal data that is transferred from the EU to a WTO member. Consequently, the principle of accountability cannot constitute an alternative measure because it is not the legal mechanism for data transfers that is the problem. Rather, it is the level of protection for personal data in the non-EU WTO member that is the problem. Should a level of protection that is essentially equivalent to that guaranteed within the EU not be available for the transfer of personal data to the non-EU WTO member, then the principle of accountability would not be sufficient in itself to comply with the right continuous protection of personal data.[548]

Carla Reyes has argued that using technology to enforce data protection laws would increase compliance and decrease the impact on international trade.[549] It is unclear however to what extent technological measures would be considered as reasonably available alternatives by the WTO adjudicative bodies. Should the adjudicative bodies choose to consider technological measures as reasonably available measures, then the EU may attempt to show that technological measures do not allow it to achieve the level of protection it requires and, therefore, cannot be a genuine alternative.[550] The EDPB already provided guidance on the limitations of technological solutions to comply with the right to continuous protection of personal data in Article 8 CFR.[551] For example, the EDPB stated that if a data exporter transfers personal data to a cloud service provider which requires access to the data in the clear in order to execute the task assigned *and* the power granted to the public authorities of the recipient country to access transferred data (such as for surveillance purposes) goes beyond what is necessary and proportionate in a democratic society, then the "current state of the art [is] incapable of envisioning an effective technical

[546] This is the case for digital services such as cloud computing services, social network services, IoT maintenance services, and digital lodging arrangement platform services that cannot be supplied without systematic, structural, and continuous cross-border flows of personal data. See Sect 4.3.3.2.

[547] Velli (2019), p. 889; Mishra (2019), pp. 16–17; Yakovleva and Irion (2016), pp. 206–207; cp. Kuner (2009), pp. 269–272.

[548] Mishra (2019), p. 17; Bennett (2012), pp. 40–43.

[549] Reyes (2011), p. 33.

[550] Cp. WOT AB Report, *Brazil – Retreaded Tyres*, para. 156 (on Article XX GATT).

[551] EDPB (2020), pp. 26–27.

measure to prevent that access from infringing on data subject rights."[552] The EDPB added that in the given scenario,

> where unencrypted personal data is technically necessary for the provision of the service by the processor, transport encryption and data-at-rest encryption even taken together, do not constitute a supplementary measure that ensures an essentially equivalent level of protection if the data importer is in possession of the cryptographic keys.[553]

This assessment must be taken into account by the WTO adjudicative bodies when they consider technological measures as reasonably available alternatives. It is difficult to say if the WTO adjudicative bodies would deviate from the guidelines provided by the EDPB. The explicit reference to the EU's desired level of protection in the guidelines—an essentially equivalent level of protection—indicates that a deviation would have to be justified with great effort and in-depth technological assessments, also with regard to the regime of government access to the transferred personal data in the respective WTO member. There is much to suggest that such technological measures would *not* be considered reasonably available alternatives. The interference with the MFN treatment obligation should therefore satisfy the necessity test in Article XIV(c)(ii) GATS.

4.4.4.1.2 Chapeau

Any interference with the MFN treatment obligation based on adequacy decisions (Sect. 4.4.4.1.2.1) and appropriate safeguards (Sect. 4.4.4.1.2.2) must also satisfy the *chapeau* requirements of Article XIV GATS.

4.4.4.1.2.1 Adequacy Decisions Versus Appropriate Safeguards

The examination under the *chapeau* requires an assessment of whether the conditions prevailing in the countries between which the measure allegedly discriminates are the same. The AB has underlined that only conditions that are relevant for the purpose of establishing arbitrary or unjustifiable discrimination in the light of the specific character of the measure should be considered.[554] In particular, conditions relating to the policy objective under the applicable subparagraph of Article XIV GATS are relevant.[555] It can be assumed that for the purposes of privacy in the digital sphere, the same conditions prevail in all WTO members. The impact of the processing of personal data of individuals can be expected to be the same regardless of the physical location of the individual. Similarly, the AB confirmed the panel's finding in *Brazil – Retreaded Tyres* "that the health impact of remoulded tyres imported from MERCOSUR countries and their European counterparts can be

[552] Ibid.

[553] Ibid., 27.

[554] WTO AB Report, *EC – Seal Products*, para. 5.299 (on Article XX GATT).

[555] Ibid., para. 5.300 (on Article XX GATT).

expected to be comparable."[556] In contrast, Neha Mishra focuses on the "regulatory culture of privacy" in different WTO members to establish same conditions.[557] The reports of the WTO adjudicative bodies, however, do not support such a focus on the regulatory culture when establishing same conditions for the purposes of the *chapeau*.

In cases in which the same conditions prevail, the analysis of whether discrimination is arbitrary or unjustifiable within the meaning of the *chapeau* must focus on the cause of the discrimination, or the rationale put forward to explain its existence.[558] The AB relied on a number of factors in making this determination:

> (i) a 'rigid and unbending requirement' that countries exporting shrimp into the United States must adopt a regulatory programme that is essentially the same as the United States' programme; (ii) the fact that the discrimination resulted from the failure to take into account different circumstances that may occur in the territories of other WTO Members, in particular, specific policies and measures other than those applied by the United States that might have been adopted by an exporting country for the protection and conservation of sea turtles; and (iii) the fact that, while the United States negotiated seriously with some WTO Members exporting shrimp into the United States for the purpose of concluding international agreements for the protection and conservation of sea turtles, it did not do so with other WTO Members.[559]

In addition, one of the most important factors in the assessment of arbitrary or unjustifiable discrimination is the question of whether the discrimination can be reconciled with—or is rationally related to—the policy objective with respect to which the measure has been provisionally justified under the paragraphs of Article XIV GATS.[560] In *US – Shrimp*, the AB highlighted that the measure treated shrimp caught using methods identical to those employed in the US differently from shrimp caught in the US or other certified countries, solely because they have been caught in the waters of countries that have not been certified by the US.[561] The AB found that this discrimination was "difficult to reconcile with the declared policy objective of protecting and conserving sea turtles."[562] Another important factor in the assessment of arbitrary or unjustifiable discrimination is the question of whether the application of the measure at issue allows for any inquiry into the appropriateness

---

[556] WTO AB Report, *Brazil – Retreated Tyres*, para. 217 (on Article XX GATT); WTO Panel Report, *Brazil – Retreaded Tyres*, para. 7.270 (on Article XX GATT).

[557] Mishra (2019), pp. 19–20.

[558] WTO AB Report, *EC – Seal Products*, para. 5.303 (on Article XX GATT) with reference to WTO AB Report, *Brazil – Retreaded Tyres*, para. 226 (on Article XX GATT).

[559] Ibid., para. 5.305 (on Article XX GATT) with reference to WTO AB Report, *US – Shrimp*, paras 163–164, 166, 172 and 177 (on Article XX GATT).

[560] Cp. ibid., para. 5.306 (on Article XX GATT).

[561] WTO AB Report, *US – Shrimp*, para. 176 (on Article XX GATT).

[562] Ibid. (on Article XX GATT).

of the regulatory program given the conditions prevailing in the concerned countries.[563]

An interference with the MFN treatment obligation based on adequacy decisions seems to satisfy many of the factors for finding arbitrary or unjustifiable discrimination. Third countries must adopt a regulatory program for the protection of personal data that is essentially the same as in the EU and there is not much flexibility regarding the level of protection for personal data when it comes to regular adequacy decisions. In this regard, it is important to note that all WTO members should have the same opportunities to obtain an adequacy decision.

First, the assessment must be the same for all WTO members. This is why many adequacy decisions underline in the recitals that

> any decision based on Article 25(6) of Directive 95/46/EC should be made and enforced in a way that does not arbitrarily or unjustifiably discriminate against or between third countries where like conditions prevail, nor constitute a disguised barrier to trade, regard being had to the Community's present international commitments.[564]

However, as has been noted, there are some content-related inconsistencies between the different existant adequacy assessments.[565] This could be problematic under the standards of the *chapeau* depending on the extent of these inconsistencies. In spite of this, the mandatory review process in Article 45(9) GDPR of the older adequacy decisions under the GDPR addresses such inconsistencies because the legal requirements in the GDPR are much more detailed than they were in Directive 95/46/EC. The GDPR simply does not leave room for such inconsistencies anymore.

Second, the EU must undertake a serious, good faith effort to assess the level of a country's data protection measures when formally asked for an adequacy decision by a WTO member. Here, the AB also underlined that

> rigorous compliance with the fundamental requirements of due process should be required in the application and administration of a measure which purports to be an exception to the treaty obligations of the Member imposing the measure and which effectively results in a suspension *pro hac vice* of the treaty rights of other Members.[566]

In *US – Shrimp* the AB criticized the US for not providing formal notice for a denied application nor an explanation of the reasons for the denial.[567] This was compounded by the fact that the US further offered no formal legal procedure for reviewing or appealing a denial.

I would argue that an assessment of a country's level of protection for personal data by an independent EU institution such as the Article 29 WP or the EDPB would

---

[563] WTO AB Report, *EC – Seal Products*, para. 5.337 (on Article XX GATT) with reference to WTO AB Report, *US – Shrimp*, para. 165 (on Article XX GATT); WTO AB Report, *US – Gasoline*, 27 (on Article XX GATT); cp. Kuner (2017), p. 34; Bhagwati (2004), pp. 153–158.

[564] This is an example taken from Recital (4) Commission Decision 2003/821/EC of 21 November 2003 on the adequate protection of personal data in Guernsey, [2003] OJ L 308/27.

[565] See Sect. 3.2.1.3.

[566] WTO AB Report, *US – Shrimp*, para. 182 (on Article XX GATT).

[567] Ibid., para. 183 (on Article XX GATT).

constitute a serious, good faith effort to assess the level of data protection in a third country. An external non-governmental assessment—such as the ones conducted by the Research Centre on IT and Law at the University of Namur (CRID) for Burkina Faso, Mauritius, Tunisia, and Morocco in 2010—might not be enough because the findings are not legitimated by an official governmental institution. At the same time, an opinion of the Article 29 WP or the EDPB cannot be reviewed or appealed. Nevertheless, it provides a detailed explanation of the reasons for the denial of an adequacy finding that should be sufficient.

It is necessary to distinguish the situation adjudicated in *US – Shrimp* from hypothetical situations concerning the EU's personal data protection regime. The effect of the measure in *US – Shrimp* was "a rigid and unbending standard by which United States officials determine whether or not countries will be certified, thus granting or refusing other countries the right to export shrimp to the United States."[568] In contrast to this, the interferences with the MFN treatment obligation caused by EU adequacy decisions still allow structural, systematic, and continuous cross-border flows of personal data on the basis of Article 46 GDPR and cannot be construed as an export prohibition.[569] The trade restrictive effect of the measure is not comparable in the EU case and therefore the implicit due process standards of the *chapeau* should be satisfied. As long as every WTO member asking for an adequacy decision receives an assessment by the EDPB, the interference with the MFN treatment obligation caused by EU adequacy decisions does not amount to arbitrary or unjustifiable discrimination under the *chapeau*.[570]

With regard to the prohibition on disguised restrictions on trade, the AB acknowledged that it is often difficult to prove the hidden factors marking a disguised protectionist measure: "Although it is true that the aim of a measure may not be easily ascertained, nevertheless its protective application can most often be discerned from the design, the architecture, and the revealing structure of a measure."[571]

An interference with the MFN treatment obligation based on adequacy decisions could be considered a disguised restriction on trade if WTO members interested in obtaining an adequacy decision do not receive any kind of assessment of their level of protection for personal data. In sum, I find that there is no disguised restriction on

---

[568] WTO AB Report, *US – Shrimp*, para. 163 (on Article XX GATT).

[569] Where the instruments providing appropriate safeguards in Article 46 GDPR are not available, a potential export prohibition for digital services that require structural, systematic, and continuous transfers of personal data could be reconciled with the policy objective of protecting privacy under Article XIV(c)(ii) GATS.

[570] Should the WTO adjudicative bodies not follow the assessment submitted here, the European Commission would potentially need to start issuing negative adequacy decisions subject to judicial review. Such negative adequacy decisions would have negative consequences for the use of the instruments in Article 46 GDPR because the decision would consist of an official determination that the level of protection for personal data is not essentially equivalent to that guaranteed within the EU. Complainants should thus be aware that a negative adequacy decision could require data controllers and supervisory authorities to suspend or ban all data transfers from the EU to third countries with a negative adequacy decision.

[571] WTO AB Report, *Japan – Alcoholic Beverages II*, 29 (on Article XX GATT).

international trade in cases in which a third country is subject to an assessment of the EDPB.

The *chapeau* analysis will be different when a special framework adequacy decision—such as the invalidated Decision (EU) 2016/1250, the Privacy Shield adequacy decision—is in force. Currently, there are no special framework adequacy decisions in force, but the EU started the process of adopting a new special framework adequacy decision for the US covering the Transatlantic Data Privacy Framework.[572] The AB clarified in *US – Shrimp (Article 21.5 – Malaysia)* that the *chapeau* does not require the conclusion of an agreement in order to avoid arbitrary or unjustifiable discrimination.[573] Rather, it is simply necessary that all countries be provided with similar opportunities.[574] Accordingly, the EU is bound to provide all countries with similar opportunities to negotiate a special framework adequacy decision if the EU adopts a new one. The standard of a good faith effort to negotiate a special framework adequacy decision would need to be assessed against the efforts made in the special framework adequacy decisions in force, or former special framework decisions.[575] Comparable resources must be invested, and comparable energy must be devoted.[576] This would set a high standard given the efforts made by the European Commission to negotiate the Privacy Shield or the Transatlantic Data Privacy Framework with the US. Should the EU once again adopt a special framework adequacy decision, it would amount to an interference with the MFN treatment obligation if the EU does not provide all WTO members with similar opportunities.[577]

4.4.4.1.2.2 Appropriate Safeguards Versus Derogations

The interference with the MFN treatment obligation based on the instruments providing appropriate safeguards in Article 46 GDPR amounts to an export prohibition for certain services.[578] Such an interference with the MFN treatment obligation may occur in cases in which supervisory authorities in EU member states make use of their corrective powers to ban or suspend data transfers in order to safeguard the right to continuous protection for personal data in Article 8 CFR. In these cases, the EU would be able to make a *prima facie* case that there is no arbitrary or unjustifiable discrimination for two reasons. First, the interference with the MFN treatment obligation can be reconciled with the measure's policy objective under Article XIV(c)(ii) GATS. Second, the due process requirements are fulfilled because

[572] European Commission (2022a); European Commission (2022b).

[573] WTO AB Report, *US – Shrimp (Article 21.5 – Malaysia)*, para. 134 (on Article XX GATT).

[574] Ibid., para. 122 (on Article XX GATT).

[575] Ibid., para. 133 (on Article XX GATT), with reference to WTO Panel Report, *US – Shrimp (Article 21.5 – Malaysia)*, para. 5.71 (on Article XX GATT).

[576] Ibid., para. 122 (on Article XX GATT).

[577] Bygrave (2002), p. 198.

[578] See Sect. 4.3.3.2.

any decision of supervisory authorities can be subject to judicial review. Nevertheless, two scenarios are imaginable that could still lead to arbitrary or unjustifiable discrimination:

- The first scenario relates to inconsistencies among the supervisory authorities of different EU member states. For example, if the French supervisory authority prohibits a Chinese service supplier to use "instruments providing appropriate safeguards," but the Dutch supervisory authority does not. This divergence is not reconcilable with the policy objective of securing compliance with the right to continuous protection of personal data in Article 8 CFR. A scenario like this is possible when supervisory authorities do not coordinate the use of their corrective powers for data transfers, for example by using the voluntary consistency mechanism in Article 64(2) GDP, or when they do not implement the results of the voluntary consistency mechanism, in which case the EDPB could still issue a legally binding decision according to Article 65(1)(c) GDPR.[579]
- The second scenario relates to inconsistencies regarding the actions of a single supervisory authority in comparable situations. This scenario would arise if for example the French supervisory authority prohibits a Chinese service supplier to transfer personal data from the EU to China on the basis of Article 46 GDPR because of fundamental rights considerations, but at the same time a Russian service supplier is still allowed to transfer personal data from the EU to Russia on the basis of Article 46 GDPR when similar fundamental rights concerns exist with regard to those data transfers. The complainant would have to show that the data transfers to Russia on the basis of Article 46 GDPR would undermine the declared policy objective of securing compliance with the right to continuous protection of personal data in Article 8 CFR.

Should a complainant be able to show the existence of either scenario, it might be possible to rebut the EU's *prima facie* case of consistency. In such cases, interferences with the MFN treatment obligation based on the instruments providing appropriate safeguards in Article 46 GDPR would amount to arbitrary or unjustifiable discrimination under the *chapeau*.

With regard to the standard of disguised restriction on trade, the the EU could make a *prima facie* case for compliance by referring to the independence of supervisory authorities according to Article 8(3) CFR.[580] Where supervisory authorities use their corrective powers in reaction to a complaint lodged with them, there cannot be a disguised restriction on international trade. Where they use their corrective powers on their own initiative, a complainant would have to show that the relevant decision was not motivated by the protection of the right to continuous protection for personal data in Article 8 CFR.

[579] See Sect. 3.3.3.1.3.

[580] See Sect. 2.2.2.4.

4.4.4.2 Interference with the Domestic Regulation Obligation

One aspect of the EU regulation of data transfers that interferes with the domestic regulation obligation in Article VI GATS can be provisionally justified under the privacy exception in Article XIV(c)(ii) GATS (Sect. 4.4.4.2.1), but it does not satisfy the requirements of the *chapeau* in Article XIV GATS (Sect. 4.4.4.2.2).

4.4.4.2.1 Privacy Exception

Interferences with the domestic regulation obligation must be provisionally justified under the privacy exception in Article XIV(c)(ii) GATS. The first type of interference occurs because special framework adequacy decisions are usually negotiated with a WTO member that would otherwise not qualify for an adequacy decision (Sect. 4.4.4.2.1.1). The second type of interference occurs when the use of corrective powers by different EU member supervisory authorities results in a fragmentation of conditions for the use of instruments providing appropriate safeguards in Article 46 GDPR across the EU (Sect. 4.4.4.2.1.2).

4.4.4.2.1.1 Interference Based on Special Framework Adequacy Decisions

The first type of interference has a significant impact on the overall administration of the EU regulation of data transfers because it essentially introduces an additional legal mechanism for data transfers that is not available to all WTO members. To justify this interference, it must be demonstrated that the respective measure is designed to secure compliance with the GDPR and the right to continuous protection of personal data in Article 8 CFR.[581] The ECJ has invalidated both of the special framework adequacy decisions that the European Commission has negotiated so far. The most important reason for the invalidations was that the decisions did not comply with the right to continuous protection for personal data in Article 8 CFR. It is therefore not even entirely clear whether these special framework adequacy decisions would have satisfied the first standard.

Furthermore, it must be demonstrated that the respective measure is necessary to secure compliance with the GDPR and the right to continuous protection of personal data in Article 8 CFR.[582] This requires a weighing and balancing test. It must take into account the importance of the objective pursued, the measure's contribution to that objective, and the trade restrictiveness of the measure.[583] Securing compliance

[581] WTO AB Report, *Argentina – Financial Services*, para. 6.202; WTO Panel Report, *Argentina – Financial Services*, paras 7.592–7.593; see Sect. 4.4.4.1.1.

[582] Ibid.

[583] WTO Panel Report, *Argentina – Financial Services*, paras 7.659, 7.661 with reference to, among others, WTO AB Report, *EC – Seal Products*, para. 5.169 (on Article XX GATT) and WTO AB Report, *US – Gambling*, paras 306–307.

with the right to continuous protection for personal data is of the utmost importance because it is a constituent part of the fundamental right to data protection in Article 8 CFR. If a special framework adequacy decision is actually found to secure compliance with the right to continuous protection for personal data, it can be assumed that its contribution to that objective is high. Moreover, the trade restrictiveness of special framework adequacy decisions is not very high because instruments providing appropriate safeguards also allow structural, systemic, and continuous cross-border flows of personal data. If a specific special framework adequacy decision actually complies with the right to continuous protection of personal data in Article 8 CFR, the interference with the MFN treatment obligation should satisfy the necessity test in Article XIV(c)(ii) GATS.

4.4.4.2.1.2 Interference Based on Corrective Powers of Supervisory Authorities

The second type of interference with the domestic regulation obligation occurs when the use of corrective powers by supervisory authorities results in a fragmentation among EU member states of the conditions for data transfers using instruments providing appropriate safeguards in Article 46 GDPR. Supervisory authorities must use their corrective powers to safeguard the right to continuous protection of personal data. The corrective powers are designed to secure compliance with the right to continuous protection of personal data. This objective is of the utmost importance.[584] While the use of the corrective powers is essential for the compliance with the right to continuous protection of personal data, the trade restrictiveness of a fragmentation among EU member states as regards the conditions for data transfers with instruments providing appropriate safeguards is quite high. Consequently, reasonably available alternative measures must be assessed.

The ECJ has addressed the issue of fragmentation in in *Schrems 2*.[585] Here the Court highlighted that the voluntary consistency mechanism in Article 64(2) GDPR enables supervisory authorities to request an opinion from the EDPB when deciding whether to suspend or ban data transfers to a third country.[586] The ECJ also emphasized the possibility for the EDPB in Article 65(1)(c) GDPR to adopt a legally binding decision, should a supervisory authority not follow an opinion of the EDPB.[587] However, the consistency mechanism in Article 64(2) GDPR is not a water-tight solution because it is voluntary. A requirement to use the mandatory consistency mechanism in Article 64(1) GDPR would be a reasonably available alternative measure that is consistent with the GATS because it guarantees the impartial application of these powers and preserves for the EU its right to achieve the desired level of data protection. Supervisory authorities must already communicate a draft decision to the EDPB for an opinion when they approve BCRs based on

[584] Mishra (2019), p. 14.

[585] ECJ, *Schrems 2*, para. 147.

[586] Ibid.

[587] Ibid.

Article 64(1)(f) GDPR. The list for the mandatory consistency mechanism in Article 64(1) GDPR would have to be extended with decisions to ban or suspend data transfers according to Article 58(2)(f) and (j) GDPR. Should the use of corrective powers by supervisory authorities lead to an interference with Article VI:1 GATS because the voluntary consistency mechanism could not prevent the fragmentation among EU member states for the use of instruments providing appropriate, it cannot be considered necessary for the purposes of Article XIV(c)(ii) GATS.

4.4.4.2.2 Chapeau

Any interference with the domestic regulation obligation in Article VI GATS based on special framework adequacy decisions must also be justified under the *chapeau* of Article XIV GATS. The analysis of whether discrimination is arbitrary or unjustifiable within the meaning of the *chapeau* must focus on the cause of the discrimination, or the rationale put forward to explain its existence.[588] I have shown above that an interference with the MFN treatment obligation in Article II GATS based on special framework adequacy decisions amounts to arbitrary or unjustifiable discrimination in cases in which other WTO members do not have similar opportunities to negotiate such a special framework for an adequacy decision. The same is true for the interference with the impartiality standard in Article VI:1 GATS. As long as special framework adequacy decisions are in force and the EU does not provide all WTO members with similar opportunities to negotiate such a solution, the interference with the domestic regulation obligation based on special framework adequacy decisions constitutes arbitrary and unjustifiable discrimination and cannot be justified under the *chapeau* of Article XIV GATS.

4.4.4.3 Interference with the Market Access Obligation

Interferences with the market access obligation in Article XVI:2(a) and (c) GATS can be provisionally justified under the privacy exception in Article XIV(c)(ii) GATS (Sect. 4.4.4.3.1) and the EU can also make a *prima facie* case of consistency with the *chapeau* of Article XIV GATS (Sect. 4.4.4.3.2).

4.4.4.3.1 Privacy Exception

There is an interference with the market access obligation in Article XVI:2(a) and (c) GATS in cases in which supervisory authorities restrict the cross-border flow of

[588] WTO AB Report, *EC – Seal Products*, para. 5.303 (on Article XX GATT) with reference to WTO AB Report, *Brazil – Retreaded Tyres*, para. 226 (on Article XX GATT).

personal data *and* structural, systematic, and continuous cross-border flows of personal data are a necessary element of the cross-border supply of a service covered by the EU's market access commitments.[589] First, it must be demonstrated that the respective measure is designed to secure compliance with the GDPR and the right to continuous protection of personal data in Article 8 CFR.[590] I have concluded above that the use of corrective powers by supervisory authorities is designed to secure compliance with the right to continuous protection for personal data in Article 8 CFR.[591]

Second, it must be demonstrated that the respective measure is necessary to secure compliance with the GDPR and the right to continuous protection of personal data in Article 8 CFR. The weighing and balancing test must take into account the importance of the objective pursued, the measure's contribution to that objective, and the trade restrictiveness of the measure.[592] The objective of securing compliance with the right to continuous protection for personal data is of the utmost importance and the use of corrective powers by supervisory authorities is essential for compliance with the right to continuous protection for personal data. Nevertheless, the trade restrictiveness of the interference with the market access obligation in Article XVI:2(a) and (c) GATS is high because the use of corrective powers results in a zero quota for the services at issue. Consequently, reasonably available alternative measures must be assessed.

In contrast to the interference with the domestic regulation obligation, the mandatory consistency mechanism in Article 64(1) GDPR does not constitute a reasonably available alternative measure that could mediate the interference with Article XVI:2(a) and (c) GATS. Nor could the principle of accountability constitute an alternative measure.[593] In addition, the corrective powers in Article 58(2)(f) and (j) GDPR already foresee temporary measures in cases where non-compliance with the right to continuous protection for personal data can be improved. I conclude that there are no reasonably available alternative measures and that therefore the use of corrective powers by supervisory authorities can be provisionally justified under the privacy exception in Article XIV(c)(ii) GATS.

---

[589] This is the case for digital services such as cloud computing services, social network services, IoT maintenance services, and digital lodging arrangement platform services that cannot be supplied without systematic, structural, and continuous data transfers. See Sect. 4.3.3.2.

[590] WTO AB Report, *Argentina – Financial Services*, para. 6.202; WTO Panel Report, *Argentina – Financial Services*, paras 7.592–7.593; see Sect. 4.4.4.1.1.

[591] See Sect. 4.4.4.2.1.

[592] WTO Panel Report, *Argentina – Financial Services*, paras. 7.659, 7.661 with reference to, among others, WTO AB Report, *EC – Seal Products*, para. 5.169(on Article XX GATT) and WTO AB Report, *US – Gambling*, paras 306–307.

[593] See Sect. 4.4.4.1.1. Neha Mishra also argued that a WTO panel will most likely refrain from considering the accountability principle due to the absence of international standards on data privacy and cybersecurity. Mishra (2019), p. 18.

4.4.4.3.2 Chapeau

Interferences with the market access obligation in Article XVI:2(a) and (c) GATS must also be justified under the *chapeau* of Article XIV GATS. The analysis of whether discrimination is arbitrary or unjustifiable within the meaning of the *chapeau* must focus on the cause of the discrimination, or the rationale put forward to explain its existence.[594] The EU would be able to make a *prima facie* case that there is no arbitrary or unjustifiable discrimination for two reasons. First, the use of the corrective powers by supervisory authorities can be reconciled with the policy objective under Article XIV(c)(ii) GATS. Supervisory authorities make use of their corrective powers to ban or suspend data transfers in cases in which data exporters infringe the right to continuous protection for personal data in Article 8 CFR. Second, the due process requirements are satisfied because all decisions of the supervisory authorities are subject to judicial review.

Nevertheless, two scenarios could still lead to arbitrary or unjustifiable discrimination. First, when a complainant successfully shows that supervisory authorities in different EU member states maintain different regimes for services and service suppliers for the same WTO member. Second, when a complainant successfully shows that a single supervisory authority in an EU member state selectively uses its corrective powers to discriminate against certain WTO members.

The EU would also be able to make a *prima facie* case that there is no disguised restriction on trade by referring to the independence of supervisory authorities according to Article 8(3) CFR.[595] Only when a complainant can successfully show that the use of the corrective powers by supervisory authorities is not motivated by the protection of the right to continuous protection for personal data can there be a finding of disguised restrictions on international trade.

4.4.4.4 Interference with the National Treatment Obligation

Finally, the aspects of the EU regulation of data transfers that interfere with the national treatment obligation in Article XVII GATS can also be provisionally justified under the privacy exception in Article XIV(c)(ii) GATS (Sect. 4.4.4.4.1) and the *chapeau* of Article XIV GATS (Sect. 4.4.4.4.2).

4.4.4.4.1 Privacy Exception

Interferences with the national treatment obligation must be provisionally justified under the privacy exception in Article XIV(c)(ii) GATS. The first interference is

[594]WTO AB Report, *EC – Seal Products*, para. 5.303 (on Article XX GATT) with reference to WTO AB Report, *Brazil – Retreaded Tyres*, para. 226 (on Article XX GATT).

[595]See Sect. 2.2.2.4.

based on the instruments providing appropriate safeguards in Article 46 GDPR because foreign service suppliers must comply with the conditions of their use in addition to the other rules in the GDPR (Sect. 4.4.4.4.1.1). The second interference is based on the use of the corrective powers of supervisory authorities (Sect. 4.4.4.4.1.2).

4.4.4.4.1.1 Interference Based on Appropriate Safeguards

It must be demonstrated that the use of instruments providing appropriate safeguards in Article 46 GDPR is designed to secure compliance with the GDPR and the right to continuous protection of personal data in Article 8 CFR.[596] These instruments must be attributed a lower level of compliance with the right to continuous protection of personal data than adequacy decisions. At the same time, the trade restrictiveness of an interference with the national treatment obligation is not very high. The use of the instruments in Article 46 GDPR is a regulatory burden, but they still allow structural, systematic, and continuous data transfers. It is thus not clear whether it is necessary to look into alternative measures that are reasonably available and achieve the same level of protection with respect to the objective pursued.

Should the adjudicative bodies of the WTO decide to look into alternative measures, it seems sensible to address the principle of accountability again with regard to the national treatment obligation.[597] The scholars who submit that it could present a less restrictive alternative refer to a text by Christopher Kuner from 2009: "An Alternative Standard for International Data Transfers."[598] In this text, Kuner argues that it is necessary to investigate what legal mechanisms could ensure that data exporters remain accountable and responsible for data processing once personal data have been transferred outside the EU. He suggests that "[t]his might include reliance on liability concepts under national law, *or* use of data transfer mechanisms that are already recognized, such as BCRs or the use of standard contractual clauses for International Data Transfers."[599] This scholarship overlooks the fact that the instruments in Article 46 GDPR—which also existed under Directive 95/46/EC—already work with the principle of accountability. The contractual solutions foreseen in Article 46 GDPR include liability concepts. For example, BCRs have to specify the liability by the data exporter established on the territory of an EU member state for any breaches of the BCRs by any member of the group of enterprises not established in the EU according to Article 47(2)(f) GDPR and Clause 6 of the standard data protection clauses adopted with Decision 2010/87/EU also entail

[596] WTO AB Report, *Argentina – Financial Services*, para. 6.202; WTO Panel Report, *Argentina – Financial Services*, paras 7.592–7.593; see Sect. 4.4.4.1.1.

[597] I have argued above—concerning the MFN treatment obligation—that the principle of accountability would not be a reasonably available alternative measure that achieves the same level of protection with respect to the objective pursued in cases in which the right to continuous protection for personal data cannot be ensured with the instruments in Article 46 GDPR. See Sect. 4.4.4.1.1.

[598] Velli (2019), p. 889; Yakovleva and Irion (2016), pp. 206–207. Kuner (2009), pp. 269–272.

[599] Kuner (2009), p. 270.

detailed rules on liability. I thus argue that there are no alternative measures that are reasonably available and achieve the same level of protection with respect to the right to continuous protection for personal data. The interference with the national treatment obligation based on instruments providing appropriate safeguards therefore satisfies the necessity test in Article XIV(c)(ii) GATS.

4.4.4.4.1.2 Interference Based on Corrective Powers of Supervisory Authorities

The second interference with the national treatment obligation is based on the use of corrective powers by supervisory authorities. To justify this interference, it must be demonstrated that the respective measure is designed to secure compliance with the GDPR and the right to continuous protection of personal data in Article 8 CFR.[600] Furthermore, it must be demonstrated that the respective measure is necessary to secure such compliance. The corrective powers are designed to secure compliance with the right to continuous protection of personal data but because of the trade restrictiveness of the decision of a supervisory authority to use corrective powers to suspend or ban data transfers to a third country is high, reasonably available alternative measures must be assessed.

I submit that there are no alternative measures that would achieve the same level of protection. The GDPR itself already entails a scaled set of corrective powers in Article 58(2)(f) and (j) GDPR. A supervisory authority may only suspend data transfers according; it may impose a temporary limitation or ban on data transfers; and it may impose a definitive limitation or ban on data transfers. The national treatment violation caused by the corrective powers of supervisory authority would therefore satisfy the necessity test in Article XIV(c)(ii) GATS.

4.4.4.4.2 Chapeau

Interferences with the national treatment obligation in Article XVII GATS based on appropriate safeguards (Sect. 4.4.4.4.2.1) and the corrective powers of supervisory authorities (Sect. 4.4.4.4.2.2) must also be justified under the *chapeau* of Article XIV GATS.[601]

4.4.4.4.2.1 Interference Based on Appropriate Safeguards

The EU would be able to make a *prima facie* case that there is no arbitrary or unjustifiable discrimination in the interference with the national treatment obligation based on the instruments providing appropriate safeguards in Article 46 GDPR. The

---

[600] WTO AB Report, *Argentina – Financial Services*, para. 6.202; WTO Panel Report, *Argentina – Financial Services*, paras 7.592–7.593; see Sect. 4.4.4.1.1.

[601] WTO AB Report, *EC – Seal Products*, para. 5.303 (on Article XX GATT) with reference to WTO AB Report, *Brazil – Retreaded Tyres*, para. 226 (on Article XX GATT).

interference can be reconciled with the policy objective under Article XIV(c)(ii) GATS. The transfer of personal data presents a risk for individuals in the EU because information about them leaves the EU where the GDPR applies and can be enforced. This is the rationale of the discrimination because in contrast, domestic services and service suppliers do not necessarily require data transfers.

The EU would also be able to make a *prima facie* case that there is no disguised restriction on international trade because services and service suppliers in the EU must also use these instruments when they transfer personal data to a third country. Accordingly, the interference with the national treatment obligation can be justified under the *chapeau* of Article XIV GATS.

4.4.4.4.2.2 Interference Based on Corrective Powers of Supervisory Authorities

The EU would also be able to make a *prima facie* case that there is no arbitrary or unjustifiable discrimination in the interference with the national treatment obligation based on the corrective powers of supervisory authorities. Supervisory authorities make use of their corrective powers to ban or suspend data transfers where data exporters infringe the right to continuous protection for personal data in Article 8 CFR.

Nevertheless, a complainant could, as Svetlana Yakovleva and Kristina Irion suggest, try to rebut the *prima facie* case and argue that the EU applies double standards when it comes to foreign internet surveillance.[602] Should supervisory authorities—and ultimately the ECJ—require a higher standard for internet surveillance in third countries than applicable for the EU member states, then the interference with the national treatment obligation based on the corrective powers of supervisory authorities would amount to arbitrary and unjustifiable discrimination. Such a double standard could not be reconciled with the policy objective with respect to which the measure has been provisionally justified under the paragraphs of Article XIV GATS. However, I showed above that there are no double standards for foreign internet surveillance and the EU member states are bound to comply with the same requirements as third countries.[603]

The EU would also be able to make a *prima facie* case that there is no disguised restriction on trade by referring to the independence of supervisory authorities according to Article 8(3) CFR.[604] Only when a complainant can successfully show that the use of corrective powers by supervisory authorities is not motivated by the protection of the right to continuous protection on personal data can there be a finding of a disguised restriction on international trade. The interference with the national treatment obligation caused by the corrective powers of supervisory authorities can therefore be justified under the *chapeau* of Article XIV GATS.

---

[602] Yakovleva and Irion (2020b), p. 11.

[603] See Sect. 2.4.3.

[604] See Sect. 2.2.2.4.

4.4.5 Summary

The justification of interferences with GATS obligations caused by the EU's fundamental rights-based regulation of personal data focuses on the general exceptions in Article XIV. The economic integration exception in Article V GATS could be relevant to justify interferences with the MFN treatment obligation if the EU concluded a trade agreement with every country that has an adequacy decision. The security exception in Article XIV *bis* GATS is only relevant in situations of heightened tension or crisis. Finally, the confidentiality exception in Paragraph 5(d) of the Annex on Telecommunications can only justify interferences with the provisions of the annex.

I find that most of the interferences with GATS obligations can be provisionally justified under the general exceptions in Article XIV GATS. Only one interference fails provisional justification under the privacy exception in Article XIV(c)(ii) GATS: The interference with the domestic regulation obligation in Article VI:1 GATS caused by a fragmented application of the corrective powers of different supervisory authorities among EU member states. The trade restrictiveness of such a fragmentation is high. Subjecting the decisions of supervisory authorities to a mandatory consistency mechanism in Article 64(1) GDPR could be a reasonably available alternative measure that is consistent with the GATS because it guarantees the impartial application of these powers and preserves for the EU its right to achieve its desired level of protection for personal data.

In addition, some of the provisionally justified interferences fail the assessment under the *chapeau* of Article XIV GATS:

- The interference with the MFN treatment obligation based on regular adequacy decisions amounts to arbitrary or unjustifiable discrimination should a WTO member that asks for an adequacy decision not receive an assessment by the EDPB concerning the level of protection for personal data.
- The interference with the MFN treatment obligation as well as the interference with the domestic regulation obligation caused by special framework adequacy decisions—if and when a new special framework adequacy decision comes into force (e.g. the Transatlantic Data Privacy Framework with the US)—also amounts to arbitrary or unjustifiable discrimination insofar as the EU does not provide all WTO members with similar opportunities to negotiate a special framework adequacy decision.
- The interference with the market access obligation based on restrictions to use the instruments providing appropriate safeguards in Article 46 GDPR amounts to arbitrary or unjustifiable discrimination if different supervisory authorities in different EU member states maintain different regimes for service supplies in the territory of the same WTO member, or if a single supervisory authority in an EU member state selectively uses its corrective powers for certain WTO members and not for others and thereby undermines the right to continuous protection of personal data.

4.5 Conclusion

The rules of the multilateral trading system of the WTO can be used as proxies to distinguish legitimate regulation from protectionism. When applied to the EU's fundamental rights-based regulation of data transfers, they allow for the legal assessment of the line between data protection and data protectionism. The analysis above shows that the regulation of data transfers is largely compatible with WTO law. Seven interferences with obligations in the GATS have been identified. Most of them are justifiable under the privacy exception in Article XIV(c)(ii) GATS. The history of the privacy exception shows that the EC negotiated the WTO's trade agreement on services with great foresight. The EC pushed for the adoption of a privacy exception during the negotiations of the GATS with a view to its future data protection framework. Nevertheless, some aspects of the EU system for data transfers need further attention because they may not be justifiable under the privacy exception in Article XIV(c)(ii) GATS.

The first aspect concerns the application of adequacy decisions. Adequacy decisions interfere with the MFN treatment obligation in Article II:1 GATS. The AB maintained that the *chapeau* of the general exceptions demands "rigorous compliance with the fundamental requirements of due process."[605] This includes formal notice for a denial of an application or an explanation of the reasons for the denial.[606] This interference with the MFN treatment obligation would amount to arbitrary or unjustifiable discrimination under the *chapeau* should a WTO member ask the EU for an adequacy decision and not receive an assessment by the EDPB. In order to comply with WTO law, the European Commission must ask the EDPB for an assessment of the level of protection for personal data in a third country when a third country asks for an adequacy decision, or, alternatively, issue a negative adequacy decision itself.

The second aspect concerns special framework adequacy decisions such as the invalidated Decision (EU) 2016/1250, the Privacy Shield adequacy decision. Special framework adequacy decisions are often tailor-made solutions for countries that otherwise would not qualify for a regular adequacy decision. They interfere with the MFN treatment obligation and the impartiality standard of the domestic regulation obligation. Should a new special framework adequacy decision come into force, this interference would amount to arbitrary or unjustifiable discrimination under the *chapeau* if the EU does not provide all WTO members with similar opportunities to negotiate a special framework for an adequacy decision. To comply with WTO law, the European Commission will have to stop negotiating special framework adequacy decision unless it is ready to initiate such negotiations with all interested WTO members. Since the EU already works towards adopting a special framework

[605] WTO AB Report, *US – Shrimp*, para. 182 (on Article XX GATT).

[606] Ibid., para. 183 (on Article XX GATT).

adequacy decision for the Transatlantic Data Privacy Framework with the US, an unjustifiable violation of the MFN treatment obligation is foreseeable.[607]

The third aspect concerns the administration of the corrective powers of supervisory authorities. The ECJ confirmed that supervisory authorities must suspend or ban transfers of personal data in cases in which the right to continuous protection of personal data in Article 8 CFR cannot be guaranteed and the data exporter refuses to take action.[608] The suspension or ban of data transfers may lead to an interference with the MFN treatment obligation and the market access obligation. These interferences amount to arbitrary or unjustifiable discrimination under the *chapeau* if the administration of the corrective powers is inconsistent. For example, when supervisory authorities in different EU member states maintain different regimes for services and service suppliers in the same WTO member, or when a supervisory authority in an EU member state selectively uses its corrective powers for data transfers to certain WTO members and not for data transfers to other WTO members where similar deficiencies regarding data protection exist, and the selective use of the corrective powers thereby undermines the right to continuous protection of personal data. Such a fragmented use of the corrective powers of supervisory authorities also interferes with the impartiality standard of the domestic regulation obligation. The interference does not satisfy the necessity test of the privacy exception. Currently, supervisory authorities are not obliged to coordinate the use of their corrective powers. They *may* use the voluntary consistency mechanism in Article 64(2) GDPR to ask for an opinion from the EDPB, which all supervisory authorities should then implement. A requirement to use the mandatory consistency mechanism in Article 64(1) GDPR would be a reasonably available alternative measure that is consistent with the GATS because it guarantees the impartial application of these powers and preserves for the EU its right to achieve the desired level of protection. This would require a change in the GDPR. Supervisory authorities must be aware that they are responsible for complying with WTO law and use their corrective powers accordingly.

With regard to the interferences with the market access obligation and the interferences with the national treatment obligation, it is important to note that allegations that the EU maintains a higher standard for internet surveillance in third countries than applicable for EU member states do not challenge the compliance of the regulation of data transfers with the *chapeau* of the general exceptions. There are no double standards for foreign internet surveillance. The EU member states are bound to comply with the same requirements as third countries in the assessment of their level of protection for personal data.[609]

From the perspective of WTO law, the design of the EU system for data transfers does not constitute data protectionism. However, the analysis has revealed that the European Commission and the supervisory authorities in the EU member states must

---

[607] European Commission (2022a); European Commission (2022b).

[608] ECJ, *Schrems 2*, para. 113.

[609] See Sect. 2.4.3.

make sure the system is applied without protectionist side effects. The Commission must treat third countries equally when it comes to adequacy assessments and the supervisory authorities must coordinate their corrective powers and use them consistently in the same or similar situations. Lastly, special framework adequacy decisions should not be adopted as WTO law would then require the EU to offer the same possibilities to all other WTO members.

References

Bibliography

Anuradha RV (2018) Technological Neutrality: Implications for Services Commitments and the Discussions on E-Commerce. Centre for WTO Studies Working Paper. New Delhi

Bartels L (2015) The Chapeau of the general exceptions in the WTO GATT and GATS Agreements. A reconstruction. Am J Int Law 109(1):95–125

Barth S, de Jong MDT (2017) The privacy paradox – Investigating discrepancies between expressed privacy concerns and actual online behavior – A systematic literature review. Telematics Inform 34(7):1038–1058

Batura O (2013) The WTO legal framework for telecommunications services and challenges of the information age. In: Hermann C, Krajewski M, Terhechte JP (eds) European yearbook of international economic law. Springer, Heidelberg, pp 201–234

Bennett CJ (2012) The accountability approach to privacy and data protection: assumptions and caveats. In: Guagnin D, Hempel L, Iten C et al (eds) Managing privacy through accountability. Palgrave Macmillan, New York, pp 33–48

Bhagwati J (2004) In defense of globalization. Oxford University Press, New York

Blouin C, Gobrecht J, Lethbridge J, Singh D, Smith R, Warner D (2006) Trade in health services under the four modes of supply: review of current trends and policy issues. In: Blouin C, Drager N, Smith R (eds) International trade in health services and the GATS. Current issues and debates. The World Bank, Washington DC, pp 203–234

Bogdanova I (2019) The WTO Panel Ruling on the National Security Exception: Has the Panel 'Cut' the Baby in Half?, EJIL:Talk!, 12 April 2019. https://www.ejiltalk.org/the-wto-panel-ruling-on-the-national-security-exception-has-the-panel-cut-the-baby-in-half/. Accessed 3 Jan 2021

Brehmer JH (2018) Data localization: the unintended consequences of privacy litigation. Am Univ Law Rev 67(3):927–969

Brin S, Page L (1998) The anatomy of a large-scale hypertextual web search engine. Comput Netw ISDN Syst 30(1):107–117

Bronckers M, Larouche P (2008) A review of the WTO regime for telecommunications services. In: Kern A, Mads A (eds) The World Trade Organization and trade in services. Martinus Nijhoff Publishers, Leiden/Boston, pp 319–380

Burri M (2015) The international economic law framework for digital trade. Zeitschrift für Schweizerisches Recht 135(2):10–72

Burri M (2019) Understanding and shaping trade rules for the digital era. In: Elsig M, Hahn M, Spilker G (eds) The shifting landscape of global trade governance. Cambridge University Press, Cambridge, pp 73–106

Burri M (2021) Towards a new treaty on digital trade. J World Trade 55(1):77–100

Bygrave L (2002) Data protection law. Approaching its rationale, logic and limits. Kluwer, The Hague

Chander A (2020) Is data localization a solution for Schrems II? J Int Econ Law 23:1–14
Chander A, Le UP (2015) Data nationalism. Emory Law J 64(3):677–739
Chen I-C (2018) Government internet censorship measures and international law. LIT, Zurich
Cimino-Isaacs CD, Fefer RF, Fergusson IF (2020) WTO: Ministerial Delay, COVID-19, and Ongoing Issues. Congressional Research Service In Focus. Washington DC
Cisco (2019) Cisco Visual Networking Index: Forecast and Trends, 2017–2022. San Jose
Collins D (2019) The public international law of trade in legal services. Cambridge University Press, Cambridge
Conrad CR (2011) Processes and production methods (PPMs) in WTO law: interfacing trade and social goals. Cambridge University Press, Cambridge
Cottier T, Delimatsis P (2008) Article XIVbis GATS. In: Rüdiger W, Stoll P-T, Feinäugle C (eds) WTO – Trade in services. Max Planck commentaries on World Trade Law. Martinus Nijhoff, Leiden, pp 329–348
Cottier T, Molinuevo M (2008) Article V GATS. In: Rüdiger W, Stoll P-T, Feinäugle C (eds) WTO – trade in services. Max Planck commentaries on World Trade Law. Martinus Nijhoff, Leiden, pp 125–164
Cottier T, Delimatsis P, Diebold N (2008) Article XIV GATS. In: Rüdiger W, Stoll P-T, Feinäugle C (eds) WTO – Trade in Services. Max Planck Commentaries on World Trade Law, Martinus Nijhoff, Leiden, pp 287–328
Crosby D (2016) Analysis of data localization measures under WTO service trade rules and commitments. The E15 Initiative Policy Brief. Geneva
Delimatsis P, Molinuevo M (2008) Article XVI GATS. In: Rüdiger W, Stoll P-T, Feinäugle C (eds) WTO – Trade in Services. Max Planck commentaries on World Trade Law. Martinus Nijhoff, Leiden, pp 367–395
Dörr O (2018a) Article 31. General rule of interpretation. In: Dörr O, Schmalenbach K (eds) Vienna Convention on the law of treaties. A commentary, 2nd edn. Springer, Heidelberg, pp 559–616
Dörr O (2018b) Article 32. Supplementary means of interpretation. In: Dörr O, Schmalenbach K (eds) Vienna convention on the law of treaties. A commentary, 2nd edn. Springer, Heidelberg, pp 617–633
Drake WJ, Nicolaidis K (1992) Ideas, interests, and institutionalization. "Trade in Services" and the Uruguay Round. Int Organ 46(1):37–100
Erixon F, Hindley B, Lee-Makiyama H (2009) Protectionism online: internet censorship and international trade law. ECIPE Working Paper No. 12/2009, Brussels
European Commission (2022a) European commission and United States joint statement on trans-Atlantic data privacy framework. 25 March 2022. https://ec.europa.eu/commission/presscorner/detail/en/IP_22_2087. Accessed 30 Oct 2022
European Commission (2022b) Questions & answers: EU-U.S. data privacy framework. 7 October 2022. https://ec.europa.eu/commission/presscorner/detail/en/qanda_22_6045. Accessed 30 Oct 2022
Fefer RF (2020) Internet Regimes and WTO E-Commerce Negotiations. Congressional Research Service Report. R46198. Washington DC
Ferracane MF (2017) Restrictions on Cross-Border data flows: a taxonomy. ECIPE Working Paper 1/2017. Brussels
Ferracane MF (2018) Data flows and national security: a conceptual framework to assess restrictions on data flows under GATS security exception. Digital Policy, Regulation and Governance. https://doi.org/10.1108/DPRG-09-2018-0052. Accessed 3 Jan 2021
Gao H (2008) Annex on telecommunications. In: Rüdiger W, Stoll P-T, Feinäugle C (eds) WTO – Trade in services. Max Planck commentaries on World Trade Law. Martinus Nijhoff, Leiden, pp 683–711
Gao H (2011) Google's China problem: a case study on trade, technology and human rights under the GATS. Asian J WTO Int Health Law Policy 6(2):347–385

Gao H (2012) Googling for the trade–human rights nexus in China: can the WTO help? In: Burri M, Cottier T (eds) Trade governance in the digital age. Cambridge University Press, Cambridge, pp 247–275

Garcia-Israel K, Grollier J (2019) Electronic commerce joint statement: issues in the discussion phase. CUTS, Geneva

Gasser U, Palfrey J (2012) Fostering innovation and trade in the global information society: the different facets and roles of interoperability. In: Burri M, Cottier T (eds) Trade governance in the digital age. Cambridge University Press, Cambridge, pp 123–154

Hamari J, Sjöklint M, Ukkonen A (2016) The sharing economy: why people participate in collaborative consumption. J Assoc Inform Sci Technol 67(9):2047–2059

Hodson S (2019) Applying WTO and FTA disciplines to data localization measures. World Trade Rev 18(4):579–607

Hon WK, Millard C, Walden I (2011) The problem of 'personal data' in cloud computing: what information is regulated?—the cloud of unknowing. Int Data Priv Law 1(4):211–228

Hufbauer GC, Lu Z (2019) Global E-Commerce talks stumble on data issues, privacy, and more. Peterson Institute for International Economics Policy Brief. Washington DC

ICTSD (2017) Debating the Future of E-Commerce and Digital Trade in Buenos Aires. Bridges 21(40). http://www.ictsd.org/bridges-news/bridges/news/debating-the-future-of-e-commerce-and-digital-trade-in-buenos-aires. Accessed on 14 May 2022

Irion K, Yakovleva S, Bartl M (2016) Trade and privacy: complicated bedfellows? How to achieve data protection-proof free trade agreements. Independent study commissioned by BEUC et al. Amsterdam

Ismail Y (2020) E-commerce in the World Trade Organization: history and latest developments in the negotiations under the Joint Statement. International Institute for Sustainable Development and CUTS International, Geneva

ITU (2019) Measuring digital development. Facts and figures 2019, Geneva

Kariyawasam R (2007) International economic law and the digital divide. A New Silk Road? Edward Elgar, Cheltenham

Keller P (2011) European and international media law: liberal democracy, trade, and the new media. Oxford University Press, Oxford

Kelsey J (2019) Understanding the European Union's understanding on computer and related services. Third World Network, Penang

Korolov M (2018) It's Cool, It's Well Wired, and It's Staying in the EU. Data Center Knowledge, 6 February 2018. https://www.datacenterknowledge.com/europe/it-s-cool-it-s-well-wired-and-it-s-staying-eu. Accessed 3 Jan 2021

Krajewski M (2003) National regulation and trade liberalization in services. The legal impact of the general agreement on trade in services (GATS) on national regulatory autonomy. Kluwer, The Hague/London/New York

Krajewski M (2008) Article VI GATS. In: Rüdiger W, Stoll P-T, Feinäugle C (eds) WTO – Trade in Services. Max Planck commentaries on World Trade Law. Martinus Nijhoff, Leiden, pp 167–196

Krajewski M, Engelke M (2008) Article XVII GATS. In: Rüdiger W, Stoll P-T, Feinäugle C (eds) WTO – Trade in Services. Max Planck Commentaries on World Trade Law. Martinus Nijhoff, Leiden, pp 396–420

Kuner C (2009) Developing an adequate legal framework for international data transfers. In: Gutwirth S, Poullet Y, de Hert P et al (eds) Reinventing data protection? Springer, Heidelberg, pp 263–273

Kuner C (2015) Extraterritoriality and regulation of international data transfers in EU data protection law. Int Data Priv Law 5(4):235–245

Kuner C (2017) The Internet and the Global Reach of EU Law. University of Cambridge Faculty of Law Research Paper No. 24/2017

Lang A (2011) World Trade law after neoliberalism. Reimagining the global economic order. Oxford University Press, Oxford

Lapid K (2006) Outsourcing and offshoring under the general agreement on trade in services. J World Trade 40(2):341–364
Le Bouthillier Y (2011) Article 32 Convention of 1969. In: Corten O, Klein P (eds) The Vienna Conventions on the law of treaties. A commentary. Vol. I. Oxford University Press, Oxford, pp 841–863
Lo C-F (2013) The proper interpretation of 'Disguised Restriction on International Trade' under the WTO: the need to look at the protective effect. J Int Disp Settlement 4(1):111–137
Luff D (2004) Current international trade rules relevant to telecommunications services. In: Geradin D, Luff D (eds) The WTO and global convergence in telecommunications and audio-visual services. Cambridge University Press, Cambridge, pp 34–50
Luff D (2012) Convergence - a Buzzword to remain? In: Burri M, Cottier T (eds) Trade governance in the digital age. Cambridge University Press, Cambridge, pp 65–90
Makulilo AB (2013) Data protection regimes in Africa. Too far from the European 'adequacy' standard. Int Data Priv Law 3(1):42–50
Mantilla BS, Pehl A (2020) National security exceptions in international trade and investment agreements. Justiciability and Standards of Review. Springer, Heidelberg
Marchetti JA, Mavroidis PC (2011) The genesis of the GATS (General Agreement on Trade in Services). Eur J Int law 22(3):689–721
Marín Durán G (2017) Untangling the international responsibility of the European Union and its member states in the World Trade Organization post-Lisbon: a competence/remedy model. Eur J Int Law. 28(3):697–729
Mathew B (2003) The WTO Agreements on telecommunications. Peter Lang, Bern
Matsushita M, Schoenbaum TJ, Mavroidis PC, Hahn M (2015) The World Trade Organization. Law, practice, and policy, 3rd edn. Oxford University Press, Oxford
Mattoo A, Meltzer JP (2018) International data flows and privacy: the conflict and its resolution. J Int Econ Law 21(4):769–789
Mattoo A, Wunsch-Vincent S (2004) Pre-empting protectionism in services: the GATS and outsourcing. J Int Econ Law 7(4):765–800
Meltzer JP (2019) Governing digital trade. World Trade Rev 18(1):23–48
Mishra N (2016) Data localization laws in a digital world. Data protection or data protectionism? Public Sphere 2016:135–158
Mishra N (2019) Privacy, cybersecurity, and GATS Article XIV: a new frontier for trade and internet regulation? World Trade Rev 19(3):1–24
Mitchell AD, Hepburn J (2017) Don't Fence Me In: reforming trade and investment law to better facilitate cross-border data transfer. Yale J Law Technol 19:182–237
Mitchell AD, Neha M (2018) Data at the docks: modernizing international trade law for the digital economy. Vanderbilt J Entertain Technol Law 20(4):1073–1134
Molinuevo M (2008) Article XX GATS: schedules for specific commitments. In: Rüdiger W, Stoll P-T, Feinäugle C (eds) WTO – Trade in Services. Max Planck Commentaries on World Trade Law. Martinus Nijhoff, Leiden, pp 445–464
Molthan AL, Case JL, Venner J, Schroeder R et al. (2015) Clouds in the Cloud. Weather forecast and applications within cloud computing environment. Bull Am Meteorol Soc 96(8):1369–1379
Muller G (2017) Troubled relationships under the GATS: tensions between market access (Article XVI), national treatment (Article XVII), and domestic regulation (Article VI). World Trade Rev 16(3):449–474
Munin N (2010) Legal guide to GATS. Kluwer, Alphen aan den Rijn
Nadakavukaren Schefer K (2009) Dancing with the devil: a heretic's view of protectionism in the WTO legal system. Asian J WTO Int Health Law Policy 4(2):423–443
Nartova O (2008) Article XXI: modification of schedules. In: Rüdiger W, Stoll P-T, Feinäugle C (eds) WTO – trade in services. Max Planck commentaries on World Trade Law. Martinus Nijhoff, Leiden, pp 465–479
Newman AL (2009) Protectors of Privacy. Regulating personal data in the global economy. Cornell University Press, New York

Oesch M (2018) Switzerland and the European Union. Schulthess, Zurich
Oesch M, Burghartz AO, Manikulam V (2020) The Jurisprudence of WTO Dispute Resolution (2019). Swiss Rev Int Eur Law 2:265–294
Panizzon M (2006) Good Faith in the Jurisprudence of the WTO. Hart, Portland
Pauwelyn J (2005) *Rien ne Va Plus?* Distinguishing domestic regulation from market access in GATT and GATS. World Trade Rev 4(2):131–170
Peng S-y (2011) Digitalization of services, the GATS and the protection of personal data. In: Sethe R, Heinemann A, Hilty RM et al (eds) Kommunikation. Stämpfli, Bern, pp 753–769
Perez Asinari MV (2003) The WTO and the protection of personal data. Do EU measures fall within GATS Exception? Which future for data protection within the WTO e-commerce Context? Paper presented at the 18th BILETA Conference: Controlling Information in the Online Environment. London
Public Citizen (2015) Only One of 44 Attempts to Use the GATT Article XX/GATS Article XIV "General Exception" Has Ever Succeeded: Replicating the WTO Exception Construct Will Not Provide for an Effective TPP General Exception. Washington D.C
Reyes CL (2011) WTO-compliant protection of fundamental rights. Lessons from the EU privacy directive. Melbourne J Int Law 12(1):1–36
Roseman D (2003) Domestic regulation and trade in telecommunications services: experience prospects under the GATS. In: Mattoo A, Sauvé P (eds) Domestic regulation & service trade liberalization. The World Bank, Washington DC, pp 83–108
Rothstein P (2008) Moving all-In with the World Trade Organization: ignoring adverse rulings and gambling with the future of the WTO. Georgia J Int Comp Law 37(1):151–180
Ruotolo GM (2018) The EU data protection regime and the multilateral trading system. Where dream and day unite. Quest Int Law 51(6):5–29
Saluzzo S (2017) Cross border data flows and international trade law. The relationship between EU data protection law and the GATS. Diritto del Commercio Internazionale 31(4):807–829
Sargsyan T (2016) Data localization and the role of infrastructure for surveillance, privacy, and security. Int J Commun 10:2221–2237
Schneier B (2014) Espionage vs. Surveillance. Blog Schneier on Security. 14 May 2014. https://www.schneier.com/blog/archives/2014/05/espionage_vs_su.html. Accessed 3 January 2021
Sen N (2018) Understanding the role of the WTO in international data flows: taking the liberalization or the regulatory autonomy path? J Int Econ Law 21(2):323–348
Shaffer G (2000) Globalization and social protection: the impact of EU and international rules in the ratcheting up of U.S. Privacy standards. Yale J Int Law 25(1):1–88
Shapiro E (2003) All is not fair in the privacy trade: the safe harbor agreement and the World Trade Organization. Fordham Law Rev 71(6):2781–2821
Sorel J-M, Boré Eveno V (2011) Article 31 Convention of 1969. In: Corten O, Klein P (eds) The Vienna Conventions on the law of treaties. A commentary, vol I. Oxford University Press, Oxford, pp 804–837
South Centre (2009) The Draft GATS Domestic Regulation Disciplines. Analytical Note of October 2009. SC/AN/TDP/SV/12
Stelly R (2019) Countries Table Proposals, Talks Continue on WTO E-Commerce Rules, Disruptive Competition Project. 23 August 2019. http://www.project-disco.org/21st-century-trade/082319-countries-table-proposals-talks-continue-on-wto-e-commerce-rules/. Accessed 3 Jan 2021
Stephenson SM (1999) Approaches to Liberalizing Trade in Services. World Bank Policy Research Paper 2107. Washington DC
Stoddart J, Chan B, Joly Y (2016) The European Union's adequacy approach to privacy and international data sharing in health research. J Law Med Ethics 44(1):143–155
Susskind R (2013) Tomorrow's lawyers: an introduction to your future. Oxford University Press, Oxford
Svantesson DJB (2020) Article 3. Territorial scope. In: Kuner C, Bygrave L, Docksey C (eds) The EU general data protection regulation (GDPR). Oxford University Press, Oxford, pp 74–99

Tinawi E, Berkey JO (2000) E-Services and the WTO: The Adequacy of the GATS Classification Framework. Institute for Agriculture & Trade Policy. https://www.iatp.org/documents/e-services-and-the-wto-the-adequacy-of-the-gats-classification-framework. Accessed 14 May 2022

Trachtman JP (2003) Lessons for the GATS from existing WTO rules on domestic regulation. In: Mattoo A, Sauvé P (eds) Domestic regulation & service trade liberalization. The World Bank, Washington DC, pp 57–82

Tuthill L (2016) Cross-border data flows: what role for trade rules? In: Sauvé P, Roy M (eds) Research handbook on trade in services. Edward Elgar, Cheltenham, pp 357–382

Tuthill L, Roy M (2012) GATS classification issues for information and communication technology services. In: Burri M, Cottier T (eds) Trade governance in the digital age. Cambridge University Press, Cambridge, pp 157–178

UNCTAD (2015) International Trade in ICT Services and ICT-Enabled Services. Proposed Indicators from the Partnership on Measuring ICT for Development. UNCTAD Technical Notes on ICT for Development N°3. Geneva

Urquhart L, Lodge T, Crabtree A (2019) Demonstrably doing accountability in the Internet of Things. Int J Law Inform Technol 27(1):1–27

Usman A, Chander A (2015) Information Goes Global: Protecting Privacy, Security, and the New Economy in a World of Cross-border Data Flows. E15 Expert Group on the Digital Economy Think Piece. E15 Initiative. Geneva

Van den Bossche P, Zdouc W (2017) The law and policy of the World Trade Organization, 4th edn. Cambridge University Press, Cambridge

Velli F (2019) The issue of data protection in EU Trade Commitments: cross-border data transfers in GATS and bilateral free trade agreements. Eur Pap 4(3):881–894

Villiger ME (2009) Commentary on the 1969 Vienna Convention on the law of treaties. Brill, Leiden/Boston

Voon T (2019) The security exception in WTO law: entering a new era. Am J Int Law Unbound 113:45–50

Wang C (2019) Invocation of National Security Exceptions under GATT Article XXI: Jurisdiction to review and standard of review. Chinese J Int Law 18(3):695–712

Weber R (2012) Regulatory autonomy and privacy standards under the GATS. Asian J WTO Int Health Law Policy 7(1):25–48

Weber R, Burri M (2012) Classification of services in the digital economy. Schulthess, Zurich

Willemyns I (2018) The GATS (In)consistency of Barriers to Digital Trade. KU Leuven Centre for Global Governance Studies Working Paper No. 207. September 2018

Willemyns I (2019) GATS classification of digital services – does 'The Cloud' have a silver lining? J World Trade 53(1):59–81

Wojtan B (2011) The new EU model clauses: one step forward, two steps back? Int Data Priv Law 1(1):76–80

Wolfrum R (2008), WTO – services. In: Rüdiger W, Stoll P-T, Feinäugle C (eds) WTO – trade in services. Max Planck Commentaries on World Trade Law. Martinus Nijhoff, Leiden, pp 71–91.

Wouters J, Coppens D (2008) GATS and domestic regulation: balancing the right to regulate and trade liberalization. In: Kern A, Mads A (eds) The World Trade Organization and trade in services. Martinus Nijhoff Publishers, Leiden/Boston, pp 207–263

WTO (2019a) World Trade Report 2019. The future of services trade. Geneva

Wu T (2006) The World Trade Law of censorship and internet filtering. Chicago J Int Law 7(1): 263–287

Wunsch-Vincent S (2006) The Internet, cross-border trade in services, and the GATS: lessons from *US-Gambling*. World Trade Rev 5(3):319–355

Yakovleva S (2020) Privacy protection(ism): the latest wave of trade constraints on regulatory autonomy. Univ Miami Law Rev 74(2):416–519

Yakovleva S, Irion K (2016) The best of both worlds. Free trade in services and EU law on privacy and data protection. Eur Data Protect Law Rev 2(2):191–208

Yakovleva S, Irion K (2018) The Interface Between Trade and Privacy: How to Reconcile the European Union Governance of Personal Data Flows with External Trade. ASIL Conference Paper

Yakovleva S, Irion K (2020a) Pitching trade against privacy- reconciling EU governance of personal data flows with external trade. Int Data Priv Law 10(3):1–21

Yakovleva S, Irion K (2020b) Toward compatibility of the EU trade policy with the general data protection regulation. Am J Int Law Unbound 114:10–14

Zacharias D (2008) Article I GATS. In: Rüdiger W, Stoll P-T, Feinäugle C (eds) WTO – Trade in services. Max Planck commentaries on World Trade Law. Martinus Nijhoff, Leiden, pp 31–69

Zhang R (2015) Covered or not covered: that is the question - Services classification and Its Implications for Specific Commitments under the GATS. WTO Staff Working Paper. Geneva

Jurisprudence

ECJ, AG Opinion, *Schrems 2:* ECJ, Opinion of AG Saugmandsgaard Øe delivered on 19 December 2019, *Schrems 2*, C-311/18, EU:C:2019:1145

ECJ, *Airbnb Ireland:* ECJ, Judgment of 19 December 2019, *Airbnb Ireland,* C-390/18, EU:C:2019:1112

ECJ, *Asociación Profesional Élite Taxi*: ECJ, Judgment of 20 December 2017, *Asociación Profesional Élite Taxi*, C-434/15, EU:C:2017:981

ECJ, *Google Spain and Google*: ECJ, Judgment of 13 May 2014, *Google Spain and Google*, C-131/12, EU:C:2014:317

ECJ, *Google v. CNIL:* ECJ, Judgment of 24 September 2019, *Google v. CNIL*, C-507/17, EU:C:2019:772

ECJ, *Schrems 2:* ECJ, Judgment of 16 July 2020, *Facebook Ireland and Schrems*, C-311/18, EU:C:2020:559

ECJ, *Uber France:* ECJ, Judgment of 10 April 2018, *Uber France,* C-320/16, EU:C:2018:221

GATT Panel Report, *US – Section 337 of the Tariff Act of 1930:* GATT Panel Report, *US – Section 337 of the Tariff Act of 1930*, 7 November 1989, 36S/345

GATT Panel Report, *US – Spring Assemblies*, GATT Panel Report of 26 May 1983, *US – Spring Assemblies*, 30S/107

GATT Panel Report, *US – Tuna (Canada):* GATT Panel Report of 22 February 1982, *US – Tuna (Canada)* 29S/91

IHC, *Schrems 2:* IHC, Judgment of 3 October 2017, *Data Protection Commissioner v. Facebook Ireland and Schrems*, 2016 No. 4809 P 8

WTO AB Report, *Argentina – Financial Services:* WTO AB Report of 14 April 2016, *Argentina – Measures Relating to Trade in Goods and Services,* WT/DS453/AB/R

WTO AB Report, *Brazil – Retreated Tyres:* WTO AB Report of 3 December 2007, *Brazil – Measures Affecting Imports of Retreaded Tyres*, WT/DS332/AB/R

WTO AB Report, *Canada – Autos:* WTO AB Report of 31 May 2000a, *Canada – Certain Measures Affecting the Automotive Industry*, WT/DS139/AB/R and WT/DS142/AB/R

WTO AB Report, *Canada – Periodicals:* WTO AB Report of 30 June 1997a, *Canada – Certain Measures Concerning Periodicals,* WT/DS31/AB/R

WTO AB Report, *China – Publications and Audiovisual Products:* WTO AB Report of 12 August 2009, *China – Measures Affecting Trading Rights and Distribution Services for Certain Publications and Audiovisual Entertainment Products*, WT/DS363/AB/R

WTO AB Report, *EC – Asbestos:* WTO AB Report of 12 March 2001a, *European Communities – Measures Affecting Asbestos and Asbestos-Containing Products*, WT/DS135/ AB/R

WTO AB Report, *EC – Bananas III:* WTO AB Report of 9 September 1997b, *European Communities – Regime for the Importation, Sale and Distribution of Bananas*, WT/DS27/ AB/R

WTO AB Report, *EC – Seal Products:* WTO AB Report of 22 May 2014, *European Communities – Measures Prohibiting the Importation and Marketing of Seal Products*, WT/DS401/AB/R
WTO AB Report, *Indonesia – Import Licensing Regimes:* WTO AB Report of 9 November 2017, *Indonesia – Importation of Horticultural Products, Animals and Animal Products*, WT/DS477/AB/R
WTO AB Report, *Japan – Alcoholic Beverages II:* WTO AB Report of 4 October 1996a, *Japan – Taxes on Alcoholic Beverages* WT/DS8/AB/R
WTO AB Report, *Korea – Various Measures on Beef:* WTO AB Report of 11 December 2000b, *Korea – Measures Affecting Imports of Fresh, Chilled and Frozen Beef*, WT/DS161/AB/R
WTO AB Report, *Turkey – Textiles:* WTO AB Report of 22 October 1999, *Turkey – Restrictions on Imports of Textile and Clothing* Products, WT/DS34/AB/R
WTO AB Report, *US – Gambling:* WTO AB Report of 7 April 2005, *United States – Measures Affecting the Cross-Border Supply of Gambling and Betting Services,* WT/DS285/AB/R
WTO AB Report, *US – Gasoline:* WTO AB Report of 29 April 1996b, *United States – Standards for Reformulated and Conventional Gasoline,* WT/DS2/AB/R
WTO AB Report, *US – Shrimp:* WTO AB Report of 12 October 1998, *United States – Import Prohibition of Certain Shrimp and Shrimp Products*, WT/DS58/AB/R
WTO AB Report, *US – Shrimp (Article 21.5 – Malaysia):* WTO AB Report of 22 October 2001b, *United States – Import Prohibition of Certain Shrimp and Shrimp Products*, Article 21.5 DSU – Malaysia, WT/DS58/AB/RW
WTO AB Report, *US – Stainless Steel (Mexico):* WTO AB Report of 30 April 2008, *United States – Final Anti-Dumping Measures on Stainless Steel from Mexico*, WT/DS444/AB/R
WTO Panel Report, *Argentina – Financial Services:* WTO Panel Report of 30 September 2015, *Argentina – Measures Relating to Trade in Goods and Services,* WT/DS453/R
WTO Panel Report, *Argentina – Hides and Leather:* WTO Panel Report of 19 December 2000a, *Argentina – Measures Affecting the Export of Bovine Hides and the Import of Finished Leather*, WT/DS155/R
WTO Panel Report, *Brazil – Tyres:* WTO Panel Report of 17 December 2007, *Brazil – Measures Affecting Imports of Retreaded Tyres*, WT/DS332/R
WTO Panel Report, *China – Electronic Payment Services:* WTO Panel Report of 16 July 2012, *China – Certain Measures Affecting Electronic Payment Services*, WT/DS413/R
WTO Panel Report, *China – Publications and Audiovisual Products:* WTO Panel Report of 12 August 2009, *China – Measures Affecting Trading Rights and Distribution Services for Certain Publications and Audiovisual Entertainment Products*, WT/DS363/R
WTO Panel Report, *Dominican Republic – Import and Sale of Cigarettes:* WTO Panel Report of 26 November 2004a, *Dominican Republic — Measures Affecting the Importation and Internal Sale of Cigarettes*, WT/DS302/R
WTO Panel Report, *EC – Asbestos:* WTO Panel Report of 18 September 2000b, *European Communities – Measures Affecting Asbestos and Asbestos-Containing Products*, WT/DS135/R
WTO Panel Report, *EC – Bananas III:* WTO Panel Report of 22 May 1997, *European Communities – Regime for the Importation, Sale and Distribution of Bananas*, WT/DS27/R/ECU
WTO Panel Report, *EC – Bananas III (Article 21.5 – Ecuador):* WTO Panel Report of 12 April 1999, *European Communities – Regime for the Importation, Sale and Distribution of Bananas*, Article 21.5 DSU – Ecuador, WT/DS27/R/ECU
WTO Panel Report, *EC – Biotech:* WTO Panel Report of 21 November 2006a, *European Communities – Measures Affecting the Approval and Marketing of Biotech Products*, WT/DS291/R
WTO Panel Report, *EC – IT Products:* WTO Panel Report of 21 September 2010a, *European Communities and its Member States – Tariff Treatment of Certain Information Technology Products,* WT/DS375/R
WTO Panel Report, *EC – Selected Custom Matters:* WTO Panel Report of 16 June 2006b, *European Communities – Selected Customs Matters*, WT/DS315/R
WTO Panel Report, *Mexico – Telecoms:* WTO Panel Report of 2 April 2004b, *Mexico – Measures Affecting Telecommunications Services*, WT/DS204/R

WTO Panel Report, *Russia – Traffic in Transit:* WTO Panel Report of 5 April 2019, *Russia – Measures Concerning Traffic in Transit*, WT/DS512/R

WTO Panel Report, *Thailand – Cigarettes (Philippines):* WTO Panel Report of 15 November 2010b, *Thailand – Customs and Fiscal Measures on Cigarettes from the Philippines*, WT/DS371/R

WTO Panel Report, *US – Gambling:* WTO Panel Report of 10 November 2004c, *United States – Measures Affecting the Cross-Border Supply of Gambling and Betting Services*, WT/DS285/R

WTO Panel Report, *US – Hot Rolled Steel:* WTO Panel Report of 28 February 2001a, *United States – Anti-Dumping Measures on Certain Hot-Rolled Steel Products from Japan*, WT/DS184/R

WTO Panel Report, *US – Shrimps:* WTO Panel Report of 15 June 2001b, *United States – Import Prohibition of Certain Shrimp and Shrimp Products*, Article 21.5 DSU – Malaysia, WT/DS58/RW

WTO Panel Report, *US – Underwear:* WTO Panel Report of 9 November 1996, *United States – Restrictions on Imports of Cotton and Man-Made Fibre Underwear*, WT/DS24/R

Documents

Article 29 WP (2001) Opinion 03/2001 on the level of protection of the Australian Privacy Amendment (Private Sector) Act 2000. WP40. 26 January 2001

Article 29 WP (2018b) Guidelines on consent under Regulation 2016/679. WP 259 rev.01. 28 November 2017 as last revised and adopted on 10 April 2018

Article 29 WP (2018c) Guidelines on Article 49 of Regulation 2016/679. WP 262. 6 February 2018

CNIL (2017) Compliance Package. Connected Vehicles and Personal Data, October 2017

EDPB (2018) Guidelines 2/2018 on derogations of Article 49 under Regulation 2016/6793. 25 May 2018

EDPB (2020) Recommendations 02/2020 on the European Essential Guarantees for surveillance measures. 10 November 2020

European Commission (2017) Communication on Exchanging and Protecting Personal Data in a Globalised World. COM(2017) 7 final. 10 January 2017

European Commission (2020) Active WTO Dispute Settlement Cases: European Commission, General Overview of Active WTO Dispute Settlement Cases Involving the EU as Complainant or Defendant, of Cases under Bilateral Agreements and of Active Cases under the Trade Barriers Regulation. Ref. Ares(2020)2149313. 21 April 2020,

European Commission/IMF/OECD/United Nations/World Bank (2009) System of National Accounts 2008, ST/ESA/STAT/SER.F/2/Rev.5

GATT (1970) Working Party Report, Border Tax Adjustments. L/3464. BISD 18S/97. 2 December 1970

GATT (1989) GNS, Note on the Meeting of 5-9 June 1989. MTN.GNS/23. 11 July 1989

GATT (1990a) GNS, Communication from the European Communities, Proposal by the European Community, Draft General Agreement on Trade in Services. MTN.GNS/W/105. 18 June 1990

GATT (1990b) GNS, Working Group on Telecommunications Services, Note on the Meeting of 5–6 June 1990. MTN.GNS/TEL/1. 27 June 1990

GATT (1990c) GNS, Working Group on Telecommunications Services, Note on the Meeting of 9–11 July 1990. MTN.GNS/TEL/2. 6 August 1990

GATT (1990d) GNS, Draft Multilateral Framework for Trade in Services. MTN.GNS/35. 23 July 1990

GATT (1990e) GNS, Working Group on Telecommunications Services, Note on the Meeting of 10–12 September 1990. MTN.GNS/TEL/3. 12 October 1990

GATT (1990f) GNS, Working Group on Telecommunications Services, Note on the Meeting of 15–17 October 1990. MTN.GNS/TEL/4. 30 November 1990
GATT (1990g) TNC, Draft Final Act Embodying the Results of the Uruguay Round of Multilateral Trade Negotiations, Revision. MTN.TNC/W/35/ Rev.1. 3 December 1990
GATT (1990h) GNS, Working Group on Professional Services, Note on the meeting of 30-31 July 1990. MTN.GNS/PROF/1. 29 August 1990
GATT (1991) TNC, Draft Final Act Embodying the Results of the Uruguay Round of Multilateral Trade Negotiations. MTN.TNC/W/FA. 20 December 1991
GATT Secretariat (1970) Group of Negotiations on Services, Draft Multilateral Framework for Trade in Services. MTN.GNS/35. 23 July 1990
GATT Secretariat (1991) Service Sectoral Classification List. MTN.GNS/W/120. 10 July 1991
GATT Secretariat (1993) Scheduling of Initial Commitments in Trade in Services: Explanatory Note. MTN.GNS/W/164. 3 September 1993
UN (1991) Provisional Central Product Classification. ST/ESA/STAT/SER.M/77. New York
UN (2012) UNGA Res 66/100. UN Doc. A/Res/66/100. 27 February 2012
UN (2015a) Department of Economic and Social Affairs, Statistics Division, Central Product Classification (CPC) Version 2.1, ST/ESA/STAT/SER.M/77/Ver.2.1. Geneva
UN (2015b) Department of Economic and Social Affairs, Statistics Division, Meeting of the Expert Group on International Statistical Classifications, New York, 19-22 May 2015, New issues requiring guidance in the Central Product Classification (CPC). ESA/STAT/AC.289/20. 12 May 2015
WTO (1998a) Ministerial Conference, Declaration on Electronic Commerce of 20 May 1998, WT/MIN(98)/DEC/2. 20 May 1998
WTO (1998b) General Council, Work Programme on Electronic Commerce. WT/L/274. 25 September 1998
WTO (1998c) Committee on Regional Trade Agreements, Establishment of the European Union, Communication from the European Communities and their Member States. WT/REG39/1. 24 April 1998
WTO (1999a) Work Programme on Electronic Commerce, Council on Trade in Services, Progress Report to the General Council. S/L/74. 27 July 1999
WTO (1999b) Work Programme on Electronic Commerce, Council on Trade in Services, Interim Report to the General Council. S/C/8. 31 March 1999
WTO (1999c) Work Programme on Electronic Commerce, Submission of the United States. WT/COMTD/17. 12 February 1999
WTO (1999d) Work Programme on Electronic Commerce, Council on Trade in Services, Progress Report to the General Council. S/L/74. 19 July 1999
WTO (1999e) Committee on Regional Trade Agreements. Note on the Meetings of 29–30 April and 3 May 1999. WT/REG/M/22. 4 June 1999
WTO (2000) Work Programme on Electronic Commerce, Council for Trade in Services, Communication from the European Communities and their Member States. S/C/W/183. 30 November 2000
WTO (2001) Council on Trade in Services, Guidelines for the Scheduling of Specific Commitments und the General Agreement on Trade in Services (GATS). S/L/92. 28 March 2001
WTO (2007) Committee on Specific Commitments, Communication from Albania, Australia, Canada, Chile, Colombia, Croatia, the European Communities, Hong Kong China, Japan, Mexico, Norway, Peru, the Separate Customs Territory of Taiwan, Penghu, Kinmen and Matsu, Turkey and the United States, Understanding on the scope of coverage of CPC 84 - Computer and Related Services. TN/S/W/60, S/CSC/W/51. 26 January 2007
WTO (2009) Working Party on Domestic Regulation, Room Document, Draft Disciplines on Domestic Regulation Pursuant to GATS Article VI:4, Second Revision, Informal Note by the Chairman of 20 March 2009

WTO (2011) Committee on Specific Commitments, Informal Discussion of Classification Issues on Computer and Related Services (CRS) on 10 March 2011, Summary by the Chairperson. JOB/SERV/44. 4 April 2011
WTO (2012) Council for Trade in Services, Report of the Meeting held on 23 March 2012, Note by the Secretariat. S/C/M/109. 21 May 2012
WTO (2014a) Committee on Specific Commitments, Report of the Meeting held on 18 September 2014, Note by the Secretariat. S/CSC/M/71. 15 October 2014
WTO (2014b) Work Programme on Electronic Commerce, Council for Trade in Services, Communication by the United States. S/C/W/359. 17 December 2014
WTO (2015a) Committee on Specific Commitments, Report of the Meeting held on 18 March 2015, Note by the Secretariat. S/CSC/M/72. 2 April 2015
WTO (2015b) Council for Trade in Service, Report of the Meeting held on 18 March 2015, Note by the Secretariat. S/C/M/122. 1 May 2015
WTO (2016) Committee on Specific Commitments, Report of the Meeting held on 5 October 2016, Note by the Secretariat. S/CSC/M/77. 21 November 2016
WTO (2017) Ministerial Conference, Joint Statement on Electronic Commerce of 13 December 2017. WT/MIN(17)/60. 13 December 2017
WTO (2019b) Joint Statement on Electronic Commerce. WT/L/1056. 25 January 2019
WTO (2019c) Joint Statement on Electronic Commerce, EU Proposal for WTO Disciplines and Commitments Relating to Electronic Commerce, Communication from the European Union INF/ECOM/22. 26 April 2019
WTO (2019d) Joint Statement on Electronic Commerce, Communication from China. INF/ECOM/19. 23 April 2019
WTO (2019e) Joint Statement on Electronic Commerce, Communication from the United States. INF/ECOM/23 RESTRICTED. 26 April 2019
WTO (2019f) Working Programme on Electronic Commerce, Council for Trade in Services. The Economic Benefits of Cross-Border Data Flows. Communication from the United States. S/C/W/382. 17 June 2019
WTO (2019g) Trade in Services, European Union Schedule of Specific Commitments. GATS/SC/157. 7 May 2019
WTO (2020) WTO Electronic Commerce Negotiations. Consolidated Negotiating Text – December 2020. INF/ECOM/62/Rev.1 RESTRICTED. 14 December 2020. https://web.archive.org/web/20210212083531/https:/www.bilaterals.org/IMG/pdf/wto_plurilateral_ecommerce_draft_consolidated_text.pdf. Accessed 21 May 2022
WTO (2021a) WTO Joint Statement Initiative on E-commerce. Statement by Ministers of Australia, Japan and Singapore. December 2021. https://www.wto.org/english/news_e/news21_e/ji_ecom_minister_statement_e.pdf. Accessed on 21 May 2022
WTO (2021b) Negotiations on e-commerce advance, eyeing a statement at MC12. https://www.wto.org/english/news_e/news21_e/ecom_10nov21_e.htm. Accessed on 21 May 2022
WTO (2022a) E-commerce negotiations resume with call for intensified efforts in 2022. https://www.wto.org/english/news_e/news22_e/jsec_04feb22_e.htm. Accessed on 21 May 2022
WTO (2022b) E-commerce talks resume following summer break, Mauritius joins the initiative. https://www.wto.org/english/news_e/news22_e/ecom_16sep22_e.htm Accessed 30 Oct 2022

Chapter 5
Restrictions on Data Transfers and Trade Agreements

In reaction to the stalemate in the multilateral trading system, international governance of digital trade has gradually shifted toward bilateral and regional trade agreements. This allowed countries to start to regulating cross-border flows of personal data outside the WTO framework. The first section of this chapter traces the development of data flow clauses in the trade agreements of the EU, the US, and other countries. It also looks at the negotiations of the big trade agreements in the late 2010s, such as the TTIP, the TiSA, and the TPP (Sect. 5.1). The second section outlines the scope for data flow clauses in the trade agreements of the EU based on different legal requirements stemming from the architecture of EU law, the GDPR, and other regulations. These requirements include the primacy of fundamental rights over international law with regard to the right to continuous protection of personal data in Article 8 CFR, the accommodation of the legal mechanisms for the transfer of personal data in the GDPR, the inclusion of cooperation mechanisms on the basis of Article 50 GDPR, and the ban of data localization requirements beyond data protection and privacy concerns. These legal requirements are necessary to consider when drafting data flow clauses for EU trade agreements (Sect. 5.2). The third section of this chapter offers and analyzes four potential designs for data flow clauses for EU trade agreements (Sect. 5.3). The fourth section is dedicated to the analysis of the EU model data flow clauses that the European Commission introduced as a template for future trade negotiations in 2018 (Sect. 5.4).

5.1 Data Flow Clauses in Trade Agreements

The first section of this chapter is dedicated to the development of data flow clauses in trade agreements over the last two decades.[1] The EU was the first to address cross-border flows of personal data in its trade agreements. Over time, the EU tried

[1] See generally Burri (2021), pp. 26–41.

T. Naef, *Data Protection without Data Protectionism*, EYIEL Monographs - Studies in European and International Economic Law 28,
https://doi.org/10.1007/978-3-031-19893-9_5

different methods to accommodate its data protection regime (Sect. 5.1.1). On the international plane, the development of data flow clauses was significantly influenced by the negotiations of the big trade agreements in the 2010s, such as the TTIP, the TiSA, and the TPP (Sect. 5.1.2). The US started to include comprehensive data flow clauses in trade agreements only after they withdrew their signature from the TPP. Currently, the US aggressively tries to commit its trading partners to the free flow of personal data across borders (Sect. 5.1.3). Four examples of trade agreements from other countries complete the overview (Sect. 5.1.4).

5.1.1 Development in EU Trade Agreements

The EU has been the pioneer in including data flow clauses in its trade agreements.[2] The following trade agreements of the EU represent the most important milestones in the development of data flow clauses: The EU-Algeria Association Agreement from 2002 (Sect. 1.1), the EU-CARIFORUM Economic Partnership Agreement from 2008 (Sect. 1.2), the EU-Canada Comprehensive Economic and Trade Agreement (CETA) from 2016 (Sect. 1.3), and the EU-Japan Economic Partnership Agreement (JEEPA) from 2018 (Sect. 1.4).

5.1.1.1 EU-Algeria Association Agreement

The earliest provision addressing cross-border data flows in a trade agreement can be found in the EU-Algeria Association Agreement (AA) from 2002.[3] The EU-Algeria AA does not contain a chapter on electronic commerce or digital trade. The provision on cross-border data flows is located in the chapter on competition and other economic matters:

> **Article 45**
> The Parties undertake to adopt appropriate measures to ensure the protection of personal data in order to eliminate barriers to the free movement of such data between the Parties.

It is remarkable that the EU and Algeria qualify data protection as a contributing factor to eliminating barriers to cross-border data flows in their AA.[4] Prior, the protection of personal data or privacy was normally included as a legitimate public policy objective that legitimated deviations from other obligations in a trade

[2]Contra Yakovleva (2020), p. 487.

[3]Euro-Mediterranean Agreement establishing an Association between the European Community and its Member States, of the one part, and the People's Democratic Republic of Algeria, of the other part, 22 April 2002 [2005] OJ L 265/1.

[4]Willemyns (2020), p. 237.

agreement.[5] Article 45 EU-Algeria AA reflects EU-style data protection. The provision implies that cross-border flows of personal data are possible under the condition that an adequate level of protection for personal data be preserved.

5.1.1.2 EU-CARIFORUM Economic Partnership Agreement

The EU tried a new approach in the EU-CARIFORUM Economic Partnership Agreement (EPA) from 2008.[6] Article 119 EU-CARIFORUM EPA in the electronic commerce chapter of the trade agreement outlines the objective and the principles of the chapter. In the second paragraph, Article 119 connects electronic commerce with data protection:

> **Article 119 Objective and principles**
> 2. The Parties agree that the development of electronic commerce must be fully compatible with the highest international standards of data protection, in order to ensure the confidence of users of electronic commerce.

The provision does not directly address cross-border flows of personal data, but it mentions electronic commerce that relies on such data flows. The provision implies that cross-border flows of personal data are possible under the condition of the presence of an adequate level of protection for personal data. More specifically, the provision refers to the "highest international standards of data protection." The EU-CARIFORUM EPA also includes a full chapter on data protection to flesh out these standards. Article 197 describes the general objective of the chapter on data protection:

> **Article 197 General Objective**
> 1. The Parties and the Signatory CARIFORUM States, recognising:
>   (a) their common interest in protecting fundamental rights and freedoms of natural persons, and in particular their right to privacy, with respect to the processing of personal data;
>   (b) the importance of maintaining effective data protection regimes as a means of protecting the interests of consumers, stimulating investor confidence and of facilitating transborder flows of personal data;

[5] For example, Article XIV(c)(ii) GATS. See Sect. 4.2.1.4.2.1.

[6] Economic Partnership Agreement between the CARIFORUM States, of the one part, and the European Community and its Member States, of the other part, 16 December 2017, OJ L 289/I/3 [2008]. Another EPA that entails a separate chapter on data protection is the Interim Agreement with a view to an Economic Partnership Agreement between the European Community and its Member States, of the one part, and the Central Africa Party, of the other part, 17 December 2007 [2009] OJ L 57/1.

(c) that the collection and processing of personal data should be accomplished in a transparent and fair manner, with due respect accorded to the data subject,

agree to establish appropriate legal and regulatory regimes, as well as appropriate administrative capacity to implement them, including independent supervisory authorities, in order to ensure an adequate level of protection of individuals with regard to the processing of personal data, in line with existing high international standards.[7]

2. The Signatory CARIFORUM States shall endeavour to implement the provisions of paragraph 1 as soon as possible and no later than seven years after the entry into force of this Agreement.

In line with Article 8 CFR, Article 197 EU-CARIFORUM EPA underlines the fundamental rights aspect of data protection in paragraph 1(a) and combines it with the facilitation of cross-border data flows in paragraph 1(b).[8] The provision commits the parties to establish a data protection regime, as well as appropriate administrative capacity, including independent supervision, in order to ensure an adequate level of protection within a relatively short period of time. This is the first time that an EU trade agreement specifically refers to an adequate level of protection for individuals regarding the processing of personal data. Even if the provision refers to existing "high international standards," it is evident that the chapter on data protection specifically reflects EU-style data protection regulation. The data protection principles and the conditions for enforcement mechanism that follow in Article 199 EU-CARIFORUM EPA are a start to ensure a high standard of data protection when correctly implemented.[9]

The chapter on data protection is complemented with rules on cooperation in Article 201 EU-CARIFORUM EPA. They underline the importance of cooperation to facilitate the development of an adequate level of protection for personal data:

Article 201 Cooperation

1. The Parties acknowledge the importance of cooperation in order to facilitate the development of appropriate legislative, judicial and institutional frameworks as well as an adequate level of protection of personal data consistent with the objectives and principles contained in this Chapter.

---

[7] Such standards are those included in the following international instruments:

(i). Guidelines for the regulation of computerised personal data files, modified by the General Assembly of the United Nations on 20 November 1990;

(ii). Recommendation of the Organisation for Economic Cooperation and Development Council concerning guidelines governing the protection of privacy and trans-border flows of personal data of 23 September 1980.

[8] Fontoura Costa (2020), p. 487.

[9] Ibid., 489.

The second paragraph of Article 201 entails a list of areas in which the parties agree to cooperate. For example, the list includes the exchange of information and expertise, assistance in drafting legislation, guidelines and manuals, and assistance with the design and implementation of compliance initiatives aimed at economic operators and consumers. Nevertheless, it would have been useful to also include compliance initiatives aimed at public authorities. Overall, the EU implemented essential parts of its data protection regulation in the EU-CARIFORUM EPA and used the trade agreement to lay the basis for an improvement of the level of protection for personal data in the contracting parties' legislative, judicial, and institutional frameworks.

5.1.1.3 EU-Canada Comprehensive Economic and Trade Agreement

The EU abandoned the approach taken in the EU-CARIFORUM EPA and chose yet another approach in the CETA from 2016.[10] The CETA does not include a general provision on the free flow of personal data across borders. This can be explained by the fact that Canada already had an adequacy decision from the EU. This means that the transfer of personal data from the EU to commercial organizations in Canada was already possible without the need for further safeguards.[11] Yet the CETA does not include substantive rules on data protection either. Article 16.4 CETA on trust and confidence in electronic commerce only entails a very general reference to the regulation of data protection:[12]

> **Article 16.4 Trust and confidence in electronic commerce**
> Each Party should adopt or maintain laws, regulations or administrative measures for the protection of personal information of users engaged in electronic commerce and, when doing so, shall take into due consideration international standards of data protection of relevant international organisations of which both Parties are a member.

The reference to international organizations is limited to the standards of the UN and the OECD as Canada is not a party to Convention 108, and the EU member states are not members of APEC. The OECD Privacy Guidelines pursue economic rather than broader normative goals of protecting personal data.[13] The provision recognizes data protection as a necessary condition for spurring international trade

[10] Comprehensive Economic and Trade Agreement (CETA) between Canada and the European Union and its Member States, 30 October 2016 [2017] OJ L 11/23.

[11] Wolfe (2019), p. 73; Greenleaf (2018), p. 208.

[12] Streinz (2019), p. 335.

[13] Yakovleva (2018), p. 496. Cp. Sect. 3.1.1.2.1.

and does not acknowledge its fundamental rights character as Article 197.1(a) of the EU-CARIFORUM EPA did.[14]

Moreover, the CETA does not restrict national or regional regulations even if they might interfere with the free flow of personal data across borders in fields covered by the agreement.[15] The provision on cross-border flows of personal data concerning financial services in Article 13.15(2) CETA exempts EU data protection law from the scope of the CETA chapter on financial services:[16]

> **Article 13.15 Transfer and processing of information**
> 2. Each Party shall maintain adequate safeguards to protect privacy, in particular with regard to the transfer of personal information. If the transfer of financial information involves personal information, such transfers shall be in accordance with the legislation governing the protection of personal information of the territory of the Party where the transfer has originated.

The CETA clearly makes a distinction between domestic data protection regulation and international trade law.[17] The CETA does not contain any data protection obligations and there are no rules for cross-border flows of personal data in the trade agreement. The EU was careful to keep separate the regulation of data protection and trade rules.[18] In addition, the EU started to shield its rules for the transfer of personal data from other obligations in the CETA as is evidenced by the provision on financial services in Article 13.15(2) CETA.

5.1.1.4 EU-Japan Economic Partnership Agreement

In the negotiation of the JEEPA, the EU was faced with Japanese demands—likely inspired by the concurrent negotiations of the TPP—to include a general provision on cross-border flows of personal data.[19] The EU was reluctant to include such provisions and resisted the Japanese demands until the end. Indeed, this disagreement emerged as the last big hurdle to the conclusion of the JEEPA.[20] After five years of negotiations, the two parties achieved agreement at the EU-Japan Summit in 2017. In a joint declaration, Prime Minister Shinzo Abe and Commission President

---

[14] Cp. Wunsch-Vincent (2008), p. 520.

[15] Berka (2017), p. 179.

[16] Yakovleva and Irion (2020), p. 14.

[17] Irion and Bartl (2017), p. 5.

[18] But see Burri (2017), p. 107.

[19] Streinz (2019), p. 335. The EU also declined in 2013 to grant India what it called "data secure status" as part of the proposed trade agreement. According to Graham Greenleaf that would have meant the recognition of completely inadequate laws in India as being adequate. See Greenleaf (2014), pp. 432–433.

[20] Mucci et al. (2016).

Jean-Claude Juncker stressed the importance of ensuring "a high level of privacy and security of personal data as a fundamental right and as a central factor of consumer trust in the digital economy, which also further facilitate mutual data flows, leading to the development of digital economy."[21] They indicated that their respective data protection reforms offered new opportunities for simultaneous findings of adequacy. The JEEPA was successfully concluded in July 2018.[22] In the end, the parties settled on a *rendez-vous* clause:

> **Article 8.81 Free flow of data**
> The Parties shall reassess within three years of the date of entry into force of this Agreement the need for inclusion of provisions on the free flow of data into this Agreement.

In 2019, the EU Commission adopted an adequacy decision for Japan.[23] The EU has thus continued to treat data protection and international trade law as two separate tracks with little middle ground. Only after the negotiations with Japan were effectively concluded did the Commission reach an internal compromise on a new template for horizontal provisions for cross-border data flows and data protection.[24]

5.1.2 Development in the Mega-Regional Trade Agreements

On the international plane, the development of data flow clauses was significantly influenced by the negotiations of the big trade agreements in the 2010s. The negotiations of the TTIP between the EU and the US were never completed but they showed how the two parties clashed over the issue of cross-border flows of personal data (Sect. 5.1.2.1). The multilateral negotiations of the TiSA were not completed either. The proposals of the US for a data flow clause triggered a defensive reaction from the EU (Sect. 5.1.2.2). In contrast, the multilateral negotiations for the TPP saw the inclusion of an intricate data flow clause, which was also integrated in the Comprehensive and Progressive Agreement for the Trans-Pacific Partnership (CPTPP) after the US withdrew its signature from the TPP (Sect. 5.1.2.3).

---

[21] European Commission (2017b).

[22] Agreement between the European Union and Japan for an Economic Partnership, 17 July 2018 [2018] OJ L 330/3.

[23] Commission Implementing Decision (EU) 2019/419 of 23 January 2019 pursuant to Regulation (EU) 2016/679 on the adequate protection of personal data by Japan under the Act on the Protection of Personal Information, [2019] OJ L 76/1.

[24] Streinz (2019), p. 335. See Sect. 5.4.

5.1.2.1 Transatlantic Trade and Investment Partnership

The TTIP was a proposed trade agreement between the US and the EU. While the idea for such an agreement had been circulating for more than a decade, formal negotiations only started in 2013. Several negotiation rounds took place in the following years and efforts to wrap-up negotiation in late 2016—before the new US administration took office—failed. The negotiations were subsequently halted by US President Donald Trump. After the US left the Paris Agreement on Climate Change, the Council of the EU decided in 2019 that the negotiating directives for the TTIP had become obsolete.[25]

In the beginning of the negotiations, EU Justice Commissioner Viviane Reding stated that data protection issues had been cut out of the TTIP as a result of "a political decision by the US and EU."[26] She also warned against bringing data protection to the trade talks at a conference in Washington D.C., indicating that the US would not be very happy with the exclusion of cross-border flows of personal data under the TTIP. She said that "[t]here are challenges to get [the TTIP] done and there are issues that will easily derail it. One such issue is data and the protection of personal data."[27] Nevertheless, US Trade Representative Michael Froman never publicly said that data protection should be off the agenda.[28]

The leaked draft text of the TTIP from 2016 did *not* include a provision on cross-border flows of personal data.[29] The leaked EU note on the tactical state of play in the TTIP negotiations from March 2016 summarized that "[d]iscussions on e-commerce covered all proposals except for the provisions on data flows and computing facilities." Nevertheless, the note also indicated that "[t]he US signaled that progress on [...] key EU interests might be accelerated if discussions on data flows and computing facilities also advanced faster." It is safe to assume that cross-border flows of personal data were repeatedly a topic on the agenda. This is probably also the reason why the European Parliament asked the Commission to ensure that the EU's *acquis* on data privacy was not compromised through the liberalization of data flows.[30] The Parliament recommended that a comprehensive and unambiguous horizontal self-standing provision based on Article XIV GATS should be incorporated into the TTIP to fully exempt the existing and future EU legal framework on the protection of personal data.[31] Interestingly, the recommendations of the Parlia-

[25] Council of the EU (2019), Article 3.

[26] Fleming (2013). See also European Commission (2013a).

[27] European Commission (2013b).

[28] Fleming (2013).

[29] The negotiation documents were leaked by Wikileaks. The documents are available on their website.

[30] European Parliament (2015), Article 2(b) xii.

[31] Ibid.

ment allowed the negotiation of a data flow clause *if* the full application of data protection rules on both sides of the Atlantic was guaranteed.[32]

The negotiations of the TTIP confirm that the EU once again decided to separate the regulation of data protection from international trade law and to shield its rules for the transfer of personal data from other obligations in trade agreements. It is questionable whether the US would ever have agreed to a trade agreement without rules enabling cross-border flows of personal data. Such rules have become more important for the US when the Privacy Shield was invalidated and the possibility to use the instruments in Article 46 GDPR has become unsure. They will continue to be important because eventually the adequacy decision for the new Transatlantic Data Privacy Framework, which is currently in preparation, will be challenged and its validity will not be evident.[33]

5.1.2.2 Trade in Services Agreement

Due to the lack of progress in the negotiations at the WTO, some WTO members formed a sub-group called the Really Good Friends (RGF) in 2012 to discuss the possibility of a services liberalization agreement. Led by the US and the EU, the RGF consisted of more than 20 countries including Australia, Canada, Japan, the Republic of Korea, Switzerland, Colombia, and Mexico. Negotiations for the TiSA started immediately after the formation of the sub-group. Over 20 full negotiation rounds took place in Geneva in the following years. Just as with the TTIP, efforts to wrap-up the negotiations in late 2016 failed. The negotiations are currently suspended and the future of the TiSA is unclear.

One of the reasons why the TiSA was not successfully concluded were the controversies over rules on cross-border flows of personal data.[34] A leaked US negotiation document from 2014 titled "Proposal of New Provisions Applicable to All Services" suggested the inclusion of a provision on movement of information:[35]

> **Article X.4**
> No Party may prevent a service supplier of another Party from transferring, accessing, processing or storing information, including personal information, within or outside the Party's territory, where such activity is carried out in connection with the conduct of the service supplier's business.

---

[32] Ibid.

[33] noyb (2022).

[34] Yakovleva (2018), p. 496.

[35] The negotiation documents were leaked by Wikileaks. The documents are available on their website.

This proposal for a data flow clause in the TiSA did not include any exception for the protection of personal data.[36] According to other leaked negotiation documents from 2015 and 2016, the provision was later included as Article 2 in the negotiating text of the TiSA Annex on Electronic Commerce. The annotated negotiation documents show that many countries considered exceptions or conditions for this provision, so as to allow more flexibility for domestic regulation. For instance, Hong Kong proposed that "[t]here should be a balance between free movement of information across border and protection of personal data. Advancing the former cause should be without prejudice to safeguarding the latter right."[37] Switzerland also proposed to include safeguards that "[e]ach party applies its own regulatory regime concerning the transfer of data and personal data by electronic means."

The leaked negotiation documents also indicated that the TiSA Annex on Localization sought to ban "local presence" and other "local performance" requirements. It is unclear whether restrictions on cross-border flows of personal data based on domestic data protection regulation would have been included in this ban. The exceptions do not mention data protection related safeguards.

The European Commission did not comment on the data flow clauses in the negotiation documents because it was waiting for the final agreement on the Privacy Shield with the US before addressing the issue of cross-border flows of personal data in the TiSA negotiations. Nevertheless, the European Parliament took a firm stand on the regulation of cross-border flows of personal data in the TiSA. It recommended that the Commission take a cautious approach to the negotiation of chapters concerning data and privacy protection. It suggested the incorporation of a comprehensive, unambiguous, horizontal, self-standing, and legally binding provision based on Article XIV GATS, which would fully exempt the existing and future EU legal framework for the protection of personal data from the scope of the TiSA.[38] Negotiations have not been resumed since 2017.

5.1.2.3 Comprehensive and Progressive Agreement for Trans-Pacific Partnership

The TPP was a trade agreement between Australia, Brunei, Canada, Chile, Japan, Malaysia, Mexico, New Zealand, Peru, Singapore, Vietnam, and the US signed in 2016. It was not ratified and could not enter into force because US President Donald Trump withdrew the US signature from the TPP in 2017. The remaining countries negotiated a new trade agreement called the CPTPP that incorporated most of the provisions from the TPP and entered into force in 2018.

---

[36] Berka (2017), p. 180; Kelsey and Kilic (2014), pp. 15–16.

[37] Burri (2017), p. 124.

[38] European Parliament (2016), Paragraph 1(c)ii., iii. and v.

The US significantly shaped the design of the provision on cross-border flows of personal data during the negotiations of the TPP, which was integrated without changes into the CPTPP:

Article 14.11 Cross-Border Transfer of Information by Electronic Means

1. The Parties recognize that each Party may have its own regulatory requirements concerning the transfer of information by electronic means.
2. Each Party shall allow the cross-border transfer of information by electronic means, including personal information, when this activity is for the conduct of the business of a covered person.
3. Nothing in this Article shall prevent a Party from adopting or maintaining measures inconsistent with paragraph 2 to achieve a legitimate public policy objective, provided that the measure:
   (a) is not applied in a manner which would constitute a means of arbitrary or unjustifiable discrimination or a disguised restriction on trade; and
   (b) does not impose restrictions on transfers of information greater than are required to achieve the objective.

The first paragraph of the provision introduces the data flow clause by recognizing the differences between regulatory regimes for cross-border flows of personal data. The second paragraph entails the obligation to allow cross-border flows of personal data by electronic means for the conduct of business. This is the first time a provision explicitly formulates a commitment to the free flow of personal data across borders. Nevertheless, the third paragraph allows derogations from this obligation for legitimate public policy objectives under two conditions. It can be assumed that data protection and privacy qualify as legitimate public policy objectives under this provision. The first condition for the derogation demands compliance with the standards that can also be found in the *chapeau* of Article XIV GATS. The second condition refers to restrictions that should not be greater than *required* to achieve the objective pursued by the measure in question. It is not entirely clear what kind of standard the second condition foresees. The use of the word required might imply that the test should be easier than a necessity test. However, only the English and the Spanish version of the CPTPP use language that does not hint at a necessity test. The French version clearly refers to a necessity test.

In addition, the parties recognize in Article 14.8 CPTPP that the economic and social benefits of protecting the personal data of users of electronic commerce as well as the contribution that this makes to enhancing consumer confidence in electronic commerce. However, the parties do not refer to the fundamental rights character of data protection. It must be assumed that the CPTPP, which is the only mega-regional trade agreement in force, is likely to set international standards for data flow clauses in future trade agreements.

5.1.3 Development in US Trade Agreements

Although the US was not the first mover when it came to data flow clauses in trade agreements, they have extensively pursued this option in more recent years. The trade agreement with the Republic of Korea from 2012 was the first attempt by the US to get some form of commitment to the free flow of personal data across borders (Sect. 5.1.3.1). The US intensified their efforts to include strong obligations for cross-border flows of personal data in the negotiations of the TTIP, the TiSA, and the TPP. After the withdrawal of its signature from the TPP, the US started to include stronger obligations on cross-border flows of personal data in trade agreements such as the United States-Mexico-Canada Agreement (USMCA) from 2018 (Sect. 5.1.3.2) and the US-Japan Digital Trade Agreement from 2019 (Sect. 5.1.3.3).

5.1.3.1 US-South Korea Free Trade Agreement

The trade agreement with the Republic of Korea from 2012 (KORUS) was the first US trade agreement to include a provision on the free flow of personal data across borders.[39] The provision on cross-border information flows is located in Article 15.8 of the e-commerce chapter in the KORUS:

> **Article 15.8 Cross-Border Information Flows**
> Recognizing the importance of the free flow of information in facilitating trade, and acknowledging the importance of protecting personal information, the Parties shall endeavor to refrain from imposing or maintaining unnecessary barriers to electronic information flows across borders.

The provision refers to personal data, but the importance of protecting it is put in strong contrast with a call on the parties to endeavor to refrain from imposing or maintaining unnecessary barriers to cross-border flows of personal data. There are no further indications as to what constitutes a "necessary" or "unnecessary" barrier in the KORUS. It is also not clear whether domestic rules on cross-border flows of personal data are considered necessary or not. Because the language used in the provision is not actionable,[40] it is uncertain if one party could use it to challenge another party's restrictions on cross-border flows of personal data.[41]

Article 15.8 of the e-commerce chapter in the KORUS is the first attempt by the US to include some form of commitment to the free flow of personal data across borders. Two other US trade agreements from 2012—one with Colombia and one with Panama—do not contain any similar provisions.

[39] Wu (2017), p. 23; Aaronson (2015), p. 687.

[40] Yakovleva (2020), p. 487; Wu (2017), p. 23; Burri (2019), pp. 95–96; Aaronson (2015), p. 687.

[41] Aaronson and Townes (2012), p. 6.

5.1.3.2 United States-Mexico-Canada Agreement

The US actively participated in the negotiations of the TPP and signed the trade agreement in 2016. One year later, President Donald Trump decided to withdraw the US signature.[42] In consequence, the US used the renegotiation of the North America Free Trade Agreement in 2018 to set new standards for data flow clauses in their trade agreements.[43] The provision on the cross-border transfer of information by electronic means is located in Article 19.11 of the digital trade chapter in the USMCA:

> **Article 19.11 Cross-Border Transfer of Information by Electronic Means**
> 1. No Party shall prohibit or restrict the cross-border transfer of information, including personal information, by electronic means if this activity is for the conduct of the business of a covered person.
> 2. This Article does not prevent a Party from adopting or maintaining a measure inconsistent with paragraph 1 that is necessary to achieve a legitimate public policy objective, provided that the measure:
>   (a) is not applied in a manner which would constitute a means of arbitrary or unjustifiable discrimination or a disguised restriction on trade; and
>   (b) does not impose restrictions on transfers of information greater than are necessary to achieve the objective.[44]

Compared with Article 15.8 KORUS, Article 19.11(1) USMCA is an actionable provision that uses strong language to install an obligation on the parties to refrain from prohibiting or restricting the cross-border transfer of information, including personal information, for the conduct of business.[45] The exception in Article 19.11(2) USMCA require the party imposing a prohibition or restriction on cross-border flows of personal data to justify its measures. The exceptions present a significant burden for any regulation of cross-border flows of personal data. A measure inconsistent with Article 19.11(1) USMCA must be necessary for a legitimate public policy objective and not be applied in a manner which would constitute a means of arbitrary or unjustifiable discrimination, or a disguised restriction on trade. These conditions are

---

[42] Removing the US from the TPP was one of President Donald Trump's first decisions in office. Nevertheless, the administration of President Barack Obama significantly shaped the design of the provision on cross-border data flows during the negotiations of the TPP.

[43] The USTR mentions the establishment of "rules to ensure that NAFTA countries do not impose measures that restrict cross-border data flows and do not require the use or installation of local computing facilities" in the official summary of objectives for the NAFTA renegotiation. See USTR (2017), p. 9.

[44] A measure does not meet the conditions of this paragraph if it accords different treatment to data transfers solely on the basis that they are cross-border in a manner that modifies the conditions of competition to the detriment of service suppliers of another Party.

[45] Willemyns (2020), p. 237.

similar to the general exceptions in Article XIV GATS.[46] However, there is an additional condition in Article 19.11(2)(b) USMCA entailing a separate necessity test that is qualified in a footnote. Differential treatment of data flows solely on the basis that they are cross-border in a manner that modifies the conditions of competition cannot satisfy the additional necessity test in Article 19.11(2)(b) USMCA.[47] This qualification in the footnote seems to be difficult to satisfy with domestic data protection rules that entail legal mechanisms for the transfer of personal data with separate requirements.[48]

There are some essential differences between Article 14.11 CPTPP and Article 19.11 USMCA. The CPTPP introduces the provision on cross-border flows of persona data with a recognition of the differences between regulatory regimes. Such an accommodating introductory clause is absent from the USMCA. Furthermore, the *chapeau* of the derogations in the CPTPP does not include a necessity test like the USMCA does. The English version of the CPTPP refers to restrictions that should not be greater than *required* to achieve the objective. The USMCA also entails a second necessity test, which is further qualified in a footnote. It seems that the USMCA is less permissive than the CPTPP of restrictions on cross-border flows of personal data for data protection or privacy. The data flow clause in the USMCA is in line with the US digital trade agenda. It is an expression of the US view that data protection is an impediment to digital trade and therefore in need of justification.[49]

In addition, the provision on cross-border data flows in Article 19.11(1) USMCA takes precedence over a long and detailed provision on personal information protection in Article 19.8 USMCA:

Article 19.8: Personal Information Protection

1. The Parties recognize the economic and social benefits of protecting the personal information of users of digital trade and the contribution that this makes to enhancing consumer confidence in digital trade.
2. To this end, each Party shall adopt or maintain a legal framework that provides for the protection of the personal information of the users of digital trade. In the development of this legal framework, each Party should take into account principles and guidelines of relevant international bodies,[50] such as the *APEC*

[46] See Sect. 4.2.1.4.2.

[47] Svetlana Yakovleva has noted that despite the differences between US- and EU-led trade agreements, they have one trait in common: "they are not formulated as non-discrimination provisions." This is not entirely correct when looking at the qualification in the footnote in Article 19.11(2)(b) USMCA, which entails such a non-discrimination obligation. See Yakovleva (2020), p. 497.

[48] See also Streinz (2019), p. 332.

[49] Ibid., 334.

[50] For greater certainty, a Party may comply with the obligation in this paragraph by adopting or maintaining measures such as comprehensive privacy, personal information or personal data protection laws, sector-specific laws covering privacy, or laws that provide for the enforcement of voluntary undertakings by enterprises relating to privacy.

Privacy Framework and the *OECD Recommendation of the Council concerning Guidelines governing the Protection of Privacy and Transborder Flows of Personal Data (2013).*

3. The Parties recognize that pursuant to paragraph 2, key principles include: limitation on collection; choice; data quality; purpose specification; use limitation; security safeguards; transparency; individual participation; and accountability. The Parties also recognize the importance of ensuring compliance with measures to protect personal information and ensuring that any restrictions on cross-border flows of personal information are necessary and proportionate to the risks presented.
4. Each Party shall endeavor to adopt non-discriminatory practices in protecting users of digital trade from personal information protection violations occurring within its jurisdiction.
5. Each Party shall publish information on the personal information protections it provides to users of digital trade, including how:
   (a) a natural person can pursue a remedy; and
   (b) an enterprise can comply with legal requirements.
6. Recognizing that the Parties may take different legal approaches to protecting personal information, each Party should encourage the development of mechanisms to promote compatibility between these different regimes. The Parties shall endeavor to exchange information on the mechanisms applied in their jurisdictions and explore ways to extend these or other suitable arrangements to promote compatibility between them. The Parties recognize that the *APEC Cross-Border Privacy Rules* system is a valid mechanism to facilitate cross-border information transfers while protecting personal information.

The provision on personal information protection uses weak language for the substantive protection for personal data.[51] While Article 19.8(1) USMCA recognizes the contribution of data protection to enhancing consumer confidence in digital trade, it does not mention data protection as a fundamental right. According to Article 19.8(2) USMCA, the parties should adopt a legal framework that provides for the protection of personal data. However, a footnote clarifies that sector-specific laws or laws that provide for the enforcement of voluntary undertakings by enterprises are enough to comply with this obligation.[52] This approach is tailored to the US patchwork regulation concerning data privacy.[53] It is evident that such a legal framework for the protection of personal data does not have to include the public sector and extend to internet surveillance practices. Even though Article 19.8(3) USMCA entails important data protection principles and highlights the importance of ensuring compliance with measures to protect personal data, it also underlines that any restrictions on cross-border flows of personal information must be necessary and

---

[51] Streinz (2019), p. 334.

[52] Geist (2018).

[53] Wolfe (2019), p. 74.

proportionate to the risks presented. This is a reference to the obligations on cross-border data flows in Article 19.11 USMCA, which accordingly takes precedence over the protection of personal data. Finally, Article 19.8(6) USMCA encourages the parties to promote compatibility between different legal approaches to data protection and explicitly recognizes that the APEC Cross-Border Privacy Rules system based on the accountability principle is a valid mechanism for cross-border data flows.

5.1.3.3 US-Japan Digital Trade Agreement

The US-Japan Digital Trade Agreement was signed in 2019, along with the US-Japan Trade Agreement. The provisions on digital trade from the USMCA have been included, almost *verbatim*, in the digital trade agreement with Japan. It seems that these provisions have become the model for data flow clauses in future US-led trade agreements.[54] Article 11 of the US-Japan Digital Trade Agreement even entails the same restrictive qualification in the footnote of the exception to the prohibition of restrictions on cross-border data flows.

5.1.4 Development in Non-EU/US Trade Agreements

Trade agreements without the EU or the US as a party also include data flows clauses. Four recent examples show the development of data flow clauses outside the EU and the US: the Costa Rica-Colombia trade agreement from 2013 (Sect. 5.1.4.1), the Mexico-Panama trade agreement from 2014 (Sect. 5.1.4.2), the China-Republic of Korea trade agreement from 2015 (Sect. 5.1.4.3), and the Sri Lanka-Singapore trade agreement from 2018 (Sect. 5.1.4.4).

5.1.4.1 Costa Rica-Colombia Trade Agreement

The Costa Rica-Colombia trade agreement was signed in 2013. It is one of many trade agreements that uses regulatory cooperation to facilitate cross-border flows of personal data:[55]

[54] Yakovleva and Irion (2020), p. 13. These provisions are also included in the US proposal for the electronic commerce negotiations at the WTO. See Sect. 4.2.4.4.

[55] Willemyns (2020), p. 237; Wu (2017), p. 23.

Artículo 16.7 Cooperación

1. Reconociendo la naturaleza global del comercio electrónico, las Partes afirman la importancia de
   b) compartir información y experiencias sobre leyes, regulaciones, y programas en el ámbito del comercio electrónico, incluyendo aquellos relaci-onados con privacidad de datos, confianza del consumidor, seguridad en las comuni-caciones electrónicas, autenticación, de-rechos de propiedad intelectual, y gobierno electrónico;
   c) trabajar para mantener los flujos transfronterizos de información como un elemento esencial en el fomento de un entorno dinámico para el comercio electrónico;

The trade agreement between Costa Rica and Colombia does not go beyond a declaration of intent on cooperation. Very often such provisions on cooperation are "just the equivalent of trade negotiators throwing in the towel on an issue where no perceivable consensus is apparent, or inserting verbiage to provide some filler to a given treaty text."[56] This is also apparent in the provision on the protection of personal data:

Artículo 16.7 Protección de la Información Personal

1. Las Partes procurarán adoptar o mantener leyes, regulaciones o medidas administrativas para la protección de la información personal de los usuarios que participen en el comercio electrónico. Las Partes podrán tener en cuenta las normas internacionales y los criterios de las organizaciones internacionales pertinentes sobre la materia.
2. Las Partes harán sus mejores esfuerzos para intercambiar información y experiencias en cuanto a sus regímenes domésticos de protección de la información personal.

In this case, the parties advise each other to endeavor to adopt data protection laws and only commit to do their best to exchange information about them. Nevertheless, the two countries acknowledge the importance of data protection for the users of electronic commerce.

5.1.4.2 Mexico-Panama Trade Agreement

The Mexico-Panama trade agreement was signed in 2014. It stands out as a trade agreement between two developing economies with a binding commitment on cross-border flows of personal data:

[56] Lacey (2020), p. 202.

> **Artículo 14.10 Flujo Transfronterizo de Información**
> Cada Parte permitirá que sus personas y las personas de la otra Parte transmitan información electrónica, desde y hacia su territorio, cuando sea requerido por dicha persona, de conformidad con la legislación aplicable en materia de protección de datos personales y tomando en consideración las prácticas internacionales.

In this case, the two parties agreed to allow transmissions of electronic information to and from their territory in accordance with data protection legislation and following international practices.[57] The reference to data protection legislation and international practices is open to different interpretations. It could indicate that the commitment to cross-border flows of personal data in the trade agreement is subject to domestic legislation that regulates such data flows for the protection of personal data. It could also mean that domestic legislation should accommodate the obligation on cross-border flows of personal data under consideration of international practices. The provision on data protection in the Mexico-Panama trade agreement does not resolve the ambiguity of the interpretation:

> **Artículo 14.8 Protección de Datos Personales**
> Las Partes fomentarán la adopción o mantenimiento de leyes y regulaciones para la protección de los datos personales de los usuarios del comercio electrónico. Las Partes tomarán en consideración las prácticas internacionales que existen en esta materia.

The provision encourages the parties to adopt or maintain data protection legislation and requires them to consider international practices when doing so. In any case, the provision is subject to general exceptions like those in Article XIV GATS, which were included in Article 19.2(2) Mexico-Panama trade agreement *mutatis mutandis*.[58]

5.1.4.3 China-Republic of Korea Trade Agreement

The China-Republic of Korea trade agreement was signed in 2015. The two parties address data protection with a rather weak provision:

> **Article 13.5 Protection of Personal Information in Electronic Commerce**
> Recognizing the importance of protecting personal information in electronic commerce, each Party shall adopt or maintain measures which ensure the protection of the personal information of the users of electronic commerce and share

[57] Wu (2017), p. 23.

[58] Monteiro and Teh (2017), p. 50.

information and experience on the protection of personal information in electronic commerce.

In this case, the two parties recognize the importance of protecting the personal data of users of electronic commerce.[59] It is interesting that China included a provision on data protection, a value it does not seem to implement domestically.[60] It is also notable that the provision includes an obligation to share information and experiences on the protection of personal information in electronic commerce. This seems like a cooperation commitment in order to address any obstacles that may arise in the cross-border flow of personal data between the two countries.

5.1.4.4 Sri Lanka-Singapore Trade Agreement

The Sri Lanka-Singapore trade agreement was signed in 2018. The influence of the CPTPP on the data flow clause in the Sri Lanka-Singapore trade agreement cannot be overlooked—even if Sri Lanka is not a member of the CPTPP.[61] The provision on cross-border flows of personal data in the electronic commerce chapter of the Sri Lanka-Singapore trade agreement is essentially the same:

Article 9.9 Cross-Border Transfer of Information by Electronic Means

1. The Parties recognise that each Party may have its own regulatory requirements concerning the transfer of information by electronic means.
2. Each Party shall allow the cross-border transfer of information by electronic means, including personal information, when this activity is for the conduct of the business of a covered person.
3. Nothing in this Article shall prevent a Party from adopting or maintaining measures inconsistent with paragraph 2 of this Article to achieve a legitimate public policy objective, provided that the measure is not applied in a manner which would constitute a means of arbitrary or unjustifiable discrimination or a disguised restriction on trade.

However, an important difference between the data flow clauses in the Sri Lanka-Singapore trade agreement and the CPTPP can be found in the exception. The condition in the CPTPP that a measure may not impose restrictions on transfers of information greater than required to achieve its legitimate objective is not replicated in Article 9.9(3) of the Sri Lanka-Singapore trade agreement. The Sri Lanka-Singapore trade agreement is more permissive of restrictions on cross-border flows of personal data. Restrictions must be adopted to achieve a legitimate public policy objective such

---

[59] Ibid., 51–52.

[60] Willemyns (2020), p. 238; Weber et al. (2020), p. 569.

[61] Cp. Burri (2017), p. 128.

as the protection of personal data and they have to satisfy the conditions that can also be found in the *chapeau* of the general exceptions in Article XIV GATS.

5.1.5 Summary

The first data flow clauses in EU and US trade agreements illustrate their respective positions on data protection-based restrictions for cross-border flows of personal data perfectly. The EU sees data protection as a precondition for trade whereas the US perceives it as a potential trade barrier akin to data protectionism. In line with its digital trade agenda, the US pushed for a binding commitment on cross-border flows of personal data in the negotiations of the mega-regional trade agreements in the 2010s. After the US withdrew its signature from the TPP, it used the USMCA to set new standards for data flow clauses. The USMCA is currently the trade agreement with the strongest obligation on cross-border flows of personal data.[62] It prohibits the parties from restricting the free flow of personal data and imposes strict conditions for exceptions, including the standards from the *chapeau* of Article XIV GATS and two necessity tests, one of which is further qualified in a footnote. This provision has become the model for US-led trade agreements. At the same time, the provision in the CPTPP has become the model for new trade agreements of its members, as the Sri Lanka-Singapore trade agreement from 2018 shows.

The EU tried different approaches in its trade agreements. It used the EU-CARIFORUM EPA from 2008 to underline the fundamental rights character of data protection. This agreement committed the parties to establish a data protection regime, as well as appropriate administrative capacity, including independent supervision, in order to ensure an adequate level of protection and facilitate cross-border flows of personal data. In contrast, the CETA from 2016 only contains a very general reference to data protection. The CETA clearly makes a distinction between domestic data protection regulation and international trade law.[63] The CETA does not contain any data protection obligations anymore, and it includes no rules for cross-border flows of personal data. The EU separated the regulation of data protection from trade rules.[64] In addition, the EU started to shield its rules for the transfer of personal data from other obligations in the CETA as the provision on cross-border flows of personal data concerning financial services in Article 13.15(2) CETA shows.

---

[62] Willemyns (2020), p. 237.

[63] Irion and Bartl (2017), p. 5.

[64] But see Burri (2017), p. 107.

5.2 Legal Requirements for Data Flow Clauses in EU Trade Agreements

The second section of this chapter is dedicated to the legal requirements for data flow clauses in EU trade agreements. The architecture of EU law, the right to continuous protection of personal data in Article 8 CFR, the GDPR, and other regulations impose requirements upon the EU for the inclusion of data flow clauses in trade agreements. The most important requirement is the primacy of fundamental rights over international law (Sect. 5.2.1). In addition, data flow clauses in EU trade agreements should accommodate legal mechanisms for the transfer of personal data in the GDPR (Sect. 5.2.2). The GDPR also encourages the EU to develop means for cooperating with third countries in the field of data protection (Sect. 5.2.3). Finally, the GDPR and Regulation (EU) 2018/1807 on a framework for the free flow of non-personal data in the EU entail requirements for a ban on data localization obligations of third countries that are not motivated by data protection or privacy (Sect. 5.2.4).

5.2.1 Respecting the Primacy of Fundamental Rights Over International Law

The first legal requirement for data flow clauses in EU trade agreements is the primacy of fundamental rights over international law. This requires a brief explanation of the relationship between primary EU law and international law (Sect. 5.2.1.1) before it is possible to discuss the implications for data flow clauses in EU trade agreements (Sect. 5.2.1.2).

5.2.1.1 The Relationship of Primary Union Law and International Law

Primary Union law is above international law in the hierarchy of the legal order in the EU (Sect. 5.2.1.1.1). The ECJ has two important competences with regard to this subordination of international law: The Court can *a priori* examine the lawfulness of a proposed international agreement according to the opinion procedure in Article 218(11) TFEU (Sect. 5.2.1.1.2) and the Court can *a posteriori* review the lawfulness of an international agreement with regard to the EU Treaties in an annulment procedure according to Article 263 TFEU or in a preliminary ruling procedure according to Article 267(b) TFEU (Sect. 5.2.1.1.3).

5.2.1.1.1 Hierarchy in the Legal Order

Primary Union law is derived from the EU Treaties, the Charter based on Article 6(1) TEU since the adoption of the Lisbon Treaty in 2009, and the general principles of law established by the ECJ.[65] The EU Treaties do not regulate *expresis verbis* the hierarchical position of international agreements within the legal order of the EU.[66] Article 216 TFEU only states that international agreements concluded by the EU are binding upon the institutions of the Union and on its member states. The ECJ endorsed early on that international agreements concluded by the EU form an integral part of Union law from the moment of their entry into force.[67]

5.2.1.1.2 A Priori Examination of International Agreements by the European Court of Justice

An important competence of the ECJ with regard to the subordination of international law is that the Court can *a priori* examine the lawfulness of a proposed international agreement according to the opinion procedure in Article 218(11) TFEU: any member state, the European Parliament, the Council or the Commission may seek the opinion of the ECJ on the compatibility of a proposed international agreement with the EU Treaties.[68] This examination also extends to the Charter and the general principles of law established by the ECJ.[69] Should the ECJ find an incompatibility, the proposed agreement may only enter into force if it is amended.

5.2.1.1.3 A Posteriori Review of International Agreements by the European Court of Justice

Another important competence of the ECJ with regard to the subordination of international law is that the Court can *a posteriori* review the lawfulness of an international agreement with regard to the EU Treaties in an annulment procedure according to Article 263 TFEU or via a preliminary ruling procedure according to Article 267(b) TFEU.[70] This review power also extends to the Charter and the general principles of law established by the ECJ.

---

[65] Craig and de Búrca (2017), p. 111; Lenaerts and Van Nuffel (2011), p. 753.

[66] Mohay (2017), p. 157; van Rossem (2009), p. 194; Van Vooren and Wessel (2014), p. 211, 221; Lenaerts and Van Nuffel (2011), p. 817.

[67] ECJ, *R. & V. Haegeman v Belgian State*, para. 5; Van Vooren and Wessel (2014), p. 211; Eeckhout (2011), p. 327.

[68] Cp. ECJ, Opinion 2/15, para. 305 and ECJ, Opinion 1/15, para. 232; Mohay (2017), p. 153; see generally Craig and de Búrca (2017), pp. 369–371; Eeckhout (2011), pp. 268–274.

[69] Cp. ECJ, Opinion 1/17, para. 237 and ECJ, Opinion 1/15, para. 119; Cremona (2020), p. 3, 10.

[70] Cp. ECJ, *Western Sahara Campaign UK*, paras 36–37; ECJ, *Parliament v. Council and Commission*, paras 67–70 and ECJ, *Germany v. Council*, para. 72. Importantly, the annulment by the

The ECJ has previously annulled decisions of the Council approving an international agreement because of a breach of the general principles of Community law. In *Germany v. Council*, the ECJ annulled the first indent of Article 1(1) of Council Decision 94/800/EC of 22 December 1994 approving the Framework Agreement on Bananas concluded by the EC and certain third countries, because it violated the general principle of non-discrimination.[71] Article 264 TFEU holds that if an action is well-founded, the ECJ should declare the act concerned to be void and, if the Court considers this necessary, state which of the effects of the act that has been declared void should be considered as definitive. The power to determine the date at which the annulment of the act becomes effective and to what extent is important to prevent the annulment from resulting in a legal vacuum.[72]

An annulment by the ECJ merely invalidates the internal act of conclusion of an international agreement with the consequence that the agreement is inapplicable within the EU but remains valid on the international plane.[73] When the ECJ annulled Council Decision 2004/496/EC of 17 May 2004 approving the PNR agreement with the US and the underlying adequacy decision, the Court recognized that the EC cannot rely on its own law as a justification for not fulfilling the agreement, which remains applicable for a period of 90 days from termination thereof, and preserved the effect of the decision on adequacy until the end of that period.[74]

5.2.1.2 Implication for the Design of Data Flow Clauses

Any EU international trade commitment must respect the provisions of the EU Treaties and the Charter.[75] This includes the right to data protection in Article 8 CFR. In order to ensure the lawfulness of a data flow clause, the European Commission must respect Article 8 CFR when negotiating trade agreements. This also concerns the right to continuous protection of personal data that is transferred from the EU to a third country, which is an unwritten constituent part of Article 8 CFR. It is therefore important to recognize and state in a trade agreement that the protection of personal data is a fundamental right, and that the protection of personal data must continue when it is transferred across borders.

There are two options for the EU to deal with the primacy of fundamental rights over international law when negotiating data flow clauses in trade agreements. The

ECJ merely invalidates the internal act of conclusion of an international agreement with the consequence that the agreement is inapplicable within the EU but remains valid on the international plane. Peters (1997), p. 76; see generally Eeckhout (2011), pp. 292–298.

[71] ECJ, *Germany v. Council*, para. 72.

[72] Cp. ECJ, *Parliament v. Council*, para. 88 and ECJ, *Commission v. Council*, para. 57; Barents (2004), p. 259.

[73] Peters (1997), p. 76.

[74] ECJ, *Parliament v. Council and Commission*, paras 68–74.

[75] Van Waeyenberge and Pecho (2014), p. 752; Gstöhl and Hanf (2014), p. 745 fn. 61.

first option does not include a commitment to the free flow of personal data across borders and focuses on carving-out data protection from an agreement. The second option includes a commitment to the free flow of personal data across borders and focuses on aligning this commitment with the right to continuous protection of personal data. Should a commitment to the free flow of personal data be integrated into a trade agreement of the EU, it must guarantee that the transfer of personal data can be restricted should the level of protection for personal data not be essentially equivalent to that guaranteed within the EU in cases in which personal data is transferred to a contracting party or parties. This is especially important in cases in which foreign internet surveillance practices capture personal data that is transferred from the EU to the surveilling third country.

5.2.2 Accommodating the Legal Mechanisms for Data Transfers

The accommodation of the legal mechanisms for the transfer of personal data in the GDPR is the second legal requirement for data flow clauses in EU trade agreements. This requires a brief explanation of the relationship between secondary Union law and international law (Sect. 5.2.2.1) before it is possible to discuss the implications for data flow clauses in FTAs of the EU (Sect. 5.2.2.2).

5.2.2.1 The Relationship of Secondary Union Law and International Law

International law is above secondary Union law in the hierarchy of the legal order in the EU (Sect. 5.2.2.1.1). The ECJ may review secondary Union law in light of an EU international agreement in an annulment procedure according to Article 263 TFEU or in a preliminary ruling procedure according to Article 267(b) TFEU. However, the ECJ has not always acknowledged international agreements concluded by the EU as a standard for the review of secondary Union law. The question of review has been linked to the issue of the direct effect of international agreements (Sect. 5.2.2.1.2).

5.2.2.1.1 Hierarchy in the Legal Order

Subject to the EU Treaties, institutions of the Union and its member states are bound by international agreements through Article 216 TFEU. International law holds a superior position in the hierarchy of the EU legal order than secondary Union law.[76] Given the primacy of international law over secondary Union law, the courts of the EU and its member states must ensure that secondary Union law and national legislation is interpreted as far as possible in conformity with the obligations contained in international agreements concluded by the EU.[77] However, a conforming interpretation is not possible in circumstances in which secondary Union law or national legislation clashes with an international agreement, and in which conformity would lead to an interpretation *contra legem.* [78]

5.2.2.1.2 Review of Secondary Law in Light of International Agreements by the European Court of Justice

It follows from the hierarchy of the EU legal order that the lawfulness of secondary Union law, which is contrary to an EU international agreement, may be reviewed by the ECJ in an annulment procedure according to Article 263 TFEU or in a preliminary ruling procedure according to Article 267(b) TFEU.[79] However, the ECJ has not always acknowledged international agreements concluded by the EU as a standard for the judicial review of secondary Union law. The question of review has been linked to the issue of direct effect of international agreements.[80]

Direct effect exists when the contracting parties so indicate in the terms of an agreement.[81] Until recently, it was rare that the EU and the other contracting party or parties addressed the issue of direct effect in a trade agreement.[82] Given the lack of presumption of direct effect in international agreements that are binding on the EU, it is often left to the ECJ to decide whether a provision has direct effect or not. The ECJ has repeatedly pointed out that the interpretative liberty to determine direct effect in international agreements is based on the fact that agreements contain no explicit provisions on the issue. The ECJ stressed that in conformity with the principles of international law, "Community institutions which have the power to negotiate and conclude an agreement [...] are free to agree with that country what effect the provisions of the agreement are to have in the internal legal order of the contracting

[76]Cp. ECJ, *IATA and ELFAA*, para. 35 and ECJ, *Commission v. Germany*, C-61/94, para. 52; Lenaerts (2010), p. 519; see generally Barnard and Peers (2017), p. 196; Van Vooren and Wessel (2014), p. 211; Lenaerts and Van Nuffel (2011), pp. 862–863.

[77]Van Waeyenberge and Pecho (2014), p. 752; see generally Van Vooren and Wessel (2014), pp. 238–240; Eeckhout (2011), pp. 355–357.

[78]ECJ, AG Opinion, *Rízení Letového Provozu*, para. 58; Lenaerts (2010), p. 519.

[79]Mohay (2017), p. 159; Craig and de Búrca (2017), pp. 371–372; Lenaerts and Van Nuffel (2011), pp. 871–873.

[80]Van Waeyenberge and Pecho (2014), p. 753; Craig and de Búrca (2017), pp. 368–369; Eeckhout (2011), p. 297.

[81]ECJ, *Portugal v. Council*, para. 34.

[82]Cp. Van Waeyenberge and Pecho (2014), p. 753.

parties."[83] In the absence of an agreement between the contracting parties on the effect of the provisions of the agreement in the internal legal orders, the ECJ considers whether the nature or broad logic of an agreement precludes direct effect, and, whether the provision in question is, as regards its content, unconditional and sufficiently precise.[84]

The EU started to depart from its conventional approach in 2010 by breaking the silence with regard to the direct effect of trade agreements in the internal legal order.[85] The Council Decision approving the trade agreement with the Republic of Korea explicitly stated that the agreement shall not be construed as conferring rights or imposing obligations which can be directly invoked before Union or member state courts.[86] Subsequently concluded trade agreements have usually included a general clause with similar effect.[87] For example, Article 30.6(1) CETA provides that nothing in the agreement should be construed as conferring rights or imposing obligations on persons other than those created between the parties under public international law, nor as permitting the agreement to be directly invoked in the domestic legal systems of the parties. Such a provision prevents a trade agreement from being directly invoked before Union and member states courts. It also blocks the possibility of using a trade agreement as a standard for the judicial review of secondary Union law.

5.2.2.2 Implications for the Design of Data Flow Clauses

The possibility to review the legal mechanisms for the transfer of personal data in the GDPR for compatibility with a data flow clause in a trade agreement depends on the direct effect of the provision and the trade agreement in question. As long as a Council decision approving the trade agreement, or the agreement itself, entails a provision that excludes direct effect of the agreement, then the legal mechanisms for data transfers in the GDPR cannot be reviewed for their compatibility with the trade agreement in question. The inclusion of such a provision is important to safeguard the EU regulation of data transfers from potential challenges.

Recital (102) GDPR explicitly allows the conclusion of international agreements which involve the transfer of personal data to third countries, insofar as such

[83] ECJ, *Air Transport Association of America*, para. 49; ECJ, *Kupferberg*, para. 17.

[84] ECJ, *FIAMM*, para. 110; ECJ, *Intertanko*, para. 45; ECJ, *IATA and ELFAA*, para. 39; ECJ, *International Fruit Company*, paras 19–20; see generally Lenaerts and Van Nuffel (2011), p. 865; Van Vooren and Wessel (2014), pp. 227–233.

[85] Semertzi (2014), p. 1127.

[86] Article 8 Council Decision 2011/265/EU of 16 September 2010 on the signing, on behalf of the European Union, and provisional application of the Free Trade Agreement between the European Union and its Member States, of the one part, and the Republic of Korea, of the other part [2011] OJ L 117/1.

[87] Semertzi (2014), p. 1131.

agreements do not affect the GDPR and include an appropriate level of protection for the fundamental rights of the data subjects:

> This Regulation is without prejudice to international agreements concluded between the Union and third countries regulating the transfer of personal data including appropriate safeguards for the data subjects. Member States may conclude international agreements which involve the transfer of personal data to third countries or international organisations, as far as such agreements do not affect this Regulation or any other provisions of Union law and include an appropriate level of protection for the fundamental rights of the data subjects.

Data flow clauses of the EU should be designed in a way that accommodates the legal mechanisms for the transfer of personal data in the GDPR as an implementation of the trade agreement. Data flow clauses should not replace the legal mechanisms for the transfer of personal data in the GDPR because these mechanisms provide the necessary details for safe, cross-border flows of personal data. I have already argued that a commitment to the free flow of personal data across borders in an EU trade agreement must guarantee that such data flows can be restricted in case the level of protection for personal data is not essentially equivalent to that guaranteed within the EU when personal data is transferred to the contracting party or parties. This is important to safeguard decisions of supervisory authorities to ban or suspend data transfers according to Article 58(2)(f) and (j) GDPR, especially on the basis of instruments providing appropriate safeguards in Article 46 GDPR.

5.2.3 Including Cooperation for the Protection of Personal Data

The inclusion of a provision on cooperation for the protection of personal data is the third legal requirement for data flow clauses in EU trade agreements. A provision in Chapter V of the GDPR on transfers of personal data is specifically dedicated to international cooperation for the protection of personal data:

> **Article 50 International cooperation for the protection of personal data**
> In relation to third countries and international organisations, the Commission and supervisory authorities shall take appropriate steps to:
>
> (a) develop international cooperation mechanisms to facilitate the effective enforcement of legislation for the protection of personal data;
> (b) provide international mutual assistance in the enforcement of legislation for the protection of personal data, including through notification, complaint referral, investigative assistance and information exchange, subject to appropriate safeguards for the protection of personal data and other fundamental rights and freedoms;
> (c) engage relevant stakeholders in discussion and activities aimed at furthering international cooperation in the enforcement of legislation for the protection of personal data;

(d) promote the exchange and documentation of personal data protection legislation and practice, including on jurisdictional conflicts with third countries.

Article 50 GDPR clearly encourages the EU to develop the means for cooperating with third countries in the field of data protection. The proliferation of data protection laws around the world, as well as the extraterritorial dimension of EU data protection law, make it necessary for the EU to interact with other data protection systems, both politically and legally.[88] The provision entails that the Commission has the broadest powers to engage in tasks relating to international outreach and cooperation in the field of data protection.[89] The Commission has already announced that it "will continue to engage actively in dialogue with its international partners, at both bilateral and multilateral level, to foster convergence by developing high and interoperable personal data protection standards globally."[90]

Article 50(a) and (b) GDPR focus on cross-border enforcement of legislation for the protection of personal data. Article 50(c) GDPR stresses that relevant stakeholders should be engaged in these discussions. Article 50(d) GDPR refers more generally to the promotion of exchange on data protection legislation. Recital (116) GDPR underlines that the Commission and the supervisory authorities should exchange information and cooperate in activities related to the exercise of their powers with competent authorities in third countries, based on reciprocity and in accordance with the GDPR. With regard to the transfer of personal data, the powers of the Commission include among other things the adoption of adequacy decisions, and the powers of the supervisory authorities include among other things corrective actions in the form of a suspension or a ban on data transfers using instruments providing appropriate safeguards such as standard data protection clauses. The two examples require assessments of the level of protection for personal data that is transferred to a third country. These assessments must be independent. However, cooperative instruments in a trade agreement could facilitate a dialogue to improve the level of data protection in a third country in which the existing protection is not considered to be adequate.[91] In addition, the Commission and the supervisory authorities are also responsible for approving the new data transfer instruments and providing appropriate safeguards in the GDPR, such as codes of conduct and certifications. It could be useful to establish cooperative instruments in a trade agreement to exchange information on how these mechanisms work.

The EU has already included provisions on cooperation for the protection of personal data in Article 201(1) of the EU-CARIFORUM EPA from 2008.[92]

[88] Kuner (2020), pp. 858–859.

[89] Ibid., 860.

[90] European Commission (2017a), p. 11.

[91] Cp. Mancini (2020), p. 205; But see Robert Wolfe arguing that "a trade agreement might not be the best vehicle for regulatory cooperation [. . .], if the objective is some form of equivalence." Wolfe (2019), pp. 65–66.

[92] See Sect. 5.1.2.2.

> The Parties acknowledge the importance of cooperation in order to facilitate the development of appropriate legislative, judicial and institutional frameworks as well as an adequate level of protection of personal data consistent with the objectives and principles contained in this Chapter.

However, the EU also changed its approach to cooperation for the protection of personal data in later trade agreements. Although the CETA is an innovation when it comes to regulatory cooperation, data protection is not considered at all. The Cooperation Forum established by the CETA creates a formal mechanism to facilitate dialogue between Canadian and EU regulatory authorities. Chapter 21 of the CETA on regulatory cooperation encourages regulators to exchange experiences and information and identify areas in which cooperation could occur. All cooperation is voluntary and regulators in the EU and Canada retain their power to adopt legislation according to Article 21.2(4) and (6) CETA. Nevertheless, the chapter on regulatory cooperation in the CETA does not apply to electronic commerce.[93]

It can be observed that interest in regulatory cooperation with the EU in the field of data protection is high. Notably, the UK's proposal on a future partnership in the exchange and protection of personal data with the EU from 2018 advocated a partnership that includes "ongoing regulatory cooperation between the EU and the UK on current and future data protection issues, building on the positive opportunity of a partnership between global leaders on data protection."[94]

It is important to distinguish between two types of regulatory cooperation. Aaditya Mattoo describes regulatory cooperation that could be far-reaching and lead to harmonization or mutual recognition on the one hand, and regulatory cooperation that only involves greater mutual understanding of how regulatory discretion in each jurisdiction will be exercised on the other hand.[95] The latter form of cooperation is less intense, but it is equally valuable because it lends predictability to trade relations.

Regulatory cooperation for the protection of personal data in the EU must respect and guarantee the right to continuous protection for personal data in Article 8 CFR and accommodate the legal mechanisms for data transfers in the GDPR. Within these limits, regulatory cooperation may be used to improve the continuous protection for personal data that is transferred to third countries. The GDPR acknowledges in Recital (101) that flows of personal data to and from countries outside the EU are necessary for the expansion of international trade. Cooperation for the protection of personal data in trade agreements should not be seen as a red line, even if data protection is a fundamental right in the EU and its content is not negotiable. The Commission recently wrote in its communication on a European strategy for data

[93] However, regulatory cooperation for the protection of personal data could indirectly take place by means of regulatory cooperation on cross-border trade in services which is subject to regulatory cooperation according to Article 21.1 CETA. Cross-border flows of personal data are closely related to trade in services. Accordingly, cooperation on regulatory matters pertaining to data protection might not be totally excluded. Mancini (2020), p. 199.

[94] HM Government (2017), para. 22.

[95] Mattoo (2015), p. 7.

from 2020 that it is convinced that international cooperation must be based on an approach that promotes the EU's fundamental values, including protection of privacy.[96] It is of paramount importance that regulatory cooperation for the protection of personal data is led by data protection experts and not conducted by trade officials.[97] The EU should advance its own data protection rules as the baseline and conceive regulatory cooperation as a tool to reach greater convergence on data protection standards.[98]

5.2.4 Banning Other Data Localization Obligations

Some data localization obligations in third countries are not motivated by data protection or privacy. The European Commission observed in its communication on a European strategy for data from 2020 that "European companies operating in some third countries are increasingly faced with unjustified barriers and digital restrictions."[99] These restrictions may concern personal data but also non-personal data. The requirement to ban data localization obligations that are not motivated by data protection or privacy can be found in the GDPR and in Regulation (EU) 2018/1807 on a framework for the free flow of non-personal data in the European Union.[100]

With regard to personal data, Article 1(3) GDPR states that the free movement of personal data within the Union shall be neither restricted nor prohibited for reasons connected with the protection of natural persons with regard to the processing of personal data. If an EU member state imposes localization requirements on personal data that are not motivated by data protection or privacy, then they will have to be assessed against the provisions on the fundamental freedoms and the permitted ground to derogate from those freedoms in the TFEU.[101] For example, the exceptions in Article 52(1) TFEU enable EU member states to retain restrictions on the free movement of services in respect of public policy, public security, and public health. Recital (101) GDPR acknowledges that flows of personal data to and from countries outside the Union are necessary for the expansion of international trade. It implies that restrictions on cross-border flows of personal data that are not motivated by data protection or privacy should also be banned on the international level wherever possible. Such a ban, however, must be accompanied with exceptions

---

[96] European Commission (2020), p. 23.

[97] Mancini (2020), p. 200; Irion and Bartl (2017), p. 10.

[98] Mancini (2020), p. 205.

[99] European Commission (2020), pp. 23–24; see also Mancini (2020), p. 205; Hodson (2019), p. 581; Peng and Liu (2017), pp. 187–192.

[100] Regulation (EU) 2018/1807 of the European Parliament and of the Council of 14 November 2018 on a framework for the free flow of non-personal data in the European Union [2018] OJ L 303/59.

[101] European Commission (2019), p. 13; see for example ECJ, *Commission v Grand Duchy of Luxemburg*, paras 90–91.

similar to those in EU law. The Commission observed in its Communication for a European strategy for data from 2020 that, without prejudice to the EU's framework for the protection of personal data, the "free and safe flow of data should be ensured with third countries, subject to exceptions and restrictions for public security, public order and other legitimate public policy objectives of the European Union."[102] Such a solution can be applied to trade agreements.

The restriction of cross-border flows of non-personal data is a subject that has not been addressed in this research so far. There should be data protection in trade agreements without data protectionism in the form of restrictions on cross-border flows of non-personal data. In 2018, the EU adopted Regulation (EU) 2018/1807 on a framework for the free flow of non-personal data in the EU. The regulation aims to ensure the free flow of non-personal data within the Union by establishing rules relating to data localization requirements. Recital (18) Regulation (EU) 2018/1807 states that data localization requirements in the EU represent a clear barrier to the free provision of data processing services across the Union.[103] This is why, according to Article 4(1) Regulation (EU) 2018/1807, data localization requirements in the EU are prohibited—unless they are justified on grounds of public security in compliance with the principle of proportionality. The prohibition of data localization requirements in the EU are far-reaching. Recital (13) Regulation (EU) 2018/1807 explicitly states that, given the large amounts of data which public authorities handle, it is of the utmost importance that public authorities lead by example and refrain from imposing data localization requirements when they use data processing services.

The prohibition of data localization requirements for non-personal data in the EU should be replicated in trade agreements. However, the exceptions should not be limited to public security. Recital (18) Regulation (EU) 2018/1807 clarifies the intention of the regulation to limit the justification for data localization requirements in the EU to public security in Article 4(1) Regulation (EU) 2018/1807:[104]

> In order to give effect to the principle of free flow of non-personal data across borders, to ensure the swift removal of existing data localisation requirements and to enable, for operational reasons, the processing of data in multiple locations across the Union, [...] Member States should only be able to invoke public security as a justification for data localisation requirements.

Panos Koutrakos argues that public security is most closely associated with what is traditionally understood as the core of national sovereignty, that is, the sphere of

[102] European Commission (2020), pp. 23–24.

[103] Article 3(5) Regulation (EU) 2018/1807 defines data localization as any obligation, prohibition, condition, limit or other requirement provided for in the laws, regulations or administrative provisions, which imposes the processing of data in the territory of a specific Member State or hinders the processing of data in any other Member State.

[104] Somaini (2020), p. 88.

activity within which the state has primary responsibility to protect its territory and citizens.[105] The Council summarized that public security

> presupposes the existence of a genuine and sufficiently serious threat affecting one of the fundamental interests of society, such as a threat to the functioning of institutions and essential public services and the survival of the population, as well as by the risk of a serious disturbance to foreign relations or the peaceful coexistence of nations, or a risk to military interests.[106]

Kristina Irion argues that the public security exception is too narrow because it precludes EU member states from taking measures that can be justified on grounds of public policy or the protection of health of humans, animals or plants.[107] This should be considered in the exceptions to the data flow clauses in EU trade agreements.

5.2.5 Summary

The scope for data flow clauses in EU trade agreements is determined by several legal requirements stemming from the architecture of Union law, the GDPR, and other regulations. The most important requirement is the primacy of fundamental rights over international law. Any data flow clause in an EU trade agreement must respect the right to continuous protection of personal data found in Article 8 CFR. The ECJ has two important competences with regard to the subordination of international law: The Court can *a priori* examine the lawfulness of a proposed international agreement according to the opinion procedure and the Court can *a posteriori* review the lawfulness of an international agreement in an annulment procedure or in a preliminary ruling procedure. Furthermore, data flow clauses in EU trade agreement should be designed in a way that can accommodate the legal mechanisms for the transfer of personal data in the GDPR. The data flow clauses should *not* replace the legal mechanisms for the transfer of personal data in the GDPR because these mechanisms provide the necessary details for safe data transfers. In addition, the Council decision approving a trade agreement, or the trade agreement itself, should include a provision that precludes the direct effect of the agreement to formally exclude the review of the legal mechanisms for the transfer of personal data in the GDPR for their compatibility with the trade agreement in question. The data flow clauses should also include a provision on cooperation for the protection of personal data in line with the objectives of Article 50 GDPR. Lastly, Recital (101) GDPR acknowledges that flows of personal data to and from countries outside the Union are necessary for the expansion of international trade. This implies that restrictions on cross-border flows of personal data that are not

105 Koutrakos (2016), p. 192.

106 Council of the EU (2017), Recital (12a).

107 Irion (2018), p. 9.

motivated by data protection or privacy should be banned. Such a ban must be accompanied with exceptions similar to those in place in EU law.

5.3 Designs for Data Flow Clauses in EU Trade Agreements

The third section of this chapter is dedicated to the design of data flow clauses in EU trade agreements. There are two options to deal with the primacy of fundamental rights over international law in cases in which the EU negotiates data flow clauses for a trade agreement.[108] The first option does not include a commitment to the free flow of personal data across borders and focuses on carving-out data protection from an agreement. The second option includes a commitment to the free flow of personal data across borders and focuses on aligning this commitment with the right to continuous protection of personal data in Article 8 CFR. The following suggestions for the design of data flow clauses in EU trade agreements all include a commitment to the free flow of personal data across borders. Such a commitment by the EU must guarantee that data transfers can be restricted if the level of protection for personal data is not essentially equivalent to that guaranteed within the EU when personal data is transferred to the contracting party or parties. This section introduces four suggestions for the design of data flow clauses in EU trade agreements and describes their advantages and shortcomings with regard to the legal requirements described above.[109] The four suggestions are: a data flow obligation with a privacy exception (Sect. 5.3.1), a data flow obligation with an adequacy exception (Sect. 5.3.2), a data flow obligation with an adequacy condition (Sect. 5.3.3), and a data flow obligation with data protection obligations (Sect. 5.3.4).

5.3.1 Data Flow Obligation with a Data Protection Exception

The first suggestion for an EU data flow clause consists of a data flow obligation and a data protection exception. The combination of a data flow obligation and a data protection (or privacy) exception is also used in the CPTPP, the Sri Lanka-Singapore trade agreement, the USMCA, and the US-Japan Digital Trade Agreement. Nevertheless, there are certain crucial differences between these trade agreements. For example, the data flow obligations in Article 14.11(2) CPTPP and in Article 9.9(2) Sri Lanka-Singapore trade agreement are worded positively (each party shall allow the cross-border transfer of personal data), whereas the data flow obligations in Article 19.11(1) USMCA and in Article 11(1) US-Japan Digital Trade Agreement

[108] See Sect. 5.2.1.2.

[109] The designs do not address cooperation for the protection of personal data and the banning of other data localization requirements in detail.

are worded negatively (no party shall prohibit or restrict the cross-border transfer of personal data). For a data flow obligation in a EU trade agreement, it would be advisable to follow the CPTPP model and provide a positively worded obligation that focuses on allowing cross-border flows of personal data and to refrain from an explicit prohibition to restrict such data flows. The positive obligation leaves more room to accommodate the legal mechanisms for the transfer of personal data in the GDPR.

Two paragraphs should precede the data flow obligation in the design of the clause. The first paragraph should recognize and state that the protection of personal data is a fundamental right, and that the protection of personal data must continue when it is transferred across borders. The second paragraph should recognize and state that the parties may have their own regulatory requirements concerning the transfer of personal data. The data flow obligation must be read and interpreted in light of these two paragraphs. With regard to the EU regulation of data transfers, these two paragraphs and the data flow obligation could accommodate the legal mechanisms for the transfer of personal data. This includes—in the absence of an adequacy decision according to Article 45 GDPR—the instruments providing appropriate safeguards according to Article 46 GDPR and the derogations in Article 49 GDPR.

The data protection exception must cover restrictions on cross-border flows of personal data that are imposed because of the level of protection for personal data existing in the third country contracting party for the transferred data. Such an exception should be applicable when the European Commission revokes or the ECJ invalidates an adequacy decision for a contracting party, and when a supervisory authority in an EU member state uses its corrective powers in Article 58(2)(f) and (j) GDPR to suspend or ban transfers of personal data to a contracting party.

There are important differences in the formulation of such an exception among the existing data flow clauses in trade agreements. These differences are decisive for the justification of restrictions on cross-border data flows for data protection or privacy. The least permissive exceptions can be found in Article 19.11(2) USMCA and Article 11(2) US-Japan Digital Trade Agreement. According to these exceptions, measures that are inconsistent with the data flow obligation must be necessary to achieve a legitimate public policy objective, they may not constitute a means of arbitrary or unjustifiable discrimination or a disguised restriction on trade, and they may not impose restrictions that are greater than necessary to achieve the objective. The last condition constitutes a second necessity test and is further qualified in a footnote. Measures do not meet the second necessity test if they accord different treatment to cross-border flows of personal data solely on the basis that they are cross-border in a manner that modifies the conditions of competition to the detriment of a covered person. This qualification makes it difficult to accommodate legal mechanisms for the transfer of personal data that require additional safeguards for cross-border flows of personal data. It is not certain if the EU regulation of data transfers could be justified under the exceptions in Article 19.11(2) USMCA and Article 11(2) US-Japan Digital Trade Agreement because of the second necessity test.

The most permissive exception can be found in Article 9.9(3) Sri Lanka-Singapore trade agreement. Any restriction on the cross-border flow of personal data to achieve a legitimate public policy objective must not be applied in a manner which would constitute a means of arbitrary or unjustifiable discrimination, or a disguised restriction on trade. This version of an exception is suitable for the EU. The exception does not entail a necessity test. A necessity test could potentially put pressure on the legal mechanisms for data transfers in the GDPR. The absence of a necessity test allows the parties to have their own regulatory systems for cross-border flows of personal data. The standards of arbitrary and unjustifiable discrimination and disguised restrictions on trade should be easy to satisfy for the EU in a bilateral trade agreement, as long as the EU regulation of data transfers is applied in good faith and respects due process. In a multilateral trade agreement, it is important for the Commission and the supervisory authorities to apply the EU regulation of data transfers equally in comparable situations to all contracting parties. As long as this is the case, these standards should not be a problem in a multilateral trade agreement either. Against this background, the first design for a data flow clause with a data flow obligation and a data protection exception could look like this:

Data Flow Clause Design One

1. The Parties recognize that data protection is a fundamental right and that the protection of personal data must continue when it is transferred across borders.
2. It is recognized that each Party may have its own regulatory requirements concerning the transfer of personal data.
3. The Parties allow the cross-border transfer of personal data when this activity is for the conduct of the business of a covered person.
4. Nothing in this Article shall prevent a Party from adopting or maintaining measures inconsistent with paragraph 3 of this Article to protect the privacy or the personal data of individuals, provided that the measure is not applied in a manner which would constitute a means of arbitrary or unjustifiable discrimination or a disguised restriction on trade.

The advantages of any trade agreement that includes a commitment to the free flow of personal data is the reciprocity of the commitment. The GDPR only regulates the transfer of personal data from the EU to third countries. Inbound flows of personal data are not guaranteed but can be addressed in a trade agreement. The disadvantage of this design for a data flow clause is that the justification for a restriction on cross-border flows of personal data lies with the defendant. Should a contracting party challenge an EU restriction on cross-border flows of personal data, the EU would have to prove that the restriction is for the protection of personal data. However, the proof seems to be easy on the basis of a reflected decision by the Commission or a supervisory authority.

5.3.2 Data Flow Obligation with an Adequacy Exception

The second suggestion for the design of a data flow clause in EU trade agreements consists of a data flow obligation and an adequacy exception. There is no model for such a data flow clause in any current trade agreement. It is a design for a data flow clause that is tailored to EU-style data protection, but should also be acceptable to the contracting parties. Just as the previous design, the first paragraph should recognize and state that the protection of personal data is a fundamental right and that the protection of personal data must continue when it is transferred across borders. The second paragraph should recognize and state that the parties may have their own regulatory requirements concerning the transfer of personal data. The third paragraph should entail the data flow obligation and the fourth paragraph should entail the adequacy exception. The second design for a data flow clause with a data flow obligation and an adequacy exception could look like this:

Data Flow Clause Design Two

1. The Parties recognize that data protection is a fundamental right and that the protection of personal data must continue when it is transferred across borders.
2. It is recognized that each Party may have its own regulatory requirements concerning the transfer of personal data.
3. The Parties allow the cross-border transfer of personal data when this activity is for the conduct of the business of a covered person.
4. Nothing in this Article shall prevent a Party from adopting or maintaining measures inconsistent with paragraph 3 of this Article to guarantee that transfers of personal data only take place subject to an adequate level of protection.

The language used in the adequacy exception would accommodate restrictions on data transfers in cases in which the protection for personal data that is transferred to a contracting party is not adequate to EU standards. The ECJ defined in *Schrems* that an adequate level of protection for personal data is a level of protection that is essentially equivalent to that guaranteed within the EU.[110] The adequacy exception is a strong expression of the right to continuous protection of personal data in Article 8 CFR and accommodates the legal mechanisms for the transfer of personal data in the GDPR. However, international agreements must be interpreted according to the rules in Articles 31-33 VCLT. It is possible that an interpretation of the term "adequate level of protection" on the basis of the VCLT leads to different results than the interpretation in EU law, which could undermine the right to continuous protection of personal data in Article 8 CFR.[111] The situation is even more complicated

[110] ECJ, *Schrems*, para. 73.

[111] Svetlana Yakovleva argues that given the fragmentation of standards on privacy and data protection and the absence of a single reference point, the interpretation of terms such as "adequate" or "appropriate" have no precise obligational content. Yakovleva (2018), p. 195.

because the level of protection guaranteed within the EU is subject to developments in Union law.

This disadvantage of the second design could be resolved with a reference in a footnote that the definition of an adequate level of protection is up to each party. This does not have to weaken the commitment to the free flow of personal data as long as the contracting parties maintain a rule-based system to determine when transfers of personal data may or may not take place based on the level of protection for personal data, and as long as such determinations are open to judicial review. For example, in the EU the independent supervisory authorities have the power to suspend or ban data transfers in cases in which the protection for personal data is not essentially equivalent to that guaranteed within the EU. However, the use of this power is subject to judicial review. It is suggested that the second design is a valid option when the contracting parties have a similar system in place. Without a similar system, the data flow obligation could easily be circumvented with political decisions by a contracting party with a protectionist agenda.

Another disadvantage of this design is—similar to the first design—that the justification for a restriction of data flows lies with the defendant. Should a contracting party challenge an EU restriction on cross-border flows of personal data, the EU would have to prove that the level of protection for personal data that is transferred to the contracting party is not adequate. While this proof is more difficult than the one required in the first design, the respective decisions by the Commission or a supervisory authority provide a good basis to satisfy the burden of proof.

5.3.3 Data Flow Obligation with an Adequacy Condition

The third suggestion for the design of a data flow clause in EU trade agreements combines a data flow obligation with an adequacy condition. It is similar to the second design but instead of integrating the adequacy criterion in the exception, it is formulated as a condition for the commitment to the free flow of personal data in paragraph 3. The third design could look like this:

Data Flow Clause Design Three

1. The Parties recognize that data protection is a fundamental right and that the protection of personal data must continue when it is transferred across borders.
2. It is recognized that each Party may have its own regulatory requirements concerning the transfer of personal data.
3. The Parties allow the cross-border transfer of personal data when this activity is for the conduct of the business of a covered person and the level of protection for the personal data that is transferred is adequate.

The advantage of this design over the second design is that the defendant does not bear the burden of proof because the criterion for an adequate level of protection is not integrated as an exception. Should a contracting party challenge an EU restriction on cross-border flows of personal data, it must also prove that the level of protection for personal data that is transferred from the EU to its territory is adequate. However, there is a similar disadvantage as in the second design concerning the interpretation of an "adequate" level of data protection according to the rules of the VCLT. A solution could be a provision on cooperation that establishes a dialogue on adequate protection for personal data. The documentation of that dialogue could be used as a supplementary means of interpretation according to Article 32 VCLT.

5.3.4 Data Flow Obligation with Data Protection Obligations

The fourth suggestion for the design of a data flow clause in EU trade agreements entails different obligations: a data flow obligation and several data protection obligations. The design of the data flow clause is the same as the third design with an adequacy obligation and an adequacy condition, but in addition to the data flow clause, the trade agreement in this fourth design would have a separate chapter on data protection. This chapter should entail several data protection obligations that are the basis for an adequate level of protection for personal data.

The fourth design builds upon the approach taken by the EU in the EU-CARIFORUM EPA and the EU-Central Africa EPA.[112] These trade agreements each have a separate chapter on data protection. The chapters define important terms such as "personal data" and the "processing of personal data" as well as "data controller." It is especially important that the term data controller also includes public authorities to incorporate internet surveillance practices within the scope of the agreement. The chapters also include an agreement between the contracting parties that the legal and regulatory regimes should include content principles such as purpose limitation, data quality and proportionality, transparency, security, rights of access, rectification and opposition as well as rules on onward transfers of personal data and sensitive data. The agreement between the contracting parties also extends to the establishment of enforcement mechanisms to ensure a good level of compliance, to provide support and help to individual data subjects in the exercise of their rights, and to provide appropriate redress to injured parties. In spite of these first attempts by the EU to formulate the conditions for an adequate level of protection for personal data in trade agreements, the EU seems skeptical to go further with substantive data protection obligations in trade agreements. During a meeting of the WTO Council for Trade in Services in 2015, a representative of the EU recalled the Union's position that "trade agreements should not go beyond affirming those general principles and should not set substantive standards on personal data protection."[113]

---

[112] See Sect. 5.1.1.2.

[113] WTO (2015), para. 4.30.

Svetlana Yakovleva argues that the EU Treaties require that the negotiation and conclusion of trade agreements be guided by the universality and indivisibility of human rights and fundamental freedoms, respect for human dignity and principles of the UN and international law, and—in order to remain faithful to these requirements—that the EU maintain its autonomy to protect personal data as a fundamental right, and not just as an instrument to generate consumers' trust.[114] While this position can be agreed with, it does not eliminate the possibility of including data protection obligations in a trade agreement. The European Commission stated that "[i]n particular, an adequacy finding is a unilateral implementing decision by the Commission in accordance with EU data protection law, based on the criteria therein."[115] However, the EU does not explain why the inclusion of data protection obligations in trade agreements is a red line. An explanation could be the loss of authority over the interpretation of such obligations and standards. I would argue, however, that as long as the data flow clause accommodates the legal mechanisms for the transfer of personal data in the GDPR, including the ability of the Commission to take and revoke adequacy decisions and the power of supervisory authorities to suspend or ban the transfer of personal data, then the inclusion of data protection obligations in trade agreements would not undermine the fundamental right to continuous protection of personal data.

The advantage of the fourth design over the third design is that the trade agreement itself provides the basis for the expectations of an adequate level of protection for personal data with the data protection obligations in a specific chapter of the trade agreement. A provision on cooperation should be added that establishes a dialogue on adequate protection for personal data. The documentation of that dialogue could be used as supplementary means of interpretation according to Article 32 VCLT.

5.3.5 Summary

There are different possibilities for designing data flow clauses, should a commitment to the free flow of personal data across borders be integrated into an EU trade agreement. Any design for a data flow clause in a trade agreement of the EU must respect the legal requirements for data flow clauses discussed in the previous section. The four suggestions that were presented in this section all respect the primacy of fundamental rights over international law, which includes the primacy of the right to continuous protection for personal data in Article 8 CFR, and accommodate the legal mechanisms for the transfer of personal data in the GDPR. The first design combines a data flow obligation with a general data protection exception. The second design uses a more specific adequacy exception. The disadvantage of these designs is that

[114] Yakovleva (2018), p. 480.

[115] European Commission (2017a), p. 9, fn. 42.

the justification for a restriction on cross-border flows of personal data lies with the defendant. The EU would have to prove that a measure is taken for the protection of personal data that is transferred to the contracting party (in case of the first design) or that the level of protection for personal data in the territory of the contracting party is not adequate (in case of the second design).

The third design combines a data flow obligation with an adequacy condition. In this design, the parties allow the cross-border transfer of personal data when the level of protection for the personal data that is transferred is adequate. The advantage of this design is that the EU would not bear the burden of proof because the criterion of an adequate level of protection is not integrated as an exception. The term "adequate level of protection," however, might have a different meaning in trade agreements than in EU law based on interpretations according to the VCLT. This could provoke problems with the right to continuous protection of personal data in Article 8 CFR. A footnote referring to an autonomous definition of the term could prevent such problems. Another solution could be a provision for cooperation that establishes a dialogue on adequate protection for personal data. The documentation of that dialogue could be used as a supplementary means of interpretation according to Article 32 VCLT. The fourth design for a data flow clause is the same as the third design with an adequacy obligation and an adequacy condition, but in addition a separate chapter on data protection. The advantage of the fourth design over the third design is that the trade agreement itself provides the basis for the expectations of an adequate level of protection for personal data with the data protection obligations in a specific chapter of the trade agreement.

5.4 The Model Data Flow Clauses for EU Trade Agreements

The fourth section of this chapter is dedicated to the model data flow clauses for EU trade agreements. In January 2018, the European Commission endorsed horizontal provisions for cross-border data flows and personal data protection as a model for the future negotiation of trade agreements. A team led by the First Vice-President of the European Commission, Frans Timmermans, has looked into how best to advance the EU's data protection interests in trade negotiations.[116] The result of these efforts are analyzed in this section.[117] The EU opted for an approach that does not include a

[116] The EU has already included these clauses in its proposals for currently negotiated trade agreements with New Zealand, Australia, Chile, Mexico, Indonesia, and Tunisia, as well as in its proposal for the recent WTO negotiations on electronic commerce. See European Commission (2018).

[117] Apart from the document containing the text of the horizontal provisions for cross-border data flows and personal data protection, there are no other official documents from the European Commission on the development, background or interpretation of the model data flow clauses for EU trade agreements.

commitment to the free flow of personal data across borders.[118] The EU model data flow clauses address data protection as a fundamental right (Sect. 5.4.1), introduce a ban on data localization requirements not motivated by data protection or privacy (Sect. 5.4.2), carve-out space for the regulation of data protection from the scope of trade agreements (Sect. 5.4.3), and reject regulatory cooperation in the field of data protection (Sect. 5.4.4).

5.4.1 *Addressing Data Protection as a Fundamental Right*

Article B of the EU model data flow clauses is dedicated to the protection of personal data and privacy. The first paragraph of Article B addresses data protection and privacy as fundamental rights:

> **Article B Protection of personal data and privacy**
> 1. Each Party recognises that the protection of personal data and privacy is a fundamental right and that high standards in this regard contribute to trust in the digital economy and to the development of trade.

The first paragraph of Article B creates a common understanding among the contracting parties of data protection as a fundamental right.[119] The paragraph does not include the different written constituent parts of the right to data protection in Article 8 CFR, which would have been helpful to clarify the scope of the right to data protection. The paragraph also does not specifically refer to the importance of guaranteeing the protection of personal data in cases in which it is transferred across borders. Moreover, the right to continuous protection for personal data is not mentioned. The first paragraph simply constitutes an acknowledgment of the fundamental rights status of the protection of personal data and privacy. This acknowledgment is also connected to the fostering of trust in the digital economy and to the development of trade.[120] A similar rationale was used in Article 45 EU-Algeria AA from 2002, which was the earliest provision addressing cross-border flows of personal data in an EU trade agreement.[121] This paragraph in the EU model data flow clauses continues the EU's narrative according to which high standards of data protection are a precondition, and not a barrier, to international trade.

The only definition in Article B of the EU model data flow clauses concerns personal data:

---

[118] See Sect. 5.2.1.2. Cp. Mancini (2020), p. 195.

[119] Streinz (2019), p. 336.

[120] Velli (2019), p. 893.

[121] See Sect. 5.1.2.1.

> **Article B Protection of personal data and privacy**
> 3. For the purposes of this agreement, 'personal data' means any information relating to an identified or identifiable natural person.

It was not considered necessary to include other definitions because the EU model data flow clauses do not entail obligations nor recommendations for domestic regulatory regimes to include data protection principles or enforcement mechanisms like the EU-CARIFORUM EPA from 2008 did. The EU removed all substantive reference to data protection principles from its model data flow clauses and did not include any data protection obligations. This might be a missed opportunity to create a deeper understanding of and commitment to the "high standards of data protection" that are referenced in the first paragraph of Article B. In addition, the EU could have used the term "adequate level of data protection" instead of "high standards of data protection" to be in line with the EU regulation of data transfers.

5.4.2 *Banning Data Localization Requirements*

Article A of the EU model data flow clauses addresses cross-border data flows without a distinction between personal and non-personal data:

> **Article A Cross-border data flows**
> 1. The Parties are committed to ensuring cross-border data flows to facilitate trade in the digital economy. To that end, cross-border data flows shall not be restricted between the Parties by:
>   (a) requiring the use of computing facilities or network elements in the Party's territory for processing, including by imposing the use of computing facilities or network elements that are certified or approved in the territory of a Party;
>   (b) requiring the localization of data in the Party's territory for storage or processing;
>   (c) prohibiting storage or processing in the territory of the other Party;
>   (d) making the cross-border transfer of data contingent upon use of computing facilities or network elements in the Parties' territory or upon localisation requirements in the Parties' territory.
> 2. The Parties shall keep the implementation of this provision under review and assess its functioning in 3 years following the entry into force of this Agreement. A Party may at any time propose to the other Party to review the list of restrictions listed in the preceding paragraph. Such request shall be accorded sympathetic consideration.

Article A of the EU model data flow clauses entails a commitment to the free flow of data across borders. In addition, it specifically bans data localization requirements such as the use of domestic computing facilities for the processing and storage of data. However, an explicit carve-out in paragraph 2 of Article B of the EU model data flow clauses—which is addressed more below—ensures that the anti-localization provision cannot be directed against data protection and privacy rules.[122]

Article A of the model clauses is a manifestation of the EU's opposition to digital protectionism. The European Commission highlighted in a communication from 2017 on exchanging and protecting personal data in a globalized world that "European companies operating in some third countries are increasingly faced with protectionist restrictions that cannot be justified with legitimate privacy considerations."[123]

Data localization requirements in third countries are often motivated by privacy or security considerations.[124] While privacy-based data localization is allowed according to Article B of the EU model data flow clauses, it must be assumed that security-based data localization will be subject to general and security exceptions that are usually part of trade agreements. For example, the general exception in Article 28.3(2)(a) CETA applies to the electronic commerce chapter of the CETA and provides that nothing in the agreement shall be construed to prevent the adoption or enforcement by a party of measures necessary to protect public security or public morals or to maintain public order.[125] This exception for public security, public morals, and public order is further qualified in footnote 33 of the CETA and may only be invoked in cases in which a genuine and sufficiently serious threat is posed to one of the fundamental interests of society. It is suggested that such an exception could not be used to justify data localization that is presented as a protection of public security, but that is applied with a protectionist agenda. Similarly, a national security exception such as entailed in Article 28.6(b)(ii) CETA—echoing the language of Article XIV *bis* GATS—could not be used to generally justify security-based localization requirements. It is only applicable for the protection of essential security interests in time of war or other emergencies in international relations.[126] The ban on data localization in Article A of the EU model data flow clauses could therefore successfully prohibit security-based localization requirements for personal and non-personal data pursued by a contracting party with a protectionist agenda.

In addition, the application of general exceptions to the ban of data localization practices in Article A of the EU model data flow clauses allows derogations for measures adopted for the protection of human, animal or plant life and health. The absence of such an exception in Regulation (EU) 2018/1807 on a framework for the

---

[122] Streinz (2019), p. 336; Yakovleva (2020), p. 495.

[123] European Commission (2017a), p. 3.

[124] Sargsyan (2016), p. 2222; Chander and Le (2015), pp. 718–721; Castro (2013), p. 1.

[125] Subject to the requirement that the measures are not applied in a manner which would constitute a means of arbitrary or unjustifiable discrimination between the parties where like conditions prevail, or a disguised restriction on trade in services.

[126] See Sect. 4.4.2.

free flow of non-personal data in the EU for non-personal data has been criticized.[127] Considerations for the protection of human, animal or plant life and health would therefore be covered in a trade agreement.

5.4.3 Carving-Out Space for the Regulation of Data Protection

The second paragraph of Article B of the EU model data flow clauses is the most important one for the restriction of cross-border flows of personal data:

> **Article B Protection of personal data and privacy**
> 2. Each Party may adopt and maintain the safeguards it deems appropriate to ensure the protection of personal data and privacy, including through the adoption and application of rules for the cross-border transfer of personal data. Nothing in this agreement shall affect the protection of personal data and privacy afforded by the Parties' respective safeguards.

The second paragraph of Article B allows the parties to adopt and maintain regulations for the protection of personal data and privacy, including rules for cross-border flows of personal data. It emphasizes that rules for cross-border flows of personal data are an integral part of the safeguards for the protection of personal data and privacy. The first sentence of paragraph 2 incorporates a subjective appropriateness test similar to that employed in national security exceptions.[128] Under this sentence, the parties enjoy wide discretion in determining what they deem appropriate to ensure the protection of personal data and privacy. This is opposed to the objective necessity test that can be found in Article 19.11(2) USMCA. In addition, the second sentence of paragraph 2 entails a complete carve-out for data protection and privacy safeguards. This means that nothing in the trade agreement may affect the safeguards for the protection of personal data and privacy adopted and maintained by the parties. Article B of the EU model data flow clauses is formulated in a way that makes restrictions on cross-border flows of personal data on the basis of the EU regulation of data transfers *a priori* not subject to the prohibition in Article A on restricting cross-border data flows.[129] Article B is a water-tight provision for any domestic data protection rule affecting cross-border flows of personal data. With this provision, the European Commission may keep its promise that EU data protection rules are not subject to trade negotiations.[130]

---

[127] Irion (2018), p. 9; see Sect. 5.2.4.

[128] Yakovleva (2020), p. 496.

[129] Ibid., 495.

[130] European Commission (2017a), p. 9.

At the same time, the carve-out for data protection and privacy safeguards may also be problematic. Jacqueline Yin stresses that the carve-out allows the parties to introduce data protectionism under the guise of data protection.[131] Similarly, Federica Velli argues that the carve-out could result in uncertainty for digital service suppliers inside and outside of the EU.[132] The EU model data flow clauses have no solution for data protection rules motivated by a protectionist agenda. For example, a requirement that a copy of all personal data must be stored in the jurisdiction in which it was collected before its transfer abroad is possible under the EU model data flow clauses in cases in which a contracting party declares that the requirement is necessary to safeguard data protection and/or privacy. The same is true for a requirement that the processing of personal data must take place in the jurisdiction in which it was collected before it is transferred abroad.

The EU model data flow clauses show that the EU treats data protection and international trade law as two separate tracks with little or no middle ground.[133] The EU uses international trade law to immunize its own regulation of data protection in the second paragraph of Article B. At the same time, the EU encourages contracting parties to adopt high data protection standards in the first paragraph of Article B. It does not use international trade law to establish obligations to substantiate high data protection standards. It uses EU law—in particular, the right to continuous protection for personal data in Article 8 CFR and the legal mechanisms for the transfer of personal data in the GDPR—to push third countries indirectly into adopting high data protection standards.

5.4.4 Rejecting Regulatory Cooperation for Data Protection

Article X of the EU model data flow clauses addresses cooperation on regulatory issues with regard to digital trade. The third paragraph of Article X rejects regulatory cooperation in the field of data protection:

Article X Cooperation on regulatory issues with regard to digital trade

1. The parties shall maintain a dialogue on regulatory issues raised by digital trade, which shall inter alia address the following issues:
   - the recognition and facilitation of interoperable cross-border electronic trust and authentication services;
   - the treatment of direct marketing communications;
   - the protection of consumers in the ambit of electronic commerce; and
   - any other issue relevant for the development of digital trade.

[131] Yin (2018).

[132] Velli (2019), p. 893.

[133] See Sect. 5.1.2.

2. Such cooperation shall focus on exchange of information on the Parties' respective legislation on these issues as well as on the implementation of such legislation.
3. For greater certainty, this provision shall not apply to a Party's rules and safeguards for the protection of personal data and privacy, including on cross-border data transfers of personal data.

Article X does not simply leave data protection out of the list of issues for cooperation and dialogue. The third paragraph of Article X explicitly mentions that the protection of personal data and privacy, including rules for cross-border flows of personal data, is excluded from cooperation.[134] Scholars and interest groups have underlined that this is a shortcoming. For example, the European Services Forum (ESF) bemoans the EU model data flow clauses for establishing that regulatory cooperation does not cover cross-border flows of personal data.[135] The ESF considers that this is a missed opportunity for the EU to better explain the GDPR. The EU should not hesitate to use a cooperation mechanism to promote its approach to data protection simply because a forum for dialogue is non-binding. Federica Velli also stresses that this exclusion prevents influences or negotiations to lower data protection standards, while at the same time underlining that the rejection of regulatory cooperation for data protection is a missed opportunity to promote the EU's position and discuss new developments in digital trade.[136] Similarly, Isabella Mancini emphasizes that the EU overlooked that data protection is an issue that arises across several diverse fields.[137] Finally, Mira Burri underlines that as the complexity of the data-driven society rises, enhanced regulatory cooperation seems indispensable for moving forward, since data issues cannot be covered by the mere 'lower tariffs, more commitments' stance in trade negotiations but entail the need for reconciling different interests and the need for oversight.[138]

It is not completely understandable why the EU explicitly excluded data protection from regulatory cooperation in trade agreements. Digital trade increasingly relies on cross-border flows of personal data and global divergences hamper trade. The EU could use regulatory cooperation mechanisms to nudge convergence while guaranteeing high standards of protection for the right to data protection in Article 8 CFR.[139] The EU should conceive regulatory cooperation as a venue to reach greater convergence for data protection standards. It has also been shown that Article 50 GDPR encourages the EU to develop means for cooperating with third countries. Previous EU trade agreements like the EU-CARIFORUM EPA and other trade agreements between third countries like the Costa Rica-Colombia trade agreement

[134] Streinz (2019), p. 336.

[135] ESF (2018), p. 2.

[136] Velli (2019), p. 893.

[137] Mancini (2020), p. 200.

[138] Burri (2021), p. 41.

[139] Ibid., 204.

include such cooperation provisions. The European Commission has stated in its recent communication on a European Strategy for Data from 2020 that it is convinced that international cooperation must be based on an approach that promotes the EU's fundamental values, including the protection of privacy.[140] Regulatory cooperation can be framed and organized in way that safeguards the right to continuous protection of personal data in Article 8 CFR.

5.4.5 Summary

The EU model data flow clauses underline the fact that high data protection standards contribute to trust in the digital economy and to the development of trade. In addition, the first paragraph of Article B creates a common understanding of data protection as a fundamental right. However, the paragraph does not include the different written constituent parts of the right to data protection in Article 8 CFR. Doing so would have been helpful to clarify its scope. The EU chose a strategy for its model data flow clauses that does not entail a commitment to the free flow of personal data across borders. The second paragraph of Article B allows the parties to adopt and maintain regulations for the protection of personal data and privacy, including rules for cross-border flows of personal data, without any conditions. The EU uses international trade law to immunize its own regulation of data protection. Nothing in the trade agreement may affect the safeguards for the protection of personal data and privacy adopted and maintained by the parties according to the second paragraph of Article B. At the same time, the EU model data flow clauses offer no solution to address protectionist data protection rules. As long as a contracting party justifies its restrictions on cross-border flows of personal data with the protection of personal data and privacy, they are exempt from the trade agreement. This is a consequence of completely excluding data protection rules from trade negotiations. The ban on data localization in Article A of the EU model data flow clauses concerns localization requirements based on other reasons than data protection or privacy. The ban is useful to target security-based data localization requirements motivated by a protectionist agenda. Considering that the EU model data flow clauses immunize data protection rules in the EU, it is not entirely clear why Article X of the EU model data flow clauses explicitly excludes data protection from regulatory cooperation. Article 50 GDPR challenges the EU to develop means for cooperating with third countries. Previous EU trade agreements like the EU-CARIFORUM EPA and other trade agreements between third countries like the Costa Rica-Colombia FTA include such cooperation provisions. The EU should conceive regulatory cooperation as a venue to reach greater convergence for data protection standards, precisely because it emphasizes in the first paragraph of

[140] European Commission (2020), p. 23.

Article B that high data protection standards also contribute to trust in the digital economy and to the development of trade.

5.5 Conclusion

In reaction to the stalemate in the multilateral trading system, international governance of digital trade has gradually shifted to bilateral and regional trade agreements.[141] It is therefore not surprising that countries have started to regulate cross-border flows of personal data outside the WTO in bilateral and regional trade agreements.

The EU has tried different approaches to address data protection and cross-border flows of personal data in its trade agreements over the past 20 years. The EU started to qualify data protection as a contributing factor in the elimination of barriers to cross-border data flows in the EU-Algeria AA from 2002. The EU then went on to underline the fundamental rights character of data protection and commit all involved parties to establishing data protection regimes, as well as appropriate administrative capacities, including independent supervision, in order to ensure an adequate level of protection and facilitate cross-border flows of personal data in the EU-CARIFORUM EPA from 2008. Then came a clear break with this strategy. The CETA from 2016 makes a clear distinction between domestic data protection regulation and international trade law.[142] The CETA does not contain any data protection obligations and there are no rules for cross-border flows of personal data in the trade agreement. In short, the EU separated the regulation of data protection from trade rules. The EU continued to do this in the EU-Japan EPA from 2018. Here, the parties agreed on a *rendez-vous* clause in the agreement and settled the issue with reciprocal adequacy decisions based on domestic data protection law. The EU's opposition to include a commitment on cross-border data flows was also a stumbling block in the negotiations of the TiSA and the TTIP in the late 2010s. In contrast, the CPTPP from 2018 or US-led trade agreements such as the USMCA from 2018 entail binding commitments for the cross-border flow of personal data. The USMCA imposes strict conditions on exceptions, including the standards from the *chapeau* of Article XIV GATS and two necessity tests. In contrast, the CPTPP leaves more room to accommodate data protection or privacy-based restrictions on cross-border flows of personal data.

The EU's reluctance to commit to the free flow of personal data across borders in trade agreements might be explained through an appeal to Union law: the right to continuous protection for personal data in Article 8 CFR, the GDPR, and other regulations impose requirements upon the EU. The most important requirement is the primacy of fundamental rights over international law in the EU. Any data flow

[141] López González/Ferencz, OECD Report 2018, 15.

[142] Irion and Bartl (2017), p. 5.

clause in an EU trade agreement must respect the right to continuous protection of personal data in Article 8 CFR. Furthermore, data flow clauses in an EU trade agreement should be designed in a way that accommodates the legal mechanisms for data transfers in the GDPR. The data flow clauses should not replace the legal mechanisms for the transfer of personal data in the GDPR because these mechanisms provide the necessary details for safe data transfers. The framework for data flow clauses also requires the inclusion of a provision on cooperation for the protection of personal data in EU trade agreements in line with the objectives of Article 50 GDPR. Recital (101) GDPR acknowledges that flows of personal data to and from countries outside the EU are necessary for the expansion of international trade. This implies that restrictions on cross-border flows of personal data that are not motivated by data protection or privacy should be banned.

However, there are different possibilities for combining these requirements with a commitment to the free flow of personal data across borders and integrating them in data flow clauses of EU trade agreements. Four suggestions for the design of data flow clauses in EU trade agreements were presented and all foregrounded the primacy of fundamental rights over international law from the perspective of EU law and all accommodated the legal mechanisms for the transfer of personal data in the GDPR.

The first design combines a data flow obligation with a general data protection exception. The second design uses a more specific adequacy exception. The disadvantage of these designs is that the justification for a restriction on cross-border flows of personal data lies with the defendant. The EU would have to prove that a measure is taken for the protection of personal data that is transferred to the contracting party (in case of the first design) or that the level of protection for personal data in the contracting party is not adequate (in case of the second design). The third design combines a data flow obligation with an adequacy condition. The parties allow the cross-border transfer of personal data in cases in which the level of protection for the transferred personal data is adequate. The advantage of this design is that the defendant does not bear the burden of proof because the criterion of an adequate level of protection is not integrated as an exception. However, the term "adequate level of protection" might have a different interpretation in trade agreements than in EU law based on interpretations according to the VCLT. This could provoke problems with the right to continuous protection for personal data in Article 8 CFR. A footnote referring to an autonomous definition of the term could prevent such problems. Another solution could be a provision on cooperation that establishes a dialogue on adequate protection for personal data. The documentation of that dialogue could be used as supplementary means of interpretation according to Article 32 VCLT. The fourth design for a data flow clause is the same as the third design with regards to containing an adequacy obligation and an adequacy condition, but it also has a separate chapter on data protection. The advantage of the fourth design over the third design is that the trade agreement itself provides the basis for an adequate level of protection for personal data.

The EU model data flow clauses, which the European Commission endorsed as a model for future negotiation of trade agreements in January 2018, do not contain a commitment to the free flow of personal data across borders. Rather, they create a common understanding of data protection as a fundamental right without specifying its scope and underline that high data protection standards contribute to trust in the digital economy and to the development of trade. The EU model data flow clauses allow the parties to adopt and maintain regulations for the protection of personal data and privacy, including rules for cross-border flows of personal data, without any conditions. The EU uses international trade law to immunize its own regulation of data protection. Nothing in the trade agreement may affect the safeguards for the protection of personal data and privacy adopted and maintained by the parties. At the same time, the EU model data flow clauses offer no solution for addressing protectionist data protection rules. As long as a contracting party justifies its restrictions on cross-border flows of personal data under the protection of personal data and privacy, they are exempt from the trade agreement. The ban on data localization in the EU model data flow clauses only concerns localization requirements based on other reasons than data protection or privacy. This is useful to target security-based data localization requirements motivated by a protectionist agenda. Considering that the EU model data flow clauses immunize data protection rules in the EU, it is not entirely clear why they explicitly exclude data protection from regulatory cooperation. The EU should conceive regulatory cooperation as a venue to reach greater convergence for data protection standards, precisely because it emphasizes that high data protection standards also contribute to trust in the digital economy and to the development of trade. To combat data protectionism, while protecting its own data protection standards, the EU would be better advised to use one of the four proposed designs for data flow clauses.

References

Bibliography

Aaronson SA (2015) Why Trade Agreements are not setting information free: the lost history and reinvigorated debate over cross-border data flows, human rights, and national security. World Trade Rev 14(4):671–700

Aaronson SA, Townes MD (2012) Can trade policy set information free? Trade agreements, internet governance and internet freedom. George Washington University Policy Brief. Washington DC

Barents R (2004) The autonomy of community law. Kluwer Law, The Hague

Barnard C, Peers S (2017) European Union law, 2nd edn. Oxford University Press, Oxford

Berka W (2017) CETA, TTIP, TiSA and data protection. In: Griller S, Obwexer W, Vranes E (eds) Mega-Regional Trade Agreements: CETA, TTIP, and TiSA: new orientations for EU external economic relations. Oxford University Press, Oxford, pp 175–186

Burri M (2017) The governance of data and data flows in trade agreements: the pitfalls of legal adaptation. UC Davis Law Rev 51(1):65–133

Burri M (2019) Understanding and shaping trade rules for the digital era. In: Elsig M, Hahn M, Spilker G (eds) The shifting landscape of global trade governance. Cambridge University Press, Cambridge, pp 73–106

Burri M (2021) Data flows and global trade law. In: Burri M (ed) Big data and global trade law. Cambridge University Press, Cambridge, pp 11–41
Castro D (2013) The false promise of data nationalism. The Information Technology & Innovation Foundation. Washington DC
Chander A, Le UP (2015) Data nationalism. Emory Law J 64(3):677–739
Craig P, de Búrca G (2017) EU law, 6th edn. Oxford Academic, Oxford
Cremona M (2020) The Opinion procedure under Article 218(11) TFEU: reflections in the light of Opinion 1/17. Europe World A Law Rev 4(1):1–11
Eeckhout P (2011) EU external relations law, 2nd edn. Oxford University Press, Oxford
Fleming J (2013) Reding warns data protection could derail US trade talks. Euractive. 30 October 2013. https://www.euractiv.com/section/digital/news/reding-warns-data-protection-could-derail-us-trade-talks/. Accessed 3 January 2021
Fontoura Costa JA (2020) Data protection in international trade law. In: Moura VD, de Vasconcelos CS (eds) Data protection in the internet. Springer, Heidelberg, pp 479–517
Geist M (2018) How the USMCA falls short on digital trade, data protection and privacy. Washington Post. 3 October 2018. https://www.washingtonpost.com/news/global-opinions/wp/2018/10/03/how-the-usmca-falls-short-on-digital-trade-data-protection-and-privacy/. Accessed 3 January 2021
Greenleaf G (2014) Asian data privacy laws: Trade and human rights perspectives. Oxford University Press, Oxford
Greenleaf G (2018) Free Trade Agreements and data privacy. Future Perils of Faustian Bargains. In: Svantesson DJB, Kloza D (eds) Trans-Atlantic data privacy relations as a challenge for democracy. Intersentia, Cambridge, pp 181–212
Gstöhl S, Hanf D (2014) The EU's Post-Lisbon Free Trade Agreements: commercial interests in a changing constitutional context. Eur Law J 20(6):733–748
Irion K (2018) Public Security Exception in the Area of non-personal Data in the European Union. Research paper commissioned by the European Parliament Committee on the Internal Market and Consumer Protection. Amsterdam
Irion K, Bartl M (2017) The Japan EU Economic Partnership Agreement: Flows of Personal Data to the Land of the Rising Sun. Research paper commissioned by the European Parliamentary Group GUE/NGL. Amsterdam
Kelsey J, Kilic B (2014) Wikileaks Briefing on US TISA proposal on E-commerce, technology transfer, cross-border data flows and net neutrality. Washington DC
Koutrakos P (2016) Public Security Exceptions and EU Free Movement Law. In: Koutrakos P, Shuibhne NN, Sypris P (eds) Exceptions from EU Free Movement Law. Bloomsbury, Oxford, pp 190–217
Kuner C (2020) Chapter V transfers of personal data to third countries or international organisations (Articles 44-50). In: Kuner C, Bygrave L, Docksey C (eds) The EU general data protection regulation (GDPR). Oxford University Press, Oxford, pp 755–862
Lacey SBC (2020) Reality check: the lack of consensus on new trade rules to govern the digital economy. J World Trade 54(2):199–218
Lenaerts K (2010) Droit international et monisme de l'ordre juridique de l'Union. Revue de la faculté de droit de l'Université de Liège 46(4):505–520
Lenaerts K, Van Nuffel P (2011) European Union law, 3rd edn. Thomson Reuters, Sweet & Maxwell, London
López GJ, Ferencz J (2018) Digital trade and market openness. OECD Report, Paris
Mancini I (2020) Deepening trade *and* fundamental rights? Harnessing data protection rights in the regulatory cooperation chapters of EU Trade Agreements. In: Weiß W, Furculita C (eds) Global politics and EU Trade Policy. European yearbook of international economic law. Springer, Heidelberg, pp 185–207
Mattoo A (2015) Services Trade and Regulatory Cooperation. E15 Initiative Think Piece. Geneva
Mohay Á (2017) The status of international agreements concluded by the European Union in the EU legal order. Pravni Vjesnik 33(3-4):151–164

Monteiro J-A, Teh R (2017) Provisions on electronic commerce in regional trade agreements. WTO Working Paper, Geneva

Mucci A, Cerulus L, von der Burchard H (2016) Data fight emerges as last big hurdle to EU-Japan trade deal. Politico. 12 August 2016. https://www.politico.eu/article/eu-japan-trade-deal-caught-up-in-data-flow-row-cecilia-malmstrom/. Accessed 3 January 2021

noyb (2022) New US executive order unlikely to satisfy EU law. 7 October 2022. https://noyb.eu/en/new-us-executiveorder-unlikely-satisfy-eu-law. Accessed 30 October 2022

Peng S-y, Liu H-w (2017) The legality of data residency requirements: how can the trans-pacific partnership help? J World Trade 51(2):183–204

Peters A (1997) The position of international law within the European community legal order. German Yearb Int Law 40:9–77

Sargsyan T (2016) Data localization and the role of infrastructure for surveillance, privacy, and security. Int J Commun 10:2221–2237

Semertzi A (2014) The preclusion of direct effect in the recently concluded EU Free Trade Agreements. Common Mark Law Rev 51(4):1125–1158

Somaini L (2020) Regulating the dynamic concept of non-personal data in the EU: from ownership to portability. Eur Data Protect Law Rev 6(1):84–93

Streinz T (2019) Digital megaregulation uncontested? TPP's model for the global digital economy. In: Kingsbury B, Malone DM, Mertenskötter P et al (eds) Megaregulation contested: global economic ordering after TPP. Oxford University Press, Oxford, pp 312–342

USTR (2017) Summary of Objectives for the NAFTA Renegotiation. November 2017. Washington D.C. https://ustr.gov/sites/default/files/files/Press/Releases/Nov%20Objectives%20Update.pdf. Accessed 22 May 2022

van Rossem JW (2009) Interaction between EU law and international law in the light of *Intertanko* and *Kadi*: The Dilemma of norms binding the member states but not the community. Netherlands Yearb Int Law 40:183–227

Van Vooren B, Wessel RA (2014) EU external relations law. Cambridge University Press, Cambridge

Van Waeyenberge A, Pecho P (2014) Free Trade Agreements after the Treaty of Lisbon in the light of the case law of the Court of Justice of the European Union. Eur Law J 20(6):749–762

Velli F (2019) The issue of data protection in EU trade commitments: cross-border data transfers in GATS and Bilateral Free Trade Agreements. Eur Pap 4(3):881–894

Weber PA, Zhang N, Wu H (2020) A comparative analysis of personal data protection regulations between the EU and China. Electr Commer Res 20(3):565–587

Willemyns I (2020) Agreement forthcoming? A comparison of EU, US, and Chinese RTAs in times of plurilateral E-Commerce negotiations. J Int Econ Law 23(1):221–244

Wolfe R (2019) Learning about digital trade: privacy and E-Commerce in CETA and TPP. World Trade Rev 18(1):63–84

Wu M (2017) Digital trade-related provisions in regional trade agreements: existing models and lessons for the multilateral trade system. ICTSD and IDB Overview Paper. Geneva/Washington DC

Wunsch-Vincent S (2008) Trade rules for the digital age. In: Panizzon M, Pohl N, Sauvé P (eds) GATS and the regulation of international trade in services. Cambridge University Press, Cambridge, pp 497–529

Yakovleva S (2018) Should fundamental rights to privacy and data protection be a part of the EU's international trade 'Deals'? World Trade Rev 17(3):477–508

Yakovleva S (2020) Privacy protection(ism): the latest wave of trade constraints on regulatory autonomy. Univ Miami Law Rev 74(2):416–519

Yakovleva S, Irion K (2020) Pitching trade against privacy- reconciling EU governance of personal data flows with external trade. Int Data Priv Law 10(3):1–21

Yin J (2018) Cross-Border Data Continues to Flow under the USMCA. DisCo. 5 October 2018. http://www.project-disco.org/21st-century-trade/100518-cross-border-data-under-the-usmca/#.XGcDCpNKiL4. Accessed 3 January 2021

Jurisprudence

ECJ, AG Opinion, *Rízení Letového Provozu*: ECJ, Opnion of AG Mengozzi, *Rízení Letového Provozu,* C-335/05, EU:C:2007:103

ECJ, *Air Transport Association of America:* ECJ, Judgment of 21 December 2011, *Air Transport Association of America*, C-366/10, EU:C:2011:864

ECJ, *Commission v. Council*: ECJ, Judgment of 11 September 2003, *Commission v. Council,* C-211/01, EU:C:2003:452

ECJ, *Commission v. Grand Duchy of Luxembourg*: ECJ, Judgment of 19 June 2008, *Commission v Grand Duchy of Luxemburg*, C-319/06, ECLI:EU:C:2008:350

ECJ, *FIAMM*: ECJ, Judgment of 9 September 2008, *FIAMM*, C-120/06 P and C-121/06 P, EU: C:2008:476

ECJ, *Germany v Council*, ECJ, Judgment of 5 October 1994, *Germany v Council*, C-280/93, EU: C:1994:367

ECJ, *Germany v. Council (Bananas)*: ECJ, Judgment of 10 March 1998, *Germany v. Council,* C-122/95, EU:C:1998:94

ECJ, *IATA and ELFAA*: ECJ, Judgment of 10 January 2006, *IATA and ELFAA*, C-344/04, EU: C:2006:10

ECJ, *International Fruit Company:* ECJ, Judgment of 12 December 1972, *International Fruit Company*, C-21 to 24/72, EU:C:1972:115

ECJ, *Intertanko:* ECJ, Judgment of 3 June 2008, *Intertanko*, C-308/06, EU:C:2008:312

ECJ, *Kupferberg*, ECJ, Judgment of 26 October 1982, *Kupferberg*, C-104/81, EU:C:1982:362

ECJ, Opinion 1/15*:* ECJ, Opinion 1/15 of 26 July 2017, *Draft agreement between Canada and the European Union*, EU:C:2017:592

ECJ, Opinion 2/15*:* ECJ, Opinion 2/15 of 16 May 2017, *Free Trade Agreement between the European Union and the Republic of Singapore*, EU:C:2017:376

ECJ, Opinion 1/17*:* ECJ, Opinion 1/17 of 30 April 2019, *Comprehensive Economic and Trade Agreement between Canada, of the one part, and the European Union and its Member States, of the other part (CETA)*, EU:C:2019:341

ECJ, *Parliament v. Council and Commission*: ECJ, Judgment of 30 May 2006, *Parliament v. Council and Commission*, Joined Cases C-317/04 and C-318/04, EU:C:2006:346

ECJ, *Portugal v. Council*: ECJ, Judgment of 23 November 1999, *Portugal v. Council,* C-149/96, EU:C:1999:574

ECJ, *R. & V. Haegeman v. Belgian State*: ECJ, Judgment of 30 April 1974, *R. & V. Haegeman v. Belgian State*, C-181/73, EU:C:1974:41

ECJ, *Schrems:* ECJ, Judgment of 6 October 2015, *Schrems*, C-362/14, EU:C:2015:650

ECJ, *Western Sahara Campaign UK:* ECJ, Judgment of 27 February 2018, *Western Sahara Campaign UK,* C-266/16, EU:C:2018:118

Documents

Council of the EU (2017) Proposal for a Regulation of the European Parliament and of the Council on a framework for the free flow of non-personal data in the European Union. 2017/0228 (COD). 19 December 2017

Council of the EU (2019) Decision authorising the opening of negotiations with the United States of America for an agreement on the elimination of tariffs for industrial goods. 6052/19 LIMITE. 9 April 2019

ESF (2018) Commission's Proposal on Cross-border data flows in Trade Agreements. Letter to Kiril Yurukov, Chair of TPC Services and Investments. 12 June 2018

European Commission (2013a) Press Release. European Commission calls on the U.S. to restore trust in EU-U.S. data flows. 27 November 2013. https://ec.europa.eu/commission/presscorner/detail/en/IP_13_1166. Accessed 22 May 2022

European Commission (2013b) Viviane Reding. Speech - Towards a more dynamic transatlantic area of growth and investment. 29 October 2013. https://ec.europa.eu/commission/presscorner/detail/de/speech_13_867. Accessed 22 May 2022

European Commission (2017a) Communication on Exchanging and Protecting Personal Data in a Globalised World. COM(2017) 7 final. 10 January 2017

European Commission (2017b) Joint Declaration by Mr. Shinzo Abe, Prime Minister of Japan, and Mr. Jean-Claude Juncker, President of the European Commission. STATEMENT/17/1917. 6 July 2017

European Commission (2018) European Commission endorses provisions for data flows and data protection in EU trade agreements. Daily News. 31 January 2018

European Commission (2019) Communication Guidance on the Regulation on a framework for the free flow of non-personal data in the European Union. COM(2019) 250 final. 29 May 2019

European Commission (2020) Communication, A European strategy for data. COM(2020) 66 final. 19 February 2020

European Parliament (2015) Resolution of 8 July 2015 containing the European Parliament's recommendations to the European Commission on the negotiations for the Transatlantic Trade and Investment Partnership (TTIP) [2017] OJ C 265/35

European Parliament (2016) Resolution of 3 February 2016 containing the European Parliament's recommendations to the Commission on the negotiations for the Trade in Services Agreement (TiSA) [2018] OJ C 35/21

HM Government, The exchange and protection of personal data, A future partnership paper, 24 August 2017

WTO (2015) Council for Trade in Service, Report of the Meeting held on 18 March 2015, Note by the Secretariat. S/C/M/122. 1 May 2015

Part III
Epilogue

Chapter 6
Concluding Remarks: Data Protection Without Data Protectionism

Many states recognize, at least on paper, that data protection and privacy are important values. Nevertheless, they diverge quite jarringly on what the correct level or design of such protection should be.[1] In particular, there is deep disagreement about when data protection crosses the line and becomes data protectionism. In this book, I have shown—using the example of EU law—where the line between data protection and data protectionism in international trade law currently is, and how it can, or should be redrawn.

The first part of this book explored EU-style data protection, its application to cross-border flows of personal data, and its consequences. EU data protection law centers around the fundamental right to data protection enshrined in Article 8 CFR. The right to data protection was integrated into the CFR alongside the right to private life to strengthen the protection of fundamental rights in light of changes in society, social progress, and scientific and technological developments.[2] I argued in Chap. 2 that the right to data protection in Article 8 CFR has an extraterritorial dimension that applies to cross-border flows of personal data. The extraterritorial dimension of Article 8 CFR affords individuals in the EU continuous protection of personal data—essentially equivalent to that guaranteed within the EU—in the case that personal data is transferred from the EU to a third country. I suggested that this right to continuous protection of personal data is an unwritten constituent part—in addition to the six written constituent parts—enshrined in Article 8 CFR. The right to continuous protection of personal data applies, for example, when personal data that is transferred to a third country could be the target of internet surveillance practices in a third country. In cases in which continuous protection of personal data cannot be

[1] Yakovleva (2020), p. 476; Schwartz and Peifer (2017), pp. 178–179; Aaronson (2015), pp. 682–683.

[2] Rodotà (2009), p. 80.

T. Naef, *Data Protection without Data Protectionism*, EYIEL Monographs - Studies in European and International Economic Law 28,
https://doi.org/10.1007/978-3-031-19893-9_6

guaranteed, the export of personal data from the EU must be restricted to accord with this unwritten constituent part of Article 8 CFR.

At the same time, the right to continuous protection of personal data found in Article 8 CFR is not absolute and can be limited according to Article 52 (1) CFR. In Chap. 3, I analyzed the possibilities of such limitations. However, as I showed, no lawful limitations are possible in cases in which systematic, structural, and continuous data transfers take place to a third country that does not provide a level of protection for personal data that is essentially equivalent to that guaranteed within the EU. The interference with Article 8 CFR caused by systematic, structural, and continuous data transfers fails the proportionality assessment in Article 52(1) CFR. Neither the freedom of expression in Article 11 CFR nor the freedom to conduct a business in Article 16 CFR can justify this interference. I thus concluded that the legal mechanisms in Articles 45 and 46 GDPR *cannot* be used for systematic, structural, and continuous data transfers to third countries that do not provide a level of protection that is essentially equivalent to that guaranteed within the EU. My fundamental rights analysis demonstrates that only the derogations in Article 49 GDPR—which do not allow for systematic, structural, and continuous data transfers—can be used to limit the right to continuous protection of personal data in Article 8 CFR. Occasional data transfers using the contract-based derogation and the consent-based derogation in Article 49 GDPR may take place even if the third country of destination does not provide an adequate level of protection. However, these derogations both require some sort of agreement from the data subject for the transfer of their personal data and the data subject must be informed about the risks of the data transfers in question. Taken together, this means that the EU fundamental rights-based regulation of data transfers can have highly restrictive effects.

The second part of this book examined the relationship of the EU fundamental rights-based regulation of data transfers and international trade law. It covered the compatibility of current EU regulation with WTO law and the possibility to accommodate such regulation in new trade agreements. In Chap. 4, I identified seven interferences caused by the EU regulation of data transfers with obligations in the GATS. Most of these interferences are justifiable under the privacy exception in Article XIV(c)(ii) GATS. My analysis also showed that the EC negotiated the GATS with great foresight. The negotiation documents reveal that the EC pushed for the adoption of a privacy exception with a view to its future data protection framework. Nevertheless, I argued that some aspects of the EU regulation of data transfers do not find justification under the privacy exception in Article XIV(c)(ii) GATS. This concerns due process requirements in cases in which a third country requests an adequacy decision according to Article 45 GDPR; special framework adequacy decisions for countries that otherwise would not qualify for a regular adequacy decision such as the invalidated Decision (EU) 2016/1250, the Privacy Shield adequacy decision for the US, or the planned adequacy decision for the Transatlantic Data Privacy Framework between the EU and the US; and inconsistencies in the use of the corrective powers to ban or suspend data transfers in Article 58(2)(f) and (j) GDPR by the supervisory authorities in the EU member states. Consequently, I found that the EU fundamental rights-based regulation of data transfers is compatible with WTO law *as long as* the due process requirements are complied with, no special framework adequacy decisions are adopted, and the supervisory authorities in the EU member states use their corrective powers actively and consistently to enforce the right to continuous protection of personal data.

Due to their importance for international trade, cross-border flows of personal data are also the subject of multiple, current negotiations in international trade law. While multilateral trade negotiations at the WTO move slow and compromise is increasingly more difficult, bilateral and regional trade agreements have become an important forum to address data flows on the international plane. I showed in Chap. 5 that the EU must respect several requirements when negotiating data flow clauses in trade agreements. The most important requirement is the primacy of fundamental rights over international law, which includes the right to continuous protection of personal data enshrined in Article 8 CFR. Yet I also criticized the EU model data flow clauses, which the European Commission endorsed as a model for future negotiations of EU trade agreements in 2018, for not committing to the free flow of personal data across borders and refusing to establish regulatory cooperation in the field of data protection. As an alternative, I proposed four new designs for a data flow clause that respect the primacy of the right to continuous protection of personal data in Article 8 CFR while still entailing a commitment to the free flow of personal data across borders and regulatory cooperation between the contracting parties in the field of data protection. The four designs further the opportunity to reach greater convergence for high data protection standards on the international plane.

The EU fundamental rights-based regulation of data transfers proved to be a good example to illuminate the line between data protection and data protectionism according to WTO law. It allowed me to show that even very high data protection standards—such as in the EU—can be compatible with the GATS when consistently applied. At the same time, the EU regulation of data transfers was also a good example to show how the line between data protection and data protectionism can or should be redrawn. The architecture of EU law gives primacy to fundamental rights over international law. The EU thus cannot negotiate data flow clauses in trade agreements that compromise its high data protection standards. The four designs of data flow clauses that I introduced combine a commitment to the free flow of personal data across borders with high data protection standards and therefore offer a new avenue for data protection without data protectionism.

Nevertheless, even if I portrayed the EU fundamental rights-based regulation of data transfers as a good example to assess the line between data protection and data protectionism, the EU regulation of data transfers also faces challenges. One of the biggest challenges today lies in the enforcement of the right to continuous protection of personal data. Fragmented enforcement clashes with EU data protection law and international trade law. Recital (10) GDPR entails one of the goals of EU data protection law:

> Consistent and homogenous application of the rules for the protection of the fundamental rights and freedoms of natural persons with regard to the processing of personal data should be ensured throughout the Union.

This applies to the transfer of personal data in the same way it applies to all other data processing operations. In addition, Article 8 CFR guarantees that everyone has the right to the protection of his or her personal data regardless of his or her place of residence in the EU. This means that the protection of personal data transferred from the EU to a third country must be the same in every EU member state and without variation regardless of the destination country. In short, *no* inconsistencies can be reconciled with EU data protection law. Moreover, inconsistent enforcement of the EU fundamental rights-based regulation of data transfers could lead to arbitrary or unjustifiable discrimination according to the standards in the chapeau of Article XIV GATS and therefore constitute a violation of WTO law. This is because such inconsistencies cannot be reconciled with the overall policy objective of securing compliance with the right to continuous protection of personal data in Article 8 CFR, which is covered by Article XIV(c)(ii) GATS.

The matter of enforcement of the EU's fundamental rights-based regulation of data transfers requires increased attention. In the end, it is the individual supervisory authorities of the EU member states that are responsible for enforcing the right to continuous protection of personal data in Article 8 CFR. Until recently, the enforcement of this right has been slack. Following the judgment of the ECJ in *Schrems 2* on 16 July 2020, however, the enforcement of this right has been put in the spotlight. In this judgment, the ECJ explicitly stated that the exercise of the powers to suspend and prohibit data transfers set out in Article 58(2)(f) and (j) GDPR are not simply optional, but an obligation that the supervisory authorities in the EU member states have to fulfill in cases in which the level of protection required by EU law cannot be ensured.[3] In short, supervisory authorities *must act* to remedy violations of the right to continuous protection of personal data, and they must act *consistently*. This concerns two situations in particular: First, the different supervisory authorities must adopt the same policy for data transfers to a specific third country (consistency among the different supervisory authorities). Second, every supervisory authority must adopt the same policy for data transfers to all third countries that pose similar threats to fundamental rights in order not to discriminate against certain countries (consistency within the individual supervisory authorities).

The *Schrems 2* judgment has put the individual EU supervisory authorities to the test. In the months following the decision, the judgment has seemed to have had little effect on data transfers in practice. Some of the largest EU data exporters maintain that they will continue to use standard data protection clauses for the transfer of personal data from the EU to the US, despite the clear indication by the ECJ that this is not sufficient. For example, Microsoft stated that they would update their contractual clauses and use strong encryption, but otherwise not change their practices.[4] This has left the supervisory authorities in the EU struggling to fulfil their "new" responsibilities.[5] Many of the supervisory authorities are underfunded and

[3] ECJ, *Schrems 2*, para. 121; ECJ, AG Opinion, *Schrems 2*, para. 144.

[4] Brill (2020).

[5] Clark (2020).

understaffed.[6] And while some supervisory authorities have acted to regulate the transfer of personal data from the EU to the US, others have not.[7] In any case, even those which have acted have so far only offered general statements and few guidelines. For example, the DPC of Ireland stated that "the application of the [standard data protection clauses] transfer mechanism to transfers of personal data to the United States is now questionable."[8] Supervisory authorities have not really used their corrective powers to remedy the violations outlined in *Schrems 2*.

On 10 November 2020, the EDPB adopted recommendations on measures that supplement transfer tools to ensure compliance with *Schrems 2*.[9] However, the EDPB identified two common scenarios in which no effective compliant measures could be found. [10] It is important to stress that the findings in *Schrems 2* not only concern data transfers to the US, but are applicable to data transfers to all third countries, some of which might also not provide a level of protection of personal data essentially equivalent to that guaranteed within the EU. It is now up to the EU—and specifically the supervisory authorities in the individual EU member states—to increase their efforts to enforce the right to continuous protection of personal data in Article 8 CFR.[11] The current situation undermines EU data protection law and any attempt to address specific data transfers only—such as transfers to the US, for example—risks violating international trade law. To remedy the current situation, a comprehensive and coordinated course of action is required. I have shown in this book that the consistency mechanism in Article 64 GDPR could offer a potential remedy although others may be necessary as well. How the supervisory authorities meet this challenge is a topic to follow-up on in future research.

Overall, this book has shown that restrictions on cross-border flows of personal data oriented toward protecting fundamental rights—such as laid out in EU data protection law—comply with international trade law and thus should not be interpreted as protectionist when applied consistently. This is clear from the fact that restrictions oriented toward protecting fundamental rights would disappear if third countries implemented stronger uniform data protection legislation and followed international human rights law pertaining to surveillance practices. In EU data protection law, data transfers are allowed as long as these rights are guaranteed. Ultimately, this means that the EU fundamental rights-based regulation of data transfers can be justifiably considered as data protection *without* data protectionism.

---

[6]Ibid.

[7]The IAPP Resource Centre collects guidance on *Schrems 2* from the supervisory authorities and governments as it comes out. See IAPP (2020).

[8]DPC (2020).

[9]EDPB (2020), p. 5.

[10]Ibid., 26–27.

[11]The individual supervisory authorities will also have to deal with an increasing number of complaints regarding data transfers. For example, the NGO "none of your business" (noyb) filed 101 complaints against Google Analytics and Facebook Connect integrations from webpages by EU controllers. See noyb (2020).

References

Bibliography

Aaronson SA (2015) Why Trade Agreements are not setting information free: the lost history and reinvigorated debate over cross-border data flows, human rights, and national security. World Trade Rev 14(4):671–700

Brill J (2020) New steps to defend your data, Microsoft On the Issues. 19 November 2020. https://blogs.microsoft.com/on-the-issues/2020/11/19/defending-your-data-edpb-gdpr/. Accessed 3 Jan 2021

Clark S (2020) GDR analysis: European regulators buckling under Schrems pressure. Global Data Rev 6 August 2020. https://globaldatareview.com/article/gdr-analysis-european-regulators-buckling-under-schrems-pressure. Accessed 1 June 2022

IAPP (2020) DPA, and government guidance on "Schrems II". 23 December 2020. https://iapp.org/resources/article/dpa-and-government-guidance-on-schrems-ii-2/. Accessed 3 Jan 2021

noyb (2020) 101 Complaints on EU-US transfers filed. 17 August 2020. https://noyb.eu/en/101-complaints-eu-us-transfers-filed. Accessed 3 Jan 2021

Rodotà S (2009) Data protection as a fundamental right. In: Gutwirth S, Poullet Y, de Hert P et al (eds) Reinventing data protection? Springer, Heidelberg, pp 77–82

Schwartz PM, Peifer K-N (2017) Transatlantic data privacy law. Georgetown Law J 106(1): 115–179

Yakovleva S (2020) Privacy protection(ism): the latest wave of trade constraints on regulatory autonomy. Univ Miami Law Rev 74(2):416–519

Jurisprudence

ECJ, AG Opinion, *Schrems 2:* ECJ, Opinion of AG Saugmandsgaard Øe delivered on 19 December 2019, *Schrems 2*, C-311/18, EU:C:2019:1145

ECJ, *Schrems 2:* ECJ, Judgment of 16 July 2020, *Facebook Ireland and Schrems*, C-311/18, EU:C:2020:559

Documents

DPC (2020) DPC statement on CJEU decision. 16 July 2020

EDPB (2020) Recommendations 02/2020 on the European Essential Guarantees for surveillance measures. 10 November 2020

About the Author

Dr. Tobias Naef studied political sciences at the University of Zurich (BA) and law at the University of Bern (BLaw/MLaw) with a focus on European and International Economic Law. Afterwards, he started a doctorate at the University of Zurich and worked as a research fellow for Prof. Matthias Oesch. He was a visiting researcher at the University of Amsterdam Institute for Information Law, the Lauterpacht Centre for International Law at the University of Cambridge and the Wilson Center in Washington D.C. Upon the conclusion of the dissertation, he first worked as a lawyer for data protection and digitalization on a legislative project at the Swiss Federal Office for Customs and Border Security. Currently, he works as a lawyer for the Data Protection Commissioner of the Canton Zurich.

T. Naef, *Data Protection without Data Protectionism*, EYIEL Monographs - Studies in European and International Economic Law 28,
https://doi.org/10.1007/978-3-031-19893-9

MIX
Papier aus verantwortungsvollen Quellen
Paper from responsible sources
FSC® C105338

If you have any concerns about our products,
you can contact us on
ProductSafety@springernature.com

In case Publisher is established outside the EU,
the EU authorized representative is:
Springer Nature Customer Service Center GmbH
Europaplatz 3, 69115 Heidelberg, Germany

Printed by Libri Plureos GmbH
in Hamburg, Germany